Encyclopedia of
American Forest and Conservation History

Editorial Advisory Board

Encyclopedia of
American Forest
and
Conservation History

RICHARD C. DAVIS

Editor

VOLUME ONE

Macmillan Publishing Company, New York
Collier Macmillan Publishers, London

The Free Press, a division of Macmillan, Inc.
866 Third Avenue, New York , N.Y. 10022

Collier Macmillan Canada, Inc.

Library of Congress Catalog Card Number: 83-811

Printed in the United States of America

printing number
1 2 3 4 5 6 7 8 9 10

Library of Congress Cataloging in Publication Data
Main entry under title:

Encyclopedia of American forest and conservation history.

Includes index.
1. Forests and forestry—United States—History—
Dictionaries.   2. Forest conservation—United States—
History—Dictionaries.   I. Davis, Richard, C., 1939–
SD143.E53   1983   333.75′0973   83-811
ISBN 0-02-907350-2 (set)
ISBN 0-02-907750-8 (v. 1)
ISBN 0-02-907770-2 (v. 2)

We gratefully acknowledge the use of several tables, as specified in the text.

The preparation of this volume was made possible in part by a grant from the Program for Research Tools and Reference Works of the National Endowment for the Humanities, an independent federal agency.

The Forest History Society is a nonprofit, educational institution dedicated to the advancement of historical understanding of man's interaction with the North American forest environment. It was established in 1946. Interpretations and conclusions in FHS publications are those of the authors; the institution takes responsibility for the selection of topics, the competence of the authors, and their freedom of inquiry.

Editorial and Production Staff

Charles E. Smith, *Publisher*
Elly Dickason, *Project Editor*
Morton I. Rosenberg, *Production Manager*
Joan Greenfield, *Designer*

Contents

List of Articles

Preface

The goal in compiling the *Encyclopedia of American Forest and Conservation History* has been to produce the standard, authoritative guide and reference to the history of forestry, conservation, forest industries, and other forest-related subjects in the United States. We trust that the first encyclopedia for this field of knowledge will be the single most useful reference tool on the desks or bookshelves of practitioners in the field, and that persons in forest-related professions and occupations will make frequent use of it in any pursuits that contain a historical dimension. Needless to say, high school and college libraries will want to add the *Encyclopedia* to their collections.

Forest resources and forest industries have been vital to America's economic, social, and cultural development since the earliest English settlers along the eastern seaboard sent home cargoes of timber and forest products. Throughout the colonial period—from the oldest centers of habitation to the cutting edge of the westward moving frontier—woodlands were the dominant feature of the American landscape. Forest bounty was instrumental in shaping American institutions—although in earlier times such resources seemed limitless and were largely taken for granted. Grievances arising from British forest policy coalesced with other complaints to produce a revolutionary spirit culminating in independence and nationhood.

Through subsequent periods in American history, forest resources (including timber, range, wildlife, and watershed) played even more conspicuous roles in national development, providing necessary ingredients for industrial growth and strategic materials in time of war. Toward the end of America's wooden age, about a century ago, fear of "timber famine," wildlife extinction, and other resource shortages combined with a growing appreciation of the nation's natural heritage to prompt new attitudes toward the forest, leading to the growth of forestry as a science and a profession, to public management and protection of vast forest tracts in the West and later in the East, and to a new spirit of

xxv

cooperation among forest industries, which today stake their future on the careful management and renewability of such resources. In recent decades, popular interest in ecology, environmental quality, outdoor recreation, and the preservation of scenery and wilderness has added a broader dimension to the American experience, which is still being shaped by its forests. New issues, perspectives, and competitions have complicated a once fairly simple story of people's economic utilization of natural resources.

The outlines of this forest inheritance are well known to scholars and interested laymen through dozens of general works and monographs of varying quality. The *Encyclopedia* will not supplant this literature. Rather, it aims both to deepen and to broaden the user's knowledge of the field by presentation of incisive and authoritative articles on every topic of significance to the American forest heritage. These articles are supplemented by bibliographies, statistical material, and appendices.

This historical encyclopedia is the work of historians, foresters, and subject specialists from many fields. Some authors are eminent scholars, others are experienced practitioners who have written about their career specialties. All authors were selected because of their ability to write authoritatively within carefully designed guidelines about specific topics.

The articles themselves were prepared expressly for the *Encyclopedia;* no reprints of earlier works are included. These articles range in length from several hundred to several thousand words and provide useful summaries of hundreds of topics of value to the specialist needing to check a fact, as well as the layman who seeks an introductory look at a subject. The articles are both factual and interpretive; that is, authors were asked to do more than describe the history of their specialty by including commentary and insights on significant facts.

Determination of article length provided an opportunity for bias to appear, for judgments on importance are subjective, indeed. Decisions on topics to include or exclude also tested objectivity. Advice on both matters was received from the *Encyclopedia's* Advisory Board and a long list of colleagues. Also, authors frequently convinced us that their assignment deserved more space or was better divided into two articles. Ultimately, however, it is the staff that must accept credit or blame for content and scope.

Major articles have been signed by their authors, who are listed in the Directory of Contributors. Their listed affiliation usually pertains to the position held at the time the article was written; in the case of retirees, the primary employers during active years are shown. The generally briefer articles without signatures were prepared by Forest History Society staff and consultants. Wherever possible, references for further reading have been included.

The articles are arranged in alphabetical order with suitable cross-references and so-called blind entries. For example, users interested in Forest Entomology will find the article alphabetized under forest but with an additional entry under Entomology *see* Forest Entomology. Within each article, other main entries appear in small capital letters; for example, in the article on the U. S. Forest Service, Gifford PINCHOT and the MULTIPLE USE-SUSTAINED YIELD ACT appear in small capitals to indicate that there is a separate article on each of these topics. In addition, the Index serves as a guide to the myriad topics within the *Encyclopedia* as well as to many topical and conceptual ideas.

The photographs were selected from the Forest History Society Media Archives. This invaluable collection derives from many sources, principally the American Forest Institute, the U. S. Forest Service, and the Weyerhaeuser Company. Although the Society has the right to use freely and to make available to others all photographs in its collection, regardless of source, credit has usually been given to the originating institution.

Many reference works were consulted as part of the editorial process. Invaluable were Elbert L. Little, Jr., *Checklist of United States Trees*, USDA Handbook No. 541 (1979), for common and scientific names of trees; Henry B. Steer, *Lumber Production in the United States, 1799–1946*, USDA Misc. Bull. No. 669 (1948); and *Statistical Abstracts of the United States* (1979). The American Forest Products Industries, now American Forest Institute, published *Forest Facts*, a series of booklets treating important lumber-producing states. The U. S. Forest Service has produced an immense forestry literature; especially valuable are its Resource Bulletins. Two other frequently consulted books were Samuel T. Dana, *Forest and Range Policy* (1956), and Ralph K. Widner, ed., *Forests and Forestry in the United States* (1968). *North American Forest and Conservation History: A Bibliography* (1977) by Ronald J. Fahl is the single most important bibliography for the field.

The five appendices contain valuable statistical, tabular, and cartographic information. Appendix I shows the establishment, change of name, or discontinuation of every forest reserve and national forest created since 1891, including the legal citation for each action. Appendix II provides similar information for the national parks. Appendix III is a chronological list of all federal statutes mentioned in any of the articles and includes date of enactment, U. S. Statute at Large number, official and common name, if any, and a brief description of the law's intent. Appendix IV is a chart showing the heads of the three dominant natural resource agencies—U. S. Forest Service, National Park Service, and Bureau of Land Management—in the context of the cabinet officers under whom they served and also by presidential administrations.

Appendix V is a historical atlas containing eighteen maps. Beginning with a general representation of the major American ecosystems, the maps become progressively more specific. The final map uses the Tahoe Basin on the California–Nevada border to represent how a complex political overlay, assembled by more than a century of decisions and superimposed over a varied terrain, causes nearly insoluble land management problems.

FOREST HISTORY SOCIETY

Acknowledgments

A project of this scope and complexity obviously required the talents of many. The 203 authors who contributed signed articles are listed in the Directory of Contributors along with their affiliations and the titles of their articles. Forest History Society Research Associate Richard C. Davis for three years served as general editor, which included major responsibilities for article design and author selection.

From its inception, the *Encyclopedia* has benefited from an Advisory Board consisting of William R. Burch, Jr., Marion Clawson, Thomas R. Cox, Susan L. Flader, Peter A. Fritzell, Richard G. Lillard, Oliver H. Orr, Harold T. Pinkett, Norman I. Wengert, Michael Williams, and Herbert I. Winer. In addition to this legion of talent are many who shared their expertise by critiquing article drafts; they are listed below.

Essentially every member of the Forest History Society staff contributed to the Encyclopedia. Executive Director Harold K. Steen and Director of Program Development Ronald J. Fahl were responsible for overall project design; Steen also authored several articles, assembled the atlas, and selected the photographs. Fahl recommended authors and contributed bibliographic suggestions throughout the project. Librarian Mary E. Johnson supplied Davis with reference assistance, authored several articles, compiled Appendices I, II, and III, and assisted with photograph selection. Assistant Editors Lorraine Kashara and Karen Burman edited and proofed the bulk of the articles; Karen Burman also provided major help with the index. Editorial Associate Richard W. Judd reworked many articles and is also an author. Secretary Kaye Ronda and free lancer Ann Bennett typed and retyped the prodigious manuscript. Library Assistants Kathryn A. Fahl and Nancy Marquez tabulated volumes of data. Finally, consultant Joseph R. Conlin authored many of the unsigned articles, as well as contributing major articles of his own.

The staff of The Free Press offered firm but patient guidance through the

Encyclopedia's final stages; their professionalism was impressive. Special thanks are due to Charles E. Smith, Claude Conyers, Colin Jones, Elly Dickason, and David Biesel.

Major financial support was received from the National Endowment for the Humanities, grant #RT-0053-79-735. Other generous supporters included the American Conservation Association, the Laird, Norton Foundation, Macmillan Publishing Company, Dr. and Mrs. William T. Weyerhaeuser, and the Forest History Society Publications Fund.

Reviewers

Lester E. Anderson, Thomas F. Armstrong, John W. Barry, H. Arnold Barton, Alfred X. Baxter, M. Gary Bettis, Larry Biles, Kenneth O. Bjork, Nelson M. Blake, W. S. Bromley, Arthur A. Brown, Ronald Brown, David Bruce, Marlin H. Bruner, Robert E. Buckman, Erwin Bulgrin, Roy M. Carter, Craig C. Chandler, Charles E. Clark, Norman H. Clark, Robert F. Collins, William K. Condrell, Thomas C. Croker, Jr., Clifford H. Cunningham, Richard Drake, John Drew, Wilmon H. Droze, John A. Eisterhold, Ivan M. Elchibegoff, Paul W. Gates, William Gove, Calvin Gower, Frank Graham, Jr., Robert D. Graham, W. D. Hagenstein, H. Duane Hampton, W. M. Hearan, Richard W. Hemingway, Robert L. Herbst, G. Melvin Herndon, Nollie Hickman, Willard Hurst, W. H. Hutchinson, Donald Hutslar, Wilbur R. Jacobs, David James, George M. Jemison, Charles Johnson, Holway R. Jones, Bruce Kilgore, William F. Kimes, Fred B. Kniffen, Peter Koch, Edward W. Kuenzi, Fred Lape, Kenneth W. Laub, Richard G. Lillard, Raymond E. Lindgren, Elbert L. Little, Jr., Thomas A. Lund, Thomas K. McGraw, John N. McGovern, Donald MacKay, Franklin D. Mahar, Michael Malone, Ervin Mancil, Thomas G. Manning, Louis G. May, Sharon R. Miller, Mark E. Neithercut, Richard C. Nordholm, David D. Olson, Sherry H. Olson, John R. Osgood, Alexis J. Panshin, Charles S. Peterson, Virgil Peterson, Clinton Phillips, Paul Pitsenbarger, A. Earl Plourde, Richard Polenberg, Boyd L. Rasmussen, Elmo Richardson, John W. Rowe, J. C. Ryan, Henry Savage, Jr., Edmund A. Schofield, Michael Sherwood, Frank E. Smith, George R. Staebler, Wallace Stegner, Ronald L. Stuckey, Raymond F. Taylor, Roger C. Thompson, Robert M. Utley, Linda D. Vance, Frank B. Vinson, J. V. K. Wagar, Norman I. Wengert, Philip L. White, Herbert I. Winer, Robin W. Winks, Neil Wissing, Donald E. Worster, Walker D. Wyman, Graeme Wynn, Otis E. Young, Heber W. Youngken, Jr., Robert L. Youngs, Duane F. Zinkel.

Encyclopedia of

American Forest and Conservation History

ADIRONDACK PARK

New York State's Adirondack Park contains approximately 6 million acres of private and public land which, since 1973, has been subject to rigorous land use control. Approximately 38 percent of the park consists of NEW YORK STATE FOREST PRESERVE lands which are protected under a provision of the state constitution; the balance of land in the park is privately held in ownerships ranging from small lots to holdings of over 100,000 acres. The Adirondack Park encompasses the entirety of Hamilton and Essex counties and portions of ten other northern counties of New York State.

The Adirondack Park was originally created by law in 1892 to "be forever reserved, maintained and cared for as ground open for the free use of all people for their health and pleasure, and as forest lands necessary to the preservation of the headwaters of the chief rivers of the State, and a future timber supply." The park was delineated on certain state maps by a blue line which encompassed a total area of 2,807,760 acres, only 551,093 acres of which consisted of state-owned lands. Technically, only the state holdings within the designated area constituted the park. In 1893, the islands of Lake George, lying outside of the original blue line, were added to the park.

The park boundary was enlarged in 1912 to encompass 4,054,000 acres; at the same time, all of these lands, both public and private holdings, were legally recognized as forming the Adirondack Park.

Until the creation of a land use planning and regulatory body, the Adirondack Park Agency, in 1971, the Adirondack Park constituted little more than an expression of legislative intent relative to a large block of land in northern New York. Although the park provided a locus for the concentration of state acquisition efforts in building up the forest preserve, few laws or regulations governed the character of the park in any positive way. A significant exception was the passage of a so-called signboard law in 1924. This was designed to conserve "the natural beauty of the Adirondack Park" by requiring that, except in special circumstances and within incorporated villages, signs or billboards within the Adirondack Park not be erected on premises other than those upon which a business was actually conducted. This law survived a test of constitutionality in 1940.

In 1931, the Adirondack Park was again enlarged, this time to 5.6 million acres, including much of the western shoreline of Lake Champlain and the entirety of Lake George. An additional 93,500 acres of land, most of it to the north, were added to the park in 1956, and in 1972 a further expansion of the boundary brought in the balance of Essex County, more of Lake Champlain to the east, and all of Valcour Island.

The genesis of a more positive character for the Adirondack Park lay in a 1967 proposal by Laurance S. ROCKEFELLER and associates to form an Adirondack Mountains National Park from approximately 1.7 million acres of land in the central Adirondacks. The concept was vehemently rejected by a broad range of interest groups and led to the appointment of the Temporary Study Commission on the Future of the Adirondacks by Governor Nelson A. Rockefeller in the fall of 1968. Two years later, the commission, under the chairmanship of Harold K. Hochschild, submitted 181 recommendations to the governor, the most important of which called for the creation of a planning and regulatory agency to insure the future integrity of the Adirondack Park.

The Adirondack Park Agency was created by law in 1971; it was given interim private land use controls and was charged with devising a series of plans for future use of the park. In 1972, the agency prepared a state land master plan which the governor approved; that same year, significant portions of Adirondack waterways became the first elements in a new state wild, scenic, and recreational rivers system. The following year, the agency submitted a comprehensive private land use and development plan to the New York State Legislature, which approved it, following considerable debate and amendment.

In its entirety, the Adirondack Park is larger than the combined acreage of the two largest national parks in the United States, but, to a greater extent than most parks, it attempts to incorporate both public and private holdings in a comprehensive planning program. The Adirondack Park encompasses not only the vast majority of New York State Forest Preserve lands but also a permanent population in excess of 100,000, and over 100 units of local government.

FURTHER READING: Frank Graham, Jr., *The Adirondack Park: A Political History* (1978).

WILLIAM K. VERNER

AFFORESTATION

In contrast to reforestation, the reestablishment of trees on previously forested lands, afforestation, as here used, is the planting of trees on lands which have not supported tree growth in historical times. Of the 2.27 billion acres of land area in the United States, 33 percent was forested in 1980; in the contiguous forty-eight states, the area of the original forest was estimated at less than 1 billion acres, or about half of the total. East of the Great Plains, only relatively small land areas were never in forest. These include tracts of very shallow, rocky soils such as the glades of the Ozarks, the serpentine barrens of Pennsylvania, and the eastern extension of the prairie-plains grasslands into Minnesota, Iowa, Missouri, and Illinois.

The bulk of previously unforested lands is therefore west of 96 degrees longitude. These lands include a good share of the cropland acreage in the Great Plains and most of the arable grassland and the nonarable nonforest. Thus the possibilities for afforestation in the United States are largely limited to the subhumid-to-arid western areas where past environmental conditions made forest establishment impossible. However, much of this western region is too dry and the soils are too heavy to permit successful tree establishment and growth.

The aim of afforestation is to provide an upper level of vegetation on lands that contain only low vegetation in order to protect soils, crops, humans, and animals from wind and dessication and to transform areas from desolate and often forbidding wasteland into productive and more habitable areas. Although many plantations will serve only protective and aesthetic purposes, they can under favorable conditions produce lumber, fuelwood, pulpwood, fodder, essential oils, and other products.

There are two main types of tree plantations in afforestation: (1) long, narrow strips of trees called windbreaks or SHELTERBELTS, and (2) blocks of trees covering larger areas. Windbreaks or shelterbelts are usually less than 100 feet wide and are mostly planted on or adjacent to agricultural lands to protect soils, crops, people, homes, orchards, livestock, wildlife, and transportation rights-of-way. Such plantings reduce wind velocity and therefore create more favorable environments on their leeward sides. They also beautify the landscape and can screen highway noise.

Blocks of trees and shrubs are planted to stabilize sand dunes, to reclaim strip-mined lands, to stabilize gullied areas, to protect livestock during severe storms, to provide habitat enclaves for wildlife, and to produce wood and other tree products. These blocks also serve as amenity plantings because they improve the landscape of otherwise desolate areas and can often provide areas for recreation, such as camping and picnicking.

Afforestation, even under favorable climatic and soil conditions, requires much more work than planting in forested areas to create the kind of environment that will enable young trees to survive and grow, especially in the first few years. The selection of planting sites is of paramount importance and should concentrate first on the most favorable situa-

Furrows of jackpine planted in Nebraska in 1919 to create a forest. Forest Service Photo.

tions where soil is deepest and has the ability to hold moisture and permit rapid root growth. Sites should be classified by a soil scientist working with the forester, so that the most adverse sites can be avoided.

Most planting sites will need preparation in advance to eradicate competing vegetation and small herbivores and to provide moisture storage. Most of the regions suitable for afforestation in the United States have developed lists of the most suitable species and seed sources for local conditions of climate and soil. Drought hardiness and the ability to withstand excessive wind in addition to temperature extremes are the desirable characteristics in species to be used. In addition, species for moderately alkaline or saline soils must be carefully selected. Selection of the species for northern latitudes of the Great Plains and Great Basin will be slightly different than for the middle or southern latitudes of those regions.

The nearest native species often prove best, although introduced species such as Siberian elm, Siberian pea tree, Russian olive, and Russian mulberry have been highly successful in the Great Plains. Conifers of greatest use are ponderosa pine and the junipers, particularly Rocky Mountain juniper and eastern redcedar, all very drought resistant. Quality of stock also includes the presence of mycorrhizae on root systems to enhance nutrient and moisture uptake. Most afforestation projects need stock with mycorrhizae because most sites in previously nonforested areas do not contain the proper species of fungi for the tree species being planted. For the most adverse sites in afforestation, container-grown planting stock is superior and gives a higher survival, more so than bare-root stock.

Protection of trees from fire, grazing animals, and small mammals, especially rodents, is essential for success in afforestation. Fencing is often needed, and poisoning or trapping rodents is necessary if trees are to survive the first few years. Many decades of experience were needed to learn successful techniques of site preparation, the proper choice of tree and shrub species, the best age and balance of tops to roots of planting stock, planting techniques and equipment, irrigation methods, and the desirable amount of care and control of competing vegetation.

Tree planting on the prairies began in the 1840s

and 1850s with the setting out of Osage-orange hedges by settlers in Ohio and Iowa. By the late 1850s, most of the counties in eastern Kansas and Nebraska had established tree groves and belts. The Nebraska territorial legislature in 1861 enacted the first of a series of laws providing tax relief to landowners who planted trees. ARBOR DAY was begun by the Nebraska State Board of Agriculture in 1872. Railroads crossing the Plains States were keenly interested in encouraging tree planting by settlers and during the late 1870s established a number of demonstration plantations there. Official encouragement for tree planting on the plains came from the GENERAL LAND OFFICE in the 1870s in the hope of improving the climate. Congress enacted the Timber Culture Act in 1873, offering 160 acres of land to any person who would plant and maintain 40 acres in trees over a period of ten years. Although the act was amended several times, it proved technically infeasible for pioneer farmers to undertake widespread plantations successfully, and the act was subject to abuse as it allowed parties to obtain virtual control of the land for at least thirteen years. Trade in relinquishments was brisk. The act was repealed in 1891. Under the Timber Culture Law, 43.5 million acres were entered but only 10.9 million went to patent, mostly in the Dakotas, Nebraska, and Kansas. The contribution to afforestation was meager.

In the 1970s, less than 3 percent of the land in the Great Plains region was in natural forest, around 35 percent was cropland, and the remainder was grassland pasture or range, except for a considerable acreage in cities, towns, and roads and highways. In this region, less than 1 percent of the cultivated land was in field windbreaks or shelterbelts. Planting of these began in 1935 with the Shelterbelt (Prairie States Forestry) Project, which ended in 1942. This practice continued in a gradually decreasing amount until by the 1970s field windbreak plantings constituted a very minor part of ongoing tree-planting efforts. However, there remained an estimated need for ten times the existing mileage of field belts to protect croplands adequately. Much of the region lacking effective windbreak protection is in the far western areas of the Great Plains, where average annual precipitation is fifteen inches or less and the successful establishment of trees is a relatively rare occurrence.

In the grassland areas of the Great Plains, particularly the Nebraska sandhills, block plantations have been used effectively for livestock protection and to control sandy blowouts on the range. The most successful afforestation effort in the United States took place here, beginning in 1891 with experiments on

three acres of private land in Holt County. The U. S. Division of Forestry supplied the trees. The survival of some of these trees encouraged the agency in 1902 to undertake a much larger project near Halsey, Nebraska, which was continued through 1965. Block plantations of ponderosa pine, jack pine, and eastern redcedar covered about 26,000 acres until a devastating lightning fire occurred in the spring of 1965, destroying nearly 16,000 acres of these plantations. Since then, no more block plantings have been made, only sufficient plantings to provide wooded conditions for recreational sites and along roadways.

A smaller afforestation project was begun by the U.S. FOREST SERVICE in 1906 in the southwestern Kansas sandhills, but this effort was terminated in 1915 after failure from drought. In the Denbigh sand dunes areas of North Dakota, the Forest Service also established a small afforestation effort between 1931 and 1941. This project was a success in growing several species of pines and larches, to the extent that sawlogs were harvested from it in the late 1970s.

FURTHER READING: Carlos G. Bates and Roy G. Pierce, *Forestation of the Sand Hills of Nebraska and Kansas* (1913). Wilmon H. Droze, *Trees, Prairies, and People: A History of Tree Planting in the Plains States* (1977). A. Y. Goor and C. W. Barney, *Forest Tree Planting in Arid Zones* (2nd ed., 1976). Raymond J. Pool, "Fifty Years on the Nebraska National Forest," *Nebraska History* 34 (Sept. 1958): 139–179. J. H. Stoeckeler, "Afforestation," in R. N. Kaul, ed., *Afforestation in Arid Zones*, Monographiae Biologicae 20 (1970), pp. 268-346. World Meteorological Organization, *Windbreaks and Shelterbelts* (1964).

RALPH A. READ

AIRCRAFT CONSTRUCTION

Wood has always been a favorite material for aircraft construction, today ranging from use in building replica aircraft and home-built sport airplanes to use in the construction of wind tunnel models for aerodynamic research. Wood continues in use for certain aeronautical equipment, especially laminated propellers for older general aviation aircraft.

Wood was long the most popular material for aircraft construction because of its high strength-to-weight ratio and because of the ease with which it could be worked. Furthermore, in the early twentieth century there was a large number of craftsmen skilled in wood-working. In the 1890s, the German Otto Lilienthal built a number of hang gliders of willow frames covered with linen fabric. American civil engineer Octave Chanute introduced the so-called bridge-truss method to glider construction, favoring

Assembling hull frames for wooden airplane, 1943. American Forest Institute Photo.

the use of airfoil-shaped ribs attached to spruce spars running from wing tip to wing tip. The Wright brothers utilized the excellent flexural property of wooden structures to incorporate the principle of "wing warping" to give their machines adequate lateral (rolling) control.

By 1909, the general configuration of the modern airplane had been established: it consisted of an externally braced monoplane or biplane having a wooden frame braced with wires to withstand flight loads. The structure made extensive use of glued joints, steel brackets, and plywood gussets and external coverings, with doped linen or muslin fabric covering. Major structural elements, such as wing spars and fuselage longerons, were usually fabricated from spruce, but ash was also popular for wing ribs and engine mounts. In America, some designers—notably Glenn Curtis—used bamboo for tailbooms. Propellers were often laminated and carved from walnut. Wooden aircraft require considerable care to maintain flight-worthy condition, another factor that mitigated against their general longevity.

A major development was the employment of so-called monocoque (single-shell) stressed-skin construction, first advocated by the Swiss engineer Ruchonnet in 1911 and first applied to aircraft by the French designer Louis Bechereau in the Deperduissin series of racers (1912–1913). These aircraft featured a hickory frame over which a three-layer skin of tulip-

wood was attached by pins and glue. A thin cloth stiffener was laid over each layer of tulipwood. The result was a surprisingly light yet very rugged structure that endowed the aircraft both with a smooth external shape and a large and unobstructed internal area. It was, however, expensive and time-consuming to create and was not widely employed, though this concept influenced the development of the all-metal monocoque airplane when designers replaced wood with metal. During World War I, wooden monocoque aircraft (such as the German *Albatros* fighter) appeared, as did wooden cantilever wing construction.

The ability of military aircraft of the 1920s to achieve relatively high maneuvering loads resulted in designers favoring fabric-covered metal structures and later, in the 1930s, all, or nearly all, metal-built aircraft. Thereafter, wood as a primary structural material for aircraft disappeared rapidly. In part, this was due to the Allied experience in World War I. Britain, for example, had found wood demands too great for her industry and after the war asked aircraft design teams essentially to redesign their wooden aircraft as metal ones. Wood also was a fire hazard, particularly on aircraft of the day with its heavily doped and varnished structure. Wood was prone to severe damage and deterioration from the elements and from insects and other pests. The availability of aluminum, with its excellent load-bearing characteristics, spurred further the trend toward the all-metal air-

Craftsmen at the Forest Products Laboratory in Madison, Wisconsin, study wooden propeller design during World War I. Forest Service Photo.

plane. This trend enjoyed great public support following the death in 1931 of Knute Rockne in the crash of a wooden-winged transport that had experienced structural failure.

Nevertheless, wood continued to make an appearance on certain advanced aircraft, notably the 1927 Lockheed Vega, which reintroduced the European monocoque tradition for both wood and metal aircraft, the 1935 Hughes H-1 racer, which used mixed wood and metal construction, and the excellent De Havilland Mosquito fighter-bomber of World War II. Perhaps the greatest example of the woodworker's craft in the history of aviation technology was the immense Hughes-Kaiser HK-1 Flying Boat, an eight-engine seaplane more popularly known as the "Spruce Goose," although its structure was in fact largely birch. The HK-1, although it completed only one brief flight, brought the state of wooden aircraft construction to a very high art. However, it remains a historical curiosity—indeed, its failure to win acceptance was due, in part, to the use of wood and not metal in its construction.

There have been other aircraft, including some turbojet-driven airplanes, that have made use of wood, primarily as a surface covering material. Methods of bonding have changed dramatically, from animal-base glues to epoxy and composite bonding substances. Nevertheless, by the 1980s, wooden aircraft were anachronistic and outside the mainstream of major technical development.

RICHARD P. HALLION

AIR POLLUTION AND FORESTS

Forests act as both sources and sinks of air pollution. As a source, a forest may produce visible smoke from fires; however, such events are relatively sporadic and short-lived sources of pollutants. Forests also are a continuing source of evaporation of mostly invisible pollution consisting of hydrocarbon compounds from leaf and stem tissues. The bluish-gray haze observed over humid southeastern forests often is the result of scattering of light by submicroscopic aerosol particles formed by photooxidation of these evaporated terpenes and subsequent polymerization of the oxidized molecules.

As a sink, forests absorb suspended particles (condensation nuclei, made up of hygroscopic substances) from the atmosphere. Scientists studying in the Black Hills of South Dakota have concluded that the forest vegetation participates in the reduction of Aitken particle (with radii less than 0.1 microns) concentrations by as much as 50 percent compared to the atmosphere of the adjacent prairie. This is the so-called green area filtration effect. The use of trees as screens against toxic particulate and gaseous pollutants has been widely advocated, although the health of many tree species declines as pollutant concentrations or exposure times increase. The major air pollutants causing damage to forest species are ozone, sulfur dioxide, hydrogen fluoride, and particulates. This list is in order of decreasing importance with respect to areal extent of adverse effects that may be expected to result from particular incidents of pollution.

Ozone is formed in the atmosphere by a complex series of reactions between nitrogen dioxide (NO2) and hydrocarbons, driven by ultraviolet light. The NO2 originates from any combustion process; the hydrocarbons are typically derived from gasoline and its combustion products. Injurious concentrations of NO2 and peroxyacetyl nitrate (PAN) are present with ozone in smog, but injury directly attributable to NO2 or PAN is rarely confirmed on forest species under field conditions. Air masses with concentrations of ozone high enough to cause injury to trees can be transported as much as seventy miles from the source area in a single day; several consecutive days of air stagnation can result in ozone buildups encompassing several states. The other major pollutant gases, typically emitted from point sources, are less likely to cause such widespread damage. Sulfur dioxide derives from sources such as coal and oil-burning power plants and metal smelters or ore-roasting facilities. Hydrogen fluoride is emitted mainly from aluminum reduction plants, phosphate fertilizer plants, and brick kilns. Particulate pollutants, such as cement dust, are dispersed over shorter distances than gases.

Occasional damage is caused by hydrogen chloride, chlorine, and ammonia. (Hydrogen chloride results from the burning of any chlorine-containing organic compounds, such as vinyl chloride; chlorine and ammonia may be released when storage tanks are ruptured.) Injury from these pollutants can be devastating, but the affected area is usually small.

Acid rain, resulting mainly from atmospheric transformations of sulfur oxides into sulfuric acid, has aroused widespread concern. In recent years, rainfall has become more acidic over extensive areas of the northeastern United States, Canada, and northern Europe. As the acidity of lake and stream waters has increased, fisheries have been eliminated. There has been no definite demonstration of effects of acid rain on terrestrial plants and animals, however.

The responses of tree species and tree communities to pollutants are historically documented in the United States. For example, damage over a period of years from sulfur dioxide (mainly originating from copper smelters) has occurred near Copper Basin, Tennessee, beginning in 1865; Kellogg, Idaho, since 1890; Redding, California, since 1903; Anaconda, Montana, since 1884; and Trail, British Columbia, since 1896. Smog pollution continues at Copper Basin and Kellogg, and some emission control strategies have been implemented. In 1980, the closure of the Anaconda smelter was announced in part because of the huge investment that would have been required for air pollution control equipment. Damage from hydrogen fluoride was noted near Spokane, Washington, about 1943, and at Columbia Falls, Montana, beginning around 1955. Long-term damage from smelter fumes is illustrated near Redding, California, where the Kennett smelter ceased operation in 1919 after killing the pine, oak, Douglas-fir, and other plant cover on over 100 square miles of surrounding mountainsides. When this watershed became of particular value thirty years later with the construction of Shasta and Keswick dams, extensive reforestation projects were undertaken on the eroding, still-barren hillsides in order to protect the reservoirs from siltation.

Examples of ozone-caused damage are the emergence tipburn and chlorotic dwarf diseases of eastern white pine (*Pinus strobus*). Emergence tipburn (dieback of emerging needles, observed throughout the range of eastern white pine) was first described in 1908, but ozone was not identified as the probable cause until the early 1960s. A combination of low concentrations of both ozone and sulfur dioxide are believed to result in the chlorotic dwarf disease of eastern white pine.

Another example of ozone damage is the X-disease of chlorotic decline of ponderosa pine (*P. ponderosa*), observed about 1956 in the San Bernardino National Forest east of Los Angeles. By the early 1970s, ozone was identified as the cause. Damage to companion species is recognized as well. Such ozone damage is now found in four other California national forests as well as in the SEQUOIA AND KINGS CANYON NATIONAL PARKS. Ozone effects in the San Bernardino National Forest include decreases of ponderosa stem growth ranging up to 40 percent and significant growth loss by white fir (*Abies concolor*) and California black oak (*Quercus kelloggii*). The mortality rate of ponderosa pine in severely damaged areas has increased up to four times, because weakened trees are killed by bark beetles. The most severely damaged pine trees produce fewer cones, and there is greater accumulation of leaf litter beneath these trees; both factors tend to inhibit seedling establishment. There is evidence that the course of forest succession will lead to species mixtures that are less fire tolerant.

The pattern and areal extent of injury observed has led to some general conclusions. Injury around point sources of pollution, as at Anaconda, Montana, usually results in a concentric pattern of high, intermediate, and low pollutant dose effects, moving from the source outward. Mountain terrain has a strong influence on the shape of the concentric zones of injury. For example, from Trail, British Columbia, tree damage extended fifty-two miles southward along the course of the

Columbia River. The width of the damaged area varied from one and one-half to ten miles, depending on the topography of the valley and tributary drainages. The extent of injury is 226,000 acres at Anaconda, 120,000 acres at Kellogg, Idaho, and up to 14,000 acres at Columbia Falls, Montana.

The urban sources of oxidant air pollution in California affect about 140,000 acres in two southern California national forests and as much as 1,500,000 acres in the Sequoia and Sierra national forests and Sequoia and Kings Canyon national parks. In both the northeastern and southeastern states, entire regions of forested land may be subject to adverse concentrations of oxidant air pollution, judging from reports of injury to eastern white pine and other sensitive species. Ozone effects on sensitive species have increased, particularly in the Blue Ridge Mountains of Virginia, as emissions from the eastern metropolitan corridor have increased.

Interdisciplinary studies view primary and secondary effects of pollutant damage in the context of ecological systems and seek to identify vulnerable connections in the systems. Simulation models can help predict the long-range effects of chronic pollutant damage. With greater understanding, tree improvement projects and silvicultural prescriptions may be helpful in ameliorating some effects of chronic pollutant exposure. However, Canadian experience at Sudbury, Ontario, where sulfur dioxide has caused extensive damage, shows that it is very expensive and sometimes impossible to restore a satisfactory forest cover.

Air pollution was legally of only local and state concern until passage of the federal Clean Air Act of 1963. Legislation of 1967 and 1970 changed the emphasis from standards based on the sources of emissions to standards based on concentrations of pollutants in the atmosphere. In 1970, federal jurisdiction over air pollution control programs passed from the Department of Health, Education, and Welfare to the Environmental Protection Agency. Subsequent legislation, reflecting a concern for energy conservation, has tended to relax emission control requirements.

FURTHER READING: T. T. Kozlowski, "Impacts of Air Pollution on Forest Ecosystems," *Bioscience* 30 (Feb. 1980): 88-93. P. R. Miller and J. R. McBride, "Effects of Air Pollutants on Forests," in J. B. Mudd and T. T. Kozlowski, eds., *Responses of Plants to Air Pollution* (1975). G. Scurfield, "Air Pollution and Tree Growth," *Forestry Abstracts* 21 (July 1960): 339-347, 21 (Oct. 1960): 517-528. D. C. West, S. G. McLaughlin, and H. H. Shugart, "Simulated Forest Response to Chronic Air Pollution Stress," *Journal of Environmental Quality* 9 (Jan. 1980): 43-49.

PAUL R. MILLER

ALABAMA FORESTS

When large-scale lumbering operations began in Alabama in the 1880s, an expansive forest covered 80 percent of the state's 33,029,760 acres. Primarily the forest consisted of pine trees, but there were also immense stands of oak, hickory, and other hardwoods.

Alabama's forests are divided into ten regions that correspond to both physical geography and tree type dominance. The coastal pine belt along the southern part of the state yields longleaf pine and was the state's first center of forestry activity. The central pine belt of loblolly and shortleaf extends from the Georgia boundary to Mississippi and lies just above the fertile Black Belt region of the state. The coal region of north-central Alabama is also a section where pine predominates.

Hardwood forests are found in the state's two most fertile areas, the Black Belt of central Alabama and the Tennessee Valley of north Alabama. The hardwood trees found there include oak, yellow-poplar, sweet and tupelo gum, cottonwood, magnolia, and hickory. The remaining regions of Alabama are mixed forests of pine and hardwoods.

In 1778, botanist and explorer William BARTRAM traveled through the eastern and southern portions of what would later become the state of Alabama. Bartram noted vast groves of pine trees that were being utilized for the production of pitch near the port city of Mobile. He referred frequently to forests of dogwoods and other hardwoods that he observed as he traveled northeast toward Georgia.

Despite such natural resources, a lumber industry in Alabama was practically nonexistent before 1860. The farmers, who comprised a large portion of the population, viewed the forests as an obstacle to be overcome while clearing fields and pastureland. The small amount of lumber cut for export was located necessarily near navigable streams that flowed south to Mobile, where the wood was shipped to market. The primitive road system in the state at that time prohibited overland transportation.

Following the Civil War, commercial interest in the Alabama forests increased for several reasons. The timberlands of the Northeast and Great Lakes areas, which had supported the lumber industry for so long, were diminishing, and new forest resources were needed to sustain production. Alabama was in need of economic assistance and many state officials were eager to attract industry. To an extractive industry such as forestry, Alabama's low property taxes were appealing. Finally, Alabama had a large labor force that was accustomed to rigorous work. Labor was also inexpensive and unorganized, which further enhanced its attraction to lumber interests.

NAVAL STORES production constituted the first great forest industry in Alabama, peaking about the mid-1870s. In 1880, the state exported 497,456 barrels of turpentine and rosin, and 3,630,009 gallons of spirits of turpentine. By the 1950s, only about 20 percent as much turpentine and rosin was being produced each year as had been supplied seventy years earlier.

During the 1880s, the lumber industry was entrenched in Alabama. The harvesting technique consisted of stripping the valuable timber from the land and then moving the entire operation to the next site. In certain cases, lumber companies provided housing for their employees in the form of railroad boxcars so that moving was made easier. The clearcutting technique left the land ravaged and open to the destructive natural forces of wind and water. It was these methods, though, that allowed Alabama lumbermen to become leading producers of American lumber in the early twentieth century.

The state's reported annual lumber production passed 1 billion board feet in 1899 and reached its peak of 2,235,738,000 feet in 1925. Southern yellow pine accounted for nearly 91 percent of that figure, and Alabama ranked fifth among the states as a lumber producer. Lumber output declined during the Depression and did not again touch 2 billion board feet until World War II.

In 1907, the Alabama legislature created the State Forestry Commission in response to public concern over the wanton destruction of forests for commercial purposes. The commission encouraged landowners to replant trees on their cutover land. Poorly funded, the commission had little power. Six of the seven members were public officials who tended to be preoccupied with their other duties.

Not until 1923 did the legislature take positive steps toward sound forest management and conservation. The amended law set qualifications for members of the commission, provided for a professionally trained state forester, and levied a license fee on the forest industry. The funds derived from licensing gave the commission more ability to plan and execute its programs.

In 1927, the legislature authorized the forestry commission to conduct a survey to locate the best sites for a system of state parks. Three years later,

the first of twenty-one state parks was established. The state park system offers different features at each park, ranging from mountainous terrain in the north to coastal fishing and swimming in the south. The construction of facilities at many of the parks was done by the CIVILIAN CONSERVATION CORPS, which established work camps at each of the park sites in the 1930s. In 1980, the parks ranged in size from less than 100 acres to more than 10,000.

The Alabama National Forest was established in 1918 from lands purchased under the WEEKS ACT, as were the Talladega and Conecuh national forests in 1936. The Alabama became the Black Warrior in 1936 and received its present name, the Bankhead, in 1942. In 1959, another unit, the Tuskegee National Forest, was established on submarginal farmlands acquired for reforestation under the Bankhead-Jones Act. In 1980, the four national forests in the state totaled 635,000 acres. Eight state forests in Alabama covered over 14,000 acres at that time.

Forestry education in Alabama has been offered since 1945 at Alabama Polytechnic Institute (now called Auburn University).

FURTHER READING: Roland Harper, "The Forest Regions of Alabama," *Southern Lumberman* (Apr. 5, 1913). Richard Massey, Jr., "A History of the Lumber Industry in Alabama and West Florida, 1880–1914," Ph.D. dissertation, Vanderbilt University (1960).

DOWE LITTLETON
WAYNE FLYNT

ALASKA FORESTS

The forests of Alaska, which in 1977 covered 120 million acres or 33 percent of the state, form two natural divisions separated by the St. Elias and Chugach mountains in southeastern Alaska.

The coastal forest of 13 million acres (5.7 million ranked as having commercial value) receives heavy precipitation and has a relatively mild climate. The major forest trees are western hemlock and Sitka spruce. Western redcedar and Alaska yellow-cedar are also found, with mountain hemlock in some areas, particularly toward the north. Other species include silver fir, alpine fir, and alder. The relief is rugged, and the heavily timbered area extends up the mountain slopes to an elevation of 1,500 to 2,000 feet, with some lodgepole pine and mountain hemlock in the muskeg areas of the higher elevations. The lush forest supports a rich understory of shrubs such as huckleberry, thimbleberry, and the aptly named devilsclub.

The interior forest of 106 million acres (22 million with commercial value) varies in density from fairly heavily timbered streambeds to more sparsely wooded benchlands and uplands. It is a mosaic of forest types created by a variety of soils, the presence or absence of permafrost, and fire. Timber of commercial size, including aspen, cottonwood, balsam poplar, paper birch, black spruce, and white spruce, is found in the valleys of the Susitna, Yenta, Tanana, Yukon, and Kuskokwim rivers and on nearby benchlands.

Aboriginal use of the forests in the coastal area differed from the interior. On the coast, the presence of abundant food gave the Haida, Tlingit, and Chilkat Indians opportunity to cultivate the arts. Exploiting the abundant growth of western redcedar, these tribes developed a unique wooden civilization. With cedar planks they built community houses of post and lintel construction; they carved totem poles from cedar, made boxes of wood sewn together with spruce roots, and made huge seagoing canoes of cedar trunks. In the interior, the Athabascan Indians used the products of the forest for shelter and fuel. The forests were shaped, however, by fire, caused either by lightning or by the Indians who used it for signaling, hunting, clearing land, gumming canoes, dividing trunks for rafting, combating insect pests, and entertainment.

Although the Russians used some timber for construction purposes and shipbuilding, there was little commercial forest utilization in the nineteenth century. Even after the American purchase in 1867, the lumber industry languished because of distance from markets, competition from the Puget Sound area, and the difficulty of the Alaskan terrain. Hand logging methods predominated. Logs were simply felled on the steep slopes (often directly into the water) and rafted full-length to the mills. In 1889, the territory produced only 6.5 million board feet of timber, and as late at 1902 only three steam donkey engines were being used to haul logs in southeastern Alaska.

The industry developed slowly in the twentieth century, initially concentrating on high-grade spruce in the densely timbered coastal area. By 1919, Alaskan mills sawed 21.6 million board feet annually. Production for the interwar years peaked in 1922 at 56.8 million board feet. During the 1930s, lumbermen cut hemlock, western redcedar, and Alaska yellow-cedar, in addition to spruce. About 20 percent of the state's lumber production met local needs for fish-trap piling, wharf piling, packing cases, barrels, mine timbers, and railroad ties. The rest, particularly the hemlock, was used for local construction, with small amounts exported from the territory. In the interior, wood was used mainly for heating and as fuel for riverboats. Until World War II, wood was processed by small, scattered sawmills and shinglemills.

Beginning in 1913, the U. S. FOREST SERVICE made a number of unsuccessful attempts to encourage pulpwood manufacture in the territory's overaged forests; the first large mill was not established until after World War II. During the war, Sitka spruce was logged and rafted to the Puget Sound area to be manufactured into British bombers. This operation prompted new interest in Alaskan forests and led to the establishment of the Ketchikan Pulp Company in 1954. Later in the decade, the Department of State, fearing that Japan would turn to Siberia for timber to rebuild its cities, worked with the Forest Service to encourage Japanese investment in Alaskan mills. As a result, mills were established at Sitka to produce pulp and at Wrangell to produce hemlock cants.

Despite a harvest that increased from 285 million board feet of timber in 1959 to 581 million board feet in 1969, Alaska's state and federal forestlands were producing well below their capacity in the 1960s. In the southeastern region, 90 percent of the commercial forest consisted of overmature, uneven-aged hemlock and Sitka spruce, and only 5 percent supported evenaged young growth produced by earlier logging.

The first step toward forest protection in Alaska came with the establishment of the small Afognak Forest and Fish Culture Reserve on Afognak Island, proclaimed by President Benjamin Harrison in 1892. The Alexander Archipelago Forest Reserve, consisting of 4.5 million acres on islands off the coast of southeastern Alaska, was created by President Theodore ROOSEVELT in 1902. Gifford PINCHOT, head of the Bureau of Forestry, sent William A. Langille to examine the new forest and to make a reconnaissance of other Alaskan regions. Langille's 1904 report, the first detailed scientific examination of the Alaskan forests, resulted in creation of the Chugach and Tongass national forests between 1907 and 1909. The two forests, covering about 26.7 million acres along the southeastern coast and including the earlier Afognak and Alexander reserves, extended over 1,000 miles from Dixon Entrance to Cook Inlet. Later they were considerably reduced in area, particularly by the elimination of 5.7 million acres of untimbered land from the Chugach in 1915.

The small Forest Service staff in Alaska managed timber harvests for the local market and encouraged some export trade. Protection of fish, game, and Alaskan antiquities was a high priority. The Forest Service designed cutting practices that would protect salmon runs and undertook research of Alaskan big

Experimental block-cutting on Prince of Wales Island near the Hollis camp of the Ketchikan Pulp & Paper Company, 1958. Forest Service Photo.

game species. The Sitka and Old Kasaan national monuments were created in 1910 and 1916 to protect Indian relics. In the 1930s, the CIVILIAN CONSERVATION CORPS built truck roads, trails, and shelter cabins in the national forests, fought fires, and restored and preserved totem poles and community houses. Fire control in the interior forests, recommended by Langille in 1904, began in 1939 with the creation of the Alaska Fire Control Service under the GENERAL LAND OFFICE. Before that year, approximately 5 to 8 million acres of the interior forest burned annually. Working together with Regional Forester B. Frank Heintzleman, the DEPARTMENT OF THE INTERIOR created a fire-fighting program based on the use of airplanes. By 1946, the average annual burn in the interior forests was less than 1 million acres.

In the lower forty-eight states, public land policy has followed the conventional stages of disposal, in which land was sold or given away to individuals, corporations, or states; reservation, in which selected lands were retained for public use as national parks, forests, or wildlife refuges; custodial management, in which these lands were given minimal protection against fire and trespass; and intensive management, in which the lands were brought to full productivity or classified for special use. In Alaska, the stages of management came in a different order. Reservation of public lands took place first, followed by custodial management, which continued until after World War II. Then came a shift to intensive management brought about partly by the coming of large mills to Alaska, partly by an increase in population, and partly by new federal legislation.

Intensive management was accompanied by disposal of lands to the state and to native corporations and was followed by the latest phase: new reservations.

Intensive management by the Forest Service began in the 1950s, prompted by increases in lumber and pulp and paper production. The Alaskan Forest Research Station was established with headquarters at Juneau, field offices at Hollis, and later a branch on the campuses of the University of Alaska in Fairbanks and Anchorage. Under Raymond F. Taylor, the station began studies on reseeding in clearcuts and on the effects of logging on salmon runs. In cooperation with other state and federal agencies, studies were made of the impact of mill waste on water quality and the marine habitat. Increased tourism led to efforts to regulate cutting, so that it would not be visible from cruise ships.

Alaskan statehood in 1959 brought about changes in timberland ownership patterns. Previously, 99 percent of Alaska had been owned by the federal government —80 percent of the federal lands under the administration of the BUREAU OF LAND MANAGEMENT and the rest in national parks, monuments, preserves, and forests. The new state received a grant of 103 million acres of vacant and undesignated land, to be selected over a period of twenty-five years. The Alaska Department of Natural Resources was set up to manage state lands, and the process of selection began. By 1968, 26 million acres had been transferred to the state; some of this land was taken from within the national forests, but more of it came from Bureau of Land Management lands. As a result, Alaska secured some excellent state forests and was able to establish a magnificent set of six state parks, which included 2.6 million acres in 1980. At that time, the state also owned sixty-one other recreation and historic areas. In close cooperation with the Forest Service, the Division of State and Private Forestry encouraged timber production on state and national forests. The state also began the disposal of public lands to individuals and corporations, much of it going for homesteads, building lots, and business ventures.

Conflicts between federal and state agencies and various interest groups slowed the transfer of federal lands during the 1960s, and in 1971 pressure from native Alaskan groups resulted in passage of the Alaska Native Land Claims Settlement Act. To resolve aboriginal land claims, Congress provided native groups with a $1 billion cash settlement and the right to select 44 million acres from a pool of around 116 million acres of federal land, much of it in the national forests.

The 1971 act sparked a controversy that was not resolved until 1980. Section 17(2)(d) authorized the secretary of the interior to withdraw from consideration by the state or native Alaskans up to 80 million acres of federal land for study as possible national parks, refuges, forests, and wild and scenic rivers. Congress was given until 1978 to make recommendations for disposal of the so-called d-2 lands. Immediately after passage of the act, the state filed for transfer of 77 million federal acres. Although the state's claim was denied by the Department of the Interior, federal courts allowed the transfer of 44 million acres. The following year, Interior Secretary Rogers Morton withdrew most of the remaining unreserved Alaska lands.

When Congress failed to meet the December 1978 deadline for designating the federal lands, President Jimmy Carter, acting under the 1906 Antiquities Act, placed 56 million acres of d-2 lands in seventeen new national monuments. The president instructed Interior Secretary Cecil Andrus to withdraw 40 million acres under the emergency authority prescribed in the 1976 FEDERAL LAND POLICY AND MANAGEMENT ACT and place them in twelve national wildlife refuges. Secretary of Agriculture Robert Bergland was directed to withdraw an additional 11 million acres in the Tongass and Chugach national forests. Thus, approximately 107 million acres of d-2 lands were set aside by executive decree, pending congressional legislation.

After considerable deliberation, Congress reached agreement, and on December 2, 1980, President Carter signed the Alaska National Interest Lands Conservation Act. The act classified a total of 104 million acres as parks, preserves, monuments, refuges, and forests, doubling the size of the nation's park, wildlife refuge, and wild and scenic rivers system. A 56.4 million acre set-aside tripled the nation's wilderness area. The act established five new national parks covering 26 million acres, fifteen national wildlife refuges covering 53.7 million acres, and four new national preserves and monuments totaling 11.7 million acres. Mount McKinley National Park, renamed Denali (the Athabascan name meaning "the great one"), received 3.76 million additional acres, and additions to the Arctic National Wildlife Range, Yukon Flats National Wildlife Refuge, and the Yukon Delta National Wildlife Refuge totaled 31.2 million acres. The Katmai National Monument, established in 1918, was redesignated as a park and preserve and expanded by 1.35 million acres, bringing its total acreage to 5.64 million. The Bureau of Land Management retained jurisdiction over 2.22 million acres in the Steese National Conservation Area and the White Mountains National Recreation Area.

Concern by the forest industries centered on the

lands in the southeastern national forests. Although a total of 3.35 million acres was added to the Chugach and Tongass national forests, the 1980 act reduced the size of the allowable yearly cut from 520 million board feet to an estimated 420 million board feet. The reduction was perceived by the forest industry as a workable compromise.

The early 1980s saw increasing federal and state cooperation in forest management, increased forest and wildlife research, particularly in game and fish habitat, increased recreational use of the forest resources in both southeastern Alaska and the interior, and the emergence of a mixed pattern of forestland ownership and management, like that which existed in the lower forty-eight states.

FURTHER READING: B. Frank Heintzleman, "The Forests of Alaska," *Trees: The Yearbook of Agriculture* (1949), pp. 361-372. Royal S. Kellogg, *The Forests of Alaska* (1910). Harold J. Lutz, *Aboriginal Man and White Man as Historical Causes for Forest Fires in the Interior of Alaska* (1959), and *Early Forest Conditions in the Alaska Interior: An Historical Account with Original Sources* (1963). Lawrence W. Rakestraw, *A History of the United States Forest Service in Alaska* (1981).

LAWRENCE W. RAKESTRAW

ALBRIGHT, HORACE MARDEN (1890–)

Born on January 6, 1890, in Bishop, California, Horace Albright grew up surrounded by extraordinary examples of mountain scenery and unspoiled natural beauty. He graduated from the University of California in 1912, then joined the staff of Secretary of the Interior Franklin K. Lane. In 1915, he became special assistant to Stephen T. MATHER, a wealthy Chicago businessman and conservationist who had volunteered to work with Lane on the administration of the national parks.

Mather and Albright became the founding fathers of the NATIONAL PARK SERVICE (NPS). They were instrumental in the drafting and passage of the National Park Service Act of 1916, which institutionalized aesthetic conservation or preservationist values in the federal government. Together they pioneered the distinctive administrative style and early conservation policies of the NPS. Both were preservationists who believed in the importance of saving grand examples of natural beauty. Both were pragmatic and effective politicians who knew how to cultivate strong support in Congress and in the field. Under their leadership, the NPS came to rival the FOREST SERVICE in political clout and breadth of program. The two agencies became competitors within the federal establishment and remained so for the next fifty years.

Albright served as assistant director of the NPS until 1919 and as superintendent of YELLOWSTONE NATIONAL PARK during the 1920s. While superintendent, he retained the office of field assistant to the director. In 1929, he succeeded Mather as director and custodian of the "Mather tradition" in the NPS. He won strong support for the national park projects that bore the distinctive Albright stamp. These included the inauguration of a large new HISTORIC PRESERVATION program, the placing of all park superintendents under civil service, the strengthening of interpretive and educational activities, the establishment of the GRAND TETON NATIONAL PARK, Carlsbad Caverns National Park, and GREAT SMOKY MOUNTAINS NATIONAL PARK, and the authorization of Death Valley and Colonial national monuments.

During the "Hundred Days" of Franklin D. ROOSEVELT's first term, Albright participated in a whirlwind of federal conservation activities. He became a close associate of Secretary of the Interior Harold ICKES. He served as one of the principal figures in the founding of the CIVILIAN CONSERVATION CORPS. He arranged for NPS jurisdiction over all parks and monuments in the District of Columbia and all Civil War battlefields and burial grounds.

In August 1933, with the NPS thriving, Albright resigned from government service to become vice-president and general manager of the United States Potash Company, a mining enterprise headquartered in New York. His career as a business executive lasted until his retirement in 1956.

Although Albright devoted most of his time after 1933 to the mining business, he maintained a substantial involvement for the next twenty-five years with the NPS and the CONSERVATION MOVEMENT generally, helping each succeeding director and secretary of the interior and most of the national CONSERVATION ORGANIZATIONS in their dealings with Congress or the White House. He persevered with John D. ROCKEFELLER, Jr., in the protracted Jackson Hole Battle and eventually saw Jackson Hole included in the national park system. He served as the first president of RESOURCES FOR THE FUTURE and helped restore Colonial Williamsburg.

His important achievements in national park administration and policymaking and his persistent efforts, spanning five decades, in behalf of aesthetic conservation earned him a place in the front rank of twentieth-century American conservationists.

FURTHER READING: Robert Shankland, *Steve Mather of*

the National Parks (1954). Donald C. Swain, *Wilderness Defender: Horace M. Albright and Conservation* (1970).

DONALD C. SWAIN

ALGER, RUSSELL A. (1836–1907)

Russell Alexander Alger was born in Medina County, Ohio, on February 27, 1836, the second oldest of Russell and Caroline Alger's four children. The family knew nothing but poverty, and in 1848 both parents died of illnesses.

Young Alger was raised by a stern uncle, who impressed upon the boy the value of hard work. Struggling to survive, Alger acquired a rudimentary education, taught school for a time, then studied law, and in 1860 moved to Grand Rapids, Michigan, to seek his fortune in lumbering. Initially, he enjoyed modest prosperity, but a pre-Civil War financial panic ruined his business, leaving him deeply in debt.

With the outbreak of the Civil War, Alger joined the army as a captain of volunteer cavalry. His subsequent military performance was truly distinguished. In June 1863, he was promoted to colonel and given command of the Fifth Michigan Cavalry Regiment which saw much heavy fighting at Gettysburg, Trevillian Station, and elsewhere. In all, Alger fought in sixty-five battles and skirmishes and was wounded twice. He resigned from the army in September 1864 for health and personal reasons. After the war, his exceptional war service was further recognized by brevet promotions to brigadier and major general.

Returning to Michigan, Alger became involved in the logging industry along the Huron shore. He was the leading partner in several successive firms, the best known of which was Alger, Smith, and Company, formed in 1881. The company specialized in the production of long timber, a type much in demand for heavy construction and ships' masts and spars. Alger was one of the first timber barons in Michigan to build a railroad into his pineries (1877), thus enabling his company to operate around the year. By 1900, Alger, Smith had depleted its best timber tracts in Michigan, and the company transferred its operations to the rich pine forests near Duluth, Minnesota. Within a few years, Alger, Smith was the leading timber producer on the Superior shore. The general also owned major interests in several other lumbering firms, including the Alger-Sullivan Timber Company in Alabama, the Manistique Lumber Company in Michigan, two redwood companies in California, and the Laurentide Pulp Company in Quebec. The success of these businesses, as well as many of Alger's other investments, made him a millionaire many times over by the turn of the century.

Because of his prominence as a war hero and business leader, friends encouraged Alger to run for governor of Michigan in 1884. Although he had no political experience, he won the Republican nomination and the election. Alger was a cautious, conservative chief executive who believed in applying strict business principles to government. The most difficult problem of his administration was the Saginaw Valley lumber mill strike of July and August 1885. When violence erupted in Saginaw and Bay City, Alger immediately sent in the requested state troops, and he also visited the strike area to urge both sides to use moderation. Critics charged that Alger, out of sympathy for fellow owners, had ordered in the militia for the sole purpose of breaking the strike. In all probability, however, the governor's strong stand preserved life and property and hastened the settlement of the strike. Alger retired from office in 1887, having decided not to seek a second term.

The following year, Alger was one of the leading candidates for the Republican nomination for president of the United States, and in 1889 he was elected commander-in-chief of the Grand Army of the Republic (GAR). As head of the large and influential GAR, he successfully led the fight to secure improved pension legislation for Civil War veterans.

In the presidential campaign of 1896, the general organized a group of Civil War heroes to stump the Midwest for William McKinley, sound money, and prosperity. Because of Alger's campaign services, his business success, and his prominence in the Republican party, McKinley after his election appointed him to the cabinet as secretary of war.

When war came with Spain in 1898, the War Department was placed under tremendous pressure to mobilize, train, equip, and transport a large army to widely separated battle fronts in the Caribbean and the Philippines. The department met these responsibilities reasonably well, but there were problems. The press attacked the secretary for "Algerism," and General Nelson Miles, commanding general of the army, charged that Alger and the commissary general had supplied the men in the field with "embalmed beef," which had caused much sickness among the troops. Two investigating commissions concluded that Miles's allegations were false.

While still secretary of war, Alger announced his candidacy for the United States Senate. As a consequence, the president asked him to resign from the cabinet in August 1899. The general decided against running for the Senate, however, and instead devoted most of the next two years to his business affairs and to writing *The Spanish-American War,* a book in which he recounted the work of the War Department and the army during the war. Upon the death of Senator James McMillan in 1902, the Michigan legislature elected Alger to serve out McMillan's unexpired term. In failing health for several years, Alger died on January 24, 1907, on the eve of his retirement from the Senate.

FURTHER READING: Rodney E. Bell, "A Life of Russell Alexander Alger, 1836-1907," Ph.D. dissertation, University of Michigan (1975). George W. Hotchkiss, *History of the Lumber and Forest Industry of the Northwest* (1898). Carl Kauffman, *Logging Days in Blind River* (1970). Frederick Logan Paxson, "Alger, Russell Alexander," in Allen Johnson, ed., *Dictionary of American Biography* (1928), I:179-180.

RODNEY E. BELL

AMERICAN FOREST INSTITUTE

In 1926, the NATIONAL LUMBER MANUFACTURERS ASSOCIATION (NLMA) initiated a National Lumber Trade Extension (NLTE) campaign intended to raise contributions of $5 million over a period of five years for the purpose of expanding domestic lumber markets. In the early years of the Depression, the number of subscribers dwindled, and in 1932 NLMA created a subsidiary organization with the name American Forest Products Industries, Inc. (AFPI), to handle its lumber and forest products promotion work including NLTE activity. AFPI, the direct forerunner of the American Forest Institute, was a nonprofit membership corporation incorporated under the laws of Delaware. Its members were its trustees, a committee of lumbermen who were among the NLTE subscribers. The new organization also provided a means whereby regional associations or forest industries companies interested in specific projects for the development and promotion of wood uses could join with other interested groups in establishing funds for such purposes.

In 1933, the AFPI trustees incorporated a subsidiary called Timber Engineering Company (TECO). TECO was a commercial corporation wholly owned by AFPI and assigned to develop ideas and inventions for the improvement and extension of the uses of lumber and timber products. European timber connector patents, which NLMA had previously acquired, were assigned to TECO, and TECO set about testing and ultimately manufacturing and promoting the use of these connectors, which enabled an expansion in the construction uses of heavy timbers.

NLMA adopted a new plan to govern its relationship to AFPI in 1935. The members of NLMA's executive committee became the trustees of AFPI; NLMA took over general trade promotion activities, leaving AFPI with special trade promotion and research projects including TECO; and the residue of the NLTE fund was turned over to AFPI. This organizational relationship remained essentially unchanged for the next eleven years.

During the 1940s, AFPI embarked upon a public relations campaign that, over a period of several years, would change the whole thrust of the organization's activities. Determined to reverse opinion surveys, which revealed that only 6 percent of the American public thought the forest industries were doing a "progressive" job, AFPI launched a program in 1941 intended both to teach the public that industry was continuously growing and protecting timber crops and to stimulate the forest products industries to adopt forest practices deserving of public approval. This program was distinguished from AFPI's trade promotion work in that it was not designed to sell forest products but rather to create public confidence in the management of the forest products industry under private enterprise. It was AFPI's task to lead industry's defense against attempts to have the U. S. FOREST SERVICE assigned authority over the REGULATION OF FOREST PRACTICES on private lands. In order to free AFPI to concentrate on this public relations work, NLMA and AFPI were separated in 1946. At that time, AFPI's remaining trade promotion programs, including TECO, were transferred to NLMA.

The base of forest industry participation in AFPI expanded in the following year to include pulp and paper manufacturers in addition to timber companies. AFPI began to provide programs and services through regional offices in 1949, with particular emphasis on the Southern states. By the next decade, AFPI was operating nationwide programs through forestry, education, industry, and editorial divisions. Its first state-level committee of forest industry companies was started in 1952, by which time ten field offices were in operation in addition to the Washington, D.C., headquarters. To cope with new trends in forest management and provide this information to more people, AFPI created its national technical forestry committee in 1958.

AFPI's secondary and primary education and youth programs date from 1947 with its first sponsorship of 4-H Club forestry awards. Subsequently, AFPI provided instructional materials on forest resources, teacher's guides, and workshops. By 1952, its teaching aids reached about half of America's schools. AFPI's editorial services provided articles for magazines ranging from leading national publications to small house organs. The editorial division also issued news releases, photographs, and newspaper advertising mats.

AFPI assumed national sponsorship of the Keep America Green program for forest fire prevention. This program originated in the Pacific Northwest in 1941 when local citizens founded a Keep Washington Green committee and Oregon residents followed a few months later with a similar program. By the 1950s, Keep Green committees were active in forty-eight states and AFPI could point to a reduction of more than 90 percent in the national incidence of forest fire. The Keep Green program aimed to promote the public's feeling of responsibility for fire and to support effective fire protection. The program operated through state central committees which coordinated the operations of county or community committees.

The tree farm movement, which encouraged private landowners to practice forest-management techniques, also began in Washington State in 1941 and quickly spread to other states. AFPI took over the program's national coordination in 1942, and with AFPI's independence four years later the American Tree Farm System expanded rapidly.

Late in 1947, the Alabama Forestry Council organized a "More Trees for Alabama" educational program improvement in woods management. Under AFPI sponsorship, the More Trees for America program was established in other states within a few years. With such slogans as "Busy Acres" and "Cash Crops from Your Woods," the program was aimed primarily at farmers and other private landowners with forests smaller than the ten acres needed for certification under the tree farm program. The First National Farm Woodlot Conference, held in 1953, led to a growth of "how to do it" programs and publications on forest management for woodlot owners and tree farmers.

Waves of environmental concern confronted AFPI in the 1960s and 1970s. AFPI in 1961 sponsored its first conference on land use, the decade's central forestry topic. In the same year, AFPI began regular public opinion sampling on forest resource questions. By mid-decade, the organization could measure considerable progress made over the preceding quarter-century. Timber being planted exceeded that being cut by a comfortable margin. There were 30,000 tree farms in 1966. More than 330,000 copies of AFPI literature were being used in schools each year.

AFPI became the American Forest Institute (AFI) in 1968. AFI continued to help the public understand the industry's positions on environmental and forest-resource issues such as water quality, productivity,

wilderness, and multiple use. It strengthened its regional programs early in the 1970s by absorbing the Southern Forest Institute. The AFI periodical poster "GreenAmerica," which began publication in 1972, combined the graphic arts with an informative text to give a balanced view of forest-resource issues. By 1980, it reached nearly 250,000 subscribers. AFI also sought to reach opinion leaders through paid advertising and television and radio public-service spots, and through its regional offices, news bureaus, and a corps of 2,400 communicators within the industry. The Tree Farm System in 1980 had almost 40,000 members with nearly 80 million acres. "Project Learning Tree," an innovative educational program that showed elementary and secondary school students the importance of forest resources, was active in twenty-nine states. AFI in 1980 had more than seventy forest industry member companies.

JAMES BEEK

AMERICAN FOREST PRODUCTS INDUSTRIES

See American Forest Institute

AMERICAN FORESTRY ASSOCIATION

At the close of the 1875 annual meeting of the American Pomological Society in Chicago, a group of twenty-five horticulturists and nurserymen formed the American Forestry Association, at that time the only organization in the country primarily concerned with forest conservation. The gathering had been called by John Aston Warder of Ohio, a former medical doctor who had left his practice for horticulture. As U.S. commissioner to the 1873 International Exhibition in Vienna, Warder had written a report on forestry in Europe. From 1875 to 1882, he served the new association as president. Reflecting the interests of its founding members, the association remained largely interested in tree culture and planting. In 1882, Warder, together with the German-trained forester Bernhard E. FER-NOW, pioneer Minnesota conservationist Christopher C. Andrews, chief of the U.S. Division of Forestry Franklin B. HOUGH, and others, formed the American Forestry Congress to work toward a broader national policy of forest conservation. At the first annual meeting of the congress later the same year, the American Forestry Association merged into the new organization. George B. Loring, the U. S. commissioner of agriculture who had just been elected president of the association, became president of the congress.

The American Forestry Congress teamed up with the American Association for the Advancement of Science in pursuing the adoption of federal legislation drafted by Fernow in 1887 for the establishment and management of forest reservations under public ownership—principles which were later included in the FOREST RESERVE ACT of 1891 and the FOREST MANAGEMENT ACT of 1897. Before that happened, the congress in 1889 changed its name to the American Forestry Association (AFA), and it incorporated under that name in 1897.

To foster public understanding of the economic importance of forests and advance the conservation of forest and related resources, the AFA in 1905 sponsored an American Forest Congress in Washington, D.C. President Theodore ROOSEVELT gave the keynote address, "The Forest in the Life of a Nation," before an audience of 2,000. The congress adopted resolutions urging enactment of a number of long-sought reforms, the most important being the proposal for unification within the DEPARTMENT OF AGRICULTURE of all the forestry work of the federal government, including the administration of forest reserves. Transfer of the reserves to the custody of the Bureau of Forestry (soon renamed the FOREST SERVICE) was accomplished by federal legislation later in the same year.

A major goal of the AFA was the creation of national forests in the southern Appalachians and the White Mountains of New Hampshire. To this end, AFA coordinated the efforts of a number of regional and national organizations. The result was the WEEKS ACT of 1911, which for the first time authorized the federal government to purchase forestland for watershed protection and provided for cooperation between the federal government and the states in the protection of forests from fire. Later, AFA sponsored the McNary-Woodruff Act of 1928, which expanded appropriations for the acquisition of land for eastern national forests.

AFA effectively sponsored or worked on behalf of numerous conservation causes, among them the NATIONAL FORESTRY PROGRAM COMMITTEE, whose work led to the passage of the MCSWEENEY-MCNARY ACT of 1928; the Southern Forestry Education Project (the "Dixie Crusaders"), which between 1928 and 1931 presented lectures and films to elementary schools throughout the South in an effort to reduce the incidence of woods burning; and the use of forest and park work programs to provide employment for the nation's jobless during the Depression of the 1930s, a campaign which led to the creation of the CIVILIAN CONSERVATION CORPS.

In 1944, AFA began a survey to determine the

The American Forestry Association was a strong advocate of establishing national forests in the Appalachian Mountains. Shown here is the entrance to North Carolina's Pisgah National Forest in 1924. Forest Service Photo.

effects that war demands for forest products had had on the nation's timber resources. The reports of this Forest Resource Appraisal formed the basis for discussions of postwar forest policy at the third American Forest Congress, sponsored by AFA in Washington, D.C., in 1946. Unlike the congress of 1905, that of 1946 could form no consensus on the leading issue of its day, the recurring debate over proposed regulation of private forestry. AFA had provided a forum for this debate since the 1930s. As an organization, AFA had favored regulation by states and refused to endorse proposals for regulation by the federal government. The Forest Resource Appraisal, which asserted that the solution for timber problems lay in increased production on national forests, thus seemed a counterattack against the Forest Service. With delegates from labor organizations supporting the concept of federal regulation, the American Forest Congress debated but remained divided on this issue. Nevertheless, AFA's directors proposed and the members adopted in a national referendum a *Program for American Forestry*, which provided general recommendations and goals for CONSERVATION ORGANIZATIONS and government agencies. The *Program* was updated at subsequent American Forest Congresses sponsored by AFA in 1953 and 1975.

Public education has been AFA's chief means for attaining its objectives. Although never a lobbying body, AFA has kept the Congress and officials in resources agencies informed of its views. Education of legislators, federal and state officials, forestland owners, and educators has been the association's principal way of spreading its conservation message. AFA's chief tools have been its magazine and book publication programs. Since 1898, the association has published continuously a monthly journal. Starting as *The Forester*, the journal underwent a series of name changes before settling on *American Forests* in 1931.

The magazine's value as an instrument for advancing conservation objectives seemed diminished during the World War I years when Charles Lathrop PACK was AFA's president and the magazine concentrated on conservation education and nature lore, avoiding controversial policy questions. The most serious internal conflict in AFA's history erupted when Herman H. CHAPMAN, writing in the Society of American Foresters' *Journal of Forestry*, questioned the continued usefulness of AFA under Pack's presidency. Chapman found ready support from other foresters such as Henry S. GRAVES, William B. GREELEY, Bernhard E. Fernow, Samuel T. DANA, and Gifford PINCHOT, who either were or would become leaders of the profession. These men believed that Pack wanted to use AFA as his personal mouthpiece and intended to obtain control of the organization by using his wealth to endow its programs. After Pack's departure in 1922, AFA's journal quickly regained its reputation under a new editor, Ovid BUTLER. It became a major forum for public discussion on forest-related issues such as the proposed transfer of the Forest Service to the DEPARTMENT OF THE INTERIOR, the reform of mining laws relating to forestlands, and the preservation of wilderness.

In 1940, AFA also began to publish its *National Register of Big Trees*, a project to encourage citizens to locate and measure the country's largest specimens of native tree species. By 1980, the register listed some 650 champions.

AFA has been the leading citizens' institution for the development of policies and practices for the management of the nation's forest resources. There were 79,000 members in 1979. Policies are determined by a board of directors, the members of which, along with AFA's president and treasurer, are nominated by a committee of the board and elected by the association members attending the annual meeting.

FURTHER READING: Henry Clepper, "Crusade for Conservation: The Centennial History of the American Forestry Association," *American Forests* 81 (Oct. 1975): en-

tire issue (also issued separately, 1975) and "*American Forests:* Magazine of Record in Conservation," *American Forests* 80 (Apr. 1974): 25-55.

HENRY CLEPPER

AMERICAN NATURE ASSOCIATION

Founded in 1922, the American Nature Association (ANA) was one of several organizations endowed by Charles Lathrop PACK after his losing factional fights within the AMERICAN FORESTRY ASSOCIATION. Whereas Pack's AMERICAN TREE ASSOCIATION (with which the ANA shared offices) concentrated entirely on forestry, ANA's stated purpose was "to stimulate public interest in every phase of Nature and the out-of-doors, and . . . the practical conservation of the great natural resources of America." However, the Pack interest in the ANA meant a heavy emphasis on forestry issues. During its early years, the association collaborated in Pack's campaign to promote the planting of trees along highways and at roadside stops.

Pack's son, Arthur Newton Pack, served as ANA's president from 1926 to 1946 and edited its monthly magazine, *Nature*. Through the success of *Nature*, the ANA grew to 60,000 members at one point. However, by the 1950s its programs differed little from those of the American Tree Association and its policies were much like those of the IZAAK WALTON LEAGUE OF AMERICA. Membership declined and the ANA was formally dissolved in 1959. With the January 1960 number, *Nature* magazine was absorbed into *Natural History*, published by the American Museum of Natural History.

AMERICAN NATURE STUDY SOCIETY

The American Nature Study Society was established in 1908 by the editorial board of *Nature-Study Review* and is, therefore, the oldest environmental education association in the United States. The dominant figure of its early years was Maurice Bigelow of the Teachers College of Columbia University. His interest was in elementary education, and the society dedicated itself to improving science education in the primary schools.

Forests and forestry was one of five or six areas of emphasis in the society's research programs and its juvenile periodical, *Nature Magazine*. The society makes an annual award, the Eva L. Gordon prize, for outstanding publications in children's science literature. In the 1970s, it sponsored programs for training lay naturalists. For children it offered "wild foods weekends." The society is affiliated with the Alliance for Environmental Education and the International Union for Conservation of Nature and Natural Resources. In 1980, it claimed a membership of about 1,000 educators.

AMERICAN PAPER INSTITUTE

Combinations of American papermakers began as early as 1861 with short-lived regional efforts to control prices by restricting production. The first organizational effort that proved to be both permanent and national was the formation of the American Paper Makers Association at Saratoga, New York, in 1878. The new association was designed as a central body with regional branches. At its sixth annual meeting, held in 1883, the group was reorganized as the American Paper Manufacturers Association, with headquarters in Springfield, Massachusetts, and six divisions representing makers of writing, book, news and colored, manila, and straw wrapping papers, and paperboard. In 1887, a wood pulp division was added. The organization became the American Paper and Pulp Association (APPA) in 1897, a name which survived for the next sixty-six years.

By the early twentieth century, APPA had developed programs or positions for such issues as forest conservation, water quality, the tariff, industrial statistics, and product standardization. In 1905, APPA established a permanent headquarters in New York. Particularly during World Wars I and II and the New Deal, APPA prospered as government called upon trade associations to mobilize American industry. With the establishment of the National Recovery Administration in 1933, APPA's executive committee comprised the Paper Industry Authority, and the association was reorganized as a federation of sixteen divisional associations, each composed of companies engaged in the manufacture of some paper or pulp specialty. The increased importance of governmental affairs led to the opening of a Washington, D.C., office in the spring of 1941.

In 1964, APPA merged with the National Paperboard Association (founded in 1932) to form the Pulp, Paper, and Paperboard Institute. This group was reorganized in 1966 into the American Paper Institute (API) through the consolidation of twelve specialized pulp, paper, and paperboard trade associations (including most of the former federated or affiliated associations of APPA) into a single organization. The absorbed groups included the Writing Paper Manufacturers Association (founded in 1861); the Tissue As-

sociation (1880); Newsprint Service Bureau (1918); National Shoeboard Conference (1927); Glassine and Greaseproof Manufacturers Association (1930); Bleached Converting and Packaging Paper Manufacturers Association (1932); Kraft Paper Association (1933); Printing Paper Manufacturers Association (1933); Specialty Paper and Board Affiliates (1933); U.S. Pulp Producers Association (1933); Vegetable Parchment Manufacturers Association (1935); and the Association of Pulp Consumers (1941). Although API was organized as a direct membership association of primary pulp and paper producers, it also included provision for direct participation by converters in specific activities.

FURTHER READING: *New Horizons: A History of Seventy-five Years of the American Paper and Pulp Association* (1952). Arthur Selwyn-Brown, *American Paper and Pulp Association: Fiftieth Anniversary, 1878–1927* (1927). David C. Smith, *History of Papermaking in the United States, 1691–1969* (1970).

AMERICAN PLYWOOD ASSOCIATION

Cooperative endeavors by the softwood plywood manufacturers in the United States began with formation of the Pacific Coast Plywood Manufacturers Association in Tacoma, Washington, in 1924. That group had been intended to set up a standard grading system, develop the fir plywood market, and analyze production and distribution costs. It folded after little more than a year, and its immediate successors, the Pacific Coast Plywood Manufacturers, Inc., and the Douglas Fir Plywood Manufacturers Association, had lives nearly as brief. The Douglas Fir Plywood Association (DFPA), organized in 1933, was to prove more successful. Axel Oxholm, hired in the following year as managing director, laid the foundations of quality assurance, technical research, and advertising programs. W. E. Difford, who became managing director in 1938, enlarged the DFPA role to broad national promotion of softwood plywood. He persuaded manufacturers to turn a relatively static industry into a growth business. Difford gave impetus to the development of standards and specifications describing products of known and predictable performance and capable of satisfying a wide range of market needs. After the successful demonstration of plywood's properties in numerous demanding World War II applications, the plywood industry and its association pioneered new markets in fields like roof, wall, and floor sheathing and exterior siding. Construction systems engineered and promoted by the association took plywood to a leadership position in many sectors of residential construction, which became the largest single market for the product. Promotion also yielded excellent returns in markets ranging from concrete forming to commercial roof decks and industrial materials handling. James R. Turnbull was appointed executive vice-president of the association in 1962, and two years later the DFPA became the American Plywood Association (APA), a change which reflected the emergence of the southern pine segment of the industry, and growth of the product mix to twenty-two species besides Douglas-fir. In that year, 1964, the first overseas field promotion branch of the association was established in West Germany, to be followed later in the decade by an office in London. APA sponsored a new plywood standard in 1966, PS 1-66 (later replaced by PS 1-74) which combined three regional standards into a single document and helped confirm softwood plywood as a national product.

Bronson J. Lewis was named APA executive vice president in 1969 when Turnbull moved to the leadership of the NATIONAL FOREST PRODUCTS ASSOCIATION. Later that year, the association centralized its technical and quality laboratory functions in a new research center in Tacoma. Many new energy-efficient plywood construction systems were introduced, and the association's overseas promotion was strengthened in Europe and extended to Japan. The industry expanded rapidly in the South, while remaining relatively stable in the West.

Environmental and energy-related constraints of the 1970s encouraged improvement of raw materials utilization and the development of more fiber-efficient panels such as composites combining veneer and fiber, waferboards made with previously unusable hardwoods, and oriented-strand boards made with long, narrow flakes or strands. This new phase in the evolution of panel products was recognized by new performance standards approved in 1979 which established test methods for measuring a panel product's ability to perform a specific application regardless of the panel's configuration. This allowed added freedom in the layup of veneered panels, utilization of a greater number of species, and higher total use of available resources in suitably qualified veneered and nonveneered panels.

When the DFPA was formed in 1924, softwood plywood production was limited to one species and the annual volume was well below 1 billion square feet. In 1980, the softwood plywood industry manufactured hundreds of different plywood products made from more than seventy species, and production capacity for veneered products was close to 23 billion square feet.

W. D. PAGE

AMERICAN PULPWOOD ASSOCIATION

In 1934, the American Pulpwood Association (APA) was organized to develop consensus standards in the pulpwood industry under the National Industrial Recovery Act and to represent the industry in dealing with federal legislation and regulation. Originally, APA operated with informal ties to the American Paper and Pulp Association (see AMERICAN PAPER INSTITUTE).

APA struggled with the implications of certain labor legislation of the New Deal era which raised questions about who were independent contractors and who were employees in a number of situations, such as woods operations. As these questions were not resolved, certain provisions of the National Labor Relations and Social Security acts of 1935 and the Fair Labor Standards Act of 1937 (FLSA) were indifferently applied until after World War II.

During the war, pulpwood production labor sources declined as pulp and paper demand increased. To meet the critical woods labor shortage, APA hired a training and safety officer to prepare workers in efficient and productive hand saw and ax care, use, and safety. This marked the beginning of a continuing training and safety program. To increase productivity by mechanizing woods operations, APA sponsored a series of meetings in the major forest regions of the South, New England, and the Lake States. These conferences developed into "Technical Divisions" in each of these regions and in the Appalachian area.

After World War II, APA successfully sought a number of reforms in labor policy that would aid the pulpwood industry in meeting increased demands on its resources. Among these measures was the exemption by Congress of small logging operations (employing no more than twelve men) from the minimum wage, overtime, and record-keeping provisions of the FLSA. Another was congressional approval of common law principles for determination of independent contractor status under the National Labor Relations and the Social Security acts.

APA kept pace with the growth of the pulpwood industry, which expanded in annual production from 20 million to 70 million cords between the late 1940s and the mid-1970s. During this period, APA added its Western and Southwestern Technical divisions. APA's technical programs provided leadership, training, and information exchange as the industry shifted from the use of hand saws and axes to power chain saws, then to shears and integrated machines for felling, bucking, and limbing, and from horse and mule power to tracked or rubber-tired tractors (see LOGGING TECHNOLOGY AND TOOLS).

During the 1950s, APA assumed responsibility for the collection, compilation, and reporting of pulpwood receipts, consumption, and inventories. During this period, legislative issues seldom threatened the pulpwood industry. APA defended successfully against challenges to the twelve-man FLSA exemption, supported the NATIONAL FOREST PRODUCTS ASSOCIATION's attempt to secure passage of the McIntire-Stennis Act encouraging university research, successfully pursued amendment of the National Bank Act to allow national banks to recognize and evaluate immature forest stands, and supported other associations on legislative issues affecting forestry or forest industry. APA anticipated the Occupational Safety and Health Act of 1970 and was among the first forest industry groups to sponsor and secure acceptance by the new Occupational Safety and Health Administration of a pulpwood logging safety code. APA also sponsored internal research, including the projects examining chemical debarking and harvesting systems in the South. It sponsored the Southern Industrial Forestry Research Council, which works with the U. S. FOREST SERVICE and universities to assess forestry research needs.

As of 1980, APA, through standing and ad hoc committees, served 61 forest products companies, about 400 independent wood fiber suppliers, 49 associate members (equipment manufacturers), and a large subscriber list. APA committees work in topical areas including forest engineering and harvesting, forest management, truck and rail transportation, safety and training, and energy. APA faces new opportunities for member service resulting from environmental legislation and regulations affecting forestry and wood energy, while the old issue of determining independent contractor or employee status in woods operations has remained a major concern.

See also: PULP AND PAPER INDUSTRY.

BOB IZLAR

AMERICAN TREE ASSOCIATION

Founded in 1922, the American Tree Association (ATA) was one of the leading promoters of the ARBOR DAY tradition during the 1920s and 1930s and also an important clearinghouse for forestry information.

Its purpose was "to further forest protection and extension, and to increase appreciation of forests as natural resources essential to the sound economic future of the country." Sharing offices in Washington, D.C., with the AMERICAN NATURE ASSOCIATION and closely associated with the Charles Lathrop PACK

family throughout its history, the ATA was not a subscription organization but instead sent certificates of membership in the "Tree Planting Army" to every individual who planted a tree. ATA described itself as the Tree Planting Army's "recruiting agency" in elementary schools. By 1929, it had enlisted 129,000 "troops."

The ATA devoted itself chiefly to promoting forestry education in elementary schools during the 1920s. One of its most successful projects was the publication of the *Forestry Primer*, a fifteen-lesson introduction to the principles and profession of forestry couched in simple language. With special editions for Michigan, the Gulf States, and the Pacific Coast, the ATA eventually printed over 4 million copies of the *Primer*.

The ATA also took an interest in national forestry policy and lobbied for the passage of the CLARKE-MCNARY ACT in 1924. Collaborating with the General Federation of Women's Clubs, the ATA promoted highway beautification projects and the planting of trees as memorials. Founded on the fiftieth anniversary of Arbor Day, it immediately urged preparation for the centennial in 1972 by individual tree planting. In fact, its greatest effort came with the George Washington Bicentennial in 1932, when over 27 million trees are said to have been planted.

The ATA published the irregular *Forestry Almanac*, later called the *Forestry Directory*, which provided a comprehensive guide to forest-related activities and organizations from the 1920s through the 1940s. ATA became inactive during the 1950s.

ARBOR DAY

Following the Homestead Act of 1862, agricultural settlement invaded the treeless plains of the central United States. Early settlers, hoping to ameliorate the conditions of life and climate in these regions, brought along trees and shrubs for planting around their new homes. Both state and federal governments encouraged such endeavors. In 1868, Iowa, Kansas, and Wisconsin passed laws giving settlers bounties for tree planting. Other states, beginning with Missouri in 1870 and then Minnesota and also Maine, exempted from TAXATION lands planted to trees.

The idea of setting aside a special day to celebrate and popularize the planting of trees, orchards, and hedges originated with Julius Sterling Morton, a farmer, newspaper editor, and politician of Nebraska City. (He would later serve as secretary of agriculture in President Grover Cleveland's second administration.) At a meeting of the State Horticultural Society on January 4, 1872, Morton described or-

Arbor Day tree planting
ceremony in Omaha,
Nebraska, 1901. Nebraska
State Historical Society
Photo.

chards as "missionaries of culture and refinement."
The planting and cultivation by every farmer of orchards and flower gardens, "together with a few forest trees," he stated, would make Nebraska
"mentally and morally the best agricultural state . . .
in the American Union." On the same day, the State
Board of Agriculture adopted Morton's resolution
designating April 10, 1872, as Arbor Day, "set apart
and consecrated for tree planting in the state of Nebraska." Prizes were offered for the greatest number
of trees planted. The name "arbor" was chosen over
"sylvan" because Morton thought the latter word referred only to forest trees while "arbor" would include fruit and ornamental trees. Apparently there
was no arbor day celebrated in 1873, but in 1874 the
Nebraska Board of Agriculture resolved to make the
day an annual occurrence. Robert W. Furnas, a friend
of Morton and fellow farmer and arboriculturist,
became the first governor to call attention to Arbor
Day by official proclamation in 1875.

Kansas and Tennessee also declared Arbor Day in
1875; Minnesota followed in 1876 and North Dakota
and Ohio in 1882. Ohio's first Arbor Day was celebrated in connection with the American Forest Congress
meeting in Cincinnati. John B. Peaslee, city superintendent of schools, introduced the participation of
school children (with a parade of 60,000 of them) as well
as the practice of planting memorial trees and groves.

In 1885, the Nebraska legislature set Arbor Day on
April 22, Morton's birthday, and made it a legal holiday.
By 1920, more than forty-five states celebrated Arbor
Day. Among foreign countries which had instituted the
idea were Spain (beginning in 1896), Italy (since 1902),
England, Canada, Australia, France, Mexico, Norway,
Russia, Japan, and China.

Tree planting on Arbor Day prompted new development of parks and school grounds, street trees,
and roadside beautification. Morton had hoped that
Arbor Day activities would promote forestry: "tree-
planting and forestry may be made so popular in
American schools," he wrote in 1896, that ". . . fervid
zeal in behalf of the woodlands and the forests will at
last become, by communal heredity, an American
trait." On the other hand, Bernhard E. FERNOW, although he had earlier urged national observance of
Arbor Day, in 1916 suggested the custom may have
"had a retarding influence on practical forestry by
misleading people into thinking that tree planting
was the main issue instead of conservative management of existing forests."

With the popularity of Arbor Day declining, Howard
H. Scanlon, shade tree commissioner for Cleveland,
Ohio, in 1936 founded the Committee for National Ar-
bor Day. Scanlon sought a nationally recognized Arbor
Day to be celebrated on the last Friday of each April
and to be endorsed by both national and state legisla-

tions. Not until 1970 and again in 1972 did President Richard Nixon proclaim a national Arbor Day, however. In the latter year, the National Arbor Day Foundation was established with headquarters in Morton's old home, "Arbor Lodge," in Nebraska City. In 1982, all fifty states as well as the District of Columbia celebrated Arbor Day at various times of the year.

FURTHER READING: Harry J. Banker, "Arbor Day: The First 100 Years," *American Forests* 78 (Apr. 1972): 8–11, 60-61. Henry Clepper, "The Man Who Gave Us Arbor Day," *American Forests* 82 (Apr. 1982): 50-53, 60-62. J. Sterling Morton, "Effects of Arbor Day upon Economic Forest Planting," *The Forester* 4 (Apr. 1898): 72-73. James C. Olson, "Arbor Day: A Pioneer Expression of Concern for the Environment," *Nebraska History* 53 (Spring 1972): 1-13.

MARY ELIZABETH JOHNSON

ARBORETUMS AND BOTANICAL GARDENS

The main distinction between arboretums and botanical gardens lies in the fact that an arboretum emphasizes the growing of woody plants while in a botanical garden all types of plants are grown. For the purposes of this article, arboretums and botanical gardens will be considered as synonymous in definition. The earliest examples began as the private gardens of individuals who were intensely interested in bringing together various collections of plants. In Boston, for example, in the seventeenth century there were a number of wealthy and propertied gentlemen who established such gardens. During the eighteenth century, regions such as Pennsylvania and South Carolina were discovered to be ideal for the establishment of botanical gardens. In the twentieth century, establishing arboretums was found to be one means of preserving large private estates.

As early as 1728, John BARTRAM, the first native-born American botanist, botanical explorer, and breeder of indigenous and foreign plants, started the first large botanical garden in America at Kingsessing on the banks of the Schuylkill River, three miles from Philadelphia. He not only collected but also propagated and distributed plants, shrubs, and trees found during his many botanical expeditions in America. His book, *Observations on the Productions, Animals, and Other Matters Worthy of Notice . . .* (1751), was based in part on his experiences and travels in Pennsylvania. The Swedish botanist Carl von Linnaeus considered John Bartram to be the outstanding botanist of his time, and Bartram's collection of trees and shrubs became the best source for botanic exchange both at home and abroad.

John Bartram's cousin, Humphry Marshall, farmer and plant collector for European patrons, established a botanical garden in 1773 at Marshallton near Westchester. In 1785, he published his classic work in American botany, *Arbustum Americanum,* which provided a description of trees and shrubs native to the United States. Bernard M'Mahon, Irish-born horticulturist, seedman, nurseryman, and author of America's first great horticultural book, *American Gardener's Calendar* (1805), founded a botanical garden near the Germantown Pike, between Philadelphia and Nicetown, for the purpose of growing native plants to exchange abroad.

Probably the first botanical garden in the southeastern region of the American colonies was started at the home of Thomas Walters, along the Santee River north of Charleston, South Carolina. Drawing primarily upon his experience with the native flora found within a forty-mile radius of his home, Walters developed a manual on plants entitled *Flora Caroliniana* (1788). In 1805, the Charleston Botanic Society and Garden was established comprising indigenous and exotic plants acquired from American botanists as well as from collectors in foreign countries.

Interest in establishing botanical gardens also was evident elsewhere. For example, at the Cincinnati Horticultural Society, a testing area for native and foreign fruits and plants was instituted. Through the latter half of the nineteenth century and on into the twentieth, most arboretums and botanical gardens in the United States continued to be developed by interested entrepreneurs. To mention but a few, Henry Shaw, a businessman, founded the Missouri Botanical Garden in 1859; Joy Morton, president of the Morton Salt Company, in 1922 founded and financially supported the Morton Arboretum in Lisle, Illinois; Pierre Samuel du Pont in 1906 founded Longwood Gardens in Kennett Square, Pennsylvania; and Charles Sprague SARGENT for fifty-four years was the dedicated first director of the Arnold Arboretum in Boston.

Among the more than 150 arboretums and botanical gardens in the United States today, there is a striking variation in size, orientation of display, staff, funding, and programs. Their aims include serving as a natural conservancy as well as a field station dedicated to research and a scientific, educational, and intellectual institution. Each of these aims complements and reflects the needs of the others. Among their many functions can be listed careful documenting, labeling, and detailed recording of the collections; testing plant materials and growing conditions; developing new and improved varieties; introducing new species; providing the public with both education and information; conducting taxonomical research; sponsoring botanical explorations; maintaining slide, photograph, and library collections as well as the numerous specimens, grounds, and greenhouses. Unfortunately, strong economic and social pressures associated with metropolitan growth have caused the disappearance of such famous botanical gardens as the Elgin Botanical Garden (Columbia University, New York City), the Gray Botanical Garden (Cambridge, Massachusetts), and the Marsh Botanical Garden (Yale University, New Haven, Connecticut). Among the better known arboretums remaining in North America today are the following: Arnold Arboretum (established at Jamaica Plain, Massachusetts, 1872); Boyce Thompson Southwestern Arboretum (Superior, Arizona, 1924); Brooklyn Botanic Garden (Brooklyn, New York, 1910); Dominion Arboretum and Botanic Garden (Ottawa, Canada, 1886); Highland and Durand-Eastman Park (Rochester, New York, 1890); Fairchild Tropical Garden (Miami, Coconut Grove, Florida, 1938); Longwood Gardens (Kennett Square, Pennsylvania, 1906); New York Botanical Garden (Bronx, New York, 1895); and the Strybing Arboretum (San Francisco, California, 1937).

At the federal level, a few individuals a century ago attempted to develop an arboretum in the national capital area—one that would take its place among the world's noted botanical gardens. In 1927, Congress approved a bill that directed the secretary of agriculture, William Marion Jardine, "to establish and maintain a national arboretum for the purposes of research and education concerning tree and plant life." The necessary acquisition of land and early planting was under the co-stewardship of F. V. Coville and B. Y. Morrisen, both of the Division of Plant Exploration and Introduction. Today, the U. S. National Arboretum—one of the largest in the country, comprising 444 acres in the northeast section of the District of Columbia along the Anacostia River—conducts research on trees, shrubs, and herbaceous plants and provides the public with a variety of information regarding the nature of these plantings. In addition to the improvements of plants through introductions, breeding, and selection, the National Arboretum exchanges seeds and plant materials with other scientific institutions throughout the United States and the world, as do many other gardens in the United States. In keeping with its educational aims, many varieties of trees and shrubs are labeled and carefully documented. As with the other arboretums and botanical gardens in the country, the National Arboretum seeks to blend both aesthetically and artisti-

cally the natural and the artificial, the wild and the cultivated, the native and the foreign.

FURTHER READING: Ulysses P. Hedrick, *A History of Horticulture in America to 1860* (1950). Holden Arboretum, *The Prospective Role of an Arboretum: A Report Prepared under the Auspices of the Institute for the Study of Science in Human Affairs, Columbia University* (1972). S. B. Sutton, *The Arnold Arboretum: The First Century* (1971). Donald Wyman, comp., *The Arboretums and Botanical Gardens of North America* (1959).

ALAN E. FUSONIE

ARCHITECTURAL STYLES AND LUMBER UTILIZATION

When the American Colonies were being established in the seventeenth and eighteenth centuries, the continent of North America was in great part covered with unbroken areas of forest from the Atlantic seaboard to the Great Plains. There was scarcely any land that was not covered with trees, and there were few able-bodied men among the colonists who did not possess the skills of the carpenter. The concomitance of need, abundant resources, requisite talents, and limited capital, which long precluded the adoption of expensive masonry forms, meant that American building, from the early seventeenth to the mid-nineteenth century, was characterized by the most extensive use of timber construction in the history of the building arts.

Since mankind largely depended on wood and masonry as building materials until the Industrial Revolution, the forms of timber framing and other techniques had reached a high stage of development in Europe by the time the colonists established their first settlements. Building in wood originated in the very earliest paleolithic cultures, and the pioneer explorers found abundant evidence of that fact in the structures of native American peoples. American Indian dwellings revealed an extraordinary diversity of domed, vaulted, gabled, conical, and slab-walled forms erected from branches, shakes, or small trunks and covered with bark, sod, thatch, or skins, the enclosures ranging from simple lean-to shelters to the gabled "long houses" of the Iroquois and the sod-covered conical-domed dwellings of the Mandan cultures.

In a few cases the colonists learned from the Indians, but for the most part they brought with them the knowledge and the skills they had acquired in their native lands. Timber construction was confined very largely to the colonies of North European origin, which extended along the eastern seaboard north of Florida

Prestressed laminated wooden beams are manufactured according to specification. Forest History Society Photo.

or were centered around New Orleans. The great diversity of colonial techniques may be classified under three general headings: framed construction, the log house, and the plank house. Of these, framed construction appeared in the greatest variety of forms, all of which were derived from late medieval building in England and the northern lands of the Continent, and they were introduced into New England and the Middle Atlantic colonies during the early seventeenth century. The dominant mode, the so-called fair house or English house, consisted of a frame of heavy squared timbers of varying sizes functioning as sills, corner posts, girts (girders), floor joists, rafters, purlins, and bracing elements. Local variations derived from continental precedents took root in the Dutch colonies of the Hudson Valley and the German settlements of the Philadelphia hinterland. The connections between framing

members were nearly always the mortise-and-tenon variety.

Far to the south, around New Orleans, the French introduced special forms of quasi-framed construction. In the comparatively primitive technique known as *poteaux-en-terre*, walls consisted of massive trunklike posts set in trenches and back-filled, while in the more advanced form called *poteaux-sur-sole* the posts were set on a heavy sill, which could be protected from decay if it were kept perpetually saturated.

The elements of the medieval frame were susceptible to virtually endless variation and could be adapted to the broad vaults, gabled roofs, and spires of churches, to the wide-span floors in the assembly rooms of government buildings, and to the stout walls of palisaded forts. Throughout New England, the frame house was usually covered with clapboard siding, though shingles were widely used in the early years. The substantial houses of the Dutch and the German settlers and the great plantation houses of Virginia generally exhibited a combination of masonry bearing walls with timber frames. The framework of wood, however used, was literally a skeleton and could thus serve every kind of architectural style appropriate to the material.

The log house, or log cabin, as it is popularly called in the United States, was bearing-wall rather than framed construction, since the wall was a solid mass of timber into which openings for doors and windows had to be cut. Originating in far northern Europe among Scandinavian peoples, it was brought to America by Swedish colonists who first settled around Delaware Bay in 1638. Squared, split, or round logs, laid horizontally one above the other, could be made into a rigid box by means of notched, mortised, or dovetailed corners. The inevitable chinks between successive logs had to be stopped by clay or mixtures of clay, chips, and grass. Roof construction of boards and purlins covered with shingles was essentially that of English, Dutch, and German houses.

The plank house was the least common of colonial forms, although it was introduced at Plymouth as early as 1627; it was confined mainly to settlements in the Connecticut Valley. The walls consisted of heavy butted planks set in a grooved sill and covered with clapboard siding or, in a few cases, with battens, narrow strips of wood lying only over the joints. If a second story was added, a plate was placed over the lowermost row of planks to carry the superimposed row. Like the log house, the plank dwelling was enclosed in bearing walls that supported internal beams, joists, and rafters as well as their own weight. And also like the log structure, the plank walls offered the excellent insulating properties of a thick body of wood, provided, of course, that joints and chinks could be adequately stopped.

The heavy timber frame of medieval ancestry, rendered much more serviceable by the invention of iron nails, spikes, and bolts and the large power-driven circular saw, offered unlimited structural possibilities. Long after iron had been introduced in England, and even after its belated appearance in the United States, the column-and-girder frame of wood was steadily expanded in size and constantly altered in form for use in mills, other kinds of factories, stores, warehouses, office blocks, and the immense proliferation of buildings called forth by the railroad. Except for such odd forms as the circular engine house and the coal dock, most of the industrial and commercial structures were supported by the familiar framework of heavy posts, girders, plates, sills, beams, and rafters. The timber frame was everywhere called "mill construction," or, later, "loft space." If there was a common ancestor, it was the wood-sheathed and wood-framed Slater Mill, erected at Pawtucket, Rhode Island, in 1793.

The mill frame and its variations seemed to answer every need, but it was unmanageably heavy for use in relatively small structures subject only to modest loads, such as single-family residences. This limitation was overcome with the invention of the balloon frame, which was the creation of a Chicago surveyor, George Washington Snow, in 1832. The earliest public building to embody the new structural system was St. Mary's Church, erected in Chicago by Augustine D. Taylor in 1833. The balloon frame is composed of a dense array of studs, joists, sills, rafters, and bracing elements of such light sections (usually the standard two-by-four-inch board) as to be manageable by one man equipped with hammer, nails, and handsaw. The technique not only made possible the rapid building up of the American West but also provided the groundwork for prefabricated construction. The heavy timbers of the mill frame were eventually superseded by iron, steel, and reinforced concrete, but the balloon frame is still the fundamental technique for the building of single-family residences.

Perhaps the most conspicuous example of construction with wood during the age of its ascendancy was the timber-truss bridge, a form in which the United States led the world. The timber roof truss was a late Hellenistic invention, and in the basic forms of king-post and queen-post, it was used down through the ages wherever spans resulted in loads that exceeded the bearing capacity of simple rafters and ties. Hidden between roofs and ceilings, the truss went unnoticed except by carpenters, but when the loads and spans of bridges passed beyond the strength of traditional pile-and-beam structures, timber trusses began to proliferate in a great multitude of forms. The initiator in America of this immensely important phase of structural development was Timothy Palmer, who in 1792 revived the arched truss, invented by Andrea Palladio in the sixteenth century, for a bridge over the Merrimack River at Newburyport, Massachusetts. Palmer invented the technique of protecting the trusses of his bridges with weatherboarding and thus created the once familiar covered bridge in the United States.

The great age of the timber truss and the timber arch coincided with the early decades of railroad construction (1830–1860), but the widely used truss forms invented by such pioneers as Theodore Burr (arch-and-truss, 1817), Ithiel Town (lattice truss, 1820), and Stephen Long (double-diagonal panels, 1830) antedated the railroad era. The type that very nearly superseded all the rest was patented by William Howe in 1841. Like the Long truss, it was reduced to two diagonals in each panel, with the diagonals as compressive members and the "posts" as tension. It was adopted for rail and highway spans and canal aqueducts throughout the country, and although it was fast disappearing around 1900, it survived on rural highways in Oregon until 1960 as the result of a deliberate policy adopted by the state highway department. Ironically, the very factors that brought the timber truss bridge to its highest stage of development also spelled its undoing. The expanding railroad system demanded bridges in unprecedented numbers, but the constantly increasing train loads, the need to span the great rivers of the Mississippi Basin, and the ever present danger of fire compelled the builders to turn to iron in place of wood as a primary structural material. Although the timber trestle carried on braced bents of piling still may be found in many parts of the country, long-span arch-and-truss bridges of iron and later steel everywhere took the place of their timber progenitors.

All the essential forms of timber construction—column-and-beam frames, balloon frames, trusses, arches, and their derivatives—had been developed by the mid-nineteenth century. There was little room for further experiments in the nature of individual elements. Innovations in fastening devices, adhesives, and the shaping of wood pieces, however, led to novel structural techniques, even though the resulting forms might have followed established traditions.

Lamella or diagrid construction, in which a great number of small pieces are bolted together to form a rigid network curved to the shape of a vault or a dome, offered an inexpensive way to roof wide spans without intermediate supports. The system was introduced into the United States in 1928, when lamella vaults were used to cover the temporary auditorium erected in Houston, Texas, to house the nominating convention of the Democratic party. The technique, unfortunately, has usually been confined to temporary structures built for expositions. The development of high-strength adhesives in the twentieth century led to a revival of the timber arch through the invention of glued laminated forms. An arch composed of laminated segments can be made stronger than monoxylic pieces of equal depth by varying the direction of the grain in the successive laminae. The technique was first used in 1937 to support the roof of the municipal auditorium in Jamestown, North Dakota.

Plywood, an outgrowth of wood veneers, was invented by French craftsmen in the eighteenth century, but it was not thought to possess a structural potentiality until the mid-twentieth. In the building boom following World War II, plywood began to be used in load-bearing members such as box girders and channels. Its most extensive application to the building process has come in the formwork necessary for reinforced concrete construction.

By the end of the nineteenth century, timber had largely given way to construction in ferrous metals and concrete for large buildings. The traditional material, however, survived in many varieties of mill construction, especially in warehouses, and in the special structures required for railroad operations. As these began to disappear with changing modes of production and transportation, the demand for lumber continued to rise because of the constant and rapid expansion of the production of single-family residences. The pressure on forest resources was thus unrelenting, and since forests play an essential role in regional ecosystems, methods of conservation, reseeding, and harvesting had to be developed not only to maintain the supply of structural wood but also to preserve the major areas of forestland. The maintenance of this precarious equilibrium is one of the continuing fundamental problems faced by all advanced industrial cultures.

FURTHER READING: Carl W. Condit, *American Building Art: The Nineteenth Century* (1960), and *American Building: Materials and Techniques* (1968). James M. Fitch, *American Building: The Historical Forces That Shaped It* (1966). Hugh Morrison, *Early American Architecture* (1952). Charles E. Peterson, ed., *Building Early America* (1972).

CARL W. CONDIT

ARIZONA FORESTS

Arizona has the largest continuous stand of ponderosa pine in the United States. This forest covers the Colorado Plateau from the rim of the Grand Canyon southeasterly to the New Mexico line, a distance of 250 miles. Elevations there are 6,500 feet and above, and precipitation generally exceeds eighteen inches annually. Other small units of commercial timber occur at the upper elevations of the numerous isolated mountain ranges in the southern and eastern areas of the state and on the Kaibab Plateau north of the Grand Canyon. Ponderosa pine is replaced at the higher elevations and on cool northern slopes by Douglas-fir, white fir, and spruce. Small, pure stands of quaking aspen are found as a transition type in all forested areas above the pine zone. Volumes in the pine forest gener-

Water, timber, and forage on the Apache National Forest, 1958. Forest Service Photo.

ally run from 5,000 to 15,000 board feet per acre. The higher mixed conifer stands have volumes approaching twice that amount. There are also three types of noncommercial woodlands in Arizona: the extensive pinyon-juniper type; the cypress type (composed of both Arizona and smooth cypress); and the evergreen oak type (made up of Emory and Arizona oak). Altogether, about 19.2 million acres, or 26 percent of the state's land area, are in forest or woodland. Only 3.2 million acres are classed as commercial, and these are chiefly covered by pine, fir, and spruce.

Forest conservation in Arizona began with the proclamation of the Grand Canyon Forest Reserve in 1893 and the Prescott, San Francisco Mountains, and Black Mesa reserves in 1898. Stockmen and miners opposed these reserves, but irrigators welcomed

them, However, the appointment in 1901 of former sheepman Albert F. POTTER to administer grazing policy led to the development of amicable relations between the U. S. FOREST SERVICE and stock interests. Grazing has since been the major use of the noncommercial woodlands. In 1980, about 63 percent of Arizona's commercial forestland was within the boundaries of the state's seven national forests. Only 4 percent was in private hands, while Indian reservations contained 31 percent, leaving but a small amount in state or other public ownership.

As the state owned less than 1 percent of the forestland, Arizona was slow to establish a state forestry agency. State forestlands were managed by the Forest Service under a cooperative agreement after 1910. Not until the 1970s was a forestry division formed in the

State Lands Commission to administer forest practice laws and protect commercial forest and woodlands outside of federal jurisdiction.

There are several units of the National Park System in Arizona; the only one to hold an extensive forested area is GRAND CANYON NATIONAL PARK, established as a national monument in 1909 and enlarged several times since to 1.2 million acres.

As early as 1869, Arizona's reported lumber production reached 1.2 million board feet. Sawmills were established in the Flagstaff area in the early 1880s when the Santa Fe Railroad was constructed. Lumber output increased more or less constantly thereafter, and a century later the annual production totaled some 425 million board feet. Most of the lumber manufactured always came from ponderosa pine. By the 1950s, nearly 90 percent was shipped to markets in other states. A second major forest industry was a large pulp and paper mill opened at Snowflake in the early 1960s, the only such mill in the southern Rocky Mountain area. Its wood supply was largely ponderosa pine thinnings and chips, a by-product in the manufacture of lumber. Poles, posts, and fuel were also important products of Arizona forests. The noncommercial woodlands were long of local significance in supplying wood products, and with the energy shortage of the 1970s, they appeared important as a source of fuel. In the 1950s, a quarter of the state's manufacturing payroll came from wood- using industries.

Watershed and wildlife continue to be important contributions of the state's forests. Deer and elk are the principal big game. Forest ranges are also essential to the state's livestock industry.

Arizona forests are subject to heavy recreational use in both summer and winter. Several developed ski areas are located on the Colorado Plateau. Summer recreation in the higher, cooler elevations is important in a state where the major population centers are located in the low, hot valleys.

The first field research program of the Forest Service was the Fort Valley Experimental Forest in the Flagstaff vicinity, established in 1908—five years before statehood. Research has been conducted there continuously since that date. Another early research program was initiated on the Santa Rita Experimental Range near Tucson. Findings from work there have been applied in the management of forest ranges throughout the Southwest.

FURTHER READING: Association of State Foresters, *Forests and Forestry in the United States: A Reference Anthology*, Ralph R. Widner, ed. (1968), pp. 399-404.

DAHL J. KIRKPATRICK

ARKANSAS FORESTS

Of the 33,616,000 land acres in the state, 32 million were originally forested. About 110 species of trees were native to Arkansas and some 50 of these have had commercial value. Oak, gum, and other hardwoods with scattered areas of pine covered the Ozark Mountains and plateau of northern Arkansas. The plains to the south and southwest were a vast expanse of shortleaf and loblolly pine, laced by strips of riverbottom hardwoods. The deep soil of the broad Mississippi River bottomland along the eastern border of the state supported oak, gum, and cypress.

A steam-powered sawmill is said to have begun operation at Helena in 1826. Ozark farmers cleared tracts for agriculture and supplemented meager livings by cutting and selling white oak for barrel staves and red oak for wagon stock. The rich pineries of the southern part of the state were not extensively exploited until the 1870s and 1880s, largely because of the abundance of Lake States softwoods in national markets and because Arkansas's shortleaf and loblolly pine had not been able to compete with the longleaf pine further south. Furthermore, Arkansas lacked the financial resources needed for development of mass-production industries. However, when lumbermen could see the approaching end of the white pine of New England and the Great Lakes region, many of them turned southward, intending to follow the traditional and heretofore successful policies of complete exploitation before moving on again to another new territory. In the late nineteenth century, huge tracts of Arkansas timberland were brought under single ownerships. Some two dozen operations dominated the industry, among them the Crossett, Fordyce, Bradley, Southern, and Union Sawmill companies. By 1909, Arkansas ranked as the fifth state in lumber production, with over 2.1 million board feet of lumber cut in that year. Much of it was shipped to the cities of the upper Midwest, New York, and Pennsylvania. Production thereafter dropped gradually, settling around half of its 1909 peak by the 1920s. Except during the Depression era, annual lumber production stayed somewhat over 1 billion board feet through the 1950s. Supplying smaller mills than those which had characterized the earlier lumber boom, loggers and pulpwood cutters of the later 1930s and the 1940s took the smaller trees which once had been left behind.

Half the wood cut in the peak year of 1909 had gone for purposes other than lumber, and, unlike lumber, this production remained relatively constant thereafter. The major products included fuelwood, posts, poles

A steam skidder at work in
Arkansas, 1900. Forest
Service Photo.

and piling, dimension stock, crossties, cooperage, veneer, and (after 1923) pulpwood. Much of this production was shipped out of the state.

By the 1920s, land clearing had reduced the state's forested area to 22 million acres, of which barely 2 million were old growth (and of this, 750,000 were contained in national forests). Of the second-growth forestlands, only 5 million acres were effectively stocked. By this time, it had become evident to many lumbermen that there would be no place to go when moving time came: little old-growth timberland was available in the South, and competitors had moved in ahead of them in the West. In adopting conservation and reforestation policies, Arkansas lumbermen did what conditions forced them to do, but they did it ahead of most operators in the South. Arkansas lumbermen followed the leadership of Henry Hardtner, who had been experimenting with reforestation on his holdings in central Louisiana, and of Herman Haupt CHAPMAN and Ralph C. Bryant of the Yale School of Forestry, who trained their students on field trips to Crossett, Arkansas. Cutover timberland and abandoned agricultural land became the base for a new lumber industry in the state. Commercial forest growth has exceeded timber drain from all causes at least since the early 1950s, and forest industries have

provided one-third of the state's manufacturing payroll.

Federal forest protection in Arkansas began with the establishment of the Arkansas National Forest in the pine region in the western part of the state in 1907 (name changed to Ouachita in 1926) and the Ozark National Forest in the uplands in 1908. The small St. Francis National Forest was established from Bankhead-Jones Act reclaimed farmland in the Mississippi River bottomlands. By 1977, the National Forest System owned 2,469,000 acres in the state.

State forestry in Arkansas has been concerned primarily with the elimination of fires, traditionally set by local residents to drive game, improve the range, and destroy insect pests. Officials of some of the larger forest products companies supported formation of the Arkansas Forest Protection Association in 1928, and that organization led efforts for legislation authorizing a state forestry commission in 1931. However, no funds were made available until 1933, when Charles Gillett, state extension forester, became Arkansas's first state forester. Arkansas was the last forested state in the continental United States to accept responsibilities for forest protection. Despite help from the CIVILIAN CONSERVATION CORPS, early plans proved too ambitious, and only after repeated administrative reorganizations was Arkansas in the mid-1950s in a position to establish effective statewide fire suppression.

State action in other phases of conservation also developed slowly in Arkansas. The Fish and Game Commission was established in 1915. Arkansas's first state park, Petit Jean, was established as a small tract of only eighty acres in 1921 in response to fears that the scenic value of the area would be destroyed by logging. Later, the park was enlarged by a donation from a lumber company. In 1927, the legislature created a state park commission which moved toward eventual establishment of a system of parks.

In 1977, of Arkansas's 18,282,000 forested acres, 18,207,000 held commercial timber. Just under 15 percent of the commercial timberland was federally owned, 1 percent belonged to state or local government, and 84 percent was private.

FURTHER READING: E. Murray Bruner, *Forestry and Forest Fires in Arkansas*. Arkansas Agricultural Extension Service, Extension Circular No. 218 (1930). Fred H. Lang, "Two Decades of State Forestry in Arkansas," *Arkansas Historical Quarterly* 24 (Autumn 1965): 208-219.

CORLISS C. CURRY

ARMY CORPS OF ENGINEERS

The Second Continental Congress appointed Colonel Richard Gridley the first chief engineer on June 16, 1775. Four years later, in March 1779, Congress authorized the establishment of a Corps of Engineers. Shortly after the end of the Revolution in 1783, the corps was disbanded. When Congress authorized new coastal fortifications in 1794, President Washington turned for help to French engineers. He appointed Stephen Rochefontaine the head of a Corps of Artillerists and Engineers to plan and construct the fortifications. Rochefontaine, at the president's urging, also began to set up a military engineering school at West Point, New York. This became the foundation of the United States Military Academy, formally established by Congress in 1802. At that time, Congress agreed to President Jefferson's request that a separate Corps of Engineers be reconstituted. Thus, the continuous history of the corps dates back to March 16, 1802, when Colonel Jonathan Williams was appointed chief engineer and the first superintendent of West Point.

The corps's involvement in civil works began in 1824. Congress passed two bills, one to remove sandbars and snags from the Mississippi and Ohio rivers, the other to order a survey of roads and canals "of national importance, in a commercial or military point

of view." The corps's responsibilities to insure the navigability of major rivers expanded in the coming years.

After the Civil War, the corps also contributed to some early flood control efforts, although the official justification for such work remained the preservation of inland navigation. Only in 1917, when Congress authorized flood control work on the Mississippi and Sacramento rivers, did the federal government become explicitly involved in flood control work. The corps's work on the Mississippi tremendously increased in 1928, when, following a disastrous flood on the lower river, Congress passed the Mississippi River and Tributaries Act. Eight years later, on June 22, 1936, Congress declared "that flood control on navigable rivers or their tributaries is a proper activity of the Federal Government in cooperation with States, their political sub-divisions, and localities thereof." It authorized the corps to construct reservoirs in a number of river basins throughout the country, considerably expanding the corps's flood control responsibilities. As federal agencies became more involved in multipurpose water resource development—flood control, navigation, irrigation, hydroelectric power, and water supply—it became necessary to demarcate each agency's obligations. The Flood Control acts of 1936, 1938, and 1944 mandated specific functional and geographical areas of responsibilities for the corps, the BUREAU OF RECLAMATION, and the DEPARTMENT OF AGRICULTURE (Soil Conservation Service), insuring coordination and reducing the disruptive bureaucratic conflicts.

These conflicts dated back to the beginning of the twentieth century and included a controversy between foresters and engineers over the effects of forestation on river flows. Many conservationists, led by Gifford PINCHOT, argued that forestation was a flood prevention device. They proposed to President Theodore ROOSEVELT that the federal government purchase timberland reserves to reduce flood flows and improve navigation during droughts. General Hiram Chittenden, an engineer officer who had won national acclaim for his construction of a road system in YELLOWSTONE NATIONAL PARK that attempted to reconcile WILDERNESS PRESERVATION with public access, opposed Pinchot. Chittenden argued that there was no scientific evidence that deforestation caused greater floods. This raised a cry from conservationists who accused the corps of opposing good forestry practices. This was not the case; neither Chittenden nor any of his fellow engineer officers opposed sound forest conservation, and many were in favor of the creation of the NATIONAL PARK SERVICE. What they did oppose, however, was the proposition that deforestation affected streamflow. In the end, nevertheless, the foresters won; Congress in 1911 enacted the WEEKS ACT, which approved federal–state cooperation in acquiring lands as national forests in order to improve streamflow.

As the corps's flood control and hydroelectric functions grew, so did its regulatory activities. Legislation to prevent obstructions to navigation can be traced back to 1890. It was the 1899 Refuse Act (Section 13 of the Rivers and Harbors Act) that firmly established the corps's authority to require permits before anything could be dumped, deposited, or constructed in any United States navigable waterway.

The corps administered the 1899 Act to protect only the navigability of the nation's rivers until 1969 when the corps changed its regulations to include other factors besides navigation in determining permit eligibility. These encompassed fish and wildlife, conservation, pollution, aesthetics, ecology, and the general public interest. Corps attempts to eliminate water pollution accelerated once the NATIONAL ENVIRONMENTAL POLICY ACT was implemented on January 1, 1970, and in response to mounting public concerns about the problem. On April 7, 1971, the corps implemented the first nationwide program to regulate the discharge of pollutants into the country's waters.

Many of the corps's regulatory functions resulted from procedures established by the 1972 Federal Water Pollution Control Act, which significantly modified corps responsibilites. A stringent permit program to control water pollution was established, but although the corps retained some responsibility in this field, the program came under the administration of the Environmental Protection Agency. However, the corps was authorized to regulate the discharge of dredged and fill material into navigable waters.

Over the years, the corps has been called upon to undertake a variety of missions in its civil works program. It has supported emergency relief activities, provided hurricane flood protection, and conducted numerous studies related to beach erosion, water supply problems, water quality control, aquatic plant growth, and drainage problems. Two of its major roles have been in outdoor recreation and in fish and wildlife conservation and enhancement. Approximately 2.5 million acres of corps land have been used primarily for fish and wildlife purposes, and of this one-fifth has been managed by other federal and state agencies in cooperation with the corps.

The corps has also been involved in forest management. Since World War II, it has worked closely with the Soil Conservation Service to insure proper drainage of watershed areas. In 1980, the corps owned over 600,000 acres of forest, of which nearly a fourth was administered by other federal, local, and private agencies. In addition, the corps, employing professional foresters, managed approximately 1.5 million acres of forest on military installations.

FURTHER READING: Albert E. Cowdrey, "Pioneering Environmental Law: The Army Corps of Engineers and the Refuse Act," *Pacific Historical Review* 46 (Aug. 1975): 331-349. Gordon B. Dodds, *Hiram Martin Chittenden: His Public Career* (1973), and "The Stream-Flow Controversy: A Conservation Turning Point," *Journal of American History* 56 (June 1969): 59-69. W. Stull Holt, *The Office of the Chief of Engineers of the Army: Its Non-Military History, Activities, and Organization* (1923). Daniel A. Mazmanian and Jeanne Nienaber, *Can Organizations Change? Environmental Protection, Citizen Participation, and the Corps of Engineers* (1979). Frank N. Schubert, *Vanguard of Expansion: Army Engineers in the Trans-Mississippi West, 1819–1879* (1980).

MARTIN REUSS

ASIAN IMMIGRANTS AND AMERICAN FORESTS

Asian immigrants have made an enormous contribution to the economic development of the Pacific Slope where they have mostly settled. Measured against the total forest labor force, the number of Asians employed in western woods and mills is small. Those who did labor in the forests and mill towns proved courageous, working often in the face of racial prejudice expressed in vigilante action and refusals to offer long-term employment. The language barrier and growing unionism with an anti-Asian bias kept Asian workers out of certain jobs and held them at unskilled levels. Employment opportunities elsewhere led Asians to seek other careers.

The first Chinese laborers in the American forests were no doubt those who in 1788 accompanied John Meares to the Pacific Northwest where they hewed a cargo of ship's spars and timber for export to the Orient. Later, Chinese immigrants worked in mills on Puget Sound and Willapa Bay. During the 1880s, local Knights of Labor chapters were active in efforts to drive Chinese from the area and successfully did so in Tacoma. Although some millmen welcomed Chinese workers because of their cheapness, others considered them inefficient and hard to work with because of language and cultural barriers. Chinese were often assigned to the lath-making machines or some similar task where they could work as a full crew. Labor contractors in Seattle, Astoria, and elsewhere often supplied seasonal crews of Chinese to lumber mills, just as they did for salmon canneries and other such enterprises. The hostility that the Chinese met from white laborers was a forerunner of that met later by other Asians.

Japanese and East Indians were working throughout the Pacific Northwest in the early twentieth century finding easy employment at first because there was a general labor shortage. The East Indians had moved south from Vancouver, British Columbia, during 1907 following race riots in that city, to work in the Bellingham and Tacoma mills and woods. White workers in Bellingham immediately commenced hostility, and in September the East Indians were forced to flee. Three years later, a similar outbreak occurred at St. Johns (now a part of Portland, Oregon) where white citizens drove out East Indian workers. After 1917, East Indians were not admissible to the United States and those remaining in mill towns fled to California or British Columbia.

By 1910, about 2,500 Japanese were employed by Washington and Oregon lumber companies, comprising only 4 percent of the industry's work force. In 1913, there were 1,248 Asians in Washington mills and another 12 were found in logging camps. Japanese workers also encountered mob violence in the Northwest mill towns. In June 1913, white workers forced the Japanese out of Darrington, Washington, and in June 1925 the activites of Toledo, Oregon, mill-workers led the Japanese ambassador to protest the treatment of his countrymen. After the restrictive immigration act of 1924, the number of Japanese forest workers continued to decline. The northwestern Japanese congregated into clearly identifiable groups in a few mill communities. The Japanese in mill towns such as Port Blakely, Washington, had sought employment as a group and not individually. Companies built separate bunkhouses for them which were partitioned into apartments as the men gained wives. By 1940, only 483 Japanese worked in Washington. Two

hundred of them lived in Longview, employed by two companies.

The U. S. FOREST SERVICE reported in 1927 that it had no evidence of Japanese or Chinese working in California's forest industry. By 1940, only six Japanese worked in California's mills. and one was in the woods.

With World War II, the United States government removed the Japanese from the Pacific Coast states, closing their forest labor careers. After the war, Asians did not return to work in forest labor in significant numbers. The more recent Asian arrivals have congregated in urban centers, not seeing forest labor as an employment opportunity.

H. BRETT MELENDY

ASSOCIATION FOR CONSERVATION INFORMATION

Founded in 1938 as the American Association for Conservation Information, the organization has been expanded to accommodate Canadian applicants for membership. In 1980, the association included sixty-eight state and provincial professionals of conservation-oriented agencies—wildlife, fish and game, and some forestry services. As its name implies, the Association for Conservation Information is primarily an educational organization, sponsoring workshops, informational programs for both adults and children, and especially publicity for conservation in the mass media, particularly television. It makes annual awards for contributions to conservation consciousness and provides consultation services for states, provinces, and localities that do not maintain official conservation programs. It publishes the *Balance Wheel* bimonthly from its Denver, Colorado, editorial offices.

AUDUBON SOCIETY

See National Audubon Society

B

BALLINGER-PINCHOT CONTROVERSY

The Ballinger-Pinchot controversy began as a public event in August 1909 when a field agent of the GENERAL LAND OFFICE, Louis Glavis, approached President William Howard Taft with a document containing damaging accusations against Secretary of the Interior Richard Achilles Ballinger. Glavis obtained direct access to Taft by means of letters of introduction and support from the influential Chief Forester Gifford PINCHOT. Glavis charged that as commissioner of the General Land Office under Theodore ROOSEVELT, as a private attorney in Seattle after his resignation, and as secretary of the interior, Ballinger had improperly attempted to assist a group of thirty-three persons known as the Cunningham claimants, some his personal friends, to obtain title to coal lands in Alaska despite evidence that they had illegally agreed to combine with the Morgan-Guggenheim syndicate, a notorious trust widely believed to have a stranglehold on the Alaskan economy. After a month of deliberation and study, Taft exonerated Ballinger of any wrongdoing and Glavis was dismissed from public service. In November, after Glavis had made his charges public in an article in *Collier's Weekly*, Taft imposed an order of silence on government officials in a futile effort to quell the storm of criticism.

In January 1910, when it became apparent that a congressional investigation of the DEPARTMENT OF THE INTERIOR was in the offing, Ballinger demanded that it also encompass the activities of the U. S. FOREST SERVICE. In response, Gifford Pinchot ordered his subordinates to make a clean breast of their role. For the first time, it was publicly revealed that the original charges of Glavis and his article for *Collier's* were prepared with the active assistance of Forest Service officers and that over the fall the publicity section of the service had provided the press with a steady flow of material damaging to Ballinger. Taft dismissed Pinchot after the chief forester had defied the silence order by defending his subordinates and criticizing the president in a letter to Senator Jonathan P. Dolliver, chairman of the Committee on Agriculture. In the investigation that followed, Ballinger was cleared by the Republican majority, but his reputation was irretrievably damaged. The counsel for *Collier's*, Louis Brandeis, succeeded in proving that the administration had attempted to cover up the extent to which Taft's exoneration of Ballinger had actually been prepared in the Department of the Interior. Though innocent of the Glavis charges, Ballinger had lost his usefulness in the Taft administration; within a year he retired.

The antagonism between Pinchot and Ballinger was rooted in policy disputes that dated from the time when both served as bureau chiefs under Theodore Roosevelt. As commissioner of the General Land Office, Ballinger was often out of sympathy with resource policies promoted by bureaus in the Interior and Agriculture departments. He was in fact a declared enemy of the most creative concept to emerge in the Roosevelt Conservation Movement, of which Pinchot considered himself the principal architect: the multiple-purpose use of resources under terms that permitted continuous government regulation. As secretary of the interior, Ballinger threatened the implementation of this concept. His predecessor, James R. Garfield, had set aside thousands of acres on the public domain, believed to be useful for development as hydroelectric power sites under the authority of the Reclamation Act of 1902, which insured that ownership would remain in the government. The next step, which Garfield had no time to implement, was to have been a short-term lease and permit system under the authority of the Right-of-Way Act of 1901 that would have permitted continuous development and regulations similar to the existing program in the national forests. Ballinger, however, restored these sites, then withdrew them again from all forms of entry including the Right-of-Way Act of 1901, thus effectively blocking any program of continuous development and regulation.

Ballinger had been a strong bureau chief but jealous in all matters of jurisdictional prerogative. Because the Land Office and Forest Service shared overlapping jurisdictions, disputes between their chiefs were inevitable. When Ballinger became secretary of the interior, he was revealed as the enemy of another central pillar of the conservation movement: the coordinated program between bureaus in the same or different departments. The Roosevelt administration had solved the problem of overlapping jurisdictions by implementing a series of makeshift arrangements, informal agreements between the Interior and Agriculture departments. Pinchot was especially vulnerable here. The Transfer Act of 1905 gave the secretary of agriculture—in reality the Forest Service—full authority to administer the forest reserves, but it left questions involving land titles or criminal prosecution in the Interior Department, that is, the General Land Office. An informal agreement in 1905 allowed the Forest Service to make the final determination in matters affecting land title, but Secretary Ballinger blocked Pinchot's attempt to have the secretary of agriculture assume the functions which the Department of the Interior still performed under the Transfer Act of 1905. He also canceled an agreement between the Forest Service and the Office of Indian Affairs that permitted the foresters to manage the forests on Indian reservations.

Their competition for the presidential ear was the most important issue between Ballinger and Pinchot. This too was perhaps inevitable. Pinchot's relationship with President Roosevelt, his position as a virtual member of the cabinet in resource matters, had been the source of his strength. It enabled him to speak on the bureau level with almost presidential authority and to move with imperial ease across the lines separating bureau and departmental jurisdictions. As a symbol of his predecessor's most cherished policies, Pinchot was a personal and political problem for Taft, to be handled with care; the president dreaded the thought of estrangement from Roosevelt. Pinchot forced the issue by insisting on the same privileges he had enjoyed under Roosevelt. Taft was really closer in outlook to Ballinger, and as secretary of war he too had chafed under Pinchot's "meddling" in War Department affairs. On issue after issue he was forced to choose between Pinchot and Ballinger. Backing the Glavis charges was an all or nothing toss of the dice for Pinchot. When the president once again sided with Ballinger, the forester took his case to the public.

FURTHER READING: Paolo Coletta, *The Presidency of William Howard Taft* (1973). Samuel P. Hays, *Conservation and the Gospel of Efficiency: The Progressive Conservation Movement, 1890–1920* (1959). M. Nelson McGeary, *Gifford Pinchot: Forester Politician* (1960). James Penick, Jr., *Progressive Politics and Conservation: The Ballinger-Pinchot Affair* (1968). Elmo R. Richardson, *The Politics of Conservation: Crusades and Controversies, 1897-1913*, University of California Publications in History, vol. 70 (1962).

JAMES LAL PENICK, JR.

BARK PRODUCTS

Except for cork, which was imported, and such varieties of bark as were used in the tanning of leather and for other special purposes such as cascara used for medicinal purposes, tree bark was almost a total waste until well into the twentieth century. Where trees were not stripped before they were removed from the woods, the bark was not accounted in scaling and was used either as a rather unsatisfactory fuel or discarded, to become a nuisance and a source of water pollution around sawmills. Beginning in the 1930s, efforts were made at various times to manufacture and market compressed-fuel briquettes from pulpwood bark, sometimes mixed with sawdust. None of these products achieved widespread commercial success. By

Plastinail is the tradename of a bark derivative with nailable qualities. Here it is being used to make a box-car floor. Weyerhaeuser Company Photo.

1920, a very limited amount of redwood bark was marketed as ornamental mulch and some pulpwood barks were used in the manufacture of wallpaper and other specialty paper products. However, its extremely low value made it generally too expensive to ship and still return a profit to the producer.

During the late 1930s, The Pacific Lumber Company of San Francisco inaugurated a program of research into the possible uses of redwood bark and devised a process of "exploding" it, a cheap means of shredding the material into fibrous strands. "Palco Wool" proved to be an excellent, low-cost insulation material with a thermo-conductivity of .25 BTU. It

was well-suited to insulating large refrigerated areas which did not require extremely low temperatures such as cold storage facilities.

Douglas-fir bark has been found to have a variety of potential commercial uses when it is mechanically separated into three fractions: cork flakes, fiber, and amorphous powder. These products have been marketed in the Pacific Northwest by the Weyerhaeuser Company as "Silvacon" (a word coined by joining "silva" and "economical") and variously used in making plywood adhesive and filler, in the manufacture of tannin, in oil-well drilling muds, and, in combination with asphalt, cork, and rubber, in the new composition floorings of the 1940s and 1950s. During the 1970s, Bohemia Lumber Company of Eugene, Oregon, began using Douglas-fir bark in the manufacture of wax, in a finely divided bark powder marketed as a plywood glue extender, and in a granulated cork product.

Perhaps the most conspicuous use of bark in the 1960s and 1970s and, in terms of using what was previously total waste, the cheapest use of it was as mulch, paving for footpaths and driveways, and other ornamental uses in both residential and commercial landscaping. Long used for such purposes in timber growing areas, the raw, broken bark became a commercial commodity with the expansion of suburbia and public parks in the third quarter of the twentieth century. The packing of it provided a means of cost-free, nonpolluting waste disposal for sawmills; transportation costs accounted for the major part of the retail price.

FURTHER READING: J. Alfred Hall, *Utilization of Douglas-fir Bark* (1971).

BARTRAM, JOHN (1699–1777), AND WILLIAM BARTRAM (1739–1823)

John Bartram was America's first native-born naturalist. A poorly educated but prosperous farmer at Kingsessing on the Schuylkill River near Philadelphia, Bartram shared his love of plants with notable city folk such as James Logan and Benjamin Franklin. These friends provided Bartram with access to scientific books. Bartram verified Logan's pioneer conclusions on plant hybridization and he proposed to Franklin the organization of the American Philosophical Society. Bartram found a lifelong patron in the London merchant Peter Collinson. The seeds and plants which Bartram sent to Collinson enlarged the gardens and lawns of many collectors, and a number of European and American naturalists who corresponded with Collinson were encouraged by him to write also to Bartram.

Bartram undertook several journeys to collect specimens for these correspondents, and he sent Collinson accounts of his trips to New York in 1743 and Florida in 1765–1766. On the Florida trip he took

Baldcypress festooned with Spanish moss looks much as it did when John and William Bartram explored the Florida coast. American Forest Institute Photo.

along William, one of the younger of his eleven children.

William Bartram received the formal education which his father had lacked. William was more introspective and less practical than his father. He failed at business and at running a Southern plantation, but found his successes in the formation of friendships and in the writing of the most famous travel book to come out of eighteenth-century America. William Bartram had been so fascinated by the trip through Florida that he returned to the region for further explorations from 1773 to 1778. His expenses were met by a London physician, John Fothergill, and William repaid his patron with drawings of trees, flowers, birds, and reptiles.

The Bartrams were active naturalists during the exploratory phase of American natural science. They were interested in trees as part of the resources of the New World. In their collecting they were influenced by the tastes of their patrons, which favored the unusual more than the practical. John Bartram, however, was alert to the practical needs of settlers as well as to the aesthetic desires of European collectors. William Bartram accepted the penetration of white civilization into Indian country, but he did not follow his father's identification with the process. William thought it important to understand and appreciate the balance of nature in the wilderness, a wilderness that included Indians as well as wild animals and untamed vegetation.

The Bartram farm at Kingsessing was a mecca for naturalists from both Europe and America. Among those who visited it were Pehr Kalm, Cadwallader Colden, John Clayton, André MICHAUX, François André MICHAUX, and Thomas Jefferson. Both of the Bartrams shared their knowledge and encouragement as generously as they shared their plant specimens.

FURTHER READING: There is one adequate joint biography, Ernest P. Earnest, *John and William Bartram, Botanists and Explorers* (1940). Important letters and other information are in William Darlington, *Memorials of John Bartram and Humphry Marshall* (1849). Francis Harper has edited both John Bartram's *Diary of a Journey Through the Carolinas, Georgia, and Florida from July 1, 1765 to April 10, 1766*, American Philosophical Society Transactions, vol. 33 (1942), and the *Travels of William Bartram* (1958). Joseph Ewan has edited William Bartram's *Botanical and Zoological Drawings, 1756–1788*, American Philosophical Society Memoirs, vol. 74 (1968).

FRANK N. EGERTON

BIG CYPRESS NATIONAL PRESERVE

See Everglades National Park and Big Cypress National Preserve

BIG THICKET NATIONAL PRESERVE

On October 11, 1974, President Gerald Ford signed the act of Congress establishing an 84,550-acre Big Thicket National Preserve in southeastern Texas near Beaumont, not far from the Louisiana border. President Ford's signature ended more than twelve years of debate between timber firms and environmentalists. Lumbermen had argued that it would be economic folly to remove such a large acreage from timber production, while the environmentalists had lobbied for an even larger preserve.

Part of the problem in forging a compromise acceptable to both groups was the lack of an accepted definition of the Big Thicket. The timber companies thought of the thicket as simply the western extension of the southeastern evergreen forest which begins in Virginia and extends across the entire South. They believed it was in no way distinguished from adjacent woodlands.

On the other hand, environmentalists such as Clyde McLeod, a botany professor at Sam Houston State University in Huntsville, maintained that a particular combination of soil and moisture had created in the Big Thicket a loblolly pine–hardwood association that possessed a rich understory of evergreen and deciduous shrubs, climbing vines, and annual and perennial herbs. This association, indeed different from the surrounding woods, had once covered over 2 million acres. By the 1960s, it had been reduced to some 300,000 acres. Within it were eight major plant communities which environmentalists believed should be protected from further logging encroachment.

The NATIONAL PARK SERVICE had examined the area with preservation in mind as early as 1938, but the real drive to preserve the Big Thicket began in 1961 when Governor Price Daniel proposed setting aside a portion of the thicket as a state park. This plan was shelved after Daniel was defeated in his bid for reelection.

Daniel's initiative, however, generated support for a park, and on October 4, 1964, a group of would-be preservationists met in the small town of Saratoga to form the Big Thicket Association with Dempsie Henley from nearby Liberty as its first permanent president. A year later, Henley enlisted the support of United States Senator Ralph Yarborough for a Big Thicket National Park. In 1970, however, the Big Thicket lost its second political champion with Yarborough's defeat for reelection. By that time, a new, more aggressive element had joined the preservation movement. Determined to carry the fight to the timber firms, this element ousted Henley from leadership of the Big Thicket Association and established a new Big Thicket Co-ordinating Committee, an umbrella organization which represented a variety of groups seeking a park.

As the timber companies said, the new leaders in the preservation movement came primarily from large metropolitan areas; most were attorneys and college professors. The guiding force was A. Y. "Pete" Gunter, a philosophy professor from North Texas State University in Denton. Over the next several years, Gunter made numerous radio and television appearances and otherwise conducted a blistering public relations campaign that left the timber firms reeling. As one lumberman stated, "He whipsawed us to death."

With public sentiment growing in favor of a park, Texas politicians found a compromise. Eventually in 1974, Congressman Charles Wilson of Lufkin and Robert Eckhardt of Houston presented a bill in Congress which led to the establishment of a national preserve composed of several small tracts scattered among seven counties. The preserve protects representative samples of the wide variety of Big Thicket flora.

FURTHER READING: James Cozine, "Assault on a Wilderness: The Big Thicket of East Texas," Ph.D. dissertation, Texas A & M University (1976).

JAMES COZINE

BIOLOGICAL SURVEY

The Bureau of Biological Survey was established in 1885 as an economic ornithology section in the Department of Agriculture's Division of Entomology. In 1886, it became the Division of Ornithology and Mammalogy, and in 1896, the Division of Biological Survey. In 1905, it gained status as a bureau and so it remained until 1939, when it was transferred to the DEPARTMENT OF THE INTERIOR. In 1940, it was consolidated with Interior's Bureau of Fisheries to form the FISH AND WILDLIFE SERVICE.

As the original name implies, the agency's early emphasis was the scientific study of bird distribution and food habits in relation to agriculture. The range of study was extended to mammals when the agency began a series of biological surveys of the United States under the direction of its chief, Clinton Hart Merriam (1855–1942), using Merriam's theory of life zones in relation to temperature. The resulting series of publications, *North American Fauna*, established the bureau as an authority on mammalogy in the United States.

Wildlife regulatory functions were thrust upon the bureau by the Lacey Game and Wild Birds Preservation and Disposition Act of 1900. The Lacey Act made the interstate shipment of wildlife taken or sold in violation of state laws a federal offense. In succeeding years, the agency also administered the Alaska game laws of 1902, 1908, 1921, and 1925, the Federal Migratory Bird Law of 1913 and its successor, the Migratory Bird Treaty Act of 1918, the 1929 Migratory Bird Conservation Act, the 1934 Migratory Bird Hunting Stamp Act (Duck Stamp Act), and the 1937 Pittman-Robertson Federal Aid to Wildlife Restoration Act.

As the Biological Survey assumed heavier administrative and regulatory responsibilities during the 1920s, it became embroiled in public controversy over issues of predatory animal control programs, federal bag limits for waterfowl, and management of wildlife refuges. The agency's premise that waterfowl population was on the increase was challenged by conservationists, who charged that game bag limits were set too high. In 1927, the Biological Survey responded by initiating a comprehensive waterfowl census. The three-year study involved thousands of volunteers and pioneered the practice of bird-banding. Results showed that the waterfowl population was indeed declining, and the agency subsequently altered its position on game bag limits and the length of the hunting season. However, the ten-year controversy discredited it as an authority on the status of wildlife in the United States. During the 1930s, the Biological Survey continued its scientific work, but its primary focus shifted to regulating game laws and managing a wildlife refuge system that expanded from 1 million acres in 1932 to 9 million acres in 1940.

In addition to the erosion of its status as a scientific agency, the Biological Survey was subject to bureaucratic struggles during the 1930s between its parent, the DEPARTMENT OF AGRICULTURE, and the Department of the Interior. In 1939, under Reorganization Plan No. II, the agency was transferred to the Department of the Interior; in the following year, it was merged with the department's Bureau of Fisheries under Ira N. Gabrielson to become the Fish and Wildlife Service.

FURTHER READING: Jenks Cameron, *History of the Biological Survey* (1929, 1973). Theodore W. Cart, "'New Deal' for Wildlife: A Perspective on Federal Conservation Policy, 1933–40," *Pacific Northwest Quarterly* (July 1972): 113–120. David L. Lendt, *Ding: The Life of Jay Norwood Darling* (1979). Keir Brooks Sterling, *Last of the Naturalists: The Career of C. Hart Merriam* (1977). Donald C. Swain, *Federal Conservation Policy, 1921–1933* (1963).

BLACKS AND AMERICAN FORESTS

Black workers have made a large contribution to forest industries since colonial days. In New England

and Pennsylvania as well as Virginia and the Carolinas they logged and sawed timber and worked in the NAVAL STORES industries. As slavery expanded across the South in the nineteenth century, the large majority of black forest workers were concentrated in that region. Until World War I, about 90 percent of all blacks lived in the Southern states. Although most of the blacks in the forest industries were loggers and turpentine workers, some became highly skilled and a few were entrepreneurs. For example, Simon Gray, although a slave, was master of a Mississippi River steamboat, hauling cypress lumber and accepting payments on behalf of his owner for many years.

Between 1865 and 1920, southern yellow pine became the major construction lumber in the nation and naval stores production expanded enormously. Freedmen constituted a large proportion of the workers in these industries. Blacks were also employed in the Pennsylvania charcoal industry and the Michigan forests. The lumber company town of McNary, Arizona, had a predominantly black population. But the majority of black forest workers remained in the South until the 1920s.

In the late nineteenth century, blacks constituted about a fourth of all forest industry employees, and some of them became managers and owners. There were 195 black owners of timber companies and 111 foremen in 1910, as well as about 16,000 stevedores and longshoremen, some of whom were independent contractors. Among the nearly 200,000 blacks in work related to forest products at the time were 5,437 charcoal workers, 1,198 pulp and paper employees, 111,283 engaged in saw and planing operations, 25,525 in logging and timber, 7,162 in turpentine distilling, and 24,341 in turpentine farming.

The life of the majority of black forest workers—those engaged in unskilled logging and turpentine work—was a difficult one. Most lived and worked in company-owned communities. They worked for low wages and were charged high rents for primitive housing, exorbitant prices for purchases at the monopoly commissaries, and excessive interest for credit advances. The customs and laws of the Southern states allowed widespread abuse of forest workers. Since slavery days there was a prevailing belief among Southern whites that blacks would not work without coercion. After slavery was abolished, most Southern states enacted laws which used debt to keep blacks on the job. Usually, these statutes prohibited workers who accepted advances of credit from leaving their employers until their debts were cleared. All their supplies came from a commissary on credit. Records were kept by the company and wages were

cleared through the commissary before workers were paid. Often, the workers were still indebted after payday. Although such laws were declared unconstitutional in *Bailey* v. *Alabama* in 1911, these practices continued in many states. Testimony obtained by U. S. Commissioner Fred C. Cubberly in Dixie County, Florida, in the 1920s revealed black workers who had been kept in camps for fifteen or more years by debt. Florida's debt law was not declared unconstitutional until 1945.

Some blacks attempted to improve their situation by forming labor unions. Longshoremen were organized in most of the port towns beginning in the 1870s and some millworkers attempted collective efforts. The radical Industrial Workers of the World attempted unsuccessfully to organize both black and white timber workers in Texas and Louisiana just before World War I.

After 1918, many blacks migrated out of the South and some engaged in forest work in all regions of the nation. Conditions of employment subsequently improved for blacks as well as for forest workers generally. Blacks continued to comprise about a fourth of the total forest industries work force until the 1950s when they numbered just over 143,000. Both their number and their proportion of the forest labor force declined after that. In 1960, 76,369 blacks comprised 18.4 percent of all forest industry workers.

FURTHER READING: Pete Daniel, *Shadow of Slavery: Peonage in the South, 1901–1969* (1972). Philip S. Foner, "The IWW and the Black Worker," *Journal of Negro History* 55 (Jan. 1970): 45-57. Jeremy W. Kilar, "Black Pioneers in the Michigan Lumber Industry," *Journal of Forest History* 24 (July 1980): 142-149. John Hebron Moore, "Simon Gray, Riverman: A Slave Who Was Almost Free," *Mississippi Valley Historical Review* 49 (Dec. 1962): 474-484. Jerrell H. Shofner, "Negro Laborers and the Forest Industries in Reconstruction Florida," *Journal of Forest History* 19 (Oct. 1975): 180-191. Joseph E. Walker, "Negro Labor in the Charcoal Industry of Southeastern Pennsylvania," *Pennsylvania Magazine of History and Biography* 93 (Oct. 1969): 466-486. Curtis W. Wienker, "McNary: A Predominantly Black Company Town in Arizona," *Negro History Bulletin* 37 (Aug.-Sept. 1974): 282-285.

JERRELL H. SHOFNER

BOONE AND CROCKETT CLUB

In December 1887, Theodore ROOSEVELT invited a number of his sportsman friends and relatives to a dinner party in Manhattan at which he proposed the creation of a hunting-conservation organization. The idea for such an association had originated in conversations between Roosevelt and his friend George Bird GRIN-

NELL, editor of *Forest and Stream Weekly* and the leading sportsman-conservationist of his day. Roosevelt's recommendation was accepted by those present at the dinner, all of whom were prominent, wellborn New Yorkers. The club was formally organized in January 1888 and named after two of America's most famous hunters. Roosevelt was elected as the club's first president, serving until 1894. Archibald Rogers was the first secretary-treasurer.

Grinnell, Roosevelt, and Rogers formulated the club's constitution; Article II stated the organization's five purposes: "to promote manly sport with the rifle"; "to promote travel and exploration in the wild and unknown, or but partially known, portions of the country"; "to work for the preservation of the large game of this country, and, so far as possible, to further legislation for that purpose, and to assist in enforcing the existing laws"; "to promote inquiry into, and to record observations on the habits and natural history of, the various wild animals"; and "to bring about among the members the interchange of opinions and ideas on hunting, travel, and exploration; on the various kinds of hunting rifles; on the haunts of game animals, etc."

Regular membership was limited to one hundred men, all of whom had to "have killed with the rifle in fair chase, by still-hunting or otherwise, at least one individual of three of the various kinds of American large game." Members were to be thorough outdoorsmen, and not armchair naturalists. However, associate membership was extended to those who had worked for wildlife conservation but who were not big-game hunters. Regular and associate members, later prominent as conservationists, included Gifford PINCHOT, Madison Grant (who would be a founder of the SAVE-THE-REDWOODS LEAGUE), Arnold Hague of the U. S. GEOLOGICAL SURVEY, C. Hart Merriam, head of the U. S. BIOLOGICAL SURVEY, author Charles Sheldon, and lawyer/biologist George Shiras III.

With influential, upper class individuals as members and with Grinnell's *Forest and Stream* as its "natural mouthpiece," the club played a key role in bringing several nationally important conservation projects to fruition. One of its first major efforts was to promote passage of the 1894 Yellowstone Park Protection Act, which established the concept that national parks should be inviolate wildlife and wilderness sanctuaries. The club also made an important, behind-the-scenes contribution to passage of the FOREST RESERVE ACT of 1891, which authorized establishment of forest reserves by presidential proclamation.

Perhaps the club's greatest significance lay in providing the milieu in which the future leader of the conservation movement, Theodore Roosevelt, formulated many of his ideas. The advice of George Bird Grinnell was particularly important, and together the two coedited several Boone and Crockett Club books on hunting, natural history, and conservation. Most of the conservation concepts Roosevelt later implemented as president can be found in these volumes.

With the later establishment of other private conservation organizations such as the NATIONAL AUDUBON SOCIETY and the NATIONAL WILDLIFE FEDERATION, the preeminent position of the Boone and Crockett Club was taken away. Yet, the club has remained active in wildlife conservation down to the present day.

FURTHER READING: John F. Reiger, *American Sportsmen and the Origins of Conservation* (1975). James B. Trefethen, *An American Crusade for Wildlife* (1975), and *Crusade for Wildlife: Highlights in Conservation Progress* (1961). Paul Russell Cutright, *Theodore Roosevelt the Naturalist* (1956).

JOHN F. REIGER

BOTANICAL EXPLORATION AND THE DISCOVERY OF PRINCIPAL FOREST TREE SPECIES

The description of the principal forest trees and their properties began with French and Spanish explorers and naturalists in the 1530s. Jacques Cartier, who made three trips to Canada between 1534 and 1541, is credited with having been the first to identify and introduce a North American species, the northern white-cedar, into Europe in 1535. This tree was mentioned in 1558 as growing along the Atlantic Coast of what became Great Britain's North American colonies, and it was reported as being grown at Fontainebleau, near Paris, in 1576. Alvar Cabeza de Vaca, shipwrecked on the coast of Texas in 1528, published in his *Relacion y Commentaries* (1542) a description of a purgative made by the natives from the yaupon (*Ilex vomitoria*), and was the first to mention pinyon nuts. Perhaps this was the first western American tree to be identified. Sassafras entered the literature when Nicolas Monardes described some brought to him in Spain by a Frenchman who had visited Florida in 1569. Jean Ribaut and René Goulaine de Laudonnière, French Huguenot leaders who battled Spanish forces in South Carolina and Florida, noted black locusts in Georgia sometime between 1562 and 1568.

Thomas Hariot, an English polymath and protégé of Sir Walter Raleigh, first visited what is now North Carolina in 1585 and provided the earliest descriptions in English of various trees of the Southeast in his *Briefe and True Report of the New Found Land of*

Virginia (1588). The chestnut, black walnut, white-cedar, mulberry, persimmon, sweet gum, and sumac were among the forms found there by Hariot and introduced into England through his efforts.

Captain John Smith, explorer, adventurer, and colonial leader, in his *Description of New England* (1616), remarked that "oke is the chief wood" there, while Thomas Morton in his *New English Canaan* (1637) placed oaks, hickories, and chestnuts at the head of his list of the trees found. Parts of New England had been kept open by means of fire, which was utilized by the Indians in their hunting practices, for agricultural purposes, and for village sites. Consequently, the white pine, a tree sensitive to fire, was found less commonly in areas where it might otherwise have been dominant. This tree was highly prized as a source of masts for ships when colonization began. Under a series of colonial and royal acts beginning in 1668, many white pine stands were reserved to the crown for that purpose.

William Penn identified five varieties of oak and ten other forest species in the vicinity of Philadelphia as early as 1683.

Among the more prominent botanical explorers of the eastern United States in the eighteenth century was the mysterious John Lawson, an English naturalist-colonist of unknown origin. His activities as surveyor-general and promoter in North Carolina led to his death at the hands of outraged Tuscaroras. His *New Voyage to Carolina* (1709), perhaps the most notable account of travel and natural history in North Carolina published before the American Revolution, described the palmetto, several varieties of oak, tulip tree, flowering dogwood, Allegheny chinkapin, laurel, cedars, and many other trees and plants deemed by the natives to have medicinal value.

Sometimes described as a "Colonial Audubon," Mark Catesby published *Hortus Britanno-Americanus* (1737), the earliest volume in English devoted exclusively to the trees of North America. It provided descriptions of eighty-five trees and shrubs he had observed in the Southern colonies.

Pehr Kalm, a Swedish protégé of Linnaeus, traveled throughout the colonies of the Northeast between 1748 and 1751 and prepared a list of fifty-eight varieties of trees, many previously unrecorded, which was published in his *Travels in North America* (1753).

William BARTRAM, son of the celebrated John BARTRAM, naturalist and horticulturist of Philadelphia, published his famous *Travels* in 1791, recounting his explorations of the regions now embraced by the Southeastern states during the years 1773 to 1777.

He and his father were discoverers of the rare tree *Franklinia alatamaha*, a member of the tea family. Long extinct in the wild, *Franklinia* survived in cultivation only by virtue of the specimens the Bartrams gathered near the Altamaha River in Georgia. The only other tree-sized American member of the tea family, the *Gordonia*, was praised by Bartram in his *Travels*. Beginning in 1728, the Bartrams, father and son, carried on a plant-exchange business with various English correspondents, to whom they supplied seeds, cuttings, and information concerning a variety of American flora. In the process, they became part of an informal network of men and women on both sides of the Atlantic that came to be known as the Natural History Circle.

John Filson, in his *Discovery, Settlement, and Present State of Kentucke* (1784), published four years before he was killed by Indians, was perhaps the first to record some of the trees of the trans-Allegheny region, including the Kentucky coffeetree, "sugar tree" (sugar maple), cucumbertree (magnolia), buckeye, wild cherry, and black mulberry.

Humphry Marshall, proprietor of a botanical garden at Marshallton, Pennsylvania, published *Arbustum Americanum: The American Grove, or, an Alphabetical Catalogue of Forest Trees and Shrubs* (1785), the first study of American trees written by a native author and published in the United States.

The trans-Mississippi region first received attention from the French writer and adventurer Antoine Simon Le Page DuPratz, whose *Histoire de la Louisiane* (1758) listed a substantial number of tree species, and from Jonathan Carver, army officer and writer, whose *Travels in Interior Parts of America* (1778) added to the known forms.

King Louis XVI of France dispatched André MICHAUX to America in 1785 with the objective of securing seeds and seedlings from America to start renewing the depleted French forests. Michaux spent eleven years exploring the forests east of the Mississippi from Florida into Canada. He established two nurseries, one near New York and the other in South Carolina, to receive and nurture his collections for shipment to France. His *Histoire des Chênes de l'Amérique*, a study of American oaks, was published in 1801. His son François André Michaux in 1810 began publishing his beautifully illustrated three-volume work later translated as *North American Sylva* (1818-1819), in which he was primarily concerned with the practical uses of the various types of wood. The *Sylva* remained the most comprehensive reference on the American forests for many years. After the acquisition of the trans-Mississippi West,

Thomas NUTTALL added three more volumes to supplement Michaux's *Sylva* (1842–1849).

The botanical exploration of the territory that became the western United States was launched from the Pacific Coast. Father Juan Crespi, in diaries kept during an expedition to California led by Gaspar de Portolá in 1769, provides the first mention of the coastal redwood. Others credit the discovery to Archibald Menzies, a Scottish physician in the British Navy who wrote of seeing the redwood on the Monterey Peninsula in 1794 while a member of the expedition commanded by George Vancouver. Louis Née, one of the botanists on the Alejandro Malaspina expedition, published in 1801 the first description of California trees which included the coast live oak and the valley oak.

In 1792, Menzies, then visiting the Puget Sound, first collected a variety of trees from that area, including the Douglas-fir and Nootka false-cypress or Alaska yellow-cedar from Nootka Sound; a dogwood at Admiralty Inlet; western hemlock and planetree maple near present-day Jefferson City, Washington; the giant-cedar from Matia Island in the San Juans; several species of ash from the Hale Passage within sight of Mount Rainier; the madrone from a spot near Fort Vancouver in Oregon Territory; and several spruces and a cedar near the present site of Sitka, Alaska. Near the presidio of Monterey, Menzies discovered an oak, a poplar, and the California sycamore in 1794. Many of Menzies's specimens were not immediately named and described by him, leaving that measure of discovery to later workers.

The activities of Meriwether Lewis and William Clark, co-leaders of the first American expedition to the Far West, materially expanded the natural history horizons of the new nation. President Thomas Jefferson was responsible for planning their three-year expedition (1803–1806), the first of many launched and supported by the federal government. Both men had military backgrounds, a precedent followed for the next three-quarters of a century. The authorized account of their trip, the two-volume *History of the Expedition under the Command of Captains Lewis and Clark*, did not appear until 1814, and a complete account was finally published in 1904. They specifically mentioned some eighty-five varieties of trees. Of these, they have been credited with the discovery of thirty-four for which no technical descriptions had been published at the time that Lewis and Clark first found them.

Of the many other notable early nineteenth-century sylvan discoverers, several merit mention here. Edwin James, a twenty-three-year-old surgeon-botanist-

geologist and chronicler of Major Stephen H. Long's expedition to the Rockies (1819–1823), discovered the limber pine near Pike's Peak in 1820. Other species first identified by James include an elm, several oaks, a walnut, and a coffeebean tree.

Thomas Nuttall, a native of Liverpool and a printer by trade, arrived in Philadelphia in 1808. He almost immediately called on the eminent physician-naturalist Benjamin Smith Barton with a flower he sought to identify and soon found himself a willing pupil of Dr. Barton. Nuttall's unsponsored early scientific expeditions were financed by his earnings as a printer. This indefatigable many-faceted naturalist later made several expeditions to the Far West. His *Journal of Travels into the Arkansas Territory During the Year 1819* (1821) provided a picture of the botany of the Southwest. Nuttall later became curator of Harvard University's botanical garden from 1822 to 1834 and, as mentioned above, rounded out Michaux's *North American Sylva* with three additional volumes. In 1834, Nuttall's research revealed the difference between the Pacific dogwood and its eastern cousins.

David Douglas, son of a Scottish stonemason, probably was the most famous figure in the history of nineteenth-century American botany. After training as a Glasgow gardener's apprentice, he came to the attention of Sir William Hooker, professor of botany at the university there. Douglas refined his botanical learning under Hooker's guidance and received Hooker's recommendation when the London Horticultural Society sought someone to secure new North American plants for English gardens. Douglas's first expedition took him to New York and Ontario in 1823. A second voyage brought him to Oregon early in 1825 after eight months at sea with stops at various points along both coasts of South America. After two and a half years in the forests of Oregon and western Canada, Douglas returned for a brief stay in England before setting out in 1829 on his last expedition, to Oregon, California, and Hawaii, where he died in July 1834.

In the course of his thousands of miles of travel by foot, horseback, and canoe, Douglas, despite incredible vicissitudes, gathered for his sponsors numerous new botanical specimens. Among the plants he discovered in the Oregon country between 1825 and 1834 were the giant chinkapin, together with various species of oak, maple, pine, fir, and spruce.

The glamorous and mercurial explorer John Charles Fremont of the U. S. Army Topographical Engineers, during his second expedition into California in 1843–1844 identified a number of new species, including a cypress, the interior live oak, the incense-cedar, the

Joshua-tree, and the single leaf pinyon. His botanical discoveries have been memorialized in the name of a beautiful, small California tree, *Fremontia*.

Subsequently, expeditions sent forth by the U. S. Army, especially the Pacific Railroad Survey conducted by the topographical engineers in the 1850s, significantly rounded out the knowledge of the plant life of the Far West. Notable among the naturalist members of these surveys were two physicians, John Milton Bigelow and John S. Newberry. Bigelow prepared a report on the species encountered along the route followed by the 35th Parallel Survey of 1853 led by Captain Amiel W. Whipple, and he was also a participant in the Mexican Boundary Survey of 1849–1855. Newberry described the numerous forest trees found along the route of Lieutenant Robert S. Williamson's survey of the territory between the Sacramento and Columbia rivers in 1855.

During the remainder of the century, additional western forest species were discovered by the several geographical and geological surveys (and, after 1879, the unified U. S. GEOLOGICAL SURVEY), the U. S. Bureau of BIOLOGICAL SURVEY, and other federal government agencies.

FURTHER READING: Stanley W. Bromley, "The Original Forest Types of Southern New England," *Ecological Monographs* 5 Jan. 1935): 61-89. June Rainsford Butler, "America—A Hunting Ground for Eighteenth Century Botanists with Special Reference to Their Publications about Trees," *Proceedings of the Bibliographical Society of America* 32 (1938): 1-16. Paul Russell Cutright, *Lewis and Clark: Pioneering Naturalists* (1969). Richard Beale Davis, *Intellectual Life in the Colonial South, 1585–1763* (1978). Virginia S. Eifert, *Tall Trees and Far Horizons: Adventures and Discoveries of Early Botanists in America* (1965). Robert Elman, *First in the Field: America's Pioneering Naturalists* (1977). Joseph Ewan, ed., *A Short History of Botany in the United States* (1969). Joseph Kastner, *A Species of Eternity* (1977). Susan Delano McKelvey, *Botanical Exploration of the Trans-Mississippi West* (1955). Alfred Rehder, *Manual of Cultivated Trees and Shrubs* (1940). Henry Savage, Jr., *Discovering America, 1700–1875* (1979), and *Lost Heritage* (1970).

KEIR STERLING

BOTANICAL GARDENS

See Arboretums and Botanical Gardens

BOX AND CONTAINER INDUSTRY

Throughout the first half of the twentieth century, producers of wooden boxes and containers were the nation's second largest consumer of lumber. Production peaked during World War II, when about 14 billion board feet—nearly half the national lumber output—were consumed in 2,400 box plants. After the war, wooden boxes yielded to fiberboard containers, but increases in the use of hardwood pallets helped to preserve the importance of wood in shipping the country's produce. In 1970, about 15 percent of the lumber consumed in the United States was used for shipping purposes, half of this amount going into pallets.

In colonial times, cooperage was the leading container industry but wooden boxes and crates assumed increasing importance after the Revolutionary War. Early boxes were handmade from thin pieces of wood. At the end of the eighteenth century, improved woodworking machinery and mass-produced nails cheapened the manufacturing process. In the ensuing decades, industrialization and expanding transportation facilities created a strong demand for containers in a variety of sizes and specifications. During the late nineteenth century, wooden boxes and crates were used to ship almost any type of product, such as shoes, clothing, tea, vegetables and fruits, canned goods, poultry, furniture, hardware, farm implements, heavy machinery, and delicate instruments.

Veneer baskets were first produced in 1866 by James Kirby of Michigan for use by peach growers in the southern part of the state. As unit costs were lowered by mass production in the 1870s and 1880s, veneer baskets replaced the hand-woven splint variety. Used throughout the fruit and vegetable industry, veneer baskets included berry baskets, till baskets, hampers, round-stave baskets, splint or market baskets, and Climax or grape baskets. Tough yet flexible hardwoods such as ash, beech, elm, maple, birch, gum, bass-wood, poplar, and cottonwood were used in veneer baskets.

Box manufacture required wood that was light yet strong, able to hold nails, workable, and odor-free. Manufacturers prized the white pine, which in addition to these qualities presented a smooth, light surface for printing and labeling. Until 1910, white pine constituted about 50 percent of the lumber used for boxes. When the pine forests appeared to be limitless, producers of boxes and box shooks, like other forest products manufacturers, used only the best wood and wasted the remainder. Increasing scarcity and higher prices, along with increased product demand, led manufacturers to turn to lesser grades of wood. By the middle of the nineteenth century, box factories, often adjuncts to sawmills, were using slabs, edgings, trimmings, and miscuts. In the Northeast and the Lake States, second-growth pine and older trees unsuitable for construction lumber became an impor-

These wooden bushel baskets were manufactured in Maryland. American Forest Institute Photo.

tant source of box material. After 1910, pine was supplemented by red gum, spruce, cottonwood, hemlock, yellow-poplar, and indeed almost every available lumber species.

The close proximity of important industrial and fruit-growing centers, both major box users, gave eastern lumber regions preeminence in box and container production well into the twentieth century. In 1927, New England, New York, Pennsylvania, West Virginia, Virginia, and North Carolina were the largest box producing regions in the country, while major box and container consumers were Virginia, New York, Illinois, Massachusetts, California, and Pennsylvania. By 1950, the box industry had shifted partly westward, with Oregon, Washington, California, Michigan, North Carolina, and Massachusetts the leading producers. Important consumers included Florida, Texas, Washington, Oregon, Missouri, California, Virginia, and New York. Shippers of canned goods were the largest consumers of boxes, with the fruit and vegetable industries ranking second.

Standardization of the growing number and variety of boxes and containers became necessary in the early twentieth century. The Standard Baskets and Containers acts of 1916 and 1928 established the capacity for each type of container and reduced the number of containers in each category. By 1928, forty-four competing styles of berry boxes were reduced to three, while styles of till baskets were reduced from forty-four to four, and hampers from

seventy-five to nine. Private efforts to impose standards proceeded from the trade associations, including the National Association of Wooden Box Manufacturers, established in Chicago in 1900, and the California Pine Box Distributers, the Wooden Box Institute, and the Inland Empire Wooden Box Association, all founded soon after. The Pacific Coast Division of the National Association of Wooden Box Manufacturers adopted a tariff in 1928 that provided specifications for size, thickness, and tolerance for all commonly used containers. The tariff also set standards for the manufacture, assembly, and loading of nailed wooden boxes for fruits and vegetables. This Tariff Number 1 was later adopted by manufacturers and carriers across the nation.

Standardization ensured a full measure for the consumer and reduced shipping and manufacturing costs by permitting more types of product to be shipped in a given style of box. Fewer production halts for retooling allowed manufacturers to meet the growing needs of box consumers with greater assurance. Marketing was easier and carriers were able to figure shipping charges according to an average weight, a practice not possible with nonstandard containers. Precedence of other federal standards brought the repeal of the Baskets and Containers acts in 1968.

In 1905, the U. S. FOREST SERVICE began conducting laboratory tests on various wood materials and designs seeking to improve shipping containers. The testing program was expanded after completion of the Forest Products Laboratory in Madison, Wisconsin. During both world wars, the laboratory worked with the military to research and develop secure ordnance containers that conserved space and material. During World War II, the laboratory's work in boxing and crating, in interior cushioning, bracing, and cradling, and in training personnel in packing and inspection, resulted in a reduction of materiel losses due to damaged containers from 50 percent to 3 percent.

Competition from the fiberboard container industry began as early as 1910. Initially, fiberboard boxes were used for packaging while goods continued to be transported in wood, but the demand for lighter containers motivated fiberboard manufacturers to create cartons that would withstand the rigors of rail shipment. The wooden box industry's trade associations reacted by enlisting the support of rail shippers to prevent encroachment of the fiberboard shipping containers. The associations argued that wood provided better protection of the commodity and wooden boxes conserved forests because they used lower grade wood and mill wastes and were reusable, while fiber used pulp from high-grade timber. Fiberboard producers, on the other hand, pointed out that their product was lighter, easier to handle, and presented a greater deterrent to theft since tampering with sealed fiberboard boxes was more conspicuous than with the wooden variety, which could simply be nailed shut after opening.

A suit initiated by the R. W. Pridham Company, a fiberboard producer, against the Southern Pacific Railroad for discrimination against fiber boxes brought these issues before the Interstate Commerce Commission in 1911. After considering some 4,000 pages of testimony taken from box manufacturers and shippers across the country, the commission decided in favor of Pridham, thereby opening the shipping container market to the fiberboard industry.

Although the competition from fiberboard and corrugated boxes slowed the expansion of the wooden box industry, the volume of wood used for boxes did not decline precipitously until the 1960s. Manufacture of boxes and crates used 4.5 billion board feet of lumber in 1912. Consumption rose gradually until the Depression, dipped to 2.5 billion board feet, and reached 4.5 billion board feet again in 1940. Stimulated by wartime demand, wood consumption peaked at around 14 billion board feet in 1944, then dropped to 4.3 billion board feet in 1952. New developments in handling methods and a variety of new fiberboard and plastic containers with greater strength and flexibility led to sharp declines in the use of wooden boxes in the late 1950s. By 1960, only about 1.9 billion board feet of lumber were consumed in box and container production. Containerization and the

use of forklifts and increased truck transport contributed to further declines in the 1970s.

Use of wood, however, continued to be an important part of the shipping industry, with declines in wooden boxes more than offset by increases in the use of pallets. Used to facilitate mechanized handling and transport, pallets were introduced in the 1920s, and in 1938 the Navy began intensive use of pallets in its warehouse and port facilities. By 1950, 23 million pallets were produced annually, using 575 million board feet of lumber. Warehouse and handling facilities were largely geared to use of pallets by the next decade, and in 1970 production of pallets consumed around 2.9 billion board feet of lumber. Another 800 million board feet was used annually throughout the 1970s for dunnage, blocking, and bracing during shipment. Containerization—the unit shipment of a number of packages in a single container for ease of handling—brought plywood into prominent use in the shipping industry. In 1970, 2 percent of all plywood consumed in the country was used for shipping purposes. Despite its declining use in boxes, wood continued to play an important part in transporting goods and produce.

FURTHER READING: Nelson C. Brown, *Forest Products* (1950), and "Half a Century of Box Making," *The Timberman* 50 (Oct. 1949): 218-226. Hu Maxwell, "The Uses of Wood—Wood in the Manufacture of Boxes and Crates," *American Forestry* 24 (Sept. 1918): 533-554.

MARY ELIZABETH JOHNSON

BRIARWOOD PIPE BLOCKS

Although the manufacturers of smoking pipes do not rank among the leading consumers of wood products, the peculiar demands of the craft have created a minor industry of surprising size. For example, in 1950, when the population of the United States was 150 million, pipemakers consumed 14 million briarwood pipe blocks (cut from root burls), or one for every eleven people. Most of these blocks were imported, especially from southern France and Italy, where the preferred species for pipe burls, *Erica arborea*, grows abundantly. However, when access to the European product was closed by the outbreak of World War II, a burl-gathering business of some size developed in the southern and western states. Native American laurel, rhododendrons, and several varieties of California manzanita (which are closely related to *Erica arborea*) were discovered to make adequate substitutes. After the war, most American pipemakers returned for a time to European briar. When the imported product became scarcer and more expensive in the late

1960s and early 1970s, American burls once again came into favor. The harvesting of burls is a minor occupation in the southern Appalachians and California foothills.

BRITISH COLONIAL FOREST POLICIES

In the late sixteenth century, when Queen Elizabeth was using Protestantism, privateering, and commercial policy to strengthen the English nation, many of her subjects became aware that their island kingdom was being weakened by a serious forest resource crisis. Firewood, structural timbers, cooperage materials, wood-based chemicals, and many other forest products were becoming scarce and more expensive, especially in the heavily populated regions of southern England. Sporadic conservation and reforestation efforts failed because of the pressure of a growing human and animal population on a limited land base. Britain was becoming more and more dependent on northern European nations for forest supplies, and the growing English commercial and naval fleet was almost wholly dependent on Sweden for pitch and tar and on several Baltic nations for masts and spars. There was an extremely unfavorable balance of trade with these "Eastland" nations, and in an age when mercantilist ideas were in vogue it was natural that almost all of the early British colonial schemes emphasized the importance of exploiting the North American forests.

The early British mercantilists soon discovered, however, that almost all of the initial schemes for resource development in America were unrealistic. Forest-based manufacturing industries such as glass, iron, potash, tar, and pitch proved unsuccessful in pioneer Virginia, where staying alive, raising cattle, and growing grain and tobacco were the major concerns of almost every settler. In Massachusetts, a very large investment in an ironworks scheme was entirely lost. By the mid-1640s, New England did become a major exporter of red and white oak barrel staves, cedar shingles, oak beams, and white pine boards. But because of high shipping costs, few of these products ever reached the mother country. Even the strongest supporters of British mercantilism were unwilling to pay more for New England timber than for Baltic supplies.

During the formative years of the British colonial system, therefore, there was never a well-organized government effort to control the American timber economy. Growing colonial timber exports were responses to natural increases in demand in the British West Indian sugar islands and in market areas outside the British Empire—in the Azores, Madeira, the Canary Islands, and southern Europe. The British navigation acts passed during the third quarter of the seventeenth century did not prohibit any of this trade; rather, they encouraged it by stimulating shipbuilding. Even the closure of the Baltic to British timber-supply ships during the First Dutch War and the discovery of mast shipments from northern New England to the Mediterranean for Spanish warships failed to lead to the creation of timber reserves for the Royal Navy in North America or to long-term trade restrictions affecting forest products. Although the Royal Dockyards received shipments of white pine masts from New England almost every year after 1653, both the British navy and the merchant marine continued to be heavily dependent on masts and spars and completely dependent on pitch and tar from the Eastland.

It was not until the time of William and Mary that Parliament began regulation of the colonial forests. In 1691, the new royal charter for Massachusetts (which included Plymouth Colony and Maine) set aside for the Royal Navy all trees twenty-four inches or more in diameter growing on ungranted lands outside of townships. Further investigations revealed that this provision did not halt the destruction of mast trees. Pitch and tar, on the other hand, were not even being produced in the colonies in significant amounts because of high transatlantic shipping costs, the dearth of technical knowledge, and the high cost and scarcity of labor. This information, together with a highly unstable relationship with France and an attempt by the Swedish tar monopoly to restrict the supply and raise the price of pitch and tar, were the principal motivations for the passage of the Naval Stores Act of 1705. Parliament sought to overcome the labor and transportation problems inherent in pitch, tar, and turpentine production by granting generous bounties (which were also applied to masts) to merchants who delivered such products to English ports. Parliament also prohibited the shipment of all NAVAL STORES directly to foreign nations and forbade the destruction of all pitch and tar trees under a foot in diameter on all ungranted lands from New Jersey to Maine. Increased protection for mast trees was obtained under the White Pine Act of 1711, which extended the reservation provisions of the Massa-

Shown is a page from the Naval Stores Act of 1729, which applied to Scotland and the British American colonies. This act was part of the so-called Broad Arrow policy and remained in effect until the American Revolution. Forest History Society Photo.

Anno secundo

Georgii II. Regis.

An Act for better Preservation of His Majesty's Woods in *America*, and for the Encouragement of the Importation of Naval Stores from thence; and to encourage the Importation of Masts, Yards, and Bowsprights, from that Part of *Great Britain* called *Scotland*.

WEREAS by an Act passed in the Eighth Year of His late Majesty's Reign [instituted, An Act giving further Encouragement for the Importation of Naval Stores, and for other Purposes therein mentioned] it is enacted, That no Person or Persons whatsoever, within any of His Majesty's Colonies of Nova Scotia, New Hampshire, the Massachusets Bay, the Province of Main, Rhode Island, and Providence Plantation,

3   7 D 2

chusetts Charter to all ungranted lands both within and outside of townships in all the northern colonies covered by the legislation of 1705.

The bounty system for pitch and tar proved highly profitable for New England shipowners who delivered naval stores to England. The enormous growth in the manufacturing portion of this industry, however, took place amid the stands of longleaf pine in the Carolinas, and not in the northern colonies where the trees had been protected and where much experimental work was carried on without a great deal of success. Although Carolina tar was not always of high quality and the Royal Navy continued to rely almost exclusively on the Swedish product, the Navy Board paid bounties of over a million pounds sterling before the Revolution.

The British government reduced trade deficits with the Eastland by encouraging the importation of American naval stores for its commercial fleet. By eliminating import duties on colonial construction and cooperage timber, Britain further reduced its balance of payments with the Baltic nations, especially during the third quarter of the eighteenth century. Bounties and the elimination of import charges, however, could not solve the problem of maintaining a long-term reserve of white pine for masts for the Royal Navy. The contract system for naval masts meant that acquisition and shipment of these timbers were the business of a very small number of politically well-connected merchants. Furthermore, mechanical improvements in the white pine industry, especially the widespread use of water-driven reciprocating gang saws, meant that potential mast trees were being turned into boards at a rapid rate at a time when naval demands were increasing. The destruction of valuable trees, the continual conflict between the surveyor-general of the king's woods and the mill operators, and the open rebellion of Massachusetts lawyers and politicians who claimed that the first white pine act did not apply to Maine, finally provoked Parliament into passing the White Pine Act of 1722. This was a poorly framed law that attempted to protect several thousand trees for the navy by reserving all white pines, regardless of dimension, that grew on ungranted lands outside all townships from New Jersey to Nova Scotia. To aid the surveyor in enforcing the act, penalties for unauthorized cutting were recoverable in admiralty court. The burden of proof as to where a tree was felled was shifted from the enforcing officer to the lumberman. The act also forbade the shipment of lumber to ports outside the Empire—a provision that was totally ignored and finally modified in 1765 to allow pine boards and oak staves to be shipped to the important markets in southern Europe.

Lumbermen sought to avoid the mast law by creating "paper townships" in the wilderness, but Parliament responded to this strategy with the White Pine Act of 1729. The act extended the mast reservation to all ungranted lands inside and outside all towns and colonies. This legislation seemed to close a major loophole, but there were so many confusing and contradictory concepts regarding land grants, titles, and "public" and "private" property in the colonies that it actually created more opportunities for legal challenges. Another provision reserving all white pines twenty-four or more inches in diameter on private land in Massachusetts and Maine that had been transferred from the public to the private domain after October 6, 1690, added more confusion to the issue of the continuity of land titles. It also led to a renewal of the charge that much of the mast legislation violated the Massachusetts Charter of 1691.

The mast laws intensified bitter political conflicts over the control of land in the northern colonies. In New England, proprietors of town lands and wilderness tracts used the local courts to sue each other, royal officials, and licensed mast contractors for trespass. There was, at times, open defiance and even violence against heavy-handed enforcement by the crown's agents. At other times, royal governors and surveyors issued licenses freely or chose not to enforce the letter of laws that affected the livelihood of so many forest dwellers.

While Benning WENTWORTH was surveyor-general and governor of New Hampshire (1743–1766), most large mill operators in northern New England had almost free access to the woodlands. Beginning in 1766, however, John Wentworth, the new governor and surveyor, attempted to set stricter but more reasonable standards. He pressed for a policy of setting aside relatively small but carefully defined tracts of white pine rather than continue with the unworkable blanket reservation set up by Parliament. Wentworth proved to be the most competent and tactful but also the least successful of all the king's surveyors in New Hampshire and Maine. Operating in an era of widespread defiance of parliamentary taxation and military occupation, he found that "the great cries and oppositions for the word liberty" encouraged open defiance of the mast laws. His legal battles with the Kennebec Proprietors over the mast lands of eastern Maine were viewed by the radicals in that organization as part of a larger conspiracy aimed at destroying all traditional English liberties. Even before Lexington and Concord, most forestlands were outside of his control, and many of his deputies were arrested by revolutionary governments. Mast shipments to the mother country ceased after the spring of 1775, and Wentworth fled to Boston. Later, as the surveyor of the king's woods in Canada, his proposals for setting aside relatively small but carefully guarded mast reservations were accepted by the British government. These measures were of great value to the Royal Navy during the French Revolutionary Wars.

FURTHER READING: Robert Greenhalgh Albion, *Forests and Sea Power: The Timber Problem of the Royal Navy, 1652–1862* (1926). Charles F. Carroll, *The Timber Economy of Puritan New England* (1973). Jere R. Daniell, *Experiment in Republicanism: New Hampshire and the American Revolution, 1741–1794* (1970). Gordon E. Kershaw, *The Kennebeck Proprietors, 1749–1775* (1975). Joseph J. Malone, *Pine Trees and Politics: Naval Stores Forest Policy in Colonial New England, 1691–1775* (1964).

CHARLES F. CARROLL

BROWER, DAVID ROSS (1912–)

David Ross Brower is one of this country's leading environmental activists. Born in Berkeley, California, on July 1, 1912, he grew up there and attended the University of California, Berkeley, in 1929–1931, dropping out to work. Learning of the SIERRA CLUB on a trip to the Sierra Nevada, he joined in 1933. Among the first in the western United States to employ pitons and rope for safety in mountain climbing, Brower became an expert climber during the 1930s and made many first ascents in the Sierra Nevada and one on Shiprock in New Mexico. He served as a first lieutenant with the Tenth Mountain Division in Italy from 1943 to 1945.

From 1935 to 1968, Brower did editorial work for the *Sierra Club Bulletin*. From 1941 to 1952, he was an editor for the University of California Press. He honed his skills in what was to become his specialty—the use of photography and prose in the service of wilderness and environmental preservation.

Active in conservation since 1938, Brower became the Sierra Club's first executive director in 1952. One of the earliest national battles over wilderness, and the first in which he led the club, involved the successful defense of Dinosaur National Monument (1952–1956). During the 1950s and 1960s, the club grew from a moderately activist group concerned chiefly with the Sierra Nevada to a militant, national organization. Much of this change was due to Brower's vision, effective publicity, and aggressive conservation tactics. He initiated the National Outdoor Recreation Resources Review (1956–1958), was prominent in work for the Wilderness Act (1952–1964). NORTH CASCADES NATIONAL PARK (1955–1968), and the REDWOOD NATIONAL PARK (1963–

1968); and was instrumental in saving the Grand Canyon from proposed dams (1952–1968).

Between 1959 and 1968, Brower designed and edited the club's twenty-volume Exhibit Format series. Many of these books were extensions of specific club battles. Brower was also responsible for other volumes in smaller format, such as the popular *On the Loose*, by Terry and Renny Russell (1967), which portrayed the club's general environmental ethic.

During the 1960s, two factions developed in the club and coalesced around Brower. His opponents on the board of directors disagreed with his opposition to a nuclear power plant in California's Diablo Canyon and charged him with disregard for the board's policies, fiscal overextension, and excessive militancy in defense of wilderness. He ran for election to the board, lost, and was forced to resign in May 1969.

In July 1969, he founded Friends of the Earth (FOE) in New York, with its main office in San Francisco. He was FOE's president until 1979 and is now chairman of its board. During the 1970s, FOE was somewhat more militant than the Sierra Club, especially in its antinuclear posture, but the two organizations cooperated in such projects as their Alaskan and redwood campaigns. The club gave Brower its John MUIR Award in 1977 and elected him honorary vice-president. Brower initiated and edited FOE's series, *The Earth's Wild Places* (10 volumes, 1970–1977), *Celebrating the Earth* (1972–1973), and numerous other books.

Perceiving that ecological concerns are global and a threat to peace, Brower was instrumental in establishing autonomous FOE organizations in twenty-four other countries. Under his leadership, FOE, like the Sierra Club, enlarged its efforts to include, in addition to scenic and wildlife protection, the fight against pollution, nuclear power and arms, and excessive population and economic growth. Brower was nominated for the Nobel Peace Prize in 1978 and 1979.

FURTHER READING: David Brower, *Environmental Activist, Publicist, and Prophet,* an oral history by Susan Schrepfer (University of California Regional Oral History Office, 1978). John McPhee, *Encounters with the Archdruid* (1971). Roderick Nash, *Wilderness and the American Mind* (rev. ed., 1982).

SUSAN R. SCHREPFER

BUNYAN, PAUL

Paul Bunyan has since the 1920s become a super-hero fixture in the American imagination. Herculean in physique and near-demigod embodiment of the North American lumberjack, this fictive giant of the forest industry rapidly emerged as a major popular culture symbol of rugged virility, physical might, ingenuity, and American occupational enterprise. Bunyan's reputed larger-than-life exploits, told through story and celebrated through mass media, are familiar to countless people of all ages. Scores of adult and juvenile literary treatments, together with commercial offshoots ranging from wood-product ads to tourist theme parks, towering statues (the best known one erected in 1937 in Bemidji, Minnesota), and annual lumberjack festivals, have all contributed to the Bunyan mystique.

In story and icon, Paul has been variously depicted as a remarkable woodchopper, river driver, foreman, timber cruiser, and woods boss—the archetype for workingman roles that have shaped the evolution of big timber harvesting. In some tales, Bunyan clears entire tracts with a single sweep of his hefty ax. In others, he feeds his crew by converting a pond into a gargantuan kettle of pea soup. Some yarnspinners claim that he once built a sawmill so tall that the smokestacks had to be hinged to clear the clouds. In one adventure Paul's dragging canthook forms the Grand Canyon. Embellishments on similar fantastic accomplishments are legion. Many of the anecdotal episodes team Paul with Babe, the Big Blue Ox. The animal is described in one account as eleven feet tall, 8,246 pounds in weight, and having a span of two ax handles and a plug of chewing tobacco between the eyes. Because Babe's horns spread sixteen feet and four inches, Bunyan had a blacksmith hinge them for ease of movement among trees. The ox is often pressed into service, hauling whole sections of timber, or pulling a river straight with one tug on a logging chain, or helping Paul dig Puget Sound. Babe's hoofprints are said to have created lakes. Other Bunyan cohorts include clerk Johnny Inkslinger, crewmen Chris Crosshaul, Shot Gunderson, and Sourdough Sam, and a host of similar comrades in keeping with woods work and the creative whimsy of Bunyania popularizers.

The Bunyan canon has analogs in world myth, epic, and prose saga. This feature has reinforced the commonplace but highly misleading characterization of Paul Bunyan as "mythological." Paul, Babe, and the allied logging corps operate in the historic past in a real-life secular and occupational context. The accounts lack the primordial setting and complex spiritual and philosophical underpinnings that typify true mythology. Instead, Bunyan stories fuse a variety of oral and literary antecedents: North American oral and printed tall-tale tradition; migratory anecdotes and legends that cluster around formidable occupational heroes, notably eccentric foremen and laborers of unusual size and strength; Scandinavian saga; personal experience narrative; folk history of lumbering personnel, work techniques and routines, camp conditions, and logging equipment on both sides of the Canadian-American border; and literary attempts to fashion an indigenous American epic in popular prose dress.

Much debate has surrounded the proportioning of Bunyan tale influences, particularly on the issue of Bunyan lore orality during the nineteenth century. Bunyan anecdotes appear to have circulated among Michigan, Wisconsin, Minnesota, Far West, and pan-Canadian lumberjacks between 1900 and 1910, and perhaps for a decade or two earlier. No one has satisfactorily established a euphemeristic precedent for Bunyan, though James Stevens (*Paul Bunyan*, 1925) asserted that the folk hero's prototype was an actual French-Canadian logger, "a mighty-muscled, bellicose, bearded giant named Paul Bunyon" who fought in the Papineau Rebellion of 1837 in the Two Mountains country, at St. Eustache. Even though it is a plausible claim, Stevens never defended it with firm historical evidence, nor have a host of perpetuators. But like the stories themselves, Bunyan's alleged French-Canadian pedigree continues to hold popular appeal that revisionist scholarship is unlikely to erode. Much less persuasive are etymological attempts to see Paul's surname as transference from *Bon (Petit) Jean*, a diminutive and much different tale character from imported Old World peasant tradition.

The details of the popularization of Bunyan stories, on the other hand, are well documented. In the United States, published Bunyan anecdotes first emerged on July 24, 1910, in a *Detroit News-Tribune* Sunday supplement column by James MacGillivray. The journalist set down fragmentary Bunyan anecdotes personally heard in Michigan lumber camps. In 1914, in what was to be the seminal treatment, Red River Lumber Company adman William B. Laughead turned the lore to the promotional needs of his Minneapolis firm, which was expanding its operations to the West Coast. Laughead's pamphlet, *Introducing Mr. Paul Bunyan of Westwood, Cal.*, though limited in circulation to lumber industry management and dealers, inspired the author to follow up with a reworked and expanded version in 1922, known alternately under the titles *The Marvelous Exploits of Paul Bunyan* and *Paul Bunyan and His Blue Ox.* Laughead gave name to Babe and invented Inkslinger along with those fictional coworkers previously identified. The public edition found a ready audience;

its success opened the door to free borrowing and competitive elaboration on motifs by Esther Shephard (*Paul Bunyan*, 1924) and James Stevens (*Paul Bunyan*, 1925). Subsequent derivations have poured forth. They included poetry (as in works by Carl Sandburg and Richard Wilbur), an operetta (by W. H. Auden, 1941), Bunyan anthologies (such as Harold Felton's *Legends of Paul Bunyan*, 1947), and filmstrips for schoolchildren.

Paul Bunyan material continues to flow in and out of print. Bunyan "lies" typically build outward from reality to fanciful impossibility. Among loggers the yarns measure and challenge one's familiarity with the facts of their occupation. Lumberjacks who tell the stories among peers delight in this playful test of ingroup knowledge and experience; the accounts bemuse seasoned woodsmen at no cost to camaraderie or alienation of gullible neophytes. Woods storytellers also relish opportunities to expose nonloggers to Bunyan lore.

In all, Paul Bunyan material is collective fantasy about an occupational superhero every bit fitted for his expansive forest arena and America's mid-twentieth century work ethos of large-scale, time-saving productivity. It is likely that Paul Bunyan will be transformed into an ecologically concerned forester if the giant is to remain viable for future generations of conservation-minded Americans.

FURTHER READING: Earl C. Beck, *They Knew Paul Bunyan* (1956). Robert D. Bethke, *Adirondack Voices: Woodsmen and Woods Lore* (1981). Richard M. Dorson, *American Folklore* (1959), and *America in Legend* (1973). Edith Fowke, "In Defense of Paul Bunyan," *New York Folklore* 5 (1979): 43-51. Daniel Hoffman, *Paul Bunyan, Last of the Frontier Demigods* (1966). W. H. Hutchinson, "The Caesarean Delivery of Paul Bunyan," *Western Folklore* 22 (Jan. 1963): 1-15.

ROBERT D. BETHKE

BUREAU OF LAND MANAGEMENT

The U. S. Bureau of Land Management (BLM) was formed in 1946 through a merger of the GENERAL LAND OFFICE (GLO) and the Grazing Service, both of which were then located in the DEPARTMENT OF THE INTERIOR. During the 134 years between its establishment and its absorption in BLM, the GLO supervised the transfer of over 1 billion acres of federal public lands into state and private ownership. The Taylor Grazing Act of 1934, which assigned to the Department of the Interior responsibility for organizing and administering grazing districts on suitable public rangeland, represented a major modification of the historic policy of disposing of the public domain. A Division of Grazing was established within the Office of the Secretary; in 1939, this division became a bureau of the department, the Grazing Service.

Administratively, the GLO and the Grazing Service were disparate organizations. GLO was centralized, quasi-judicial, and ministerial, carrying out prescriptive duties with relatively little exercise of administrative discretion. The Grazing Service was highly decentralized. Its small field force, deployed across the public lands in the Far West, adjudicated grazing privileges and adjusted grazing use to range capacity as a first step to land rehabilitation.

Nevertheless, the GLO and the Grazing Service both held responsibility for multiple-use lands of the Department of the Interior, and, to assure greater use of the resources and more efficient administration, the two bureaus were merged into the BLM in accordance with Plan 3 of the Reorganization Act of 1945. BLM's primary responsibility has been management of the public lands, the residual portion of the public domain which had neither been transferred out of federal ownership nor specifically assigned to some other governmental administrative jurisdiction. BLM also has responsibility for administration of the mineral estate which underlies the public lands, the national forests, and many other categories of lands, including acquired lands and former public lands where mineral rights were reserved to the United States. A major BLM responsibility has been preparation of environmental and economic analyses, plans, and schedules for leasing oil and gas on the Outer Continental Shelf and conducting lease sales. BLM also conducts cadastral surveys and maintains land status records of the public lands and the numerous reservations created from them, including the national forests.

After 1948 BLM moved away from the historically ministerial public lands administration toward a largely discretionary management by trained natural resource professionals under the direction of cabinet and subcabinet officers. BLM adapted the FOREST SERVICE's multiple-use principle to the arid and semi-arid lands; it also adopted Gifford PINCHOT's requirement that on-the-land officials have both the authority and the responsibility to make land-use decisions. The public lands and the national forests are adjacent and to some extent intermingled; their respective uses are similar and the users are often the same individuals. Since about 1960, the BLM and the Forest Service have deliberately sought to coordinate their policies at all management levels.

It was only with passage of the FEDERAL LAND POLICY AND MANAGEMENT ACT OF 1976 (FLPMA) that BLM was given an unequivocal statutory basis for its public land management policy. The 1934 Taylor Act had provided for management of natural resources on public land "pending its final disposal." To some the phrase meant the old policy of transfer of public lands into private ownership; to others it provided an argument against federal investment in land administration or rehabilitation. FLPMA, however, clearly prescribed retention of public lands in federal ownership as the rule and made transfer a carefully circumscribed exception. FLPMA proclaimed multiple use, sustained yield, and environmental protection as guiding principles for public land management.

In 1980, BLM's forestland jurisdiction in the Far West exclusive of Alaska totaled 26 million acres, 4 million of which were intensively managed for timber production. These intensively managed forestlands comprised 2.5 million acres of Oregon and California Railroad Revested Lands and 1.5 million acres in northern California and northern Idaho. The remaining 22 million BLM acres outside of Alaska were managed with less intensity, with soil and water conservation and wildlife habitat as important considerations along with the supply of minor forest products such as fence posts and fuelwood for local consumption.

At the beginning of 1980, BLM managed 91 million acres of forestland in Alaska, where intensive forest management had been deferred until state selection, native claims, and expansion of the national parks, national forests, and national wildlife refuges could be reconciled. After this was accomplished with passage of the Alaska National Interests Lands Conservation Act of 1980, BLM's Alaska forest holdings were reduced to 63 million acres, including 5 million classified as commercial.

Altogether, at the end of 1980, BLM managed 90 million acres of forest, which covered 36 percent of its land jurisdiction. The allowable timber cut in 1980 for all BLM land was 1.2 billion board feet.

BLM is organized as a standard trilevel decentralized bureau, with national headquarters in Washington, D.C.; eleven state offices; and fifty-six district offices. There are also four Outer Continental Shelf offices covering Alaska, the Pacific, the Gulf of Mexico, and the Atlantic. In 1980, BLM had a total of 5,800 permanent employees, about 17 percent of whom were in forest management.

FURTHER READING: Marion Clawson, *The Bureau of Land Management* (1971). Samuel Trask Dana and Sally K. Fairfax, *Forest and Range Policy: Its Development in the United States* (2nd ed., 1980). E. Louise Peffer, *The Closing of the Public Domain: Disposal and Reservation Pol-*

icies, 1900–50 (1951). William Voigt, Jr., *Public Grazing Lands: Use and Misuse by Industry and Government* (1976).

JERRY A. O'CALLAGHAN

BUREAU OF OUTDOOR RECREATION AND HERITAGE CONSERVATION AND RECREATION SERVICE

The Bureau of Outdoor Recreation (BOR) was established in 1962 by Secretary of the Interior Stewart L. UDALL following the recommendations of the OUTDOOR RECREATION RESOURCES REVIEW COMMISSION. Udall reassigned to BOR some of the NATIONAL PARK SERVICE responsibilities derived from the Park, Parkway, and Recreation Area Study Act of 1936. Principally, BOR was expected to provide leadership and promote coordination of the nation's outdoor recreation programs and to prepare a National Plan for Outdoor Recreation. Following the so-called Treaty of the Potomac, a joint letter to President John F. Kennedy in which Secretary Udall and Secretary of Agriculture Orville Freeman agreed to cooperate in regard to recreational use of lands controlled by their respective departments, Congress passed the Outdoor Recreation Act of 1963. This act did not specifically refer to BOR, but it did clarify the authority of the secretary of the interior over the functions assigned to BOR. Later, one of BOR's chief missions was to carry out the DEPARTMENT OF THE INTERIOR'S responsibilities under the Land and Water Conservation Fund Act of 1964. Additional functions were served under a number of other laws, including the Federal Water Project Recreation Act of 1965, the Wild and Scenic Rivers Act of 1968, and the National Trails System Act of 1968.

Under the Land and Water Conservation Fund Act, BOR administered a program of matching grants to the states and their subdivisions for recreation planning, land acquisition, and facility development. The fund, under BOR's administration, also supported acquisition of federal lands and water areas for recreational purposes. BOR promoted (but never quite achieved) coordination of federal activities affecting outdoor recreation, provided technical assistance to state and local governments, and monitored recreational research. BOR coordinated studies and proposals for the national trails and wild and scenic rivers systems, reviewed the impacts of transportation projects on recreational resources, and in the early 1970s provided staff support to the Council on Environmental Quality. BOR also processed transfers of surplus federal properties to state and local jurisdictions for recreational development, and conducted programs for the conversion of abandoned railroad lands for recreation and conservation purposes.

In its central activity, the preparation of a National Plan for Outdoor Recreation, BOR was never successful. Outdoor recreation in the United States involved more than a score of federal agencies, as well as hundreds of state and local jurisdictions. Bureaucratic jealousies probably made a comprehensive plan impossible. As late as 1981, a third draft of the national plan was in circulation, with ultimate approval by all parties a doubtful prospect.

Because its activities cut across so many organizational boundaries, BOR's history was a stormy one. The National Park Service, which had long conceived of itself as the national leader in outdoor recreation, resented BOR's intrusion from the outset. Furthermore, BOR's first director was Edward C. Crafts, an energetic and opinionated veteran of the FOREST SERVICE and of several conflicts with the National Park Service.

Crafts endowed BOR with a dynamic and expansive image, but that image did not survive his departure following the inauguration of President Richard M. Nixon in 1969. BOR came under increasing attack, partly from competing agencies. The chief cause for criticism of BOR, however, was its failure to produce the national plan and to complete satisfactorily its technical assignments relating to the Alaska Native Claims Settlement Act of 1971. In addition, the fervor for outdoor recreation planning that had caused the establishment of BOR had given way by the early 1970s to concern for environmental quality. BOR stagnated.

The administration of President Jimmy Carter, inaugurated in 1977, engineered the end of BOR. Carter proposed a sweeping reorganization of federal programs for the protection of natural, historic, and recreational resources through the establishment of a National Heritage Program. Congress eventually rejected Carter's heritage program for a number of interlocking reasons, prominent among them the objections of HISTORIC PRESERVATION interests who criticized the program's blurring of distinctions between natural and cultural resources and its alteration of the Advisory Council on Historic Preservation. Unfortunately for BOR, however, Secretary of the Interior Cecil Andrus had sought to anticipate the legislative heritage program through administrative action. In 1978, Andrus abolished BOR and established the Heritage Conservation and Recreation Service (HCRS). HCRS absorbed not only the activities of BOR but also the work of the Office of Archeology and Historic Preservation and the National Natural Landmarks

Program, both units of the National Park Service. Andrus appointed Chris T. Delaporte as director of HCRS.

Morale within HCRS and the tone of its relations with other agencies were both at a low level from the start, and they deteriorated steadily. Historic preservationists believed that their concerns were being subordinated to recreational pursuits and dissipated throughout the bureau organization. They accused Delaporte of systematically purging personnel in the historic preservation programs. In 1980, the National Conference of State Historic Preservation Officers voted "no confidence" in HCRS and its director. Recreational and conservation interests also offered little visible support for Delaporte. As perhaps the last blow, Delaporte's personal behavior became the subject of scandalous revelations in the press.

The end came swiftly when the presidential administration of Ronald Reagan replaced that of Jimmy Carter, which had created HCRS. Early in 1981, Secretary of the Interior James G. Watt— who had been director of BOR from 1972 to 1975—abolished HCRS and transferred to the National Park Service the organization and its programs, excepting only the Land and Water Conservation Fund grant program, which was assigned to the Office of the Secretary. With the return of most federal recreation activity to the National Park Service, the national outdoor recreation program had come full circle.

FURTHER READING: Edwin M. Fitch and John F. Shanklin, *The Bureau of Outdoor Recreation* (1970).

DAVID A. CLARY

BUREAU OF RECLAMATION

The federal reclamation program is the outgrowth of centuries of effort by Indians, Spanish colonists, Mormons, and other groups to settle the arid American West by controlling and conserving scarce water supplies. The 1902 Reclamation Act authorized the secretary of the interior to locate, construct, operate, and maintain waterworks in the West for the purpose of irrigation agriculture, regarded as essential to regional economic development. The secretary created the Reclamation Service within the U. S. GEOLOGICAL SURVEY. (The service became a separate bureau within Interior in 1907.) The service's self-liquidating public works programs were designed to foster Western settlement through the construction of dams, canals, and other facilities. Under the service's director, Frederick H. NEWELL, twenty-five projects were undertaken within five years to tap rivers draining the forested mountains of the West, and the work of transforming the desert went rapidly forward. Structures such as Theodore Roosevelt Dam in Arizona, Arrowrock Dam in Idaho, and the Gunnison Tunnel in Colorado established Reclamation's reputation as the world's foremost builder of water conservation structures. However, after Newell's departure in 1914 it was clear that the program was not attaining its broader social objectives of Homestead Act settlement and the creation of family farms. Various factors including poor planning, declining revenues, soaring construction costs, and depressed farm prices created hardships for project settlers. Following an intensive investigation by a Fact Finders' Committee in 1923, the service was renamed the Bureau of Reclamation, and legislative and administrative reforms were implemented that alleviated many problems.

Ironically, the onset of hard times in the 1930s enabled the agency under the direction of Elwood MEAD to expand its program within the context of New Deal anti-Depression programs and incorporate multiple-purpose planning into federal water conservation and use. Public power became the "paying partner" of irrigation, and thousands of workers were employed on undertakings such as the Boulder Canyon, Columbia Basin, Colorado-Big Thompson, and Central Valley projects. The agency vastly expanded its staff and regionalized its field structure in 1943 to be more responsive to user needs. Huge dams such as Hoover, Shasta, and Grand Coulee were built, and the program was broadened into areas such as community water supply, flood control, fish and wildlife propagation, and recreation. By the early 1950s, Reclamation had become a powerful public works agency with the technical and administrative skills to advance multiple-purpose programs.

During the next thirty years, the agency's development philosophy and orientation were challenged by groups and individuals who sought to limit growth and preserve the natural environment. Its projects were also assailed on the basis of safety hazards, doubtful economic feasibility, destruction of historic and scenic areas, and adverse effects on wildlife habitat. The bureau, however, continued its construction program in endeavors such as the Colorado River Storage Project with its massive Glen Canyon Dam. Increasing emphasis was placed on the nonagricultural benefits of its projects. The agency remained a leader in water-related research, maintained a vigorous foreign activities program, gave greater attention to water quality, and launched programs into wind, geothermal, and other alternative forms of renewable energy. By the mid-1970s, emphasis was being placed on upgrading existing hydroelectric facilities and exploring the potential of low-head waterpower sources. Nevertheless, the failure of Teton Dam in Idaho in 1976 accelerated the decline of Reclamation as a builder of big dams. Environmental and economic restrictions drastically reduced opportunities for dams and related works. Reclamation, however, continued to play a major role in the planning and use of Western water and power resources. In 1979, Commissioner R. Keith Higginson changed the agency's name to the Water and Power Resources Service to denote the transformation in its policies and fundamental philosophy.

FURTHER READING: Michael C. Robinson, *Water for the West: The Bureau of Reclamation, 1902–1977* (1979). William E. Warne, *The Bureau of Reclamation* (1972).

MICHAEL C. ROBINSON

BUTLER, OVID MCQUAT (1880–1960)

Ovid M. Butler, who would become one of the nation's most influential exponents of forestry and natural resource conservation, was born July 14, 1880, in Indianapolis. Graduating from Butler University (founded by his grandfather, Ovid Butler) with the A.B. degree in 1902, Ovid M. Butler worked for three years as a newspaperman, then went to the Yale Forest School, receiving the M.F. degree in 1907.

Entering the U. S. FOREST SERVICE that year, he was assigned to the Boise National Forest in Idaho and later to the district office in Ogden, Utah, where he became chief of the Division of Forest Management. Just before World War I, Butler directed investigations for the Forest Service which resulted in publication of *The Distribution of Softwood Lumber in the Middle West* as Department of Agriculture reports 115 and 116 (1917 and 1918). The most comprehensive study of the distribution of lumber from mill to consumer made up to that time, this report brought Butler to the attention of the lumber industry. During 1916–1917, he was assistant district forester at Albuquerque, New Mexico. In 1917, he was transferred to the Forest Products Laboratory at Madison, Wisconsin, as assistant director.

On March 1, 1922, Butler was employed as forester by the AMERICAN FORESTRY ASSOCIATION (AFA) in Washington, D.C. A year later, he was named executive secretary and editor, appointments he held until his retirement in 1948. As editor of *American Forests* for twenty-five years, he gained recognition as a foremost authority on policies, public and private, affecting forestland use and management.

Early in his career with AFA, he joined forces with

his friend William B. GREELEY, forester of the United States, to advance federal-state-private cooperative programs in reforestation and fire control. This campaign culminated in the passage of the CLARKE-MCNARY ACT of 1924.

In 1932, during the depths of the Depression, Butler began advocating that the government relieve unemployment by providing jobs for men in work camps on the national and state forests and parks. Joined by other conservationists agitating for solutions to the pressing social problems of the times, Butler urged in the pages of *American Forests* and in letters to officials that the government make use of the available labor to carry on needed reforestation, road building, fire prevention, and park development on the public lands. Out of these discussions evolved the CIVILIAN CONSERVATION CORPS (CCC), created by President Franklin D. ROOSEVELT on March 4, 1933. Butler never claimed credit for conceiving the idea of the CCC, but as much as anyone he was responsible for this innovative experiment in social progress.

In 1944, under Butler's general direction, AFA launched a nationwide Forest Resource Appraisal, a fact-finding survey to determine the country's forest conditions as a result of the heavy drains on timber supplies caused by World War II. Its reports were made public through state-by-state articles in *American Forests*. Recommendations by national conservation leaders for an action program were presented at an American Forest Congress, held in Washington, D.C., in 1946, attended by some 400 delegates. The congress was influential in advancing policies for forest resource use by federal and state governments, forest products industries and associations, private landowners, research agencies, and educational institutions.

During 1927 and 1928, Butler was president of the SOCIETY OF AMERICAN FORESTERS. In 1936, he was a delegate to the World Forestry Congress in Budapest. He was long a member of the advisory board of the National Arboretum and was a member-at-large of the National Council of the Boy Scouts of America. In 1955, Butler University in Indiana, from which he had graduated in 1902, conferred on him the honorary degree of Doctor of Science.

The author of hundreds of articles and editorials on conservation subjects, Butler was author or editor of *American Conservation in Picture and in Story, Rangers of the Shield,* and *Youth Rebuilds* (all published in 1935). He was noted for an ability to set technical data forth clearly for the lay reader. Through his writings, Butler helped make conservation a household word and forestry a familiar concept. He died on February 20, 1960.

HENRY CLEPPER

CALIFORNIA FORESTS

California's present forest wealth is concentrated in the redwood-dominated northern Coast Range and the pine timber regions of the Klamath Mountains, Cascade Range, and the Sierra Nevada. Noncommercial forests and woodlands cover the southern Coast Range, the foothills around the Central Valley, the high elevation subalpine areas, the Modoc Plateau, the desert border foothills, and the Transverse and Peninsula ranges of southern California. Annual precipitation, ranging from 120 inches along the northern coast to less than 5 inches in the southeast, plays an important part in California forest distribution. Forests that originally covered about 46 million of the state's 100 million acres have been reduced to 40 million acres. About 16 million acres, half of which is in national forests and half privately owned, are productive and available for harvest.

The mixed evergreen forest of the northern Coast Range is best known for the coastal strip of redwoods, seldom over forty miles wide, that extends about 400 miles from Monterey County to Oregon. Redwood, unlike most conifers, reproduces effectively by sprouting. The species grows rapidly and produces highly prized, durable, and colorful timber. Venerated as the world's tallest tree, the redwood is preserved in several publicly owned stands, as is the closely related giant sequoia of the southern Sierra Nevada. Associated species of the northern Coast Range are Douglas-fir, tanoak, and madrone, and in the north limited quantities of grand fir, western hemlock, Sitka spruce, red alder, western redcedar, and Port-Orford-cedar. The latter yields a fragrant, durable, finely textured wood for many exacting uses, particularly boat building.

In the higher northern elevations, redwood gives way to Douglas-fir, giant chinkapin, and several oaks, and to the east, sugar, ponderosa, and Jeffrey pines. California Douglas-fir, presently third in importance after pine and true fir in terms of productive forestland acreage, was earlier regarded as inferior to the timber of the Pacific Northwest. Since the mid-1930s, it has grown in value until now it supplies more timber than any other California species.

Northern inland ranges, including the Klamath, the Cascade, and the Sierra Nevada, support a mixed conifer forest consisting of variable combinations of Douglas-fir, ponderosa and sugar pine, white fir, incense-cedar, and California black oak. Ponderosa pine, the dominant tree in the original mixed conifer forest, was the most important lumber tree in California next to redwood, until after the turn of the century. Along with Jeffrey pine, which grows in relatively pure stands on the eastern Sierra slopes, ponderosa pine was marketed as California white pine, until litigation in the 1920s forced a name change. Sugar pine, the largest of the pines, was an important source of shakes and shingles during the pioneer days, and later the soft, easily worked wood was used for cabinets and industrial stock. The durable incense-cedar has supplied fence posts, rails, shakes, and shingles locally since pioneer times, although because of brown pocket rot in overmature trees, the wood was undesirable for lumber. Today, incense-cedar is the world's principal pencil wood and is in high demand for rustic siding.

In elevations above mixed conifer stands occurs the fir forest, consisting mainly of red fir in association with white fir, lodgepole pine, and Jeffrey pine. The true firs—white, grand, and red—are second only to the pine in acreage of productive timberland. Although used locally since pioneer days, the firs were initially regarded as inferior for commercial lumber. In the 1920s and early 1930s, the U. S. FOREST SERVICE required lumbermen on national forests to cut and remove the true firs, but since there was little market for the lumber, the logs were often removed and left to rot or were burned. The consumer and thus the industry has since discarded this prejudice.

South of Santa Cruz, the mixed evergreen forest of the Coast Range loses Douglas-fir and becomes essentially a mixed evergreen-hardwood forest of tanoak, madrone, and live oak, with limited amounts of Coulter, ponderosa, knobcone, Jeffrey, and sugar pines, and in the north, Monterey and bishop pines along the coast and fir in the mountains. Monterey pine's rapid growth and high-quality wood have made it one of the most important commercial softwoods in the Southern Hemisphere, with extensive plantations in Australia, New Zealand, and South Africa. Further south, only coast live oak is found. In the Transverse and Peninsula ranges are scattered stands of the mixed conifer forest on the higher ridges. Bigcone spruce, in association with Coulter and Jeffrey pines, replaces Douglas-fir.

The subalpine forests of the California mountains consists of lodgepole pine, whitebark pine, and mountain hemlock, often with some western juniper, quaking aspen, and western white pine. Blue oak and Digger pine predominate in the foothill woodland forest around the Central Valley and at lower elevations in the Coast Ranges. Associates in various locations include both live and deciduous oaks and California buckeye. The Modoc Plateau and desert border area east of the northern Sierra Nevada consists of almost pure western juniper, but south of Lake Tahoe singleleaf pinyon pine grows in association with junipers. Bristle-cone and limber pines occur above the pinyon-juniper woodland in the White Mountains along the California-Nevada border.

Riparian forests are found along many of the streams that flow out of the mountains. At higher elevations, species include white alder, bigleaf maple, and black cottonwood, and at lower elevations, California sycamore, Fremont cottonwood, and California boxelder. Other riparian species in certain localities include valley oak, Hinds walnut, southern California black walnut, red alder, and Oregon ash.

The forests of California have been of great value to the residents of the state from the earliest days of settlement. Indians found the forests to be a bountiful wildlife habitat and gathered acorns in the oak woodlands. The Hinds walnut and southern California black walnut provided additional food sources. Spanish settlers utilized wood for small boat construction, rafters and ceiling beams, lintels, and frames. For larger structures—the missions, for example—pine and fir timbers were carted or dragged down rough roads from nearby mountains. Redwood, first reported by the Spaniards in 1769, was employed in the construction of missions in the San Francisco Bay Area before 1800 and by the Russians at Fort Ross around 1812.

The oaks served early settlers as a principal source of fuelwood; canyon live oak, the hardest and densest wood of all the oaks, was used for tools and implements. The closely related tanoak, most abundant in the northern Coast Range, was the source of tannin for the important tanning industry begun by the Russians at Fort Ross and lasting through the Spanish and early American periods. Oak was also used for furniture, religious art, barrels, yokes, saddle parts, and the vats used in the manufacture of leather and tallow.

As early as the 1820s, small amounts of lumber were being harvested along the fringes of the redwood forest at Monterey and shipped to settlements in southern California and Hawaii in conjunction with other items of trade. California's first mills contained crude water-powered up-and-down saws. In 1844, the state's first steam mill was erected at Bodega Bay, north of San Francisco. The historic mill at the site of the 1848 gold discovery on the American River was actually part of a growing lumber empire John Sutter had established along the northern Sierra front. As gold-seekers flocked to California, the infant lumber industry struggled to meet the enormous demand for mine timbers and building lumber, particularly for the growing port of San Francisco. Lumber prices skyrocketed, drawing lumber imports from as far away as Maine and stimulating local production. By the late 1850s, the Cali-

Ponderosa pine in the Sierra, showing that the redwoods are not the only large trees in California. Forest History Society Photo.

fornia industry was not only meeting local demand but also supplying a thriving export trade. Redwood City reigned as the center of the state's logging industry, which extended up the coastal redwood forest and through the northern interior pine region. Wholesale dealers in San Francisco shipped lumber to Hawaii, Australia, and the Pacific Coast of Latin America.

Redwood logging presented a number of difficult challenges. Transporting the giant logs to the mills was complicated by steep terrain and lack of snow. Early loggers simply felled or rolled the timber into nearby streams and waited for the spring floods. By

the 1880s, skid roads—logs set in the earth crossways along the hauling road and greased to reduce friction —allowed lumbermen to cut timber further away from the streams; narrow-gauge logging railroads opened up previously inaccessible inland regions. The portable steam donkey engine invented by John Dolbeer and first used near Eureka in 1881 introduced cable yarding to the redwood industry. In the next decade, lumbermen went a step further by running the cable through a block mounted on a spar tree, thus lifting one end of the log off the ground while it was being winched to the yard. By the early 1900s, a cable slung between two spar trees lifted logs entirely off the ground. The steam donkeys were replaced in the 1930s by heavy diesel tractors that permitted more flexible and efficient harvesting techniques.

Moving lumber from the mill to markets presented further problems. Since the state's northern coast lacked good harbors, ships were compelled to take on lumber directly from the dangerous headlands. Inlets known as "dogholes" provided some shelter for the small schooners that carried much of the lumber between the north coast and San Francisco. Lumber was sluiced from the bluffs to the waiting schooners down long apron chutes. During the 1880s, railroads increased the accessibility of many coastal mills, and steam schooners, which were larger, more reliable, and more maneuverable, facilitated coastal shipping. In the inland mountain ranges, particularly the Sierra Nevada, lumber and logs were transported to railheads by long flumes extending down mountain valleys from mills or logging operations at higher elevations.

Emerging during the gold rush period, California's lumber industry increased steadily until the mid-1920's. In 1868, California produced 319 million board feet of lumber, and in 1899, 737 million. Annual production reached 2 billion board feet by 1923. Output declined during the Depression, but by 1948 the state was producing over 5 billion board feet, ranking second only to Oregon in lumber production. In the peak year of 1959, its cut of over 6 billion board feet represented over 16 percent of U. S. production.

Although California had a small papermaking industry as early as 1856, it was not until after World War II that pulp and paper production assumed an important role in the state's economy. By 1968, the state's seventeen mills consumed 11.9 million tons of wood residues and chips. In addition, California produced an average of 800 million square feet of softwood plywood annually during the 1970s. Other forest products included posts and piling, shingles and shakes, furniture, wood flour, and wood preservatives. Although the number of mills in California decreased during the 1960s and 1970s, production of wood products increased, reflecting a trend toward concentration in both mills and timberland holdings.

Forestry efforts in California have been closely tied to WATERSHED MANAGEMENT. Early in the state's history, it became evident that water was critical to California's future development. Since 70 percent of the total water run-off originated on forested areas, the characteristics of the forests greatly influenced availability and quality of the state's water supply, as well as the frequency and severity of floods. Severe droughts in the late 1800s and devastating floods in

southern California following fires in watershed areas moved forward-looking citizens to take steps toward conservation of the forests. First among the states to establish a forestry office (1883) and a Board of Forestry (1885), California demonstrated an early concern for its wildland resources. At a time when most westerners objected to federal control of the forests, the California legislature, concerned about watersheds, called for increased fire fighting and forestry efforts on the state's federal forestlands. Growing public awareness of California forests brought the reestablishment of the Board of Forestry in 1905 and the appointment of California's first state forester, E. T. Allen. Over the next decade, the state developed a large, efficient fire control agency. In 1945, it began regulating timber harvesting on privately owned lands, and since 1972, it has been licensing foresters practicing in the state. By 1872, Stanford University, the University of Southern California, and the University of California all had conducted some forestry instruction, although the first viable and continuing educational program in the state was established on the Berkeley campus in 1914. Humboldt State University began forestry instruction in 1953.

State forestry efforts were supplemented by those of the federal government. Following congressional authorization in 1891, President Benjamin Harrison set aside the first California forest reserve, the San Gabriel, now part of southern California's Angeles National Forest. By 1980, California had twenty-two national forests with over 24 million acres within their boundaries. Federal forestry research in California began in the national forests around 1910. In 1912, the Forest Service Feather River Experiment Station was organized on the Plumas National Forest. Fourteen years later, the California Forest Experiment Station, successor to the Feather River station, was dedicated, with headquarters in the same building as the Division of Forestry of the University of California at Berkeley. Known as the Pacific Southwest Forest and Range Experiment Station since 1959, it has a research staff of over 100 scientists with special field units and laboratories in several other locations.

The nation's first state park was dedicated in 1864, when President Abraham Lincoln deeded Yosemite Valley and Mariposa Grove to the state of California. The land surrounding Yosemite Valley was declared a national park in 1890, and in 1905 California returned the valley itself to the federal government. In 1902, citizens led by the Sempervirens Club of San Jose and by Andrew J. Hill induced the state legislature to purchase lands for the California Redwood

State Park (now Big Basin) near Santa Cruz. In 1918, the SAVE-THE-REDWOODS LEAGUE was formed and began a campaign that resulted in the preservation of 3,000 acres of old-growth redwoods in the Humboldt and Del Norte state parks, now encompassed by the Redwood National Park. The California State Parks Commission was created in 1927 and began its tenure by approving a plan to survey the state for possible park sites under the direction of Frederick Law OLMSTED, Jr. The resulting report identified 125 sites out of 330 investigated and provided the state with a foundation on which to build a state park system.

In 1975, there were 230 park and recreation areas, comprising 843,000 acres. In addition, five national parks, eight monuments, and three recreation areas lie within the state's boundaries. State-owned forestlands, mostly in parks, include about 600,000 acres.

FURTHER READING: C. Raymond Clar, *California Government and Forestry from Spanish Days until the Creation of the Department of Natural Resources in 1927* (1959), and *California Government and Forestry II: During the Young and Ralph Administration* (1969). Samuel Trask Dana and Myron E. Kreuger, *California Lands: Ownership, Use, and Management* (1958).

ROBERT A. COCKRELL

CALIFORNIA STATE FORESTRY

Significant efforts toward government regulation of forestry began in 1883 when Assemblyman James V. Coleman of San Mateo County sponsored a joint resolution establishing the Lake Bigler Forestry Commission to investigate the rapid disappearance of timber from around Lake Tahoe (as it is now called). Despite the commission's plea, nothing was done for Tahoe's forests, but in 1885 the state did create a permanent Board of Forestry, with Coleman as its first chairman. This board was given few funds and obtained few forest protection laws. It made a general survey of the state's forests, established two tree nurseries, and published some substantial reports. Its abolition in 1893 was followed by a decade of official indifference.

The administration of Governor George Cooper Pardee beginning in 1903 saw a renewed interest in state forestry. A joint survey of the state's forests was undertaken in cooperation with the United States Bureau of Forestry. The Forest Protection Act of 1905 provided for a trained state forester and created a new Board of Forestry consisting of the governor, secretary of state, attorney general, and state forester. Edward Tyson Allen was the first holder of the new office. He was charged with coordination of fire

protection, care of state parks, cooperation with local government and individuals in planning and managing woodlands, appointment of voluntary fire wardens, and impressment of citizens to fight fire during emergencies. However, the financial burden rested upon local governments and private parties. Eventually, counties and local associations (notably in Los Angeles County) created their own forest and fire departments. The first major problems to be tackled by the state were the safe disposal of logging slash and the elimination of light burning in mature forests (not finally discredited among California timber owners until the 1920s).

California progressed slowly in practical forestland management. In 1919 the state restructured the Board of Forestry with appointees representing specific interests (the timber industry, livestock, hay and grain) and the general public, as well as the state forester. The state forester was authorized to enter cooperative agreements with local governments and landowners, and, for the first time, the state appropriated funds for fire protection. These provisions at last permitted the state to claim federal WEEKS ACT funds to support protection and place its first rangers in the field. But administrations anxious for economy in government hampered forestry work during the 1920s. New programs in insect eradication and fire patrol depended primarily upon assessments against the timberland owners.

In 1925, Californians pressured Congress to extend federal cooperation under the CLARKE-MCNARY ACT to include the protection of brush watershed. In the following year, a state constitutional amendment exempted lumber trees from property taxes for forty years after planting or natural regrowth. Eventually, with increasing population and land values, this measure began to irritate tax assessors. A yield tax law replaced it in 1975.

Governor Clement Calhoun Young's administration undertook a major revision of California government and forestry in 1927 with legislation creating a new Department of Natural Resources. Within its jurisdiction was placed the Division of Forestry, under the state forester, now relieved of supervision over state parks. The Board of Forestry, stripped of executive power, consisted of members from timber, water, agriculture, and livestock interests. The first chairman of the new board was the aging former governor Pardee, who had chaired previous boards of forestry in 1905–1907 and 1919–1923, as well as the Conservation Commission of California. This latter body in 1912 had made a report, ignored by a parsimonious legislature, upon the condition of water, forests, and minerals. But

Forest fires have long been a primary focus of California forest policy. In the early 1930s, state officials proudly demonstrated a new fire truck in the Sierra foothills. Forest History Society Photo.

in 1928 appropriations were greater than ever before. Twenty counties entered agreements whereby state rangers supervised rural and mountain fire protection.

The Great Depression brought further enhancement of forest protection and also the replacement of the pickup labor system with professional fire crews. State rangers supervised labor camps where jobless men worked for their bunk and food. These camps and later the federal CIVILIAN CONSERVATION CORPS added ranger stations, lookouts, roads, firebreaks, and other facilities. But fire suppression work still suffered from miserly state appropriations. Only after American entry into World War II were state fiscal resources made available to allow implementation of the division's Master Fire Plan of 1940 (the "Clar Plan"), which treated fire protection as a statewide problem. At last, state rangers no longer needed to beg for local assistance.

The Forest Practice Act of 1945 provided effective regulation, designating four timber regions in which landowner committees determined practice rules in cooperation with the Division of Forestry. In the same session, the legislature appropriated funds to purchase three state forests for the study of proper land management. By 1950, the division was able to assign field personnel to advise owners of small timber plots and to make recommendations for treatment of vegetation around small dams.

Although a growing population led to dramatic increases in the number of wildfires by the mid-1950s, higher worker efficiency through training and the use of aircraft and other mechanical developments kept the number of acres burned at a moderate level. In 1967, the Division of Forestry established a wildland fire training academy in the Almador County foothills. On the first day of 1977, the large division was given departmental status, and the title of state forester was replaced by that of director. By the end of the decade, the department had over 5,000 regular employees. With 225 fire stations, 74 lookouts, 7 "helitack" crews, and 13 primary air attack bases, it was directly responsible for fire protection upon some 23 million acres of timber and watershed land, and it supported protection by other agencies on an additional 9 million acres.

Forest products sold from state forests enriched

the state treasury by some $8.5 million a year, while tree nurseries operated by the department sold 5.4 million seedlings for reforestation purposes.

FURTHER READING: T. F. Arvola, *Regulation of Logging in California, 1945–1975* (1976). C. Raymond Clar, *California Government and Forestry* (2 vols., 1959, 1969).

C. RAYMOND CLAR

CANADIAN-AMERICAN RELATIONS IN THE FOREST PRODUCTS INDUSTRIES

Speaking to a commercial convention in Detroit in 1865, Nova Scotia statesman Joseph Howe observed that the timber trade between British North America and the United States, "twisted and intertwined as it is, is a trade owned . . . by the two countries." The statement remains as true in the 1980s as it was in 1865. Yet despite widespread exchange of techniques, capital, personnel, and forest products, the boundary has made a difference, giving important direction to commercial developments in both nations.

Four general factors have influenced the trade. The North American boreal forest that stretched across Canada and the United States for the most part provided similar resources along both sides of the border. The resulting similarity of forest industries intensified competition for regional markets and was thus a significant factor governing trade relations between the two nations. A second influence upon the international economy was Canada's relation to Great Britain, which Americans often had difficulty in understanding and which therefore delayed the establishment of a mature trading relationship between Canada and its neighbor to the south. Third, although the lumbering frontier generally moved in a westerly direction, the resource was unevenly distributed and its exploitation was unevenly accomplished. The westward ebb and flow of this trade, an expression of regional unity across the border, responded not only to resource availability but also to market fluctuations, advances in techniques, and political developments. Finally, the forest products industry has loomed larger in Canada's foreign trade than it has in that of the United States. A nation of abundant forest resources and a huge land area, much of which is unsuitable for agriculture, Canada relied heavily on its forest industries and continues to do so today. In the United States, greater land use competition and a more diversified industrial base resulted in a smaller role for forest products exports. Throughout Canada's history, the nation has generally found itself in a position of responding to American

markets and American political initiatives. Canadian trade has occasionally been crucial to Americans, but the American connection has always been so to Canadians.

In colonial times, England and the West Indies absorbed North American forest products, and both Canadian and American coastal settlements hardly considered trading with one another what each already had in excess. After the Revolutionary War, as settlements moved west, opportunities for exchange of forest products between the two nations improved.

Although conscious of their nationality, lumbermen chose to follow logging opportunities regardless of borders. The Saint Croix River, which served as the boundary between Maine and New Brunswick, demonstrated some of the advantages and problems of the early international trade. Since logs, regardless of their place of origin, could obviously be landed on either bank of the river, market possibilities rather than political boundaries determined the destination of the log drive. Depending upon which market brought the best returns, timber cut in either nation would be sawn at mills in Saint Andrews and Saint Stephen on the New Brunswick shore for shipment to Liverpool, or at Calais on the Maine side of the river for transport to Boston or New Orleans. Canadian and American lumbermen cooperated in rafting and log driving and on river improvements, railroad construction, and sorting booms. The commercial arrangements on the Saint Croix were typical of the ways in which trade flowed across the international boundary as the lumber industry moved west.

Lumbering operations throughout New Brunswick after the War of 1812 were international in scope. Capital arrived from Yankee sources and supplies for the lumber camps were also of New England origin. American capital had little effect on established trading patterns, however, and New Brunswick continued to export squared pine timber and deals to British markets. Indeed, Maine's representatives in Congress voted with the majority for the Tariff of 1832, with a 25 percent duty on rough lumber that would discourage any deflection of the transatlantic trade to the United States. Before 1846, relatively insignificant amounts of New Brunswick lumber were imported into the United States.

The developing international economy was not without friction. Typical of disputes along the lumbering frontier was the so-called Aroostook War, which featured more bluff and bravado than blood. This disagreement was caused by conflicting boundary claims along the Saint John River, which arises in northern Maine and emerges on the Bay of Fundy at

Saint John, New Brunswick. The eastern boundary of Maine, which today seems fairly straight and certain, was anything but that before 1842. No accurate maps of the region had been available when the 1783 Treaty of Paris outlined the boundaries of the state and province. The resulting ambiguities plagued the border region for the next sixty years. The boundary dispute became heated in the mid-1820s, when loggers from Maine and New Brunswick moved into the Aroostook and Saint John river valleys. Maine, Massachusetts (which held extensive tracts of Maine land), and New Brunswick claimed jurisdiction over the timber in the disputed territory. Repeatedly harassed by agents from both sides of the border, lumbermen brought the crisis to a head in 1839. Militias from Maine and New Brunswick were sent to the Aroostook territory, followed by federal troops and British regulars. Although no real violence took place, the threat of it encouraged diplomats to seek an early solution. The Webster-Ashburton Treaty of 1842 was the result.

In addition to determining the boundary, the treaty defined the legal trading relationship between state and province, stipulating that forest and agricultural products from the Saint John River Valley in Maine would enjoy free and open navigation upon the provincial section of the river. Article 3 of the treaty stated that "when within the province of New Brunswick, the said product shall be dealt with as if it were the produce of said province." Subsequently, a good deal of American timber was milled in the cities of Fredericton and Saint John—often by American millowners—and sold as Canadian lumber, thereby gaining free access to British markets.

Canadian-American markets also developed along the Saint Lawrence basin. As early as 1787, Britain opened the Lake Champlain-Richelieu River route to free importation of lumber, NAVAL STORES, and various agricultural products, thereby benefiting settlers in upper New York and Vermont and merchants in Quebec and Montreal at the expense of pioneers in Upper Canada. Timber moved north out of the United States on the Richelieu to the Saint Lawrence and was shipped to markets in Britain. In this case, as in others, legal decree merely legitimated an existing de facto international trade in forest products.

The movement of lumber along the waterways of this region was reversed by the canal-building era of the early nineteenth century. After the opening of the Champlain Canal in 1822, timber could be transported from Lake Champlain down the Hudson River, giving lumbermen the option of a more profitable New York market. With the completion of the Erie Canal in 1825 and the Oswego Canal connecting Lake Ontario with the Erie Canal in 1828, producers in western New York were no longer compelled by the northward flow of rivers to sell their timber in Montreal and Quebec but could also take advantage of the New York market. In Upper Canada, the Rideau Canal, connecting Ottawa with Kingston on Lake Ontario, was opened in 1832, and Canadian logs and lumber began what would be a growing movement in the direction of American markets, despite a tariff barrier of between 20 and 30 percent. The canal system, which disrupted natural waterborne commercial routes, constituted a brilliant success for New York merchants and achieved, as Hugh J. G. Aitken has observed, "what military force had failed to achieve: the destruction of Montreal's commercial empire around the lower lakes."

Exploitation of forests for both American and British markets brought a quick exhaustion of the available pine in the Maritimes, Maine, New York, and Vermont; many lumbermen in mid-career elected to move westward. Many from the American side initially relocated in southern Ontario and subsequently moved on to Michigan. As loggers migrated westward through Canada and the United States, they took with them a technology developed in an international context. Techniques of rafting, boom construction, log driving, log marks, and camp construction and types of camp food and entertainment were shared across the border.

Nevertheless, Canadian commerce remained directed largely to British ports through most of the first half of the nineteenth century. Exceptions to this mercantilist pattern occurred mainly along the inland boundary and only in response to particular local circumstances. The decade of the 1840s, however, brought an end to British preferential treatment of Canadian forest products and witnessed a fundamental change in the old relationship. Canadian producers found themselves in an uncertain world market, competing without advantages.

Seeking alternatives to British markets, Canadian lumbermen turned to ideas of free trade and to the United States. Improved transportation systems gave Canadian mills an appealing market south of the border. In the United States, interest in lowering tariff barriers was fueled by increasing costs of domestic lumber, unprecedented urban growth, and an apparent depletion of forest resources in the eastern states. In 1854, the mutual interest of the two nations was formally recognized in the Canadian-American Reciprocity Treaty which, among other things, allowed free exchange of natural products and raw materials, including boards and scantlings, between the two countries. Although the results of the treaty were less than expected, the period would be recalled later as something of a golden age of enlightened commercial relations. The treaty accentuated a general realignment of Canadian exports from Britain to the United States.

The Confederation in Canada and the Civil War in America brought new considerations and tensions to the tariff question. In 1866, the United States abrogated the Reciprocity Treaty, bringing to an end the free flow of timber and lumber across the border. The 20 percent American tariff was reinstated on lumber imports, and in response Canada levied an export duty of one dollar per thousand feet on pine sawlogs. Four years later, the United States placed sawlogs on the free list, retaining a two-dollar duty on lumber. The free import of logs helped American millowners but the tariff on lumber hurt Canadians. In 1879, Sir Leonard Tilley typified the growing nationalism and protectionist sentiment in Canada when he announced that "the time has arrived when we are to decide whether we will simply be hewers of wood and drawers of water."

No better example of changing political circumstances and the changing flow of trade in the lumber industry is found than that of relations between Michigan and Ontario. Although Michigan lumber went primarily to Chicago and Albany, square timber from the state's Upper Peninsula before the 1870s was exported through Canada to British markets. As their stocks of pine declined, Michigan mill owners began reversing this flow as early as 1851 by importing sawlogs from Ontario. By 1886, Michigan lumbermen, intent on rafting the wood to Michigan to be sawn, held stumpage on 1.75 billion feet of timber in the Georgian Bay area. In that year, Canada doubled its export duty on sawlogs to two dollars a thousand, causing some Michigan operators to relocate their mills to the Ontario shore of Lake Huron. The heavy exploitation of Canadian forests by Lake States lumbermen was resented by their Canadian counterparts, whose lumber was subject to import duties in the United States. The relationship between Ontario timber and Michigan sawmills was an important part of the tariff battles of the last third of the nineteenth century.

Even though it heard arguments against protectionism, the U. S. Special Tariff Commission in 1882 recommended that the lumber schedule be kept intact. Typical of reactions to this decision was that of the *New York World* editor who labeled the tariff a "bounty, for the rapid destruction of American forests." Similar concern that American tariff policy encouraged rapid exhaustion of American forests was expressed in Charles S. SARGENT's *Report on the Forests of North America* (1884), compiled for the Tenth Census of the United States. Sargent estimated the Lake States white pine at about 55 billion feet, and the annual harvest at 3 billion feet.

Both the American tariff and the Canadian export duty were lowered in 1890, and the flow of sawlogs across the Great Lakes increased. In 1894, despite opposition from lumber manufacturers, all American duties on lumber were eliminated. Lumbermen petitioned the Senate Finance Committee asking that the tariff be reestablished in order to "equalize the adverse conditions under which the American lumber manufacturer operates as compared with his foreign competitor." Others supported free trade, among them an ex-mayor of Saginaw, Michigan, who publicized his opposition in pamphlets directed at the Finance Committee. Protectionists prevailed in 1897, when the Dingley Tariff restored the two-dollar duty. As a result, Michigan sawmills enjoyed a brief period of renewed activity.

Unfortunately, Michigan's spurt in lumber production did not represent any increase in available local timber resources, and when Ontario responded to the Dingley Tariff in 1898 by prohibiting the export of sawlogs altogether, Michigan operators faced the choice of retiring from business or moving to Canada and enduring the provisions of the Dingley Tariff, as did their Canadian counterparts. Other provinces soon followed the Ontario example, reminding American loggers that they operated on crown timberlands at the pleasure of the Canadian government.

In general, these commercial policies over the past century have been futile as political barriers were eroded by more fundamental economic needs for interdependence. This was particularly true as farms and cities expanded across the treeless prairies, creating a continuing demand for lumber from the eastern forests in both nations. For the most part, it was the pineries of the Lake States that provided lumber to customers of the mid-continent; Canada's three great eastern lumber producing provinces—New Brunswick, Quebec, and Ontario—supplied lumber to growing cities in the East. After 1900, however, midwestern markets in both Canada and the United States were increasingly fed by the expanding lumber industry in British Columbia and the Pacific Northwest, as timber stocks were depleted in the East.

The decline in lumber production in the East coincided with the rise of the pulp and paper industry which, like lumbering, quickly developed international connections. In just seven years, from 1913 to 1920, Canadian wood pulp production doubled to a total of 1.9 million tons. Canadian pulp might have simply gone to feed mills on the American side had not Canadian policies intervened. British Columbia led the way in 1891, establishing export duties on pulpwood, and in 1897 this became national policy. In recognition of American dependence on Canadian sources, the Underwood Tariff of 1913 permitted the free entry of inexpensive paper, favoring a movement of the American pulp and paper industry to Canada, principally New Brunswick, Quebec, and Ontario. The shift in the industry was fundamental. In 1908, 65 percent of the harvest was exported as raw material, 95 percent of this volume going to the United States. In 1920, only 31 percent was exported with domestic mills consuming the rest. By the 1920s, these mills had made Canada the world's largest producer of newsprint. Over 90 percent of its newsprint exports went to the United States.

But while Canadian politics built up the Canadian newsprint industry at the expense of the American, so did American capital and management contribute to the development of that industry. The history of the New York-based International Paper Company is typical. The firm was part of a rapidly expanding industry competing for a limited supply of spruce timberlands in the northeastern United States. Spreading from New York through New England in the 1890s, International Paper Company's mills by 1898 had exhausted nearby supplies of spruce. Across the border, the spruce forests of Ontario and Quebec were ideally situated on excellent rivers, capable of supplying both transportation for pulpwood and hydroelectric power for the mills. By 1900, International Paper owned extensive Canadian timberlands and crown land licenses, and in the next two decades the ban on Canadian pulpwood exports, coupled with the removal of the tariff on newsprint, encouraged the company to relocate in Canada. In 1919, International Paper Company established at Three Rivers, Quebec, a mill that became the largest newsprint plant in the world. In 1925, the Canadian subsidiary of International Paper bought the extensive properties of the Canadian Riordon Company, with its mills, millsites, waterpower privileges, and large tracts of timberlands. That year, the company constructed a second newsprint mill at Gatineau, Quebec, and in 1930 it built a third at Dalhousie, New Brunswick. Other companies followed International Paper Company's lead, relocating a substantial part of the American newsprint industry in Canada during the 1920s.

On the West Coast, Canadian lumber production concentrated on markets in the United States in the 1910s and 1920s. Here also, Americans played an important part in the Canadian industry, particularly after 1900, by investing in timberlands and leases, sawmills, logging operations, and later pulp and paper companies. American techniques, such as skidder logging, the incline hoist, the highland yarder, the portable spar, and the use of Climax locomotives, filtered into the woods of British Columbia between 1900 and 1920.

The Depression brought a slump in this trade, and in 1930 the United States placed a tariff of one dollar per thousand board feet on softwood lumber, British Columbia's major wood export. Ironically, it was during the depths of the Great Depression that the Canadian-American tariff battles reached their most extreme levels. In 1932, the American tariff was raised to four dollars a thousand feet. Canadian lumber exports to the United States, coming mostly from British Columbia, dropped from more than 1 billion board feet in the late 1920s to 234 million in 1934. At the same time, a strong lumber market in Britain during the 1930s redirected Canadian exports overseas. By 1938, for instance, 80 percent of the lumber exported from British Columbia went to British markets.

Canadian-American interdependence was finally recognized between 1936 and 1938 with Canadian acceptance of the Reciprocal Trade Agreements, which reduced tariffs on lumber by half. Concessions on Douglas-fir and western hemlock, British Columbia's major lumber species, were limited to 250 million board feet annually. However, it was the post-World War II housing boom in the United States, rather than the tariff agreements, that revitalized American markets for British Columbia lumber and provided much of the basis for the industry's expansion into the interior of the province. By 1980, 50 percent of British Columbia's softwood lumber exports went to the United States, along with 75 percent of its newsprint and 55 percent of its pulp chips. Today, much of the West Coast lumber, pulp, and paper industries is dominated by firms that span the international border. Examples are Weyerhaeuser, which in 1975 owned the largest pulp mill in British Columbia; Crown Zellerbach, which had two mills in the interior of the province; Crestbrook Forest Industries, with joint Canadian-American-Japanese ownership; and Pope & Talbot, with operations straddling the British Columbia-Washington boundary.

An appropriate recognition of the continuing need for international exchange in the forest products industries of the two nations is the cooperation to protect forest resources along the border. Timber owners and protective associations in the Pacific Northwest joined with those in British Columbia in 1909 to establish the WESTERN FORESTRY AND CONSERVATION ASSOCIATION, which subsequently developed programs throughout western North America. In 1949, the U. S. Congress authorized the Northeastern Forest Fire Protection Compact, which provided for a united effort on the part of the New England states, New York, Quebec, and New Brunswick. Perhaps more than any other single factor, these developments symbolized the commonness of the Canadian-American forest products industry.

FURTHER READING: Douglas Rudyard Annett, *British Preference in Canadian Commercial Policy* (1948). John B. Brebner, *North Atlantic Triangle: The Interplay of Canada, the United States and Great Britain* (1945). Harold A. Davis, *An International Community on the St.*

Croix (1604–1930) (1950). Anita Shafer Goodstein, *Biography of a Businessman: Henry W. Sage, 1814–1897* (1962). Arthur Reginald Marsden Lower, *The North American Assault on the Canadian Forest* (1938), and *Great Britain's Woodyard: British America and the Timber Trade, 1763–1867* (1973). Orville John McDiarmid, *Commercial Policy in the Canadian Economy* (1946).

CHARLES E. TWINING

CARRIAGE AND WAGON BUILDING

The principal material used in the construction of carriages and wagons has always been wood. Iron, and occasionally other metals, have been used to strength-

Manufacture of horseless carriages also required wood, as this photograph of wooden parts used for the 1937 Ford stationwagon shows. Forest History Society Photo.

The interior of this streetcar was finished with white ash. Forest History Society Lantern Slide Collection.

en, brace, secure, or join wooden parts, or to provide more durable wearing surfaces, but both load-bearing members and the covering shells of horse-drawn vehicles have long been fashioned of wood. Even the axles of many eighteenth- and early nineteenth-century carriages were of wood, and, in many wagons, the wooden axle persisted until the end of the horse-drawn era. Some of the more primitive vehicles, such as the famed Red River cart of the Dakota Territory, even dispensed with metal wearing and fastening parts, and were entirely of wood. The various woods used were generally chosen for toughness and elasticity, some for lightness, and still others for bending properties. During the earlier period when carriage and wagon shops used only local lumber, availability sometimes caused substitutions to be made, so that it was not always the most suitable timber that went into vehicles.

Ash, preferably white ash, was one of the more important woods used in carriage work, and to some extent, in wagon work. It was tough and adapted to bending when steamed or boiled. It could be employed either for running-gear parts or for body framing. Oak, too, was widely used, particularly for wagon work, where it was often used to make the same components for which white ash was used in carriages. Maple was also employed in wagons, but infrequently

in carriages. Hickory could be substituted for oak or ash and was especially desirable where elasticity was important such as in spokes and rims and in wooden springs. In the case of spokes, the wood was preferably split out of the log, rather than sawed, in order to insure maximum possible strength through straightness of grain. Elm, birch, or oak was frequently used for hubs. Panel wood needed to be light and adaptable to warping into either simple or compound curves. In America, whitewood or yellow-poplar was most important for this purpose. Likewise, wagon flooring and paneling was often poplar, or white or yellow pine, while trucks and drays intended for extremely heavy use might require oak flooring.

In the nineteenth century, important technological changes slowly took place in vehicle construction. The first small evidences of this came around the 1830s but they were hardly noticeable until perhaps mid-century; the real development awaited the final quarter of the century. Gradually, the machine operator and the assembler replaced the craftsman. Sawing stock to size was the first step; later, the completed parts were fashioned by machine. Wheel spokes were machine made, and eventually the entire wheel came to be so built. Improved wood-bending machinery enabled the bending of wheel rims, thus making possible stronger and cheaper wheels. Numerous other parts were similarly bent. Finally, during the 1870s, began the process of mass production, with machines turning out large numbers of identical parts, which in turn permitted the cheap vehicle, thus opening vast new markets. The 1900 census reported 7,632 carriage and wagon building establishments in the United States, using altogether over $8.9 million worth of lumber.

New England, especially Massachusetts and Connecticut, had been the dominant carriage and wagon building center in the early nineteenth century; around the time of the Civil War the scene began to shift to the Midwest, with the states of Ohio, Indiana, Illinois, and Michigan becoming the most important. Through both eras New York remained strong, while Pennsylvania and New Jersey shared a lesser importance. By the 1890s, the industry showed some development in the Southern states, attracted by the availability of lumber. The carriage trade slowly died during the first two decades of the twentieth century, while the wagon trade lingered, in a small way, for another two decades. Even as the era closed, some of the technology passed to the infant automobile industry, for early auto bodies were sometimes of wood, as were wheels, some frames, and occasionally axles.

DON H. BERKEBILE

CARSON, RACHEL (1907–1964)

"Writing," Rachel Carson wrote, "is a lonely occupation at best." She viewed writing as "hard work" and good writing as that which tells a story "as clearly and simply as possible." Although she felt that writing as many as 1,500 words constituted "a very good day," Carson wrote *Under the Sea Wind* (1941), *The Sea Around Us* (1951), *The Edge of the Sea* (1956), and *Silent Spring* (1962), one of the most influential books in the history of conservation. Her books dealt with scientific topics, but her graceful prose attracted a readership vastly larger than the scientific community. *Silent Spring* especially captured worldwide attention, and the question of retaining an acceptable environmental quality was no longer left for specialists to answer.

Rachel Carson was born on May 27, 1907, in Springdale, Pennsylvania. She graduated from Pennsylvania College for Women (1929) and Johns Hopkins University (1932), and in later years received three honorary doctorates. In 1931, Carson accepted an appointment as staff biologist at the University of Maryland, moving to the federal Bureau of Fisheries in 1936 as an aquatic biologist. In 1949, she became editor-in-chief of the FISH AND WILDLIFE SERVICE, an agency of the DEPARTMENT OF THE INTERIOR that was formed through the merger of the Bureau of Fisheries and the BIOLOGICAL SURVEY. Three years later, she resigned to devote her time to writing.

In 1975, the AMERICAN FORESTRY ASSOCIATION polled 104 of its members, who listed Rachel Carson among the ten most influential contributors to American conservation history. Undoubtedly, this ranking resulted from *Silent Spring*, a book that is frequently used to pinpoint the substantive beginning of the ENVIRONMENTAL MOVEMENT. In *Silent Spring*, Carson focused on the overuse and misuse of chemical pesticides that had already degraded the environment and potentially could damage it in a massive way. She was gentle with foresters and the resource managers who had learned in school the advantages of natural or biological controls of insects and other pests. She was not gentle with governments, agencies, and institutions that authorized and even mandated liberal doses of an ever lengthening list of poisons to control pests.

The reaction to *Silent Spring* was mixed. Generally, resource professionals rejected it as impractical or simplistic, whether they had read it or not. Agencies stoutly resisted its influence, but with highly publicized backing from President John F. Kennedy, the federal government moved quickly to restrict use of DDT and other persistent pesticides. Regulations administered by the Environmental Protection Agency for pesticide use after 1970 are part of Rachel Carson's legacy. In 1963, she received the Conservationist of the Year Award from the NATIONAL WILDLIFE FEDERATION, and in 1969, the Interior Department renamed the Coastal Maine Refuge as the Rachel Carson National Wildlife Refuge. She died April 14, 1964.

FURTHER READING: Paul Brooks, *The House of Life* (1972). Rachel Carson, *Silent Spring* (1962). Frank Graham, Jr., *Since Silent Spring* (1970). Philip Sterling, *Sea and Earth: The Life of Rachel Carson* (1970).

CARY, AUSTIN (1865–1936)

Austin Cary was born July 31, 1865, in East Machias, Maine. At Bowdoin College, he majored in science with emphasis on botany and entomology and received the A.B. degree in 1887 and the M.A. in 1890. After graduation he did free-lance work as a land cruiser and surveyor in the northern New England woods. His research on tree growth, cutting methods, entomology, and the life cycles of northern Maine trees was published by the Maine Forestry Service and the *Paper Trade Jour-*

nal. Cary's writings helped foster an industrial interest in improved land use, tree planting, and selective tree breeding.

He traveled abroad several times, especially to the Black Forest of Germany, to study forestry practices. Upon his return in 1898, he was employed by the Berlin Mills Company in New Hampshire as the first company forester in North America and began a lengthy campaign to convert this firm and others in northern New Hampshire and western Maine to long-range planning of cutting, planting, and land use. The opposition he encountered instilled in Cary a missionary zeal; to convert the industry to his views, he began a lifelong career of speaking, writing, and traveling.

Cary held teaching positions at the Yale Forest School (1904–1905) and at Harvard (1905–1909). During this period, Cary wrote his only book, *A Manual for Northern Woodsmen* (1909). Briefly, he was superintendent of forestry in New York State (1909–1910). In 1910, however, Cary joined the U. S. FOREST SERVICE. From 1917 onward, Cary spent his entire career in the South where cutover lands, growing up to second growth, were becoming increasingly important to the paper industry during the rapid expansion that followed the widespread adoption of kraft boxes for packaging.

Cary served the Forest Service as a sort of roving extension forester. He sought to teach landowners and forestry companies to maximize their long-term profits by planning, careful cutting, regeneration of the cover, better selection of stock, and generally adopting modified German forestry practices. Along with others in the South, Cary was very successful; by the 1930s he was known as the "Father of Southern Forestry."

Cary's success was due in part to his straightforward and strong personality. He gave his message in colorful and blunt language. Although the need for governmental help in meeting the costs of refurbishing cutover lands hampered the fulfillment of Cary's dream of primarily private forestry, he correctly perceived that once private firms realized the possibility of long-term continuous profits they would introduce good forestry practices. Cary's impact on the world of the woods in New England and the South was immense. He returned to Maine after retiring from the Forest Service in 1935 and died on April 28 of the following year.

FURTHER READING: David C. Smith, *A History of Lumbering in Maine, 1861–1960* (1972). Roy R. White, "Austin Cary and Forestry in the South," Ph.D. dissertation, University of Florida (1961), and "Austin Cary, the Father of Southern Forestry," *Forest History* 5 (Spring 1961): 2-5.

DAVID C. SMITH

CATSKILL PARK

Central New York State's Catskill Park was created by law in 1904 and, since then, has served as the focus for most NEW YORK STATE FOREST PRESERVE land acquisition in the four-county Catskill region. Unlike the ADIRONDACK PARK, the Catskill Park is not subject to comprehensive land-use and development controls.

WILLIAM K. VERNER

CHAPMAN, HERMAN HAUPT (1874–1963)

One of the most influential leaders in the development of the forestry profession in the United States, H. H. Chapman was widely acclaimed as an educator, researcher, author, and defender of public and professional interests. Born in Cambridge, Massachusetts, October 8, 1874, Chapman attended the University of Minnesota where he earned bachelor of science and bachelor of agriculture degrees in 1896 and 1899, respectively, and was awarded an honorary doctor of science degree in 1947. As superintendent of the Minnesota Agricultural Experiment Station in Grand Rapids from 1898 to 1903, Chapman became impressed with the significance of forestry in rural land use and was active in promoting legislation leading to establishment of national forests in Minnesota. This interest led to his enrollment in the Yale School of Forestry, from which he received the master of forestry degree in 1904. After two years with the U. S. FOREST SERVICE, Chapman returned to Yale in 1906 as an instructor. He became Harriman professor of forest management in 1911. A prolific writer, Chapman published a series of books on *Forest Valuation* (1915), *Forest Mensuration* (1921), *Forest Finance* (1926), and *Forest Management* (1931), which served for years as standard texts in most American forestry schools. His field instruction in Louisiana led him into research on the management of southern pines. He was an early advocate of controlled burning of ground cover for fire protection and to encourage reproduction, and his experiments also induced other improvements in the silvicultural treatment of the Southern forests. On two occasions, during periods of sabbatical leave, Chapman was associated with the Forest Service. In the service's Southwest Region he was chief of forest management from 1917 to 1919, and in the Lake States he worked with the Forest Taxation Inquiry in 1926 and 1927. Following his retirement from Yale in 1943, Chapman remained active for a number of years as a consultant in forest management and policy. He died July 13, 1963.

Chapman's conviction that instruction in American forestry schools should provide an educational background comparable to that of other learned professions resulted in his leadership in developing the system of accreditation adopted by the SOCIETY OF AMERICAN FORESTERS (SAF) in 1937. He was the first chairman of the SAF committee on accrediting schools of forestry and, later, head of the society's committee on ethics, which drew up the code adopted in 1948. Chapman served as president of SAF from 1934 to 1937, and in 1948 he received the organization's highest award, the Sir William Schlich Memorial Medal. Earlier he had been active in the AMERICAN FORESTRY ASSOCIATION (AFA) as a longtime director, and he was responsible for bringing about AFA's reorganization in 1922. He was a member of the Connecticut State Park and Forest Commission from 1913 to 1948 and served as its chairman after 1938. His concern for the development of federal and state forestry policies and programs led to his continual involvement in issues affecting the public interest. He was in the forefront in recurrent fights to defend national forest policies and to oppose transfer of the Forest Service from the DEPARTMENT OF AGRICULTURE to the DEPARTMENT OF THE INTERIOR.

GEORGE A. GARRATT

CHARCOAL

The history of the charcoal industry in the United States illustrates how the needs of an emerging nation may combine with various world events, new chemical products, and new processes of chemical synthesis to affect the harvesting and utilization of forest resources. From the colonial period through much of the nineteenth century, the need for iron products required that forests be harvested for charcoal to stoke the blast furnaces. Charcoal was also required for making gunpowder, for some domestic heating and cooking, and for the smelting of other metals, but in the nineteenth century, American charcoal was largely consumed in iron manufacture. The census of 1880 showed that over 94 percent of the 74 million bushels of charcoal consumed in that year went for this use. In the twentieth century, World War I, the airplane, and the automobile created a need for chemicals produced as by-products of charcoal, such as acetone for munitions and acetate for airplane dope and automobile lacquers. Photography and bakelite also created a demand for acetate and formaldehyde from wood. Chemicals were the principal product, and charcoal became a by-product.

Charcoal is a complex mixture of residues resulting from the decomposition of wood or bark heated under conditions that severely restrict the supply of oxygen. Around 280 degrees centigrade, an exothermic reaction occurs. The usual carbonization procedure involves prolonged heating to a final temperature of 400 to 600 degrees centigrade in the absence of air. The carbon content of the resulting charcoal is around 80 percent.

United States charcoal production peaked at around 700,000 tons about 1882. The consumption of wood for charcoal probably has never been surpassed since; the 1970 and 1980 production figures are for charcoal briquets that contain char from sources other than wood, along with starch binder and other ingredients.

The charcoal iron industry in America began with the construction of an iron furnace at Falling Creek, some eighty miles from Jamestown, Virginia, about 1620. The Falling Creek furnace was destroyed in 1622; no written accounts remain of its operations. In 1645, a furnace was constructed near Saugus, Massachusetts, and it operated successfully until 1675. Additional furnaces started up in many localities near iron ore deposits. Charcoal iron works, built like plantations, included entire communities of homes, stores, and churches, along with extensive woodlands. The early furnaces were twenty to thirty feet high with a diameter of four to eight feet. They were constructed on steep hillsides so that raw material could be easily loaded through the top. These furnaces produced one to six tons of iron per day, using about one ton of charcoal for each ton of pig iron. By the end of the nineteenth century, new charcoal iron furnaces averaged sixty feet in height and had the capacity to produce 20,000 tons a year. As furnaces and iron production grew, so did the demand for charcoal. When Franklin B. HOUGH made a survey of the charcoal needs of American iron furnaces in the late 1870s, he found that they needed the harvest of 100 to 1,521 acres of woodland annually to sustain their opera-

TABLE 1. Charcoal Production for Selected Years

Year	Thousands of Tons
1850	260
1882	700
1905	266
1910	500
1920	200
1930	450
1940	250
1950	250
1960	320
1970[1]	500
1980[1]	800

1. Charcoal briquet production from all sources including wood, bark, lignite, coal, and agricultural residue.

Brick beehive charcoal kilns, Colorado, 1916. Forest Service Photo.

tions. The twenty-three furnaces reporting expected to cut over their woodlands in cycles ranging from fifteen to fifty years; to assure a permanent supply of charcoal, each furnace needed anywhere from 9,000 to 50,000 acres of woods.

After the Revolutionary War, ironmaking expanded rapidly as the colonists moved westward. The first blast furnace west of the Allegheny Mountains was built in 1790. The great iron and steel center of Pittsburgh started with a furnace constructed in 1796. Until at least 1832, all United States pig iron was made with wood charcoal. In 1850, when pig iron production was 563,000 tons from 377 furnaces, about one-half was still charcoal iron and the rest was made with coal. Charcoal iron production continued to increase until 1880 when about 800,000 tons were produced, or 14 percent of the nation's total pig iron production; about 700,000 tons of charcoal were required to produce that record figure. As larger blast furnaces were built, the use of charcoal in iron manufacture declined, in part because charcoal lacked strength adequate to support the overburden in the higher furnaces and in part because once local forests had been harvested for charcoal production, longer hauling distances increased

transportation costs. By 1892, charcoal pig iron was down to about 5 percent of total iron production, although the last charcoal blast furnace in the country did not shut down until 1945.

In the colonial period, all charcoal was produced in "earthen kilns" or "pits" made by stacking wood carefully around a central chimney (kept open with poles and small pieces of wood) and covering the pile with several inches of earth, mud, or leaves and charcoal dust. The iron industry preferred charcoal with a high crushing strength, such as was produced from dense hardwoods like maple, birch, beech, oak, and hickory. The wood was ignited through the open chimney, and the rate of combustion was controlled by using a shovel to open or close vents at the base of the mound. The progress of charcoaling operations in these pits was judged by observing the color and amount of smoke leaving the kiln. Pits ranged widely in size, containing anywhere from ten or fifteen cords up to eighty cords of wood. Those associated with the iron furnace at Hopewell, Pennsylvania, averaged thirty to forty feet in diameter and held twenty-five to fifty cords.

Nineteenth-century charcoal makers also used

TABLE 2. Yield of Various Products per Ton of Dry Wood

Intermediate Products		Final Products	
Total 100 percent spirits, gal.	5	Charcoal, lb.	600
		Noncondensable gas, cu. ft.	5,000
		C.P. methanol, gal.	3
		Methyl acetone, gal.	.7
		Allyl alcohol, gal.	.1
		Ketones, gal.	.2
		Methyl acetate, gal.	1.0
		Soluble tar, gal.	22
Settled tar, gal.	11	Pitch, lb.	66
		Creosote oil, gal.	3
Acetic acid (as 100 percent), lb.	101	Ethyl acetate, gal.	14.7
		Ethyl formate, gal.	1.3

brick or stone kilns, which were said to secure a higher yield of charcoal per cord of wood and to require less labor to operate than open pits. Brick kilns were of two types: dome or beehive shaped, holding about forty cords, and rectangular, with a capacity of about eighty cords. Their use never entirely replaced charcoal pits; when Franklin B. Hough made a survey of charcoal iron furnaces in 1876, the great majority reported making all their charcoal in open pits, chiefly because pits could be located anywhere in the woods and because it was more economical to haul charcoal than wood. Charcoal pits remained in use in some areas until after the middle of the twentieth century. According to Nelson Courtlandt Brown (1937), 672,000 bushels of charcoal were made by the open pit method in 1935, a little less than 2 percent of the nation's total production for that year.

Hardwood Distillation

The recovery of the volatile products of hardwood was started about 1812 with the collection and condensation of the gases from a beehive kiln. This process was cumbersome because of the multiple stacks required, and the gases were contaminated with combustion products resulting from air infiltrating into the kilns. The brick kiln, like the pit, was satisfactory only so long as the chief product of wood distillation was charcoal. As Hough could remark as late as 1878, "scarcely a thought has been had as to the saving of the volatile products of carbonization." However, during the course of the following decades, externally heated cast iron or steel retorts began to replace beehive kilns for charcoal production and made it feasible to collect the vapors from the carbonization of wood. Cylinders about nine feet long and holding about five-eighths to one cord of wood were used at first, but about 1895 there came into use the larger oven retort, which could

be loaded by running cars directly into the chambers. The capacity of most retort plants was in the range of 22 to 100 cords, but a few could handle up to 225 cords. They operated on a twenty-four-hour cycle, whereas brick kilns had taken fifteen to twenty-five days to complete the carbonization process. Retorts were also more efficient in the conversion of wood into charcoal. Richard Schallenberg has calculated that open pits produced from thirty-five to thirty-eight bushels of charcoal per cord of wood, brick kilns from forty-five to fifty, and iron retorts from sixty to sixty-five bushels per cord. Furthermore, the retorts recovered usable by-products in the form of crude "pyroligneous acid" and noncondensable gases ("wood gas"). The pyroligneous acid was refined to make acetate of lime, methanol (wood alcohol), and tar. The tar was burned to heat the retort, and the wood gas was burned to dry and preheat the wood. Methanol was widely used as a solvent in the production of shellacs and varnishes, in stiffening hats, and in perfumery, aniline dyes, formaldehyde, and the manufacture of explosives, and it was mixed with grain alcohol to produce denatured alcohol; the acetate of lime was used in the manufacture of wood vinegar, acetic acid, many commercial ace-

TABLE 3. Composition of Noncondensable Gas

Constituent	Volume Percent of Dry Gas
Hydrogen	2
Methane	17
Hydrocarbons	1
Carbon monoxide	23
Carbon dioxide	38
Oxygen	3
Nitrogen	16

tates, acetic ether, acetone (which in turn supplied iodoform and chloroform), and other products.

Before the rise of petrochemical production in the 1920s, all industrially important organic chemicals were distilled from wood. The recovery of acetone as a by-product of butanol fermentation decreased the importance of acetone from wood, but the biggest blow to the importance of wood chemicals came in 1925 when synthetic methanol arrived from Germany at forty-five cents per gallon, thirty-two cents below the price of pure-grade methanol from wood distillation. Commercial Solvents Corporation began the first commercial synthetic methanol production in the United States in Indiana in 1927 from carbon monoxide and hydrogen collected also as a by-product of butanol production.

In 1930, about fifty hardwood-distillation plants were still in operation, but most closed down during the Depression. In 1950, only five were still operating, and this number was reduced to one by 1960. In 1969, the last plant, located at Marquette, Michigan, closed down.

Softwood Distillation

Softwood species were also distilled, but the products were different from those obtained from hardwood species. The only commercially successful plants used longleaf pine (*Pinus palustris*) lightwood, knots, and stumps. The products were charcoal and pine tars and oils. Turpentine was refined from the oils. The yield of charcoal was 350 to 400 pounds per ton of wood. Turpentine and pine tar yields were 4 to 6 gallons and 20 to 30 gallons, respectively. The softwood distillation industry was never as large or as significant as the hardwood distillation industry. In 1919, L. F. Hawley estimated that twelve or thirteen plants were operating. The last plant, located in Louisiana, operated occasionally during the 1970s.

The construction of the ovens and methods of operation varied considerably between plants. Some were externally heated ovens, similar to those used for hardwoods, with a capacity of about ten cords. Most, however, were smaller-capacity retorts heated by internal flues. Operation varied from collecting all of the distillate externally, as for hardwoods, to collecting the volatile distillates externally and the remainder from the bottom of the kiln.

The charcoal product was used for fuel. The liquids were refined for various end uses. Turpentine was refined from the oil liquids and the remaining oil was refined for solvent, chemical, and pharmaceutical uses. The tar was used for cordage, rubber, oakum, roofing cements, and pharmaceuticals.

Recent Charcoal Production

After World War II, charcoal production began to increase to meet a demand for its use for restaurant, home, and recreational cooking fuel, which the U. S. FOREST SERVICE reported to consume over half the charcoal produced in 1956. Since most of the large wood-distillation plants had ceased operations, new sources were needed, and many small kilns were constructed in rural areas to utilize low-grade logs from woodlots and slabs and edgings from sawmills.

In 1961, the Forest Service counted 1,977 charcoal-converting units in the United States. These included 262 brick kilns, 805 concrete and masonry block kilns, 430 sheet steel kilns (mostly portable, for use in the woods), and 480 other units such as retorts and ovens. Ninety-four percent of these producing units (accounting for 98 percent of the charcoal production) were located in the eastern portion of the United States. Thirteen large producers provided 56 percent of the total production.

Traditionally, charcoal was used in lump form, often screened to remove pieces smaller than one-half inch. This practice left behind a large volume of unusable fines. The accumulation of charcoal fines, the desire to produce a uniformly sized product with uniform burning rates, and the need to supply a cleaner product for the new home and recreational markets led to the production of briquetted charcoal. The briquetting process consists of dry grinding the charcoal and mixing it with a starch solution to form a paste. The paste then goes to a double-roll rotary press which delivers the formed briquets to a continuous drier. In about three hours, the moisture content is reduced from 40 percent to less than 1 percent. The briquets may contain charcoal and starch and various amounts of coal, clay, and char from lignite or agricultural residues.

Kilns, most commonly constructed of poured concrete, are used to convert roundwood, sawmill slabs, and edgings into charcoal. They have a capacity of from 40 to 100 cords and operate on about a seven- to twelve-day cycle. Raw material in the form of sawdust, shavings, or milled wood and bark is converted to charcoal in a continuous multiple-hearth furnace commonly referred to as a Herreshoff furnace. The capacity is usually at least one ton of charcoal per hour. The yield of charcoal is about 25 percent by weight on a dry basis. The first reference to the use of the Herreshoff furnace for charcoal was reported in 1948; by 1980, there were about sixteen in operation in the United States, supplying over one-half of the wood and bark charcoal. Gases from the kilns and furnaces are burned to alleviate air pollution, sometimes with additional fossil fuel to recover heat and steam, or in afterburners to nearly eliminate visible pollution and odors.

In 1980, charcoal was nearly all consumed for cooking as charcoal briquets, although some was employed in certain metallurgical and filtration processes and horticultural uses. The market for charcoal briquets showed promise of continued growth, although the use of wood residues for fuel offered increasing competition for raw materials. No longer would unused, low-cost wood residue provide an incentive for constructing charcoal plants, and the cost of charcoal seemed likely to increase at a rate that is higher than the increase in cost of wood fuel.

FURTHER READING: Nelson Courtlandt Brown, *Forest Products: Their Manufacture and Use* (1919), and *Timber Products and Industries* (1937). A. W. Goos, M. A. Trepanier, and M. K. Johnston, "Some Experiments in Sawdust Carbonization," *Forest Products Research Society Proceedings* 2 (1948): 55-59. John Hartwig, "Control of Emissions from Batch-type Charcoal Kilns," *Forest Products Journal* 21 (1971): 49-50. L. F. Hawley, *Wood Distillation* (1923). Franklin B. Hough, *Report upon Forestry* (1878). Jackson Kemper III, *American Charcoal Making in the Era of the Cold-Blast Furnace* (n.d.). James A. Kent, *Riegel's Industrial Chemistry* (1962), contains a technical description of hardwood and softwood distillation. W. G. Nelson, "Waste-wood Utilization by the Badger-Stafford Process," *Industrial and Engineering Chemistry* 22: 312-315. Jack Rienks, "Charcoal Burner and Waste Heat Systems," *Wood Residue as an Energy Source, Forest Products Research Society Proceedings* 29 (1975): 104–106. Richard H. Schallenberg, "Evolution, Adaptation, and Survival: The Very Slow Death of the American Charcoal Iron Industry," *Annals of Science* 32 (1975): 341-358. Richard H. Schallenberg and David A. Ault, "Raw Materials Supply and Technological Change in the American Charcoal Iron Industry," *Technology and Culture* 18 (July 1977): 436-466. U. S. Forest Service, Division of Forest Economics and Marketing Research, *Charcoal and Charcoal Briquette Production in the United States, 1961* (1963).

ANDREW J. BAKER

CHARLES LATHROP PACK FORESTRY FOUNDATION

In 1930, Charles Lathrop PACK reorganized his numerous bequests on behalf of forestry as the Charles Lathrop Pack Forestry Foundation, incorporated in Washington, D.C. At that time it was the only privately endowed foundation devoted to forestry in the United States. The foundation continued Pack's support of scholarships and fellowships and financed investigations of current issues in forest management and research. Typical of these projects were studies of the application of sustained yield in the Pacific Northwest,

the effect of small sawmills on social and economic conditions in the South, and an evaluation of farm forestry extension in eastern and central farm woodlands.

Publication of the reports of some studies resulted in useful and informative monographs. Several of these were published jointly with other agencies, among them *Tropical Forests of the Caribbean* by Thomas H. Gill, published in cooperation with the Tropical Plant Research Foundation (1931), and *Selective Timber Management in the Douglas Fir Region* by Burt P. Kirkland and Axel J. F. Brandstrom, published cooperatively with the U. S. FOREST SERVICE (1936). Between 1944 and 1948, the foundation cooperated with the SOCIETY OF AMERICAN FORESTERS in a study of forest administration in nine states and commissioned studies on the marketing of forest products.

The foundation purchased demonstration forests to provide examples of scientific silviculture. These tracts were then put under the management of Cornell University, the University of Michigan, the New York State College of Forestry at Syracuse, the University of Washington, and Yale University.

Throughout the foundation's three decades of operation, Thomas H. Gill served as secretary. Henry S. GRAVES, dean emeritus of the school of forestry at Yale, was chairman of the advisory committee. Upon Pack's death in 1937, his son Randolph Greene Pack (1890–1956) became president of the foundation. Randolph expanded activity in INTERNATIONAL FORESTRY, and during his tenure the foundation supported the Mexican Institute of Renewable Natural Resources. After Randolph's death, the presidency passed to his brother Arthur Newton Pack (1893–1975) who redirected the work of the foundation toward problems of the Southwestern deserts.

HENRY CLEPPER

CHEMICALLY DERIVED WOOD PRODUCTS

The production of chemicals from wood in America had its beginning with the early colonists who leached wood ashes with water to make potash, needed for the production of soap. Americans gradually learned how to produce other substances from wood, more often than not using technology generated in Europe. As a percentage of the total chemical manufacture of the United States, the wood chemical industry peaked at the end of the first third of the twentieth century. However, the production of wood chemicals in North America (excluding chemical cellulose used for papermaking) in the 1970s still represented more than 1 billion dollars annually and held promise of substantial growth as Americans increasingly recognized the need to base their raw material needs on renewable resources. The most important chemical derived from wood at the beginning of the 1980s was cellulose, used for the production of man-made fibers, films, and plastics. This material was followed in order of importance by fractionated tall oil, sulfate turpentine, lignin products, vanillin, ethyl alcohol, torula yeast, and miscellaneous chemicals such as dimethyl sulfoxide (DMSO).

Destruction Distillation

The first major chemical process to be used on wood in the United States was destructive distillation. This process had its origin in the manufacture of CHARCOAL needed to produce iron from the colonial period until the mid-nineteenth century when anthracite coal became the predominant fuel used in the reduction of ores. In destructive distillation, wood is heated in an oven or a retort in the absence of air. The wood substance decomposes, yielding gaseous and liquid products with charcoal forming the residue. At first, charcoal was the principal product of this process, being used in the iron and chemical industries and for fuel. Gradually, the liquid products, mainly acetic acid, methyl (wood) alcohol, and acetone, became the most important items, with charcoal the by-product. In 1940, the hardwood distillation industry consumed 540,000 cords of wood to produce 4.5 million gallons of methyl alcohol, 62 million pounds of acetic acid, and 540 million pounds of charcoal. However, cheaper methods were found to synthesize alcohol and acetic acid, with the result that collection and fractionation of wood destruction distillate was essentially discontinued by the late 1960s.

Chemical Cellulose

Chemical analysis of wood shows that it is comprised of 40 to 45 percent cellulose, 25 to 30 percent hemicellulose, 25 to 30 percent lignin, and 1 to 5 percent extractives and ash. The lignin acts as the cementing substance that holds wood fibers together and must be removed to produce chemical wood pulp. The cellulose present in wood does not differ chemically from that present in other natural fibers such as cotton or flax. Chemical wood pulp fibers are less than 1/10 the length of cotton fibers, so they are not directly useful for the production of woven textiles. Since cellulose does not melt without degradation, it must be dissolved in a solvent and subsequently regenerated in order to produce a man-made textile fiber.

The man-made fiber industry had its beginning in 1884, with the production of "artificial silk" by Hilaire de Chardonnet in France. This product was made by extruding a solution of nitrocellulose dissolved in ether and alcohol through a spinneret, followed by evaporation of the solvent. Although attractive, the fibers produced from nitrocellulose were extremely flammable. During the 1890s, the cuprammonium process was perfected by Despassis and the viscose process by Cross, Bevan, and Beadle. These processes used cotton linters, a short-fibered by-product of the cotton industry, to produce "rayon." By 1925, rayon production in the United States was over 50 million pounds annually, and a new source of cellulose was needed. Cooperative research by one of the major rayon producers, E. I. du Pont de Nemours & Co., and several wood pulp producers resulted in a specially refined grade of sulfite wood pulp suitable for rayon production. This pulp was produced by the Brown Company in the eastern United States from spruce (1927) and by the Rainier Pulp and Paper Company (subsequently Rayonier, Inc.) in the West from western hemlock (1928).

Rayon production continued to expand in the United States, and with it came the need for new facilities to manufacture chemical cellulose from wood. Three sulfite mills built in Washington in the late 1920s were modified to produce rayon-grade wood pulp, and they merged to form Rayonier, Inc. In 1939, the first (and only) sulfite pulp mill in the South was built to utilize southern pine for chemical cellulose production. In the early 1950s, three large chemical cellulose plants were constructed in the Southeast by International Paper Company, Buckeye Cellulose Company, and Rayonier. Each of these plants used the newly invented prehydrolyzed-kraft pulping process, which is much less sensitive to wood species than the sulfite process. The 1950s and 1960s also witnessed a number of new sulfite chemical cellulose mills in the West, including the Cosmopolis (Washington) mill of Weyerhaeuser, the Alaska Pulp Company mill at Sitka, and the Ketchikan (Alaska) mill later owned by Louisiana-Pacific. In 1980, more than half of the production of all these mills was exported. The chemical cellulose produced was used in the rayon industry and in the manufacture of nitrocellulose for lacquers and gun cotton, cellulose ethers, and cellulose acetate fibers, films, and plastics.

The cellulose acetate industry had its beginnings during World War I when Dreyfus Brothers in England produced "dope," a cellulose acetate solution in acetone, for coating airplane wings. After the war, the Celanese Corporation in England and the United States found a method for producing acetate textile fibers. Du Pont, Tennessee Eastman, the American Viscose Company, and others subsequently entered this business. Acetate fibers were originally made from cotton linters. Pulping research at Rayonier in the late 1930s led to the development of sulfite wood pulp with high purity and whiteness suitable for acetate based on western hemlock, southeastern pine, and hardwoods. Prehydrolyzed kraft pulp for acetylation was introduced into the marketplace in 1967. Cellulose acetate fibers, film, and plastics can be produced independent of the use of petroleum; with the oil shortages of the late 1970s and 1980s, there seemed to be a good future for these products. Expansion of the rayon industry in the United States, on the other hand, seemed less promising because of the high energy consumption of the viscose process, but research on new processes is in progress in a number of major corporate and university laboratories.

Vanillin

During the first third of the twentieth century, most of the chemical wood pulp used in papermaking was produced by the acid bisulfite process (see PULP AND PAPER INDUSTRY). Wood was cooked with a solution of calcium bisulfite and sulfur dioxide, which dissolved approximately one half of the wood substance in the form of calcium lignosulfonate and wood sugars such as mannose, glucose, galactose, and xylose. These dissolved products were discharged into rivers, streams, or bays adjacent to the mills. Many sulfite pulp mills were located in relatively remote locations, and little thought was given to the consequences of this practice. As the population of the country grew and shifted to areas where pulp mills were located, it became apparent that this practice would have to be discontinued. Utilization appeared to be the best approach to effluent reduction.

Since the State of Wisconsin had the most advanced environmental concerns, it is not surprising to find the beginnings of chemical utilization in that state during the 1930s. A process for producing vanillin from sulfite pulping liquor was discovered and introduced commercially in 1934. At the end of World War II, annual production approached 500,000 pounds per year.

Vanillin is the principal flavoring ingredient in vanilla extract. The substantial growth in the processed food industry has increased the market for vanillin, as has the use of vanillin as the primary building block for important pharmaceuticals used in the treatment of hypertension and Parkinson's disease.

Additional facilities for manufacturing vanillin from lignosulfonates were installed by the Ontario Paper Company (Thorold, Ontario) and the Monsanto Chemical Company (Seattle, Washington) after World War II. In 1979, ITT Rayonier, Inc., opened a plant to produce vanillin at Hoquiam, Washington. Annual production of vanillin from pulping by-products in North America soon approached 10 to 12 million pounds, a sizable business with vanillin selling for close to five dollars a pound. However, the original objective of lignin utilization has hardly been dented by this development, since vanillin represents less than 0.1 percent of the 15 billion pounds of sulfite liquor solids produced annually in North America.

Lignin Products

As a result of substantial experimentation in private and public laboratories, chemical uses have been found for part of the lignosulfonates generated from the pulping industry. The remainder is used as fuel in recovery processes; no pulp mill in the United States still discharges its pulping liquor directly into the environment. Beginning in 1905, J. S. Robeson was successful in marketing crude and modified dry calcium lignosulfonates for use as tanning aids and as mineral and foundry core binders. This business did not expand much until the 1950s, when it was discovered that oil well drilling mud fluid additives could be made from lignosulfonates. Together with animal food pelletizing, these represented major volume markets. Total production of lignin products in 1981 approached 650,000 tons annually. The major producers of lignosulfonates were Georgia Pacific, Crown Zellerbach, ITT Rayonier, and American Can. Lignin isolated from kraft black liquor is produced by Westvaco.

Ethanol

The fermentation of sugars derived from wood has been continuously practiced in Europe and Russia for many decades, but it was only during the two world wars that these processes were of technical interest in the United States.

Immediately before World War I, three alcohol plants based on the fermentation of acid hydrolyzates from wood were built at Fullerton, Louisiana; Georgetown, South Carolina; and Port Hadlock, Washington. The first two of these operated successfully during the war but were shut down afterward for want of an economical source of wood residues. The third plant, based on a process using anhydrous sulfur dioxide, never functioned properly.

Economics favored raw materials other than wood for alcohol production until World War II. Then, the war in the Pacific cut off supplies of natural rubber and accelerated the demand for synthetic rubber. The latter was derived, in part, from butadiene synthesized from ethyl alcohol. Shortages of molasses and grain stimulated the search for other sugar sources to produce alcohol. The U. S. Forest Products Laboratory in Madison, Wisconsin, developed a process utilizing softwood sawdust. A plant was built at Springfield, Oregon, to use sawmill waste but was not completed until after the war. The process essentially involved hydrolysis of the wood, with dilute sulfuric acid in tall pressure vessels holding up to 100 tons of wood. The hydrolyzate was then neutralized with lime and fermented with yeast. Unfortunately, severe problems were experienced with the hydrolysis vessels. These complications, coupled with the lower cost of synthetic ethyl alcohol, doomed the project, and the plant was dismantled in 1949.

The federal government also subsidized a fermentation plant at the Puget Sound Pulp and Paper Company (later Georgia-Pacific) sulfite pulp mill at Bellingham, Washington. This plant utilized the wood sugars present in the sulfite pulping liquor and has operated almost continuously since World War II. During the early 1970s, the distillation equipment was improved so that a purer product could be produced. By 1981, annual production was estimated to be 5 million gallons; it was sold for blending with gasoline to make "gasohol," a motor fuel.

Torula Yeast

The sugars in spent sulfite liquor or wood hydrolyzates can be fermented with a different organism, *Candida utilis*, to produce a product commonly referred to as single cell protein (SCP) or torula yeast. This product contains over 50 percent protein and is high in the B-vitamin complex. Two plants were in operation in 1981: Wausau Paper Mills Co. at Rhinelander, Wisconsin, and Boise Cascade in Salem, Oregon. The latter began production in the early 1970s. United States SCP production at the end of the decade was about 18 million pounds a year, and the product had a diversity of uses, including flavoring products for human consumption.

Animal Feeds

Secondary treatment of pulp mill effluents also produces large quantities of mixed bacterial organisms high in protein. A pioneer effort in use of such a product for cattle fodder was begun by ITT Rayonier at Port Angeles, Washington, in 1980. Crude wood sugars, produced as a by-product of the Masonite hardboard process in Mississippi, were sold directly as a liquid concentrate for cattle feeding. This type of raw material could, of course, also be used for fermentation.

DMSO

Although it is produced in only limited quantities, DMSO warrants mention because of its interesting properties and the fact that it represents the conversion of a liability into an asset. Until the advent of the low-odor recovery furnace and other odor-abatement procedures, kraft pulp and paper mills were distinguished by unpleasant odors released into the surrounding atmosphere. These odors resulted primarily from organic sulfides produced by the chemical cleavage of wood lignin. Scientific study of the mechanism of odor formation led to the discovery of a commercial process for producing methyl mercaptan and dimethylsulfide (DMS) on a large scale from kraft pulping black liquor. Production of DMS began in 1961 at the Bogalusa, Louisiana, mill of Crown Zellerbach. DMS is oxidized to produce the powerful solvent DMSO, which has found a whole host of chemical and medicinal uses. The most interesting of these is the transporting of drugs through the skin by topical application. Applications research on DMSO was actively pursued during the 1960s and 1970s at the Camas, Washington, laboratories of Crown Zellerbach. Medical applications were carried out at the University of Oregon Medical School, Portland, Oregon.

Bark Chemicals

Hot water extraction of chestnut, oak, and hemlock bark to produce chemicals suitable for tanning leather has been practiced in the United States for more than a century. During the late 1940s, it was discovered than TANNINS were also useful for drilling shallow oil wells. Research by The Pacific Lumber Company and the Institute of Paper Chemistry in the late 1940s led to the invention of a process for alkaline treatment of waste redwood bark to produce a tannin-type drilling mud product. Simultaneously, Rayonier laboratories developed processes for producing drilling mud additives by high-temperature, bisulfite extraction of western hemlock bark. Two manufacturing plants for the latter (Hoquiam, Washington, and Vancouver, British Columbia) were built in the middle 1950s.

Lignosulfonate-derived drilling mud additives are more useful in the deep drilling now needed to produce oil and have gradually supplanted bark-derived products. The last bark extraction plant in North America was closed in 1977.

Research and Development

Much of the early basic development work leading to production of chemicals from wood and bark was carried out in European industrial laboratories. As the wood chemicals industry became important in the United States, scientific endeavor became centered in Wisconsin at the Forest Products Laboratory and University of Wisconsin at Madison, and at the Institute of Paper Chemistry in Appleton. Following World War II, research efforts spread to the state forest products laboratories of Oregon and Washington. Research and development bloomed, beginning in the 1950s, in the industrial research laboratories of Rayonier, Puget Sound Pulp and Timber, Crown Zellerbach, Marathon Paper Company, and Westvaco. Oil economics and the environmental movement essentially destroyed United States industrial research and development efforts on wood chemistry at the beginning of the 1970s; research and development in the forest products industries had to be redirected to meet pressing clean-up goals. By the late 1970s, a new appreciation of the finite availability of nonrenewable resources, coupled with rapidly escalating petroleum prices, had resulted in renewed research in wood and bark chemistry in a number of American universities. Among the leaders of this movement were North Carolina State University at Raleigh, Virginia Polytechnic Institute (Blacksburg), University of Washington (Seattle), University of California (Berkeley), Purdue University (West Lafayette, Indiana), and Georgia Institute of Technology (Atlanta).

FURTHER READING: L. C. Bratt, "Wood-Derived Chemicals: Trends in Production in the U.S.," *Pulp and Paper* (June 1979): 102–108. H. L. Hergert, "New Horizons for Cellulosics," *National Symposium on Polymers in the Service of Man* (1980), pp. 27–31. F. W. Herrick, "Chemistry and Utilization of Western Hemlock Bark Extractives," *Agriculture and Food Chemistry* 28 (Mar./Apr. 1980): 228–237. F. W. Herrick and H. L. Hergert, "Utilization of Chemicals from Wood: Retrospect and Prospect," *Recent Advances in Phytochemistry* 11 (1977): 443–515: Jet Propulsion Laboratory, *JPL Publication 79-9* (1978). R. N. Shreve, *The Chemical Process Industries* (1945).

HERBERT L. HERGERT

CHRISTMAS TREES

Evergreen trees have been used as a part of winter celebrations since ancient times. The custom of lighting the Christmas tree is usually traced back to Martin Luther. Decorated Christmas trees were introduced in America by homesick Hessian soldiers during the Revolution. Christmas trees became items of commerce in the nineteenth century; as early as 1890 some 35,000 were sold in Paris.

In the United States the Christmas tree industry has been closely associated with forestry throughout its life. In the first part of the twentieth century the trees were cut from wild stands of conifers growing primarily in the northern tier of states from New England through the Lake States to the Pacific Northwest. Many were imported from Canada. The move from wild trees to plantation-grown ones was fostered by the forestry extension services and schools of forestry. Experience with reforestation, soil stabilization plantings, and similar projects in Michigan and the other Lake States indicated that trees could be cultured and improved to provide better shaped and longer lasting Christmas trees at a lower price. Successful Christmas tree plantations were reported as early as the 1930s. By the early 1950s plantation-grown trees were dominating the market and in 1980 they accounted for over 90 percent of those sold. Most of the wild trees still cut are cultured on the stump to improve the quality—very few trees can be marketed now unless their natural style of growth has been improved.

Statistics on the Christmas tree industry are elusive. The U. S. FOREST SERVICE in 1949 estimated sales of natural trees at about 28 million, of which 21 million were believed produced in the United States. At the industry peak in the 1960s, total sales were estimated at over 40 million. There are now believed to be about 32 million Christmas trees sold annually with a retail value between 400 and 500 million dollars.

Plantations may extend over several thousand acres in the northern states and parts of the eastern and southern mountains. In the Midwest and other agricultural areas there are many more of lesser extent. Many are operated as sidelines to tree farms and agricultural farms.

A wide range of species of conifers is grown. Scotch pines have recently been the most popular, in part because of their general adaptability to a wide range of growing conditions. Others are white pines and, in smaller numbers, Austrian and Norway pines. Balsam and Fraser firs and Douglas-fir are grown in Eastern mountain areas, as are Douglas-fir and other firs in the Far West. Spruces are represented by Colorado, Norway, and, to a lesser extent, white. About half of the pines grown, especially the Scotch, are treated to hold and improve their natural color. Most of the spruces are also treated to prevent needle drop. Many new and sometimes exotic species are coming in as plantations spread to the southern and southeastern states. Virginia pines are becoming popular in the Southeast and Afghan pines in the dry areas of the Southwest.

A significant development of the 1960s and 1970s

was the increasing popularity of "choose and cut" drive-in plantations, a practice first widely publicized many years earlier when President Franklin D. ROOSEVELT allowed trees to be cut on his Hyde Park estate for $1.00 apiece. On these plantations, the retail customer selects his tree in the field, cuts and hauls it away himself, thus eliminating the need for a tree lot in town. Such farms are growing rapidly in all areas; some enjoy annual sales of many thousands of trees. Most are family operated. This method of marketing enables entry into the industry with a minimum of investment of time and money by persons with small acreage. Approximately 10 percent of Christmas trees are now sold through this type of operation. In some urban areas, this figure may go as high as 15 to 20 percent. National forests sometimes issue permits for individuals and groups to cut their own trees; these trees, of course, have not been pruned or cultured in any special way.

It has been customary in many cities to decorate a large tree, either growing or hauled in from the forest, as a community Christmas tree. New York began doing this in 1912 and Philadelphia in 1913. A National Christmas Tree has been designated in Washington, D.C., since 1923.

FURTHER READING: *American Christmas Tree Journal* (Milwaukee: National Christman Tree Association). *Christmas Trees* and *Christmas Trees from Seed to Sale* (both Lecompton, Kansas: Tree Publishers). A. M. Sowder, *Christmas Trees: The Tradition and the Trade*, U. S. Department of Agriculture, Agriculture Information Bulletin no. 94 (rev. ed., 1957). USDA, *Trees: Yearbook of Agriculture* (1949).

G. MYRON GWINNER

CIVILIAN CONSERVATION CORPS

Within a month after Franklin D. ROOSEVELT became president in March 1933, Congress passed the first social legislation to assist those most seriously afflicted by the Great Depression. This act provided for Emergency Conservation Work, better known as the Civilian Conservation Corps (CCC), although the latter title was not established by statute until 1937. Perhaps the most popular of the New Deal's agencies, the corps furnished jobs for thousands of unemployed young men (called Juniors), World War I veterans, American Indians, and, as technicians, Local Experienced Men (LEMs) who were out-of-work woodsmen.

Directed until 1939 by Robert Fechner, a labor union official, and thereafter by James McEntee, the corps was an example of interdepartmental cooperation on the national level and of effective federal–state relationships. The U. S. Department of Labor, functioning through state selection organizations, had jurisdiction over the enrollment of men, while the DEPARTMENT OF AGRICULTURE, the DEPARTMENT OF THE INTERIOR, and the ARMY CORPS OF ENGINEERS had final authority over the work done, depending upon whether it was fire fighting, reforestation, timber-stand improvement, soil conservation, wildlife restoration, land reclamation, park development, or flood control. In most areas, state forestry or parks agencies had immediate charge over these projects. The army commanded and supplied the CCC camps and supervised their recreational activities. The U. S. Office of Education helped with educational programs, while religious programs found support from local sources.

In 1935, Roosevelt raised the enrollment goal from 250,000 to 600,000 men. The corps reached a total of slightly under 560,000 in October and thereafter declined to a level of about 300,000, which it held until 1941. In an election-year attempt to cut the federal budget, the president ordered a reduction in the agency's size for 1936. It is a tribute to the corps's prestige that this caused vigorous bipartisan opposition to the plan both in Congress and in the states. The CCC was, however, to be only a Depression-era agency despite its popularity, and attempts in 1937 and 1939 to legislate permanence proved unsuccessful.

As national economic conditions improved in the late 1930s, enrollment quotas became more and more difficult to fill, even with lowered admission standards. With the outbreak of World War II in Europe, defense-related jobs became plentiful and fewer youths were prompted to join the corps; others used their CCC training to advantage when they obtained regular employment or entered the military forces. The CCC's strength gradually waned and Congress ended it in June 1942 as part of the general cutback of New Deal relief agencies.

The CCC served a dual role in saving and restoring the nation's human and natural resources. In the corps's nine-year existence, over 2.5 million men wore its forest-green uniform and benefited from its educational and job opportunities. The enrollees planted some 2.25 billion trees, built nearly 6 million erosion check dams, carried out forest-stand improvement work on 4 million acres, engaged in tree and plant disease and pest control on 21 million acres, built over 122,000 miles of truck trails, fought hundreds of forest fires, and supplied a ready source of manpower for a variety of emergency situations. Perhaps the principal contemporary criticism of the agency was that it sometimes appeared to take jobs away from local residents;

President Franklin D. Roosevelt visits the first Civilian Conservation Corps camp, located on the George Washington National Forest in Virginia, in August 1933. Seated, third from left, is Secretary of the Interior Harold L. Ickes. To the left of FDR is Henry A. Wallace, secretary of agriculture. American Forestry Association Photo.

it was also attacked by some foresters, both in industry and in the federal service, who disliked the mixing of resource conservation with social rehabilitation purposes and who felt that political selection of supervisors and foremen was inconsistent with good forestry practices. The outstanding criticism leveled by later writers has been that the CCC placed limitations on the number of black enrollees and practiced discrimination against those it did admit. Nevertheless, the widespread approval of the corps, which continues to the present, attests to its accomplishments and to the validity of the concept.

FURTHER READING: Calvin W. Gower, "The CCC Indian Division: Aid for Depressed Americans, 1933–1942," *Minnesota History* 43 (Spring 1972): 3–13. Kenneth Holland and F. E. Hill, *Youth in the CCC* (1942). Charles W. Johnson, "The Army and the Civilian Conservation Corps, 1933–

1942," *Prologue: The Journal of the National Archives* 4 (Fall 1972): 139–156. Barrett G. Potter, "The Civilian Conservation Corps and New York's 'Negro Question,'" *Afro-Americans in New York Life and History* 1 (July 1977): 183–199. Elmo R. Richardson, "Was There Politics in the Civilian Conservation Corps?" *Forest History* 16 (July 1972): 12–21. John A. Salmond, *The Civilian Conservation Corps, 1933–1942: A New Deal Case Study* (1967).

BARRETT G. POTTER

CIVIL WAR AND AMERICAN FORESTS AND FOREST INDUSTRY

The Civil War of 1861–1865 had at first a depressing and then a stimulating effect on forest industries. Recovery from the general depression following the Panic of 1857 was well under way by the autumn of

1860, but Lincoln's election, the secession of the Southern states, and the outbreak of war led to another financial crisis and business downturn the next year. As railroad building and the construction industry declined, so did the consumption and price of lumber. On the Chicago market, mixed cargo lots sold for $12 per thousand board feet in mid-October 1860 and for only about half as much in the summer of 1861. But government orders of lumber for military purposes soon took up some of the slack in demand, and by 1863 private purchases had begun to increase with the return of general prosperity. Construction now boomed in much of the North. In Philadelphia, where only nine factories were built in 1861, fifty-seven went up in 1863. In Chicago, more buildings were erected in 1864 than in any previous year. By 1864, Chicago lumber dealers were paying much the highest price yet, $23 per thousand feet, almost four times as much as in 1861. With the end of hostilities and the discontinuance of military buying, the price dropped to $10 in 1865.

During the war decade the total output of lumber increased by a larger amount than in the 1850s, though by a smaller amount than it would grow during the 1870s. The total for 1859 was 8 billion board feet and for 1869 it was 12.75 billion. Softwood production accounted for most of the increase, rising from 5.8 to 9.25 billion board feet, while hardwood production rose only from 2.2 to 3.5 billion board feet.

Some lumbering areas contributed more than others to the increasing output. By 1860, New York and Pennsylvania were each producing more than Maine, which earlier had led all the states in lumber production. During the war, Maine turned out more than ever, the exports from Bangor doubling in four years. But New York and Pennsylvania continued to outproduce Maine, though the two middle states exported much less, both consuming most of what they produced. Philadelphia even depended on Maine for some of the city's supply. Michigan and Wisconsin enlarged their output even more rapidly, and a very large proportion of it was distributed throughout the comparatively treeless states of the prairies and the plains. Chicago, the entrepot for much of the Great Lakes product, was by 1865 the largest lumber market in the world. North Carolina, long a fairly important source of lumber and the leading source of tar and turpentine, suffered from the Union naval blockade. So did Mobile, Alabama, previously a busy port for the shipment of yellow pine. Lumbering in the State of Oregon and the Territory of Washington was less affected by events in the rest of the United States than by those in California, Australia, China, and Hawaii, where the largest accessible markets were located. Still, the presence of Confeder-

ate raiders in the Pacific Ocean interfered to some extent with the West Coast trade. At the end of the war the great development of lumbering in the South and in the Far West still lay decades in the future, but the shift in the center of the business from the Northeast to the Midwest was already well under way. The postwar regional distribution of the industry is shown by the census figures for 1869. Of that year's total output, the Midwest (Great Lakes and Central states) accounted for 6.29 billion board feet, the Northeast (New England and Middle Atlantic states) for 4.5 billion, the South (excluding Tennessee) for 1.28 billion, and the Far West (Rocky Mountain and Pacific states) for only 621 million.

During the last two years of the war, employers in the industry had to contend with a labor shortage as they tried to expand their operations while workers were being drawn away by other employment opportunities and by the draft. To keep conscripted laborers, some employers helped to pay for soldier substitutes. To meet the competition of alternative jobs, all had to raise wages, and these went to unprecedented heights. For example, loggers in the pineries of northwestern Wisconsin, who had received board and $12–$25 a month in 1860 and 1861, were getting board and $3–$5 a day in 1864. To make up for the persisting scarcity of labor, employers brought in men from Canada to work in the woods, and they made increasing use of women and girls in the operation of sawmills. A large proportion of the lumberjacks were transients, and labor recruitment always posed difficulties for lumbermen who failed to find an entirely satisfactory solution when the problem was made more acute than ever by the war.

The wartime labor shortage provided an added incentive for the introduction of labor-saving methods, and improvements were made both in transportation techniques and in sawmill machinery. On Lake Michigan, where fleets of sailing vessels had carried lumber before the war, steam tugs began to pull trains of such vessels, stripped of their rigging, during the early 1860s. On the Mississippi River, lumber rafts grew progressively larger, and in 1864 steamboats began to push long strings of them, getting them to their destination in half the time and with scarcely more than half the cost. For capturing logs and directing them to sawmills on tributaries of the Mississippi, the newly invented fin boom—a chain of logs with collapsible rudders or fins—came into use in 1862. The previously invented circular or rotary saw rapidly took the place of the much less efficient "muley" saw. By 1864, the double edger, which simultaneously trimmed both edges of a board, was in widespread use. Meanwhile, machinery was being adapted to new processes, such as the making of shingles. Before the war, nearly all shingles had been made by hand; they were preferred to machine-made ones, which were still in an experimental stage. By the end of the war, machine manufacture had been perfected, and the machine-made product had largely superseded the handmade. The wartime innovations were intended to economize on labor and to speed up production, not to prevent waste. Though cutting a much thinner kerf than the rotary saw and thus saving wood, the existing band saw continued to be used almost exclusively for sawing expensive imported cabinet wood.

The Civil War gave a stimulus both to the wasteful exploitation of timber and to the movement for forest conservation. In the absence of obstructionist Southern members, the wartime Congress passed laws for the increasingly rapid disposal of the federal domain. The Homestead Act and the Morrill Act, both of 1862, made it possible for speculators to acquire vast tracts of valuable timberland inexpensively. Statutes of 1862 and 1864 provided grants to aid the construction of the Union Pacific and Central Pacific railroads, thus adding to precedents for the large-scale transfer of public lands, including forested ones, to private corporations. Already, however, a few Americans were warning against the impending destruction of the forests and were raising protests that eventually were to bring about a reversal of the government's policy. Writing during the war, the greatest of the pioneer conservationists, George Perkins MARSH, made only a passing reference to the "present rebellion" in his classic *Man and Nature* (1864). Still, Marsh's work had a profound influence on readers who were concerned about the deforestation, which the war was hastening. The book helped to inspire later legislation for the establishment of forest reserves.

FURTHER READING: There exists in print no comprehensive account of forests and forest industries as affected by the Civil War. A good treatment of the subject in the case of one state may be found in Frederick Merk, *Economic History of Wisconsin During the Civil War Decade* (1916).

RICHARD N. CURRENT

CLAPP, EARLE HART (1877–1970)

Earle Hart Clapp was born in North Rush, New York, on October 15, 1877, the son of Edwin Perry Clapp and Ermina Jane (Hart) Clapp. Deciding on a career in forestry, Clapp attended Cornell University in 1902–1903 and transferred to the University of Michigan where he studied under Filibert Roth and received the B.A. in forestry in 1905.

His first assignment in the U. S. FOREST SERVICE was as timber surveyor in Medicine Bow Forest Reserve. In 1906, his work on several reserves included the development of techniques for determining minimum prices for timber on government land.

In 1907, Clapp was appointed as chief of timber sales in the Washington office. Forester Gifford PINCHOT required his staff to gain firsthand knowledge of field conditions, so Clapp made trips to western national forests. He was promoted to associate district forester in the Southwest, where he served from 1909 to 1911, and to forest inspector as a forest management research supervisor, serving from 1912 to 1915.

A branch of research was established within the Forest Service in 1915, with Clapp as chief. Activities of the new branch included silvicultural studies by experiment stations in national forests; investigations in the Forest Products Laboratory in Madison, Wisconsin; forest industrial investigations; fire protection studies; and studies of the relationship between forests and streamflow. Clapp had dual problems with his own lack of background in research and with inadequate appropriations for the branch. Although World War I needs helped research work gain respectful recognition, there was a sharp postwar reduction in support, with the work confined to widely separated and poorly staffed units in experiment stations and in Washington, D.C.

The 1920s saw Clapp make significant contributions to the cause of federal forestry. The 1920 *Report on Senate Resolution 311* ("Capper Report"), largely Clapp's work, portrayed forest depletion as a fundamental national problem and called for coordinated national, state, and private sector efforts. Clapp's *Forest Experiment Stations* (U. S. Department of Agriculture Circular 183, 1921) proposed a series of ten regional stations and the establishment of a small central laboratory to be used by the Research Branch. A study presented to the SOCIETY OF AMERICAN FORESTERS in 1926 called for a nationwide forest survey and argued the benefits of a concentrated ten-year effort in forest research. Clapp's efforts helped build support for the enactment of the MCSWEENEY-MCNARY ACT in 1928 which endorsed research as a major Forest Service activity.

The research branch staff helped prepare the 1933 *National Plan for American Forestry: Report on Senate Resolution 175* (COPELAND REPORT). The report proposed a coordinated federal–state program which would place large areas of land suitable only for growing timber under public control. The exigencies of the Depression and infighting within President Franklin D. ROOSEVELT's cabinet doomed efforts to gain congressional approval for the report's recommendations, but the ambitious Great Plains shelterbelt project was initiated after research in one of the regional forest experiment stations.

In 1935, Clapp was appointed associate chief of the Forest Service. The death of Chief Ferdinand A. SILCOX in December 1939 led to Clapp's advancement to acting chief, a position he held until Lyle Ford WATTS was named chief in January 1943. As acting chief, Clapp continued to oppose transfer of the Forest Service to the DEPARTMENT OF THE INTERIOR, persisted in advocating federal regulation of timber cutting on private forestland, and urged the addition of 150 million acres to the national forests. During his last two years in the Forest Service, Clapp's major responsibility was to prepare a plan for a fresh appraisal of the nation's forest situation. He unsuccessfully advocated the possibility of alleviating poverty in depressed forest areas by means of reforestation activities.

After his retirement in December 1944, Clapp maintained an active interest in national forestry. He died on July 2, 1970. His competence, vision, and integrity were recognized in his election as Fellow of the SOCIETY OF AMERICAN FORESTERS, in the bestowal upon him of the society's Gifford Pinchot Medal, and in his receipt of an honorary Sc.D. from Cornell University in 1928.

NORMAN J. SCHMALTZ

CLARKE-MCNARY ACT

Named for Congressman John D. Clarke of New York and Senator Charles L. MCNARY of Oregon, the Clarke-McNary Act of June 7, 1924, resulted as a compromise following years of controversy. The law emphasized a cooperative rather than a coercive federal–private relationship, the key issues during the lengthy debates, and expanded upon several WEEKS ACT provisions.

Section 2 of the law increased the Weeks Act federal matching program with cooperating state agencies. Not only did Clarke-McNary make more federal money available to protect nonfederal forestland, but private contributions could also be added to those of the state for the purpose of match. Thus there was federal as well as state incentive to increase private protection efforts. The so-called CM-2 monies quickly became the financial mainstay of state fire protection efforts.

Section 3 of the act authorized a comprehensive study of "the effect of tax laws, methods, and practices

upon forest perpetuation." Congress charged the investigators to recommend tax legislation that would encourage the conservation and growth of timber and also to study means of insuring standing timber against loss from fire and other causes. Fred R. Fairchild of Yale University headed the decade-long tax study, which resulted in the comprehensive *Forest Taxation in the United States* (1935).

Section 6 amended the Weeks Act to include timber production, along with the earlier provision for flood control, as justification for federal land purchases. Other sections encouraged cooperative efforts for SHELTERBELTS, woodlots, and nurseries.

The act's cooperative posture to encourage voluntary adoption of conservation methods by private landowners has continued as basic federal policy. However, there have been many unsuccessful efforts to invoke federal regulation of private forestland practices; the Clarke-McNary Act grew out of one of these efforts. Gifford PINCHOT, former chief of the U. S. FOREST SERVICE and an eminent conservationist, led the proregulation faction on the grounds that voluntary efforts had been ineffective. Forest Service Chief William B. GREELEY believed that Pinchot unfairly described a complex situation and recommended that regulation of private practices be limited to state agencies. Congressman Bertrand Snell of New York sponsored the prescriptive legislation that Pinchot favored. When it became clear that Congress would not support the Snell Bill, Senator McNary held hearings nationwide and developed the cooperative legislation that bears his name.

FURTHER READING: Harold K. Steen, *The U. S. Forest Service: A History* (1976).

CLIFF, EDWARD PARLEY (1909–   )

On September 3, 1909, Edward P. Cliff was born in Heber City, Utah, where he acquired a love of the out-of-doors. One of his professors at Utah State University, Lyle Ford WATTS, was a future FOREST SERVICE chief who would continue to be a major influence on his career. After graduating in 1931, Cliff became an assistant district ranger on the Wenatchee National Forest in Washington.

In 1934, Cliff was transferred to the Portland regional office as one of the first wildlife specialists in the Forest Service. During two winters he was detailed to Washington, D.C., to collaborate in writing the *Range Plant Handbook*. In 1939, he was promoted to supervisor of the Siskiyou National Forest in coastal Oregon. Having successfully combated a serious arson problem there, he was made supervisor of the more diversified Fremont National Forest in Oregon in January 1942.

Cliff's record of wartime achievements on the Fremont earned him a promotion in 1944 to assistant chief of the Division of Range Management in the Washington Office. In 1946, he returned to Utah as assistant regional forester in charge of the Division of Range and Wildlife Management for the Intermountain Region. There he began to confront on a daily basis the service's major problem of the early postwar years: overgrazing and the stockmen's reluctance to accept livestock reductions (see GRAZING ON FORESTLANDS). These problems became especially severe in the Rocky Mountain Region. In 1950, he was assigned as regional forester in Denver, where he successfully defused the "range war."

In 1952, Cliff returned to Washington as assistant chief for the national forest system. He played a major role in developing the service's recreational program; laid the groundwork for the passage of the Multiple-Use Mining Act of 1955; and advanced the application of multiple-use management principles on the national forests.

Cliff served as chief of the Forest Service from 1962 until 1972, a decade of rapid change. Public interest in the national forests and demands for all forest products and services expanded greatly. Most national forest programs grew in size and complexity. For example, recreation use increased at the rate of 10 percent annually. A long-range FORESTRY RESEARCH program was developed and research facilities and programs were substantially enlarged. Cooperative relationships with the states were strengthened, but funding of state and private forestry activities lagged behind that for national forests and research. Total appropriations for all activities increased fourfold. Concurrently, public concern over the environment grew dramatically, and some environmental groups were becoming critical of the agency's policies. The controversy over clearcutting made the last few years of Cliff's tenure tumultuous. By the time of his retirement in 1972, he had begun to improve the balance in national forest programs by strengthening interdisciplinary planning and modifying timber-cutting guidelines. During his tenure as chief, important legislation affecting forest policy included the Outdoor Recreation Act (1963), the Wilderness Act (1964), the Wild and Scenic Rivers Act (1968), the National Trails System Act (1968), and the NATIONAL ENVIRONMENTAL POLICY ACT (1969).

After leaving the Forest Service, Cliff in 1972 began a new career as a forestry and land use consultant. The first year he worked with the National Materials Policy Commission and wrote the land use chapter of its final report and a comprehensive special report entitled "Timber—The Renewable Material." Beginning in 1973, he embarked on a series of international forestry consultancies with such organizations as the United Nations Development Program, the Food and Agricultural Organization of the United Nations, the U. S. Agency for International Development, and the International Executive Service Corps. By 1981, he had completed fourteen missions involving travel and work in twenty-one countries in Central and South America, Africa, Asia, and the Mediterranean region.

In recognition of his conservation and public service accomplishments, Cliff received many honors and awards including the Utah State University Distinguished Service Award (1958) and honorary degree of Doctor of Science (1965), U. S. Department of Agriculture Distinguished Service Award (1962), National Civil Service League Career Service Award (1968), Tuskegee Institute Distinguished Service Award (1970), American Society of Landscape Architects honorary membership (1972), International Association of Game, Fish and Conservation Commissioners' Award for Outstanding Achievement in Wildlife Habitat Management (1972), and the SOCIETY OF AMERICAN FORESTERS' Gifford Pinchot Medal for outstanding service to the profession of forestry (1973).

DENNIS M. ROTH

COLBY, WILLIAM EDWARD (1875–1964)

Born, raised, and educated in California, William Colby graduated from Hastings College of Law in 1898 and began practice in San Francisco. Between 1911 and 1937, he taught mining and water law at the University of California, Berkeley. He also made significant contributions to American conservation, particularly through his work with the SIERRA CLUB and the California State Park Commission.

Colby's association with the Sierra Club began in 1898 when he served as the first summer attendant at the club's information center in Yosemite Valley. Thereafter, he served as a club director (1900–1949), secretary (1900–1917, 1919–1946), and president (1917–1919). With the encouragement of John MUIR, Colby initiated the club's "High Trips" in 1901, both to attract members and to educate them to the value of preserving the mountain wilderness areas visited. For twenty-eight years, Colby directed these outings, attended by approximately 200 people annually.

During the first half of the twentieth century, Colby played a leading role in all of the Sierra Club's major environmental political battles. He teamed with Muir and was especially important in the successful effort to gain recession of Yosemite Valley from state to federal control and its inclusion within YOSEMITE NATIONAL PARK. However, they were unable to prevent authorization of a reservoir in the Hetch Hetchy Valley within the park. Colby, over many years, worked actively for the enlargement of the Sequoia National Park (1926) and the creation in 1940 of Kings Canyon National Park (see SEQUOIA AND KINGS CANYON NATIONAL PARKS). He also promoted the construction of the John Muir Trail, a 185-mile-long pathway along the Sierra Nevada crest from Yosemite to Mount Whitney.

Colby's association with the SAVE-THE-REDWOODS LEAGUE led to his appointment as the first chairman (1927–1936) of the California State Park Commission. Colby oversaw the expenditure of a $6 million state bond issue matched with private funds for the acquisition of extensive state park lands. Under his direction, the state park system made major advances, growing from the initial five parks to forty-nine parks and eleven historical monuments.

In 1950, after Colby retired from forty-nine years on the Sierra Club's board of directors, he was elected honorary president. In 1961, Colby was the first recipient of the club's John Muir Award recognizing outstanding contributions to the preservation of American scenic resources. In 1966, the club established the Colby Award, an annual prize for outstanding conservation work for the club.

DOUGLAS H. STRONG

COLORADO FORESTS

In the three decades after the gold rush of 1859, miners, homesteaders, cattlemen, and other pioneers progressively depleted the magnificent forests of the Colorado Rockies. In 1891 and 1892, acting under the new FOREST RESERVE ACT of 1891, the federal government attempted to halt the destruction by creating five extensive reservations totaling over 3 million acres in the state: the White River (second oldest in the nation), Pikes Peak, Plum Creek, South Platte, and Battlement Mesa. The action touched off a conflict between conservationists and anticonservationists in Colorado that raged for years.

Colorado conservationists, led by the Colorado State Forestry Association (founded in 1884), included scientists, teachers, the state's wealthiest cattlemen, civic-minded urban businessmen, and the populations of eastern slope cities dependent on western slope water. Generally, they were little interested in the aesthetics of conservation; their primary concern was protecting the vital forest watersheds. Nevertheless, on a local level they achieved little. Although the Colorado state constitution of 1876 specifically provided for enactment of laws to "prevent the destruction of forests upon the lands of the state," no effective legislation followed. Similarly, Edgar Ensign's work as Colorado's first forest commissioner (1885–1891) ended when the prodevelopment state legislature refused to appropriate further funds for his office. The modern office of state forester was not established until 1911.

The state's insurgent anticonservationists—small cattlemen, miners, homesteaders, and important political leaders—were among the most volatile in the West. Passionately individualistic and prodevelopment, they argued that it was their "mission" to convert wilderness to civilization, to utilize forest resources in the process of creating a viable economy. They also argued that the federal government had no right to interfere in their affairs or in the destiny of the state. The forest reserves were, as one settler said, "a damnable outrage," and the attitude of most pioneers toward them was actively hostile for over two decades.

In the first decade of the new century, President Theodore ROOSEVELT crushed the anticonservation movement in Colorado by creating eleven new forest reserves (nearly 9 million acres) in the state. What U. S. Senator Thomas M. Patterson called a "condition of revolt" ceased to exist by 1917. During the 1920s and 1930s, as Coloradans came to appreciate the benefits of the government's "wise use" forestry policy and the work of its CIVILIAN CONSERVATION CORPS, they remained at peace with the federal government.

In the 1970s, conflict again surfaced and continued throughout the decade. The issue, then as earlier, was whether Colorado's forests should be preserved or exploited. Conservationists persistently agitated for the expansion of wilderness areas, while mining, energy, housing, and skiing interests argued against it. At the end of the decade, Colorado had 13.8 million acres of national forest including 1.2 million acres of wilderness within its borders. There are several units of the National Park System in the state; the principal one is the 264,000-acre ROCKY MOUNTAIN NATIONAL PARK, established in 1915.

Commercially, Colorado's forests of ponderosa pine, Douglas-fir, lodgepole pine, and Engelmann spruce have provided timber for posts, poles, mine timbers, and railroad ties. Annual lumber production in 1980 totaled 157 million board feet. Of the state's total land area, 34 percent, or more than 22.6 million acres, was classified as forestland, although only 12,275,000 acres were commercial forest.

Trail riders on the Trappers Lake Trail of the White River National Forest, 1940. Forest Service Photo.

Forestry instruction in Colorado was first offered at Colorado College in Colorado Springs in 1905. The program was terminated in 1934. Colorado State University in Fort Collins established its still continuing forestry program in 1911.

FURTHER READING: G. Michael McCarthy, *Hour of Trial: The Conservation Conflict in Colorado and the West* (1977).

G. MICHAEL MCCARTHY

COMMUNITY FORESTS

Since colonial times, community-owned forests have provided a variety of public benefits ranging from watershed protection and public revenue to arboreta and wildflower sanctuaries. New England, with its strong tradition of community participation, developed and nurtured the idea of town forests in the eighteenth and nineteenth centuries. In the early twentieth century, the concept gained broader acceptance as travelers returning from Europe brought back impressions of town forests harking back to the medieval village commons.

New England's first known town forest was established in 1710, when the village of Newington, New Hampshire, set aside a tract of unallotted land for common pasturage, fuelwood gathering, and timber cutting. Newington's forest yielded building materials for the local church, the school, the parsonage, and the town hall. Revenue from timber sales supported the town's parsonage and minister and in later years liquidated the community's Civil War debt. Public profits from the forest also helped fund a village library in 1892 and a public water system in 1912. Abandoned village farms, reforested with pine, provided several New England towns with public forests. Other tracts were granted as gifts or memorials, were acquired by debt default, or were purchased as an investment for the maintenance of schools, libraries, or other public facilities.

Much of the credit for spreading the popularity of the town forest belongs to Harris A. Reynolds of the Massachusetts Forestry Association and William P. Wharton of the AMERICAN FORESTRY ASSOCIATION. Both toured the town forests of Europe shortly after the turn of the century and, upon their return, worked toward the adoption of the idea in America. Imbued with the enthusiasm of Reynolds and Wharton, the Massachusetts Forestry Association and the American Forestry Association issued bulletins, press releases, and articles promoting town forests throughout the Northeast.

In 1912 and 1913, New York and Massachusetts granted counties, towns, and villages authority to acquire and manage forests for a variety of purposes. In later years, both states offered free seedlings to participating governments. Local administrators were slow to take advantage of the acts, but by the early 1920s, several acquisitions had been made. Notably, the city of Rochester, New York, purchased an extensive tract of forest useful mainly for watershed protection, and Otsego County maintained a forest for stumpage revenue. By 1938, New York boasted 215 school forests, 213 village forests, 50 county forests, 50 city forests, and 51 town forests. Other states enacting special legislation to promote community forests during the 1910s and 1920s included Michigan, Minnesota, New Hampshire, New Jersey, Ohio, Pennsylvania, Vermont, and Wisconsin.

The form and purpose of the community forests varied according to local needs and circumstances. In Wisconsin, parcels of CUTOVER LANDS and lands abandoned by homesteaders fell to town and county governments when taxes went unpaid. Spurred by hopes of returning the land to productivity, Wisconsin offered free seedlings to county forests, resulting in 1.7 million acres of reforested county lands by 1938. Concern for watershed protection inspired other community forests. Seattle's extensive preserve, encompassing 91,350 acres on the heavily timbered Cedar River watershed, was acquired for such purposes in 1900. Intensive management began in 1924 under an appointed forester. Nurtured in a city-owned nursery, 3.9 million Douglas-fir, Sitka spruce, and western redcedar were planted on the preserve, while mature trees were harvested by timber companies under contract with the city. By 1938, Seattle had liquidated its debt for the purchase of the forest through timber sales.

During the Depression, community forests became an important source of relief for unemployed workers. Tree planting provided temporary work as well as the possibility for public profits at a later date. Jobs on community forestlands were especially important in rural New England and in the cutover districts of the Lake States. In some cases, firewood from community forests warmed the homes of families on relief. Moreover, the local forest was the scene of much activity by the CIVILIAN CONSERVATION CORPS (CCC). In Wisconsin's county forests alone, the CCC planted 32 million trees, completed nearly 2,000 miles of truck trails and 336 miles of firebreaks, and constructed 21 lookout towers and 55 recreational campsites between 1933 and 1937.

During the late 1930s, over 1,600 towns, villages, schools, boroughs, and counties owned public forests. By 1953, the number had more than doubled and included a total of 4.4 million acres. Wisconsin, with 2.2 million acres, led the nation in local government forestland, and Minnesota, with 869,000 acres, ranked second; New York, with 180,000 acres, ranked third. One of the earliest examples of multiple-use management of public forests, community forests across the country continue to provide local citizens with recreational opportunities, watershed protection, forestry experience, employment, and forest products.

RICHARD W. JUDD

COMPANY TOWNS

The term "company town" is often associated with any community that is socially and economically dominated by a single firm. More accurately, the term applies to a town that is wholly owned by a particular company: all property, homes, commercial and recreational facilities, and sometimes even the churches and schools are under its control. When this happens, managers find themselves not only operating their major businesses but also functioning as town planners, landlords, school boards, security forces, and social workers. Though such towns are popularly associated with the mining and textile industries, they also played a significant role in the development of nearly every major lumbering region in America and they were especially significant from the mid-nineteenth to the mid-twentieth century.

Most company towns were the product of economic necessity rather than of any overt paternalistic desire on the part of the company. Logging and milling operations were often set up in remote forest areas, so far from other settlements that commuting was impossible. The transient nature of logging camps, especially, made it impractical for employees to own their own homes. As a result, companies were forced to provide temporary living and other community facilities. Some logging camps, however, were surprisingly permanent, especially if they were created in the twentieth century. Ryderwood, Washington, for example, was created in 1923 by Long-Bell Lumber Company and eventually boasted a population of over 2,000. It consisted of 400 homes, three stores, a school, a church, a modern sewage-disposal plant, a community heating plant, and a water system. It cost approxi-

The town of Snoqualmie, Washington, constructed for the employees of Weyerhaeuser Company. The houses were eventually sold to the employees when company towns were being phased out. Weyerhaeuser Company Photo.

mately $1.5 million to build. Unlike most other logging towns, Ryderwood did not disappear when the 130,000-acre stand of timber had been cut over. In 1952, the company established a permanent tree farm in the area and then put the town up for sale. A California firm purchased it for $90,000, reconditioned it, and turned it into an attractive haven for senior citizens.

Most logging camps were neither as extensive and well planned nor as permanent as Ryderwood, and most full-fledged, long-lived lumber towns were therefore associated with millsites. The typical mill town was created by the company on property near the mill in order to attract and hold workers who otherwise would have no place to live. Managers usually paid better attention to designing such towns than to laying out logging camps, sometimes even providing better homes and community facilities than those of other

small towns that grew more haphazardly without the benefit of corporate planning.

The operation of a logging camp or mill town was only incidental to a company's main economic concerns, but the history of the settlement itself always reflected what was happening to the company and to the industry. If business slacked off, population dwindled. When business picked up, the town fathers might even make plans for expanding the residential area. When business failed or when timber was no longer plentiful in the region, the town usually disappeared unless other economic opportunities for its residents had moved in. In such cases, the homes were often sold to residents and the towns became permanent communities. In other cases, modern sustained-yield forest practices helped stabilize the economy and assure more permanent settlement, and some company towns became communities of homeowners at the behest of the companies themselves. Others simply disappeared as employee-tenants were encouraged to purchase homes in nearby communities.

Residents of company-owned towns were clearly more vulnerable than others to problems associated with abusive social control, excessive paternalism, and restrictions upon personal freedoms. So far as the companies were concerned, the door was open for the high prices and compulsory trading at the company store, refusing to allow employee representation on town boards, and arbitrary law enforcement. Employers could also use their landlord status to curtail the activities of union organizers by not allowing "undesirable persons" to enter company property. Furthermore, when the companies erected schools and churches and put both teachers and ministers on company payrolls, the opportunities for thought control were obvious. Such abuses frequently occurred, though many towns were also relatively free of them. Their incidence varied with the company, the era, and the region.

Some writers have suggested that company-owned towns were deliberate profit-making ventures. This is true at least in the sense that most companies made certain they did not lose money on the town. As an investment, the town was seldom if ever a major producer of revenue. Profits from rentals, stores, movies, and other company-operated facilities were usually minimal, and in many cases they were partially returned to employees through company store rebate plans. Prices were often relatively high in company stores, but this was at least partly attributable to transportation costs. In addition, in times of economic stress some companies extended liberal credit to employees in order to keep them until the mill could return to full production. There were also frequent abuses, such as forcing employees to trade at company stores or deliberately encouraging perpetual debt at the store in order to make it impossible for employees to leave the area, and thus assure a ready supply of cheap labor. It appears, however, that such abuses were not as widespread in mill towns as in mining communities.

The physical appearance of a company town often reflected prevailing social attitudes as well as certain economic necessities. Racial segregation was common, even outside the South, and in most cases black housing was of somewhat lesser quality than that provided for whites. In the South, churches and schools were also segregated so that in communities such as Elizabeth, Louisiana, two company-built schools and two company-built churches were to be seen. Homes were

One of the company stores of the Dierks Lumber Company, which was active in Arkansas and Oklahoma. American Forest Institute Photo.

always built of wood but often went unpainted. When a company did paint its houses, it usually preferred to paint them all the same color, thus adding to a drab uniformity already imposed on the residential area by a uniformity of architectural style. All this, of course, saved money. House plans ranged from those with two bedrooms, a kitchen, a living room, and sometimes a bath in the most desirable mill towns, to single-room shanties with dirt floors and few amenities in others—particularly in some logging camps. A bird's-eye view of the typical mill town would demonstrate the near total dominance of the company. The most important feature would be the mill pond full of logs, the mill standing next to it, and the drying yards not far away. The residential area, occupying as little land as possible, would seem almost incidental, making it apparent that the life of the town was absolutely dependent upon the mill. Standing in sharp contrast to the uniform employee housing would be the more pretentious, commodious home of the plant manager. Thus the very appearance of the town tended to emphasize its paternalistic nature.

Paternalism also extended to recreational facilities, as most companies built recreation halls, sponsored social clubs, and provided baseball diamonds. Some companies even hired professional ballplayers to work in the mills and at the same time improve the town teams.

In some larger communities, town management could become almost a full-time job, especially when it included human relations as well as community facilities. It was not uncommon for a kindly resident manager to become almost a father-confessor for some of his townsmen, though there were probably as many examples of the other extreme—malicious and sometimes brutal bossism. But running the town was only incidental to the company, and management usually gave it as little time as possible, especially if there were no serious social problems. In some cases, paternalistic managers used their almost unlimited powers to enforce certain standards of personal conduct—sometimes because of genuine religious or public-spirited attitudes of their own but more often simply because it was good for company business. Excessive drinking and gambling, for example, could cause lateness or absenteeism, and at least some companies attempted to stop such problems simply by forbidding these activities on company property and discharging the guilty parties. There is evidence also that some managers were motivated by a kind of class consciousness that made many of their rules a demonstration of contempt for the wage earner who, they believed, was not capable of self-discipline.

By the mid-twentieth century, various changes in the national economy and in the forest industry itself reduced the need for company-owned towns, and by the end of the 1960s practically all of them had been abandoned or sold to local residents. There were a few notable exceptions, such as Scotia, California, where The Pacific Lumber Company continued to maintain a model community. In general, however, the company town is a passing feature of the American forest industry. It was essential to the foundation of the industry in practically every part of the country, but with the economic need no longer there, there was no reason for an institution such as the company town to survive.

FURTHER READING: James B. Allen, *The Company Town in the American West* (1966). Norman Clark, *Mill Town: A Social History of Everett, Washington, Beginning to Present* (1970). Everett was not really a company-owned town, in the sense of the definition given here, but the book makes excellent reading for anyone interested in the way a lumber company totally dominated the life of a town even after it sold lots and residential structures to the residents. Edwin T. Coman, Jr., and Helen Gibbs, *Time, Tide and Timber: A Century of Pope and Talbot* (1950). Jack Held, "Scotia, the Town of Concern," *The Pacific Historian* 16 (Summer 1972): 76-92. Bernice Larson Webb, "Company Town—Louisiana Style," *Louisiana History* 9 (Fall 1968): 325-339. Curtis W. Wienker, "McNary: A Predominantly Black Company Town in Arizona," *Negro History Bulletin* 37 (Aug. 1974): 282-285.

JAMES B. ALLEN

COMPOSITION BOARD INDUSTRY

The fiberboard and particleboard industries include hardboard, insulation board, particleboard, medium-density fiberboard, cement-bonded board, and molded products. This industry is of relatively recent origin and is based on products and materials conceived in the laboratory; consequently these industries are tied closely to science and technology.

Products assembled from comminuted woody materials are made primarily from woodworking wastes, noncommercial or low value tree species, and agricultural wastes. There is some use of industrial wood waste at the present time, such as heat for energy generation. Bark, forest residues, municipal refuse, and agricultural wastes can also serve as raw material for various types of building materials.

Products of comminuted wood have some very desirable characteristics, including availability in large sheets, smooth surfaces, uniformity in properties from sheet to sheet, and freedom from localized defects. Not all products need to have smooth surfaces,

Wood pulp is formed into thick sheets and then dried, producing a 4′ x 8′ board that can be cut, drilled, and painted. Forest History Society Photo.

and ones with rougher surfaces have good application in the structural building market.

Many available products have been largely excluded from the primary structural market, because they have been unable to approach the longitudinal stiffness, dimensional stability, and long-term load-carrying ability of sawn lumber or plywood. However, the situation is changing dramatically. Combinations of aligned particles that have been manufactured with optimum geometry can yield materials equaling or surpassing the structural capability and reliability of sawn lumber and plywood. Another important factor is the ease with which properties of comminuted wood products can be modified by treatment of the particles with fire retardants, preservatives, and stabilizing impregnations.

The quality of lumber and plywood is changing, since most of the world is now in an era of small-log, short-rotation forestry. The fiber and particleboard industries can convert lower-quality raw material into high-quality products, thus overcoming the disadvantages of supply that result from modern forestry practices.

Composition board is a term that includes molded wall panels, lumber products, and composite products of veneer. In general, fiberboard and particleboard are terms that cover a group of board materials manufactured from wood or other lignocellulosic fibers or particles to which binding agents and other materials may be added during manufacture to obtain or improve certain properties. These panels are composed of two broad types, fibrous felted and particleboards. The fibrous felted board is a panel material manufactured of refined or partly refined lignocellulosic fibers. These fibers are characterized by an integral bond that is produced by an interfelting of fibers and, in the case of certain densities and control of conditions of manufacture, by ligneous bond, and to which other materials may have been added during manufacture to improve its properties.

Particleboard is a generic term for a panel produced from lignocellulosic materials (usually wood), primarily in the form of discrete pieces or particles, as distinguished from fibers, combined with a synthetic resin or other suitable binder. The end product is bonded together under heat and pressure. Other materials may have been added during manufacture to improve certain properties. Particleboards are further defined by the method of pressing. When the pressure is applied in the direction perpendicular to the faces, as in conventional multiplaten hot press, they are defined as flat-platen pressed; and when the applied pressure is parallel to the faces, they are defined as extruded. Virtually all particleboard is manufactured by some type of the platen method, resulting in the high quality of the panel manufactured and production efficiencies. Molded particleboard and fiberboard, however, are pressed into the desired configurations using shaped dies.

The manufacturing steps for particleboards follow the same general path. Raw material is brought into the plant and reduced to the desired particle type. Some raw material, such as planer shavings, may not need any further refining. This raw material, called the furnish, usually is dried to a moisture content of approximately 2 to 4 percent, although it may be slightly more moist when used with certain adhesives. The furnish is then sorted by sizes, depending upon the particular production process. The material then is blended with resins and wax. The normal resins used are urea-formaldehyde for protected applications and phenol-formaldehyde for unprotected or structural application. Wax is used to inhibit the pick-up of water by the finished product. After blending, the furnish is formed into mats. These mats can range from less than one inch to over twelve inches in thickness, depending on the final product requirements and the type of particle being used. Multi-opening, single-opening, continuous, or stack presses are used to produce a platen-pressed board. Extruded boards are produced by having the furnish forced through a hot die. The finished boards are then cooled and trimmed, sanded, cut to size as required, and moved to the marketplace.

Dry-process fiberboard is made using techniques similar to those for making particleboard. Wet-process fiberboard, however, differs from the dry-process techniques in that the forming process is similar to paper technology, where the wood fibers are treated and formed into a mat in a slurry condition. In 1914, Carl G. Muench developed a process that is still used for producing an insulating board (a low-density fiberboard) out of wood fibers. The fibers are worked into a slurry in a huge head box and then are metered out onto a continuously moving screen. The water is drained away from the screen, leaving a damp mat of interlaced fibers. This material is then oven dried, which yields the sheets of board. This system has also been successfully used in converting bagasse (the residual sugar cane stalk after the sugar has been extracted) into insulation board.

Wet-process hardboard is a refinement of the insulation board manufacturing process. William H. MASON discovered the process accidentally in 1924. The process is similar to that used for the insulation board, except that after the mat is formed it does not go into an oven for drying. Instead, it is hot pressed

into its final density. A screen is used on the bottom of the mat to allow the moisture to escape during the pressing operation. The board's strength is obtained from the interlacing of the fibers developed during felting and by the rebonding of the lignin to the fibers that occurs during the hot pressing of the damp mats. Additives can be used to improve the properties of this board, called Masonite after its inventor.

One of the first, if not the first, platen-pressed type particleboards was started by Farley and Loetscher Manufacturing Company in 1935 in Dubuque, Iowa. They used an eleven-opening press but pressed four boards in each opening, resulting in forty-four boards per pressing. These boards were used as core material to which high-pressure thermosetting plastic laminate was applied. The pilot plant ran until 1942, when it was discontinued because of difficulties in producing plastic sheet material near a dusty particleboard plant and because the company did not have enough raw material for developing a full-scale plant.

F. Pfhol was awarded a Swiss patent in 1936 for a type of particleboard. This is the best known European patent in the particleboard industry. He also obtained a patent in Czechoslovakia in 1936 on "boards for cabinet makers and carpenters." The Dyas Wood Products Industry, Ltd., in Czechoslovakia bought the rights to this patent and, after one and a half years of experimental work, designed and built a crude production line. Commercial production ended with the start of World War II.

In 1938 and 1940, Torfitwerke G. A. Haseke obtained patents on methods of producing particleboard. In 1941, this company erected a commercial wood particleboard plant in Bremen, Germany, that is generally considered to be the first operational plant.

The extrusion method of producing particleboard was initially developed in Germany by Otto Kreibaum in 1947–1949. Several plants were built in the United States based on this original European concept; similar developments were introduced independently in the United States. This manufacturing method did not become important because of inherent problems with board properties and the small production capacities.

In the mid-1960s, the medium-density fiberboard was developed, using high-quality fiber generated by recently developed pressurized refiners. A high-quality board is produced with smooth surfaces and what are known as "tight edges" needed for furniture applications. Particleboards, on the other hand, have a rather porous edge and must be treated with plastic or other filler materials or edge-banded with wood before it can be used for finished products.

Mineral-bonded building products started in 1914.

They were developed in Radenthein, Austria, under what is known as the Heraklith method. Portland cement and gypsum are used as the binders. This product has good acoustical, thermal, fungal-resistant, and fire-resistant properties. It is made with a particle called wood wool or EXCELSIOR and wood flakes. Lightweight building blocks can also be produced using planer shavings or other wood particles and mineral binders.

FURTHER READING: Thomas M. Maloney, *Proceedings of the Washington State University Particleboard Symposium* (1967–1980), and *Modern Particleboard & Dry-Process Fiberboard Manufacturing* (1977). A. A. Moslemi, *Particleboard* (1974). A. J. Panshin, E. S. Harrar, W. J. Baker, and P. B. Proctor, *Forest Products: Their Sources, Production, and Utilization* (1950).

THOMAS M. MALONEY

COMPTON, WILSON MARTINDALE (1890–1967)

Wilson Compton, who is probably the most important figure in the history of the lumber trade association movement, was born in Wooster, Ohio, on October 15, 1890. He attended the College of Wooster and then went on to Princeton University where he earned a Ph.D. degree in the department of history, politics, and economics. Compton taught economics at Dartmouth for one year before taking an appointment with the Federal Trade Commission and pursuing a law degree at Hamilton College. During this period, Compton published a number of articles in professional journals about the economic difficulties of the lumber industry. His perceptive understanding of the problems of lumbermen and his kindred work with the Federal Trade Commission finally brought an invitation from the newly reorganized NATIONAL LUMBER MANUFACTURERS ASSOCIATION (NLMA) to serve as the association's first secretary-manager. Compton's selection proved to be an auspicious one for the organization.

Compton served as secretary-manager of NLMA from 1918 until 1944 when he left the organization to become president of Washington State College in Pullman. He served as the president of the college until 1951 when he resigned to accept a position with the U. S. State Department's policy planning staff. He quit the State Department job two years later after differences with Senator Joseph McCarthy. Between 1953 and his official retirement from public life in 1959, Compton was director of the Council for Financial Aid to Education. He spent most of the remaining years of his life in his native Wooster, Ohio, where he died on March 7, 1967.

Wilson Compton's ideas and strategies have powerfully influenced the activities and policies of organized lumbermen in the twentieth century. In his twenty-six-year career with the NLMA, Compton took an organization plagued with excessive and bitter rivalries and a lack of cooperation and molded it into an aggressive, forward-moving association which placed emphasis on united action and cooperative work with government agencies. Under Compton's guidance, NLMA rearranged and standardized its procedures for collecting fees and used its publicity department to promote a more positive image for the lumber industry. He continued to build upon his reputation as a spokesman for organized lumbermen when he helped resolve the demobilization problems after World War I. Both FOREST SERVICE officers and private lumber operators praised Compton for his efforts to lessen competitive rivalries in the industry and to direct attention to national problems. Government agencies plied Compton's office with offers and requests for cooperative public and private programs—a strong indication of the national association's increasingly important role in the nation's economic life. There is little doubt that Compton's open cooperation and collaboration with government agencies enhanced the influence of NLMA among most lumbermen.

Compton was one of the more prominent of all trade association leaders throughout the 1920s and 1930s. He believed that excessive competition was destructive to the conduct of rational and efficient business activity and advocated trade association cooperation and merger and consolidation of corporate enterprise as a means to achieve a stable and orderly economic environment. His numerous publications and public statements testify to a fertile, restless, and creative mind. Compton was a proponent of progressive capitalism and a severe critic of unregulated competition. His views about government–industry cooperation made him a controversial figure in an industry split between modernists and operators who still clung to the laissez-faire competitive world of the nineteenth century.

During Compton's years with NLMA, many of the organization's most progressive and forward-looking programs were initiated. In addition to the strong working relationship established with the federal government, Compton strengthened and broadened the association's public relations and trade promotion programs; expanded its technical, research, and engineering capabilities; and made the organization's work on fire insurance and lumber standards more efficient. He formed both American Forest Products Industries and the Timber Engineering Company as subsidiaries of the national association and enlarged and created other affiliates of the parent organization as need and circumstance dictated.

Wilson Compton was a skilled diplomat who enjoyed the respect (although not always agreement) of his colleagues in the trade association world. His significant contributions are revealed primarily through the personal letters and comments of his contemporaries, his own public statements and numerous publications, and the continuation of the major institutions which he helped to conceive and to mold.

WILLIAM G. ROBBINS

CONFERENCE OF GOVERNORS, 1908

At the suggestion of Frederick H. NEWELL, chief engineer of the Reclamation Service, President Theodore ROOSEVELT invited the governors of each state and territory to a conference at the White House on May 13–15, 1908. Governors or their representatives of fifty-two states, territories, and dependencies accepted the presidential invitation, as did the Cabinet, members of the Supreme Court, many congressmen and senators, representatives of seventy associations, twenty-one from the press, and fifty-two guests.

Newell, W J McGee, and Gifford PINCHOT organized the event, which was divided into sessions on mineral, land, and water resources. Steel magnate Andrew Carnegie gave the keynote address on minerals, railroader James J. Hill opened the session on land, and former California governor George C. Pardee led off the final group with a paper on irrigation. Roosevelt had characterized the conservation of natural resources as "the most weighty question now before the people of the United States." Of the nearly fifty speakers, most responded to the presidential sense of urgency with thoughtful papers; a few opted for florid and empty rhetoric. The conferees recom-

Governors, scientists, and industrialists assembled for a group photograph during their 1908 conference at the White House. President Theodore Roosevelt, seated ninth from left in the front row, chaired the conference, and Chief Forester Gifford Pinchot, standing second from left in the last row, was its principal architect. Forest Service Photo.

mended that the president call similar conferences in the future, that each state appoint a conservation commission, that forest and water policies and laws be adopted or enacted that would enhance conservation, and, finally, that laws be enacted that would prevent the waste of human lives and minerals in the mines. In response, Roosevelt created a National Conservation Commission and appointed McGee, Overton W. PRICE of the U. S. FOREST SERVICE, George W. Woodruff of the DEPARTMENT OF THE INTERIOR, Joseph A. Holmes of the GEOLOGICAL SURVEY, and Pinchot as chairman. In 1909, the commission released an exhaustive, three-volume report on the state of the nation's natural resources.

Historians have made much of the fact that certain factions of the conservation community were either underrepresented or excluded from the Governors' Conference. John MUIR of the SIERRA CLUB, for example, was not invited. Robert A. Long, a nationally prominent lumberman from Missouri, was the only official spokesman for the forest industries. However, Texas lumberman W. Goodrich Jones represented Governor T. M. Campbell, and the printed proceedings include a supplement with a paper by lumberman Frank H. Lamb of Washington. The supplement also includes a paper by Samuel Gompers, "Conservation in Relation to Labor." Nonetheless, the roster was not balanced and clearly was dominated by views that were compatible with Pinchot's.

The conference had a significant effect on the course of conservation. In fact, Henry Clepper (1968) maintains that it was "the single greatest stimulus to resource preservation and management" in U. S. history. The conference gave wide publicity to the conservation of natural resources and made the concept of conservation politically acceptable at both federal and state levels; forty states responded by establishing conservation commissions or similar bodies. When Congress passed the WEEKS ACT in 1911, which authorized federal matching funds to states for specified forestry purposes, thirty-six states had forestry agencies or departments; obviously, at least some of these agencies existed because of enlightened governors. Governors' conferences have continued on an annual basis, but no longer at the White House and no longer focusing solely on conservation.

FURTHER READING: Henry Clepper, "The First White House Conference on Natural Resources," *American Forests* 74 (May 1968): 28-31, 50-51. W J McGee, *Conference of the Governors of the United States* (1908). Charlotte Wittwer, "The 1908 White House Governor's Conference," *Environmental Education* 1 (Summer 1970): 142–145.

CONGRESSIONAL COMMITTEES AND FEDERAL FORESTLANDS

In 1885, Woodrow Wilson pointed out that "Congress on the floor is Congress on public exhibition, while Congress in its committee rooms is Congress at work." Although not mentioned in the Constitution, the committee system was established by the First Congress in 1789. Since then, much of the work of writing legislation, developing comprehensive policy, and overviewing execution of the laws has been done by various congressional committees. The House and Senate initially relied upon select committees, assuming that standing committees would accrue dangerous powers over the years. In the first decade of the nineteenth century, however, standing committees were deemed acceptable and by 1899, forty-nine standing committees had been established in the Senate alone. The Legislative Reorganization Act of 1946 reduced the number of standing congressional committees, although new issues and concerns over the next decades prompted several additions to the shortened list.

From time to time, select committees are formed to deal with matters of a topical nature, and subcommittees to the standing committees complete the division of labor. Although the number of standing committees has been reduced in the twentieth century, the number of subcommittees, select committees, and special committees has grown. In 1976, the Senate alone compelled its 100 members to fill 1,999 committee positions, an average of twenty assignments each, although the work load has never been evenly distributed.

Legislation and policy innovation on matters relating to forestlands have been the subject of many of these committees. Twelve Senate committees, for instance, handle policy matters in the field of forestry, environmental protection, and natural resources, while seven more have secondary responsibilities. Those committees with major responsibilities in forest policy are Agriculture and Forestry, and Interior and Insular Affairs; Public Works handles many environmental issues. In the House, the Agricultural Committee and the Committee on Interior and Insular Affairs are of primary importance.

Of the sixteen standing Senate committees formed in 1816, the most prominent in matters relating to forests and public domain was the Committee on Public Lands. Public Lands dealt with entry to the federal lands; through the century, policy decisions relating to land grants and forfeitures, land titles, improvements on federal land, homesteads, timber and stone lands, mining claims, and matters relating to game animals, birds, and fish on the public lands came before the committee. After 1891, Public Lands also received jurisdiction over forest reserves created out of the public domain.

Both House and Senate Public Lands committees had jurisdiction over national parks created out of the public domain and have considered legislation to establish such parks as Yellowstone, Yosemite, Wind Cave, and Petrified Forest. Preservation of prehistoric sites and natural objects of interest on public lands also fell under their purview. In 1905, for instance, the Senate Public Lands Committee reported a bill to create national monuments to preserve two groves of Big Trees (*Sequoia gigantea*) in California and in 1906 considered legislation resulting in the Antiquities Act.

In 1921, Public Lands committees in the House and Senate were combined with several related committees, gathering under their jurisdictions matters such as geologic survey, Indian affairs, territories, mines, and irrigation. During the 1946 reorganization, the committees were again amalgamated with others and in the next session were retitled Interior and Insular Affairs, to describe more accurately their new jurisdictions. Of the six major subcommittees within Senate Interior and Insular Affairs, three—Parks and Recreation, Water and Power Resources, and Public Lands—were concerned in significant ways with forestlands. At a January 24, 1975, committee organizational meeting, the crucial Public Lands Subcommittee was retitled Environment and Land Resources. Three years later, Senate Interior and Insular Affairs was retitled Energy and Natural Resources.

The House Committee on Interior and Insular Affairs also acquired additional jurisdiction in forest-related policy after 1946. Its subcommittees on Environment, National Parks and Recreation, Water and Power Resources, Indian Affairs, and Public Lands all have responsibilities for forested lands. The National Parks and Recreation Subcommittee reviews all matters dealing with the National Parks System. The Environment Subcommittee examines the environmental impacts of any laws or programs under the jurisdiction of the committee as a whole; Indian Affairs is concerned with forests on Indian reservations or lands regulated according to Indian treaties, and Public Lands has authority over forest reserves created from the public domain and over the National Wilderness Preservation System.

In other forest-related issues, the agricultural committees of the House and Senate acquired primary jurisdiction. The House established its Agricultural Committee in 1820, but it was not explicitly given authority over the subject of forestry until 1880. However, the Senate Agricultural Committee, formed in 1825, assumed responsibility for public forestlands immediately. Considering the committee's vast scope in the twentieth century, it is ironic that a minority of senators had originally opposed the formation of Senate Agriculture on the grounds that congressional power to legislate in regard to agriculture and forests was limited to those lands within the District of Columbia. Between 1857 and 1863, Senate Agriculture was actually abolished. In the pre-Civil War period, however, it was largely responsible for the final wording of much landmark federal legislation, including the federal Timber Reservation Act of 1827 and the Timber Trespass Act of 1831.

Granting cabinet status to the DEPARTMENT OF AGRICULTURE in 1889 was itself a matter put before the Agriculture Committee. Three years after the creation of a forestry division in the Department of Agriculture in 1881, "forestry" was added to the Senate committee's name. After 1911, the committee was given jurisdiction over all subjects relating to timber and forest resources other than those created from the public domain. The committee also exercised powers to protect migratory birds and formulated acts that established refuges for that purpose. In 1913, the committee reviewed the Weeks-McLean Bill that placed all migratory game and insectivorous birds within the custody and protection of the federal government. The bill, declared unconstitutional, was replaced in 1918 by the Migratory Bird Treaty Act.

After 1880, the scope of the House Agricultural Committee's concerns closely paralleled that of the Senate group; its jurisdiction included forestry in general as well as national forests purchased after 1911 under the WEEKS ACT but not those created from the public domain. In 1971, the House committee's scope was broadened in matters relating to the development, use, and administration of the national forests. A variety of critical issues that came to a head in the 1970s—watershed protection, sustained-yield timber management, and forest fire prevention—were debated in the Agricultural Committee.

Overlap between Interior and Insular Affairs and Agriculture has been common in both House and Senate. Although the two committees cooperated at times by jointly reporting bills, the jurisdictional problems have frequently led to bureaucratic conflicts, especially in regard to wilderness areas. In the early 1970s, House Speaker John McCormack worked out an arrangement under which Agriculture would deal with wilderness areas east of the 100th meridian and Interior and Insular Affairs with those to the west. This proved unworkable, however, and during the Ninety-Third Congress, both committees prepared an Eastern Wilderness Bill.

In addition to Senate and House standing committees, select committees have played an important part in the history of forestry and conservation. Among the most significant was the Senate Select Committee on Reforestation. When the United States entered World War I, the federal government effectively suspended its forest conservation campaign in favor of maximum short-range production. The results of this and further neglect during postwar readjustment prompted several forest industry organizations to join in the National Forestry Program Committee (NFPC) and work for a redefinition of national goals, particularly in the matter of reforestation.

In 1923, partly as a result of NFPC's work, the Senate organized its Select Committee on Reforestation and directed it to formulate a "comprehensive national policy" for timberlands and timber production. The committee was chaired by Charles L. MCNARY of Oregon. In addition to five Senate members, all from leading timber-producing states, the committee worked closely with Congressman John D. Clarke of New York, a leading advocate of reforestation, and named William B. GREELEY, chief forester of the U. S. FOREST SERVICE, a member ex officio. The select committee held exhaustive hearings in Washington and in sixteen important lumber-producing states. An active staff supported by private forestry associations gathered voluminous testimony on all aspects of the nation's forest reserves.

The committee found that only 469 million acres of forest or potential forestland remained out of an estimated original forested area of 822 million acres. Members were particularly disturbed that 75 percent of the virgin growth and 60 percent of the total forest acreage was located in the Rocky Mountain and Pacific states. The eastern half of the country, they found, was in dire need of reforestation.

Based on its studies, the committee recommended the far-reaching reform of national forestry policy that became the CLARKE-MCNARY ACT of 1924. The committee proposed that the United States immediately adopt as its goal an increase in the "rate at which timber is produced on the land suited to this form of use." To implement this policy, the committee recommended extending federal forest ownership where special public interests (watershed, for example) existed and removing obstacles to private timber growing as far as practicable. The committee called

for $2.5 million for federal–state cooperation in fire prevention; $100,000 annually for the distribution of seeds and seedlings, again in cooperation with the states; $100,000 in matching funds for the purposes of assisting farmers and other landowners in developing woodlots, windbreaks, and other forest growth; and the purchase of cutover land for future reforestation by the Forest Service. Though somewhat modified, these recommendations were incorporated into the final act.

At times joint committees of the House and Senate have also been responsible for forest-related legislation. Among the most controversial was the Committee to Investigate the Department of the Interior and the Forest Service—the so-called Ballinger-Pinchot Committee. Charges by Gifford PINCHOT against Secretary of the Interior Richard A. Ballinger, stemming from the disposition of coal lands in Alaska, and Pinchot's subsequent dismissal as chief of the Forest Service, prompted a joint resolution of Congress on January 19, 1910, designating a committee to investigate the affair. The committee consisted of six members of the Senate, appointed by the president, and six members of the House, elected by that body. The committee, chaired by Senator Knute Nelson of Minnesota, convened on January 26, 1910, and conducted hearings through June 13. It collected several volumes of documents and heard testimony from thirty-three individuals, including Ballinger, Pinchot, and Louis R. Glavis, Pinchot's chief confidant.

The committee was torn by political factionalism and maneuvering, which resulted in a minority report censoring Ballinger, issued by four Democratic members. The majority report, however, supported the secretary of the interior, concluding that the charges against him were motivated by differences in broad policy matters relating to forestry and conservation and by competition between the Interior Department and the Forest Service. In addition to exonerating Ballinger, the report recommended that the federal government lease (but not sell) the Alaska coal lands. The joint committee referred the report to the House Committee on Agriculture, which reported it without amendment. Although the report cleared Ballinger of charges, it did nothing to settle the coal claims; the issue continued to plague the Taft administration. A bill to settle the claims was introduced in the House by Ballinger and Taft in June 1910. It was taken up by the Committee on Public Lands but failed to pass. The land claims were eventually canceled by Ballinger's successor. Ironically, the controversial claims ultimately proved of little value.

A second controversial joint committee was the Congressional Committee on Forestry, formed in 1938 in response to a growing awareness that forests were a vital national concern. Chaired by John H. Bankhead of Alabama, the committee of five senators and five representatives held hearings in seven major forest regions—Idaho, Florida, Alabama, New York, California, Oregon, and Wisconsin—and in Washington. On March 24, the committee presented Congress with its report, titled *Forest Lands of the United States.* The report reviewed the forest situation in the United States, reaffirmed the need for stronger industry measures, and made several recommendations for intensifying cooperative measures to prevent depletion of private and public forests.

The committee called for further forestry activity under existing administrative structures. It recommended increased funding under the Clarke-McNary Act and extension of the act to cover forest pests and diseases on private and state-owned forests and to provide seeds and seedlings for all landowners. The committee recommended that the Cooperative Farm Forestry Act of May 18, 1937, be continued and expanded. Finally, the committee recommended a credit system for long-term, low-interest loans to private foresters, again through administrative facilities already available.

Meeting during a period of intense strain between the Forest Service and the lumber trade associations over matters relating to national forest policy, the committee skirted the subject of federal regulation of private forestlands, although it did formulate a plan by which intermingled public and private holdings could be managed for sustained-yield harvest. The committee recommended regulation of nonfederal forestlands by the states, again compromising the polarized demands of the Forest Service and the trade associations. When Senator Bankhead introduced his Forestry Omnibus Bill in the fall of 1941, neither the Forest Service nor industry representatives found it much to their liking. Lacking support from either side, the bill died in committee.

To relate the various committees' shifting positions on forest and conservation matters would be to treat the entire history of American federal forestry. Recommendations from individual committees are altered from one year to the next in response to public opinion, the policy of the executive branch, and even slight changes in personnel. For example, in 1907, the Senate Agricultural Committee advocated barring the president from proclaiming additional forest reserves in six western states. (Congress accepted the recommendation, but President Theodore ROOSEVELT rushed 16 million acres of forestland into national forests before the law went into effect.) In 1911, with minor changes in membership, the same committee reviewed and recommended passage of the conservationist Weeks Act. Similar swings characterize the history of other committees.

Committees other than those discussed here shared in the division of responsibilities for the nation's forestlands. The Committee on Appropriations, for example, reported the Sundry Civil Appropriations Act of July 1, 1898, which made the first appropriation ($75,000) for protection and administration of the forest reserves. In recent years, subcommittees of the House and Senate Committees on Banking and Currency have been concerned with the price of lumber and played an important role in the ill-fated National Timber Supply Act of 1969. The 1980 edition of the National Wildlife Federation's *Conservation Directory* (pp. 1-3) listed the following committees and subcommittees with responsibilities relating to forest and conservation:

U.S. Senate Committees:

Committee on Agriculture, Nutrition and Forestry. Responsibilities include, among other things, forestry, forest reserves and wilderness areas other than those created from the public domain; watersheds; soil conservation; and food from fresh waters. Subcommittees include, among others, Environment, Soil Conservation and Forestry; and Agricultural Research and General Legislation.

Committee on Appropriations. Responsibilities include all matters relating to appropriations for the support of the government. Subcommittees include Agriculture and Related Agencies; Interior and Related Agencies; Energy and Water Development.

Committee on Commerce, Science and Transportation. Committee is concerned with inland waterways (except construction), testing related to toxic substances, other than pesticides.

Committee on Energy and Natural Resources. Concerns include energy policy; energy regulation and conservation; public lands and forests, including farming and grazing thereon, and mineral extraction therefrom; national parks, recreation areas, wilderness areas, wild and scenic rivers, historic sites, military parks and battlefields, and, on the public domain, preservation of prehistoric ruins and objects of interest; and mining claims and mineral conservation. Subcommittees include Parks, Recreation, and Renewable Resources.

Committee on Environment and Public Works. Responsibilities include environmental policy; environmental research and development; fisheries and wildlife; water resources; flood control and improvements of rivers and harbors; public works, bridges, and dams; water pollution; regional economic development; and environmental protection and resource utilization and conservation. Subcommittees include Environmental Pollution; Water Resources; Transportation; Regional and Community Development; and Resource Protection.

House of Representatives:
Committee on Agriculture. Concerns include insect pests and protection of birds and animals in forest reserves; agriculture generally; agricultural colleges and experiment stations; soil conservation; forestry in general and forest reserves other than those created from the public domain; and rural development. Subcommittees include Forests; Conservation and Credit; and Rural Development and Special Studies.

Committee on Appropriations. Committee considers appropriations for the support of the government. Subcommittees include Agriculture; Rural Development and Related Agencies; Energy and Water Development; and Interior and Related Agencies.

Committee on Interior and Insular Affairs. Concerns include forest reserves and national parks created from the public domain; forfeiture of land grants and alien ownership; geological survey; irrigation and reclamation; Indian lands; military parks and battlefields, and national cemeteries administered by the secretary of the interior; mineral resources of the public lands; mining interests generally; conservation on the public lands; preservation of prehistoric ruins and objects of interest on the public domain; public lands generally. Subcommittees include Energy and the Environment; National Parks and Insular Affairs; Water and Power Resources; Mines and Mining; and Public Lands.

Committee on Interstate and Foreign Commerce. Committee is concerned with inland waterways. Subcommittees include Energy and Power, and Health and the Environment.

Committee on Merchant Marine and Fisheries. Concerns include coastal zone management; and fisheries and wildlife, including research, restoration, refuges, and conservation. Subcommittees include Fisheries and Wildlife Conservation, and the Environment.

Committee on Public Works and Transportation. Concerns include flood control and improvement of rivers and harbors; public works for the benefit of navigation, including bridges and dams; water power; and oil and other pollution of navigable waters. Subcommittees include Economic Development, and Water Resources.

Committee on Rules. Grants rules outlining conditions for floor debate on legislation reported by regular standing committees.

Since World War II, issues in forestry and conservation have grown more complex; the committee system and its responsibilities for these matters reflect this complexity.

RICHARD W. JUDD
JOSEPH R. CONLIN

CONIFER-LEAF PRODUCTS

Pine needles were commonly stuffed into mattress bags by pioneers and even second- and third-generation farmers in pine country from Maine to California. Another traditional use of longleaf pine needles in the nineteenth century was the making of woven baskets, bowls, trays, and ladies' hats, a recreation revived by 4-H clubs in the South during the 1920s.

Pine needles have also served as a fuel and a mulch. Southeastern strawberry growers continue to prefer them for the latter purpose. Commercial processing of the needles for agricultural purposes became a minor industry in Mississippi in the 1930s. Cut to a uniform size, fanned clean, and sprayed with a disinfectant oil, the needles (called "pine straw") were marketed as a litter for chicken coops and other livestock operations. The processed needles absorbed moisture without matting, masked odors, and if composted after discarding made a general-use fertilizer as rich as most chemical preparations. The expense of harvesting and the development of synthetic substitutes for the litter limited the growth of even this minor industry.

Fresh needles and small twigs of pines, redcedar, white-cedar, black and white spruce, eastern hemlock, junipers, and other conifers (as well as laurel and eucalyptus leaves) have been steam-distilled to provide aromatic essential oils for use in perfumes and deodorants, cleaning fluids, salves and liniments, soap, insecticides, furniture polish, and other goods. Chemically, these oils are composed of mixtures of terpenes and their derivatives. The conifer-needle distillation industry was an old one in Europe and, although always quite small, dates at least from the 1870s in the United States. Of the pines, longleaf supplies the most suitable needles for distillation, yielding about one pound of oil for every 250 pounds of foliage. One to two hundred pounds of northern white-cedar needles and twigs may provide a pound of distilled cedar needle oil. As recently as the late 1970s, homemade stills produced cedar oil in northern Vermont, New York, Ontario, and Quebec, providing seasonal employment for a handful of rural workers. At that time, only about 4,400 gallons of cedar needle oil were produced a year.

Indians and nineteenth-century pharmacists brewed cedar needle tea for use as a stimulant. It is said to have been rich in vitamin C, but it was later banned by the Food and Drug Administration because in some cases it caused irritation to the lining of the stomach.

CONNECTICUT FORESTS

When Reverend Thomas Hooker migrated from Massachusetts to Connecticut in 1635, the land was almost completely covered with dense mixed forests, about half of which consisted of chestnut, followed by smaller quantities of oak, hemlock, ash, elm, maple, and white pine. In northwestern Connecticut grew stands of sugar maple, beech, and yellow birch. Indians had cleared large tracts of land close to waterways for agricultural purposes and had reduced the proportion of conifers in other regions by burning the forests to facilitate hunting. By 1750, the rapidly growing European population had cleared two-thirds of the land for agriculture and only the rockiest and steepest third remained in forest. Most of the remaining forest was repeatedly coppiced to fill the demand for FIREWOOD and industrial CHARCOAL. As early as 1730, wood in some localities was in such short supply that towns enacted ordinances against building wooden fences. In order to protect the supply of valuable wood products such as pine masts, barrel staves, and cedar fence posts, the harvest of certain kinds of trees was regulated by 1715.

Agriculture expanded in Connecticut until the middle of the nineteenth century, at which time the forest cover was reduced to less than 30 percent of the state's 3,135,000 acres. Since then, agricultural decline has reversed this trend, and by the mid-1960s forests had reclaimed two-thirds of the state. Even though the forest area increased, the quality of the forest continued to deteriorate until well into the twentieth century. Short-rotation firewood coppice cutting was common as late as 1930 and the wildfires often associated with this practice favored sprouting hardwoods and discouraged hemlock and white pine. In addition to losses from heavy cutting, Connecticut suffered the disastrous blight of 1910–1920 which destroyed the chestnut, the state's most productive and valuable hardwood. The Great Hurricane of 1938 destroyed most of the remaining old-field white pine in eastern Connecticut.

Lumbering also encroached upon the forests. Heavy use of portable steam sawmills between 1880 and 1930 reduced the remaining old timber and old-field white pine. Lumber production in Connecticut peaked in 1909 at 168 million board feet and then decreased rapidly. At the peak, 74 percent of the lumber was hardwood; chestnut alone supplied 46 percent. In 1918, only 64 million board feet were produced from all species, and in 1932 only 8 million. However, after World War II lumber production gradually increased again, and in 1980 the state produced 70 million board feet and some 500,000 cords of firewood.

There are few areas in the United States where people have used forests longer or harder than in Connecticut. However, because of the state's heavy rainfall and stable soils, most of the twentieth century has seen major natural recovery of the forests. Natural reforestation was complemented by some of the earliest forestry programs in America.

In 1900, Connecticut appointed Walter Mulford as state forester, the first such official in the United States. Concurrently, Mulford became forester of the Connecticut Agricultural Experiment Station in New Haven. Early state forestry efforts focused on education, demonstration, and research. To promote these objectives, small state forests were acquired. In 1905, a basic system of FIRE CONTROL was mandated by the legislature, vesting responsibility for fire control in the state forester/state forest fire warden.

The year 1900 witnessed the founding of the Yale Forest School under an endowment from the family of Gifford PINCHOT. This was the nation's first graduate school of forestry; its first director was Henry S. GRAVES. Related educational and extension activities commenced in 1901–1902 at what is now the University of Connecticut at Storrs, which established its department of forestry in 1923.

Forestry at the state level was encouraged by the

Connecticut Forestry Association, founded by Reverend Horace Winslow in 1895 at Simsbury. In 1928, the organization became the Connecticut Forest and Park Association and enlarged its objectives to include support for parks and RECREATION.

Originally, Connecticut's foresters felt that the benefits of good forest management were self-evident and that, if forestry was properly demonstrated and promoted, appropriate private endeavors would follow. As this proved somewhat naive, foresters assumed a more aggressive role. State forestry and park activities were consolidated in 1921 under the direction of a new volunteer board, the State Park and Forest Commission, and to this commission the Connecticut Agricultural Experiment Station transferred all of its forestry functions except research. Austin F. Hawes, who had been state forester from 1904 to 1909, returned to that post in 1921, where he served until 1944. Through an energetic training program, judicious appointments of town fire wardens, and increased state and federal financing, a highly effective fire-control organization was built and annual fire losses were reduced to insignificance.

Although Connecticut's first park, the Israel Putnam Memorial Campground, was established in 1887, strong interest in parks and recreation developed somewhat later. In 1911, a temporary State Park Commission was established to draw up plans to acquire and maintain state parks. The commission became permanent in 1913 and many wooded inland parks have since been acquired. In 1925, an autonomous Commission on Forests and Wildlife was created with separate funds for the acquisition of lands for forests, parks, and wildlife management. This agency acquired over 100,000 acres during the next two decades. Limited funds made it easier to acquire heavily cutover, upland forests than the waterfront properties most desired by the parks program. However, most of the park management activity has been concentrated on swimming areas, especially along Long Island Sound.

The Depression era brought a major expansion of park and forest activities. By the time the CIVILIAN CONSERVATION CORPS had been founded, Connecticut already had its own state-operated program, upon which some of the national program was modeled. Land acquisitions proceeded rapidly and the federal Resettlement Administration transferred substantial areas, especially in eastern Connecticut, to the state on ninety-nine-year leases.

During the 1940s, the progress of the Park and Forest Commission was impeded by contention within the agency between partisans of recreation and those of forestry. This land use conflict was muted somewhat in 1971 by adoption of a program first envisioned by State Forester Harry A. McKusick, in which all of the state's wildland conservation activities were consolidated on a regional basis within the Division of Conservation and Preservation of a Department of Environmental Protection. This new agency combined the state's various natural resource and environmental regulatory functions into a single public authority. Under this reorganization the State Park and Forest Commission was abolished.

In 1975, Connecticut had 234 state park, forest, and recreation areas comprising 191,000 acres; of this, about 180,000 acres were managed for timber production and other commercial purposes. The federal government at the same time managed only about 2,000 acres of forest in Connecticut, while 1,659,000 acres of commercial forest remained in private hands. Nonfarm, nonindustry proprietors owned 65 percent of this private commercial forest.

During the 1970s, fiscal restraint and new political priorities limited progress in the area of parks and forestry. In addition, during the late 1970s lumbering and fuelwood cutting underwent a major revival. It remained to be seen whether the institutions that had come into being could forestall another sequence of overexploitation, neglect, and recovery.

FURTHER READING: Articles on the forest history of Connecticut have frequently appeared in *Connecticut Woodlands*, published quarterly by the Connecticut Forest and Park Association since 1936. Of particular interest is the seventy-fifth anniversary issue (vol. 35, Spring 1970) devoted to the history of the state's forests and forestry.

DAVID M. SMITH
JOHN E. HIBBARD

CONSERVATION FOUNDATION

The Conservation Foundation was founded in 1948 by Fairfield Osborn, George E. Brewer, and Samuel H. Ordway, Jr. The purpose of the foundation is to promote knowledge about the earth's resources, including forest resources. It has no members but solicits funds from other foundations, individual donors, and government support programs in order to conduct research, grant fellowships, and prepare educational material, particularly films and other audiovisual media. Supporting foundations include RESOURCES FOR THE FUTURE, the Environmental Defense Fund, and the Environmental Law Institute.

In cooperation with Encyclopedia Britannica Films, the foundation produced several films in the landmark *Living Earth* series in 1948 and, in 1949, *The Living Forest* series. These films were the basis of popular education in conservation and forestry for a generation of schoolchildren.

In 1977, the foundation published *The Lands Nobody Wanted* by William E. Shands and Robert G. Healy. The report analyzed the 24 million acres of national forest land in the eastern United States, which had been acquired through purchase since the WEEKS ACT was enacted in 1911.

Together with the U. S. FOREST SERVICE, the Conservation Foundation operates the Pinchot Institute for Conservation Studies at Milford, Pennsylvania (the former Pinchot estate). Foundation headquarters are in Washington, D.C.

CONSERVATION MOVEMENT

A considerable body of legislation existed by the late colonial period to regulate the use of natural resources. Despite or perhaps because of these regulations, following independence, a general abundance of natural wealth combined with the individualistic spirit of American society to encourage exploitative practices. During the course of the nineteenth century, however, an increasing number of individuals came to accept the notion that the physical bounds of geography and natural resources on the continent would soon be reached. It seemed clear that nature's bounty could not sustain American civilization much longer unless more conservative resource utilization practices were adopted.

Although its antecedents may be traced to earlier European conservation practices, the American conservation movement had multiple domestic origins. Industrialization increased resource use, leading to fears of future scarcity. A growing number of individuals trained in the biological and engineering sciences observed, evaluated, and described the impacts of resource depletion. They believed that democratic government seemed continually threatened by the increasing concentration of ownership of the nation's resources in the hands of a few individuals. Meanwhile, high birth and immigration rates caused the population to double and redouble, increasing future competition for resources. On an ominous note, the Census Bureau announced the closing of the frontier in 1890: there would be no more "free land" to act as a safety valve against social unrest. Rising concern for human welfare suggested that a more thoughtfully planned administration of the remaining public domain was needed to assure widespread distribution of the benefits of natural resources. Post-Civil War nationalism enhanced the acceptability of the concept of federal stewardship over natural resources, while the subsequent emergence of the United States as a world power provoked interest in husbanding the material resources required for economic and military stamina.

Also developing during the latter half of the nineteenth century was a distinct popular movement for the protection of natural beauty. Its champions would preserve nature both for its own sake, reflecting the transcendentalist spiritual tradition, and as a means of recreating and refreshing the human psyche, jaded by the conditions of urban and industrial life. Although the advocates of these ideas regarded themselves as conservationists, their preservationist programs sometimes reinforced and sometimes competed against the movement for commodity or utilitarian conservation. Similarly, proponents of utilitarian conservation were not always in accord with one another on the purposes or methods, on the respective roles of federal or state government, nor on the primacy of the government or private sectors.

As a popular movement on the national level, conservation was highlighted first in the Progressive reform era of the early twentieth century and again, with partly different economic underpinnings, during the New Deal of the 1930s. In the three decades after World War II, both conservation and preservation tended to either compete with or be subsumed under an emerging ENVIRONMENTAL MOVEMENT, which combined many of the old interests with a more general concern for maintaining the quality of life.

Early Forest Conservation

Forestry, the first of the resource-management professions, seemed particularly appropriate to the reform spirit of the late nineteenth century; Gifford PINCHOT believed that "conservation began with forestry." More specifically, conservation as a national policy began with nineteenth-century fears of a timber famine. During that century, the lumberman's frontier had advanced through New England into the Great Lakes region, dipped into the South, and was poised to move into the Pacific Northwest. "Cut out and get out" timber removal and unchecked forest fires had stripped many regions of their only valuable economic resource. The apparent abundance of resources as well as the nineteenth-century economic tradition that gave industry unimpeded access to resources and gave private property virtual sanctity against government regulation, had determined this outcome. Gradually, however, reform-minded citizens and public officials began to question whether the profit motives of a free market would for long coincide with those of a nation, or if there would be any certainty for future commodity supplies unless the federal government established the priorities.

The United States Commissioner of Patents predicted in his annual report for 1849 that "the waste of valuable timber in the United States will hardly begin to be appreciated until our population reaches 50,000,000. Then the folly and shortsightedness of this age will meet with a degree of censure and reproach not pleasant to contemplate." Other articles on the harmful long-term effects of forest destruction appeared in the reports of the commissioners of patents and of agriculture during the 1850s and 1860s. The most influential treatise on the subject was *Man and Nature* by George Perkins MARSH (1864, revised 1874), which described in detail the diverse effects of forest depletion upon civilization in the Mediterranean region.

Before 1873, federal legislation dealing with timber had been concerned primarily with securing an adequate supply for naval construction purposes. Most states and territories had passed laws concerning forest fire control, although these were scarcely enforced. Since the colonial period, government regulation of forest industries had been virtually forgotten. Sporadic state and private attempts to encourage tree planting, beginning early in the nineteenth century, culminated in the widespread adoption of ARBOR DAY, first observed in Nebraska in 1872. The federal government ventured into this area with the Timber Culture Act of 1873, which offered 160 acres to any settler who would plant 40 of them in trees. Such measures sought to solve the timber problem by encouraging private initiative: the more trees planted by individuals, the less would be the shortfall in national timber supplies. Emphasizing arboriculture, these measures did nothing to promote wise management of existing forests.

Many individuals saw a need for a more positive forest policy. By 1876, the American Association for the Advancement of Science and the AMERICAN FORESTRY ASSOCIATION (the latter formed the previous year by concerned botanists and horticulturists) had persuaded Congress to appropriate funds for a federal forestry agent. Franklin B. HOUGH, hired to fill this new position, compiled three detailed reports between 1877 and 1882 that provided a wealth of data on forest conditions and utilization. Other relatively reliable information on American forests and their depletion became available when the Tenth Census published the *Report on the Forests of North America* (1884), compiled by Charles S. SARGENT, director of Harvard's Arnold Arboretum. These reports supported the recommendations made since the 1860s by several GENERAL LAND OFFICE commissioners and Carl Schurz (secretary of the interior, 1877–1881) that essential modifications were required of the land laws as they related to timberlands. The PUBLIC LAND COMMISSION of 1879 also contributed to the pressure for reform by proposing that the government sell timber while retaining the land, so that it might in the future continue to produce forest crops.

When in 1891 Congress repealed the Timber Culture Act and revised other land laws, a brief amendment authorized the president to reserve forestlands from entry under the land laws. This enactment constituted a major departure from the tradition that the government held the public domain for the purpose of disposing of it to private interests. It had the support of most of the citizens and agencies that had voiced support for a forest policy up to that time. Some 38 million acres of forest reserves were set aside under Presidents Harrison and Cleveland. However, no provision was made for their management or protection. The purposes and administration of these reserves were debated until 1897, when Congress passed the second major forestry legislation as an amendment of the annual Sundry Civil Appropriations Act. Known generally as the FOREST MANAGEMENT ACT, the new law defined the purposes of the national government in the conservation of public forests: "to improve and protect the forest, . . . securing favorable conditions of water flows, and . . . a continuous supply of timber." In linking forests and streamflow, the act reflected as much concern over erosion, domestic water supplies, river and harbor development, irrigation, and flood control as over timber. The subsequent establishment of many of the forest reserves at higher elevations was due to the influence of mountain ranges on water supply and the fact that these particular timberlands, not always supporting the richest growth, had not yet left the public domain for private ownership. In the 1897 act lay the roots of the federal stewardship, judicious use, multiple-purpose development, and commodity utilization advocated by forest conservationists of the succeeding decade. Lovers of nature and outdoor RECREATION supported the establishment of forest reserves, but, from the standpoint of contemporary foresters and conservationists, the inherent beauty later considered to be a national asset was incidental to economic value.

With passage of the Forest Management Act, federal forest administration became the responsibility of the General Land Office (GLO) of the DEPARTMENT OF THE INTERIOR; ironically, all the forestry expertise in the federal government at that time was in the DEPARTMENT OF AGRICULTURE's Division (later Bureau) of Forestry, which since 1886 had been headed by the German-born and trained Bernhard E. FERNOW. The first United States citizen educated in forestry, Fernow had been closely involved in the deliberations preceding the forest legislation of 1891 and 1897 and had earned scientific stature for American forestry by instituting research on the physical properties of wood. He also attempted to educate the public and the timber industry on the practicality and profitability of proper timber harvest procedures. The GLO necessarily relied on Agriculture for technical advice until 1901, when it set up its own Division of Forestry under Filibert Roth, who had been trained by Fernow. By 1905, however, another European-trained forester, Gifford PINCHOT, who had followed Fernow in the Department of Agriculture, succeeded in having the forest reserves transferred from Interior to his own department. Emphasizing "service" over "bureaucracy," Pinchot also had his bureau renamed the FOREST SERVICE. Two years later, to abolish any hint that they were reserved from commodity utilization, Pinchot had the title of forest reserves changed to that of national forests.

The consolidation of federal forestry activity in the Department of Agriculture had been one of the principal recommendations of the American Forest Congress sponsored in Washington, D.C., by the American Forestry Association in January 1905. Attended by leaders of lumbering, mining, grazing, irrigation, education, and government, the congress sought to achieve broader understanding of the relationship between forestry and industry and to advance the conservation of the forest as a permanent resource. As the largest meeting held up to that time concerning forestry and forest management, the congress highlighted the important place which these subjects had achieved in the economic life of the nation.

Water Conservation

Effective utilization of arid lands in the western states, where successful agriculture depended upon irrigation, constituted another area where traditional land-disposal policies proved inadequate. Before turning toward a policy of federal stewardship, the reclamationists experimented with legislation offering incentives toward a private solution to the arid lands problem, such as the Desert Land Act of 1877, which offered claimants up to 640 acres if they would irrigate it. (That effort was similar to the way the forerunners of forest conservation had tried to solve the timber supply problem with measures like the Timber Culture Act of 1873.) John Wesley Powell, who studied the arid lands for the Department of the Interior, concluded in his *Report on the Lands of the Arid Region of the United States* (1878) that before being disposed of, the public domain should be classified according to its

best use. Seeing that the Desert Land Act had done more to encourage speculation than irrigation, Congress eventually took Powell's advice. In 1888, it authorized the survey of sites suitable for irrigation waterworks and the reservation of irrigable lands until they could be opened to orderly homesteading by executive proclamation. Powell, then director of the GEOLOGICAL SURVEY, accordingly withdrew millions of acres; but a storm of protest led Congress to reopen irrigable lands within two years.

Reclamationists were slower than forest conservationists in accepting federal control of resources. The Interstate Irrigation Congress, held in Salt Lake City in 1891, debated the issue of federal control and recommended that irrigable public land be ceded to the states. Congress responded with the Carey Act of 1894, which offered to each of the arid states and territories up to 1 million acres of such lands as they were able to settle, irrigate, and cultivate within ten years. Although more than 1 million acres eventually went to patent under the Carey Act, the law's initial slow progress in encouraging reclamation cast doubt upon the ability of states or smaller governments to undertake successfully extensive impoundment and diversion projects. Indeed, reclamationists welcomed the creation of federal forest reserves to protect the watersheds around the heads of streams, and by 1900, the National Irrigation Association dropped its demand for cession of irrigable lands to the states. Congress, increasingly favorable toward federal lands stewardship, passed the Newlands Act of 1902, authorizing the secretary of the interior to locate, construct, operate, and maintain works for the storage, diversion, and development of water for reclamation. To carry out these duties, the secretary organized the Reclamation Service under the leadership of Frederick H. NEWELL within the Geological Survey.

Progressive Conservation

Gifford Pinchot, however, was the central figure in the agitation for conservation that turned a movement previously of interest mainly to resource managers and users into a national political crusade capturing the imagination of much of the American public in the Progressive era. With the exception of President Theodore ROOSEVELT, whose unqualified support insured the success of many of Pinchot's programs, perhaps no other name has been so consistently linked to the helm of American conservation as that of Pinchot. The programs also benefited from a close working arrangement between Forester Pinchot and Roosevelt's secretary of the interior, James R. Garfield. But Pinchot held an intransigent belief that resources existed in order that they might be utilized for human economic welfare. This view eventually placed him at odds with people like John MUIR whose commitment to conservation sprang from an interest in recreation in a primeval setting. Even before he obtained control of the forest reserves, Pinchot had proposed that the administration of national parks be consolidated in his agency, so that their resources might be properly utilized. When the city of San Francisco applied for a permit to construct reservoirs in YOSEMITE NATIONAL PARK, Pinchot endorsed the move and thus shocked many who did not believe that Hetch Hetchy's water was as valuable as its scenic beauty. This cleavage between conservation and preservation generated support for the establishment of a new NATIONAL PARK SERVICE in the Department of the Interior, eventually created in 1916.

Both utilitarian conservation and aesthetic preservation advanced during Roosevelt's presidential terms. Roosevelt withdrew from private entry a large amount of public domain: he added over 141 million acres to the national forests before 1907; closed nearly 80 million acres of coal deposits (later reopening almost half of them when further study indicated the absence of coal); closed 4.7 million acres of potash deposits and 4 million acres containing oil. Other presidential withdrawals accumulated as the Reclamation Service implemented its program. For the most part, Roosevelt's actions looked toward enactment of legislation that would enable the resources to be brought into use while title to the lands and control over utilization would remain with the government. On the side of preservation, Roosevelt supported the congressional withdrawal of nearly 214,000 acres from development in five new national parks, and following passage of the Antiquities Act of 1906, he established sixteen NATIONAL MONUMENTS. He also gave attention to the protection of wildlife with the creation of four large game refuges and fifty-one bird reservations.

When the Roosevelt administration imposed charges on grazing privileges and the use of coal and waterpower sites, opposition arose in the West. Early in 1907, while approving the change in name of forest reserves to national forests, Congress began to reassert its own authority over the public lands by abolishing the Forest Service's special receipts fund and by canceling the executive power to create or enlarge reservations in six western states. Attempts to organize support for an anticonservationist policy culminated in June, when western political leaders gathered for the Denver Public Lands Convention at the call of the Colorado legislature and Governor Henry Buchtel. Most of the delegates spoke for Colorado and Wyoming stockraising and mining interests, who wanted the

public lands ceded to the states and all nonforest lands eliminated from the national forests. U. S. Senator Henry Moore Teller of Colorado succinctly expressed the feelings of western settlers and others intent upon developing resources: "We cannot remain barbarians to save timber." But divided opinion among delegates from elsewhere in the West and a formidable presentation by Pinchot prevented the convention from formulating a strong anticonservationist program.

Thereafter, Pinchot and the president turned increasingly toward the public for support, whipping up a popular fervor which justified the name "conservation crusade." Together with Frederick Newell of the Reclamation Service and W J McGee, a former protégé of John Wesley Powell in the Geological Survey, Pinchot instigated a series of conferences and commissions that focused the nation's attention on his conception of conservation. In this view, resources were to be developed and used without waste for the common good of present and future generations. The goal of conservation was to be "the greatest good of the greatest number for the longest time"; the method was to be an integrated program for all natural resources, giving each its proper treatment in relation to the whole. Pinchot later credited McGee, "the scientific brains of the new movement," with developing much of the theoretical underpinning of conservation.

The Pinchot men persuaded Roosevelt to establish an Inland Waterways Commission in 1907. That body was to design multiple-purpose development of river basins, coordinating irrigation, navigation, flood control, and hydroelectric power. From it, Pinchot and his allies secured a resolution requesting that the president call a conference of state governors and other prominent citizens to publicize and arouse national support for their unified philosophy of conservation of mineral, land, and water resources.

This CONFERENCE OF GOVERNORS, the first gathering in the nation's history of the chief executives of the states, met in May 1908 in the White House. Roosevelt addressed the issue in his opening remarks: "We are coming to recognize as never before the right of the Nation to guard its own future in the essential matter of natural resources." Participating were thirty-eight governors and their aides, representatives of the territories and of seventy national organizations, and prominent industrialists, cabinet members, congressmen, scientists, engineers, public officials, and labor leaders. Pinchot and McGee controlled the proceedings, coordinating publicity and writing speeches for some of the participants. Almost all of the speakers focused on the economic side of conservation; only a few, particularly J. Horace

MCFARLAND of the American Civic Association and George F. Kunz of the American Scenic and Historic Preservation Society, advocated the preservation of wildlife and scenic beauty.

The conference made recommendations for the continuation of existing laws and the enactment of new ones protecting the timber supply, preventing soil erosion, protecting waterflow, providing for the protection and replacement of private forests, and conserving mineral resources. The Governors' Conference also recommended that future conferences be called to assure continued cooperation between the states and the nation, and that conservation commissions be established for the nation and for each state. By mid-1909, forty-one states had carried out this last suggestion.

Roosevelt followed up the success of the Conference of Governors by calling for a North American Conservation Conference. In February 1909, representatives of Canada, Newfoundland, Mexico, and the United States met in Washington, D.C., to consider mutual interests in the conservation of natural resources. Pinchot, Secretary of State Robert Bacon, and Secretary of the Interior James R. Garfield attended for the United States. Although no public sessions were held, the North American conference adopted a declaration of principles based on public ownership and social responsibility. Maintaining that conservation was too big a job for any nation acting alone, the North American conference called upon Roosevelt to sponsor a World Conservation Conference. This call had been anticipated by Roosevelt and his advisers, and invitations had been sent to fifty-one nations and accepted by thirty when Roosevelt's successor in the White House, William Howard Taft, canceled the plan.

Following the recommendations of the Conference of Governors, Roosevelt appointed a National Conservation Commission in June 1908. The commission was composed of representatives of the resource agencies of government and of members of Congress friendly to the conservation cause. Pinchot was chairman. With the aid of the governmental departments, the commission compiled the most comprehensive inventory that had yet been made of the natural resources of the United States. Completed by December, the commission's three-volume report contained few entirely new proposals, but it did present Pinchot's concepts in the form of a recommendation for a comprehensive policy.

To receive the report of the commission, Roosevelt in December 1908 convened a Joint Conservation Conference (or Second Governors' Conference) attended by twenty governors, representatives of eleven others, members of twenty-six of the new state conservation commissions, and spokesmen for sixty national organizations. The Joint Conference expressed great enthusiasm for the work of the National Conservation Commission and recommended that its work be continued. Nevertheless, Congress was becoming increasingly wary of the Roosevelt administration, which had appointed seven separate commissions to study national problems and provide expert information enabling the executive to act where the legislative branch would not. In March 1909, Congress refused appropriation to cover the work of the National Conservation Commission and prohibited federal officials from aiding the work of any executive commission that lacked specific legislative authorization. The formal work which had begun with the Conference of Governors thus came to an end.

When William Howard Taft replaced Theodore Roosevelt in the White House in 1909, the force behind the organized conservation movement was lost. Congressional opposition was strong, and neither the new president nor the members of his cabinet were committed to the cause in the way that Roosevelt had been. Taft generally favored the conservation policies of his predecessor and kept Pinchot on, but he gave the forester no privileges beyond those of other bureau chiefs. Pinchot, accustomed to exercising wide powers and convinced of the moral rightness of his cause, eventually became involved in public criticism of Taft's secretary of the interior, Richard A. Ballinger (see BALLINGER-PINCHOT CONTROVERSY). Taft discharged Pinchot for disrupting orderly administration, but Pinchot flaunted his dismissal as evidence that his charges had been correct. Triumphantly he carried on the conservation crusade outside the government.

Already in the summer of 1908, Pinchot had organized a Conservation League of America to serve as a pressure group on behalf of his programs in Congress. The league, presided over by Walter L. Fisher (later appointed secretary of the interior upon Ballinger's retirement in 1911), was a loose coalition of established organizations, primarily waterways associations. Pinchot soon found it inadequate for his purposes. He tried briefly to exploit the American Forestry Association (AFA) as a substitute but found it uninterested in sidetracking its traditional forestry objectives in order to champion Pinchot's broad-ranging unified conservation program.

In the summer of 1909, Pinchot organized the National Conservation Association (NCA), a membership group like AFA, backed by Pinchot's private wealth and staffed with his friends and protégés. NCA's secretary until 1912 was Thomas R. Shipp, who had done public relations work for the Forest Service, the Inland Waterways Commission, and the

Governors' Conference; he was followed by Harry Slattery, formerly Pinchot's private secretary. NCA's first treasurer was Overton W. PRICE, former associate forester who had been fired along with Pinchot. Other staff members included lifelong friends and former Forest Service colleagues. Initially, President Charles Eliot of Harvard University served as NCA president, but when Pinchot left federal employment in January 1910, he became president of NCA and Eliot served as honorary president. NCA was essentially Pinchot's personal vehicle for a muckraking campaign to "save" the Pinchot-Roosevelt conservation program.

As a popular movement, NCA was not successful. Pinchot had initially hoped for a membership of 50,000 to 100,000, but in fact the rolls probably never passed 2,500. Pinchot's dominance of NCA and his close ties to Roosevelt's political aspirations led the public to doubt the organization's objectivity. In an attempt to bolster membership, NCA started a journal, *American Conservation*, in 1911, but abandoned it within the year, turning the subscription lists over to AFA's *American Forestry*.

Pinchot's particular interests at the time led NCA to be identified primarily with waterpower and mineral leasing policies. Its principal activity was congressional lobbying. Among its projects was an unsuccessful fight for the Capper bill to regulate private forestry in 1920, and, in the same year, successful support for the Federal Water Power Act and the Mineral Leasing Act. Two years later, Pinchot was elected governor of Pennsylvania. With its chief supporter's energies thus occupied, NCA was dissolved in 1923 and its membership absorbed into AFA.

Pinchot's personal views on the conservation movement also played an important role in the National Conservation Congress, an annual forum for the exchange of ideas, experiences, and problems among state, private, and federal conservation leaders, first called by the Washington (State) Conservation Association in Seattle in 1909. The congress's first session adopted perhaps the broadest statement of purpose of any conservation organization: "to act as a clearing house for all allied social forces of our time, to seek to overcome waste in natural, human, or moral forces." By the following year, some participants in the congress were complaining that it was but a political scheme to support both the Republican insurgency against Taft and Theodore Roosevelt's aspirations for reelection. Pinchot's partisans were successful until 1913 in focusing the congress's programs on national legislative issues, particularly in regard to fees charged utilities for hydroelectric

power sites. The anti-Pinchot faction tried to resurrect the congress in 1916, but that was its last meeting. The congress left a legacy of bitterness toward Pinchot and his political brand of conservation.

Despite the acrimony that accompanied these final efforts to organize conservation under Pinchot's leadership, major tenets of his program by 1910 had been enacted into law and incorporated in the programs of federal (and many state) agencies responsible for resource administration. In his book, *The Fight for Conservation* (1910), Pinchot remarked that "official opposition to the conservation movement, whatever damage it has done or still threatens to the public interest, has vastly strengthened the grasp of conservation upon the minds and consciences of the people." Conservation principles became an element in public education; *The Conservation of Natural Resources in the United States*, by Charles R. Van Hise (1910), was only the first of a number of texts on the subject.

Touring the West after his dismissal, Pinchot found expressions of support for his policies. In the 1910 elections, conservation showed promise as a political issue, particularly in the election of Hiram Johnson as governor of California and of Miles Poindexter as U. S. senator from Washington. But in the national elections of 1912, Roosevelt, who regarded the conservation policy as the outstanding accomplishment of his previous term, lost to Woodrow Wilson, who had little interest in natural resource policy. Wilson's secretary of the interior, Franklin K. Lane, adeptly continued conservation policies without experiencing many of the political eruptions of the past. The benefits of federal resource administration had been well demonstrated, and even to many westerners the alternative of state control seemed to promise only a return to relative chaos.

Nevertheless, Pinchot's concept of unified conservation had been proved to be more of a public relations device than an operating program. In the 1910s and 1920s, forestry, reclamation, waterpower development, flood control, waterways improvement, and mineral leasing each continued to make substantial progress in its own way, but the partisans of each measure feared that a broader program might obscure their specific needs. Wildlife and natural beauty, neither an important part of the Pinchot program, also developed their own conservation programs concurrently, each with its separate, although overlapping, following.

Conservation in the 1920s
Federal resource agencies during the 1920s continued to collect scientific data and to draft plans for the use of resources, which would set the background

for more aggressive governmental actions in the following decade. Moreover, the Reclamation Service's Boulder Canyon project, authorized in 1928 with the support of the incoming Hoover administration, was to be the first large federal conservation project based on multiple-purpose objectives.

A major theme of the Republican administrations of the 1920s was government cooperation with private enterprise: federal agencies discarded the concept of resource regulation in favor of providing services to the state and private sectors. This orientation characterized such important legislation as the CLARKE-MCNARY ACT of 1924, the McNary-Woodruff Act of 1928, and the MCSWEENEY-MCNARY ACT of 1928, all vigorously supported by the National Forestry Program Committee, a group set up in 1920 to represent the major forestry organizations and forest product associations.

During the 1920s, progress in resource conservation seldom came from initiatives by the nation's political leadership. Herbert Hoover, the first president after Theodore Roosevelt to hold a personal interest in conservation, attacked the problem of what to do with the remaining public lands by having Congress in 1930 authorize the creation of the Committee on Conservation and Utilization of the Public Domain. Under the chairmanship of James R. Garfield, who had been Roosevelt's secretary of the interior, the committee recommended in 1931 that the unreserved and unappropriated public lands should be granted to the states, a plan failing to appeal even to the western states, which shunned the added responsibility. Equally unsuccessful was the Timber Conservation Board, which Hoover appointed in 1930 to study the problem of chronic overproduction in the forest industries, following a suggestion originating with Wilson Compton of the NATIONAL LUMBER MANUFACTURERS ASSOCIATION. Although the board, chaired by Secretary of Commerce Robert P. Lamont, produced a valuable statistical report on *The Forest Situation in the United States* (1932), its recommendations for sustained-yield forestry on both private and public lands led to no legislative or administrative result. The crusading spirit of the Progressive conservation movement did not reappear in the 1920s.

Conservation under the New Deal

Franklin D. ROOSEVELT entered the White House in 1933 with the national economy in a shambles and a dust bowl plaguing the midlands. Federal conservation during the Progressive era had been a remedy against the depletion of resources; during the New Deal, it was also intimately linked to economic recovery and unemployment relief. When accepting the presidential nomination, Roosevelt had blamed the lack of a national land policy for both the threat of soil erosion and the threat of timber famine: "It is clear that economic foresight and immediate employment march hand in hand in the call for reforestation of these vast areas." From the start, the second Roosevelt made conservation one of the major elements of his administration.

The conservation measures adopted during the New Deal were carried out by the established government bureaus as well as by a wide range of emergency social and economic planning programs. The CIVILIAN CONSERVATION CORPS, created in 1933, was both a means of removing the unemployed from the streets and of expanding manpower for ongoing conservation programs such as fire protection, reforestation, and the building of access roads and recreational facilities. Similarly, under the Public Works Administration and the Works Progress Administration, swamps were drained, river and stream beds improved, and federal funds were provided for the control of erosion. The National Industrial Recovery Act (NIRA) of 1933 led to the adoption in the next year of a Forest Conservation Code that required the industry to formulate and enforce forest practices rules. The Shelterbelt Project, or Prairie States Forestry Project, started by the Forest Service under a presidential directive in 1934, planted millions of trees in strips adjacent to farmlands in order to alter wind patterns and thus restrain the loss of topsoil that was helping to create a class of bankrupt farmers. The TAYLOR GRAZING ACT, also of 1934, set up the mechanism for the federal administration of the remaining public domain. The Soil Conservation Act of 1935 permanently established federal policy for the control and prevention of soil erosion. The Pittman-Robertson Federal Aid in Wildlife Restoration Act of 1937 authorized federal cooperation with the states in wildlife conservation. The Bankhead-Jones Farm Tenant Act of the same year provided for federal acquisition and reforestation of submarginal or abandoned farmland.

The New Deal program that came closest to carrying the dual concepts of federal stewardship and judicious use of natural resources to full implementation was the TENNESSEE VALLEY AUTHORITY (TVA), created in 1933. This program provided for such multipurpose resource use as had been advocated by the Inland Waterways Commission a quarter of a century earlier. TVA offered something for every conservationist, whether his concerns included reclamation, irrigation, prevention of soil erosion, forestry, navigation, energy, wildlife, outdoor recreation, or social welfare. Individuals dispossessed from land inundated by TVA reservoirs were expected to reach a higher standard of living through employment in the massive construction projects. Eventually, TVA's low-cost electrical power and improved river navigation were to induce manufacturers to relocate or expand into the region, continuing local prosperity. Until World War II interrupted this course of events, TVA enthusiasts had projected similar regional federal conservation projects to revitalize the economies elsewhere in the country.

On the whole, however, during the New Deal period, as J. N. DARLING, then head of the BIOLOGICAL SURVEY, remarked in 1935, "conservation as a national principle has no substance or coordination." Fourteen federal and many state agencies had conservation programs, but, as Darling added, "collisions are frequent." Reclamationists ran afoul of the defenders of parks and wildlife; the National Park Service competed with the Forest Service for control of millions of acres of land; proposals for preserving wilderness ran head on against the aspirations of both recreationists and commodity developers; renewed proposals for Forest Service regulation of industrial timber production were countered by a private tree farm movement and a vigorous industrial public relations campaign denouncing federal regulation as "socialistic."

The New Deal did set up an administrative framework for comprehensive and continuing conservation planning. This was the National Planning Board, originally appointed by Roosevelt in 1933 to assist the administrator of public works in carrying out NIRA programs. (In 1934, the board became directly advisory to the president and its name was changed to National Resources Board; it became the National Resources Committee in 1935 and the National Resources Planning Board from 1939 until its termination in 1943.) From its inception until 1939, the board was dominated by Secretary of the Interior Harold L. ICKES. Upon taking office as secretary, Ickes had confessed to Pinchot: "I am a Gifford Pinchot conservationist. I learned the principles of conservation at your feet, just where T. R. learned his" (Polenberg, 1966, p. 104). The board promoted integrated thinking in respect to the interrelationships between resources; however, its deliberations led to few specific administrative or legislative programs.

For the coordination of federal conservation activities, Ickes was more interested in merging all resource agencies into an enlarged Department of the Interior under a new title, the Department of Conservation. His efforts to achieve this reorganization only added to the disruption of the ideal of conservation as a unified concept. In particular, Ickes's repeated attempts after 1935 to have the Forest Service transferred to Interior brought permanent enmity between the secretary and his former mentor, Pinchot, and set off the most vitriolic quarrel among conservationists since the Hetch Hetchy dispute more than twenty-five years earlier. Nevertheless, in part because of such administrative empire building, the New Deal period was characterized by unprecedented levels of federal involvement and expenditures on behalf of most phases of conservation. Even Pinchot was willing to concede in 1937 that "no other administration, since that of Theodore Roosevelt, has done so much for conservation as that of Franklin Roosevelt."

Conservation, Preservation, and Environmentalism

Movements to conserve natural resources for the general economic welfare began in the mid-1870s; programs for the preservation of natural beauty, wildlife, and outdoor recreation in a natural environment are of similar vintage. Within the federal government, these latter values led to the creation of such bureaus as the National Park Service and the FISH AND WILDLIFE SERVICE, much as the interests of utilitarian conservationists were largely served by the Forest Service and the Reclamation Service, among other agencies. Politically, utilitarians and preservationists clashed in the Hetch Hetchy controversy of the 1910s, in several projects for expansion of the national park system at the expense of the national forests between the wars, and again from the late 1940s through the 1960s over a number of proposed reclamation projects and forest management issues. Thereafter, the concept of protecting the quality of the total human environment for both material and nonmaterial values, having taken new form as the environmental movement, challenged both utilitarianism and preservation as the dominant theme in conservation.

The environmental movement was in part a popular crusade that arose in response to the apparent inability of government to reconcile the conflicting priorities of utilitarianism and preservation. Much like the early conservation movement in the nineteenth century, however, environmentalism was a political and social movement based on the assumption that applied concepts of stewardship and judicious use of limited resources were essential for the survival of American society.

FURTHER READING: James Leonard Bates, "Fulfilling American Democracy: The Conservation Movement, 1907–1921," *Mississippi Valley Historical Review* 44 (June 1957): 29-57. Jenks Cameron, *The Development of Governmental Forest Control in the United States* (1928).

Thomas R. Cox, "The Stewardship of Private Forests: The Evolution of a Concept in the United States, 1864–1950," *Journal of Forest History* 25 (Oct. 1981): 188–196. Whitney R. Cross, "Ideas in Politics: The Conservation Policies of the Two Roosevelts," *Journal of the History of Ideas* 14 (June 1953): 421-438, and "W J McGee and the Idea of Conservation," *Historian* 15 (Spring 1953): 148–162. Samuel Trask Dana, *Forest and Range Policy: Its Development in the United States* (1956). Samuel P. Hays, *Conservation and the Gospel of Efficiency: The Progressive Conservation Movement, 1890–1920* (1959). G. Michael McCarthy, *Hour of Trial: The Conservation Conflict in Colorado and the West, 1891–1907* (1977). M. Nelson McGeary, *Gifford Pinchot: Forester-Politician* (1960). Roderick Nash, *Wilderness and the American Mind* (1967, rev. 1982). Edgar B. Nixon, comp., *Franklin D. Roosevelt & Conservation, 1911–1945* (1957). Sherry H. Olson, *The Depletion Myth: A History of Railroad Use of Timber* (1971). E. Louise Peffer, *The Closing of the Public Domains: Disposal and Reservation Policies, 1900–1950* (1951). Gifford Pinchot, *Breaking New Ground* (1947). Richard Polenberg, *Reorganizing Roosevelt's Government: The Controversy over Executive Reorganization, 1936–1939* (1966). Elmo R. Richardson, *The Politics of Conservation: Crusades and Controversies, 1897-1913* (1962). Harold K. Steen, *The U.S. Forest Service: A History* (1976). Donald C. Swain, *Federal Conservation Policy, 1921-1933* (1963).

GARY CRAVEN GRAY

CONSERVATION ORGANIZATIONS

The CONSERVATION MOVEMENT in the United States has long been associated with membership organizations that promote public policies and educate and arouse their members and the wider public to action. In earlier years these organizations tended to be composed of leaders, often scientists and professionals, who took responsibility for promoting conservation objectives. But over the course of the twentieth century, and especially after 1960, they arose more from the general interests of citizens, developed mass memberships, and imparted a strong grass-roots flavor to organized conservation efforts.

Before 1960, conservation organizations were associated with the drives for efficiency in the development and management of forests, water, soil, and wildlife. The oldest continuously active conservation organization is the American Fisheries Society founded in 1870. The oldest one concerned with forests is the AMERICAN FORESTRY ASSOCIATION (AFA), formed in 1875, which pioneered in urging the establishment of federal forest reserves in the last quarter of the nineteenth century and in the twentieth promoted forest production, sustained-yield harvest, professional training for foresters, forestry

research, and more intensive management. Allied institutions were concerned with state forests and state forest policy. The earliest of these was the Minnesota Forestry Association, organized in 1876. The AFA encouraged the proliferation of similar organizations: between 1885 and 1901, fourteen states formed forestry associations, the most important being those established in Pennsylvania (1886) and New Hampshire (1901). Still others formed later. These groups were concerned with the role of forests in watershed protection, tended to attract people for that reason as well as for wood production, and in earlier years were sometimes known as "forests and waters" groups. They were small in membership and served primarily a leadership role. The same could be said of the BOONE AND CROCKETT CLUB (1888), ostensibly a small hunting and exploring group, several of whose members held key positions in government and elsewhere.

Also serving largely a leadership role were the Soil Conservation Society of America (1945), which brought together technical soil experts concerned with the implementation of the Soil Conservation Act of 1935, and the WILDLIFE SOCIETY (1936), composed of wildlife professionals. But these two emerging conservation interests, which came to the fore in the 1930s, also developed strong citizen components. The National Association of Soil Conservation Districts (1947) brought together leaders of rural community soil conservation efforts. A later organization, the National Watershed Congress (1954), while closely linked with soil conservation groups, served more to bring together those who promoted rural development through wetlands drainage and upstream reservoirs and helped to identify soil conservation with development at a time when the new environmental phase of the conservation movement was turning programs in a different direction. State wildlife organizations, initially in the form of groupings of local hunting or fishing clubs, were formed primarily to work toward the control of water pollution. These were brought together in 1936 into the NATIONAL WILDLIFE FEDERATION, which was the most clearly grass-roots conservation organization of the time.

While these organizations were setting the dominant tone of the conservation movement, others were more concerned with outdoor recreation and the protection of forested land from development in order to maintain its natural and aesthetic qualities. One, the SIERRA CLUB, was formed in 1892 by John MUIR and a small group of mountain climbers and others fond of the Sierra Nevada and anxious to protect the newly established YOSEMITE NATIONAL PARK. The club became deeply involved in political action to establish national parks, prevent the destruction of wild rivers by dam building, promote wilderness designations, and advance an increasingly wide range of conservation and environmental issues. Until 1950, the club remained primarily a California group, but soon after it expanded its membership and interests to the nation at large. Similar western hiking clubs, such as the Mazamas of Oregon (1894), the Mountaineers of Washington (1906), and the Colorado Mountain Club (1912), carried out like activities in their own regions but did not develop into the national force that the Sierra Club came to be. Such groups formed the FEDERATION OF WESTERN OUTDOOR CLUBS in 1932. In the eastern states, too, aesthetic and recreational interests were expressed in organizations such as the Appalachian Mountain Club (1876) and the Association for the Protection of the Adirondacks (1901). A broadening of purpose was shown by the change of the name of the Connecticut Forestry Association (formed in 1895) to the Connecticut Forest and Park Association in 1927 and that of the Massachusetts Forestry Association (formed 1898) to the Massachusetts Forest and Park Association in 1930.

National organizations had similar aesthetic and natural environment objectives. The National Parks Association was formed in 1919 by Stephen T. MATHER, first director of the National Park Service, to provide public support for that program. Lesser known, but of considerable importance before World War I, was the American Civic Association, formed by J. Horace MCFARLAND in 1906 to prevent the national parks from being absorbed by the U. S. FOREST SERVICE and to fight for a separate administration. In later years, the wilderness movement, closely allied to the national park spirit, grew in order to foster establishment of wilderness areas, Robert MARSHALL formed the WILDERNESS SOCIETY in 1935 to promote this cause. The society became increasingly active in the years after World War II, leading the fight for the Wilderness Act of 1964. Two more specialized national organizations, the IZAAK WALTON LEAGUE OF AMERICA, formed in 1943, and the later Trout Unlimited (1958), both originating as fishermen's groups, played important roles in outdoor recreation objectives, such as the protection of the Boundary Waters Canoe Area and the development of the new outdoor recreation program which emerged in the late 1950s.

These organizations were still relatively small as the new environmental phase of the conservation movement began to grow in force in the 1960s. Those concerned with natural and aesthetic values, such as the Sierra Club and the Wilderness Society, made especially rapid membership gains after 1960. The National Parks Association changed its name in 1971 to the NATIONAL PARKS AND CONSERVATION ASSOCIATION, seeking to take on a broader range of issues. Even more striking was the rapid growth of the Audubon Societies. The National Association of Audubon Societies, organized in 1905 to foster a concern for protecting birds from commercial exploitation, had tended to generate separate state organizations which went their own ways and did not work effectively on the national scene. Reorganized in 1940 as the NATIONAL AUDUBON SOCIETY, it underwent a significant revival, grew rapidly, and by the end of the 1970s reached 360,000 members. It brought to conservation issues an emphasis especially on appreciative or nonconsumptive uses of wildlife, as opposed to hunting, and tended to benefit from the very rapid growth of public interest in "nongame" wildlife activities.

This environmental phase brought new points of view into conservation affairs which presented some of the older organizations with new challenges. The AFA did not feel comfortable with the growing interest in outdoor recreation in the 1960s and especially feared that it would restrict the use of forestlands for wood production. It drew back from the objectives of the NATIONAL PARK SERVICE as expressed in its ten-year program, "Mission 66," adopted in 1956, which called for doubling the facilities in the national parks, and opposed early moves for the preservation of wild rivers such as the Allagash in Maine. It was the last of the older conservation organizations to become reconciled to the wilderness legislation debated by Congress between 1956 and 1964. AFA continued to associate itself with older styles of conservation, emphasizing sustained-yield wood production, and, while losing members over its opposition to wilderness, gained more among woodland owners interested in tree farming, industrial forestland owners, and the timber industry. Along with many of its state counterparts, AFA feared much of the environmental movement, expressed the more limited interest in wood production, and remained aloof from many newer environmental activities. By the late 1970s, it was referred to at times in the nation's capital as a "trade association" rather than a conservation organization.

The National Wildlife Federation (NWF) went through a different history. Although it remained based upon the state organizations of hunters and fishermen, as a national federation of these groups it also developed a new category of individual membership for individuals interested in wildlife. By 1980, the NWF had reached over three-quarters of a million individual members. These were far more interested in appreciative uses of wildlife and related issues of environmental pollution. Some state wildlife affiliates remained interested only in hunting and fishing and shunned connections with the newer appreciative wildlife enthusiasts, but others sought out cooperation and took up the newer issues. The Pennsylvania Federation of Sportsmen was an example of the first; the Michigan United Conservation Clubs, of the second. At the national level, the National Wildlife Federation took an aggressive stance which brought it into active cooperation with many of the newer trends of the time. Because of its interest in wildlife habitat it could readily find common ground with both wilderness-type organizations and those interested in pollution.

Even more important was the spate of new groups that arose in the late 1960s and throughout the 1970s. Some of these were organizations based in Washington, D.C., to lobby for new conservation laws, such as Environmental Action (1970), the Environmental Policy Center (1972), and Defenders of Wildlife (a descendant of the Anti-Steel-Trap League founded in 1925). Two notable specialized organizations served as environmental litigation groups, bringing a variety of legal actions especially against administrative agencies for failing to implement new laws; these were the Environmental Defense Fund (1967) and the Natural Resources Defense Council (1970). Especially active in a wide range of issues in the nation's capital was Friends of the Earth, formed in 1969 by David BROWER after he was dismissed as executive director of the Sierra Club. Friends of the Earth remained small, some 25,000 members, but had a keen political sense and was impelled vigorously by Brower's infectious inspiration. The American Rivers Conservation Council (1973) was formed to protect free-flowing streams, and the Public Lands Institute (1977), located in Washington, D.C., was organized to deal with western public lands issues. A little known, but growing, organization was the Oceanic Society (1969), concerned with coastal and ocean issues, which by 1980 had reached over 60,000 members. In the background of these membership groups, playing somewhat more of a leadership role as technical experts, were the Conservation Foundation (1948), which had already proven influential among conservation opinion leaders, and its offspring, the Environmental Law Institute (1970).

Even more significant, however, was the degree to which conservation organizations arose rapidly at the regional and state levels. Whereas most of the vigorous activity had previously taken place in national organizations, the new grass-roots citizen component spawned a host of local and state groups. Some of these, such as the Oregon Environmental Council (1968) and the Maryland Conservation Council, dealt with legislative and administrative issues, keeping members abreast of public matters in their own states. Some dealt with regional concerns such as the protector of the western deserts, the Desert Protective Council (formed in 1954). Within the West, new statewide wilderness organizations arose to deal with issues in specific states such as California, Oregon, Washington, New Mexico, Wyoming, and Utah, and a new national group, the American Wilderness Alliance, was established in Denver in 1978.

Beyond all this, one could describe an almost uncountable number of local organizations that grew up to deal with particular environmental conservation problems. Some died when the issue was resolved, but many continued, often in the form of separate groups, but equally often as local branches of national organizations such as Trout Unlimited, the Sierra Club, the Audubon Society, and the NATURE CONSERVANCY. Some sought to protect a particular park or wetland from destruction by the building of a highway or the siting of an industrial facility. Others formed to protest pesticide spraying of mosquitoes in suburban areas or spruce budworm in Maine. Some organized to protect a free-flowing stream from construction of a dam and still others emerged when citizens joined together to protect their local community from a hazardous waste site or other threat of environmental degradation.

Through this survey of conservation organizations one can observe two major trends. First was the long-term shift in composition from professional leaders to the general public; as one moved into the environmental era of conservation activities, the grass-roots component of organizations rose steadily. This accounts for the enormous range and variety of groups formed. Second were the changing objectives which these organizations reflected. While some groups continued effectively to further the earlier goal of efficient resource development in matters of forests, water, soil, and wildlife, newer groups placed more emphasis on the conservation of the environment surrounding people in work, home, and play in order to maintain a level of quality of air, water, and land that would enhance daily human life. These historical trends can be read dramatically through the lives of the conservation organizations themselves.

SAMUEL P. HAYS

CONSULTING FORESTRY

The growth of American forestry has provided increasing opportunities for self-employed foresters who serve as consultants by providing professional advice and services for fees. As early as 1893, Gifford PINCHOT opened an office in New York City in order to be available as a consulting forester. In this capacity he made surveys of the forestlands of several wealthy owners in the Adirondacks and prepared plans for the application of forestry principles in the management of their lands. As a consultant for the State of New Jersey, he prepared a report recommending improved methods of forest-fire control and assessing the state's timber resources. Unlike Pinchot's consulting services, which were concerned primarily with SILVICULTURE, most early consulting forestry work dealt with determination of the volume of the timber on areas being traded or logged by wood-using industries. This emphasis was evident, for example, in the pioneering consulting work of Austin CARY in New Hampshire and Maine during the 1890s.

By the 1920s, the number of consulting foresters had slowly increased and their work tended to extend beyond timber cruising to varied silvicultural investigations. The consulting firm established by David T. MASON in Portland, Oregon, in 1921, typified the new interests. The firm soon became engaged in the development of forestry programs for several redwood properties and began to recommend application of the principle of sustained yield. In more recent years, consulting firms have usually provided the following services: timber valuation and appraisal, forest management plans, silvicultural and utilization recommendations, and timber volume and quality estimates. These services were provided mainly to owners of large forest tracts, but they became increasingly employed by smaller nonindustrial owners as well, particularly after the rise of the tree farm movement in the 1940s. Such services may involve brief consultations on specific problems, possibly with foresters permanently employed by industrial owners, or long-term study and management of forest properties. They may include work in locating sites for new industrial developments and in appraising domestic and foreign timber investments.

Public agencies often encourage and assist in the development of consulting forestry by recommending consulting foresters to prospective clients, providing lists of consultants, and disseminating results of forest research. Such agencies provide educational programs on forestry opportunities and thereby stimulate forest landowners to seek professional guidance from consultants.

In 1910, there were probably fewer than a dozen consulting foresters in the United States. By 1950, there were some 150 firms providing advice and services and employing more than 200 foresters. During the 1970s, there were approximately 1,000 consulting foresters or about 12 percent of the total of privately employed foresters in the country. The growth of consulting forestry has been stimulated to a great degree since the 1930s by the need of forest products industries for technical assistance to increase efficiency and profits, especially in expanding pulp and paper production operations and in the need of commercial forestland owners for specialized managerial services.

FURTHER READING: There is no detailed history of American consulting forestry, but useful references to the subject appear in Henry Clepper, *Professional Forestry in the United States* (1971), and Norman Munster and Arthur Spillers, "Consulting Foresters," USDA, *Trees: Yearbook of Agriculture* (1949).

HAROLD T. PINKETT

CONTAINER INDUSTRY

See Box and Container Industry

CONVICT LABOR IN FOREST INDUSTRIES

Leasing of convicts to private companies began long before the Civil War and was not limited to the Southern states, but it was in the South after 1865 that state and county prisoners constituted a large portion of the labor force in the lumber and naval stores industries (see LUMBER INDUSTRY: SOUTHERN STATES and NAVAL STORES). Without a tradition of supporting public institutions and with depressed economies, the former Confederate states began leasing their prisoners to avoid the costs of internment facilities. Many counties followed suit. At the same time, the lumber and naval stores industries were expanding rapidly in the region. Although they competed with mining, railroad, and agricultural interests in seeking to obtain convict labor, large firms engaged in the forest industries often obtained contracts entitling them to all the prisoners of a state for a specified period, usually two years. Sometimes they subleased some of them, but in any case there was little control by the state over the way the companies employed the prisoners. Since logging and turpentine camps were usually isolated far out in the woods, camp managers and woods riders were free to handle prisoners as they saw fit. Absentee owners, many from Northern states and England, rarely questioned the methods as long as they were profitable.

County leases were even more conducive to abuse. Company agents frequently contracted with sheriffs to supply specified numbers of prisoners. Since many county prisoners received short sentences, sheriffs were often obliged to use creative methods to make their quotas. As vagrancy was a punishable crime, blacks and whites alike traveled at great risk wherever they were not well known. Once enmeshed in the system, prisoners were often kept in the camps by debt peonage. Although holding a person to labor for debt was a violation of the United States statutes, the law was made ineffective by the Supreme Court's decision in the 1904 Clyatt case.

Conditions varied from camp to camp, but all were grim. Prisoners were chained at night, and in some turpentine camps they worked in chains. They were always under control of armed guards, and dogs were used to find the occasional runaways. Whipping was a common punishment for many infractions, including the inability to work fast enough. Workdays were often fourteen hours, and the work was heavy and exhausting.

Demands for the cessation of convict leasing came from reformers in the early twentieth century. Some states enacted better controls, and some began building prisons. Since counties and states were beginning to build roads, that soon seemed to be a better way to use prisoners than to lease them to private firms. Exposés of horrible abuses reached national attention in the early 1920s when Martin Tabert's murder in a Florida convict camp triggered many investigations. Several states had already ended the leasing system and the others soon followed. Although collusion between local officials and some employers kept many people in debt peonage in logging and turpentine camps for another thirty years, official leasing ended shortly after World War I. Because of the informality of much of the system, reliable statistics are unavailable, but more than 10,000 convicts were working in the Southern forests during most of the years just before the war.

FURTHER READING: Pete Daniel, *The Shadow of Slavery: Peonage in the South, 1901–1969* (1972). Daniel A. Novak, *Wheel of Servitude: Black Forced Labor After Slavery* (1978). J. C. Powell, *American Siberia, or, Fourteen Years' Experience in a Southern Convict Camp* (1891). Jerrell H. Shofner, "Forced Labor in the Florida Forests: 1880–1950," *Journal of Forest History* 25 (Jan. 1981): 14-25.

JERRELL H. SHOFNER

COOPERAGE INDUSTRY

"Cooperage is the science of making barrels, kegs, tubs, pails, and other containers of pieces of wood known as staves and heading bound together by hoops" (Brown 1937, p. 199). Cooperage is a very ancient art, dating to the beginning of the Christian era and even earlier. The trade is divided into two broad divisions: tight and slack cooperage. This classification is made on the basis that tight cooperage has the ability to hold liquids, and slack cooperage is generally used to contain flour, sugar, and other solid materials.

The beginning of the American cooperage industry can be traced to *Mayflower* passenger John Alden. He was hired as a cooper at Southampton, where the *Mayflower* was outfitted. Early American cooper shops like Alden's were usually backroom or shed operations, in which a cooper with hand tools was able to make two or three barrels a day.

The century following the Revolutionary War was a time of rapid growth, and the demand for all types of cooperage began to exceed the productive capacity of the hand shops. This insufficiency of supply became very evident after the first oil well was drilled near Titusville, Pennsylvania; oil was transported in wooden barrels. In the first year of its discovery, 2,000 wooden oil barrels were required; by 1863, more than 3 million barrels were used to ship oil. The oil industry spread from Pennsylvania into New York and other states, creating an unprecedented demand for barrels. During this time, hand shops were converted to large mechanized cooperage plants.

The cooperage industry reached its greatest productivity about 1900. The wooden barrel was almost universally used as a shipping container and was known as the king of packages. Cooperage manufacturers annually consumed an estimated 1.8 billion board feet of wood during this time, and approximately 60 percent of this volume was processed into slack barrels. The hardwood species preferred for slack cooperage included oak, gum (red, tupelo, and black), maple, ash, elm, beech, birch, cottonwood, and basswood; yellow pine, Douglas-fir, and ponderosa pine were among the preferred softwoods. White oak, because of its impermeable nature, strength, workability, and excellent seasoning qualities, is preeminently the best tight cooperage wood. Limited amounts of red oak, red gum, and white ash have been used in tight barrels for liquids.

By the 1960s, changes in consumer buying habits, new packaging techniques, and a system of freight rates based upon the gross weight of packages encouraged the development of lightweight containers made of materials other than wood. Steel, aluminum, corrugated paper, and fiberboard containers resulted in a greatly reduced demand for wood cooperage. Timber usage has now dropped to an estimated 200 million

Bundles of 100 chestnut staves are ready for assembly into barrels. Forest History Society Lantern Slide Collection.

board feet per year, and almost all of it is white oak for tight cooperage.

The last remaining significant markets for wooden barrels in the United States are for aging bourbon whiskey and wine. White oak and redwood are used exclusively for this purpose. The bourbon industry averaged filling 2,010,212 barrels per year from the repeal of Prohibition in 1933 through 1973. Since that time, the average per year has been 1,202,748 barrels. This decrease can be attributed to barreling at a higher proof while marketing at a lower proof. In the early 1980s, barrels were being made to contain fifty-three gallons instead of the previous standard of fifty gallons.

American white oak is a preferred species as an aging container for spirits in other countries as well. Exports account for an estimated 40 to 50 million board feet annually of white oak shipped as staves and heading pieces to the United Kingdom, Spain, Canada, Japan, and other nations.

The outlook for the future of the cooperage industry is probably limited to spirit and wine aging. The wine market appears to be increasing while spirits, including bourbon and scotch, are static or even declining.

FURTHER READING: Nelson C. Brown, *Timber Products and Industries* (1937). Franklin E. Coyne, *The Development of the Cooperage Industry in the United States, 1620–1940* (1946). Hu Maxwell, "The Uses of Wood: Wood Used in the Cooperage Industry," *American Forestry* 25 (July 1919): 1206–1216.

DAVID M. MEEKS

COOPERATIVE FORESTRY

Cooperative forestry today involves a broad scope of activities. National and international cooperation among research institutions, public and private, is widespread; closer ties are being forged with users of research results through sophisticated planning processes and feedback mechanisms. Public land managers are seeking ever closer cooperation among their respective agencies in planning, technical communications, policy development, and standardization. In the state and private forestry field, a complex interrelationship of public and private agencies and programs comprises cooperative arrangements for 37 million acres of nonfederal public forestland, 65 million acres of industrial land, and 238 million acres of nonindustrial private land.

Although cooperative efforts have been moving ahead at an accelerated pace, there are still and probably always will be conflicting goals and objectives among the many hundreds of public and private organizations engaged in forest conservation activities and the formulation of forest policies. However, improved communications, induced by improved cooperation, have resulted in better understanding of the various views of all concerned.

The core of public state and private forestry programs is the unique partnership of the U. S. FOREST SERVICE and cooperating state and territorial forestry agencies. This federal–state partnership carries out major programs on nonfederal public and private lands in rural fire prevention and protection, forest pest management, forest management and use, forest products utilization, tree seedling production, tree improvement, and forest resources planning and development.

Other federal, state, and local agencies are also involved. Most cooperative state extension services and land grant colleges and universities conduct educational programs for woodland owners, forest products processors, and other forest users. The Soil Conservation Service provides conservation plans to rural landowners, with recommendations for woodland uses and soil mapping, watershed planning and operations, resource conservation and development projects, and related soil and water activities—all contributing to forest conservation. The Agricultural Stabilization and Conservation Service offers cost-sharing programs, and the Farmers Home Administration loan programs aid nonindustrial private forest owners with tree planting, timber stand improvement, and other special forest practices. State conservation districts cooperate with state foresters in the protection, management, and use of forestlands and resources on privately owned lands in their districts. A number of youth and adult employment and training programs of the Department of Labor are used by state foresters for forest conservation programs on nonfederal public lands. Many counties, cities, and other local governments carry out forest protection and management programs of various kinds, often in cooperation with federal and/or state agencies.

In the private sector, a notable advance has been the growth of the body of professional consulting foresters. From only a handful after World War II, the ranks had swelled to a thousand or more by 1980. Also in the private sector, the forest industries offer technical forestry services to nonindustrial private forest owners and sponsor tree farms in most states.

Some historians may differ, but this remarkable cooperative effort began when President Abraham Lincoln signed An Act to Establish a Department of Agriculture on May 15, 1862. This act included a charge to "acquire and diffuse among the people of the United States useful information on subjects connected with agriculture in the most general and comprehensive sense of that word, and to procure, propagate, and distribute among the people new and valuable seeds and plants." A further charge was "to acquire . . . all information concerning agriculture by means of books and correspondence, and by practical and scientific experiments."

Concurrently, many midwestern states and territories passed laws to encourage tree planting. Nebraska was among the first, in 1861, followed by Iowa, Kansas, Dakota Territory, Minnesota, and Missouri. Michigan and Wisconsin were the first states to set up study commissions to look into forest protection needs (1867). In 1872, Nebraska proclaimed the first ARBOR DAY.

In 1873, William M. Brewer offered regular lectures in forestry at Yale University, but an equally noteworthy event was Franklin B. HOUGH's address delivered at the annual meeting of the American Association for the Advancement of Science, held in Portland, Maine. Hough's paper, entitled, "On the Duty of Governments in the Preservation of Forests," eventually resulted in a rider to an appropriation act for fiscal 1877, approved August 15, 1876, which constitutes the beginning of the Forest Service of today. This proviso, engineered by Congressman Mark H. Dunnell of Minnesota, directed the commissioner of agriculture to expend $2,000 for forestry investigations and inquiries and to report to Congress. This study was the beginning of General Forestry Assistance funds, which are appropriated for Forest Service use to this day.

Commissioner of Agriculture Frederick Watts appointed Hough on August 10, 1876, to carry out this program. Hough produced three impressive volumes, abstracting the forestry knowledge of the Western world, presenting statistics on foreign commerce, and recommending actions to advance forestry in the United States. In 1881, a Division of Forestry was established in the DEPARTMENT OF AGRICULTURE. Hough, until then a "forestry agent," was named chief.

In 1875, the AMERICAN FORESTRY ASSOCIATION was founded in Chicago, largely through the work of John A. Warder of Ohio. This citizens' association has been instrumental in the support of numerous advances in state and private forestry throughout the past century.

During the tenures of Nathaniel EGLESTON (1883–1886) and Bernhard E. FERNOW (1886–1898) as chiefs of the Division of Forestry, federal activities in the state and private forestry field were practically nil. Fernow, the first trained forester to hold public office, did make some notable advances in forestry research and forestry education. But it remained for his successor, Gifford PINCHOT, to give real impetus to state and private forestry at the federal level.

Earlier, Pinchot had turned down a job with the Division of Forestry, upon completion of his forestry studies in Europe, to undertake development of a forest management plan for the Biltmore Forest in North Carolina. This forest, established by George W. Vanderbilt, is recognized as the first managed forest in the United States. In 1898, Pinchot replaced Fernow as chief of the Division of Forestry. In the appropriation act approved March 1, 1899, the division was authorized for the first time "to advise the owners of woodlands as to the proper care of the same." In an act approved on March 21, 1901, the division achieved bureau status and was authorized to set up five field offices.

Shortly after taking office, Pinchot issued Division of Forestry Circular No. 21, offering technical assistance to lumber companies. The service proved popular. By 1905, some 11 million acres of private land had been or were being studied. In 1899, Circular No. 22 offered planning assistance for tree planting on private lands. By 1904, 334 plans for planting more than 13,000 acres had been prepared. In 1905, the unit of private lands was in the management division, and cooperative tree planting was a unit in the extension division. In 1908, a separate Office of State and Private Cooperation was established in Forest Service headquarters.

State forestry, meanwhile, underwent many years of agonizing birth pains, at least in the view of many of its early advocates. California had acquired the Yosemite Valley and Mariposa Big Trees Grove in 1866 as a state park, the first state park and first dedication of forestland in the nation. In 1885, New York established the Adirondack and Catskill Forest Preserves and created a forest commission. That same year, California, Ohio, and Colorado each passed a law authorizing a state forestry agency, but only New York's endured. In 1887, Kansas established an Office of Commissioner of Forestry. In 1891, Maine's Forest Commission was established, the forerunner of the Maine Forest Service. In 1895, Pennsylvania established a Bureau of Forestry, which achieved department status in 1901. At the dawn of the twentieth century, New Hampshire, Minnesota, and Michigan rounded out the seven states with forestry agencies.

In the first decade of the 1900s, the Forest Service began cooperative projects with several states. Passage of the WEEKS ACT in 1911 gave added emphasis to this cooperation by providing authority for federal–state cooperation in fire protection. By 1924, twenty-nine states had cooperative agreements with the Forest Service under this legislation.

Cooperative extension forestry, through the land grant colleges and universities, began in 1914 with passage of the Smith-Lever Act. This law provided for outreach educational activities for people not attending participating universities. The nature of extension work has changed little through succeeding years.

In 1920, the NATIONAL ASSOCIATION OF STATE FORESTERS was founded at a meeting in Harrisburg, Pennsylvania. Today, the executive committee of this association serves as adviser to the secretary of agriculture in matters related to the most recent cooperative forestry legislation.

The CLARKE-MCNARY ACT of 1924 was a milestone in the history of cooperative forestry. This law not only strengthened the Weeks Act provision for cooperation in forest fire protection but also included provisions for cooperative tree planting and forestry extension programs. Within five years of passage, thirty-eight states had cooperative fire protection agreements with the Forest Service, and thirty-one states had cooperative extension forestry programs. Growth of extension forestry was particularly noteworthy, since only four states had such programs in 1924. Many new state tree nurseries were established as a result of the Clarke-McNary Act. By 1930, almost 26 million trees were shipped out from state nurseries for field planting.

The 1930s brought the Great Depression, severe drought, and President Franklin D. ROOSEVELT. Under Roosevelt's leadership, the Prairie States Forestry Project (Shelterbelt), TENNESSEE VALLEY AUTHORITY, Soil Conservation Act of 1935, Agricultural Conservation Program, Cooperative Farm Forestry Act (Norris-Doxey Act) of 1937, and other conservation measures were launched. Each of these was the progenitor of programs in existence today.

The Tennessee Valley Authority was established by Congress in May 1933. It has been a model of cooperative forestry, transforming an abused and neglected forest resource into an economic and social asset for the thousands of owners of small tracts that comprise almost all of the forestland base.

The shelterbelt project was directly responsible for passage of the Cooperative Farm Forestry Act in 1937. Support for the shelterbelt program was kept alive and strengthened by broadening its concept of private landowner assistance nationwide. The Cooperative Forest Management Act of 1950 strengthened the program of private landowner assistance and added provisions for assistance to operators and processors of forest products.

In 1933, the Soil Erosion Service was set up in the DEPARTMENT OF THE INTERIOR. In 1935, it was transferred to the Department of Agriculture and formally established as the Soil Conservation Service (SCS) through passage of the Soil Conservation Act. In its early years, the service was very active in providing forestry assistance to small landowners. As state forestry agencies grew in their ability to provide similar services, the forestry aspect of the SCS program was reduced to its current level of providing conservation planning, including forestland use recommendations, to farmers and other private landowners.

The Agriculture Conservation Program provided cost-sharing for farmers. Tree planting and timber stand improvement practices originally were authorized as erosion control measures. In 1973, the Agriculture and Consumer Protection Act authorized the Forest Incentives Program, offering cost-sharing to nonindustrial forestland owners for carrying out forestry measures to provide for production of timber and other benefits.

The American Tree Farm Program was launched in 1941 by the American Forest Product Industries, Inc. (now AMERICAN FOREST INSTITUTE). At that time, some 650 professional foresters were employed by forestry firms. In the ensuing years, this number has increased at least tenfold. Many of the forest industries conduct cooperative forestry programs with private landowners in their operating areas, providing genetically improved planting stock, forest management planning assistance, and selective harvesting programs.

With passage of the Cooperative Forest Management Act of 1950, service forestry in the states burgeoned. Within ten years, forty-six states and Puerto Rico had adopted the program. By the early 1980s, all fifty states, Guam, Puerto Rico, and the Virgin Islands participated.

In 1947, Congress enacted the Forest Pest Control Act and made the Forest Service responsible for the management of forest pests on all ownerships, greatly enhancing cooperative programs. By the 1980s, all fifty states had adopted legislation that permits federal–state cooperation in insect and disease control.

Small watershed and flood control programs are carried out in cooperation with the Forest Service, state foresters, SCS, and soil conservation districts throughout the United States. The Forest Service, through state foresters, is responsible for the forestry aspects of these programs.

The Rural Development Act of 1972 authorized the secretary of agriculture to develop a three-year pilot Rural Community Fire Protection Project. This program has extended Forest Service–state forester cooperation to thousands of local fire departments in communities of less than 10,000 population.

The Cooperative Forestry Assistance Act of 1978 brought together and broadened legislation that had been enacted in the previous three decades. Under this legislation, the secretary of agriculture is authorized to provide financial and technical assistance to state foresters to develop genetically improved tree seeds; procure, produce, and distribute tree seeds and seedlings; plant trees; plan and implement forestry measures on nonfederal lands; protect and improve watersheds; and provide technical and financial forestry assistance to private forestland owners, vendors, operators, wood processors, and public agencies.

The act also broadened insect and disease control to cover protection of wood products. A new section provided authority for urban forestry assistance. Rural fire prevention and control included authority for cooperation with local fire-fighting forces and a special rural fire disaster fund to supplement authority available under the Federal Disaster Act. There are also provisions for (1) forest resources planning by the states to consolidate overall forestry planning activities under the umbrella of the FOREST AND RANGELAND RENEWABLE RESOURCES PLANNING ACT; (2) organization management assistance for state cooperators; and (3) technology implementation assistance for state foresters and other state agencies. It also provides for consolidated payments to states based on state forest resource programs developed by the state.

The Renewable Resources Extension Act of 1978 provided for an expansion of forestry extension activities. The act called for development of a five-year "Renewable Resources Extension Program" to direct and guide state extension directors in the development of similar state level programs. This act contains a September 30, 1988, "sunset" clause.

The 1970s were noteworthy for numerous efforts to seek a common ground among forestland owners, forest industry, various conservation organizations, and public agencies for building effective cooperative forestry programs. These efforts are ongoing. However, the 1980s may well usher in a new national consciousness of the importance of the privately owned forestlands in the United States.

FURTHER READING: Henry Clepper, *Professional Forestry in the United States* (1971). Samuel Trask Dana, *Forest and Range Policy* (1956). Jay P. Kinney, *Development of*

Forest Law in America (1917). Harold K. Steen, *The U.S. Forest Service: A History* (1976). Ralph R. Widner, ed. *Forests and Forestry in the American States* (1968).

RICHARD L. KNOX

COPELAND REPORT

A National Plan for American Forestry was issued by the U. S. Senate on March 13, 1933. This two-volume, 1,677-page study had been prepared by the U. S. FOREST SERVICE and described and evaluated all aspects of forestry for both the public and private sectors. It was compiled under the direction of Assistant Chief Earle H. CLAPP and was named for Senator Royal Copeland of New York, who had introduced a resolution requesting the information.

The study provided a blueprint for New Deal forestry and included analyses of timber, water, range, recreation, and wildlife resources. It also dealt with FORESTRY RESEARCH and federal–state cooperative programs. The modern concept of multiple use received its first substantive treatment. Throughout the 1930s, references to the Copeland Report appeared in a full range of studies and reports, attesting to its usefulness. An objective measure of the degree of its implementation is made difficult by the tumultuous context of the Depression and approaching World War II.

The report received mixed reviews, for its recommendations offended certain sectors of the forestry community. Some foresters opposed the idea of becoming politically active, preferring to view their profession as an application of the natural sciences. Industrial readers were disappointed by the scathing rebuke they suffered, as part of Forest Service rationale for its recommendations, for example, to purchase $50 million worth of private forestland per year under the aegis of the CLARKE-MCNARY ACT. The report also recommended federal regulation of logging private land, a volatile issue until the 1950s.

Most evaluations, however, were complimentary. The AMERICAN FORESTRY ASSOCIATION judged the report to be an "extraordinarily able analysis of the forest situation in this country." Much more than a historical oddity, the Copeland Report offers a state-of-the-art view of American forestry and forestland issues during the 1930s.

FURTHER READING: *A National Plan for American Forestry* (1933). Harold K. Steen, *The U. S. Forest Service: A History* (1976).

CORK

Cork is the outer bark or phellum of an evergreen oak, *Quercus suber*. Because its natural function is purely protection and its removal under proper circumstances does not damage the cambium, harvesting the bark does not kill nor apparently shorten the life of the tree. Since antiquity, cork has been used by seafarers and fishermen for floats and, after the invention of the glass bottle in the seventh century, as a stopper. The best quality cork is still used for these purposes as well as, in the machine age, for gaskets and other high-pressure sealers. Inferior cork is ground and used in a wide variety of compositions. In the twentieth century it was combined with asphalt, rubber, and synthetics in the manufacture of flooring and other building materials. Cork was the most common insulating material in the early days of refrigeration and is still used for that purpose to some extent, usually in combination with other materials.

Naturally, *Quercus suber* flourishes in a rather narrow range of climate, elevation, and soils on the shores of the Mediterranean, especially in Spain and Portugal. As early as 1790, the acorns of the tree were planted in the southeastern United States. In 1858, the U. S. Patent Office sponsored a large-scale attempt to introduce the tree to the South and to California where several thousand cork oaks were planted in twenty-one counties. Again in 1904, the University of California made substantial plantings in parks and along roadways. In 1940, Woodbridge Metcalf, a Berkeley scientist, stripped 166 of 300 *Quercus suber* in Chico, California, but with ambivalent results. In the same year, C. E. McManus of Baltimore launched a campaign to promote the planting of the tree in the southeastern United States.

The most intensive campaign to develop the cork oak in the United States was begun in 1942 when, in cooperation with the University of California, the U. S. FOREST SERVICE systematically planted, thence monitored, 4,500 acorns in the foothills ringing the Central Valley and the Los Angeles basin. The Forest Service hoped the tree would flourish in badly burnt districts but the result was a disappointment.

However, the cork oak did quite well in most areas where the native live oak flourished and in 1949 a census found 4,000 mature trees in California, 40 in Arizona, and 60 in the Southeast.

This was not enough to excite the interest of the cork manufacturers' industrial association, the Cork Institute of America, and most companies continued to import their materials. Although the trees reproduce easily, may be harvested decennially for 100 to 150 years, and grow on land otherwise of limited use, the harvesting of cork is a tedious manual operation requiring some skills. Given the high costs of labor and the relatively low value of raw cork, importation remained more attractive. In 1980, the United States was still the world's largest consumer of the product although the number of companies using it had declined drastically. With only seven members remaining in the 1960s, the Cork Institute itself dissolved.

CUTOVER LANDS

This term is generally used to describe coniferous forestlands from which the marketable timber has been removed. It came into use in the 1880s and 1890s, particularly in the Lake States, where lumbermen usually took the pine first and years later returned to cut such hemlock and hardwoods as could be marketed. The cutover lands were the result of commercial lumbering operations. They were not lands cleared for farming. The term early came to carry the connotation that these lands presented special difficulties in being converted into productive farms, and, accordingly, they represented something new in the history of land occupation and farm making in America, where it had come to be assumed that wherever large trees had grown, fine productive fields could and would be made. It seemed almost a law of nature that the plow followed the ax.

Since most of the land of the eastern United States was covered by forests, stumps and stumplands were a part of the farmers' westering experience from Jamestown and Plymouth Rock to the prairies of Illinois. The farm makers who pushed inland from the Atlantic Coast faced a monumental, often lifelong task of clearing the land of trees and brush to make fields for planting.

The number and state of decay of the stumps in roadway, field, or village square mirrored the age and progress of a settlement. During the early years, large stumps in a village or near a crossroads served as plat-

In areas where agriculture followed closely behind logging, land was converted from one productive use to another with minimal dislocation. In other areas, lumbermen provided cleared land far in excess of agricultural needs, and these often abandoned "cutover lands" became a problem for government to solve. Louisiana Forestry Commission Photo.

forms for preachers, politicians, peddlers, auctioneers, and others. Figurative uses of the word stump multiplied in the American language and many of those usages still remain. Politicians, for example, still take to the stump or stump the country, although they travel by airplane and speak in auditoriums. Most Americans will admit that they have been stumped from time to time.

This process of farm making is also reflected in the agricultural census, first taken in 1850. Farms were counted and the number of acres in each farm reported. The land in farms was recorded as "improved" or "unimproved." This rudimentary land classification continued to be used until 1925, although in 1870, at least four decades after settlers had entered the western prairies, the census divided unimproved land in farms into woodland and other lands. Thus it could probably be said that by 1870 the men in Washington, D. C., who directed the census had discovered that not all farms were made by clearing off the forests.

However, in the great movement of land occupation west of the Appalachians, it was little noticed that in the forests of New England and upper New York, where lumbermen had cut the pine and moved on, there was much difficulty in making farms where forests had been removed. Pine stumps seemed indestructible and impervious to rot. Talleyrand, who engaged in some land speculation in New England and New York in the mid-1790s, denounced the lumberman as interested only in cutting down the trees, then leaving without regret, "If in leaving he does not forget his axe." Perhaps it was natural for lumbermen to cut and get out. Everybody knew that the forests of America were limitless and inexhaustible. There was no need to husband resources. Beyond New England were the forests around the Great Lakes and before those were cut, the even more magnificent forests of the West Coast had come into view.

The forests of northern Michigan, northern Wisconsin, and northeastern Minnesota provided some of the finest trees for lumber encountered by Americans in the western march. The spreading settlement that pushed beyond the wooded lands into the prairies and plains of the Mississippi Valley, the rising cities, the constantly improving transportation network in the interior, and the rapidly advancing lumbering technology all combined to provide a growing market for the Lake States lumbermen. Most were little interested in seeing their cutover lands transformed into farms. Indeed, many wanted no farm settlers on the land until they had taken what they wanted, because settlers would increase taxes by demanding roads, schools, and other services. Moreover, this cutover land was not attractive to farm makers. It was often covered with the tangled debris left by the logger and dotted by defective pine and other useless trees. The soil was too often sandy, full of rocks and stones, or badly drained. Worst of all, the pine stumps seemed incapable of rotting. They had to be grubbed or blasted out. Added to all this, fires often ran unchecked in the cutover and made the land even more unattractive to the farmer. In 1897, Filibert Roth, a member of the U. S. Division of Forestry, surveyed forestry conditions in northern Wisconsin and was appalled by what he saw. "Logging," he wrote, "has been carried on in almost every town of this region, and over 8 million of the 17 million acres of forest are cutover lands, largely burned over and waste brush lands, and one half of it as nearly desert as it can become in the climate of Wisconsin."

By the 1890s, it was becoming clear to businessmen and politicians that the forests of the Lake States were disappearing. Many had assumed that farm makers would occupy the cutover lands naturally and thus provide a new economic base for the once forested northern counties. But land seekers continued to be drawn to the western plains, and the lengthening lists of tax-delinquent land suggested that farmers needed to be encouraged to settle in the cutover. Encouragement came from all sides from the 1890s to the early 1920s. During these decades, a vast amount of energy was expended in finding ways of attracting farmers. A host of agencies, some public, some private, were created to carry this cause forward. States established immigration agencies and counties voted money for advertising. Lumber companies, railroads, chambers of commerce, land colonization companies, real estate companies and agents all joined in producing propaganda and seeking other means to promote land settlement of these empty cutover lands.

In Wisconsin, for example, the College of Agriculture was brought into the campaign. In 1896, the dean of the college brought together a settler's guide dealing with the "agricultural opportunities" of the area. The book, *Northern Wisconsin: A Handbook for the Homeseeker*, was widely used. Over 50,000 copies were circulated during the first two years after publication. Later, the college established branch experiment stations in the north, and with the creation of the system of county agricultural agents, the first eleven county agents served in the cutover lands.

For several decades many assumed that pine stumps were the most serious obstacle to converting the cutover lands into farms. The College of Agriculture, the U. S. DEPARTMENT OF AGRICULTURE, and private agencies worked separately and together to find quick, cheap, easy ways of removing stumps—a task they never accomplished. The end of World War I promised an abundance of surplus explosives and for a few years hopes were high that, with cheap explosives and high farm prices, the cutover land would at last be converted. In 1921, Dean Harry L. Russell estimated that in Wisconsin alone, with 8.5 million acres of land available, 100,000 new farms could be made in a region of "adequate rainfall and good soil." However, the collapse of farm prices and the mounting farm surpluses of the 1920s spelled an end to forty years of farm promotion in the cutover of the Lake States. A similar story unfolded in the logged-off lands of Washington, Oregon, California, and the southern yellow pine region.

In 1928, B. H. Hibbard and associates published a study of *Tax Delinquency in Northern Wisconsin.* In seventeen of the northern counties of Wisconsin, only 6 percent of the land was actually in crops. Over 80 percent of the land remained in brush. Tax delinquency had been mounting steadily since 1921, and no buyers could be found for tax warrants. The land was reverting to the counties. Hibbard observed that it would take 400 years, at the present rate of progress, to convert the cutover into farms.

In 1931, W. A. Hartman and J. D. Black published a pamphlet, *Economic Aspects of Land Settlement in the Cut-over Region of the Great Lakes States,* which dealt with progress of farm making in the whole region. The picture was as bleak as that presented by Hibbard three years earlier. After forty years of promotion and propaganda carried on by public and private agencies, it seemed clear that the plow was not going to follow the ax into the cutover.

From the time of the Great Depression on, those concerned with the vast expanse of the cutover lands talked less about farm settlement and more about making the best possible use of these lands. Reforestation, frustrated early in the century by those who farmed, was actively promoted by creating agencies for fighting forest fires, by reforming the forest tax laws, and by encouraging the establishment of county, state, and federal forests along with commercial reforestation of suitable lands. In Wisconsin, removal of isolated farm settlers was combined with provision for rural-land zoning and the encouragement of recreational use of some of the lands. These developments indicated that work was going forward toward using the lands for purposes suited to their quality and location. Progress was slow, but it did take place.

With a logged-off area of 156 million acres by the 1920s, the yellow-pine district of the South also faced a cutover land problem. Leadership was taken up by the Southern Pine Association (SPA) which, in cooperation with the Southern Settlement and Development Organization, the U. S. departments of Agriculture and Interior, and other groups, sponsored a Cut-Over Land Conference of the South in New Orleans in 1917. Following World War I, the SPA, lumbermen, regional development associations, and railroads sought to attract settlers from the North, war refugees from Europe, and returning army veterans to the Southern cutover lands. The problems encountered by the new farms were similar to those seen in the Lake States. Southern advocates of reforestation, such as Henry Hardtner of Louisiana, quickly dismissed the agricultural movement as a "skin game" to sell unfit land. A movement for reforestation gradually replaced interest in agricultural use of the Southern cutovers by the 1930s. As Southern lumbermen became aware of the value of second-growth forests, they lobbied for favorable taxation and other government policies that would encourage reforestation and continual timber production.

FURTHER READING: The United States Department of Agriculture, a number of agricultural college experiment stations, and many private agencies have published innumerable pamphlets on land clearing and stump removal, as well as material on farm making in the cutover and logged-off land. A short list of useful books and pamphlets includes *Northern Wisconsin: A Handbook for the Homeseeker* (1896); *"The Dawn of a New Constructive Era": Being the Full and Complete Report of the Cut-Over Land Conference of the South* (1917); B. H. Hibbard and others, *Tax Delinquency in Northern Wisconsin* (1928); W. A. Hartman and John D. Black, *Economic Aspects of Land Settlement in the Cut-over Region of the Great Lakes States* (1931); O. B. Jesness, *A Program for Land Use in Northern Minnesota* (1935); Raleigh Barlowe, *Administration of Tax Reverted Lands in the Lake States* (1951); and William N. Sparhawk and Warren D. Brush, *The Economic Aspects of Forest Destruction in Northern Michigan,* U.S. Department of Agriculture Technical Bulletin No. 92 (1929). U. P. Hedrick, *Land of the Crooked Tree* (1948), recalls the author's youth in the Michigan cutover. Arlan Helgeson, *Farms in the Cutover: Agricultural Settlement in Northern Wisconsin* (1962), describes the prodigious efforts put forth in Wisconsin to convert the cutover into farms. Vernon Carstensen, *Farms or Forests: Evolution of a State Land Policy for Northern Wisconsin* (1958). Richard White, *Land Use, Environment, and Social Change: The Shaping of Island County, Washington* (1980), sketches attempts to convert Puget Sound stumpland into farms. For efforts to solve the cutover lands problem in the South, see James E. Fickle, *The New South and the "New Competition": Trade Association Development in the Southern Pine Industry* (1980).

VERNON CARSTENSEN

DANA, SAMUEL TRASK (1883–1978)

Born in Portland, Maine, on April 21, 1883, Samuel T. Dana graduated from Bowdoin College in 1904 and received the M.F. degree from Yale Forest School in 1907. Joining the U. S. FOREST SERVICE in that year, he served in the Office of Silvics in Washington, D.C., the only unit in the service then devoted wholly to research. Upon American entry into World War I, Dana was commissioned as a captain in the U. S. Army and was assigned to help determine military needs for wood products. On his return to the Forest Service after the war, Dana became assistant chief of the Branch of Research. He served as forest commissioner of the State of Maine (1921–1923), then returned to the Forest Service as director of the newly established Northeastern Forest Experiment Station. In 1927, Dana was designated as the first dean of the University of Michigan School of Forestry and Conservation (School of Natural Resources after 1950). Under Dana's deanship, the school markedly expanded its educational offerings and research programs in forestry and other professional natural resources curricula, such as wood technology, fisheries management, and wildlife management. Students were drawn from all over the world. On his retirement in 1953 as dean emeritus, Dana was internationally known as the doyen of education in natural resources in its broadest aspects.

Retirement provided Dana with opportunities to engage in other professional activities. In 1956, he published his landmark book, *Forest and Range Policy: Its Development in the United States*, which has remained the definitive historical treatise on its subject. For the AMERICAN FORESTRY ASSOCIATION (AFA) he was senior author of two state studies, *California Lands* (1958) and *Minnesota Lands* (1960). For the SOCIETY OF AMERICAN FORESTERS (SAF) he was senior author of an appraisal of *Forestry Education in America: Today and Tomorrow* (1963).

Dana contributed to the work of many professional organizations and other agencies. He was president of SAF during 1935–1936 and editor-in-chief of the *Journal of Forestry* from 1928 to 1930 and again from 1942 to 1945. He was adviser to the secretary of agriculture on strip-mining policy; consultant to the Forest Service on research; a frequent consultant to AFA: a member of the OUTDOOR RECREATION RESOURCES REVIEW COMMISSION; consultant to the Bureau of Outdoor Recreation; and adviser on forestry education to the University of Florida, North Carolina State University, and Yale University.

For Dana's contributions to education, to his profession, and to society, honorary doctorates were conferred on him by Bowdoin College, the University of Michigan, and Syracuse University. Dana was a recipient of the Sir William Schlich Memorial Medal from SAF; the Distinguished Service Award of the American Forest Products Industries; and, from AFA, the John Aston Warder Medal as the individual who had done most for forest conservation over the longest period of time. He was a fellow of the FOREST HISTORY SOCIETY. He headed the United States delegation to the First World Forestry Congress in 1926, and forty years later, at the sixth congress in Madrid, he was presented with the medal for outstanding service in international forestry.

FURTHER READING: Henry Clepper, "A Salute to Samuel T. Dana at 90," *Journal of Forestry* 71 (Apr. 1973): 200-202.

HENRY CLEPPER

DARLING, JAY NORWOOD (1876–1962)

Born on October 21, 1876, in Norwood, Michigan— the source of his middle name—Jay "Ding" Darling grew up in Sioux City, Iowa, and considered himself an Iowan the remainder of his life. During his youth in the Sioux City area and on summer visits to an uncle's Michigan farm, Darling enjoyed the outdoors and kindled a lifelong love for hunting and fishing.

In 1900, he graduated from Beloit College, Wisconsin, where he had developed an interest in biology, and began drawing political cartoons for the *Sioux City Journal*. In 1906, he joined the *Des Moines Register and Leader* (later the *Register and Tribune*) and remained there until his retirement in 1949, except for a brief term at the *New York Globe* from late 1911 until early 1913. From 1916 until 1949, his work was also syndicated by the *New York Herald Tribune* and appeared in more than 100 daily newspapers circulated to millions of readers throughout the nation. He became famous as "Ding," the contraction of his last name with which he signed his cartoons.

Darling was influential in persuading the Iowa legislature to set up a State Fish and Game Commission in 1931, and he served as one of the first fish and game commissioners. In 1932, he helped to fund an experimental Cooperative Wildlife Research Unit at Iowa State College (later Iowa State University). The unit became a model which eventually influenced the establishment and practice of fifty wildlife and fisheries research units at land-grant universities in twenty-nine states. Darling also had a major role in the merger of Iowa's Fish and Game Commission and Park Commission into a State Conservation Commission in 1935. His efforts also resulted in a biological survey of the state, conducted by Aldo LEOPOLD in the 1930s. The resulting "Twenty-Five Year Plan" for conservation in

Iowa was long considered a model for organizing similar programs in other states.

In 1934, Darling originated the idea of the federal duck stamp and designed the first in the series. Sales of the stamps during the next forty-six years totaled more than $160 million and made possible the purchase of 2 million acres of prime waterfowl habitat. Also in 1934, Darling was appointed by President Franklin D. ROOSEVELT to the position of chief of the Bureau of Biological Survey, forerunner of the FISH AND WILDLIFE SERVICE. As chief of the survey, Darling instituted reforms that gave the formerly lethargic agency new visibility and respect. He cracked down on game hogs, formed and dramatically enlarged the national wildlife refuge system, and gathered resources for wildlife protection on a scale previously unheard of. He also designed the familiar "flying goose" symbol that today marks every federal wildlife refuge.

As a result of his experience with the survey, Darling realized that associations concerned with conservation were not organized to exert political influence as opposing forces were. In response, following his resignation from the survey in 1935, he led in the creation of the NATIONAL WILDLIFE FEDERATION and served as the group's first president.

Darling not only was honored with two Pulitzer prizes for his cartooning but also received scores of awards for his accomplishments in conservation, including the Audubon Medal and the Roosevelt Medal. He was named cochairman, with Walt Disney, for National Wildlife Week, 1962, but he died on February 12, a few weeks before the observance.

Darling, like other conservationists, sometimes felt that he preached to a largely indifferent public. He once likened conservation awards to "giving medals to generals who lose all their battles." Darling spent many winters on Sanibel Island, Florida, where he helped establish a wildlife refuge which later became part of the federal system and in 1978 was dedicated as the Jay N. "Ding" Darling National Wildlife Refuge.

FURTHER READING: David L. Lendt, *Ding: The Life of Jay Norwood Darling* (1979). J. N. Darling, *Ding's Half Century* (1962).

DAVID L. LENDT

DELAWARE FORESTS

When William Penn sailed up the Delaware River in 1682 to assume proprietary control of "Penn's Woods," he marveled at the lush forest stands, unrivaled in his native England. Forest growth once covered more than half of the land area in the present State of Delaware. In 1980, the forested area was 385,000 acres, about one-third of the state's land. The timber varies from mixed hardwoods in the north through a transitional growth to pure loblolly pine stands in the southern portion of the state.

The utilization of the forest probably began early in the eighteenth century when the Delaware colonists exported to England shipments of bark and roots from pine, cherry, and other species for medicinal purposes. Soon, the colonists were making their own lumber and ships from the plentiful oak and pine, and shingles and shakes from the cypress and cedar. As colonization increased, sawmills sprang up at the headwaters of the many small streams feeding into Delaware Bay. Many of the state's older cities and towns owe their existence to these sawmill-gristmill complexes. Forest products developed in the ensuing years included CHARCOAL for the smelting of bog iron, wood fruit baskets and boxes made from redgums and tulip trees, and pilings, poles, veneer, pulpwood, and barrel stock. The state had an important wood container and spoonwood industry until the advent of plastics; the last basket mill closed in the mid-1960s. The lumber industry in Delaware reached its peak production of 55 million board feet in 1910; it was something over 15 million board feet annually in the 1970s.

In 1974, 48 percent of the private commercial forest in Delaware was owned by farmers. Public ownership made up almost 4 percent and the forest industry holdings about 8 percent. Another 40 percent of the commercial timberland was held by miscellaneous private concerns. A 1974 U. S. FOREST SERVICE study reported that Delaware maintained the highest average volume of growing timber per acre of commercial timberland of any state east of the Mississippi River.

During the first decade of the twentieth century, the Forest Service surveyed Delaware's forestlands and made recommendations for forest management, but the state lacked funds to carry out these suggestions. In 1925, the Delaware Federation of Women's Clubs was instrumental in getting a bill through the legislature authorizing a forest study commission. This led, in turn, to the creation in 1927 of a State Forestry Department directed to protect Delaware's forests, advise woodland owners on management practices, establish a tree nursery, and acquire lands for state forests. This department in 1970 became the Delaware Forest Service, a unit of the State Department of Agriculture. By 1980, state forests totaled 6,300 acres. In 1937, the Delaware State Park Com-

mission was created and by 1981 it managed eleven units totaling over 8,900 acres.

W. F. GABEL

DENDROLOGY

Although literally meaning "the study of trees," dendrology in the United States has been concerned largely with taxonomy, the identification and classification of trees within the appropriate plant families, genera, and species. To European explorers and colonists, America presented a rich and complex array of woody species, some of which were of genera known in Europe, while others were entirely new. This flora stimulated both the expanding science of botany in Europe and the creativity of the colonists in developing new uses for these new species. "Botanizers" who roamed North America, often well in advance of settlement, contributed to the early history of dendrology. The period, lasting for more than 100 years, between the activities of John BARTRAM in the Southeast and those of David Douglas on the Pacific Coast, was an era of collection and identification.

In the nineteenth century, dendrological interest shifted to a stocktaking of the nation's forests, their location, composition, state of health, and economic significance. Ushered in by Asa Gray, this second phase in the history of dendrology was highlighted by contributions from many of the major names of American botany, including George Engelmann, William Trelease, Liberty Hyde Bailey, and Nathaniel Lord Britton. The field was dominated by the vigor, force, and accomplishments of Charles S. SARGENT, the country's first, and perhaps greatest, dendrologist. As director of the Arnold Arboretum at Harvard University after 1873, Sargent was charged with growing as many types of plants as possible and teaching the "knowledge of trees." He succeeded in teaching a nation, directly or indirectly. In 1879, from the contributions of many regional experts and his own field experience, Sargent drafted for the Tenth Census the first comprehensive publication on the North American forests and their products. The data in this *Report on the Forests of North America* (1884) significantly influenced early forestry legislation. Sargent's fourteen-volume *Silva of North America* (1891–1902) remains a standard source for most American dendrological works. Sargent made the Arnold Arboretum the nerve center of North American dendrology; the *Journal of the Arnold Arboretum*, devoted to the taxonomy of ligneous plants, remains the most respected publication of its kind.

By the early twentieth century, the U. S. FOREST SERVICE and its predecessors had assumed leadership in developing uniform and stable scientific and common tree names. George B. Sudworth was in charge of Forest Service dendrology work from 1886 until his death in 1927. Sudworth compiled a number of influential volumes, including *Forest Trees of the Pacific Slope* (1908). His *Nomenclature of the Arborescent Flora of the United States* (1897) was the first of a series of standard references leading to the *Checklist of United States Trees (Native and Naturalized)* (1979). More recently, Forest Service dendrological work was continued by William A. Daton and, later, Elbert L. Little, Jr.

From the beginning of forestry instruction in American universities, dendrology was a required course in the curriculum. At first, the subject was largely concerned with the taxonomy of the major forest species and the field identification of the woody vegetation during both growing and dormant seasons, while information on the utility and silvical relationships of particular species was presented in courses on wood science and silvics respectively. As these fields matured, such specific information tended to be presented in dendrology. A recent sample of catalog descriptions of dendrology courses showed that about one-half indicated a coverage of economic or silvical characteristics.

Currently, a common dendrological "package" of a given species consists of its (1) scientific and common names; (2) varieties, ecotypes, and common hybrids; (3) morphological description of botanical features and habit; (4) average and maximum size and age; (5) range, common associate species; (6) relative tolerance and growth patterns and rates; (7) site and environmental patterns; (8) economic significance and utilization; and (9) important environmental hazards. Contributors of this information include ecologists, silviculturists, taxonomists, and biosystematists. Such information is used by foresters, land managers, botanists, and naturalists. Dendrology, however, as attested by the publication of guides to woody plants from Humphry Marshall's *Arbustum Americanum: The American Grove* (1785) onward, has long had an enduring attraction and utility for the layman. As the storehouse of accumulated information about the basic units of a major natural resource, dendrology is a common meeting ground of many and often diverse groups.

FURTHER READING: William A. Dayton, "What is Dendrology?," *Journal of Forestry* 43 (Oct. 1945): 719-722, and "Historical Sketch of U. S. Forest Service Botanical Activity, 1905–1954," *Journal of Forestry* 53 (July 1955): 505-

507. William M. Harlow, Ellwood S. Harrar, and Fred M. White, *Textbook of Dendrology* (6th ed., 1979). Elbert L. Little, Jr., "Dendrology," *McGraw-Hill Encyclopedia of Science and Technology* (1960). Charles S. Sargent, *Silva of North America*, vol. 1 (1891), pp. v-ix.

FRED M. WHITE

DEPARTMENT OF AGRICULTURE

On May 15, 1862, President Abraham Lincoln signed the act establishing a Department of Agriculture in the United States government. This legislation was the first of a series of agricultural reform laws to encourage family farming and the settlement of the West. The others, passed within two months of the department legislation, were the Homestead Act, the Transcontinental Railroad Act, and the Morrill Land Grant College Act. According to its enabling act, the new department was "to acquire and to diffuse among the people of the United States useful information on subjects connected with agriculture in the most general and comprehensive sense of that word, and to procure, propagate, and distribute among the people new and valuable seeds and plants." This law remains the basic authority of the department. Isaac Newton, a Pennsylvania dairy farmer, became the first commissioner of agriculture. (It was not until 1889 that the department attained cabinet rank and was headed by a secretary.) Newton laid out a plan of work and launched a research program. Research continued to be the dominant activity for several decades under his successors, although some regulatory activities began in 1884.

Influenced by Franklin B. HOUGH, a New York physician and statistician, Congress appropriated $2,000 in 1876 to appoint "a man of proved attainments in the Department of Agriculture to study and report on forest supplies and conditions." Hough received the appointment and completed a report which led to further congressional support for forestry investigations in the department. A Division of Forestry was established in 1881, and in 1886 Bernhard E. FERNOW became its chief. Trained as a forester in Germany, Fernow was the department's first professional forester. Fernow promoted the forestry legislation of the 1890s until he was succeeded by Gifford PINCHOT as chief of the division in 1898. In advancing the work of forestry within the deparment, Pinchot had the support of James "Tama Jim" Wilson, secretary of agriculture for sixteen years beginning in 1897. Wilson made his department the foremost agricultural research establishment in the world. He surrounded himself with a group of able, aggressive scientists, who established a series of new agencies dedicated primarily to research. In addition to the Bureau of Animal Industry and the Weather Bureau, which had been established earlier, the new agencies included the Bureau of Plant Industry, the Bureau of Entomology, the Bureau of Chemistry, the Bureau of Soils, the Bureau of Biological Survey, the Office of Public Roads, and the Office of Experiment Stations.

In 1901, Wilson made Pinchot's division the Bureau of Forestry. The Bureau was still a research agency until Pinchot persuaded Congress and President Theodore ROOSEVELT to transfer the forest reserves from the DEPARTMENT OF THE INTERIOR to Agriculture in 1905. On July 1, 1905, the bureau was redesignated the FOREST SERVICE. Renamed national forests in 1907, the reserves have continued to be the responsibility of the Forest Service and the Department of Agriculture.

During the first three decades of the twentieth century, the dominant responsibilities of the Department of Agriculture were research, regulation, and education. Then the Great Depression and the New Deal led to what has been called "the new department." During the 1930s, a series of action programs administered by new agencies under the leadership of Secretary of Agriculture Henry A. Wallace made the department an important force in American economic life. The price support and adjustment program, administered by the Agricultural Adjustment Administration, was the keystone to this change. It has continued, under somewhat different names for programs and agencies, into the 1980s.

Other new agencies of the 1930s included the Soil Conservation Service (transferred from the Department of the Interior in 1935, where it had been known as the Soil Erosion Service), the Federal Surplus Commodities Corporation, the Farm Security Administration (later the Farmers Home Administration), the Federal Crop Insurance Corporation, the Rural Electrification Administration, and the Farm Credit Administration. In addition to forest conservation, the department was now responsible for soil conservation. The department not only was charged with encouraging food production but it also was responsible for getting food to needy people. In addition to providing economic stability for farmers through price support and adjustment, the department also supervised programs to improve the lot of poorer farmers and to improve the quality of rural life.

After the 1930s, the department underwent major reorganizations, but its functions remained somewhat the same. The transfer of the Forest Service to a new department was proposed by both President Richard Nixon and President Jimmy Carter, but each time the proposal was withdrawn. The emphasis given departmental programs has changed from the 1930s to the 1980s. During the 1950s, the price support and adjustment program accounted for about three-fifths of the department's expenditures; by the 1970s, the food stamp and related programs absorbed about the same proportion of the total funds. Although the department had almost the same number of permanent employees in 1980 that it had in 1950 (about 85,000), in 1980 more were employed in food distribution and in meat and poultry inspection and other regulatory duties, and fewer were working in research and price support programs.

FURTHER READING: Gladys L. Baker et al., *Century of Service: The First 100 Years of the United States Department of Agriculture* (1963). Wayne D. Rasmussen and Gladys L. Baker, *The Department of Agriculture* (1972).

WAYNE D. RASMUSSEN

DEPARTMENT OF THE INTERIOR

The Department of the Interior is the country's principal conservation agency, with responsibility for much of the nation's federally owned public lands and natural resources, as well as for the native American reservation communities and for the people living in island territories under American administration. The role of the department has changed a great deal since its creation in 1849, when it was viewed as general housekeeper for the government.

There long had been need for an agency such as the Department of the Interior, but the Mexican War and the addition of new territory forced the issue. In an annual report of 1848, Secretary of the Treasury Robert J. Walker pointed out that the State Department had little to do with the Patent Office, which it controlled, and the War Department had little interest in supervision of Indians or pensions. He spoke of the many tasks under his jurisdiction not related to public finance, and discussed in particular the Treasury Department's control of the Land Office. He recommended a department to handle these and other functions, and Congress, on March 3, 1849, passed an act to establish the Department of the Interior. The plan of the new department was simple. In contrast to the State Department, responsible for foreign affairs, Interior was to be the "Home Department."

The role of the Department of the Interior has nowhere been more apparent than in the units making up the agency. In 1849, the newly established department's responsibilities included the GENERAL LAND OFFICE, the Office of Indian Affairs, the Pension Office, the Patent Office, the Office of the Commissioner of Public Buildings, charitable and penal institutions in the District of Columbia, the census of the United States, and the accounts of marshals and other officers of the federal court system.

As the years passed, the importance of the department increased. Interior helped make certain that the railroads, so important for unifying the country in the nineteenth century, conformed with the laws involving the disposal of the public lands granted them by Congress. Interior supervised the Indians, once they were brought under control, and attempted to better their lives by improving reservations, setting up schools, and introducing modern medical techniques. The Bureau of Education, forerunner of a later department, became part of Interior in 1867. National parks became part of Interior's domain. The first park, YELLOWSTONE NATIONAL PARK, was established in 1872, and the next year Interior took responsibility for the territories of the United States. In 1879, the U. S. GEOLOGICAL SURVEY was created to conduct the classification of the public lands and the examination of their geological structure, mineral resources, and products. There were many unrelated functions, for Interior became a department of miscellany, the most likely place for any new government activity. Minor duties included control of the Freedman's Hospital and Asylum in Washington and supervision of Howard University, established in 1867.

As the century ended, the responsibilities continued to change. The Interstate Commerce Commission emerged from Interior. The Department of Justice, created in 1870, ended Interior's jurisdiction over accounts and expenses of district attorneys, marshals, and other court officers. Interior lost duties with the creation of the Bureau of Labor in 1888, and the Census Bureau went to the new Department of Commerce and Labor in 1903.

With the turn of the century, another of Interior's responsibilities became important: conservation. The era of cheap land—land that settlers misused and discarded—was, by and large, over. President Theodore ROOSEVELT saw the need to preserve resources, both mineral and land, and though conservation was not new with him, Roosevelt placed government agencies behind the idea. He determined that the government should help the people take care of their lands and reclaim arid land by means of irrigation. The Reclamation Service was established in 1902 to construct and operate water storage and diversion works in the arid and semi-arid lands in the Western states. Like land and railroad policies, conservation involved the department in politics—some Westerners wanted conservation of natural resources, others wanted exploitation. Still, the conservation movement

continued to gain support. With the creation of the Bureau of Mines in 1910, Interior collected information on the mining industry and inspected and regulated mines throughout the United States.

During the Wilson administration, the NATIONAL PARK SERVICE was created in 1916, giving increased status to the country's national parks, though the service later gained additional responsibilities covering RECREATION and historical sites. During World War I, as the problem of national resources became acute, Interior was charged with their allocation and protection. In the 1920s, Interior continued reclamation and conservation activities and became involved in politics because of the Teapot Dome Scandal.

It was with the New Deal and Secretary of the Interior Harold L. ICKES that the modern department began to come into being. In addition to serving as secretary from 1933 to 1946, Ickes was petroleum administrator during World War II. He conducted the campaign to ration gas and oil and came to be called the Czar of Petroleum, a title which apparently did not displease him. His duties brought the department prestige and power in the field of conservation of natural resources. Meanwhile, transfer to the department in 1939 of the Bureau of Biological Survey and the Bureau of Fisheries, later split into Commercial Fisheries and Sport Fisheries and Wildlife, gave Interior control of other functions, taking duties from both the DEPARTMENT OF AGRICULTURE and the Department of Commerce, though the Bureau of Commercial Fisheries was transferred back to Commerce in 1970. In 1946, the BUREAU OF LAND MANAGEMENT was established by merging the GENERAL LAND OFFICE (dating from 1812) and the Grazing Service (created in 1934), with responsibility for management of millions of acres of public land.

One hundred and thirty-one years after its founding in 1849, the department still exercised jurisdiction over vast sections of federal land—over 500 million acres—and administered the Bureau of Indian Affairs, which carried out the government's trust responsibilities for the Indian reservations. In addition, as noted in the *United States Government Manual, 1979–1980,* the department oversees "the conservation and development of mineral and water resources; mine health and safety training; the conservation, development, and utilization of fish and wildlife resources; the coordination of Federal and State recreation programs; the preservation and administration of the Nation's scenic and historic areas; the operation [on Interior lands] of Job Corps Conservation Centers and Youth and Young Adult Conservation Corps Camps, and coordination of other manpower and youth training programs; the reclamation of arid lands in the West through irrigation; and [until 1979] the management of hydroelectric power systems," as well as administering governmental affairs in Guam, American Samoa, the Virgin Islands, and the Trust Territory of the Pacific Islands, and the programs provided by the federal government to Alaskan native people.

Specifically, the Department of the Interior in 1980 administered the Bureau of Indian Affairs, the Heritage Conservation and Recreation Service (abolished in 1981), the United States Fish and Wildlife Service, the National Park Service, the BUREAU OF RECLAMATION, the Bureau of Land Management, the Office of Water Research and Technology, the Office of Coal Leasing Planning and Coordination, the Office of Youth Programs, the Office of Territorial Affairs, the Bureau of Mines, the United States Geological Survey, the Office of Minerals Policy and Research Analysis, the Ocean Mining Administration, the Office of Surface Mining Reclamation and Enforcement, and the Office of Outer Continental Shelf Program Coordination.

A number of these agencies and much of the focus of the modern Department of the Interior had been established in the last twenty-five years. For example, the Office of Minerals Policy and Research Analysis, which oversees minerals research and policy development in the department, was set up in 1976; the Ocean Mining Administration, responsible for developing policy for mining in deep seabed areas, dates from 1975; and the Office of Surface Mining Reclamation and Enforcement, which establishes minimum standards for regulating the effects of surface coal mining, was established in 1977. These agencies gave a new focus to the department's activities in the minerals area and, combined with such older agencies as the Bureau of Mines and the United States Geological Survey, which had been given expanded responsibilities in recent years, resulted in the department being the primary government agency in the conservation of the country's mineral wealth. Other new offices in the department were Water Research and Technology, Territorial Affairs, Outer Continental Shelf Program Coordination, and Youth Programs. To be sure, some of the new offices, such as the short-lived Heritage Conservation and Recreation Service, resulted from reorganization, but others were the product of new responsibilities, especially in the conservation area.

During its more than 130 years of existence, the Department of the Interior has been involved in controversies, some of which have damaged the department's reputation. In its early years, there were claims that the department was a nest of patronage. Like other government agencies, it was dominated by political appointees before development of the Civil Service. There were scandals involving the Bureau of Indian Affairs and the General Land Office. In fact, the scandals in the General Land Office helped influence the Congress and President Theodore Roosevelt in 1905 to approve transfer of administration of the forest reserves from Interior to the Department of Agriculture.

Controversies and scandals in the area of conservation have damaged the department's reputation the most. The BALLINGER-PINCHOT CONTROVERSY during the Taft Administration, which pitted Secretary of the Interior Richard Ballinger against the nation's forester, Gifford PINCHOT, concerned commercial access to resources on lands in the public domain and led to a feeling among many observers that the department was anticonservationist. But it was because of the Teapot Dome Scandal of 1921–1923 that the department suffered its darkest hour. Former Secretary of the Interior Albert Fall went to jail and the department's reputation with conservationists reached a low point. Memories of these two controversies thwarted Ickes's efforts during the New Deal to transfer the Forest Service to his department and to make Interior into a Department of Conservation and Public Works. After 1923, other controversies arising from the conflicting demands of developers and preservationists have plagued the department, especially during the Eisenhower administration, but the department eventually became what Ickes had hoped— the Nation's "Department of Conservation." In the final third of the twentieth century, the Department of the Interior continues as the guardian of much of the country's natural wealth.

What then are the differences between the department of 1849 and the department of 1980? Many are implicit in the above account of the department's maturity. Policies of the department still gain political attention and occasionally stir controversy. Yet most Americans now favor beautification and conservation of natural and historic sites. They are against water pollution and support the national parks. The secretaries since the 1920s have made an effort to arouse public support behind the department. Interior is much less a "Department of the West" than formerly. It is concerned with water supplies threatened by drought in the Northeast, recreation and historic sites in the East, and renovation of the nation's capital, tasks different from the days when Interior dealt primarily with Indians and reclamation in the West.

FURTHER READING: For a general survey, see Eugene P. Trani, *The Secretaries of the Department of the Interior, 1849–1969* (1975), which has an extensive bibliography on the department. Information on current organization is in "The Department of the Interior," *United States Government Manual, 1979–1980* (1980), pp. 322-350.

Eugene P. Trani

DEVOTO, BERNARD AUGUSTINE (1897–1955)

A self-styled "literary department store," Bernard DeVoto was one of the most versatile and prolific American writers of the twentieth century: a novelist, historian, critic, journalist, editor, and teacher. As a widely read columnist for *Harper's Magazine*, he became an early model of the conservationist "watchdog," waging what historian Arthur Schlesinger called "a long and remarkable campaign to save the West from itself."

DeVoto was born on January 11, 1897, in Ogden, Utah, the only child of Florian DeVoto, an Italian Roman Catholic, and Rhoda Dye DeVoto, a descendant of Morman pioneers. His childhood experience of religious tension grew into a lifelong distaste for all orthodoxies of belief. After high school in Ogden and one year at the University of Utah, he was admitted to Harvard where, after brief service in World War I, he took his bachelor's degree in 1920.

Between 1922 and 1927, Bernard DeVoto taught English at Northwestern University. In 1923, he married one of his students, Helen Avis MacVicar. While living in Evanston he published his first two novels, both bitter accounts of western life, and began his career as social critic, writing for H. L. Mencken's *American Mercury.* Returning to Cambridge in 1929, DeVoto taught at Harvard while continuing to establish the broad parameters of his literary career. In 1932, he published a controversial volume of social history, *Mark Twain's America.* He continued to write fiction but became best known for his penetrating essays on the social and political issues of the day.

Leaving Harvard in 1936, DeVoto served as editor of *The Saturday Review* for two years. As curator of the Mark Twain Papers from 1938 until 1946, he edited two volumes of Twain's previously unpublished work and furthered the research on the West that would lead to his great historical trilogy, his most lasting contribution to American letters. In 1943, he published *Year of Decision: 1846,* a narrative rendering of the forces of Manifest Destiny. *Across the Wide Missouri* (1947), a history of the pioneering fur traders, earned DeVoto the Pulitzer and Bancroft prizes. *The Course of Empire* (1952), which critics have rated among the best and best-written histories of the West, won the National Book Award.

For the last twenty years of his life, writing the monthly "Easy Chair" column for *Harper's,* DeVoto employed his historical sense and critical acuity, his ironic wit and persuasive colloquial style in a wide-ranging series of outspoken commentaries upon the American scene. His guises were numerous: historian, traveloguer, literary critic, political analyst. He was at his best when he took up his pen in angry defense of civil liberties or the environment.

DeVoto's knowledge of the West's economic and ecological peculiarities, his love of controversy, and his command of a national audience combined to make him a powerful spokesman for conservation interests. Constantly reminding his readers that "this is *your* land we are talking about," he frequently used the "Easy Chair" as an educational forum on the public domain and the threats to it from stockmen, loggers, and power companies. In the late 1940s, his exposé effectively stopped an attempted "landgrab" by western stockmen. For a six-year term beginning in 1948, he was a member of the Advisory Board on National Parks, Historic Sites, Buildings, and Monuments, and until his death on November 13, 1955, he remained the national parks' most outspoken public advocate. Insisting that protection of the wilderness was an urgent national issue, DeVoto distinguished himself as a pioneer of modern conservationism.

FURTHER READING: A selection of DeVoto's conservation essays is reprinted in *The Easy Chair* (1955). A thorough biography, *The Uneasy Chair* (1974), has been written by Wallace Stegner who also edited DeVoto's *Letters* (1975). A complete bibliography of DeVoto's works is included in *Four Portraits and One Subject: Bernard DeVoto* (1963).

Glenn Q. Snyder

DIMENSION STOCK

The cutting of dimension stock has been a profitable sideline of American hardwood mills since the middle of the nineteenth century. By sawing to size the edgings, trimmings, round-edged timber, and ends on order from wood-finishing industries, mills in New England, the Appalachians, and the Lake States cut down drastically on waste and shipping costs for consuming industries. By 1900, large hardwood mills produced dimension stock as an integral part of their operation.

The regional names given to dimension stock are almost as varied as the products made from it: squares, blanks, billets, cleats, bolts, cut-to-size stock, spool stock, brush stock, chair stock, vehicle stock, leg stock, handle blanks. ("Cut stock" usually referred to dimension stock in softwoods.) The machin-

Pine molding stock is resawn into rough molding strips before final shaping according to customer specifications. Weyerhaeuser Company Photo.

ery used to convert dimension stock is also varied: planers, borers, shapers, lathes, mortisers, dry kilns, and glue spreaders.

Few finishing industries preferred bulk lumber to precut blocks. Since the turn of the century, most small hardwood products and even custom items have been made from dimension stock. Among them were bobbins and shuttles; pulley blocks; patterns for molding; carriage and later automobile parts; baseball bats, tennis rackets, and other hardwood athletic equipment; musical and scientific instruments; spokes, ladder rungs, penholders, pencils, poles, and most wood for lathe work; domestic woodenware, toothpicks, handles for tools of all kinds, toys, and so on. Although virtually all varieties of hardwood (and some softwoods) are manufactured into dimension stock, the most common varieties used for the purpose have been hickory, ash, maple, and basswood.

FURTHER READING: A. T. Panshin et al., *Forest Products* (2nd ed., 1962).

DIVISION OF FOREST INSECT INVESTIGATIONS

The Division of Forest Insect Investigations was established in 1902 with an appropriation of $5,800. Its functions were slightly altered several times by acts of Congress, and jurisdiction over it was transferred in several reorganizations of the executive departments in 1904, 1933, and 1935. Financial support was also erratic, rising to as high as $253,000 in 1940 (this included some CIVILIAN CONSERVATION CORPS money), declining to $150,000 in 1944, and rising to a level of $500,000 by the 1950s. In 1953, the secretary of agriculture dissolved the bureau of which the Division of Forest Insect Investigations was a part and distributed its functions among several branches of the Agricultural Research Service. Most of these functions are presently carried out by the U. S. FOREST SERVICE.

During its independent existence, the division was an extremely active and productive bureau. It sponsored important research into damage caused by pine bark beetles (*Dendrocotonus*) and, in cooperation with the Forest Service, NATIONAL PARK SERVICE, and state agencies, found ways to prevent (by its own estimate) $10 million annual damages to both forests and cut timber.

FURTHER READING: A. G. Hall, "Silent Saboteurs," *American Forests* 59 (Feb. 1953): 8–11, 46–69. U. S. Department of Agriculture, *Insects: Yearbook of Agriculture* (1952), pp. 444-449, 462-468.

DRURY, NEWTON B. (1889-1978)

Newton Drury's career underscores the dependence of the early park movement on the new field of public relations counsel. Born in San Francisco on April 19, 1889, Drury became student body president and a leader of the campus progressives at the University of California, Berkeley. After graduation in 1912, he taught at the university and was assistant to its president, Benjamin Ide Wheeler. In 1919, he and his brother Aubrey formed the Drury Brothers Company, an advertising and public relations agency. That same year, the organizers of the SAVE-THE-REDWOODS LEAGUE, many of whom knew Drury from the university, asked Drury Brothers to manage the league. Newton Drury became executive secretary in charge of publicity and fund raising.

The league combined state and private funding. Through the early 1920s until success was attained in 1927, Drury campaigned for league-inspired legislation authorizing a California State Park Commission, a park site survey, and a park bond issue. In 1928, he coordinated a referendum which secured approval by the electorate of one of California's first statewide bond issues. All revenue from the bond issue was to be matched with private subscription, which Drury secured for the redwoods by soliciting memorial grove donations; he eventually obtained $3 million from the Rockefellers alone. Following the bond referendum, the State Park Commission hired Drury as its land acquisitions officer, a post he filled for eleven years.

Seeking a proved administrator committed to park preservation, Secretary of the Interior Harold L. ICKES offered Drury the position of director of the NATIONAL PARK SERVICE in 1933 and again in 1940, when Drury accepted. In this federal office from 1940 to 1951, Drury opposed such inappropriate entertainment traditions as the nightly tossing of a "fire fall" over the wall of Yosemite Valley and the feeding of the bears in Yellowstone, but he was unable to stop either practice. Some preservationists criticized Drury for a perceived

willingness to compromise in 1943 and 1947 when loggers sought to cut spruce timber in OLYMPIC NATIONAL PARK. Ickes and others interpreted Drury's diplomacy as weakness. In 1951, Secretary of the Interior Oscar Chapman suggested Drury resign as director, apparently in large part because of Drury's opposition to the BUREAU OF RECLAMATION's proposed dam at Echo Park in Dinosaur National Monument. Drury's departure caused a brief scandal within the park movement.

Upon his return to California, Drury was appointed by Governor Earl Warren as chief of the State Division of Beaches and Parks, where he served until 1959, when he returned to the league. After World War II, accelerated logging of redwoods and the rising stumpage rates rendered state and private park funding increasingly inadequate. In the 1960s, Drury led the league in a low-key campaign for a REDWOOD NATIONAL PARK. The battle was marred by bitter opposition from industry and differences between the militant SIERRA CLUB and the league under Drury's moderate leadership. The club and the league, however, joined forces in urging expansion of the park after its establishment in 1968. Drury was executive secretary of the league until 1971, president from 1971 to 1975, and chairman of the board of directors from 1975 until his death on December 14, 1978. He was known for his unassuming nature, his constancy, and his moderation in dealing with opponents.

FURTHER READING: Newton Drury, *Parks and Redwoods, 1917 to 1971*, an oral history by Amelia Roberts Fry and Susan R. Schrepfer (University of California Regional Oral History Office, 1972).

SUSAN R. SCHREPFER

DUBOIS, JOHN (1809-1886)

John DuBois was a leading figure in Pennsylvania's lumber industry during its heyday. The second of thirteen children, DuBois was born in Owego, New York, where his father (also named John) farmed and ran a small sawmill. Young John went to work in his father's mill at the age of fifteen. By the time he was nineteen, he was in charge of his father's lumber rafts, floated down the North Branch of the Susquehanna River to market each year. He proved a shrewd businessman, selling his first rafts for more than the going price. In 1838, John and two brothers, David and Ezekiel, purchased a millsite and timberland on Lycoming Creek, north of Williamsport, Pennsylvania. The enterprise prospered, encouraging further investments.

The late 1840s were pivotal for John DuBois and for lumbering in Pennsylvania. James H. Perkins persuaded John and David DuBois and their partner, Elias S. Lowe, to join in building a giant log boom on the West Branch of the Susquehanna at Williamsport. In 1846, the state legislature chartered the Susquehanna Boom Company. Controlling a majority of the stock, John DuBois became president. Operations began in 1850, although a permanent boom was not in place until a year later. In spite of opposition by raftsmen threatened by log drives, the boom was repeatedly enlarged and improved, spurring lumber production on the West Branch. Within two decades, Williamsport had become the nation's leading lumber-producing center. Among the mills served by the boom were those of John DuBois, including a large steam sawmill located across the river from Williamsport in DuBoistown.

Another brother, Matthias, became DuBois's main partner in 1848. Matthias was a good business manager, and John was inventive and hard driving. They prospered until Matthias's death in 1853. Subsequently, DuBois found himself overextended. In 1863, he bought out his remaining partner, Lowe, whom he blamed for the financial problems, and liquidated assets to pay off debts. DuBois also gave up control of the boom company, having tired of complaints about its management.

Gradually, DuBois rebuilt. The new management of the boom charged exorbitant fees, and DuBois soon allied with his erstwhile critics to combat the company. Then, in the early 1870s, recognizing the dwindling supplies of timber tributary to Williamsport, he moved to the present-day town of DuBois, just west of the Allegheny divide. There he built a large sawmill which he supplied with logs first by water, then by railroad. Steadily, his interests at DuBois expanded, coming to include three sawmills, a box factory, machine shop, store, hotel, tannery, 100 houses for workmen, and 1,200 acres of cleared farmland. As at Williamsport, DuBois's competitiveness led to friction. Nevertheless, at his death in 1886, his lumber operations were among the state's largest.

DuBois was a lifelong bachelor; after he died, control of his interests passed to a nephew, John E. DuBois. Except in 1860 when he built a mill at Havre de Grace, Maryland, to saw logs that had escaped when the Susquehanna Boom broke, John DuBois had concentrated his efforts in Pennsylvania. His nephew, by contrast, invested in lumbering in Mississippi, South Carolina, and Oregon, but disposed of these holdings before his death in 1934, when John E. DuBois, Jr., took over. By then, lumbering was virtually over in Pennsylvania. A small sawmill owned by John E. DuBois, Jr.,

was still cutting in DuBois in the 1970s; its capacity was a mere 8,000 board feet a day, a far cry from the time when DuBois operations had been among the industry's largest.

FURTHER READING: *American Lumbermen* (first series, 1905), pp. 67-69. Benjamin F. G. Kline, Jr., *Dinkies, Dams, and Sawdust* (1975), pp. 1201-1226.

THOMAS R. COX

DYEWOODS

Among the useful plant materials sought by the earliest European naturalist-explorers who visited North America were woods from which coloring matter could be extracted. Although the United States proved to have an abundant supply of woods suitable for imparting a more or less permanent color in textiles, their commercial possibilities were never fully exploited.

At least as far back as the sixteenth century, logwood and brazilwood were exported to England from South and Central America. In 1770, Lord Sheffield reported that among dye materials exported from the West Indies and South Carolina were a large quantity of indigo and some sassafras from North America. Among the dyewoods imported to North America were annatto, fustic, and logwood, as well as barwood and other African dyewoods.

Black oak bark was the most important native-grown dye material used in the United States and exported during the nineteenth century. One source indicates that it was first shipped to England from Wilmington, Delaware, before the American Revolution. However, its commercial possibilities were not exploited until Edward Bancroft, author of *Experimental Researches Concerning the Philosophy of Permanent Colors* (Philadelphia, 1814) started to promote it in 1781. Bancroft called yellow dye derived from black oak leaves "quercitron" (from *Quercus nigra*, Linn., now known as *Q. velutina)*. The greatest concentration of yellow dye was found in the bark's cellular coat and somewhat less in its cortical or interior part. Bancroft obtained a British patent in 1785 for quercitron's exclusive use and application to alum-mordanted wool, silk, and calico printing. In 1804, an American patent was issued to Thomas Benger for an improvement in preparing the bark in a more marketable form. In the second edition of his *Practical Treatise on Dyeing and Calico Printing* (1846), Clinton G. Gilroy stated that black oak had almost completely superseded the use of fustic (*Chlorophora tinctoria*) because of its beauty and low cost, although at that time black oak's main use in

French, English, and Scottish establishments was as the ground for brown and pale green lightweight muslins.

Butternut (*Juglans cinerea*) and black walnut (*J. nigra*), both of which yield excellent fast brown dyes, were used extensively in the United States by both professional and home dyers. The earliest recorded use of butternut dyeing in the American colonies was in 1669, when a sample of dyed fabric was sent to the Royal Society in London by Governor Winthrop of Connecticut.

Alder (*Alnus*), maple (*Acer*), and white oak (*Q. alba*) barks and sumac (*Rhus*), because of their high tannin content, were frequently used as mordants, as well as to achieve neutral-colored gray or tan dyes. Sumac was so important that both domestic and imported sumac twigs were used in American dyehouses. Frequently mentioned as a local, but impermanent, source of reds was pokeweed (*Phytolaccaceae*). Yellow and orange colors were produced by white ash (*Fraxinus americana*) and sassafras (*Sassafras albidum*) barks and Osage-orange (*Maclura pomifera*).

Asa Ellis, a dyer writing in 1798, lamented America's dependence on imported dyestuff, a sentiment reiterated frequently in the late eighteenth and nineteenth century. If the United States government would "encourage some able chemist to explore the qualities of our . . . woods, barks, shrubs," Ellis hoped, "the advantages, [which] our rising nation might derive, would soon indemnify us for the extra expense." Nevertheless, the United States did not even impose a tariff on imported dyewoods until 1846.

The use of dyewoods and other natural dye materials diminished during the second half of the nineteenth century as the quantity of cheaper and more dependable supplies of aniline dyes increased and as their color range broadened. However, one American dyewood processing firm continued to export quercitron and flavine extracts of oak bark to large dye-stuff manufacturers in Germany and Switzerland until the advent of World War I. The United States is said to have used more than 100,000 tons of dyewoods annually in the period before World War I.

The last efforts to revive the commercial production of dyewoods occurred during World War I, when supplies of German aniline dyestuffs were cut off as these chemical industries were converted to the production of explosives. A "dyestuff famine" took place in 1915 and 1916 until American manufacturers of synthetic dyestuffs reached volume production. For the last time, the United States textile industry turned to natural dyes. Logwood (*Haematoxylon campechianum*) and its derivative, hematine; fustic bark from Mexico and Central America; quercitron and flavine; hypernic, a derivative of brazilwood; sumac; cutch (*Acacia catechu* or *Areca catechu*); and gambier (*Uncaria gambir*) were all once more in demand. The army's orders for certain colored textiles added to civilian needs, increasing production of dyewoods manifold. There was also an attempt to utilize Osage-orange mill waste as a commercial dyestuff. This material had long been used in Texas on a modest scale; unfortunately, though it produced a good color, the high cost of shipping it to East Coast manufacturers made it impractical.

Since the 1920s, dyewoods have been imported on a very small scale for use in textile crafts.

FURTHER READING: Rita J. Adrosko, *Natural Dyes and Home Dyeing* (1971). Charles R. Delaney, "The Manufacture, Use, and Newer Developments of the Natural Dyestuffs," *The Journal of Industrial and Engineering Chemistry* 10 (Oct. 1918): 798-801. F. W. Kressman, "Osage Orange: Its Value as a Commercial Dyestuff," *The Journal of Industrial and Engineering Chemistry* 6 (June 1914): 462-464. U. S. Tariff Commission, *Census of Dyes and Coal-Tar Chemicals 1917*, Tariff Information Series No. 6 (1918).

RITA J. ADROSKO

ECOLOGICAL SOCIETY OF AMERICA

Founded in 1915 as an association of academics and professional ecologists, the Ecological Society of America was also devoted to popular education in the then obscure science of the relationship of organisms to their environment. Until the environmentalist movement of the 1970s inspired a widespread interest in ecology, the organization remained a tiny association of educators, research scientists, and the few professional ecologists employed by private industry. Until 1950, there were fewer than 1,000 members but by 1980, it had grown to 6,000 members, a fair size among professional associations.

The society holds an annual meeting and has published two scholarly journals and a newsletter since its first years of existence: *Ecology, Ecological Monographs,* and the *Bulletin of the Ecological Society of America.* It regularly sponsors two awards for its members: the George Mercer Award for outstanding papers in the field of ecology, and the Eminent Ecologist Citation for long and distinguished activity in the field of ecology. Although the Ecological Society took note of current ecological issues in the 1970s and early 1980s and was consulted by government agencies and congressional committees, it has remained a scientific, professional organization, not involved in political action.

FURTHER READING: Robert L. Burgess, "The Ecological Society of America: Historical Data and Some Preliminary Analyses," in F. N. Egerton and R. P. McIntosh, eds., *History of American Ecology* (1977).

ECOLOGY AND FORESTS

Ecology is the study of the interactions of organisms with each other and with their environment. The word *Oekologie* was coined by the German zoologist Ernst Haeckel in 1866. The science became formally organized around 1900, although various ecological topics had been investigated since antiquity within the context of natural history studies.

Observations of ecological relationships have been recorded in America since the early European explorations. Over time, such accounts have become more detailed and analytical. Thomas Hariot (or Harriot), in his *Briefe and True Report of the New Found Land of Virginia* (1588) described inland sites as more favorable to tree growth than were the lands along the coast, with "the Soyle to bee fatter; the trees greater and to growe thinner; the grounde more firme and deeper mould."

Captain John Smith remained longer in America than had Hariot, and the characterizations of the coastal regions of Virginia and Massachusetts contained in

Twelve years after a fire, the young forest takes over the site amidst the remains of its predecessor. Weyerhaeuser Company Photo.

his *Generall Historie of Virginia, New-England, and the Summer Isles* (1624) conveyed an idea of vegetation and animals. Late in the seventeenth century, the French explorer Baron de Lahontan recorded his impressions of New France in his *Nouveaux Voyages . . . dans l'Amérique Septentrionale* (1703). His description of Lake Erie has some of the characteristics of an ecological survey. The abundance of sturgeon, whitefish, trout, deer, beaver, and turkey gave an impression of paradise; all the shores were "deck'd with Oke-Trees, Elms, Chesnut-Trees, Walnut-Trees, Apple-Trees, Plum-Trees, and Vines which bear their fine clusters up to the very top of the Trees, upon a sort of ground that lies as smooth as one's Hand."

John Lawson's *New Voyage to Carolina* (1709) indicated the kinds of forests that grew on sandy soils, low and wet lands, and highlands of North Carolina. Mark Catesby's travels in the same region to study and collect plants and animals resulted in his *Natural History of Carolina, Florida, and the Bahama Islands* (1729–1747) which included full-page, hand-colored engravings. He noted that "the Northern Continent of America is much colder than those Parts of Europe which are parallel to it in Latitude." In eastern Carolina, he found three main soils, differing in texture and in water content but identified by the plants growing on them as *"Rice Land, Oak* and *Hiccory Land,* and *Pine Barren Land."*

John BARTRAM, an intellectual Pennsylvania farmer, was America's first resident naturalist. He recorded observations on plant life, soils, moisture, and elevations in letters and in journals he kept during trips to Lake Ontario in 1743 and through the Carolinas, Georgia, and Florida in 1765–1766. In his second journal, Bartram offered interpretations of the relationship between forests and soils.

Among European naturalists who visited Bartram was Pehr Kalm, a student of the Swedish naturalist Carl Linnaeus. Kalm had been sent to America to find plants likely to have usefulness in Scandinavia. In his *Travels into North America* (3 vols., Swedish, 1753–1761; English, 1770–1771), Kalm correlated the occurrence and the habitats of plants. Kalm's observations were detailed enough to be called ecological life histories: *Rhus glabra* he found to be the most common sumac, growing "like a weed in this country, for if a corn-field is left uncultivated for some few years together, it grows on it in plenty, since the berries are spread every where by the birds." This is among the earliest observations on plant succession. Kalm also realized that particular soils favored certain plants, which in turn, he thought, might serve to indicate good soil for crops.

William Bartram, who had accompanied his father John to Florida in the 1760s, returned to the Southern woodlands in the following decade and later published *Travels Through North & South Carolina, Georgia, East & West Florida* (1791). His descriptions carried ecological surveys to a new level of precision.

America's climate was of vital concern to settlers, who were alert to any changes therein. John Clayton of Tidewater Virginia wrote in 1688 that he had "been told by very serious Planters, that 30 or 40 years since, when the Country was not so open, the Thunder was more fierce." He believed that the climate could be favorably modified by draining swamps and clearing the woods. In 1748, Pehr Kalm, who thought similarly, questioned elderly residents in the middle colonies and in Canada, most of whom agreed that formerly the winters had been colder.

Hugh Williamson, a physician, hypothesized in the *Transactions* of the American Philosophical Society (1771) that land cleared for cultivation would reflect into the air more heat than would the forest, thereby increasing warmth in winter. Because heat rises, he also thought that clearing woodland would not necessarily make the summers hotter. Thomas Jefferson also briefly discussed the amelioration of the climate in his *Notes on the State of Virginia* (1788), stating that rivers once known to freeze over in winter seldom did so any longer and that, because snow no longer accumulated in the mountains, flooding had ended.

In 1772, Joseph Priestley discovered that plants restore oxygen to the atmosphere. Trees were henceforth seen as more than merely useful providers of fuel, lumber, and shade. The Marquis François Jean de Chastellux, who visited the United States in the early 1780s, expressed doubt of the wisdom of the Americans' rapid elimination of their forests. Several American physicians published papers in the 1780s and 1790s echoing this concern. Samuel Williams, in his *Natural and Civil History of Vermont* (1794), tried to test such arguments by quantifying the evidence for the climatic influence of forests. He noted that the rainfall figures in North America were about twice those

for Europe at the same latitude, a difference he assumed to be caused by the great amounts of water evaporating from America's forests. By simple experiments he calculated that an acre of forest would emit 3,875 gallons of water and 14,774 gallons of "air" to the atmosphere in twelve hours. Williams measured a difference of 10 or 11 degrees in the temperature of the soil ten inches below the surface in an open field and in a Vermont forest in the summer. He concluded that this supported the belief that winters had increased in warmth by 10 or 11 degrees since the settlement of America.

Down to the end of the eighteenth century, there seems to have been virtual agreement that the American climate was becoming milder as the land was brought under cultivation from forests and swamps. However, in 1799, in a study of the relationship between climate and disease, Noah Webster challenged the evidence for climatic change that Jefferson, Williams, and others had offered.

Phenology is a branch of ecology dealing with the relation between climate and periodic biological activity. This term for what had earlier been called the "calendar of flora" was first used in German in 1853 and in English in 1875, but phenological studies long predated adoption of the name. Kalm, who sought information of value for raising American plants in Europe, in 1749 began to note seasonal changes in plants; he compared these data with meteorological tables he compiled for the Philadelphia area. While serving as an American diplomat in France, Jefferson made investigations similar to those Kalm had made in America. Samuel Williams seems to have planned a comprehensive investigation of climate and phenology in America, for in 1786 he sent to prospective observers a plan (never carried out) for collecting such data.

The published accounts of North American explorers, such as those of the Lewis and Clark expedition or of Henry R. Schoolcraft, never matched in importance the contribution to ecological knowledge resulting from the South American explorations of Alexander von Humboldt. Although the Swiss-born naturalist Louis Agassiz was eager to follow Humboldt's example in scientific exploration, and the expedition which he led to Lake Superior resulted in a more thorough natural history survey than had appeared after previous expeditions (*Lake Superior*, 1850), Agassiz lacked Humboldt's curiosity about environmental influences on the distribution of species. In identifying the plants from the region, Agassiz obtained the assistance of Asa Gray, who had already become interested in the striking similarities between mountain plants in America and Japan. Gray was to explain these similarities from the 1850s through the 1870s with concepts of competition, extinction, and evolution developed by Charles Lyell and Charles Darwin.

In 1803, Benjamin Smith Barton discussed *calendaria florae* in his *Elements of Botany*, America's first textbook of botany. He apparently believed that these tabulations of information could provide the basis for a science of ecology and that, if the clearing of forests and draining of swamps was changing the climate, the evidence would appear in changes in the timing of seasonal phenomena. Compilations of weather data made by the Surgeon General's office beginning in 1816, the GENERAL LAND OFFICE in 1817, and the State University of New York in 1835 sometimes included phenological information. In 1855, Franklin B. HOUGH began publishing accumulated data from New York and shortly thereafter data collected by the Smithsonian Institution. This material provided an unprecedented opportunity for phenology, although no one drew any significant ecological conclusions from it.

Henry David Thoreau's understanding of ecological relationships is evident in his "Natural History of Massachusetts" (1842) and "The Succession of Forest Trees" (1860). Thoreau believed himself to be the first to make a comprehensive study of forest propagation. He discussed the means by which the seeds of different species were disseminated and explained that pines are succeeded by oaks because young oaks can grow in the shade of pine trees, whereas young pines cannot; but pines spring up when an oak forest is cut, because young pines can grow in an open field, while young oaks grow best in shade.

While serving as United States ambassador first to Turkey and then to Italy, George Perkins MARSH observed the long-term effects of man's impact on the environment. In 1864, he published *Man and Nature*, a treatise on the balance of nature and man's upsetting of this balance. The third chapter, "The Woods," encompassed one-third of the book. Although Marsh never conducted research in any forest, no American had earlier synthesized so well a knowledge of botany, meteorology, and geography in relation to the natural economy and the impact of deforestation upon the land. Marsh's book encouraged some Americans to seek the rational management of natural resources, and the *Report upon Forestry* (1877) prepared by Franklin B. Hough for the DEPARTMENT OF AGRICULTURE illustrated the necessity of ecological knowledge for forest management.

John Wesley Powell, in the report of the Geographical and Geological Survey of the Rocky Mountain Region (1878), explained the importance of matching land use with environmental conditions. He had found that rainfall was usually the limiting factor on tree growth in the intermontane West. He attempted to identify lands that could realistically be expected to maintain forests and those that could not. His ecological observations, like Hough's, assumed the necessity of scientific knowledge as a basis for practical decisions.

Questions about FOREST INFLUENCES upon the environment were obviously important, but they were not easily answered. Nevertheless, an 1893 report by forester Bernhard E. FERNOW and meteorologists M.W. Harrington, Cleveland Abbe, and George E. Curtis marshaled evidence of the relationships of forests to local climates, droughts, and floods. Although proof was lacking, existing evidence seemed to support the claim that forests had favorable influences in these environmental considerations.

Biological control was the first area of ecological investigation in which American naturalists took the lead. In 1905, after other methods had failed to eliminate the European gypsy moth from the forests around Medford, Massachusetts, U. S. Department of Agriculture entomologists L. O. Howard and W. F. Fiske attempted to introduce the moth's natural predators into the infested area. Their effort led to the publication of a monograph on the moth and its parasites (1910) but not to the elimination of the moth. This failure discouraged research on biological control in the East, though not in California, where it had succeeded in limiting the invasion of a citrus scale insect in 1888.

Throughout the nineteenth century, phytogeographers had described the composition and geographical range of types of vegetation (such as tundra, northern coniferous forests, and tropical rain forests). Plant ecologists, who extended these descriptions to local plant associations, in the twentieth century became embroiled in controversy over how to understand and describe such phenomena. A coastal plains pine forest, for example, was easily distinguished from a piedmont deciduous forest, but whereas some ecologists were impressed by the uniformity of each of these throughout its range, others were equally impressed by the degree to which the species within each changed from one end of its range to another.

Frederick E. Clements, who wrote *Plant Succession* (1916), held that associations were definite, classifiable entities with developmental histories controlled by climate and that, unless sidetracked by events such as fires, each would reach a stable climax community. This perspective was strengthened in a widely used text written by Clements and John E.

Weaver, *Plant Ecology* (1929). The persistence of Clements's influence is illustrated by E. Lucy Braun's *Deciduous Forests of Eastern North America* (1950). Henry A. Gleason, on the other hand, in the *Bulletin of the Torrey Botanical Club* (1926), maintained that superficially similar associations differed from place to place. Successional patterns seemed less fixed to him than they did to Clements. Gleason recognized no real climax communities. Before 1950, Gleason had few supporters, but by 1975 most academic ecologists had abandoned Clements's perspective for Gleason's.

Because modern plant ecology arose out of phytogeography rather than from practical concerns, foresters had to solve many of their own ecological problems. Furthermore, the total number of plant ecologists in the United States before 1950 was not large, and not all of them did research in forests. Consequently, plant physiologists, pathologists, and entomologists also made many important contributions to forest ecology. With the introduction of FORESTRY AS A PROFESSION in America, foresters began studying plant ecology under the name of "silvics." Fernow and the U. S. FOREST SERVICE began using that term in 1905, and in 1917 the SOCIETY OF AMERICAN FORESTERS defined it as "(1) that branch of ecology which treats of the life of trees in the forest, and (2) the life history, requirements, and general characteristics of a forest tree from the point of view of silviculture."

In 1928, James W. Toumey published his classic text, *Foundations of Silviculture upon an Ecological Basis.* He drew upon succession studies by Clements and others and asserted that with the ecologists' insights foresters could better control the kinds of stands that replaced the cut forest. After Toumey's death, his text was revised by Clarence F. Korstian (1937), and it remained standard until Stephen H. Spurr published *Forest Ecology* in 1964 (revised by Spurr and Burton V. Barnes in 1973).

Beginning in 1909, the Forest Service's own research stations also played a significant role in advancing forest ecology. Concern for the relation of forests to climate declined, except for the hope of diminishing prairie winds with SHELTERBELTS. However, foresters did continue to investigate the unresolved question from the nineteenth century of the relation of forests to water supply, particularly when the traditional wisdom was challenged by the ARMY CORPS OF ENGINEERS early in the twentieth century. In the 1950s, the Forest Service's experiment stations began compiling life histories of the forest trees within their respective regions. These studies were first published as pamphlets, but in 1965 H. A. Fowells collected and revised them under the title *Silvics of Forest Trees of the United States.* Both Fowells's handbook and the silviculture texts illustrated the blending of theoretical and applied plant ecology for the practical management of America's forests.

FURTHER READING: Richard H. Boerker, "A Historical Study of Forest Ecology: Its Development in the Fields of Botany and Forestry," *Forestry Quarterly* 14 (1916): 380-432. Frank N. Egerton, ed., *American Plant Ecology, 1897–1917* (1977), and *History of American Ecology* (1977). Ashley L. Schiff, *Fire and Water: Scientific Heresy in the Forest Service* (1962). Robert H. Whittaker, "Classification of Natural Communities," *Botanical Review* 28 (Jan.-Mar. 1962): 1-239 (reprinted separately, 1977).

FRANK N. EGERTON

EDGE, MABEL ROSALIE (1877–1962)

Born on November 3, 1877, into a wealthy New York family, Mabel Barrow married Charles Noel Edge, an engineer, in 1909. She returned from several years of European travel in 1913 and promptly became an ardent campaigner on behalf of woman suffrage. Later, a love of bird watching led her into the NATIONAL AUDUBON SOCIETY, but in 1929 she became disaffected with that organization after reading Willard G. Van Name's pamphlet, *A Crisis in Conservation,* which accused the society of being enmeshed in entangling alliances with firearms manufacturers. Mrs. Edge joined with Van Name, an official of the American Museum of Natural History, who had achieved prominence for his exposé, *Our Vanishing Forest Reserves* (1929), and with Irving Brant, a midwestern journalist and editor (and later biographer of James Madison), to form the Emergency Conservation Committee (ECC). The ECC was founded with the limited intention of reforming the Audubon Society, and its work apparently helped force the resignation of T. Gilbert Pearson from the society's presidency in 1934.

The ECC continued, however, with broader goals. It was less a membership organization or even a real committee than a name under which the indefatigable Mrs. Edge carried out a series of one-woman conservationist campaigns. Almost single-handed, she secured the creation of the Hawk Mountain Wildlife Sanctuary in Pennsylvania, the first refuge intended specifically to benefit birds of prey. (Privately owned, Hawk Mountain was administered by an association headed by Mrs. Edge.) She also led a bitter, four-year fight with several lumber companies, which resulted in the founding of OLYMPIC NATIONAL PARK in Washington State. Mrs. Edge was a leading figure in the movement to add 6,000 acres of old-growth sugar pine forest to YOSEM-

ITE NATIONAL PARK in 1937 and in the alliance that sponsored the establishment of Kings Canyon National Park (see SEQUOIA AND KINGS CANYON NATIONAL PARKS) in 1940.

She criticized other conservationists nearly as much as she cooperated with them, however. An absolute preservationist, she eventually came to regard all conservation organizations but the ECC as "limited and discriminating": they concentrated their efforts on a particular species or region and were not devoted to the protection of nature in general. Mrs. Edge tended to lump them all with the lumber industry as enemies to be warred upon. For thirty years, her ECC carried on feuds with other groups.

By 1948, Brant had left the ECC and Mrs. Edge had quarreled with Van Name. She worked on alone, financed by her own inherited fortune and small contributions (although the ECC is said to have claimed as many as 900 adherents in the late 1940s). When she died on November 30, 1962, the ECC ceased to exist. Single-minded, inflexible as a point of principle, Mrs. Edge was also extremely effective, "the only honest, unselfish, indomitable hellcat in the history of conservation," according to Van Name.

FURTHER READING: Maurice Broun, *Hawks Aloft: The Story of Hawk Mountain* (1949). Stephen Fox, *John Muir and His Legacy: The American Conservation Movement* (1981). Frank Graham, Jr., *Man's Dominion: The Story of Conservation in America* (1971).

EGLESTON, NATHANIEL HILLYER (1822–1912)

Nathaniel Egleston was born into an old New England family in Hartford, Connecticut, on May 7, 1822. A graduate of Yale Divinity School and a prominent Congregational minister, Egleston, a resident of Williamstown, Massachusetts, developed an interest in conserving forests. Upon the merger of the AMERICAN FORESTRY ASSOCIATION and the American Forestry Congress at Montreal in 1882, Egleston was elected a vice president of the combined organization, while the presidency went to his fellow Massachusetts resident, U. S. Commissioner of Agriculture George B. Loring. In May 1883, Loring appointed Egleston chief of the U.S. Division of Forestry; this action appears to have been an act of favoritism to a friend by which Loring demoted the energetic and prolific Franklin B. HOUGH, whom he disliked.

Conscientious and sincere in promoting forestry, Egleston composed a number of pamphlets and articles on the subject for such magazines as *Harpers, Atlantic,* and the *New Englander.* In his first annual report to Loring, he said that action should be taken to ensure that the extensive forestlands owned by the federal government were properly cared for and were used for the general welfare. He also recommended that the federal government establish forestry schools and forest experiment stations.

However, Egleston proved to be a weak administrator. Gifford PINCHOT was merciless in his later evaluation of him, and Egleston was apparently not well regarded by Loring's successor as commissioner of agriculture, Norman J. Colman, who had been appointed by President Grover Cleveland. Colman did not ask Egleston for a program for his division, nor did Egleston offer one, and a year later Cleveland arranged for Bernhard E. FERNOW's appointment as chief. Egleston appears to have been relieved rather than upset when he was replaced by the more qualified Fernow, and he remained with the division until 1898. He died on August 24, 1912.

FURTHER READING: Harold K. Steen, *The U. S. Forest Service: A History* (1976), pp. 20-21. *National Cyclopaedia of American Biography*, 13 (1906), pp. 340-341.

FRANK J. HARMON

ENTOMOLOGY

See Forest Entomology

ENVIRONMENTAL MOVEMENT

In the late 1950s and early 1960s, a new set of public concerns began to take shape which came to be called the "environmental movement." This differed markedly from the older "CONSERVATION MOVEMENT," expressing objectives of environmental quality and ecology rather than efficient material resource development and management, and constituting a broad, mass movement far more than did earlier conservation efforts.

These new concerns arose out of the massive social and economic changes that took place in American society after World War II. Much of this came from the rising standard of living of the American people and the growth of amenities, as distinguished from earlier preoccupation with necessities and conveniences, as an increasing aspect of leisure time and consumption patterns. As with advanced industrial societies generally, Americans began to place less emphasis in their lives on work, and more on home, family and leisure, and the quality of these nonwork activities. One aspect of these new values and objectives was a higher quality of one's surrounding environment, the air, water, and land.

The memory of unregulated logging followed by fire and erosion added fuel to the environmental movement. This photograph was taken in Colorado in 1915. Forest Service Photo.

At the same time that these new values came to be important to a large segment of Americans, modern technology developed a new capability for environmental disruption. The scale of industrial plants, electrical generating utilities, highways, surface mining, housing developments, and transmission lines grew so rapidly that these often appeared to constitute massive threats and intrusions into either residential communities or places where one enjoyed recreational and leisure-time activities. At the same time, the use of chemicals increased markedly. Chemical waste often got into the air, water, and land to inflict harm on people, plants, and animals to such an extent that it seemed out of control. Much of the environmental movement arose from attempts by people to protect the environment they knew and prized from such degradation.

These twin objectives—enhancement and protection of one's environment—often gave rise to a broader concern for the long-run viability of the physical and biological world upon which sustained human institutions depended. Much environmental degradation seemed to disrupt normally functioning biological processes, to change ecosystems in undesirable ways, to destroy plant and animal species, to diminish agricultural and wildlands through rapid development and suburbanization. As the 1970s wore on, there was increasing concern about the exhaustion of the supply of material resources and especially energy. Many began to argue that there were "limits to growth," that the carrying capacity of the earth was finite, and that rapid population growth, personal consumption, and waste in industrial production endangered the long-run viability of human society.

Few of these concerns had appeared earlier in the conservation movement, which had focused primarily on resource development. In fact, much of the new environmental movement was at odds with the earlier conservation concerns. In forestry, conservation had stressed sustained-yield wood production, whereas the environmental movement thought of the forest as an environment for home, work, and play rather than as a source of commodities. The environmental demand for wilderness designations and aesthetic management met with severe opposition from professional foresters interested primarily in wood production. In the development of water resouces, which had earlier played a major role in conservation activities, the construction of dams and channelization and dredging of streams met with vigorous environmental opposition because of preference for free-flowing streams and natural wetland systems. Beyond this, the interest in air and water quality were quite new concerns which had not been a part of earlier conservation activities at all.

The environmental movement began to take shape in the late 1950s and early 1960s largely around objectives associated with public land management. Outdoor RECREATION had grown rapidly after World War II and, by the late 1950s, had led to the creation of the OUTDOOR RECREATION RESOURCES REVIEW COMMISSION which outlined a variety of possible programs.

The Wilderness Act of 1964 created a national system of wilderness areas, and in 1968 new acts provided for a national system of hiking trails and WILD AND SCENIC RIVERS. At the same time, a special fund to finance outdoor recreation, the Land and Water Conservation Fund, was created in 1964 to provide money for outdoor recreation activities at both the federal and the state levels. All these activities continued vigorously into the 1970s. The wilderness movement, for example, continued to expand and to gather even more vigorous support than it had in the early 1960s; its most significant effort in these years was the drive to designate wilderness areas in Alaska.

In the 1960s, the new concern about pollution began to take shape. One can trace the interest in both air and water pollution back to earlier decades, but these were localized and limited efforts, and it was not until the late 1950s that communities began to demand that special steps be undertaken to reduce both kinds of degra-

dation. Much of the initial interest was aesthetic; smoke made cities unattractive, and raw sewage floating in streams, such as the Potomac River at Washington, D.C., was both unsightly and offensive to human smell. Federal laws passed in the 1960s provided a significant underpinning for a new management program for both air and water; they became a comprehensive federal attack when the Clean Air Act and the Clean Water Act were passed in 1970 and 1972. More and more, these programs came to emphasize the adverse effects of pollution on human health as well as on fish and other biological life.

New concerns absorbed an increasing amount of attention from the environmental movement in the 1970s. One arose from the adverse impact of harmful chemicals. The concern for pesticides had arisen much earlier, in the late 1950s, and had been emphasized especially by Rachel CARSON in her book, *Silent Spring* (1962). In the 1970s, this was extended to

This 160-foot diameter device at the Bellingham, Washington, plant of Georgia-Pacific Corporation treats 20 million gallons of pulp mill waste per day. Georgia-Pacific Photo.

harmful chemicals to which workers were exposed in the workplace, to chemicals escaping from industrial plants to contaminate the air and water, and to the presence of many toxic waste dumps from which chemicals leaked into water supplies and the air. The other involved the question of energy supplies. Almost every form of energy production and conversion gave rise to some environmental harm, such as the destruction of a wild river by a dam, stream pollution from surface mining, or the dangers of atomic energy. By the time of the first interruption of Middle East oil supplies in the winter of 1973–1974, the environmental movement had developed an alternative energy program that would increase supplies and at the same time be far more environmentally benign. It emphasized greater efficiency in energy use—conservation, a moratorium on nuclear power, rapid development of photovoltaic solar energy, and the use of coal, under strict controls and safeguards, as an interim source.

Throughout the 1970s, environmental affairs took on an international scope. Environmental problems increasingly appeared to be transnational and global: the pollution of seas, such as the Mediterranean, shared by several nations, the "transboundary" flow of air pollution within Europe or between Canada and the United States, the pollution of the oceans from oil spills, the depletion of the ocean fishery and the destruction of tropical forests, the feared imbalance between population and food supply and the build-up of carbon dioxide in the atmosphere. This concern was spearheaded by the United Nations Conference on the Environment, held in Stockholm, Sweden, in 1972, and the subsequent establishment of the United Nations Environment Program. Citizen organizations such as the SIERRA CLUB, the NATIONAL AUDUBON SOCIETY, and the Natural Resources Defense Council developed special international programs, and environmental professionals in the United States participated actively in research and writing about them, often jointly with their counterparts in other nations. By 1980, two reports gave these issues sharp focus: one, a *World Conservation Strategy*, prepared by the World Wildlife Fund, and the other, *The Global 2000 Report to the President*, drawn up by the U. S. Council on Environmental Quality.

The environmental movement was popular and mass based; it arose far less from the institutional leaders of society and far more from the general public as people in many places and many walks of life sought to enhance and protect their environment. These popular demands gave rise to legislation, but they also stimulated much more public influence through the courts and in administrative decision making. Several environmental groups hired lawyers and financed litigation on behalf of environmental objectives, often seeking to restrict the environmentally harmful effect of development sponsored by federal agencies. The courts gave "standing" to individuals to protect their environmental rights, and many laws provided that citizens could sue to enforce them. Administrative agencies found themselves challenged directly by citizens who demanded actions more in tune with environmental objectives. One extremely useful environmental process was the environmental impact statement, provided in the NATIONAL ENVIRONMENTAL POLICY ACT of 1969, in which each federal agency had to assess the environmental impact of its actions and propose alternatives that might be environmentally preferable. Much litigation took place under this requirement, which served to modify somewhat the practices of some federal agencies.

The management of the public lands was especially influenced by public involvement. Strong citizen interest in designation of wilderness areas on the national forests gave rise to the first major role of the public in the formation of administrative environmental policy. Plans for wilderness, and later for general forest management, were prepared in draft form which then were circulated for public comment. At various stages in the decision-making process, public meetings for input from citizens were held. These became the pattern for environmental impact statements which the courts required; they were mandated for all forest plans and for the various plans in the administrative districts of the BUREAU OF LAND MANAGEMENT. Administrative agencies responded to these persistent citizen demands for policies favorable to their views by developing a host of procedures for involving the public. The FOREST SERVICE was perhaps most involved in this process. In the wilderness review procedure known as RARE II, completed in 1979, over 264,000 letters or other responses were received by the Forest Service.

The environmental movement did not proceed without considerable opposition. This came especially from those in both public and private life who were committed to material development objectives and who looked upon environmental objectives as secondary and often unnecessary. Whereas environmentalists looked upon their gains as merely a modest beginning, developmentalists considered them to be "extreme." Public development agencies, while privately resistant to environmental demands—a resistance displayed by their constant effort to limit citizen input into administrative decision—sought to convey a stance of acceptance. Many private businessmen were more explicitly hostile. While accepting some environmental innovations, they increasingly developed political strategies to thwart and turn back many gains. As the environmental movement came on stronger in the late 1960s and early 1970s, developmental groups were momentarily stunned and reacted in disbelief. Soon, however, they began to organize in opposition and did so effectively throughout the decade. Often they were able to blunt legislation considerably by influencing administrative choices in implementing laws. And they used the courts even more frequently than did environmentalists in pressing their case. Throughout the 1970s, this opposition succeeded in holding back many environmental objectives.

To most environmental issues there was a highly technical context; many matters of land management, air and water pollution, and the ecological effects of chemical pollutants depended on technical questions of fact. Hence scientific investigations played a critical role in environmental debates. This provided the environmental movement with a significant opportunity, of which it took full advantage, to bring into debates much technical information which institutional leaders in government, corporations, and even scientific organizations tended to overlook. But in this task the environmental movement was also at a disadvantage, for the discovery, acquisition, transfer, and application of information in decision making was often costly, and business corporations and government enjoyed far greater resources. This inequality in political influence which the environmental movement faced was symptomatic of the way in which the new political inequality in American society turned heavily on inequality in the access to and use of technical information.

Even though developmental opposition had become a formidable force by the late 1970s, the environmental movement also remained strong. Public opinion studies indicated that concern for air and water pollution remained high, that a large majority of Americans felt that forests should not be cut further, that deserts should be protected from development and motorized intrusion, that wildlife habitat should be retained in the face of development and that wetlands should be protected. The views of institutional leaders in government and the professions as well as in private business did not always reflect these attitudes, giving rise to the conviction by environmentalists that only through continued public pressure could the environmental gains of the 1960s and 1970s be maintained and furthered. This popular element, so absent in the earlier conservation movement, was the vehicle by which changing public values in the advanced industrial society of the United States were translated into public policy.

FURTHER READING: Lynton K. Caldwell, Lynton R. Hayes, and Isabel M. MacWhirter, *Citizens and the Environment: Case Studies in Popular Action* (1976). Environmental Defense Fund and Robert H. Boyle, *Malignant Neglect* (1979). Michael Frome, *Battle for the Wilderness* (1974). Ronald Inglehart, *The Silent Revolution: Changing Values and Political Styles Among Western Publics* (1977). Harvey Lieber, *Federalism and Clean Waters* (1975). Ian L. McHarg, *Design with Nature* (1969). Ralph Nader and John Abbotts, *The Menace of Atomic Energy* (1979). Rice Odell, *Environmental Awakening: The New Revolution to Protect the Earth* (1980). Frank J. Popper, *The Politics of Land-Use Reform* (1981). Joel Primack and Frank von Hippel, *Advice and Dissent: Scientists in the Political Arena* (1974). Joseph L. Sax, *Mountains Without Handrails: Reflections on the National Parks* (1980). Anne W. Simon, *The Thin Edge* (1978). Richard J. Tobin, *The Social Gamble* (1979). The best compilation of environmental affairs during the 1970s is contained in the annual reports of the Council on Environmental Quality (1970–1981).

SAMUEL P. HAYS

EVERGLADES NATIONAL PARK AND BIG CYPRESS NATIONAL PRESERVE

In 1979, Everglades National Park contained just under 1.4 million acres of unique subtropical vegetation, making it the third largest American national park. The park represents almost one-fifth of the geographical area known as "Everglades," a region drowned by a shallow sheet of water moving slowly southwestward from Lake Okeechobee to Florida Bay. Most of this region is covered by waist-high sawgrass interspersed with hammocks or forested islands of pine, mahogany, cypress, palm, and oak. On the coast are dense growths of mangroves, important as spawning grounds for shrimp and other marine life. The park preserves a habitat for many rare species of animals, birds, and fish. These include alligators, crocodiles, manatees, anhingas, egrets, herons, and spoonbills. From the time of European discovery and subsequent Spanish colonization, people dreamed of draining the Everglades for the purpose of turning the swamplands into an agricultural paradise. Since 1900, the State of Florida and the United States government have spent large sums for drainage and flood control with the result that vast tracts in the northern Everglades have been opened to sugar culture, vegetable growing, and cattle raising.

In the nineteenth century, virtually the only visitors to the lower Everglades were commercial hunters, especially plume hunters who sought the feathers of egrets and other exotic birds to decorate women's hats. During the 1890s, however, naturalists began to visit the region and report on its extraordinary plant and animal life. Fearful that lumbermen and farmers would destroy the natural beauty, the Florida Federation of Women's Clubs induced the Florida legislature and the Florida East Coast Railroad to set aside land for a small wild preserve. Royal Palm State Park, administered by the Federation, was opened in 1916. This tract, originally only 1,920 acres, formed the nucleus of what later became Everglades National Park.

During the 1920s, conservationists in the Miami area formed the Everglades National Park Association led by Ernest Coe to agitate for the establishment of a much larger reserve. In 1929, Congress authorized the secretary of the interior to investigate the feasibility of such a park and in 1934 passed a bill authorizing a maximum boundary within which state and private lands might be acquired for the Everglades National Park. This was signed into law by President Franklin D. ROOSEVELT on May 30, 1934.

Because of the Great Depression and other problems, neither Congress nor the Florida legislature was willing to make the appropriations necessary for land purchases and park development. To reduce costs and overcome the opposition of land speculators, the park was reduced in size from a projected 2 million acres to 1.4 million acres. With these obstacles removed, President Harry Truman formally opened Everglades National Park on December 6, 1947.

Some of the land left out of Everglades National Park when its boundaries were redrawn lay within the Florida Keys; the rest was in the region to the northwest of the park known as the Big Cypress Swamp. Higher in elevation than the Everglades, Big Cypress Swamp had a more prairielike appearance and consisted of numerous stands of centuries-old cypress along with palm, pine, and oak. During the Seminole wars, it was the last refuge for the Seminole and Mikasuki tribes. At the beginning of the twentieth century, lumber companies purchased large tracts of the marshland and prepared to harvest the timber. Oil exploration began near the swamp community of Pinecrest in 1939, and four years later Humble Oil and Refining Company brought in the first commercially successful well in Sunniland. Other land developers busily sold Northern customers Florida swampland in the Big Cypress. These interest groups united to keep the Big Cypress Swamp from inclusion in the Everglades National Park.

Whereas a portion of the Everglades was protect-

ed, Big Cypress was open to exploitation. Lumber companies exhausted the resources of cypress and pine by 1957. Oil and gas production grew with new finds, however, and discoveries continued in the 1980s. Land development and land fraud also continued.

A new type of land development occurred when the Dade County Port Authority in 1967 began a search for a site to construct a supersonic jetport. In September 1968, clearing began on a thirty-nine-square- mile location in the Big Cypress Swamp. Conservation organizations, fearing that development of the jetport would destroy the major source of water for Everglades National Park, joined in opposition, and in August 1969, the secretary of the interior, the secretary of transportation, and the governor of Florida together halted construction until appropriate ecological studies were undertaken. The majority of these studies concluded that the completion of the jetport would do irreversible damage to the Big Cypress Swamp, and federal, state, and local authorities agreed on January 15, 1970, to a so-called jetport pact, which stopped further development and renewed a search for another site.

The jetport controversy served as a catalyst to efforts to protect Big Cypress. Both the legislative and executive branches of the United States government undertook to protect the valuable watershed. President Richard Nixon in November 1971 announced that his administration planned to introduce legislation in Congress to acquire the Big Cypress Swamp. The purpose of the legislation was to protect the rare flora and fauna of the swamp and to maintain the area as a vital water source for the Everglades. Despite this commitment by the administration, congressional delegations from Florida, and conservation groups, federal action was not taken on the proposal until after the Florida legislature in 1973 passed an act designating Big Cypress as an area of critical concern. This state legislation allocated $40 million to assist the federal government in any land acquisition. Congress responded by passing an act authorizing federal expenditures of $116 million and establishing Big Cypress National Preserve. President Gerald Ford signed the bill into law on October 11, 1974.

Designation as a national preserve acknowledges that the land is far from pristine. The legislation allows continuation of oil and gas exploration, various nontraditional recreational activities, traditional activities of the Seminole and Mikasuki Indians, and private landownership under federal regulation. The goal of the legislation is to protect the area from further drainage and provide a perpetual water supply for Everglades National Park. In 1979, the preserve contained 570,000 acres of which 232,000 were in federal ownership. The state-designated area of critical concern where development is strictly regulated includes the federal preserve and an additional 288,000 acres.

FURTHER READING: Luther J. Carter, *The Florida Experience: Land and Water Policy in a Growth State* (1974). Marjorie Stoneman Douglas, *The Everglades: River of Grass* (1947). Junius E. Dovell, "A History of the Everglades of Florida," Ph.D. dissertation, University of North Carolina (1947). Charlton W. Tebeau, *Man in the Everglades: 2000 Years of Human History in the Everglades National Park* (1968).

JOHN C. PAIGE

EVOLUTION AND DISTRIBUTION OF AMERICAN FORESTS

Certain characteristics of North American forests have their roots in the geologic past, so that a historical approach provides a useful perspective for understanding their present character. In this endeavor it is not necessary to delve back farther than the early part of the Cenozoic era, which began approximately 75 million years ago. Many modern plant genera and even some species of modern trees may have been living then.

The Eocene Epoch

In late Eocene time the North American continent supported no mountains, and whatever ranges of hills existed were inadequate to exert significant influence on the climatic pattern, such as our mountains do at present. Seas had encroached on the continental margins, and their temperature-ameliorating influence, when added to the relative flatness of the land, prevented extremes of climatic conditions. Latitudinal belts of climate and of forest vegetation were far more regular than they are today.

The frost line undoubtedly occurred far north of its present position, for tropical tree genera such as *Ficus* (fig), *Laurus*, *Persea*, and *Sabal* (palmetto) had a place in forests which occupied approximately two-thirds of the present United States. The frost-free

Cenozoic Era

Eocene Epoch	began 60 million years ago
Oligocene Epoch	40 million years
Miocene Epoch	26 million years
Pliocene Epoch	13 million years
Pleistocene Epoch (Ice Age)	2.5 million years
Postglacial Epoch	12,000 years

character of this region can be inferred not only from the kinds of trees in the fossil assemblages but also from the fact that nearly 90 percent of the broad-leaved woody species had smooth leaf margins. This proportion is similar to that in the modern Amazon forests and very different from that in the present temperate forests where tooth-margined leaves prevail. Also, the Eocene trees were well burdened with vines, again as in tropical forests. Curiously, these tropical trees always grew intermingled with genera now characteristic of temperate forests, such as *Corylus* (hazel), *Betula* (birch), *Castanea* (chestnut and chinkapin), *Alnus* (alder), and *Pinus* (pine). Since trees in these genera nearly all require a chilly season to stimulate each new increment of growth, the climate must have been cool enough in winter to meet their requirements, yet lacked frost to which the tropical trees are sensitive. Modern conditions like these occur at the southern tip of Florida, where tropical trees are able to endure occasional light frosts and yet winters are cool enough to satisfy the needs of many temperate-zone trees.

The tropical elements in Eocene forests dropped out at about the latitude of the northern tier of states, allowing familiar temperate zone trees such as *Fagus* (beech), *Acer* (maple), *Tilia* (basswood), *Quercus* (oak), *Pinus*, *Tsuga* (hemlock), *Thuja* (arborvitae), and *Sequoia* to dominate in a broad belt stretching across most of Canada and Alaska. Most of these trees can endure long periods of temperature well below freezing, but they require considerable heat in summer to complete their growth and metabolic processes. Only across the northern fringe of the continent, from Alaska to Greenland, was summer heat inadequate for temperate zone forest, and so only a few genera of trees such as *Abies* (fir), *Pinus*, *Betula*, *Populus* (cottonwood and poplar), and *Corylus* contributed to the forest vegetation of that arctic fringe.

The Oligocene Epoch

Late Eocene time was a period of maximum warmth, with plants achieving their most northern distribution limits. Subsequently, starting with the Oligocene epoch, there were erratic variations in climate through millennia, but the general trend was one of lowering temperatures.

The frost line receded southward rather rapidly, resulting in most tropical trees dying out except in the southern tier of states. Summer heat must not have declined proportionately, for temperate forest still persisted in Alaska.

A second major feature of Oligocene time was the

start of significant uplift in the Rocky Mountain region. Whatever hilliness had been there earlier had no great effect on rainfall distribution, but now the ridges became high enough to intercept moisture as it was carried from west to east by the prevailing air streams of the westerlies. The more rain fell on the windward slopes of the Rockies, the less was carried over the crest to keep the east slope and adjacent plains moist, so that in Oligocene time drought east of the Rockies caused the elimination of closed forest, with either savanna, or possibly even steppe, developing in the rain shadow of the Rockies.

The Miocene Epoch

Continued cooling during Miocene time resulted in the temperate forest retreating southward, allowing the impoverished but cold-tolerant forest that had been confined to arctic latitudes to spread southward and become a subarctic belt.

As the transcontinental belt of temperate forest was forced southward, it encountered the dry area just east of the Rockies, and, as drought had intensified and expanded over even a larger area by Miocene time, the temperate forest split into segments moving southward on either side of the arid tract. The western segment encountered more adversity, for an uplift of the Sierra Nevada axis made the intermountain area too dry for the moisture-adapted mesophytic temperate forest but suitable for xerophytic (that is, adapted to survive seasons of considerable dryness) woodland and scrub to extend northward from Mexico between the Sierra Nevada and the Rockies. Despite the splitting of temperate mesophytic forest, in Miocene time it still retained its rich complement of both angiosperm and gymnosperm trees in both the eastern and western segments.

The Pliocene Epoch

Further climatic cooling allowed the subarctic forest characterized by *Abies, Picea, Pinus*, and *Betula* to expand as a broad belt across Canada, with tundra developing on the northern margin of the continent which had become too heat-deficient for any trees.

Temperate forest plants east of the midcontinental steppe were able to continue their southward migrations and maintain harmonious relationships with temperature conditions since the eastern half of the continent still had abundant rainfall the year around, and the north–south orientation of the Appalachians kept these mountains from acting as a barrier to southward migration. However, the southern climate proved increasingly incompatible for most of the evergreen coniferous elements of this eastern segment of temperate forest, and they came to play relatively minor roles, and these mainly in the northern part of the temperate belt. These persisting conifers include *Tsuga, Thuja, Pinus*, and *Chamaecyparis* (whitecedar). Even *Sequoia*, which had been an especially widespread member of the early Cenozoic temperate forest, disappeared in the east. Tropical trees retained but precarious footholds on the southern fringes of North America.

Those temperate forest plants that had become segregated west of the midcontinental arid lowlands found adequate moisture mostly in a narrow strip of land west of the Cascade-Sierra axis, but as continental cooling tended to force them southward down this strip, they encountered aridity spreading northward from southern California and Mexico. Lowering temperatures in the proximity of the Pacific Ocean reduced the summer heat supply, but at the same time they kept the winters from becoming very cold. Sunny days, especially in autumn and spring, permitted photosynthetic activity in plants that kept their leaves in winter and so were equipped to take advantage of them. Evergreen conifers found such a climate very favorable. On the other hand, many deciduous trees, such as *Fagus, Tilia, Liquidambar* (sweetgum), *Carya* (hickory), and *Ulmus* (elm), which stood leafless during those favorably warm periods, were unable to get sufficient heat during the cool summers, and so died out in the west. Only a few broadleaved trees such as *Juglans* (walnut), *Platanus* (sycamore), and *Cercis* (redbud) were able to survive in the west by taking advantage of mainly stream-margin habitats which enabled them to extend south into the warmer but dry latitudes. As the temperate mesophytic forest in the west lost most of its broadleaf components during Pliocene time, conifers such as *Sequoia, Tsuga, Thuja, Chamaecyparis, Pseudotsuga* (Douglas-fir), and *Abies* assumed dominance. *Pseudotsuga* almost alone among these trees retained substantial representation in the mountains of the Cordillera, taking advantage of an elevational range that is high enough to avoid the dryness of the basal plains and foothills, but below the chilly subalpine belt where *Picea* (spruce) and *Abies*, filtering down from the north, were the prevailing dominants.

The expanding aridity of the southwest which so hampered the southward migration of temperate-zone mesophytes allowed a gradual differentiation of chaparral scrub and woodland in sections where the winters were not too cold, and woodland or forest in foothills where aridity was not so intense but winters were cold. The very lowest and driest areas became desert from New Mexico to southern California and southward in Mexico, with steppe developing to the north. In contrast to the temperate mesophytic and subarctic forests, which spread southward during early Cenozoic time, the xerophytic vegetation of the foothills and basal plains expanded northward from Mexican origins.

During the chilling that brought about the southward plant migrations, the mountains of western North America were lifted higher and higher. As their summits became cool enough, tree species evolutionarily derived from the transcontinental subarctic forest extended southward down the mountains. Eventually these summits rose until the very highest ridges became too cold for any trees and became covered with alpine tundra. The *Picea-Abies* forests then became a subalpine belt on the mountain slopes.

The Pleistocene Epoch

Continental cooling climaxed during the Pleistocene epoch, with several periods so cold that ice accumulated in central Canada and radiated outward as glaciers, most of which spread about as far south as the Ohio and Missouri rivers before a warm interval caused them to waste away. Essentially all the subarctic forest and arctic tundra belts were devastated during these ice floods, but the cooling allowed most of the component species of these belts to extend southward beyond the ice and commingle with the temperate vegetation which persisted even close to the ice fronts. Thus extinction was prevented, and taxonomic stocks remained available to reconstitute the boreal vegetation as the ice melted away. In the western mountains, vegetation belts shifted to lower altitudes, and, since the lowered temperatures made the scant rainfall more effective, desert and other xerophytic vegetation temporarily became restricted in area. Along the Pacific Coast, mesophytic forest could shift southward only a short distance owing to aridity, but, since continental glaciation got no farther south than the present State of Washington, taxonomic diversity suffered very little.

In the approximately 12,000 years since the last major glacier receded, the distribution of vegetation in North America has resumed its Pliocene pattern. In about the middle of this span there was a period of abnormally high temperatures which allowed dry land vegetation to expand for a time, but even the effects of that episode have been essentially erased. The result of this 75 million-year evolutionary history of North American vegetation is a plant cover over a large part of the present United States which may be classified within eight basic types distinguished by their major features of composition and ecology: the *subarctic, subalpine, eastern temperate mesophytic, western temperate mesophytic, temperate xerophytic,* and *tropical seasonal* forests; *microphyllous woodland;* and *tropical rainforest.*

The Subarctic Forest

The transcontinental belt of subarctic forest of today extends from the east coast of Canada to the eastern foothills of the range of mountains next to the Pacific Coast. Apparently, *Picea glauca* (white spruce), *P. mariana* (black spruce), and *Larix laricina* (tamarack) are relatively intolerant of oceanic climate. *Picea* barely reached the Arctic Ocean at Norton Sound and the Mackenzie Delta, and the Pacific Ocean at Cook Inlet; *Picea mariana* and *Larix* show even less tolerance, but *Betula papyrifera* (paper birch) occurs on the coast both at Kodiak Island and British Columbia.

The same adversity of oceanic climates prevented any of these subarctic trees from pressing farther south in the inland west during glaciation. They were all eliminated west of the Rocky Mountain foothills as the last (Wisconsin) glacier swept into northern Idaho and Washington, deep in the path of the westerlies which drag oceanic influences far inland around the latitude of the international border.

East of the Rockies, *Picea glauca* responded to glacial climatic changes by spreading far south into what is now steppe, as shown by peat fossils in Texas and New Mexico. Possibly this indicates no more than interfingering by means of wetlands in the steppe region, with much of the land between the peat-accumulating lowlands remaining prairie despite better moisture relations resulting from lowered temperatures. East of the Mississippi, *Picea glauca* and other boreal trees extended equally far south, becoming intimately intermingled with broadleaved trees of the temperate mesophytic forest.

As the southern edge of Wisconsin ice melted back, trees spread northward as rapidly as land became exposed, yet some fragmentary populations of boreal species persisted well south of the ultimate line of their continuous distribution. Thus *Picea glauca* still occurs in the Black Hills of South Dakota and in southeastern Michigan, *Picea mariana* in Pennsylvania, *Larix* (tamarack) in West Virginia, and *Abies balsamea* (balsam fir) in Iowa.

Trees of the subarctic forest can endure the most extreme winter temperatures without injury, but they must have a minimum amount of summer heat. The temperature of the warmest month must average at least ten degrees centigrade or tundra covers the landscape. At their southern limits in the east, these trees are restricted to sites having the coolest microclimates, where they are most free of competition from temperate zone trees. Dryness becomes limiting in mid-continent, with boreal forest giving way to prairie in southern Canada.

Fire is an important element in subarctic environment, and its effects are evident in most landscapes. Since coniferous foliage and wood are rich in resins and low temperatures retard decomposition so that thick layers of litter and duff accumulate, hot fires may sweep the landscape after only a few warm days in summer have dried the debris.

The composition of subarctic forest is distinctive east of the Rockies. There, in places where zonal soils remain free of fire for a long time, *Picea glauca, Betula papyrifera,* and *Abies balsamea* tend to become canopy dominants. The last is the most shade-tolerant, but it also has the disadvantages of being very easily killed by fire, least adapted to cast its seeds any distance into a burned area, and short-lived after it gets there. Thus the *Picea* and *Betula* are first to crowd out the opportunistic plants that are quick to invade burned sites, and they form long-lasting members of the community.

The first fire followers usually include large amounts of *Epilobium angustifolium, Pteridium aquilinum,* or *Rubus idaeus.* A number of trees also seed in quickly and eventually crowd out the shorter plants as they lift their canopies above them. *Betula papyrifera, Populus tremuloides* (quaking aspen), *Pinus banksiana* (jack pine), *P. resinosa* (red pine), and *Picea mariana* form forests temporarily, until *Picea glauca* and *Abies balsamea* displace them. *Betula,* although primarily a temporary invader, persists in the oldest forests, maintaining its place by sprouting from the root summit after each forest fire.

Glaciation left undulating topography with varying soil texture, varying mineral content, and varying depth to water tables. Thus forest productivity differs considerably from place to place, and a very good indicator of this productivity is the composition of the relatively rich flora of herbs and shrubs beneath the trees. For example, in Quebec recognition of only fifteen species of critical indicator plants is needed to assess the productivity of forestland and ascertain the areal extent of that productivity class.

Westward and northward from the eastern foothills of the Rockies the subarctic forest has distinctive characteristics. *Abies balsamea, Pinus banksiana,* and *P. resinosa* do not occur in that section, but *P. contorta* (lodgepole pine), ecologically equivalent to *P. banksiana,* becomes an important invader of deforested sites. The forest undergrowth also has distinctive species, such as the abundant *Shepherdia canadensis* and *Lupinus arcticus,* but their value for forest productivity assessment has not been worked out.

Thus far the vegetation of zonal soils that are podzols or at least podzolic has been the focus of our attention, but glaciation left many basins in which lakes, ponds, fens, and bogs have developed, as well as large areas of nutrient-poor outwash sand and extended tracts of bedrock with only thin and interrupted films of loose material to cover it. Wetlands commonly pass through stages in which *Carex* dominates a fen, followed by shrubbery (such as *Chamaedaphne, Ledum, Vaccinium, Oxycoccus,* and *Alnus*) with *Sphagnum* as a ground cover, and finally a *Picea mariana/Sphagnum* swamp. *Pinus banksiana* and *P. contorta* exceed all other trees in their ability to form permanent forests on poor sands. Such forests are not dense, their undergrowth is impoverished, and xerophytic lichens are conspicuous. East of Hudson Bay, glaciers swept the bedrock so clean that in large areas the tree cover is broken and limited to slight depressions containing a little gravel, or moss and lichens, to serve as a rooting medium.

Beyond the northern limits of dense forest there are successively shorter and more open stands of trees as arctic timberland is approached. *Picea mariana, P. glauca, Larix, Abies,* and in the west *Populus balsamifera* (balsam poplar) may dominate this broad belt of stunted trees.

The Subalpine Forest

In the Appalachians and Rocky Mountains, tree species evolutionarily derived from those of subarctic forest dominate forest belts below alpine summits, wherever peaks and ridges attain sufficient height.

Throughout the Appalachians, *Picea rubens* (red spruce) is an important species. It is so closely related to *P. glauca* that the two hybridize over a large area astride the Canadian border. A break in the continuity of the high Appalachians occurs in Pennsylvania, and this gap corresponds to an important difference in the vegetation of the northern and southern sections. *Picea mariana* as well as *P. rubens* are important upland trees in the northern Appalachians, where *Betula papyrifera* and *Pinus resinosa* are joined by other fire followers such as *Acer rubrum* (red maple), *Populus grandidentata* (bigtooth aspen), and *Prunus virginiana* (chokecherry). In the southern Appalachians, the only important trees are *Picea rubens, Abies fraseri* (Fraser fir, closely related to *A. balsamea*), and *Betula alleghaniensis* (yellow birch), the last playing a role similar to that of *B. papyrifera* in the north. The northern Appalachians contain some bogs similar to those of the subarctic, but none of these are found in the south. In the latter area two unique types of vegetation are heath balds and grass balds. Heath balds occupy exposed and excessively drained ridges, and are dominated by medium to tall members of the heath family, such as several species of *Rhododendron, Kalmia latifolia* (mountain-laurel), and *Vaccinium corymbosum.* Grass balds cap rounded summits with a cover of grasses and sedges of a rather xerophytic stamp.

Throughout the Appalachians there are undergrowth plants of the same or closely related species as occur in subarctic forest. A few of the highest mountains in the northern Appalachians exceed the upper limits of tree growth and support alpine tundra vegetation. In the southern Appalachians there is no vestige of alpine tundra left, although during the height of glaciation the high ridges there appear to have supported it.

In the Rocky Mountain subalpine forests, *Picea engelmannii* (Engelmann spruce) and *Abies lasiocarpa* (subalpine fir) are close relatives of the subarctic dominants. In these mountains *Populus tremuloides* and *Pinus contorta* are the characteristic fire-followers, although the latter does not extend into the southern Rockies. Many high peaks and ridges support alpine tundra, and as the tree line is approached several species of pine accompany the *Picea* and *Abies: Pinus albicaulis* in the northern Rockies, *P. flexilis* (limber pine) in the central and southern Rockies, *P. aristata* (bristlecone pine) and its variety *P. longaeva* in the central section. A remarkable feature of this subalpine forest is the way in which the major dominants maintain their tall spirelike stature until they get within about 100 meters of the alpine tree line where the last individuals are extremely dwarfed and misshapen by the wind. *Populus tremuloides* not only plays the role of a fire follower in certain habitat types, but it also forms permanent and more pure stands on pockets of moist, rich soil. Subalpine forests are frequently interrupted by parks, permanently treeless areas usually of limited extent, in which heavy soils prevent tree invasion, leaving the area to a cover of grasses, or grasses with *Artemisia.*

The Sierra-Cascade mountain chain, as well as ridges next to the Pacific farther north, all come under such strong oceanic influences that neither the subarctic forest trees nor their evolutionary derivatives have been able to dominate the cold slopes just below upper tree lines. *Tsuga mertensiana* (mountain hemlock) occurs throughout these ranges, but it is accom-

panied, or locally almost displaced, by a variety of other conifers. In southern Alaska, *Chamaecyparis nootkatensis* (Alaska-cedar) is a minor codominant, and here *Picea sitchensis* (Sitka spruce) is the only important invader of deforested sites. Both *Tsuga* and *Chamaecyparis* extend southward through the subalpine belts of British Columbia, Washington, and Oregon, where the forest is enriched locally by *Abies amabilis* (Pacific silver fir) and *A. lasiocarpa.* Even more tree species form pioneer stands on devastated sites: *Abies procera* (noble fir), *Larix occidentalis* (western larch), *Picea engelmannii, Pinus contorta, Pseudotsuga menziesii* (Douglas-fir), *Pinus monticola* (western white pine), *P. albicaulis,* and *Larix lyallii.* The last two occur mainly in the upper edge of the subalpine belt where they retain permanent status in the discontinuous tree cover.

This central section of the Pacific subalpine forest, where the westerlies have a strong oceanic influence on the climates, is the only latitude where *Abies lasiocarpa* and *Picea engelmannii,* which are primarily characteristic of continental climates, extend their ranges to the Pacific coast. In the same way, *Tsuga mertensiana, Larix occidentalis, L. lyallii,* and *Pinus albicaulis*—all primarily restricted to oceanic climates—extend eastward to enrich Rocky Mountain subalpine forests at the same latitude.

In the southernmost or Californian section of the Pacific subalpine forest, *Abies magnifica* (California red fir) shares dominance with *Tsuga mertensiana.* Temporary forests here are composed mainly of *Pinus contorta, P. attenuata* (knobcone pine), *P. monticola,* and *Abies concolor* (white fir). In the dwarfed and discontinuous tree cover just below the timberline, *Pinus albicaulis, P. aristata* (bristlecone pine), *P. flexilis,* and *P. balfourianna* (foxtail pine) are added.

Bogs are common practically throughout this western subalpine belt. *Populus tremuloides* occurs on wet but not peaty soils in the central and southern sections, but it is far less ubiquitous here than in the Rockies.

The Eastern Temperate Mesophytic Forest

That part of the temperate mesophytic forest that became partitioned off into approximately the southeastern quarter of North America retained its species richness to a high degree, since there were neither east-west mountain ranges nor an arid belt to interfere with the southward migrations which compensated for Pleistocene cooling. However, relatively few of the coniferous elements of the early Cenozoic forest were retained. Survivors included several species of *Tsuga,*

Thuja occidentalis (northern white-cedar), *Chamaecyparis thyoides* (Atlantic white-cedar), *Pinus strobus* (eastern white pine), several species of *Taxus* (yew) and *Taxodium* (baldcypress), and *Torreya taxifolia*. Most of these conifers became relegated to minor roles, and most became restricted to the cooler northern perimeter of the temperate zone. Others became limited to bogs (*Chamaecyparis*, *Thuja*), swamps (*Taxodium*), or to extremely small areas where they are in danger of extinction (*Taxus floridana* and *Torreya*). In the northern margin of this forest, winter temperatures drop as low as in much of the adjacent subarctic forest, but the summers are longer with more heat units available.

Tree species in this largely broadleaved forest number in the hundreds, distributed among many genera and families. The flora finds its closest similarity with the temperate mesophytic flora of eastern Asia centered approximately on Korea. Both the American and Asian floras are far richer than the temperate mesophytic flora of central Europe. There, during glaciation, southward migration was cut short by the chain of mountains stretching from the Pyrenees eastward well into arid central Asia.

The typical tree of this American eastern temperate mesophytic forest has broad, thin leaves with toothed or lobed margins. It is deciduous, has inconspicuous flowers, and is wind pollinated. Throughout, there is a generous sprinkling of relatively short trees which define a thin second tree stratum, a feature lacking in subarctic-subalpine forests. Representatives of this lower stratum are the deciduous *Carpinus caroliniana* (American hornbeam), *Cornus florida* (flowering dogwood), *Ostrya virginiana* (eastern hophornbeam), and *Oxydendrum arboreum*, and in the south the evergreen *Ilex opaca* (American holly).

In the northern half of the forest, the dominants include *Acer saccharum*, (sugar maple), *Carya* (hickory), *Fagus grandifolia* (beech), *Quercus alba* (white oak), *Q. rubra* (northern red oak), *Tilia americana* (American basswood), and *Ulmus americana* (American elm). *Castanea dentata* (chestnut) would certainly be included in this list had it not been for a devastating fungal parasite that was accidentally introduced into the flora. Considering the forest as a whole, it is floristically the richest, and, in the deep valleys of the southern Appalachians, has the largest specimens of many of these species.

Owing to the highly flammable litter of the coniferous element in the northern reaches, the first Caucasians in the area encountered considerable tracts of temporary forest dominated by *Pinus strobus* or *P. resinosa*. These trees were the base of a thriving lumber industry until supplies became virtually exhausted.

The glaciers which extended south to approximately the Ohio and Missouri rivers left a deep mantle of loams in most places, and the fertility of these soils, coupled with abundant precipitation the year around, have given the area greater value for diversified agriculture than for forest. On the other hand, the natural forests included valuable timber trees such as *Acer saccharum*, *Castanea dentata*, *Juglans nigra* (black walnut), *Liriodendron tulipifera* (yellow-poplar), *Pinus strobus*, *Prunus serotina* (black cherry), and *Quercus alba*. Their increasing scarcity and their increasing monetary value have prompted interest in making plantations of such species in local areas where the agricultural potential is not high.

Although good soils are widespread, there are some sizable tracts of outwash sands stretching from Minnesota to New York, and the soils developed on these are so infertile that they support hardly more than *Pinus banksiana* and/or species of *Quercus*.

The western edge of this northern half of the temperate mesophytic forest was once pushed eastward and replaced for a few thousand years by prairie vegetation which borders it on the west. This occurred during a long and extremely dry period roughly midway in the interval since glaciation, as a consequence of drought and fire, which extended the prairie eastward as a peninsula terminating at the foothills of the Appalachians. Owing to subsequent increase in precipitation, most of this prairie peninsula should have been reforested naturally when Caucasians arrived. However, lightning and aboriginal burning largely prevented tree advance from Illinois westward.

Practically all broadleaved trees in the North are deciduous, but progressing southward evergreens become more and more important, and in the southern tier of states, *Magnolia grandiflora*, *Quercus virginiana* (live oak), and *Q. laurifolia* (laurel oak) are major evergreen dominants. In the South, annual burning by aborigines, a practice continued by Caucasians, replaced broadleaved trees over much of the uplands by fire-tolerant *Pinus palustris* (longleaf pine) or *P. elliottii* (slash pine). These pines provide useful timber, pulpwood, and resin, and at the same time their open spacing under frequent burning favors herbage useful for livestock and quail. Since unburned uplands would develop into closed forests of mainly *Quercus*, and since these are practically worthless for lumber, grazing, or quail management, planned burning has been recognized as a highly desirable element of land management. Careful studies have indicated no long-term adverse impacts of such management on soils. Other pines, chiefly *P. taeda* (loblolly pine) or *P. echinata* (shortleaf pine), are pioneer invaders of abandoned cropland in the south. Infertile sands support rather permanent forests of *Pinus palustris* with *Quercus laevis* (turkey oak), and extremely leached white sands have *P. clausa* (sand pine) with *Q. chapmanii* and other shrubs.

Owing to the low relief of the landscape, rivers are bordered by extensive terraces with water tables near the soil surface. The species-rich forests of these soils remain relatively free of fire influence. Ponds and the margins of slow-flowing drainageways support swamps containing several species of *Taxodium* and/or *Nyssa* (tupelo).

The Western Temperate Mesophytic Forest

A relatively arid climate kept the western segment of the temperate mesophytic forest from spreading south to the same latitude as did the eastern segment. East of the Pacific Coast ranges, moisture was also inadequate on lowlands and in foothills. The upper slopes of the interior mountains had sufficient moisture, but the heat supply became limiting not far above the foothills. Even in the remaining areas available along the coast and inland on midslopes, the temperature regimes favored only those trees that were evergreen and thus capable of using periods of warm weather during the season of frost.

One major division of this forest flora occurs on the coastal lowlands and footslopes of adjacent mountains, plus the seaward slope of the northern Rockies. A second major subdivision consists of belts at midelevation on interior mountain slopes.

In the Alaskan section of the coastal strip, rainfall is heavy but the heat supply is minimal and the flora poor in species. *Tsuga heterophylla* (western hemlock), with small amounts of *Chamaecyparis nootkatensis* form the stable forest, usually replacing *Picea sitchensis* which invades deforested or other bare land. *Populus trichocarpa* (black cottonwood) and the shrubby *Alnus sinuata* are the most conspicuous elements of the forest, and both are temporary invaders of wet soils. *Picea sitchensis*, which provides the most valuable timber, is the largest species in its genus, attaining both great size and age in this section.

The coastal strip along British Columbia and the area west of the Cascades in Washington and Oregon has far richer and more highly productive forests than in the Alaskan section. Here the major invader of logged or burned sites is *Pseudotsuga menziesii*. Much like *Picea* in the north, *Pseudotsuga* here attains great size and age and provides the most valuable timber. *Alnus rubra* (red alder), the largest species in its genus, is another important primary invader, and both it and *Pseudotsuga* are often joined by *Thuja plicata* (western redcedar) before *Tsuga heterophylla* demonstrates its competitive superiority. As in eastern North America, this western forest has a thin lower tree stratum, here variously composed of *Acer circinatum, Cornus nuttallii* (Pacific dogwood), and *Taxus brevifolia* (Pacific yew).

In valleys between mountain ranges, where precipitation is reduced, *Abies grandis* (grand fir) takes over the role played by *Tsuga* elsewhere, and under still drier conditions *Quercus garryana* (Oregon white oak) gains control. Wetlands support permanent forests of *Thuja plicata*. Within a few miles of the ocean *Picea sitchensis* and *Acer macrophyllum* (bigleaf maple) are well represented if not dominant, and many coastal dunes are stabilized by a race of *Pinus contorta*.

Although conifers became dominants throughout the western temperate mesophytic forest, this section of the coastal strip from British Columbia to Oregon contains a few broadleaved trees inherited from the early Cenozoic forest. Remnants that were able to retain a place, even though a minor one, in the cool western forests include *Acer circinatum, A. macrophyllum, Cornus nuttallii, Fraxinus latifolia* (Oregon ash), and *Quercus garryana*.

The westerlies drop much precipitation as they rise across the Cascade Range, and, although the basin just to the east supports only arid steppe vegetation, the air masses still contain so much water vapor that as they start ascending the Rockies they yield sufficient moisture to provide the west slopes with forests similar to those west of the Cascades. Here on the western slopes of the Rockies, *Tsuga heterophylla, Thuja plicata*, and *Abies grandis* play much the same roles as near the ocean. *Pinus monticola* and *Larix occidentalis*, which are minor species near the coast, here become the principal trees first to dominate deforested land. *Pseudotsuga* and *Alnus rubra* also occur here in the inland, but the varieties are smaller, and they play minor roles, as does *Pinus contorta*. Of the broadleaved group found west of the Cascades, only *Cornus nuttallii* persisted here in the interior, and it is restricted to a single small population. *Taxus brevifolia* is left as the only common member of the lower tree stratum.

A third distinctive segment of the coastal forest that is strongly dependent upon oceanic climate occurs along the coast of northern California. The single dominant here is the tall *Sequoia sempervirens* (redwood), a tree that in early Cenozoic time was widely distributed across North America and Eurasia. Most of the trees found to the north in Oregon and Washington also extend into this section, but here they are all relatively minor components of the forest, far overtopped by *Sequoia*. *Sequoia* has a longevity exceeding 2,000 years and therefore seedlings needed to replace natural death need not be abundant. As the old virgin stands are logged, relatively short rotations must be planned to continue production of this most valuable timber tree along the coast.

The most impoverished western relics of the early Cenozoic forest are found on midslopes of those mountains outside strong influences of oceanic climate. Narrow belts of such forest, of which small forms of *Pseudotsuga menziesii* (Douglas-fir) are the most characteristic trees, occur from the interior valleys of British Columbia and Alberta to Mexico, and from the interior valley of California to the east slope of the Rockies.

In California, the most competitive conifers of this belt on the mountain slopes include *Abies concolor*, *Libocedrus decurrens* (incense-cedar), and *Pseudotsuga*. Less competitive conifers which tend to form the first forests following devastation are *Pinus lambertiana* (sugar pine), *P. jeffreyi*, and, in certain valleys on the west slope of the Sierra, the massive *Sequoiadendron giganteum* (giant sequoia). These forests often have a fairly well developed lower tree stratum variously composed of *Taxus brevifolia*, the evergreen broadleaved *Lithocarpus densiflorus* (tanoak), and *Quercus chrysolepis* (canyon live oak), or the deciduous *Cornus nuttallii* and *Quercus kelloggii* (California black oak).

East of the Cascades and in areas where oceanic influence is essentially nil, the *Pseudotsuga* belt includes *Abies concolor* from southern Idaho to Arizona, and here, in the inland, fire followers include *Larix occidentalis*, *Pinus contorta*, *P. ponderosa*, *P. strobiformis* (southwestern white pine), and *Populus tremuloides*. Both *Pinus contorta* and *Populus tremuloides* also form permanent communities on special soil types. *Picea pungens* (blue spruce) is found along creeks and on stream terraces, as well as about the margins of moist meadows that frequently interrupt forest.

The Temperate Xerophytic Forest

The forests considered thus far are all derivatives of those temperate forests of early Cenozoic time that require plentiful moisture, so that then as now the gross features of their distribution reflect temperature control. Their changing geographic position through geologic time has been primarily southward. We shall next consider xerophytic forests of an entirely different origin.

South of the belt of the westerlies, the earth is encircled by the subtropical high pressure belt, centered approximately on thirty degrees north latitude. Air masses in this belt are mostly descending and radiating outward, unlike the predominantly directional movements in the westerlies to the north or easterlies to the south. Descending air becomes dry, and this is the belt in which most desert vegetation is found. Since the existence of the belt is a consequence of the polar-equatorial temperature gradient, plus atmospheric currents set up by the earth's rotation, xerophytic vegetation must always have occurred here. Dry climates are not conducive to fossilization, so we have very little direct information on the history of xerophytic vegetation. However, the present alignment of xerophytic vegetation types in somewhat concentric belts around true deserts, together with the taxonomic distinctiveness of such vegetation, suggests an ancient origin very different from that of the mesophytic forests we have considered. Much of the vegetation of the western United States has spread northward from the center of aridity. Previously it has been pointed out that the relatively mesophytic *Pseudotsuga* belt on the western mountains is limited on its lower boundary by drought, so it is appropriate to proceed by first considering the adjacent xerophytic forests of the foothills below.

Pinus ponderosa, which can invade the *Pseudotsuga* belt only after deforestation, extends downslope onto land too dry for *Pseudotsuga*, where it becomes the characteristic species of an extensive timber belt reaching from southern British Columbia into Mexico. In the vicinity of the Mexican border, it is accompanied or replaced by ecologically similar pines such as *P. engelmannii* (Apache pine), *P. leiophylla*, and, below the border, *P. durangensis*. North of this region, two varieties of *P. ponderosa* alone distinguish the belt.

All of these trees are less shade tolerant than *Pseudotsuga* and therefore form forests that are not as dense, often open enough to deserve designation as savanna. Fires do little damage except to seedlings, so they also favor the development and maintenance of savannalike stands. The undergrowth varies from perennial grasses to shrub types of varying stature. The wood of these pines is an important timber source, and the undergrowth in most places provides valuable forage.

A limited amount of *Pinus ponderosa* forest occurs around the interior valley of California where it is enriched by *Quercus kelloggii* and a number of mostly evergreen shrubs, all of which are adapted to retain their places on burned tracts.

In the Rocky Mountain foothills and adjacent mesas, savannas or open forests of distinctly shorter trees occur just below the drier edge of the *Pinus ponderosa* belt. Either *Pinus (P. cembroides, P. edulis* [pinyon], *P. monophylla* [single-leaf pinyon], or *P. quadrifolia*) or many species of *Juniperus* are the conspicuous plants. Here again, well-spaced trees favor interstitial grass and shrub cover. In the drier margin of this belt, the dominants are not only more widely spaced, but they may also be dwarfed to essentially shrub stature.

Two regional variations are to be noted. From Texas to southern California, *Cupressus arizonica* (Arizona cypress) locally enriches the tallest stratum. Then from southern Idaho and central Wyoming northward to southern Alberta, the only pine associated with *Juniperus* is *Pinus flexilis.*

The trees are all fire sensitive, but the grass and litter cover are mostly too meager to carry fires hot enough to kill the trees.

This vegetation provides no lumber, but the juniper trunks have served well as durable fence posts, the pinewood has been used for fuel, and the large pine seeds have some value as human food. Perhaps the greatest worth of the vegetation lies in the forage it produces.

The *Pinus-Juniperus* belt occurs in dry climates that have cold winters. In the southern Rockies and especially in the foothills of California and southern Oregon, equally dry areas that are not so cold support woodlands for which the appropriate though little-used term "encinal" (a Spanish word meaning oak woods) is specific. At least a dozen species of *Quercus* are involved over the wide geographic range of the type. Locally a few other conifers, such as *Pinus coulteri, P. sabiniana* (Digger pine), or *Pseudotsuga macrocarpa*, are minor constituents. Broadleaved trees such as *Arbutus* (madrone), *Lithocarpus* (tanoak), and *Vauquelinia* may also be involved.

An especially interesting feature of the arid region in which xerophytic woodlands occur is that moist stream terraces and deep ravines often contain woody plants derived from the temperate mesophytic forest of early Cenozoic time. Unlike those stopped by arid climates, these continued southward. They avoided drought by adapting to the limited habitats of moist soil that are maintained by permanent creeks flowing across the dry uplands. Some examples are: *Acer negundo* (boxelder), *Cercis occidentalis* (California redbud), *Crataegus douglasii* (black hawthorn),

Platanus wrightii (Arizona sycamore), *Prunus virginiana* (chokecherry), and *Ptelea trifoliata* (common hoptree).

Uplands in areas of chaparral scrub or steppe also support trees in riparian habitats, but *Populus* and *Salix* provide the great bulk of this vegetation.

Deserts are a special case, for there small, deeply rooted trees often occur thinly scattered over the gravelly uplands. In Arizona and New Mexico, small-leaved deciduous trees in the legume family, as in *Acacia, Cercidium* (paloverde), *Olneya tesota* (ironwood), *Parkinsonia*, and *Prosopis* (mesquite) are especially well represented. Dendritic species of cacti and *Yucca* also provide upland trees in these deserts. Such trees have negligible economic value, but terraces along the few major rivers once supported woodlands of *Prosopis* which furnished excellent FIREWOOD until these habitats were preempted for agriculture.

The Tropical Seasonal Forest

During the vast southward displacement of mesophytic forests that occurred in early and mid-Cenozoic time, frost-sensitive tropical trees became restricted to the Caribbean area. Southern Florida either retained a remnant of such vegetation or regained it after temporarily losing it during glaciation in the north.

Southern Florida is in the subtropical latitudinal belt. In this belt, drought is so severe near the west coasts of continents that desert prevails, but progressing eastward from the Pacific Coast the long dry seasons are slowly reduced in length until, at the southern tip of Florida, they last only a few months.

Such climates, throughout the world's tropics as well as on islands and peninsulas only a short distance outside the tropics, support broadleaved forests that make their vegetative growth during the rainy summers, then become inactive during the dry season except for the production of flowers. These are often called seasonal forests, in contrast to rainforest where dry spells are so short that, when the forest as a whole is considered, growth and flowering are essentially continuous throughout the year.

That part of the seasonal forest with the least rainfall has trees that mostly stand leafless during the dry cool season. At the wet margin of seasonal forest (where seasonal differences in plant activity are least pronounced), practically all trees are "evergreen." Florida, with rainfall allowing a fair sprinkling of evergreen trees, supports a semideciduous seasonal forest. Other areas of seasonal forest occur on the Caribbean Islands, in Mexico, South America, and Hawaii.

The broadleaved deciduous trees of tropical seasonal forest are neither ecologically nor taxonomically related to temperate zone deciduous trees. Their leaf margins are mostly smooth rather than being toothed or lobed, the flowers are conspicuous and either bird- or insect-pollinated, in contrast with the inconspicuous, wind-pollinated flowers of trees of northern forests. A sprinkling of palms and bamboo also occurs in tropical seasonal forest.

Many valuable trees are native to seasonal forest, including *Swietenia mahagoni* (West Indies mahogany), *Dalbergia* (rosewood), *Cedrela* (Spanish cedar), and *Chlorophora tinctora* (fustic). Species from similar forests elsewhere in the world have been planted to a limited extent in seasonal forests of the Americas, chiefly *Eucalyptus* and *Tectona grandis* (teak).

During the dry season, strong insolation dries the recently deposited blanket of leaves until the fire hazard becomes very high, so fires have always swept through these forests throughout their evolution. The fires are not hot enough to injure most trees of any size, and small individuals readily sprout from the root summit.

Where coasts and embayments are protected from significant wave action, they are muddy rather than sandy and here mangrove forest is found. Like coconut, these trees are also well adapted for saltwater dissemination and have wide distribution around the world. In south Florida and the Caribbean area, *Rhizophora mangle* (mangrove), *Avicennia germinans* (black-mangrove), *Laguncularia racemosa* (white-mangrove), and *Conocarpus erectus* (button-mangrove) are the trees of the mangrove belt, these tending to be zonally arranged with *Rhizophora*, supported by stilt roots, extending out into shallow water, and *Conocarpus* extending the belt farthest from the water's edge.

Mangrove trees have been harvested extensively around the world for CHARCOAL and tanbark, but there is growing awareness recently that the litter of these broadleaved evergreen trees, swept into the shallow coastal waters, is the essential base of food chains starting with microorganisms and progressing to the immature stages of economically important shrimp and fish that are harvested elsewhere in the seas. Belatedly, laws are being enacted to keep the remaining mangrove forests intact, owing to their importance to the fishing industry.

Puerto Rico and the Virgin Islands in the Caribbean and the Hawaiian Islands in the Pacific have many rather tall mountains, and, being in the path of the easterlies, they have a wet windward and dry leeward side. Seasonal forest occurs on slopes where

drought is not so intense. In drier areas, microphyllous woodland replaces it.

The Microphyllous Woodland

Trees of this woodland are of low stature and as the name indicates have very small leaves or leaflets. The wood is hard, the stems are crooked, usually thorny, and the plants stand leafless during the long dry season. Their canopies are closed, but they cast such a thin shade that shrubs are abundant beneath them. A highly distinctive feature of this woodland throughout its occurrence in the Americas is the thin sprinkling of arborescent cacti which show above the general canopy level. Unlike most tropical forests, palms are unrepresented. When enough litter accumulates to nourish a fire, most woody plants then coppice readily from their root summits. Grasses and other herbs, which are otherwise poorly represented, tend to flourish until a new canopy develops.

The most valuable trees of this woodland are the native *Guaiacum officinale*, producing the hard, resinous lignumvitae wood, and the naturalized Mexican tree *Haematoxylon campechianum*, the heartwood of which produces a dye that has not yet been made completely obsolete by synthetics.

The Tropical Rainforest

If microphyllous woodland occurs beyond the dry margin of tropical seasonal forest, environment beyond the wet side favors tropical rainforest. Areas with so much rainfall throughout the year that the forest as a whole shows no seasonal rhythms are relatively small and widely dispersed, for most tropical forests fall in the seasonal category. In Hawaii and in Puerto Rico and the Virgin Islands, rainforest occurs on certain windward mountain sides, and there it has been divided into lowland and montane belts.

Lowland rainforest is closed, evergreen, and has about the same percentage of plants flowering or changing their leaves each month of the year. This is taxonomically the richest and most primitive vegetation on earth. A single hectare in Malaysia, for example, proved to contain over 200 species of trees, so there could hardly be more than one individual per species. The trees have slender, straight bores with at least the lower half free of branches. Buttressed bases are common, especially on the few individuals that elevate their canopies distinctly above the general canopy level and are referred to as emergents. Many trees are too short to reach the main canopy level, and among these quite a few have the habit of producing their flowers directly from old wood, a characteristic found in temperate-zone forest in only *Cer-*

cis. The leaves of the forest as a whole tend to be larger than average, especially in plants of the undergrowth. As in seasonal forest, leaf margins are mostly smooth. Palms are common in the lower strata, and some reach the main canopy. Epiphytic vascular plants, and especially lianas, are abundant, many of the latter climbing to the tops of even the emergents. Both of these plant form types are poorly represented in most seasonal forests, especially where a large percentage of the trees are deciduous.

The lush appearance of lowland rainforest gives many people the impression that forest could be supplanted by plowed cropland, as in temperate latitudes, to obtain very high yields. This has been tried and found to be a disastrous mistake in different parts of the tropics. Lowland rainforest soils are mostly porous clays of low fertility. When leaves drop to the forest floor the warm, moist conditions favor their rapid and complete decay, with the shallow-rooted plants immediately bringing the released nutrients back into plant tissues. Most fertility is therefore contained in living tissue as a result of rapid recycling. Forest destruction involves fire which releases all nutrients and these are quickly dissipated by the high rainfall. Heat from the sun dries out the soil sufficiently that the clay hardens irreversibly, so the soil profile is ruined.

Above an altitude of about 1,000 meters, the character of rainforest is rather clearly different from that below, and the term montane rainforest is appropriate. Here there are fewer tree species, the boles are not so tall and straight, and buttresses and lianas are less in evidence. Vascular epiphytes and mosses become abundant.

On exposed ridges and knobs that rise above montane rainforest, trees are reduced to shrub size and present a smooth, dense canopy to the wind. The crooked stems and gnarled appearance of the woody plants have prompted some to refer to such vegetation as "elfinwood." Tree leaves are still smaller than those of montane rainforest, and mosses are usually quite conspicuous among the epiphytes. Low temperatures allow thick layers of litter and duff to accumulate.

Tropical rainforest appears to be the ancestral home of many families and genera, if not species, that are found in forests to both the north and south. Many trees of seasonal forest, for example, are temporary invaders of deforested rainforest sites, and some of them are evergreen only in the rainforest area. Even temperate forest has a few trees whose relatives are nearly all tropical. For example, *Diospyros virginiana* (common persimmon), *Sassafras albidum,* and *Asimina triloba* (pawpaw) are members of families best represented in the rainforest belt. They are probably examples of preadaptation to frosty climates that lingered as rainforest shifted southward during the Cenozoic era.

FURTHER READING: Rexford Daubenmire, *Plant Geography with Special Reference to North America* (1978). H. A. Fowells, *Silvics of Forest Trees of the United States,* Agriculture Handbook No. 271 (1965). Elbert L. Little, Jr., *Checklist of United States Trees (Native and Naturalized),* Agriculture Handbook No. 541 (1979).

REXFORD DAUBENMIRE

EXCELSIOR

As the incidental waste from planing, wood shavings have been used for padding and packing fragile glassware and crockery since the dawn of the carpenter's craft. However, the actual manufacture of "excelsior" is a rather recent industry. A machine for making fine, uniform coils of wood was developed in the United States in the late 1850s and excelsior was first marketed as a mattress stuffing in 1860.

"Excelsior" was originally a brand name but, because of its immediate popularity, the simplicity of the machinery involved, and the general laxity of nineteenth-century copyright law, it soon became a generic term, freely used by the approximately 200 mills that produced it in the United States at the end of the century. Although these mills were to be found in every state, the industry was concentrated in New York, Kentucky, New Hampshire, Wisconsin, and Washington.

As a commercial commodity, excelsior was paper-thin curled strands of wood, the best quality used for mattress and furniture stuffing and known as "wood wool." It was shaved to a thickness of 1/100 inch and a width of 1/64 inch. Cheaper grades, for packing, ran to 3/10 by 1/4 inches.

European nations took up the manufacture of excelsior very early and broadened its uses to include filtration and the making of "ropes" for use in the casting of iron pipe. The most desirable woods for excelsior manufacture are lightweight, odorless (or pleasantly scented), and gum and resin free. Through the early twentieth century, basswood was preferred for upholstery, but in 1920 it represented only 14 percent of the total lumber used in the industry. By 1950, when the major use of excelsior was in packing, cottonwood accounted for 50 percent of the total and various pines 40 percent. Poplar and aspen were also popular.

During the first half of the twentieth century, most automobiles and mass-produced cheap furniture were upholstered with excelsior stuffing. By 1920, the in-

Excelsior bales ready for shipment. Forest History Society Photo.

dustry consumed 100 million board feet of lumber each year. However, although a plant could be set up for very little capital and many companies which manufactured and shipped fragile commodities maintained their own excelsior machines, the number of excelsior plants declined steadily from about 200 in 1900 to 95 in 1920, 66 in 1930, and 48 in 1935. By the end of the 1940s, there were 56 American plants devoted largely or entirely to producing 150,000 tons of excelsior a year from about as many cords of wood.

In the 1960s, excelsior declined radically. It was displaced as a stuffing by new synthetic products, especially foam rubber, and as a packing by styrofoam, air-filled plastics, and other lighter, cheaper materials. In 1967, excelsior production had declined to 90,000 tons and in 1972 to 62,500 tons. Very little of this was marketed in bulk, but instead further processed into paper-wrapped pads. In 1972, the total value of excelsior manufactured in the United States was $14 million.

FARM FORESTRY

During the westward expansion and subsequent settlement of the United States, timber, although it was utilized for building materials and fuel, was generally regarded as a hindrance to agriculture. Millions of acres of timberland were gradually cleared by hand and converted to farm crops.

However, much timber was left standing, either because it was inconveniently located or because it occupied land that would have low productivity as cropland. Also, abandoned farms reverted to forests. As the pattern of public and private landownership emerged, much of this timber fell into private hands. These tracts of timber, which are generally referred to as woodlots, range in size from a few to many hundreds of acres. Usually, woodlots are contiguous to farmland.

Nationwide, 72 percent of all commercial forestland is privately owned. Fifty-nine percent of the total is in farm and miscellaneous small ownership; the remainder belongs to much larger industrial forest ownerships with more than half located in the South and the remainder divided between the North and West.

However, although farm and miscellaneous small private owners hold more growing stock than any other class of owner, their lands are probably least heavily stocked; thus, their share of total growing stock nationally is approximately 40 percent. Most foresters agree that this portion could be significantly increased through increased assistance and more intensive management. Such management could include planting denuded areas, better fire management, insect and disease controls, precommercial thinning, pruning, and fertilization.

It was not until the turn of the century that landowners, public officials, and foresters began to recognize the management potential of these woodlots. In fact, Bernhard E. FERNOW, chief of the U. S. Division of Forestry (1886–1898) anticipated that woodlot owners would opt to manage their small parcels sooner than the industrial owners, because of the pride of ownership. Fernow was in error, however, and woodlot management has remained a perplexing forestry problem.

Since the small landowner often lacked the necessary interest, training, and initial capital required, the federal government began to offer forest management assistance. The Division of Forestry offered some assistance to private landowners as early as 1898, but authorizing legislation was lacking.

Cooperative legislation began in 1911, with the passage of the WEEKS ACT, authorizing federal matching funds to enable states to protect forests on watersheds of navigable streams. This cooperation was expanded in 1924 by the CLARKE-MCNARY ACT, which extended fire management to all watersheds. Also, to bring about reforestation and the planting of farm SHELTER-BELTS, the Clarke-McNary Act authorized cooperation with the states in the construction and operation of nurseries.

The Norris-Doxey Cooperative Farm Forestry Act of 1937 made provision for public assistance in tree planting, farm forestry extension work, research, and service forestry. The act was administered at the federal level and pertained largely to farmers. Actual implementation was primarily restricted to "forest farming" demonstrations, showing how farm woodlots could be profitably managed.

The Forest Pest Control Act of 1947 authorized the federal government, alone or in cooperation with state and local agencies and private landowners, to prevent and control forest insects and diseases, irrespective of landownership. However, the necessity of equal fund matching has limited this program to forest owners with a relatively large financial resource.

The 1937 farm forestry program was repealed and replaced by the much broader Cooperative Forest Management Act of 1950 (CFM). It authorized federal cooperation with state foresters in providing technical services to small private forestland owners and operators and to small processors of roundwood. This assistance helps the small landowner to manage timber more effectively and profitably. It also helps the

Woodlots intermingled with Wisconsin farmland. Wisconsin Conservation Department Photo.

small wood processor to become more efficient. In addition, woodlot owners are given assistance in forestry projects that lead to conservation of water resources, probably the most important aspect of CFM forestry in the West. Amendments in 1972 extended CFM authority for assistance to urban areas to ensure a livable environment for urban as well as rural people.

In 1978, the Cooperative Forestry Assistance Act (CFA) codified earlier cooperative legislation. This streamlining has improved implementation and cooperation between the various federal and state agencies.

The Soil Conservation Service, which provides technical assistance under the auspices of the U. S. Agricultural Stabilization and Conservation Service, operates typically. It promotes the conservation of water as well as soil, and its services are available to the small landowner. Although funded at the federal level, the programs, such as streambed protection, stockwater impoundment, and flood control, are implemented under local leadership.

Combined federal and state help in forest management is also offered to woodlot owners through the Cooperative Extension Services. This aid is primarily educational in nature and is mainly limited to owners of relatively small tracts.

In addition to federal cooperation programs, there has been since 1941 a significant private effort. The American Tree Farm System began with the dedication of Weyerhaeuser's Clemons Tree Farm near Elma, Washington, on June 12, 1941. By 1980, there were nearly 39,000 TREE FARMS nationwide, encompassing 79.6 million acres. The AMERICAN FOREST INSTITUTE administers this program which operates at the state level under local sponsorship that may include private, state, or federal agencies.

A tree farm is defined as an area of privately owned, taxpaying forestland dedicated by its owner to the growing and harvesting of repeated forest crops. The program seeks to place more woodland under management practices that enhance growth and quality of timber and gives public recognition to outstanding private timber managers.

At the state and county levels, woodlot management is regulated by forest practice acts and ordinances. As part of an effort to eliminate an alleged need for federal control of logging on private land, states began to enact their own regulations in the 1930s. Generally called forest practices acts, this legislation requires forestland owners to obtain a permit before logging and to abide by various requirements to protect soil, water, and future timber supplies. More recently, some county governments have adopted similar forestry ordinances tailored to fit their local situations.

A great deal of activity is currently underway with regard to public assistance to private timber owners, especially on the part of state foresters under the CFA act. These programs seek to improve the management of private timber through technical forestry assistance, demonstrations and educational means, and marketing and utilization assistance. However, many foresters agree that the programs, although good in concept, are often inadequately financed. In terms of national timber supply, increased assistance to private landowners will probably be required in the future.

FURTHER READING: William A. Duerr, *Timber! Problems, Prospects, Policies* (1970). Leon S. Minckler, *Woodland Ecology: Environmental Forestry for the Small Owner* (1975). Hardy L. Shirley and Paul F. Graves, *Forest Ownership for Pleasure and Profit* (1967). Stephen H. Spurr, *American Forest Policy in Development* (1976).

GARETH C. MOON AND MICHAEL E. MOON

FEDERAL LAND POLICY AND MANAGEMENT ACT, 1976

This law, popularly referred to by its acronym—FLPMA—or as the BLM Organic Act, was enacted to give congressional clarity to a long sequence of Executive Branch decisions. The law aims to establish a mission for 450 million acres of public land in the eleven western states and Alaska, to give the BUREAU OF LAND MANAGEMENT (BLM) sufficient authority to carry out the mission, and to facilitate congressional oversight.

FLPMA addresses a wide range of issues and policies: BLM lands generally will remain in federal ownership (which effectively eliminates the concept of public domain lands); there will be periodic resource inventories; land management will be in accord with the principles of multiple use and sustained yield; the BLM is to coordinate grazing fees with the U. S. FOREST SERVICE; and 50 percent of grazing receipts will be applied to range improvement.

FLPMA moved through Congress at the same time as the NATIONAL FOREST MANAGEMENT ACT of 1976. Since the latter law resulted from extreme controversy, it received much attention, and relatively little notice was given to FLPMA in the professional and trade literature. Subsequently, however, as part of the livestock industry's long tradition of opposing federal restriction on its use of public ranges—most recently called the "Sagebrush Rebellion"—FLPMA has been widely debated.

FURTHER READING: Samuel Trask Dana and Sally K. Fairfax, *Forest and Range Policy* (2nd ed., 1980).

FEDERATION OF WESTERN OUTDOOR CLUBS

Founded in 1932 "for the promotion of the proper use, enjoyment, and protection of America's scenic, wilderness, and outdoor recreation resources," the Federation of Western Outdoor Clubs (FWOC) has actively participated in most environmental controversies in the western tier of states since its inception. In 1980, FWOC was comprised of about fifty local hiking, camping, climbing, and boating clubs and some Montana, Idaho, Washington, Oregon, and California chapters of the NATIONAL AUDUBON SOCIETY and SIERRA CLUB. In 1980, the combined membership of FWOC's associated but independent components was 150,000.

The Federation serves principally as an information exchange, publicizing environmentalist issues and activity in its semiannual *Outdoors West* (formerly *Western Outdoors Quarterly*) and at an annual convention. It generally takes a militant environmentalist stand on development issues, espousing the preservation of existing wilderness areas and the creation of new ones. FWOC appeals to both ecological and aesthetic ideals and encourages politi-

cal activism and agitation. In 1979–1980, it launched a campaign to ally the environmentalist movement with Indian tribes and labor unions with shared goals. FWOC is headquartered in Seattle, Washington.

FENCING

In the seventeenth century, whether settling in New England, the Middle Colonies, or the South, English colonists repudiated the common law provision that, although no one was obliged to build fences, an owner of livestock was accountable for trespass by his animals. Colonists regarded all unenclosed land, particularly virgin forests and grasslands, as proper common pasturage for anyone's livestock, since it was not yet feasible to produce hay. In 1632, Virginia enacted a law requiring growers to enclose their crops against livestock. After the independence of the United States in 1776, state courts and legislatures retained this "custom of commons."

Various types of fences were usually made of wood, which was relatively abundant from the colonial era until the nineteenth century. The most common type was the so-called Virginia or "worm" fence consisting of tiers of about ten or twelve-foot-long rails which interlocked with each other in a zigzag pattern along a strip of land that was perhaps ten feet in width. The best rails were of clear wood, easily split. Oak, chestnut, locust, walnut, and cedar were the preferred species. From 8,000 to 9,000 rails went into a mile of fence. Less wood and land were required in erecting rail-and-post fences in straight lines. Boards, stumps, stone, and sod were also employed to make fences. Western settlers copied eastern fence making as long as wood was available. In 1871, the U. S. DEPARTMENT OF AGRICULTURE reported that the Virginia fence was still used more widely than any other type.

By the 1850s, when wood provided over 3 million miles or 93 percent of the total length of farm fences, farmers began to struggle with what came to be known as the "fence problem" since no type was fully satisfactory for their purposes in both old and new states. Seventy-nine percent of farm fencing in 1850 was of the Virginia type, 9 percent of post-and-rail construction, 5 percent of boards, and the rest of stone. The Virginia fence was easily damaged, permitted the growth of weeds, and wasted farmland, while its rails lasted only about twenty-five years. In addition, it was increasingly expensive to replace wood fences in older states where timber supplies had become scarcer. Farmers on the Western prairies had little or no timber and were forced to import wood from states like Minnesota and

Riders reflect on the beauty of Montana's Lolo National Forest. Their interests are represented by the Federation of Western Outdoor Clubs. Forest Service Photo.

Hand-split rails are stacked in a zigzag fashion to protect the field at right from overgrazing. Forest History Society Lantern Slide Collection.

Wisconsin. In 1871, according to U. S. agricultural officials, the investment in fences nearly equaled the national debt and almost $94 million was spent annually in maintaining them.

After experiments were made with wire, Osage-orange hedges, and other fences, the problem was alleviated. In the 1870s, Joseph F. Glidden of Illinois and other inventors developed barbed wire fencing which needed wood only for posts. By the 1890s, the new fencing was widely adopted in the West where grain growers and other farmers eventually defeated cattlemen and forced them to enclose grazing grounds for livestock. Older states, too, adopted the common law provision on fencing for economic reasons. Fences were needed mainly to confine livestock in enclosures where it was now possible to feed them better.

Twentieth-century farmers did not have to face the problem of depending on wood fences. As late as 1880, wood provided 5.5 million miles or 83 percent of the farm fencing then in use. A decade later, wood provided 4.6 million miles, only 51 percent of farm fencing, while wire provided 49 percent. By 1910, only 2.1 million miles or 15 percent of farm fencing was wood, the remainder being wire.

Nevertheless, wooden posts were necessary to support wire fencing, and the making of wooden fence posts continued to be a major use of American forests. In the 1910s, while rail fences were disappearing from the countryside, 500 million fence posts were consumed annually, the equivalent of 2.5 million board feet of lumber. Where wood was available locally, fence posts were the product of farm woodlots, while commercial production—to a great extent as a by-product of the POLES AND PILING INDUSTRY or as a use for tops and the trunks of trees too small for lumber —took place in the Great Lakes States, California, eastern Virginia and North Carolina, and the Gulf Coast. Commercially produced posts went onto farms on the treeless prairies and lined thousands of miles of railroad rights-of-way.

The species largely used for posts in California and the Southwest was redwood; in the Pacific Northwest and on the plains, western redcedar; in the Midwest and Lake States, northern white-cedar (and locally produced locust, white oak, catalpa, mulberry, and hackberry); in the Northeast, northern white-cedar and chestnut; in the Appalachians, chestnut, sassafras, catalpa, and white oak; and in the South, cypress, Atlantic white-cedar, juniper, eastern redcedar, and longleaf pine. Chestnut dropped out of use during the following decades as the trees succumbed to blight.

By the 1930s, the annual production of fence posts had increased to about 600 million and, at 4.3 percent of wood consumption, constituted the fourth largest use of wood. In that decade one project alone—protection of the SHELTERBELTS being planted on the plains —called for an estimated 56 million posts. Highway right-of-way and guard posts also became important markets.

Depending upon the species, wooden posts might be expected to last anywhere from two to thirty years. About 1916, southern pine treated with creosote came into extensive use, and in the next two decades it became a major source of posts for the Midwest and South. Early important production centers were Louisiana, eastern Texas, Arkansas, and Oklahoma. Most southern pine post production came from thinnings of second growth too small for poles. Plagued with the presence on the market of large numbers of inadequately treated posts, the American Wood-Preservers Institute developed an industry standard which was approved by the U. S. Department of Commerce in 1961 and was designed to assure consumers of pressure-treated fence posts that could be expected to give over thirty years of service.

However, with competition from steel posts and stakes, the production of wooden posts became a declining industry. The U. S. Department of Agriculture measured the output of wooden posts at 306 million pieces in 1952, a figure that wavered downward to only 97.7 million in 1970.

FURTHER READING: Nelson Courtlandt Brown, *Forest Products: Their Manufacture and Use* (1919); *Timber Products and Industries* (1937); and *Forest Products* (1950). Clarence H. Danhof, "The Fencing Problem in the Eighteen-Fifties," *Agricultural History* 18 (Oct. 1944): 168–186. Earl W. Hayter, "Barbed Wire Fencing—A Prairie Invention: Its Rise and Influence in the Western States," *Agricultural History* 13 (Oct. 1939): 189–107, and *The Troubled Farm, 1860–1900: Rural Adjustment to Industrialism* (1968), chaps. 5 and 13. A. J. Panshin, E. S. Harrar, and J. S. Bethel, *Forest Products* (2nd ed., 1962). Martin L. Primack, "Farm Fencing in the Nineteenth Century," *Journal of Economic History* 29 (June 1969): 287–291.

A. WILLIAM HOGLUND

FERNOW, BERNHARD EDUARD (1851–1923)

The first professional forester to practice in North America was the German-born Bernhard E. Fernow who did more to advance the profession in the United States and Canada in its early years than any other man. Fernow was born January 7, 1851, in the province of Posen, Prussia. He received training and experience in the Prussian Forest Academy at Münden and with the Prussian forest department. Fernow immigrated to America in 1876 and in 1878 became manager for Cooper Hewitt & Company's 15,000 acres of woodland in Pennsylvania, used for making CHARCOAL.

Fernow was a leader in the American Forestry Congress and served as its secretary from 1883 to 1895, as chairman of its editorial committee, and in other positions. President Grover Cleveland made him chief of the Division of Forestry in the DEPARTMENT OF AGRICULTURE in 1886. He quickly assembled a qualified staff and started research in silviculture, pathology, wood technology, forest products, and tree planting on the Great Plains. He eventually prepared over 200 articles, addresses, and monographs, and over 50 circulars and bulletins which laid the groundwork for forestry in North America. He traveled and wrote and spoke widely to scientists, students, and the public. He was perhaps the first in America to emphasize that forestry meant manage-

ment to allow natural regeneration and provide a sustained yield of products, and that forestry should be economically practical. Federal and state governments should, he believed, manage their forest holdings, serving as a guide to lumbermen and farmers.

Fernow strongly urged college instruction in forestry, and he started and directed the first four-year forestry school in the United States (in 1898 at Cornell University) and in Canada (in 1907 at the University of Toronto). Also in 1907, Fernow taught forestry briefly at Pennsylvania State College. He lectured at the Yale Forest School in 1904. He was a major figure in promoting and establishing the Adirondack Forest Preserve and the New York Forest Commission in 1885 and in securing federal legislation in 1891 for setting aside forest reserves and in 1897 for managing them. Using legal training gained in Germany, Fernow drafted model bills for all this legislation and for forestry laws in other states, including laws for fire protection and setting up state forestry agencies. Fernow's attempt to combine practical commercial forestry on a demonstration forest in the Adirondacks with his forestry school at Cornell led to a dispute with neighboring estates who succeeded in closing his school in 1903 by persuading the governor to veto its appropriation. From 1903 to 1907, Fernow was active as a consulting forester in the Northwest, the South, Cuba, and Mexico.

Fernow started the *Forestry Quarterly* in 1902 and was its editor until its merger with the *Proceedings* of the SOCIETY OF AMERICAN FORESTERS (SAF) in 1916, whereupon he became editor of the combined publication, the *Journal of Forestry*. He wrote three books which became standard texts: *The Economics of Forestry* (1902), *A Brief History of Forestry* (1907), and *The Care of Trees in Lawn, Street, and Park* (1910). He served as president of SAF in 1914 and 1916, and was made a fellow in 1918. He helped organize and was first president of the Canadian Society of Forest Engineers in 1908, and after 1910 he served for thirteen years on the Canadian Conservation Commission. He led a drive for more parks, reserves, and research, and for better forest fire control in Canada. He was elected a vice-president of the American Association for the Advancement of Science in 1895. He received honorary LL.D. degrees from three universities (Wisconsin, 1896; Queen's, 1903; and Toronto, 1920). Fernow died on February 6, 1923.

FURTHER READING: *Journal of Forestry* 21 (Apr. 1923): 305–348. Charles E. Randall, "Fernow, the Man Who Brought Forestry to America," *American Forests* 70 (Apr. 1964): 14–16, 44, 46. Andrew Denny Rodgers III. *Bernhard*

Eduard Fernow: A Story of North American Forestry (1951). Harold K. Steen, *The U. S. Forest Service: A History* (1976).

FRANK J. HARMON

FINNISH IMMIGRANTS AND AMERICAN FORESTS

Most male Finnish immigrants to America had had experience in forest labor in their homeland, so it was natural that one of their major sources of employment in this country would be the lumber industry. In rural Finland, from which the great majority of these immigrants came, logging offered crucial supplementary income for landowners, who added to agricultural earnings by selling timber from their woodlots, and for rural workers, who found work in logging during the winter months when little was available in farming. Significant numbers of Finns worked as loggers in the forests of the Lower Peninsula of Michigan during 1870–1890, of southern Oregon (near Marshfield) beginning in the 1860s, and of northern California (Mendocino and Humboldt counties) from the 1870s. Finnish immigration did not become a mass movement until the 1890s. however, at about the time lumber operations were reaching a peak in northern Michigan, Wisconsin, and Minnesota, and it was this area that became the major center of Finnish forest workers. As these forests began to be logged out after the turn of the century, the major concentration of Finns in the lumber industry gradually shifted to the Pacific Northwest, especially to Washington and the redwood forests of northern California. Finns also found employment in lumber mills, and sizable Finnish communities grew up in such sawmill towns as Cloquet and International Falls, Minnesota; St. Ignace and Baraga, Michigan; Aberdeen, Washington; Coos Bay, Oregon; and Fort Bragg and Eureka, California.

Although Finns were accustomed to logging, working conditions in the industry in America were unfamiliar. Logging in Finland has been essentially a part of the agricultural system—an extension of the village economy—and the isolated, male-inhabited lumber camps of America seemed lonely and unattractive. Small groups of professional Finnish lumberjacks did develop, centering around towns like Duluth, Minnesota, and Seattle, Washington, where Finnish businesses such as saloons and boardinghouses arose to cater to these single, homeless men. For the great majority of Finnish-American forest workers, however, logging was simply a temporary means to a more important end: establishment in a more desirable job, or—more likely—a farm in America or Finland. Indeed, Finnish-Americans, as a group, were quite successful in settling on the land in rural America, and many of them (particularly those in places such as the northern Great Lakes region and northern California where the lumber industry was important) assured success for their farms by logging to earn extra income, a means familiar to them from the old country.

Finnish-Americans, as one of the most radical immigrant groups in America, were active within trade unions in the lumber industry. The Industrial Workers of the World (IWW) especially received broad support from Finns in logging areas. For example, Finns made up over half of about 4,000 IWW workers that went on strike in lumber camps and mill towns in Minnesota in December 1916 and January 1917. However, such a minor immigrant group as the Finns contributed so small a percentage of forest workers that they were not involved in union leadership, as they were in the mining industry where they were more heavily represented. One important exception was Santeri Nuorteva, a prominent Finnish-American radical, who served briefly in 1913 as an organizer for an American Federation of Labor union among lumber workers on the Pacific Coast.

FURTHER READING: There is a single minor published work dealing specifically with Finnish-Americans in lumbering: Walter Mattila, "The Finnish Paul Bunyans," *Finnish Emigrant Studies Series*, 8 (1973). P. G. Hummasti, *Finnish Radicals in Astoria, Oregon, 1904–1940* (1979), has a chapter on Finns and the IWW in the Pacific Northwest. John I. Kolehmainen and George Hill, *Haven in the Woods: The Story of the Finns in Wisconsin* (1951), and Hans Wasastjerna, *History of the Finns in Minnesota* (1957), contain scattered references to Finns in the lumber industries of these two states. Reino Kero, *Suuren Lännen suomalaiset* (1976), which is being translated into English, has a brief section on the Finnish-American logger.

P. GEORGE HUMMASTI

FIRE AND FOREST MANAGEMENT

Fire and life share a common chemistry, a common geographic range, and probably a common origin in lightning. Lightning fire has long been a selective force of great evolutionary significance; the sooty part of coal, fusain, is the residue of ancient fires. Most terrestrial biotas have, in some form, adapted to fire, and some even enjoy a kind of symbiosis with fire.

Fire exists within an environment of fuels, weather, and topography. When this environment is combined with a typical pattern of ignition, the result is a fire regime or regular pattern of fire occurrence.

Controlled burning to remove ground cover in Florida. Damage to pine trees is held to a minimum by burning into the wind, causing the fire to be relatively cool. Florida Forest Service Photo.

Fire and its environment shape each other. Fires burn with a typical frequency, shape, and intensity; they show an inverse relationship between size and frequency. Ecosystems, in turn, adapt to this pattern of fire, and by the nature of their adaptation tend to further shape the character of fires that burn within them.

Fire is a mechanism of decomposition and rearrangement. On a microscale, fire recycles nutrients; on a macroscale, it recycles whole groups of organisms and communities, a process known as succession. The intensity of fire is affected by the amount of fuel available to it, that is, by the amount of biomass awaiting decomposition. In cold climates, generally the rate of fuel production is small, but the rate of nonfire decomposition is still slower so litter builds up on the forest floor. Thus fires tend to be episodic but intense. In warm climates, the rate of fuel production is commonly high, but the rate of decomposition is also high; fires are typically more frequent but less intense. Where other means of decomposition are slow and fire is excluded, the essential nutrients of some systems tend to become locked up in inert reservoirs of forest litter. When fire enters the system, the nutrients are distributed. On the macroscale, fire produces a mosaic of vegetative types and a mixture of age classes instead of a decadent, homogeneous climax stand. Fire may retard successional progression or the tendency of one vegetative association to replace another. An ecosystem subject to periodic burning may be considered as a system in dynamic equilibrium rather than as one following a life cycle that tends toward a particular community.

In the United States prominent fire regimes caused by lightning occur primarily in the mountainous areas of the West, although south Florida and some other Southern states also experience lightning fire seasons. The heaviest concentration of lightning fires occurs in the ponderosa pine belt arcing across Arizona and New Mexico; summer lightning fires are also common through the Sierra Nevada, the eastern flank of the Cascades, interior Alaska, and the Northern Rockies. Fuels created by the natural growth cycle make grass available for burning on an annual basis, chaparral on a cycle of 10 to 35 years, and forests anywhere from 7 years for litter fires in ponderosa pine to 150 years in lodgepole pine. The prevalence of oak and pine forests, in particular, and their association with savannahs is closely related to the fire history of the area.

Most fires, however, are caused by man. Since at least the days of *Homo erectus*, humans have been applying fire to and withdrawing it from the natural landscape. Man is also the greatest modifier of the fire environment, particularly its fuels. It is probable that most ecosystems have been strongly influenced by man's fire policies. The very concept of "wildfire" has its basis in cultural attitudes rather than natural events.

Various people have exploited the possibilities of fire and biological adaptations to it for their own purposes. There is evidence that the American Indian, for example, used free-burning fire for hunting, surrounding, or driving game. Large "barrens" or "deserts" were maintained by fire as hunting sites. Fire was applied to the cultivation and harvest of natural grasses, berries, and nuts. It was used along the coastal plains and in interior Alaska to drive off mosquitoes and flies. It was fundamental to slash-and-burn agriculture, supplying fertilizer in ash. Fire was used as spectacle and as ritual; the Apaches were said to burn off miles of mountain landscape in the hope that the smoke would induce rain. In California, smoke was used to destroy mistletoe which invaded mesquite or oak, and in Oregon, some tribes would use smoke to cause pandora moths to drop from trees to the ground where they could be gathered as food. Fire was widely employed in war, both as a tactical weapon and as the tool of a strategic policy of scorched earth. During the Sioux wars of 1876, some half million acres were burned by the Indians to drive off cavalry units, and the desire to open up dense woods and prevent ambush was among the most common reason for firing around villages, trails, and hunting sites. With undergrowth removed by fire, traveling and hunting by stalking were also improved. Explorers and pioneers often reported reproduction springing up where Indian fire practices were terminated.

Early pioneers tended to adopt Indian fire practices—continuing fire hunting, for example; firing the woods for pasturage improvement; encouraging a shifting, slash-and-burn agriculture. The mixture of logging, land-clearing, and frontier fire habits was often responsible for holocaust fires; other conflagrations appeared where lands, previously unburned, were drained and fired. Most of the terribly destructive wildfires from the Miramichi fire of 1825 to the great Idaho fires of 1910 originated in such frontier fire practices. With more stable settlement, however, fire practices changed, but rural residents did not want fires eliminated, only better controlled. Rural fire codes and public opinion generally worked to discipline what had become promiscuous fire into more useful forms.

The management of forestlands for continuous production made it necessary to suppress many forms of earlier fire practices. Against traditional frontier and agricultural fire practices the U. S. FOREST SERVICE in the early twentieth century proposed "systematic fire protection." The most celebrated confrontation between these two systems of fire management was the "light burning" controversy in northern California, which began about 1909 and did not conclude officially until a state commission condemned light burning in 1923. Local lumbermen, in an effort to protect mature timber, had promoted "light" surface fires to reduce fuel buildup. The Forest Service, however, insisted that such fires preserved existing stands at the expense of reproduction, that the technique was more expensive and less effective than systematic fire protection, that it would dilute the forest protection message presented to the public, that it would play into the hands of herders intent on replacing forests with pasturage, and that it promoted a laissez-faire frontier economy which might pose a political threat to government conservation and professional forestry. The service insisted on a strict contrast to previous fire usage habits. Slash, for example, was not to be burned *in situ* by broadcast fire, but was to be piled and burned.

The Forest Service also proposed the extension of systematic fire protection into new regions, such as the cutover lands of the South and the remote Northern Rockies. In the early 1930s, the service debated, then officially condemned, the practice of "let burning," or leaving fires to burn in remote sites or "loose herding" them into such regions. In the South, however, the acceptance of controlled fire became part of the price of admitting the cutover pineries into industrial forestry. Beginning in 1909, Herman Haupt CHAPMAN and others both in and outside the service conducted studies over many years demonstrating the usefulness of controlled fire for the silviculture of longleaf pine, for hazard reduction, for the encouragement of more nutritious pasturage, and for the management of habitats for such wildlife as bobtail quail. In 1932, the service allowed state cooperators to control burn and still qualify for the CLARKE-MCNARY ACT program, and in 1943 the practice was extended to the Southern national forests. This debate, however, emphasized the uniqueness of the Southern fire problem, and prescribed fire was not generally promoted beyond the South despite growing evidence that it could be used advantageously in the West in the silviculture of the ponderosa pine, in hazard reduction in white pine and lodgepole pine, and in brush conversion. After studies in several Western states by Harold Weaver and Harry Kallander, the Bureau of Indian Affairs in 1948 instituted controlled burning of pine stands on the Fort Apache, San Carlos, and Hualapai reservations in Arizona.

Research on the role of fire in natural ecosystems led to experiments designed to determine the potential range for prescribed fire for all aspects of land management. The results of studies in fire ecology and prescribed fire were disseminated by the annual Tall Timbers Fire Ecology Conferences (1962–1976) and by the reports of a National Fire Effects Workshop (1978) sponsored by the Forest Service. This research supported the belief that prescribed fire could be a suitable management tool. The NATIONAL PARK SERVICE abandoned its policy of total suppression, which had been first introduced in YELLOWSTONE NATIONAL PARK in 1886 and had been followed in national parks since then except for some prescribed burning in the Everglades. In 1968, the park service revised its fire policy to divide all fires into either wildfire, which was to be suppressed, or prescribed (management) fire, which, regardless of origin, was to be encouraged. The Forest Service similarly adjusted its policy in phases between 1971 and 1978.

Prescriptions for broadcast fire in all forms of land management became commonplace. One of the great limitations on prescribed burning had been the absence of comparability between fires and hence between their effects. Research on fire physics aimed at removing this objection. Physical and mathematical models became available to predict fire spread and intensity, and fire intensity was correlated with ecological effects. The principal measurements of intensity used were fire intensity or Byram's intensity (BTUs per second per foot), which measured the flaming front, and the reaction intensity or combustion rate (BTUs per second per square foot), which measured energy release for a given unit of fuel. Most prescribed burns sought to keep Byram's intensity below fifty, although special firing techniques occasionally allowed for more intense fires without loss of control. By the early 1970s, particularly in the South, more acreage was prescription-burned than was burned by wildfire. By 1980, prescribed fire of all sorts (including slash disposal, site preparation, and natural fire) was commonly used in the Northwest, Northern Rockies, Lake States, New Jersey, and California. With its vast expanses, Alaska too had great potential for prescribed natural fire programs. The limiting factor in many regions such as the Northwest was smoke, which was subject, like other industrial effluents, to air quality standards.

FURTHER READING: Arthur A. Brown and Kenneth Davis, *Forest Fire: Control and Use* (2nd ed., 1973). T. Z. Kozlowski and C. E. Ahlgren, eds., *Fire and Ecosystems* (1974). Stephen J. Pyne, *Fire in America: A Cultural History of Wildland and Rural Fire* (1982). Ashley L. Schiff, *Fire and Water: Scientific Heresy in the Forest Service* (1962). U. S. Forest Service, *Effects of Fire . . . : A State-of-*

Knowledge Review, General Technical Reports WO-7, WO-9, WO-10, WO-134, and WO-15 (1979).

STEPHEN J. PYNE

FIRE CONTROL

Fire control is one aspect of the larger question of fire practices, or the way in which natural and man-caused fire may be used or withheld. A controlled burn to one culture may be a wildfire to another. Industrial forestry found existing agricultural and frontier fire practices unsuitable and had to create a new set of practices—much of it based on the suppression of the customs of an earlier era.

Fire control was long considered the *sine qua non* of successful forestry. Henry S. GRAVES in 1910 declared that it was 90 percent of forestry. But it was a peculiarly American problem, as Coert DuBois wrote in 1914, "American foresters have found that they have a unique fire problem, and that they can get little help in solving it from European foresters." Earle Hart CLAPP observed in 1933 that "forest fire research apparently originated in the United States, undoubtedly as the direct result of a forest-fire situation which is more serious than in almost any other country."

Agriculture had brought a form of rural fire protection. Fire was used in land clearing, in the fertilizing of shifting cultivation, in pasture improvement, hunting, and habitat maintenance, and in a variety of other ways, some of them adapted from fire practices of the American Indian. Fire codes regulated these uses, though they were dependent on local enforcement and on local volunteer crews to cope with escaped fires. Fires were rarely controlled unless they threatened farm, field, or village, and, if large, such fires quickly exceeded any effort at control. Large fires, however, were considered a temporary phenomenon of settlement: when wildlands were transformed into arable land, forest fires would disappear.

With industrialization came both the reservation of wildland from settlement and the reversion of once arable land back to forest. Traditional fire practices were suited neither for industrial forestry nor for the

A hand-powered fan psychrometer provides an empirical measure of relative humidity, one of the most important variables used to estimate the likelihood of fire ignition and to predict its rate of spread. The psychrometer uses two thermometers, one with a wet wick over its mercury bulb. The fan cools the wet bulb through evaporation; comparison of the wet- and dry-bulb temperatures provides an index of relative humidity.
American Forest Institute Photo.

preservation of forestland for its influences such as watershed. Land managers had to develop new sources of manpower, new equipment, new techniques, and new means of enforcement. They would often have to develop a region in the name of fire protection, complete with roads, trails, and communication networks. They would create policies to decide which fires to suppress and which, perhaps, to promote. The first manifestation of these needs came between 1885 and 1886, when New York created its state forest preserve in the Adirondacks, Ontario established a system of fire patrols for the provincial forests, and the U. S. Army took over the administration of YELLOWSTONE NATIONAL PARK, in part to bring fire control.

Among the earliest fire protection organizations were those formed among private timber owners. Several appeared after the 1903 and 1908 fires in the Northeast, and many after the 1902 and 1910 fires in Idaho and the Northwest. Especially where government influence was negligible or where compulsory fire patrol laws were enacted, fire protection associations became common. They appeared, for example, in California, the Lake States, Georgia, Kentucky, West

Virginia, Pennsylvania, and New Hampshire. Many private companies, moreover, entered into cooperative agreements with state or federal agencies, and permittees on the national forests were required to furnish assistance in fire control. Many of the private organizations were eventually supplanted by state forestry departments. The most famous of the private groups was the WESTERN FORESTRY AND CONSERVATION ASSOCIATION (WFCA), which was organized in 1909 as an umbrella organization for the numerous fire protection associations that had appeared in the Northwest. By 1980, the WFCA had members in eleven western states and in Canada.

Federal involvement in fire control began with the reservation of parts of the public domain from settlement. The assumption of national park administration by the U. S. Army set an important precedent, and with the FOREST MANAGEMENT ACT of 1897 the GENERAL LAND OFFICE (GLO) accepted responsibility for fire control and enforcement against trespass on the forest reserves. The Transfer Act of 1905 gave these reserves to the U. S. FOREST SERVICE, however, and modern fire protection dates from this event.

The Forest Service has assumed a central institu-

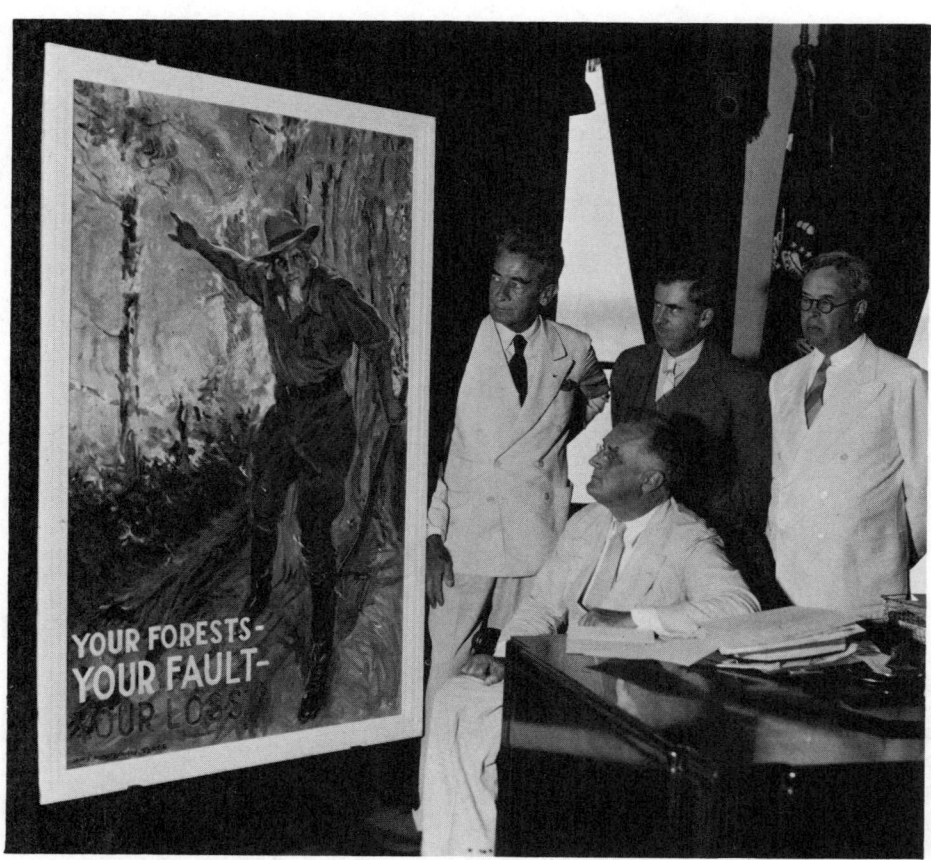

In 1937, illustrator James Montgomery Flagg contributed this now famous poster to the Forest Service's fire prevention campaign. Close examination reveals that Flagg used his own likeness for Uncle Sam. Standing at Flagg's left are Secretary of Agriculture Henry A. Wallace and Associate Chief Earle H. Clapp; seated is President Franklin D. Roosevelt. Forest History Society Photo.

In order to lessen the fuel load before the hazardous dry season, a flame thrower is used to ignite the logging debris. American Forest Institute Photo.

tional and intellectual role in fire programs at all levels of national life. Institutionally, the service has controlled the national forest system and promoted cooperative fire control programs with the states and industry. Intellectually, the service introduced the standards of professional forestry into the debate about fire policy. Popular sentiment often held that fire control was impossible in a technical sense, indefensible on economic grounds, and undesirable on environmental terms; professional forestry as represented by the Forest Service demonstrated otherwise. By the early 1960s, the Forest Service exercised a hegemony in terms of resources, scientific research, and administrative control over national wildland fire protection and cooperative rural programs.

All of the other federal landholders offer some form of fire protection. The NATIONAL PARK SERVICE's program began effectively with army administration.

For the Bureau of Indian Affairs, fire protection followed the 1910 fire season. For the FISH AND WILDLIFE SERVICE, it came with the acquisition of wildlife refuges. The TAYLOR GRAZING ACT of 1934 gave the Grazing Service responsibilities for grazing districts, primarily in the Great Basin. The Alaska Fire Control Service was established under the GLO in 1939. Reorganization of the Grazing Service and the GLO as the BUREAU OF LAND MANAGEMENT (BLM) in 1946 gave the new agency the largest federal fire program outside the Forest Service. Alaska, in the late 1950s, made the BLM a major force in federal fire protection. During the late 1970s, when BLM began to lose its Alaska lands to the state, to native corporations, and to other federal agencies, its fire-fighting role diminished.

Cooperation among the federal agencies began with agreements between the agencies and the Forest Service. The Forest Service brought the National Weather Service into fire protection. It chaired the Forest Protection Board (1927–1933), which sought to coordinate federal fire programs and informally adopted Forest Service fire policy and techniques as a standard. After the board was dissolved, the principal medium for federal cooperation during the New Deal years was the CIVILIAN CONSERVATION CORPS (CCC); during the war years, it was civil defense and military programs. With the emergence of a BLM fire organization, liaison between the DEPARTMENT OF THE INTERIOR and the Forest Service developed in two forms: the Boise Interagency Fire Center (BIFC), established in 1969 for the coordination of support services during fire emergencies, and the National Wildfire Coordinating Group, set up in 1976 for better integration of training, standards, prevention programs, and so forth. By the late 1960s, even though increasing differences in objectives among federal land agencies made the adoption of a single policy seem less attractive, cooperative fire protection was expanding its international scope in the form of fire assistance treaties with Canada and Mexico, BIFC support on large firest in Canada, and the establishment of a fire management study group within the North American Forestry Commission.

Fire protection by the states began in a number of ways. For some, like New York and Pennsylvania, it came with land acquisition. For others, like Oregon and California, it came with compulsory fire patrol laws; for New Jersey, with the adoption of tough fire codes, such as those imposed against railroads; for Maine, with the creation of its Forestry District in 1909. For all, fire protection responsibility was given to state forestry departments. For these bureaus the assumption of fire control brought political permanence. Of great significance both to the promotion of these bureaus and to a certain standardization of objectives and techniques was legislation allowing for federal state cooperation in fire protection. The WEEKS ACT of 1911 began the experiment, but it was the CLARKE-MCNARY ACT of 1924 and its amendments that were fundamental. The federal government, through the Forest Service, could administer grants-in-aid theoretically equal to the amount contributed by the states. The Forest Service would set standards and inspect for compliance. Most of the land now under protection is guarded by the states, and for this expansion of fire control the Clarke-McNary Act is largely responsible. It allowed for federal standards to be introduced without expansion of the national forest system itself, and, in turn, it led to a wide range of cooperative forestry programs. By 1966, all the states participated.

The states, too, have developed cooperative arrangements among themselves. For fire control the most important are the interstate compacts which provide for mutual assistance, shared resources, and often common training. The first was among the Northeastern states and New York (1949), followed by the Southeastern states and Southcentral states (1954), the Mid-Atlantic states (1956), and California and the Northwestern states (1978). Two still larger organizations have been superimposed over these: the Northeast Forest Fire Supervisors (1973) and the Southern Forest Fire Chiefs Association (1974). Quebec (1969) and New Brunswick (1970) have joined the Northeast Compact, and in 1971 the Northeastern states agreed to underwrite the Roscommon Equipment Center in Michigan. In the West, under the aegis of the Western Forestry and Conservation Association, interstate fire councils have been set up to coordinate research and exchange information. Among them are the California-Nevada, Intermountain, Northwest, Rocky Mountains, Southwest, and Alaska councils.

Between 1950 and 1954, under the direction of the Office of Civil Defense, the Forest Service gradually assumed responsibility for coordinating wildland and rural fire protection in the United States. The service built its national plans out of the Clarke-McNary program, but these plans now had to encompass rural as well as wildlands. A further form of assistance—also growing out of World War II—came through the Federal Excess Property Program, which gave the Forest Service priority access to surplus equipment, largely military, that it could pass on to cooperators. By the 1970s, some $200 million worth of equipment had been distributed to state and rural fire agencies. Locally the effect could be great, and nationally the success of this program became the basis for the Rural Community Fire Protection program authorized in 1972 and funded in 1976. The Forest Service directs the program through the state foresters.

Because of both its institutional relationships and its role in the dissemination of professional forestry, the fire policy of the United States Forest Service has special significance. As an event of national importance, the service's program effectively began in 1910 with two fire challenges: the light burning controversy in California and a summer of holocausts which burned some 5 million acres throughout the western forests, 3 million in the northern Rockies alone. The first event challenged the intellectual credibility of service policy, and the second attacked its technical capability. The fire control policies of the service can be dated by that agency's strategic concepts, tactical emphases, and research programs relating to four problem types of fires considered as cultural rather than natural events. These four types may be termed "frontier fire," "backcountry fire," "mass fire," and "wilderness fire."

The first of these types, "frontier fire," includes the fire practices common to the largely agricultural frontier economy which developed in the United States. Against the frontier's laissez-faire use of fire, the service during the 1910s and 1920s proposed "systematic" fire protection, dedicated to fire suppression and reliant on sound planning and administration. Fire research during this period concentrated on the investigation of fire as an economic question in forestry and as a technical problem. A period of administrative experimentation ended in 1921 with the Mather Field Conference, which standardized fire control within the service, and in 1923 with an official denunciation of light burning by a special panel, which eliminated the challenge posed by frontier fire practices as an alternative form of management. The "economic theory" was generally adopted as a policy; it called for adjusting the investment in protection to the values at risk. In the late 1920s, the Shasta Experimental Fire Forest was established as an administrative model of systematic fire protection.

The second type, "backcountry fire," includes fires occurring on forested lands remote in space or time, that is, lands in the undeveloped parts of the national forests and lands such as those in the South and Lake States that had been cut over and burned and for which fire protection over a long period could only be regarded as an investment in the future. The period 1930 to 1949 tested the geographical and financial limits toward which systematic fire control could be pushed. The guiding strategic concept was termed "hour control." This was the result of statistical analysis by S. B. Show and E. I. Kotok in furtherance of earlier work by Coert DuBois on fire occurrence and area burned. Their studies sought to identify the necessary manpower and speed of first attack in each of the broad fuel types in California, which would assure satisfactory limitation of the area burned. Comprehensive planning based on these concepts was made possible by New Deal conservation investments such as the CCC, which strengthened fire control organizations everywhere. The magnitude of CCC involvement resulted in a tactical emphasis on manpower. By 1939, inspired by the CCC demonstration, operational trials were under way with two forms of special fire suppression crews: the forty-man crew accented the power of a large, organized body of men applied toward fires that had escaped initial attack, while the smokejumpers—or "parachute firemen"—concentrated on initial attack in remote areas, a cheaper and faster form of control than a dispersed system of ground smokechasers. Research continued the interests of the earlier period, concentrating on planning and fire danger rating. However, the amplification of means at hand during the New Deal encouraged the Forest Service to extend its aims and in 1935 the service adopted the "10 A.M." policy, which stipulated control by 10 A.M. the morning following the report of a fire, or, failing that, control by 10 A.M. the next day, and so on. Faced with this mandate to control the fire overnight, foresters were justified in calling out heavy forces for the initial attack.

By the 1950s, fire research and protection strategy had taken up a third problem, that of "mass fire." Stimulated by World War II demonstrations of the effectiveness of fire as a weapon, researchers examined the atmospheric and thermodynamic relationships of high-energy fires and devised field experiments such as those used in Operation Firestop in 1954. During this period, the support previously given by the emergency conservation program of the New Deal was replaced by an alliance between foresters and military and civil defense agencies. The war years, too, developed the major national fire prevention programs—Keep America Green and the Cooperative Forest Fire Prevention Campaign (SMOKEY BEAR). At the same time, fire protection completed its state program and expanded to new limits in Alaska and in rural fire defense. Increased emphasis on equipment complemented that on manpower, and the Forest Service established two equipment development centers. By 1956, air tankers and helicopter transport were in use. The Forest Service, which had created a Division of Forest Fire Research in 1948, opened three fire research laboratories and joined the National Academy of Science Committee on Fire Research.

By the late 1960s, a fourth fire type, "wilderness fire," was becoming the focus of significant attention. Fuel modification became the strategic concept for the control of wildfire, and the preferred tool was prescribed (broadcast) fire. Research interests shifted from fire physics to fire ecology, a study that reinforced the preference for prescribed burning as a management tool. In 1971, the Forest Service modified the 10 A.M. policy to accommodate natural fires in wilderness areas and promulgated a ten-acre policy as a guide for presuppression planning. The necessity for these adjustments followed, in part, from environmental legislation, beginning with the Wilderness Act of 1964. In 1978, the service replaced the amended policy with a new one, in effect a policy of fire by prescription. Wildfires were to be suppressed and prescribed fires were to be encouraged; all fires which escaped initial attack would be evaluated separately for the determination of proper control objectives.

FURTHER READING: Arthur A. Brown and Kenneth Davis, *Forest Fire: Control and Use* (2nd ed., 1973). Stephen J. Pyne, "Fire and the Forest Service: A History of Policy and Research," *Journal of Forest History* 25 (Apr. 1981): 64-77, and *Fire in America: A Cultural History of Wildland and Rural Fire* (1982). U. S. Department of Agriculture, Forest Service, *Fire Control Notes* (1936–1973), and *Fire Management Notes* (1973–   ). Ralph R. Widner, ed., *Forests and Forestry in the American States* (1968).

STEPHEN J. PYNE

FIREFIGHTING METHODS AND EQUIPMENT

The control of fire relies on a three-part strategy: to prevent ignition, to modify the environment in which a fire burns (notably its fuels), and to attack a fire while it remains a point source, as almost all fires are in the beginning. For a fire beyond the initial stage, the techniques of fire control are as ancient as those of fire use.

In the Middle Ages, European peasants fought wildfire with brooms, rakes, fire lines, and backfires. In pre-Columbian America, Indians fought wildfire with blankets, tree boughs, and backfires. For fire protection during the agricultural settlement of America, fire control relied on a combination of European and Indian techniques. In many settled regions, rural fire codes regulated the use of fire and stipulated the means to contain those fires that escaped. In some regions unique systems evolved. On the Great Plains, this included the use of plows, horse-drawn drags, and backfires. In the East, special railroad tank cars and velocipedes came into use. In still other regions, where wildlands intermingled with rural lands, protective backfires were usually the order of the day.

All methods of direct control, however, had certain elements in common: each required rapid detection; most relied on preexisting firebreaks or fuelbreaks in the form of roads, streams, or plowed corridors; and all applied specified techniques to the perimeter of the fire—swatting flames with bags, flaps, or tree boughs; trenching a path through the fuels; backfir-

Converted seaplane drops fire-retarding chemicals to give ground crews time to suppress fire by conventional means. American Forest Institute Photo.

Mountain top lookout transmits bearing of sighted forest fire to the central dispatcher. American Forest Institute Photo.

ing along a natural or prepared break. All depended, too, on the presence of fire fighters, making the control of fire unique among the management of natural processes. To a great extent, the history of fire suppression techniques is the story of how fire fighters came to be, how they were organized, and how, in some instances, equipment came to supplement them.

With the reservation of large blocks of land from agricultural reclamation, there developed a need for a program of fire control that was not dependent, as rural fire control was, on settlement. Instead, new means of detection, alternate methods of transportation, and novel hand tools to be used by a class of people who were, by definition, not settlers all had to be invented and then organized. The experiment began in a serious way in 1885–1886 when the U. S. Army took over the administration of YELLOWSTONE NATIONAL PARK, Ontario began a system of fire patrols on its provincial forests, and New York arranged for fire protection on the lands of its Adirondack Preserve. Twenty years later, a number of private timber protective associa-

tions also entered into the experiments. Between the great fires of 1910 and the Mather Field Conference of 1921, the U. S. FOREST SERVICE pioneered the fundamentals of "systematic fire protection," a program that sought to analyze and synthesize all the elements of wildland fire control. By the 1930s, the program was being actively projected into all the wild and many of the rural lands of the United States. It is not too much to say that, for many large areas in the federal reservation system, the land was effectively settled by the paraphernalia of fire control. Since then the trend in fire control has been simply to apply greater force to the fire line in shorter time.

For detection, early experiments relied on a system of patrols, then on a network of fixed lookouts; many of these have, in turn, been replaced by aerial observation. To communicate information, portable phones were most commonly used, later supplemented by radios. The prospects of the radio prompted the Forest Service to establish a radio laboratory in Beltsville, Maryland, in 1927, and another in Portland,

A helitanker drops a load of retardant on a fire on Idaho's Nezperce National Forest, 1967. Forest Service Photo.

Oregon, ten years later. For tools, the implements of farm, mine, and logging camp were modified into such forms as the Pulaski and McLeod tools, among others. Mechanical equipment—especially for transportation—became common by the 1920s; indeed, the mountain fire truck and the modern bulldozer were invented in the late 1920s, the bulldozer by a Forest Service employee. After World War I an arrangement was made between the Army Air Service and the Forest Service to use planes for aerial reconnaissance, a popular program that continued sporadically until 1922; eventually the Forest Service and several states began to acquire planes of their own. Aircraft, indeed, became integrally related to the ambitions of fire control. From its modest beginning in 1919, the dream of an aerial delivery system for chemicals and fire fighters led to repeated experiments, notably in 1936–1939 by the Forest Service and in 1946–1947 between the Forest Service and the

army. The breakthrough came—as it did for the mechanization of fire control in general—with a massive conversion of military hardware left over from World War II and the Korean conflict. An important event in the development of modern technology, including aircraft, was Operation Firestop, a year-long, multi-agency experiment staged in southern California in 1954. Two years later, both the air tanker and the helicopter came of age as tactical fireline machinery. So significant had equipment of all sorts become to fire control that the Forest Service established two equipment development centers, and a number of eastern states combined to help fund the equipment center that Michigan had long established at Roscommon.

Originally, in lieu of a settler class that could be counted on to fight fires, the Forest Service relied on its permittees and on per diem fire guards or smokechasers; during major outbreaks, the army could be called

A specially equipped helicopter can lay fire hose much faster than ground crews. Los Angeles County Fire Department Photo.

upon, as it was in 1910. Where reserved lands mingled with rural lands, fire warden crews remained common. But particularly as systematic fire protection reached into the backcountry, a reliable, independent force was needed. The breakthrough came with the CIVILIAN CONSERVATION CORPS (CCC). Thanks to the CCC, a physical plant for fire control appeared almost overnight, and impressive complexes of fuelbreaks became a fundamental component of strategy. But equally significant was the experience with large, organized crews: directly out of the CCC experiment in 1939 came the forty-man crew, destined for large project fires, and the smokejumpers, ideally suited for initial attack on small remote fires. After World War II, a host of organized crews emerged for project fires: the Southwest Forest Fire Fighters, composed of Indians and Hispanics; the Snake River Valley crews, formed out of migrants in the Great Basin; and crews assembled from forest work projects, such as thinning, or from the manpower pools of nearby towns. Specialized crews for initial attack advanced stride for stride with their big fire counterparts—helitack crews, smokejumpers, ground tanker crews, and so on. In 1961, the Interregional Fire Suppression crew program—a rapid deployment force—was organized in conjunction with interregional supervisory and administrative teams. By 1976, the National Interagency Fire Qualifications System (NIFQS), under the concept of total mobility, brought a universal scale of evaluation and promised to make equipment and crews interchangeable nationwide on project fires. In the early 1980s the NIFQS was itself being expanded to include all types of emergency response under the National Interagency Incident Management System.

This tremendous multiplication of suppression resources meant that more fires could be hit while small; for large fires, it meant that closer work was often possible. However, the largest reason for a reduction in burned acreage was a general change in fire practices, a transformation that reduced the number of low-intensity fires routinely burning on the landscape and that eliminated the use of protective backfires set by alarmed residents. But with increased resources and power came magnified responsibilities for their management. During the 1970s, information technology became more common; the management of the suppression effort might involve more difficulties than the actual control of the fire. At the same time, new techniques were developed for special problem areas. In the postwar era, suburbs and wildlands were intermingled in many regions, most spectacularly in southern California, and this required some hybridization with the techniques of urban fire control and considerable coordination among agencies. Elsewhere, the preference for prescribed natural fire in wilderness areas removed some of the most remote and logistically troublesome areas from routine suppression. Suppression strategy, moreover, adopted generally a philosophy of wholesale fuel management as a means of reducing fire intensity, the preferred technique being prescribed broadcast fire.

FURTHER READING: Arthur A. Brown and Kenneth P. Davis, *Forest Fire: Control and Use* (2nd ed., 1973), chap. 13. Henry Clepper, *Professional Forestry in the United States* (1971), especially chap. 12, "Wings over the Forest." Harry P. Gaylor, *Wildfires: Prevention and Control* (1974). North American Forestry Commission, *Forest Fire News*, an irregular newsletter. Stephen J. Pyne, *Fire in America: A Cultural History of Wildland and Rural Fire* (1982). U. S. Forest Service, *Fire Control Notes* (later, *Fire Management Notes*), 1936– . Ralph R. Widner, ed., *Forests and Forestry in the American States* (1968).

STEPHEN J. PYNE

FIRES

See Forest Fires

FIREWOOD

The abundance of firewood hastened the settlement of the United States. Since there was no other readily available fuel in the seventeenth century, the first settlers were fortunate to live in wooded areas. No fuel shortages kept them from destroying trees to clear land for cultivation. Although trees were plentiful, they were not a cheap source of fuel. It was expensive in terms of man-hours to obtain firewood. After cutting and hauling bulky trees, men sawed and split them to proper size. Only an able axman could cut, split, and stack in a day as much as one cord consisting of a pile of wood eight feet long, four feet wide, and four feet high. This kind of labor was indispensable long after the establishment of the first settlements. Almost until the twentieth century, firewood remained the main fuel to meet the needs of an increasing population and industrial expansion.

The kind of trees used for firewood depended not only on their availability but also on their fuel value and other factors. The heaviest hardwoods such as hickory, white oak, sugar maple, beech, red oak, and birch have the most value as fuel. One cord of good dry hardwood weighs two tons and produces as much heat as a ton of anthracite coal or 200 gallons of fuel oil. Hemlock, spruce, pine, and other softwoods with a lot of pitch ignite easily and are especially useful as kindling. They are more suitable for burning in fireplaces than in kitchen stoves because regular use produces soot which clogs stovepipes. After settlements were established beyond the eastern seaboard, settlers also tried other kinds of firewood such as fir, aspen, and ponderosa pine even though oaks remained high on their lists of preferred fuels.

As long as fireplaces were used in private and public buildings, the demand for firewood remained great. It took from ten to twenty acres of woodland to supply the fuel burned by one fireplace annually. Also, a fireplace wasted 80 percent or more of its heat up a chimney. Trying to reduce this waste, Benjamin Franklin in 1744 developed the iron stove that bears his name. The Franklin stove was an open fireplace made of cast-iron plates which stood away from a chimney. The stove transmitted heat by radiation from its back and sides and by direct conduction through ducts. In spite of Franklin's efforts, however, the traditional fireplace was the main heating facility until the nineteenth century.

Besides complaining about wasteful fireplaces, in the eighteenth century Americans worried about their supply of firewood. Fuel problems were most acute in the towns of New England and the Middle Colonies where it was necessary to procure firewood at higher prices from greater distances after nearby sources were depleted. In 1750, Pehr Kalm, a Swedish traveler, observed that high fuel prices caused complaints in Philadelphia. The prices were blamed on the competition for fuel from the operators of brick kilns and iron smelters as well as on the destruction of trees in clearing land. On the eve of the American Revolution, the unknown author of the book *American Husbandry* also described the removal of trees as ruthless and observed that the demand for firewood and lumber had raised fuel prices in New England and Philadelphia to the levels that prevailed in England. Colonial legislators shared these concerns and enacted laws to protect forests and to regulate the sale of firewood. Massachusetts Bay Colony established the standard cord in 1647; New York followed in 1684, Rhode Island in 1698, South Carolina in 1738, Delaware in 1741, Georgia in 1766, and North Carolina in 1784. Massachusetts provided for official inspectors in 1655, Rhode Island in 1698, and New Hampshire in 1714. Most of the colonies enacted similar legislation. In 1772, New York passed a law prescribing the minimum size of trees that could be cut for firewood in Albany County. Meanwhile, few efforts were made to develop Virginia and Pennsylvania coal as an alternative fuel before the 1790s, so

that it was necessary to import coal from England for industrial purposes.

From the close of the American Revolution through the Civil War, the demand for firewood was intensified by the rapid growth of population and industry. While the total population rose almost tenfold, from 3.9 million in 1790 to 38.6 million in 1870, the rural sector grew at a slower rate, even though thousands of Easterners and European immigrants established farms in the West where firewood was usually available. But the almost fifty-fold increase of the urban population from a little over 200,000 to over 9.9 million meant that more Americans than before, especially in the older part of the country, were buying firewood from farmers, who sold over 5 million cords annually by 1840. Also factories and the so-called hand-and-neighborhood industries, which numbered over 123,000 in 1849 and doubled in the next two decades, were increasingly competing for the fuel supply.

Meanwhile, the development of steamboats further increased the demand for firewood. In 1807, Robert Fulton showed the applicability of steam to navigation when his steamboat, *Clermont*, made its maiden trip from New York to Albany on the Hudson River. This commercial success spurred the construction of other steamboats, which were used on the Great Lakes and the Ohio and Mississippi rivers after 1812. Steamboat captains stopped enroute to purchase firewood which settlers had cut and piled at landings. After mid-century, steamboats were moving on the waterways of the Pacific Coast.

Within two decades after the introduction of the steamboat, the demand for firewood was also increased by the development of steam railroads. The tenders of the early locomotives were flatcars with piles of wood and hogsheads of water. Until a process was developed to use blasts of air in forcing a coal fire, locomotives depended on steam produced by burning wood. In 1853, to give but a single example, there were eighteen wood storage stations along the seventy-six-mile line of the original New York Central. By the Civil War, however, coal was a serious competitor to wood for powering at least the Northern railroads, and by the 1870s coal was the dominant fuel for transportation.

During the decades after the War of 1812, when the development of railroads and steamboats coincided with urban expansion, the growing demand for firewood aroused fears of a fuel crisis. Both Noah Webster and ex-president James Madison berated Americans for destroying trees and creating thereby a scarcity of fuel. Webster feared that the lack of coal and firewood from interior districts would force New

Englanders to quit their soil. Newspaper and other writers complained that fuel was becoming not only scarcer but also costlier, particularly in Eastern towns and cities. Agricultural writers advised farmers to economize in using wood fuel because it was more expensive for them, too. Even in inland states such as Ohio and Kentucky, fuel was becoming scarcer by 1830. Since trees were in greater demand for fuel, lumber, and fencing, these critics urged landowners to plant new ones. In spite of these warnings and such efforts as those undertaken by Massachusetts to survey its forest resources in 1837, the campaign for conservation produced few tangible results. Its sense of urgency was moderated by alternative measures of relief.

The first main result of the fuel crisis was the development of stoves to replace fireplaces. While Marcus Bull of Philadelphia experimented with theories of heat to determine the relative value of different kinds of wood as fuel, inventors designed cooking and heating stoves that were more efficient than fireplaces in the use of wood. Two decades after issuing its first patent for a stove in 1793, the United States Patent Office began receiving a steady stream of applications from inventors like William T. James who was the first to develop a satisfactory cooking stove. Over 800 stove patents were issued by 1845, more than for any other object. By 1850, there were 230 foundries in thirteen states making iron castings for assembly into stoves. At this time the per capita consumption of wood declined in New England and the middle states which led other areas in adopting stoves.

Another result of the fuel crisis was the burning of anthracite coal mined in Pennsylvania. As early as 1785, Benjamin Franklin had written about the procedures for burning coal, and in 1798 Oliver Evans invented a coal-burning stove. In the 1790s, the Lehigh Coal Mine Company began delivering coal to Philadelphia, and other companies were soon promoting the use of coal stoves. Pioneer mine promoters such as Jacob Cist boasted of the economic advantages of coal over firewood. In 1820, only 365 tons were sent, mainly via canals, to market; ten years later, the output reached 181,000 tons. With construction of the Delaware, Lackawanna, and Western Railroad from the Wyoming Valley to New York by mid-century, coal became available to more Eastern consumers.

The 1870s were a national turning point in the competition of wood and coal. During this decade, the volume of firewood used by consumers reached its peak although its relative importance was declining. About three cords of wood were used for each ton of coal. This relationship was reflected in the consumption of fuel as measured by British thermal units (BTUs), each representing the quantity of heat required to raise the temperature of one pound of water one degree Fahrenheit at or near its point of maximum density (39.2 degrees). From a high of 91 percent of the BTUs produced in 1850, the share of firewood decreased to 73 percent in 1870. However, the use of wood and coal was unevenly distributed. By 1880, coal was widely burned in densely populated centers which ranged from New York to Kansas as well as San Francisco and other cities, while wood was still commonly used elsewhere.

For almost a century after the 1870s, the consumption of firewood declined as other fuels met the needs of an increasing population and expanding industrial economy. In the 1880s, over 95 percent of the firewood was used for domestic purposes, while the rest was for industries, railroads, and steamboats. Most railroads had quit using wood, and by 1900 their competition had virtually ended steamboating on rivers. Coal had gained preeminence, but even hay, corncobs, and sunflower stalks were burned by prairie farmers who lacked wood. Until the 1920s, coal kept gaining in importance, with the bituminous type used more than anthracite. Then petroleum fuels which had been gradually introduced since the 1870s gained more acceptance along with natural gas and electricity from waterpower. In the 1920s, for every cord of firewood used in homes or industries eight tons of coal were consumed. Nonwood sources produced 43 percent of the BTUs consumed in 1880, 89 percent in 1910, and 95.5 percent in 1940. By 1970, they were so dominant that firewood produced less than 1 percent of the BTUs consumed. The per capita use of wood declined steadily from 63.1 cubic feet (0.8 cords) in 1900 to 2.6 cubic feet (less than .05 cords) in 1970. Most of the wood users were farm families.

The fuel crisis of the 1970s created a new boom in firewood. After World War II, more homes and industries depended on oil for heat. Oil was also used in the process of generating electricity. Large quantities were imported from Arab nations which imposed a temporary embargo on the shipment of oil in 1973. Amid suspicions that American oil companies were also responsible for the crisis, government and private agencies sought to develop alternative sources of energy such as solar power. Industrial users of oil reconverted to coal. Homeowners resumed the use of firewood, which began rising in price. Manufacturers again made wood stoves which provided the primary or supplementary source of heat in an estimated 2 million homes by 1980. Whereas 1 percent of northern New England homes had depended primarily on wood in

1973, over 20 percent of them did so by 1980. This shift increased the national per capita use of firewood from 2.6 cubic feet in 1970 to an estimated 2.9 cubic feet by 1977.

FURTHER READING: Arthur H. Cole, "The Mystery of Fuel Wood Marketing in the United States," *Business History Review* 44 (Autumn 1970): 339–359. A. William Hoglund, "Forest Conservation and Stove Inventors, 1789–1850," *Forest History* 5 (Winter 1962): 2-8. Josephine H. Peirce, *Fire on the Hearth: The Evolution and Romance of the Heating Stove* (1951). R. V. Reynolds and Albert H. Pierson, *Fuel Wood Used in the United States, 1630–1930*, United States Department of Agriculture, Circular No. 641 (1942). David E. Schob, "Woodhawks and Cordwood: Steamboat Fuel on the Ohio and Mississippi Rivers, 1820–1860," *Journal of Forest History* 21 (July 1977): 124–132.

A. WILLIAM HOGLUND

FISH AND WILDLIFE SERVICE

The complicated organizational genealogy of the U.S. Fish and Wildlife Service began in 1871 when the independent Bureau of Fisheries was established by an act of Congress. It was later placed in the Department of Commerce and in 1939 was transferred to the DEPARTMENT OF THE INTERIOR. In the following year, it was merged with the Bureau of BIOLOGICAL SURVEY and renamed the Fish and Wildlife Service. Up to that time, the Bureau of Fisheries had been concerned primarily with commercial fishing. In 1956, the agency was divided into two bureaus—Commercial Fisheries and Sport Fisheries and Wildlife. In 1970, a major departmental reorganization transferred Commercial Fisheries to the Commerce Department. Sport Fisheries and Wildlife, renamed in 1974 the U. S. Fish and Wildlife Service, remained in Interior and was charged "to assure maximum opportunity for the American people to benefit from fish and wildlife resources as part of the natural environment."

Throughout its history, the service and its predecessors have been principally concerned with fish and with migratory birds. The forestlands under its jurisdiction are incidental to the protection of these fish and birds; the preponderance of the more than 390 national wildlife refuges are waterways and wetlands. However, the Kenai National Moose Range in Alaska, the Wichita Mountains Reserve in Oklahoma, and several wildlife sanctuaries in the Pacific Northwest are forested in part and involve the agency in forest management, including the employment of foresters.

In 1980, the Fish and Wildlife Service maintained three Job Corps Civilian Conservation Centers and 108 Youth Conservation Corps camps, some of which were involved in forest management.

FLOORING INDUSTRY

See Hardwood Flooring Industry

FLORIDA FORESTS

Forestland in Florida originally covered 27 million acres, almost 80 percent of the state's land area. Longleaf and slash pine and a variety of oaks covered most of the state, while juniper and cypress were predominant in the swamps and mangrove clung to the southern coastal areas. Most of this forest remained undisturbed well into the twentieth century.

Forest exploitation on a limited scale began in the 1760s with the production of planks, shingles, staves, and tar. During the American Revolution, Florida supplied England with lumber and NAVAL STORES, but the trade declined when Spain resumed control over the colony. Acquisition of Florida by the United States in 1819 brought some increase in activity, and by 1834 there were twenty-five mills in the vicinity of Pensacola manufacturing lumber, LATH, shingles, and staves for markets in the United States and the West Indies. Still, lumbering was limited to regions where the logs could be moved easily down rivers and streams to the mills.

Prospects for the industry changed after the Civil War, when railroads extended down the peninsula, opening the interior and connecting Florida with the rest of the nation. Since huge swampland tracts had been transferred to the state, lumbermen found land cheap and easily acquired. The state sold its lands at bargain prices and gave millions of acres to the railroads as construction subsidies. These corporations in turn sold their lands to the lumber industry. After 1870, lumber production rose sixfold from 200 million board feet a year to a peak of over 1.2 billion reported in 1909. By that time, Jacksonville had become one of the largest exporters of naval stores in the world, and Pensacola was a major lumber center; lumbering contributed about half of the state's total manufactured product. Vast turpentine operations also developed in the north Florida pinelands beginning in the 1870s. The peak year for Florida naval stores, 1908, yielded over 17 million gallons of turpentine and over 1 million barrels of rosin, almost half the rosin produced in the United States. Fifty years later Florida still produced 14 percent of the nation's naval stores.

Railroad hauling
baldcypress logs in Florida
over rails set on hand-
hewn ties. American Forest
Institute Photo.

Initially, the pine forests provided almost all of Florida's lumber, but after about 1900 specialized equipment and new logging techniques made it possible to harvest the magnificent cypress that flourished in the swamplands. Production of cypress peaked at about 200 million board feet in 1930, when it provided about 22 percent of the state's lumber output. Both pine and cypress lumber production dwindled during the Great Depression.

By 1930, destructive cut-out-and-get-out practices and rampant wildfires had reduced Florida's once bountiful forests to just 6 million acres of virgin stands. With the passing of the prime timber, the big mills closed one by one. During the 1930s, local property taxes became delinquent on as many as 12 million acres, a reflection not only of the depths of the Depression but also of the declining value of the denuded land.

By 1923, lumbermen, landowners, and other concerned individuals established the Florida Forestry Association. This organization persuaded the state legislature to create the Florida Board of Forestry in 1927. The following year, Florida's first state forester was appointed and the new state forest service began work. Its goals were FIRE CONTROL, reforestation, and promotion of sound forest management. The coming of pulp and paper mills in the 1930s, which brought sweeping changes in the structure of the forest industries, had a pronounced impact upon the young forestry movement. Pulp and paper interests could not afford to exhaust their timberlands as their predecessors had done. Although the industry was less mindful of the quality of the state's air and water resources, its leaders were ardent conservationists in their treatment of the forests. In Florida, the PULP AND PAPER INDUSTRY led the way in sustained-yield management and reforestation on their own lands and set precedents for forestry elsewhere.

Before the creation of the Florida Forest Service, the state's fire record was the worst in the nation. Cattlemen, turpentiners, and farmers burned the woods regularly, and their fires frequently escaped onto adjacent lands. Within the first year of its operation, however, the Florida Forest Service, aided by large landowners, established the state's first forest fire-protection program, intended to curb wildfires and educate citizens and industry to the value of saving the forests. Initially, the program covered only about 700,000 acres. In the mid-1930s, Florida's counties were invited to cooperate with the state in establishing fire-control units. In 1973, when the last county was brought into this program, the system encompassed more than 26 million acres of forest and wildland. Since then, annual average loss to fire on the protected wildlands has been less than 1 percent.

The first step in the Florida Forest Service's reforestation work was a seedling nursery started at the State Prison Farm at Raiford in 1928. Efforts of private landowners, particularly the pulp and paper industry, reinforced the state program after the 1930s. By the 1960s, the state led the nation in tree planting five years in a row, with more than 100 million seedlings planted annually. Since then, in much of northern Florida, pine plantations, tended and guarded against fires, have stretched for miles along the highways.

The Florida Forest Service began sponsoring traveling shows extolling the virtues of fire prevention and good management for owners of nonindustrial woodlands in the late 1920s. In the early 1940s, the state's Forest Management Assistance Program was established to help landowners. More recently, the service initiated programs in environmental education, urban forestry, and RECREATION. In 1979, income from the sale of timber, grazing, and mineral rights and from recreational use on the four state forests amounted to more than $4 million. At that time, the state forests included 306,000 acres.

Florida developed a state park system beginning in 1928 with Royal Palm Park, then managed by the General Federation of Women's Clubs. From 1935 to 1949, the park system was united with forestry under the Florida Board of Forestry and Parks. Since 1949, forestry and parks have been under separate agencies. By 1980, the state park system included seventy units totaling 155,779 acres.

As Florida was the only southeastern state with any public domain lands remaining when the federal forest reserve system was established, it became the first state in the region to have a national forest, the Ocala, dedicated in 1908. The Choctawhatchee was created in the same year but was transferred to the War Department in 1940 to become a military base. In 1980, a small portion was redesignated a national forest. The Osceola National Forest was established in 1931 and the Apalachicola in 1936. In 1980, the four forests totaled over 1 million acres, all in the pinelands of north Florida. Other large tracts of Florida lands have received federal protection in the Everglades National Park established in 1934 and the Big Cypress National Preserve established in 1974.

In the late 1970s, Florida's forests supplied about 3 million cords a year to 9 pulpmills in the state, while more than 125 sawmills, veneer mills, and other primary wood-using plants utilized about 400 million board feet of timber annually.

FURTHER READING: Archer Stuart Campbell, *Studies in Forestry Resources in Florida* (3 vols., 1932–1934). John A. Eisterhold, "Lumber and Trade in Pensacola and West Florida: 1800–1860," *Florida Historical Quarterly* 51 (Jan. 1973): 267-280. William Gober, "Lumbering in Florida," *Southern Lumberman* 193 (Dec. 15, 1956): 164–166. Clinton Newton Howard, *British Development of West Florida, 1763–1769* (1947).

JOHN M. BETHEA

FOLKLORE AND FOLK MUSIC

Folklore can be defined as the study of stories, songs, legends, beliefs, customs, and practices that have been passed on in small face-to-face groups, chiefly by oral tradition and simple observation and imitation. The study can concentrate on the items so passed on, as in the distributional study of a particular song such as "The Jam on Gerry's Rock," or it can emphasize process, the way such songs are created, performed, or learned, and what part they play in the lives of those who create and continue them. It can be historical, concerned with the way things were in the past, or it can deal with the present, with the way such material exists and functions among woodsmen and loggers today.

The fact that most studies of lumberwoods folklore have been historical and item-oriented has created the impression that folklore *is* of the past and therefore inevitably disappearing. Contemporary folklore studies in areas other than the lumber industry have shown that although much has changed, much remains the same. The process-and-function-oriented studies of present-day logging and loggers by folklorists such as Barre Toelken, by breaking free of the old historical emphasis, are once again demonstrating that the idea that folklore is dying is in itself a kind of folklore.

The fact remains that most folklore study of the lumber industry has been fiercely unbalanced in its emphasis on the song traditions of the Northeast and Middle West. Even within that emphasis, the thrust has been to collect and preserve the songs themselves. As a result, we have a series of excellent and carefully annotated collections of such songs. It can even be said that no corpus of industrial songs has ever been better collected and preserved than those of the forest. But we know far less about what part the songs played in the lives of the woodsmen. Who sang and who listened? When and where did singing occur, and under what circumstances? Why did men sing at all, and why did they sing the specific repertoire they did sing? We do have some information on these important matters, but not as much as we wish.

In spite of our deficiencies of knowledge, we do have some fine song collections available. Roland Palmer Gray's *Songs and Ballads of the Maine Lumberjacks* (1924) was the first to be published, but it is an amateurish and highly uncritical volume. Franz Rickaby's *Ballads and Songs of the Shantyboy* (1926), drawn from the author's collecting work in Michigan, Minnesota, and Wisconsin, is a first-rate work with an excellent introduction. *Minstrelsy of Maine* (1927), a compilation by Fannie Hardy Eckstorm and Mary Windslow Smyth, contains the words to many woods songs set in an intelligent and informative narrative context that helps to explain obscurities in the songs. It also explores matters of creativity and function; the classic study of "The Jam on Gerry's Rock," for example, is a chapter to itself. Many of the same songs, but this time with their melodies, appear in Phillips Barry's fine little book, *The Maine Woods Songster* (1939).

William M. Doerflinger's *Shantymen and Shantyboys* (1951), republished in 1972 as *Songs of the Sailor and Lumberman*, contains some new song material from New Brunswick and eastern Maine. However, its chief distinction is the inclusion of information on local satirical songs and on songmakers such as Larry Gorman. E. C. Beck's *Songs of the Michigan Lumberjacks* (1941) contains much local material of considerable interest, but the documentation is frequently fuzzy (Beck's later books add very little that is new, tending as they do to repeat each other heavily). *Songs of Miramichi* (1968) by Louise

Manny and James Reginald Wilson is an excellent and well-documented collection drawn chiefly from the singing of elderly woodsmen of an important central New Brunswick lumber area. Edith Fowke's *Lumbering Songs from the Northern Woods* (1970) draws on the author's extensive collecting work in Ontario and is the most completely annotated of all such collections, making it a good starting place for anyone interested in lumberwoods songs.

Several recent books have gone beyond the publication of collectanea. Edward D. Ives's *Larry Gorman: The Man Who Made the Songs* (1964), although its emphasis is still on songs, picks up Doerflinger's lead and shows that the making and singing of satirical songs played an important part in the entertainment traditions of the lumbercamps. Ives's *Joe Scott, the Woodsman Songmaker* (1978) is both a biography of a common woodsman and a study of the place of song in lumbercamp life. Robert Bethke's *Adirondack Voices: Woodsmen and Woods Lore* (1980) takes for its field the northern Adirondacks of New York and includes a great deal more than simply songs. Finally, Barre Toelken, in his *The Dynamics of Folklore* (1978), includes a substantial segment on contemporary loggers of the Northwest, considering such matters as dress, gestures, work skills, narratives, heroes, practical jokes, and language.

Since the stuff and significance of folklore is intimately bound to the patterns of everyday life, one of the best ways to study it is through the lives of common woodsmen. Several annual volumes of the Northeast Folklore Society (Orono, Maine) offer such material from the State of Maine: *Fleetwood Pride* (1967), *Me and Fannie* (1973), and *I'm a Man That Works* (1978). Two more of that society's publications, although they are not biographical, are detailed accounts of daily life: *Argyle Boom* (1976) describes day-to-day work at the log sorting gap, and *Suthin* (1977) describes the year's round for a single camp and crew in the winter of 1946–1947. Also useful is *Men of the Forest*, volume VI, number 1, of *Sound Heritage* (Provincial Archives of British Columbia, 1977), which contains several different accounts of West Coast logging life.

Several repositories contain a great deal of material on lumbercamp life and lore, much of it in the form of taped interviews with woodsmen and river drivers themselves, three of the most notable being the Northeast Archives of Folklore and Oral History (Orono, Maine), the Randall V. Mills Memorial Archive of Northwest Folklore (Eugene, Oregon), and the Aural History Programme of the Provincial Archives of British Columbia (Victoria). Anyone interested in developing detailed information on any one of the better known lumbercamp ballads should begin by looking it up by title in G. Malcolm Laws's *Native American Balladry* (1964).

EDWARD D. IVES

FOOD FROM THE FOREST

Primitive peoples in all forested parts of the world made staples of nuts, berries, roots, tubers, fungi, and forest game and fish. However, a hunting and gathering economy is practicable only in regions of extremely low population density. At an early, prehistorical stage of social and economic development on all continents, the forest was abandoned as an important source of food. While remaining vital for other necessities, the forest retreated in favor of agriculture in all civilizations. In advanced societies, forest foods are either forgotten; or disdained and resorted to only in extremity; or retained in the diet as incidentals, sometimes as delicacies, with harvesting regarded as recreational; or cultivated, ceasing to be food from the forest.

All of the original American colonies were planted in woodlands amidst a primitive population largely dependent on the forest for their diet. But only the first, Jamestown, may be said to have survived on forest food and then barely and for only two or three winters. To European settlers and Americans of later generations, the forest was a source of timber, NAVAL STORES, pelts, and hides but an obstacle in the way of an adequate food supply. Each shifting of the frontier only briefly and relatively renewed the importance of forest foods in the diet of those in the phalanx.

The most important exception to this rule was pork. Although not native to North America, hogs adapted quickly to the hardwood forests of the eastern United States into which they were released by a labor-scarce people. They flourished on the rich mast and required little or no attention. The tough "razorback" or "land pike" was rounded up or hunted like game at "hog-sticking time" and was the major source of protein in the expansion movement.

Wild meat also contributed to the American economy after the frontier had passed on. Market hunters —through shooting, trapping, and netting—made venison, wildfowl, and other game standard fare in American homes through the nineteenth century. Butcher shops offered deer haunches alongside beef

Maple syrup is produced by boiling the sap of sugar maple, as here in New York State. Forest History Society Lantern Slide Collection.

quarters, while newspapers quoted prices for ducks, woodcocks, snipe, and passenger pigeons. Although state game laws alone proved ineffective, the federal Lacey Act of 1900, prohibiting interstate trade in illegally killed wildlife, did much to curtail market hunting. Wild game was not an important element of diet in the middle of the twentieth century except in some isolated areas where both legal hunting and poaching persist as part of rural cultural patterns.

Although most of the commercially important nuts in the United States are orchard crops and not indigenous to North America, half of the 5.5 million producing pecan trees in Texas and other parts of the South and Southwest in the mid-twentieth century were wild. Pinyon nut collecting has provided employment for Indians and Mexicans from western Texas to the Pacific Coast, and quantities are shipped to eastern cities. Before devastation of the parent trees by blight, vendors selling chestnuts roasted over charcoal-burning iron pots were familiar city street scenes. Until development of cracking and kernel-separating machinery in the 1930s, the hand-cracked walnut kernel industry, using black walnuts largely from native groves, was significant in the Ozarks and in parts of Kentucky and Tennessee. Several species of blueberries and huckleberries continued in the twentieth century to be gathered commercially in New England, the Blue Ridge section of Virginia, and places in Washington, Oregon, and Montana. The Pacific plum has local importance in southwestern Oregon and northern California, especially as a food item for the Klamath Indians. Wild rice, a staple of the Chippewa Indians who gathered it on the shores of lakes on the Minnesota National Forest, was widely marketed as a breakfast food beginning in the 1920s.

The making of syrup and sugar from the sap of various species of maple trees was practiced by Indians before the European occupation of America. Colonists adopted and developed Indian practices. Ninety percent of the maple sugar and syrup manufactured is produced from the sap of the sugar maple, *Acer saccharum*. Areas of significant production are western New England, New York, Pennsylvania, the northern Appalachians, northern Ohio, and the Lake States. In 1859, the first year of census record, production totaled 1,598,000 gallons of syrup and 40 million pounds of sugar. Despite competition from cane sugar beginning in the 1860s, demand continued for maple as a luxury item. Farmers traded sugar and syrup to country storekeepers, who in turn sold it to commercial dealers. The latter met the needs of a rising market by adulteration of the product, keeping production from increasing accordingly. In conse-

quence, in 1893 producers formed a cooperative, the Vermont Maple Sugar Makers Association, to encourage sales directly to the consumer. The peak production of 4,863,000 gallons of syrup was reached in 1918.

Although forest foods are less important in the United States today than they are in many countries, new items are added from time to time to the list of those marketed. An example is torula yeast, used in the flavoring of ice cream, which began to be produced commercially in the 1960s from sulfite liquor, a by-product from the manufacture of wood pulp.

JOSEPH R. CONLIN

FOOD IN LOGGING CAMPS

Because early woods operations were isolated and a large proportion of the workers were unmarried casual laborers, the provision of food was an integral part of commercial logging from the beginnings of the business. Three, four, and on some river drives even five square meals a day were universally recognized as the employer's obligation and part of the workers' remuneration.

Food was abundant in even the most primitive Maine shanty camps. It had to be. Studies of energy consumption by occupation indicate that "there is probably no harder physical work than lumbering in the forest, particularly in winter." Fellers and buckers in the days of muscle-power logging seem to have routinely consumed 7,000 calories a day and possibly as many as 9,000.

The fare in the earliest New England camps was rude and monotonous, comprised principally of "the great trinity" of beans, pork, and bread. Pickled beef, baled codfish, sourdough biscuits, flapjacks, molasses, and tea "strong enough to float an ax" were also common, but there seem to have been little fresh meat, vegetables, and fruits served because of the difficulties of supply. However, as there is little evidence that scurvy was a widespread problem, it may be that they were provided and simply not mentioned. Cookery was as rough as the food. In New England, the meals were typically prepared by a boy or by the loggers in turns.

During the last third of the nineteenth century (somewhat later in New England), there occurred a "revolution" in the diet of American loggers, which made the workers in the industry perhaps the best-fed occupational group in the country. The food a company provided became a primary, even the principal, theater of competition for labor in both the Great Lakes region and the Pacific Northwest. Better means of supplying the camps meant fresh meats,

Loggers sit down to a hearty meal in a company-operated camp. American Forest Institute Photo.

vegetables, fruits, eggs, and milk. Meals were varied. Baking—loggers were especially fond of pies and other pastries—appears to have been exceptionally good and was taken as the measure of the professional men and women (the latter especially on the West Coast) who replaced the amateur boys and loggers. Finally, dining was taken out of the bunkhouse and given its own facility, the famous "cookhouse."

The quality of food at cookhouses after the turn of the century was often compared to what was served "at the best hotels." With wages in a district more or less uniform, a company's table became the chief attraction it set before the mercurial work force. Even when labor relations in the industry reached the nadir of 1917, the year of the great Wobbly strike and the intervention of the U. S. Army's SPRUCE PRODUCTION DIVISION, food was never an issue. That meals would be generous, varied, and well-prepared had been resolved long before. Indeed, many of the larger companies took pride in their cookhouses as an index of their social responsibility. Many devoted close attention to their food service divisions and even took a loss on them.

Other employers grumbled that "these men are the type that expect the best without reason," but they too were obligated to conform.

The most curious cookhouse custom was the nearly universal rule that there was to be no unnecessary conversation during meals. Among the various explanations that have been offered for this custom, the most convincing is that the cooks—traditionally crotchety and, if they were good, tolerated as tyrants within their precinct—insisted on it in order to move the crowd of loggers in and out of the cookhouse as quickly as possible. The cooks' workday was necessarily several hours longer than the men's and they had no desire to have it prolonged by socializing. In any event, the loggers ate quietly and quickly, bolting their huge meals in ten minutes or even less. Mills allowed only twenty minutes between the time they opened the cookhouse doors for breakfast and when they started the machinery.

The standards and customs of the lumberjack cookhouses were extended to the mill towns but, in the end, the transformation of the industry by modern forestry and the internal-combustion engine brought eating practices into line with the national norm. With tree farming, loggers ceased to be transient "casuals" and, more and more, were sedentary town dwellers who married and took their meals at home. The chain saw and the logging truck eliminated the physical need for huge feeds. Modern logging work consumes a fraction of the energy used by the handworker. Where old-fashioned camps and cookhouses survive, however, in Alaska, Canada, and here and there in the Pacific Northwest, the men continue to demand "the best" and the quality of the fare is still impressive to visitors.

FURTHER READING: Joseph R. Conlin, "Old Boy, Did You Get Enough of Pie?" *Journal of Forest History* 23 (Oct. 1979): 164–185.

JOSEPH R. CONLIN

FOREST AND CONSERVATION PUBLICATIONS

It can probably be said that the publication of George Perkins MARSH's highly influential *Man and Nature; or, Physical Geography as Modified by Human Action* in 1864 marks the beginnings of American forest conservation as well as the origin of a body of American forestry literature. The few earlier American works relating to the forest had included some botanical studies of trees, several books dealing with timber, and several which touched upon silviculture. Marsh's book for the first time convincingly demonstrated that a continuation of the plunder of the American forests for their resources would lead to their destruction with far-reaching environmental effects. Within a decade of the appearance of *Man and Nature*, there arose in America the first traces of both a professional forestry literature and a conservation literature aimed at the general public.

Forest Conservation Literature

Many nineteenth-century Americans had viewed the forest through the prose of such romantic works as Thoreau's *Maine Woods* (1864), while at the other end of the literary spectrum were equally romantic visions of the logger's life depicted in such books as J. S. Springer's *Forest Life and Forest Trees* (1851). Marsh's *Man and Nature* helped to place both views into a new perspective through a marshaling of sobering facts.

By 1875, the forest conservation movement was being represented by a national organization—the AMERICAN FORESTRY ASSOCIATION (AFA). The first publications of the AFA were its *Proceedings* (1882–1897). Between 1889 and 1897, AFA used as its offi-

cial organ *Forest Leaves*, a publication of the Pennsylvania Forestry Association. In the latter years, AFA acquired *The Forester*, first issued in 1895 as *The New Jersey Forester*. *The Forester* in 1897 was the only national monthly illustrated journal devoted to forestry, and by 1898 it became the outspoken official voice of the AFA. A flurry of title changes over the next few years reflect AFA's changing thrust. In 1902, the magazine became *Forestry and Irrigation*, published jointly with the American Irrigation Congress. By 1908, the title became *Conservation*, perhaps as a result of pressure from Gifford PINCHOT for the AFA to broaden its aims to be more in tune with Theodore ROOSEVELT's administration. But, reluctant to dilute its forestry mission, AFA in 1910 renamed its journal *American Forestry*. In 1911, *American Forestry* absorbed *American Conservation*, the short-lived voice of Pinchot's National Conservation Association, thus enlarging its readership considerably.

By 1920, the once activist *American Forestry* had drifted away from controversial forestry issues, becoming a magazine of conservation education and nature lore. But in 1923, under the direction of Ovid BUTLER, the journal again became issue-conscious. Its name became *American Forests and Forest Life* in the following year, and in 1931 simply *American Forests*, which it has remained. The journal has been a major influence in the American conservation movement by providing conservation education to a large audience of nonprofessionals and by being a forum for forest policy discussions.

Hunting and Fishing Magazines. Several hunting and fishing magazines have shown a concern for forest and WILDLIFE CONSERVATION. One of the earliest was *Forest and Stream*, founded in 1873. This New York weekly played a role in the formation of the NATIONAL AUDUBON SOCIETY and in game conservation reforms. In 1930, *Forest and Stream* merged with the well-established monthly, *Field and Stream. Field and Stream*, published since 1896, was an early advocate of wildlife conservation legislation and forest protection. A similar journal, *Outdoor Life*, was founded in 1898. Like *Field and Stream*, its pages have in a large part been devoted to short stories and sporting news, but it has also played a role in the conservation movement. In 1918, *Outdoor Life* first devoted space to a monthly conservation section, primarily aimed at game protection, and in 1923 it established an annual conservation award.

Parks Journals. Two journals dedicated to the establishment and maintenance of parks began in the early 1900s. The *Bulletin* of the National Parks Association was first issued in 1919, eventually becoming *National Parks and Conservation Magazine*. The main thrust of the journal has been the protection of the national parks and monuments system, but in more recent years it has called attention to more general conservation issues. In 1981, the title became simply *National Parks*. Another journal, *Parks & Recreation*, began in 1917 as the publication of the American Institute of Park Executives, superseding their *Bulletin* established in 1906. The magazine was once oriented toward state, national, and urban parks, but in 1966 it merged with three other journals and its present emphasis is the urban park scene.

Nature Magazines. Several magazines aimed at the "nature lover" have been influential in the formulation of forest and conservation policy and in making the general public aware of conservation issues. Some of these publications have changed over the years from rather innocuous nature magazines to militant environmental journals.

In 1887, Charles Sprague SARGENT launched a horticultural and forestry magazine, *Garden and Forest*. "Conducted" by Sargent, the publication received more praise than popularity. Sargent sought to inform his readers about all phases of plants and hoped to influence his audience on many conservation issues. The high-quality weekly ceased publication in 1897 due to financial difficulties.

In the same year that *Garden and Forest* was founded, the Audubon Society made its first attempt to establish a journal. *Audubon Magazine* was issued as a bird protection magazine at a time when songbird populations were being threatened by a millinery demand for feathers. But because of public indifference, the magazine lasted only two years. In 1896, a more successful attempt to establish a journal for the society was initiated. The magazine, *Bird-Lore*, was directed and financed by Frank M. Chapman. For thirty-six years, Chapman edited the publication mainly for bird-watchers, but in 1935 the magazine was bought by the Audubon Society and it began to evolve into a conservation publication. To reflect the new image of the journal, its name was changed in 1941 to *Audubon Magazine*, and finally to *Audubon* in 1961. In recent years, Audubon has combined nature writing and photography with a sometimes militant advocacy of environmental issues.

The *Sierra Club Bulletin* (*Sierra* since 1977) has gained a reputation as being one of the most militant of conservation journals. From its first issue in 1893 until the early 1950s, it was essentially a mountaineering publication devoted to local California conservation and preservation issues. But in the early 1950s

the club established a chapter on the East Coast, its first outside of California. In 1952, David BROWER was hired as the first full-time executive director, and the organization and the *Bulletin* rapidly began to shed its provincial character. Brower initiated the club's influential Exhibit Format Books, a powerful medium that touched a large segment of the general public. The *Bulletin* began to discuss not only preservation but also the population explosion, nuclear energy, and other environmentally sensitive issues. In 1969, Brower was fired by the club after months of infighting. Brower went on to establish an organization of even more international concern—Friends of the Earth, represented by their tabloid publication, *Not Man Apart*.

Less militant but equally tenacious, *Living Wilderness* has been the voice of the WILDERNESS SOCIETY since 1935. Like *Sierra*, *Audubon*, and *National Parks*, this preservation-oriented magazine uses photography as an important medium for carrying its wilderness message.

The Professional Literature

Until the early 1900s, the body of American professional forestry literature was quite small. The paucity of forestry publications is reflected in Bernhard E. FERNOW's *Annual Report* of the Division of Forestry for 1886 (1887), in which he lists approximately fifty American forestry publications ranging from classic botanical studies to pamphlets of state horticultural societies.

Government Publications. The federal government published some of the first substantive studies on forestry. The 1860 *Report of the Commissioner of Patents (Agriculture)* (1861) included a seminal paper by J. G. Cooper, "The Forests and Trees of Northern America, as Connected with Climate and Agriculture" (pp. 416-445). Cooper's paper was a survey of the forests and trees of America as well as an early plea to reverse the destruction of the forests. Shortly after the publication of Marsh's *Man and Nature*, the *Report of the United States Commissioner of Agriculture for 1865* (1866) included a similar work by Rev. Frederick Starr, Jr., "American Forests: Their Destruction and Preservation" (pp. 210-234). The Census Office took its first stock of the nation's forests in 1870, written by William H. Brewer and published as "The Woodlands and Forest Systems of the United States" in the *Statistical Atlas of the Ninth Census of the United States* (1874).

The first major government document on forestry was Franklin B. HOUGH's 618-page *Report upon Forestry* (1878), followed by three successive volumes through 1884. These reports established a high standard for later professional literature. In 1884, the Census Office issued a monumental survey by Charles S. Sargent, the *Report on the Forests of North America (Exclusive of Mexico)*, as volume 9 of the *Tenth Census of the United States*. This landmark publication included an engineering study of woods, a catalog of forest trees, and an economic survey of the nation's forests.

The flood of federal forestry publications began with the modest first report of the Forestry Division included in the *Report of the Commissioner of Agriculture* (1883; pp. 444-462). The first separate Forestry Division publications were its *Circulars* in 1886 and its *Bulletins* in 1887. Since these formative years, the FOREST SERVICE and the DEPARTMENT OF AGRICULTURE have continued to issue thousands of technical forestry publications, which have become a major part of the professional literature.

State-related publications were also an important part of the early literature. Some of the first American forestry documents were published by various state agricultural and horticultural societies in attempting to promote local forest propagation. An early example is W. C. Watson's paper, "Forests, Their Influence, Uses and Reproduction," *New York State Agricultural Society Transactions* 25 (1865): 288-303. Official state forestry publications first appeared in the reports of the state agricultural agencies, as, for instance, in the Connecticut State Board of Agriculture's *Annual Report* for 1877. The reports of the earliest state forestry agencies were issued in the 1880s; an example is the 1884 *Report* of the Vermont Commissioners of Forestry.

By 1900, a forester's library consisted mostly of state and federal reports, supplemented by a few books. The early 1900s saw the rise of the professional journal.

Professional Journals. The first American professional journal, *The Forestry Quarterly*, began in 1902 as a student publication of the New York College of Forestry at Cornell University, overseen by Bernhard E. Fernow, John C. Gifford, and Walter Mulford. When the college closed its doors in 1903, Fernow continued to publish the journal privately. After a decade of publication, *The Forestry Quarterly* had become a respected professional periodical, but it was not paying its own way. In 1913, business management of the *Quarterly* was taken over by the AFA, and within a year the *Quarterly* began to show a profit.

In 1917, *The Forestry Quarterly* merged with *Proceedings of the Society of American Foresters*. Like the *Quarterly*, the *Proceedings* was born and nurtured in its formative years under the direction of one person, Raphael ZON, editor-in-chief for most of its brief existence (1905–1916). With the merger of the two periodicals was born the *Journal of Forestry*, still the official organ of the SOCIETY OF AMERICAN FORESTERS (SAF). The *Journal* included a section reporting on society activities except during the period 1935 to 1942 when *SAF Affairs* was published separately. Fernow, the first editor-in-chief of the *Journal of Forestry*, set up standards fully as high as those of the technical journals published at the leading German schools. In the succeeding years, the *Journal of Forestry* has attempted to continue to serve as a medium of communication between all professional foresters. Its goal has been to serve the working professional with a broad scope of interest, avoiding highly technical discussions. To provide a medium for more technical articles, SAF in 1955 began the quarterly *Forest Science*, and for longer technical works SAF initiated the *Forest Science Monographs* series in 1959. In response to a need for regional specialization, SAF in 1977 launched its *Southern Journal of Applied Forestry*.

As the profession of forestry has segmented into specialized disciplines, so has the professional literature. Each discipline has its own literature and often includes technical journals outside the immediate sphere of forestry. Some of these specialized journals are the *Journal of Wildlife Management* (published by the WILDLIFE SOCIETY since 1937), *Journal of Range Management* (Society for Range Management, since 1948), *Forest Products Journal* (FOREST PRODUCTS RESEARCH SOCIETY, since 1947), and the *Journal of Soil and Water Conservation* (Soil Conservation Society of America, since 1946). These are only a few of dozens that could be listed.

Besides the professional journals, publications issued by academic institutions are an important contribution to the technical literature. Beginning in 1898, the New York State College of Forestry at Cornell University issued a series of *Bulletins*. The New York State College of Forestry at Syracuse has had several series of publications since 1912, and Yale University's School of Forestry issued its first technical publications in the same year. Most universities and colleges with strong forestry programs have published the results of their research through series issued at their institutions.

The Trade Literature

Most of the literature of interest to those in the lumber trades has been published in trade journals—one of the oldest and most prolific forms of forestry literature. Besides their informative value, trade journals have been influential in setting trends within the lumber industry. In their earlier years their columns also provided valuable forums for those concerned with forestry and conservation issues, and until the 1930s and 1940s many trade journals contributed substantially to the shaping of national forest policy. In more recent decades, however, most of these publications have become almost exclusively devoted to business or technical aspects of the industry, and many have become general building trade magazines.

The forerunners of the lumber trade journals were those Saginaw, Michigan, newspapers that since the 1850s had devoted much of their news and advertising space to the trade. The first specialized lumber trade publication was the *Lumberman's Gazette*, issued from Bay City, Michigan, in 1872 and edited by Henry S. Dow. This paper was absorbed in 1887 by the *Timberman*, a Chicago publication begun in 1886 by James E. Defebaugh. The *Timberman* became an important rival to another publication, the *Northwestern Lumberman*, which had been started in Muskegon by W. B. Judson as the *Michigan Lumberman and Railway Journal* in 1873 and had moved to Chicago in the following year. Until 1898, the *Timberman* and the *Northwestern Lumberman* waged many editorial battles and were fierce competitors. In that year, the two journals merged to form the *American Lumberman*, with Judson as manager and Defebaugh as editor. Over the years, this journal has shifted its emphasis, as is reflected by several title changes starting in 1946 when it became the *American Lumberman & Building Products Merchandiser*. It is now *Home Center*, a general building trades journal.

The *Lumber World Review* of Chicago was an active and progressive journal. It was formed under the editorship of Bolling Arthur Johnson in 1912 from the union of the *Lumber Review*, founded in 1897, and *Lumber World*, established in 1905. This journal urged a national timber policy and kept its readers informed of the outcomes of local, regional, and national timber congresses by publishing detailed proceedings. The *Lumber World Review* became the *Chicago Lumberman* in 1926 and eventually was absorbed by the *American Lumberman*, as were a number of other trade journals.

Several early trade journals arose in the South, not only to inform lumbermen in that region but also to direct the attention of the nation's lumber industries to the neglected timber resources of the South. The *Southern Lumberman*, established in Nashville by A. E. Baird in 1881, is the oldest United States lumber publication appearing continuously under the same name and from the same location. Having purchased the journal from the Baird family, Stanley F. Horn served as editor and co-owner from 1917 until 1980. In 1931, the *Southern Lumberman* bought the highly respected New Orleans publication, the *Lumber Trade Journal*, founded in Chicago in 1881. The *Southern Lumberman* was instrumental in promoting several neglected Southern woods and played a key role in bringing to national attention the Southern forests as a source of wood pulp for paper manufacture.

Forest Industries, one of today's leading trade journals, was formed in 1962 by the merger of two important Pacific Northwest publications—*The Timberman* and *The Lumberman*. The *Timberman* began in Portland in 1899 as the *Columbia River and Oregon Timberman*. Within a few years, the journal came to national prominence and the name was changed. It was a highly informative publication and published the *Proceedings* of the Pacific Logging Congresses beginning in 1910. *The Lumberman* began in 1889 as the *West Coast Lumberman*, the first lumber trade journal in the West. *The Lumberman* was particularly interested in innovative trends and the new equipment involved in lumber production.

The *New York Lumber Trade Journal*, founded in 1886, became a national publication but was particularly important to the East Coast lumber trade for providing regional prices of lumber and for its success in introducing new woods to the East Coast markets. The journal became *Eastern Building Materials and Lumber Trade Journal* in 1964.

Other important and long-lasting trade journals include *Northern Logger and Timber Processor*, published under several titles from Old Forge, New York, since 1951; *California Lumber Merchant* (now *Merchant Magazine*), published in Los Angeles since 1922; *Gulf Coast Lumberman*, issued from Houston since 1913; and *Mississippi Valley Lumberman*, published in Minneapolis from 1876 to 1973. Special interests are represented by such magazines as *Naval Stores Review*, published since 1890; *Cross Tie Bulletin*, published by the Railway Tie Association since 1920 and now called simply *Crossties*; and *Forest Farmer*, the publication of the Forest Farmers Association since 1940. Many other publications cover the logging, pulp and paper, and forest products fields.

Bibliographic Control of the Literature

Perhaps the most useful guide to earlier American books, reports, and articles on all aspects of American forestry is E. N. Munns's *A Selected Bibliography of North American Forestry*, 2 vols., U. S. Department of Agriculture Miscellaneous Publication 364 (1940).

This monumental compilation includes over 21,000 references arranged by subjects, with an author index. *The Dictionary Catalogue of the Yale Forestry Library*, 12 vols. (1962), also includes books, reports, and articles arranged by author, subject, or title. The forest historian will rely heavily on Ronald J. Fahl's *North American Forest and Conservation History: A Bibliography* (1977). Fahl's work includes a comprehensive subject index, and his introduction details other indexes and bibliographies useful to the historian.

For locating historical articles the abstracting journal *America: History and Life* is also helpful, as is the "Biblioscope" section of the *Journal of Forest History*. Other abstracting and indexing journals are available to locate articles, books, and reports on forestry, but most do not cover the earlier literature. *Forestry Abstracts* began in 1939, and the *Bibliography of Agriculture* in 1942. The *Agricultural Index* covers articles and reports beginning in 1916 and is useful for much of the trade literature. One can also find trade and policy discussions with the indexing publication, *Public Affairs Information Service Bulletin* (P.A.I.S.), issued since 1913. A survey of other forestry reference works is M. P. Kinch's "Standard References in Forestry," *Journal of Forestry* 76 (1978): 100-103.

Guides to governmental publications are Gerald Ogden, comp., *The United States Forest Service: A Historical Bibliography, 1876–1972* (Agricultural History Center, University of California, Davis, 1976), and C. R. Stanton, comp., *Index to Federal Scientific and Technical Contributions to Forestry Literature*, 1901–1971, 7 vols., Forestry Information Section, Information Report FIS-X-1 (Canadian Forestry Service, 1973).

Titles of journals and magazines are listed in the *Union List of Serials in the United States and Canada*, 3rd ed., 5 vols. (1965), and its continuing successor, *New Serial Titles* (1973–present). These serial references outline the histories of journals and identify libraries with holdings of the serials listed.

FURTHER READING: Nelson C. Brown, *The American Lumber Industry* (1923), pp. 255-261, "Trade Journals." Henry Clepper, "The Literature of Forestry," *Journal of Forestry* 29 (1931): 469-473. George W. Hotchkiss, *History of the Lumber and Forest Industry of the Northwest* (1898), pp. 643-649, "Lumber Journalism." Arthur B. Meyer, "The Literature of American Forestry," *American Forestry: Six Decades of Growth*, ed. by Henry Clepper and Arthur B. Meyer (1960), pp. 50-64. Frank Luther Mott, *A History of American Magazines*, 5 vols. (1930–1968). There are several published histories of individual journals; among them are the following: Henry Clepper, "The *Jour-*

nal of Forestry. An Historical Summary of the First Fifty Years," *Journal of Forestry* 50 (Dec. 1952): 899-912, and "*American Forests*. Magazine of Record in Conservation," *American Forests* 80 (Apr. 1974): 25-56. "Story of *American Lumberman*," *American Lumberman*, Sept. 11, 1948, pp. 144–147. Roger Tory Peterson, "The Evolution of a Magazine," *Audubon* 75 (Jan. 1973): 46-51. George F. Cornwall, "The First Half Century," *Timberman* 50 (Oct. 1949): 50-53, 78. "History of the *Southern Lumberman*," *Southern Lumberman* 223 (Dec. 15, 1971): 58-61.

MICHAEL P. KINCH

FOREST AND RANGELAND RENEWABLE RESOURCES PLANNING ACT, 1974

Long-term planning has been the administrative keystone for natural resource agencies since their inception, especially for the U. S. FOREST SERVICE. In 1974, Congress validated, expanded, and joined the planning process by enacting the Forest and Rangeland Renewable Resources Planning Act. Known commonly as RPA and at times as the Humphrey-Rarick Act after its congressional sponsors—Senator Hubert H. Humphrey of Minnesota and Representative John R. Rarick of Louisiana—the act contains two major elements for assessment and planning. It received major amendments in 1976 through the NATIONAL FOREST MANAGEMENT ACT.

RPA directed the Forest Service to make a comprehensive assessment of renewable forest and range resources on all ownership within U. S. jurisdiction. The first assessment was due on December 31, 1975, and was to be updated in 1979 and every ten years thereafter.

The Forest Service was to prepare a Renewable Resource Program, with decennial updates, including (1) an inventory of needs; (2) identification of specific programs; (3) statement of priorities; (4) study of personnel requirements; and (5) recommendations for objectives, needs, and goals. A very important dimension of this act is congressional intent to accept long-term commitments in support of approved programs.

FURTHER READING: Samuel Trask Dana and Sally K. Fairfax, *Forest and Range Policy* (2nd ed., 1980).

FOREST DEPLETION AND GROWTH

For more than 100 years, there has been serious concern in the United States about the depletion of the country's forest resources, and in recent decades there has been serious concern about forest depletion on a worldwide scale. The latter is feared to have adverse climatic effects, also on a worldwide scale.

A serious consideration of this subject requires careful distinction among three separate but related forestry concepts: land conversion, timber harvest, and forest depletion. Forestland may be cleared of trees and converted to residential or other urban uses or to farming. The cleared land may also be used for transportation facilities, such as highways or electric power lines. Timber may be harvested from a forest, as part of a planned rotation. Timber may also be cut and removed, with little or no concern for the future regeneration of the forest. These three concepts have in common the cutting of all or part of an existent forest stand and to this degree are similar. But only the third of these concepts may reasonably be described as forest depletion.

About half of the whole area of the forty-eight contiguous states was in what today would be classified by the U. S. FOREST SERVICE as commercial forest, meaning that it had the capacity to grow twenty-five or more cubic feet of industrial (that is, nonfuel) wood per acre annually in a fully stocked natural stand at the age of its most rapid growth. Actually, of course, none of this forest was "commercial" in an economic or business sense of the term at that early stage in history, for there existed no commercial uses of this vast forest. There were comparatively few open prairie areas in the eastern half of the United States; the rest was forested. In addition, there were extensive forests in the Rocky Mountains and along the Pacific Coast.

These original or virgin forests contained great volumes of standing timber. There were many species of trees, when the whole country is considered, and often several major species in a single locality. In this way, the forests of the New World contrasted sharply with the forests of Europe, which typically had fewer species. The trees in these old-growth forests were large, often so large as to excite the wonder and admiration of the early explorers. The average volume of wood per acre was about double what it is in the average American forest today. Occasionally, some areas in that original forest were regenerating naturally after natural fires, storms, or disease had destroyed or greatly impaired a still earlier mature stand. For the most part, however, these virgin forests of the colonial days were at a mature stage of growth, with near peak volumes of timber per acre for each site and each forest type.

These virgin forests at the colonial stage in history reflected the use that had been made of them in the several decades and centuries preceding the Europeans' arrival. The Indians had indeed used the forests as places in which to live and to hunt, but their ability to cut and utilize the trees was extremely limited. A few logs were used for structures and some wood was used for fuel, but the volumes involved were infinitesimal compared with the enormous volumes of wood in the forest. The Indians did use fire in some forested regions, as they did on the prairie, with consequent effects on tree and other vegetative cover. Nonetheless, timber depletion due to man's conscious efforts to use the forest for wood was dwarfed by the effects of natural fire, storms, insects, and diseases.

The virgin or original forests offered both great assets and serious problems to the settlers on the frontier. Although the settlers' tools were simple, even primitive, by modern standards, they were enormously more advanced than the tools of the Indians and in any case were adequate to enable the settlers to cut trees for their own use. Cabins, houses, and other structures and farm utensils and simple machines were fashioned from wood, and wood was the chief fuel for cooking and heating. In all of these ways, the ready availability of wood of many species and hence of different physical characteristics was a great asset. However, the land could not be farmed in cultivated crops until the forest had been removed. Food needs for the family, as well as need for cash crops such as tobacco, required that crops be cultivated. Moreover, the original forests were the place from which the Indians launched raids upon the settlers and hence were often feared or hated by the settlers.

By the latter part of the seventeenth century, New England pines were being harvested for sale as masts in sailing vessels and for manufacture into planking and lumber for sale in other parts of the world. The settler isolated on the forested frontier took trees from his land for his own use but, unless his land lay adjacent to a suitable stream on which logs or lumber could be floated to market, he was unable to market either logs

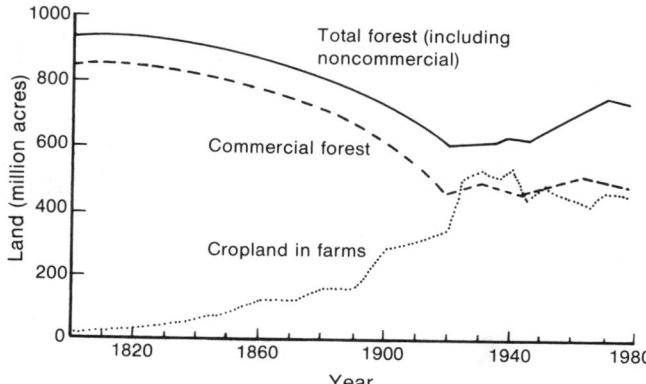

FIGURE 1.   Land in all forests, commercial forests, and cropland in farms in the United States, 1800 to 1975.

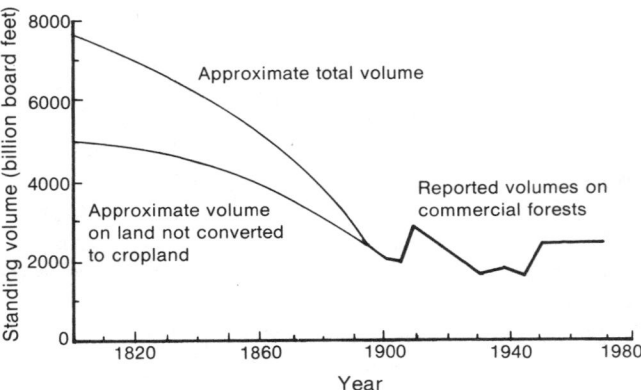

FIGURE 2. Standing volume of sawtimber at different dates in the United States, 1800 to 1977.

or lumber. In addition, the settler needed the land to grow crops, so he often cut the trees and burned them where they lay; or, to save labor, he girdled them so that they would die and ultimately fall. Some of the finest trees this continent has ever produced were thus burned where they lay after cutting. The trees were worth less than nothing in these situations; the land bare of trees was more valuable than the land covered with trees, irrespective of the kind, size, and quality of those trees.

At a comparatively early period in colonial and national history, highly localized shortages of wood for manufacture or for fuel did develop, even when on a continental scale the volume of standing timber seemed limitless. These local shortages were largely a matter of transportation cost. Thus, a few miles from the small town might be forests of zero value while at the edge of the little settlement all the easily obtainable wood had been used up.

Much of the early harvest of timber was a brutal affair, not only by the standards of the modern conservationist but also by the standards of modern commercial timber harvest. The cutting or the girdling of all the mature trees was a severe shock to the forest ecosystem. Indeed, the whole purpose of the cutting or girdling was to change the ecosystem, to get rid of the trees that shaded the land and also consumed much of the available soil moisture. Opening up the land to sunlight changed soil temperatures and soil microbiology, permitting growth of both desired plants and weeds, and modified water regimes. Often the land, bare during part of the year and typically with far less protective plant cover than the forest had provided, became subject to erosion.

As commercial forest harvest developed through the nineteenth century, it typically took from the land

all the useful or commercially valuable trees, and burned over the cleared areas, often several times. There was no concern to secure new forest regeneration; on the contrary, there was substantial effort to prevent it, especially by the use of fire. Those who thus prevented forest regrowth often felt that their actions were productive and socially desirable. There was a widespread belief that the land would go into farming. The great mistake was that much of the cleared land was not suitable for continued farming and would have been more valuable if it had reverted more quickly to forest.

The original area of what we today call commercial forest was about 850 million acres (Figure 1). As land was cleared for farming, this forest area declined, most rapidly during the nineteenth century and the first two decades of the twentieth century. Total forested area in the United States has been approximately constant since about 1920; some forest continues to be cleared for agricultural, residential, transportation, and other uses; but some land, previously cleared and farmed, has reverted to forest, especially in the eastern half of the country.

The total volume of standing timber is now about a third of what it was when settlement began (Figure 2). About half of the reduction took place on land cleared from forest and used for other purposes; about half took place on forested land harvested but allowed (or helped) to regenerate into new forests. The low point in standing volume of timber was apparently about 1930 or 1940—the available data may not be accurate enough to fix this date precisely. But there has clearly been an increase in standing volume of timber since that low point. Although timber harvest today results in much lower volumes of standing timber on the areas harvested, this loss on those areas is more than offset by the growth of new timber on other areas, and in time many of the harvested areas will have significant volumes of timber again. Except for parts of the national forests, nearly all of the original old-growth timber has been harvested; of course, logging is excluded in national parks and wilderness areas.

The large-scale depletion of forest stands and the brutal character of much of the timber harvest were in large measure responsible for the popular public demand for the establishment of the national forests, which began in 1891. Observers were shocked by the loss of the original forest. They often underestimated the ability of the forest to regenerate when given a chance. The effects of cutting were obvious and disturbing; regeneration was typically delayed. There has been a persistent tendency by foresters and others to underestimate the growth potential of American forests (Figure 3). Annual net growth was essentially zero at the beginning of the nineteenth century; growth was offset by mortality. As harvest opened up forests, some regeneration did take place, in spite of the frequent measures to prevent or inhibit it. However, net growth was comparatively low as late as 1920. Since 1920, net annual wood growth in aggregate has increased by about three and one-half times and today is substantially larger than the annual cut of timber, although there may be regional shortages.

These data make it clear that the United States is not today depleting its forests as a whole; on the contrary, forests are today being built up. Some of the growth is in species not in the greatest demand or of the greatest value. Spacing of trees on some of the regenerated forests is not optimum for maximum wood growth; some of the trees so established are not ideal in form. Also, much of the regenerated forest still has comparatively small trees. Although the regeneration is thus, from several points of view, not ideal, it is a mistake to assume that the virgin forests were ideal from a wood production viewpoint. Some of the original forests had at least some of the deficiencies noted for the new forests. The regenerated forests, with few exceptions, do provide ground cover sufficient to control soil erosion or to keep it within tolerable limits. In a great many situations, the tree species that invade a cleared site first or more aggressively than others are poor stayers—they lack competitive strength to prevail against some of the species better adapted to the site in the long run.

Two additional points should be made about these growth data. First, a substantial part of the United States is naturally forested in the sense that, if people do not interfere, trees will grow on the land. This is not to argue against efficient and competent forestry to get more wood growth of more desirable kinds and more quickly than if nature is allowed to take its course. However, it is clear that the natural regenerative capacity of American forests has been repeatedly underestimated in the past and still is by some people. Second, brutal and wasteful as the forest harvesting process was, it was a necessary step toward growth of new timber. The original stands had little or no net growth and could be made to grow only if some of the stand was removed. Most people realize that timber harvest cannot long exceed net timber growth, for inventory is thus reduced. Fewer people seem to realize that timber growth cannot indefinitely exceed harvest, because in that scenario timber stands get built up to the maximum the site will sustain. Harvest is an essential part of forestry.

These data also make it clear that a timber stand must always be viewed or evaluated in a long-term context. The characteristics of the present stand in such matters as tree species, volume and quality of wood, annual growth rates, and the like are easily seen and measured. The present stand, whether good or poor, will not endure but is constantly changing. The changes may be in desirable directions, or the reverse; the future stand may be better, or poorer. A low volume of wood now standing on a site is not, taken alone, a necessarily significant fact. The stand

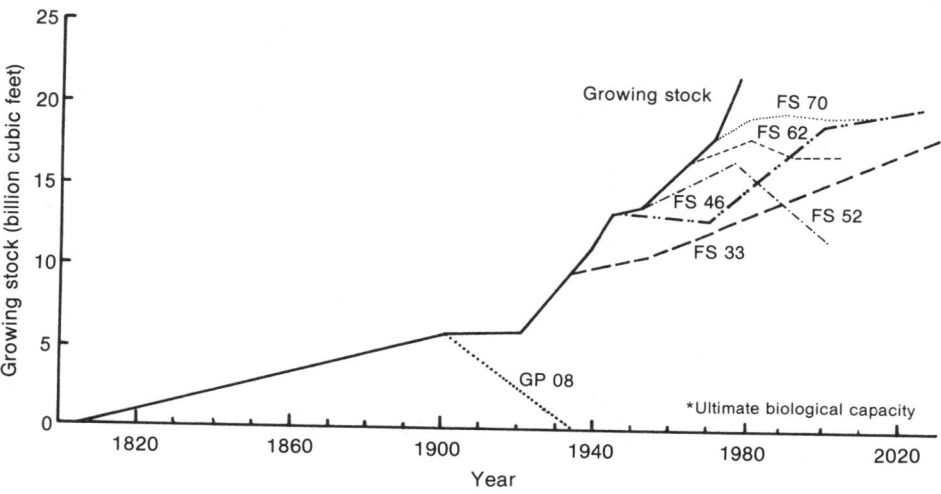

FIGURE 3. Annual net growth of timber in the United States, 1800 to 1977, and Forest Service projections of future growth made in 1933, 1946, 1952, 1962, and 1970.

SOURCE: *Science* 204 (June 15, 1979): 1171. © AAAS. Reprinted by permission.

may be young and thrifty, and the low volume natural under these circumstances. Or the stand may be thin, or unthrifty, or generally poor, with limited prospects for improvement. The present stand must always be viewed in a long-term perspective, with trends often as important as the present condition. It is only in these terms that forest depletion and growth have a real meaning.

FURTHER READING: Marion Clawson, "Forests in the Long Sweep of American History," *Science* 204 (June 1979): 1168–1174. William A. Duerr, *Fundamentals of Forestry Economics* (1960).

MARION CLAWSON

FOREST ENTOMOLOGY

The study of forest insects of economic importance to man developed with forestry and economic entomology in the late nineteenth and early twentieth centuries as part of attempts by government and scientists to make the most efficient use of natural resources in the postfrontier period. As long as wood had been abundant and cheap, waste had gone unnoticed or unheeded, but the prospective scarcity of timber encouraged efforts to control insect damage. (The *Timber Resources Review* in 1952 reported that insects caused 20 percent of the total annual growth impact —mortality plus growth loss—on American forests.)

Forest entomologists faced an enormous and complex problem. Like most land ecosystems, America's temperate forests are inhabited by a large number of insects filling a bewildering variety of niches, living on every part of the tree, from the topmost shoots to the roots, and during every life stage from seeds to dead wood. Other insects live on the insects that live on the wood, and some live on the predators and parasites. The complexity and variety of forest insect life forms meant that until the mid-twentieth century forest entomology remained largely taxonomic and biological, classifying and describing the life histories of insects. The state of the timber industry—which relied on cutting standing timber rather than raising trees from seed—also meant that forest entomologists were primarily concerned with pests of mature timber stands.

The discipline of forest entomology developed within the bureaucratic complex that grew up around the U. S. DEPARTMENT OF AGRICULTURE (USDA)—the experiment stations, land-grant universities, and other universities and private corporations that formed formal or informal ties with the various bureaus and offices of the USDA. It was a hybrid, part forestry and part entomology, and its place in the system re-

The bark of this ponderosa pine has been removed to reveal "galleries" cut by western pine beetle larvae, which weaken or kill the tree. Forest History Society Photo.

flected this division. Although federal forests were the province of the U. S. FOREST SERVICE, forest entomology was part of the Bureau of Entomology (Bureau of Entomology and Plant Quarantine after 1934). A. D. Hopkins, a pioneer in the study of bark beetles, became head of the bureau's newly formed section of forest entomology in 1904 and remained chief until 1923, when F. C. Craighead succeeded him. When the bureau was abolished in 1953, forest entomology went to the Forest Service as the Division of Forest Insect Research, while agricultural entomology went to the Agricultural Research Service.

In the same gradual fashion in which they split from economic entomology, forest entomologists acquired legal authority for control programs and appropriations to do the work. They began to concentrate on forest insects, as distinct from orchard, shade tree, and ornamental plant pests. The first legislative appropriation specifically for control of a native forest insect was for control of a bark beetle outbreak in the Pacific Northwest in 1921. Federal cooperative insect control programs were set up under the CLARKE-MCNARY ACT of 1924 and funds for forest insects and diseases were added by the MCSWEENEY-MCNARY ACT of 1928. Congress extended the federal obligation to protect forests to nonfederal lands in the Incipient Forest Pest Control Act of 1937 and gave the secretary of agriculture greater authority to control pests on private land

a decade later in the Forest Pest Control Act of 1947. This act was succeeded by the Cooperative Forestry Assistance Act of 1978, which extended the scope of cooperative work to take in stored wood and wood products.

Until the advent of DDT, forest entomologists were largely limited to indirect pest controls—the manipulation of environmental factors to suppress population growth. These methods included quarantines and inspection of planting stock to prevent the spread of insect pests; elimination of food supply by prompt salvage of dead or dying trees, disposal of logging slash and prompt utilization of cut logs; and modification of the moisture content of logs by seasoning cut lumber or floating logs in ponds. Direct controls, killing the insects involved, were impractical because of the low value of standing timber, the long growth cycle, and the expense and difficulty of treat-

Aerial application of insecticide to control an outbreak of the defoliating spruce budworm near Baker, Oregon, in 1955. American Forest Institute Photo.

ing large forest areas. Other problems of using poisonous arsenates (the only readily available compounds) also ruled against this practice. Indirect controls were also more suited for forests than agriculture, because forests, unlike field crops, were natural ecosystems, stable over comparatively long periods of time, and had natural systems of control that had evolved with the trees and the pests.

DDT, which was introduced for civilian use in 1945, changed this situation. Inexpensive, easily applied by air, toxic to a large variety of insect pests and apparently relatively nontoxic to other forms of life, DDT promised immediate control of pest irruptions, encouraged routine spraying, turned forest entomologists toward chemicals, and seemed to eliminate the need for basic biological and ecological research as a precondition for control. By 1950, forest managers were treating millions of acres a year with DDT to check a wide variety of native and imported pests. They planned even more ambitious campaigns, including one, begun in 1956, to eradicate the gypsy moth from North America.

Research topics also changed about the time DDT came on the market. Taxonomic description, which had been the main occupation of forest entomologists, was, by mid-century, sufficiently complete to allow more sophisticated studies of the ecological roles of pests. The science of ecology, which had developed rapidly in the previous generation, now offered a theoretical underpinning for forest entomology. The study of climate, population dynamics, and environmental limits made great strides in the postwar period. The focus of attention was also shifting from pests of mature timber to those of young trees, second-growth forests, and seeds. The depletion of mature forests throughout the country, the development of plantation forestry in the Lake States and the South, the increased reliance on genetics to provide superior planting stock, and the shift to intensive management and, in places, to monocultures had introduced a new set of insect problems.

By the late 1950s, forest entomology was beginning to shift away from reliance on chemicals. Even before public opposition began, it was apparent to many that blanket, routine use of DDT was no longer an acceptable practice. The sprays killed fish, affected bird populations, and could affect natural systems of control. Canadian use of DDT for the spruce budworm in the early 1950s had raised professional doubts, but serious public opposition came in the wake of the American campaign against the gypsy moth. In particular, DDT spraying on Long Island in the summer of 1957 brought public complaints, contamination of organic

farms and dairy pastures, and lawsuits. In addition, complaints about suburban sprays for the insect vector of Dutch elm disease helped bring opposition to the use of DDT anywhere and provided Rachel CARSON with the subject for *Silent Spring* (1962), a widely influential volume challenging the use of all chemical controls.

The banning of DDT and other persistent chemicals in the early 1970s and the increased attention to the environmental effects of human action have affected forest entomology, but not to the degree that they changed agricultural insect control. Forest entomologists had backed away from massive spraying by the time that public opposition to DDT and other chemicals became a major force in the late 1960s, and forest managers were, in any case, never as dependent on chemicals as agricultural entomologists. Like all pest control workers, forest entomologists must increasingly take account of the effects of their work on the ecosystem, but environmental concerns are not, or need not be, a major hindrance to forest control work. There are other pressures, though: the increased demand for forest products, the increased value of timber, and the trend toward intensive management make control of pest insects more important than ever before, and forest entomologists will need to develop more sophisticated control measures based on an even better understanding of the role of insects in the forest.

FURTHER READING: Samuel Alexander Graham and Fred Barrows Knight, *Principles of Forest Entomology* (4th ed., 1965). Thomas R. Dunlap, "The Gypsy Moth: A Study in Science and Public Policy," *Journal of Forest History* 24 (July 1980): 116–126.

THOMAS R. DUNLAP

FOREST FIRES

As events, fires are seldom singular. Large fires tend to be made of complexes of dozens of smaller blazes which blew up under the proper conditions. They often set up a cycle of reburns or type conversion which extends the effects of the original burn over a long period of time. Though October 1871, for example, is remembered for the Chicago and Peshtigo fires, these blazes were only the most spectacular among a large number that occurred at that time from Indiana to the Dakotas. The 1910 great Idaho fire engendered a cycle of subsequent burns in 1919, 1926, 1929, and later years. Oregon's Tillamook burn of 1933 set up almost equally large reburns in 1939 and 1945, and a lesser reburn in 1951. Moreover, insofar as they are cultural, as distinct from natural, events, fires may be distinguished by their type and timing. For example, different sorts of control problems accompany "frontier

Forest fires damage much more than trees. The topsoil and organic litter lost during Idaho's Roaring Canyon Fire (1939) will take generations to replace. Forest Service Photo.

fires" associated with the practice of frontier economies; "backcountry fires" in remote regions or on land that needs protection for a long time until it can be productive; "mass fires" resulting from incendiary warfare and forest conflagrations; and "wilderness fires" burning in primitive or wilderness areas (see FIRE CONTROL). Many large fires have acted as catalysts in policy formulation, and those that have been especially damaging or critically timed have acquired historical notoriety.

In the nineteenth century, large fires followed logging and land clearing, feeding on the disturbed fuels, ignited by careless fire practices of farmers and loggers, and usually occurring during periods of drought and hot weather. The first holocausts of record were the Miramichi and Piscataquis fires of 1825, which together burned perhaps 3 million acres in Maine and New Brunswick. From the late 1860s to the early decades of the twentieth century, large conflagrations swept the Lake States. The most deadly was the

1871 Peshtigo fire which covered 1.28 million acres and took over 1,400 lives in Wisconsin, while other fires occurring simultaneously burned 2.5 million acres in Michigan. The 1881 Michigan fires burned 1 million acres in the Thumb, took 169 lives, and first brought the Red Cross into civilian disaster relief. In 1894, fires covered several million acres in northwestern Wisconsin and Michigan, while a separate large fire around Hinckley, Minnesota, took 418 lives. Also famous were the 1908 fires in Wisconsin and around Metz, Michigan; the 1911 AuSable-Oscoda fires in Michigan; and the 1918 Cloquet, Minnesota, fire. These holocausts were important in the development of regional fire-protection systems and provided a lurid backdrop which early conservation reformers could point to with dramatic effect.

The 1903 and 1908 fires, which burned in an arc from Maine to upstate New York (including 637,000 acres in and around ADIRONDACK PARK), stimulated state fire organization and the establishment of private timber protective associations; prompted creation of the Maine Forestry District (1909); and contributed to agitation for the WEEKS ACT (1911), which provided both for the extension of the national forest system into the eastern United States and for cooperative fire protection between the federal and state governments. In the West, the 1902 and 1910 fires delivered a similar one-two punch. The first, sometimes called the Yacolt fire, was a series of 110 or more large fires that covered more than 1 million acres and took 38 lives in western Washington and Oregon. It stimulated the emergence of private fire-protection organizations which were consolidated under the WESTERN FORESTRY AND CONSERVATION ASSOCIATION in 1909. The 1910 fire in northern Idaho and northwestern Montana had the greatest effect on the development of a federal fire policy.

Fire problems confronting the FOREST SERVICE in August 1910 were actually of two sorts. In California, the light-burning controversy went public while throughout the national forest system some 5 million acres burned. The Big Blowup in the northern Rockies was only the most spectacular of that season. Light burning challenged both the credibility of forestry as a source of expertise on fire management and the political support for the national forest system. But it was the Big Blowup—which swept some 3 million acres, pushed the service more than a million dollars into debt, and took the lives of perhaps eighty-five fire fighters—that traumatized the young Forest Service, contributed in no small degree to the passage of the Weeks Act, and shaped service fire policy nationwide. Forestry had made fire control the *sine qua*

non of professional management and promised that the national forest system could provide it; the presence or absence of conflagrations became public tests of these premises. The 1910 fires, moreover, were the first challenge faced by Henry S. GRAVES as chief forester and were an indelible reference point in the memory of two future chiefs—William B. GREELEY and Ferdinand SILCOX, district and assistant district foresters at the time. The fires initiated, too, the effective beginning of scientific research on fire control and systematic fire-control planning, and they coincided with Frederick Clements's study of fire and lodgepole pine, which greatly advanced the understanding of fire ecology in the West. Systematic fire protection as a national policy may be dated from the fires of 1910.

A series of droughts and exceptionally large fires occurred between 1930 and 1934. The eastern coastal plain was hit hard during 1930 and 1931; even the Dismal Swamp burned. One effect in the South was that the Forest Service allowed its cooperators to practice controlled burning without disqualification under the CLARKE-MCNARY ACT program. In the West, the Matilija Fire of 1932 was the largest California fire ever recorded. The Tillamook fire of 1933 raged over 311,000 acres, bringing among other things official approval for the fire line use of the CIVILIAN CONSERVATION CORPS (CCC). The Pete King-Selway fires of 1934 became the largest fires in the northern Rockies since 1910. They revived a debate within the Forest Service about "let burning" on remote sites. But like light burning before it, let burning was condemned, and in 1935 the service promulgated its 10 A.M. Policy. However, following large fires on the Florida national forests from 1941 to 1943, the service liberalized its fire policy to permit controlled burning on the national forests, as it had permitted it earlier on the lands of cooperators in the South.

The 1947 Maine fires burned 220,000 acres of forest and led both to state reforms and to the Northeastern Interstate Forest Fire Compact (1949), an exemplar for similar compacts and fire councils. Destroying hundreds of homes and cottages near Bar Harbor, these blazes also highlighted a new problem: the mass fire burning along the interface between wildland and suburb. The mid-1950s witnessed large fires across the southern United States, culminating perhaps in 1956 with the Buckhead fire (Florida) and Malibu and Inaja fires (southern California)—eleven fire fighters perished in the latter. Because of the loss of life, the 1956 fires led to major reforms in Forest Service fire safety ranging from training to research, and they helped to give national significance to southern California fires which burned largely in chaparral rather than tall forest.

A year later, some 5 million acres burned in Alaska. This, combined with the prospect for imminent statehood, helped bring fire protection to the Alaskan interior and greatly strengthened the BUREAU OF LAND MANAGEMENT (BLM) as a fire protection organization. Lands managed by the BLM in the Great Basin were the source of several large fires centered on Elko, Nevada, in 1964. Their control required interagency action. The logistical problems that arose led to the establishment of the Great Basin Fire Center the next year and influenced the later development of the Boise Interagency Fire Center. The Swanson River-Russian River (Alaska) fires of 1969 coincided with the opening of the center.

In 1967, large fires occurred in the northern Rockies and the Northwest, and along the coastal plains of the Carolinas. The former led the Forest Service and other cooperating agencies to consider broadening the scope of the Boise Interagency Fire Center to enable emergency assistance on a nationwide basis. The same fires led the NATIONAL PARK SERVICE to examine the impact of suppression technology on primitive lands and influenced the new wilderness fire policy which the service issued in 1968. The major stimulus for reform, however, came in 1970 with costly and damaging fires in Washington (near Wenatchee) and in California (including the Laguna fire). The burned acreages were the largest on the national forest system since 1910 and resulted in several changes—a modification of policy in 1971, a shift in research directions, and inquiries which led to FIRESCOPE and the National Wildfire Coordinating Group charter (1976). FIRESCOPE applied general-systems concepts to the peculiar jurisdictional problems of southern California, treating fire as one type of incident among many and integrating the suppression resources of the many levels of government in the region. A similar combination of large fires in California and Alaska in 1977 reinforced these trends.

Among other fires of regional importance were the 1919 and 1929 burns in the northern Rockies, the 1924 fires in California, fires in the Lake States through the 1920s and 1930s, the 1952 fires in Kentucky and West Virginia (2 million acres), the 1961 fires in the Northwest and northern Rockies, the 1963 fires in the border states and New Jersey (250,000 acres on "Black Saturday" alone), the 1975 Baxter State Park fire in Maine, and the nearly annual fires in southern California from the early 1950s to the present. Fires with particular meaning for federal agencies included the 1937 Blackwater fire (Wyoming) which killed fifteen CCC enrollees and highlighted the need for development of more highly trained and organized fire crews such as the smokejumpers and the forty-man crew; the 1949 Mann Gulch fire (Montana), which killed thirteen smokejumpers and led to changes in the jumper program; and the 1969 Swanson River (Alaska) and 1976 Seney (Michigan) fires which influenced the program of the FISH AND WILDLIFE SERVICE.

Several prescribed burns, moreover, have affected policy through problems created by smoke. Among the most important were the naturally ignited Teton fires in 1971, which led to policy reanalysis by the National Park Service, and the prescribed fires along the Mogollon Rim, Arizona, ignited in autumn 1975 and again in 1979 by the Fort Apache Indian Reservation and the Forest Service; the smoke created health hazards in the Phoenix metropolitan area and led to better national recognition of smoke management as an inevitable part of controlled burning. Among the largest fires of recent years were escape fires from growing experimentation with prescribed burning. Such runaways occurred in Idaho in 1979 and Michigan in 1980.

FURTHER READING: Arthur A. Brown and Kenneth Davis, *Forest Fire: Control and Use* (2nd ed., 1973). Stewart Holbrook, *Burning an Empire* (1944). Stephen J. Pyne, *Fire in America: A Cultural History of Wildland and Rural Fire* (1982). Betty Spencer, *The Big Blowup* (1954).

STEPHEN J. PYNE

FOREST HISTORY SOCIETY

This nonprofit, tax-exempt private organization began its existence in St. Paul, Minnesota, in 1946 as the Forest Products History Foundation, a special project of the Minnesota Historical Society. Conceived by two leading University of Minnesota historians and sponsored by a prominent St. Paul lumberman, it was maintained for several years under the direction of Rodney C. Loehr. With renewed interest and financial support from local businessmen in 1952, Elwood R. Maunder was recruited to be its executive director, a position he held until 1978, when he was succeeded by Harold K. Steen. In 1953, in recognition of the broadening scope of its activities, the organization became the American Forest History Foundation, only to be renamed again in 1955, with its incorporation as the Forest History Foundation, under the nonprofit corporation act of the state of Minnesota. The present designation of Forest History Society was formally adopted in 1957.

In 1964, seeking a direct relationship with a major university, the society moved from St. Paul to New Haven, Connecticut, where, under a five-year agreement with Yale University, it was associated with the School of Forestry and the Sterling Memorial Library. The potential of larger quarters and stronger support in the West led in 1969 to its move to Santa Cruz, California, and an informal association with the local branch of the University of California.

In its role as an educational organization, the society's basic goal is related to the promotion of knowledge in the total field of North American forest-related history. To that end, it is engaged in a wide range of activities, including a continuous search for pertinent source materials, promotion of scholarly research and publication, compilation of bibliographies and other research aids, and serving as the center of an informational network. Over the years, the program has undergone distinctive changes in priorities to meet developing needs and opportunities, as in the current gradual shift in emphasis from studies of institutions and individuals to investigations of issues of national import.

As the first step toward its underlying goal, the society began in 1952 to seek out unpublished original documentary sources of man's use of the forest resource and to serve as a clearinghouse for channeling such archival materials to appropriate institutions in the regions to which they pertain. In this undertaking, it is currently cooperating with an informal network of nearly fifty research libraries and other active repositories across the United States and Canada. In addition, as an adjunct to its Santa Cruz library, the society maintains its own archival collections, comprised of depositions from organizations and individuals that have designated it as their official· repository; included are the past records of such national groups as the AMERICAN FORESTRY ASSOCIATION, AMERICAN FOREST INSTITUTE, NATIONAL FOREST PRODUCTS ASSOCIATION, NATURAL RESOURCES COUNCIL OF AMERICA, and SOCIETY OF AMERICAN FORESTERS.

The society's substantial collection of books, periodicals, manuscripts, records, photographs and slides, and other historical materials has been developed essentially as a research library, primarily intended to meet the needs of its resident staff and affiliated research associates who work on society-sponsored special projects and of visiting scholars. It also provides much of the information needed for staff response to all manner of inquiries pertaining to forest and conservation history. A significant part of the collection is the series of tape-recorded interviews assembled since 1953 in conjunction with the society's overall endeavor to gather and preserve archival records. This activity has resulted in in-depth oral interviews with more than 200 leading American and Canadian educators, foresters, conservationists, businessmen, and federal and state personnel, who have been active participants in the administration, management, and utilization of the North American forest-related resources.

The quarterly *Journal of Forest History*, the society's most visible product and the magazine of record in its field, had its beginning in 1957 as a mimeographed *Forest History Newsletter*. Changed to printed form the following year, it carried the designation *Forest History* until 1974, when the present title was adopted. The organization also cooperates in the publication of books and reference tools based on the research of its staff and various collaborators.

As one aspect of its overall effort to encourage scholarly research and writing, the society makes a number of special awards in the field of forest history. Presented annually since 1972 are two grants for published articles judged best by panels of outside evaluators. Named in memory of two of the society's founders, the Weyerhaeuser Award honors the authors of outstanding articles in the *Journal of Forest History*, the Blegen Award those appearing in other publications. In 1976, a biennial Book Award was created to honor the author of a book judged the most outstanding volume in forest and conservation history published during a two-year period; the books are nominated by their publishers and evaluated by an independent panel. Other awards and commendations may also be made occasionally in recognition of distinctive contributions to the field and the society.

The work of the society is financed by corporate and individual memberships, gifts, and bequests, all chiefly in support of its general operating budget, and research grants and contracts for special projects. Associated with the society, but independent in its administration, is the Forest History Society Endowment Fund, a nonprofit public foundation incorporated in the State of California in 1969 for the purpose of administering endowment gifts and bequests; the annual income is available for support of the society's program.

GEORGE A. GARRATT

FOREST INDUSTRIES ADVISORY COUNCIL

In 1959, the board of directors of the NATIONAL LUMBER MANUFACTURERS ASSOCIATION (NLMA) authorized establishment of an Economic Council of the Lumber Industry to take a long-range look at the industry's economic problems and produce guidelines to correct them. The council met in the following year and annually thereafter. Council members were selected each year by the presidents of NLMA from among industry leaders. The council was a forum, not an organization. It had no staff, no continuous membership, and no authority. Unlike the FOREST INDUSTRIES COUNCIL (FIC) which represented its member organizations as an advisory body, the economic council was not tied to organizational representation. Reflecting NLMA's change of name to NATIONAL FOREST PRODUCTS ASSOCIATION, (NFPA), the economic council became the Economic Council of the Forest Products Industry in January 1966. Its membership base was broadened in 1970 when pulp and paper executives were invited to participate. In 1974, it became the Economic Council of the Forest Industries. To better reflect its evolving role, in 1977 it changed its name once more to become the Forest Industries Advisory Council (FIAC).

The 1970 meeting marked the emergence of the Economic Council as a forum for the discussion of problems of immediate concern to the forest industries and as a source of guidance for FIC. "Environmental awareness" was spreading and the existing structure by which the industry represented itself to the government and the public was not working satisfactorily. The Economic Council asked FIC to undertake the redirection of the work of the AMERICAN FOREST INSTITUTE (AFI) and to improve the financing of the industry's communications programs. This was only the first of many significant cooperative projects for FIC to emanate from the deliberations of the expanded advisory council.

The success of the Economic Council and then of FIAC in identifying and appraising problems and opportunities of universal interest to the forest industries prompted revision of FIAC and FIC leadership. By 1980, a system had evolved under which the FIAC chairman served also as chairman of FIC, while his designated successors for the next two years participated as members of both councils. This arrangement afforded complete familiarity and continuity between FIAC deliberations and recommendations to FIC and FIC requests for action among its member groups.

HAROLD P. NEWSON

FOREST INDUSTRIES COUNCIL

In 1943, the American Paper and Pulp Association (APPA), the AMERICAN PULPWOOD ASSOCIATION (APA), and the NATIONAL LUMBER MANUFACTURERS ASSOCIATION (NLMA), alarmed by the prospect of extended federal controls of private enterprise through regulation, taxation, or expanded governmental ownership of timberland, formed the Forest Industries Council (FIC) as a forum to promote the exchange of views on correlated political activity, the furtherance of forest conservation programs, and the avoidance of misunderstanding and public criticism within the forest industries. FIC was the first national organization designed to coordinate the policy of the forest industries; it was intended to supplement and not to interfere with the freedom of action of the existing industrial associations.

FIC sponsored public relations programs through a number of committees and some existing organizations such as the American Forest Products Industries (AFPI) and the Forest Industries Committee on Timber Valuation and Taxation (FICTVT). As early as 1945, it was proposed that FIC assume direct control over AFPI, the industry's public information arm; this move was rejected then on the grounds that if FIC were to become an action agency it would lose its value as a policy-recommending and coordinating body, as it remained for thirty years.

During this period, APA remained a direct membership association, but evolutionary changes occurred in both APPA and NLMA. The latter expanded its scope beyond the limits of lumber manufacturing interests. First it did this through creation of such subsidiaries as AFPI and FICTVT as "special accounts" to which individual companies could subscribe whether or not these companies were members of any of the solid-wood associations within the NLMA federation. Later, after AFPI and FICTVT had become independent, the range of NLMA's concerns broadened as the nonlumber-product interests of both new and old association members became increasingly diverse. Accordingly, NLMA changed its name to NATIONAL FOREST PRODUCTS ASSOCIATION (NFPA) in 1964. Similarly, APPA reorganized into the AMERICAN PAPER INSTITUTE (API) in 1966, henceforth providing both direct membership for primary pulp and paper producers and limited participation by converters in selected API activities to which they subscribed directly. In the span of fifteen years, all three of the founding members of FIC had become organizations that could look to forest products companies for direct membership to the extent of their individual business interests and without an obligation to support activities outside their normal business. This change reflected the evolution of the product mixes of many forest products firms which sought more efficient use of wood as a raw material by increasing both diversification and specialization of product lines.

Widespread awareness of the increasing comity of interest throughout the forest industries led to wider interest in limited policy development and action programs and to an ever larger number of problems referred to FIC for consideration and recommendations. By 1970, FIC was broadened to include representation from the major regional and product organizations already within the NFPA federation, including the AMERICAN PLYWOOD ASSOCIATION, the INDUSTRIAL FORESTRY ASSOCIATION, the Southern Forest Products Association, and Western Wood Products Association, as well as the AMERICAN FOREST INSTITUTE (successor to AFPI) Wood Council, and FICTVT. With this strengthened base of industrial support, FIC was in a position to carry out new public relations programs requested by the FOREST INDUSTRIES ADVISORY COUNCIL (FIAC) during the 1970s.

The spirit of mutuality was evident as FIC member groups in only five weeks prepared and distributed a *Handbook on Environmental Information for the Forest Industry* in time for use on the first "Earth Day," April 22, 1970. Subsequent FIC joint efforts, undertaken at the request of FIAC, were equally successful. Often conducted by a single FIC member organization as the "lead" agency, these programs resulted in guidance through Congress of satisfactory Clean Water Act amendments; defeat of the Solid Waste Disposal Tax; a victory for sound federal forest management through the Monongahela legislation; passage of the Resources Planning Act; establishment of an FIC Environment and Health Council; completion of a forest productivity project; a successful effort to develop pulpwood logging safety standards; not only retention but also improvement of timber capital gains and other tax savings; and similar programs of benefit to the forest industries.

In carrying out these joint projects, the American Paper Institute (API) and NFPA became increasingly close in their operations; eventually, API environmental personnel moved in with the NFPA staff and were jointly administered. Similar close relations developed between the government affairs functions of the two associations.

The American Forest Institute (AFI) undertook to provide secretariat service for FIC and to apply its communications skills to FIC projects managed by other member groups as "lead agencies." By 1980 this arrangement had led to the logical step of FIC becoming the board of trustees for AFI.

The evolution of FIC into a more widely representa-tive organization (and the simultaneous broadening of FIAC) was indicative of a coalescence throughout the entire forest industry. Finally, the concentration in 1980 of FIC and FIAC leadership in a single individual, who during his tenure had access to advice from a representative cross section of the forest industries, provided opportunity for coordinated action such as had never before existed.

HAROLD P. NEWSON

FOREST INDUSTRIES STRUCTURE

The identity of the industries making up the wood products industries must be clearly in mind before their structures can be systematically discussed. Collectively, they are known by a variety of names, including the timber industry, the forest products industry, and the forest industries. The descriptive quality of these names varies, but they are intended to describe the industries in which the woody portion of trees, usually in the form of logs, bolts, or pulpwood, is first processed into a commercial wood product other than fuelwood. Such products include lumber, pulp, and veneer. However, the latter two products are captive of the paper and paperboard industries in the case of pulp, and the plywood industry in the case of veneer. In fact, the manufacture of pulp is regularly integrated within the same facility with the manufacture of paper or paperboard, as is the manufacture of veneer with the manufacture of plywood. Thus, paper, paperboard, and plywood are generally identified as primary wood products as they will be here. Other primary wood products include hardboard, insulation board, particleboard, poles, piling, shakes, and wood shingles. Each of these products are made from the woody or xylem portion of trees.

The opportunities for substitution among the above products in most of their individual uses are limited. For example, plywood is not a good substitute for dimension lumber in framing a house, nor is paperboard a good substitute for plywood in the making of cabinets; neither is writing paper a good substitute for containerboard in the manufacture of shipping containers. Because wood products are not usually good substitutes for one another, they are customarily looked upon as the products of separate industries. This view is consistent with the economic concept of an industry, which includes all the sellers of close substitute products who supply a common group of buyers.

Rigorous application of the concept would prompt further distinctions. For example, since the uses of hardwood lumber and softwood lumber are different and they ordinarily are not substituted for one another, the manufacture of hardwood lumber would be distinguished as an industry distinct from the manufacture of softwood lumber. For the same reasons, the hardwood plywood industry would be distinguished from the softwood plywood industry.

The above primary wood products are not of equal importance; they are rank-ordered in Table 1 in terms of their value of shipments in 1972. The five products with the largest value of shipments comprise 85.8 percent of the total. These products are clearly of special importance, as are the industries in which they are made. Therefore, subsequent discussion of the structure of the wood products industries will deal essentially with five industries: the softwood lumber industry, the softwood plywood industry, the pulp industry, the paper industry, and the paperboard industry. Collectively, they might be referred to as the principal primary wood products industries. However, for ease of exposition, the name will be abbreviated to the principal wood products industries.

Historical Background

The beginning of the lumber industry in North America can be traced to 1631 with the establishment of a commercial sawmill in Berwick, Maine. Since that time, the industry has had an important place in the development of the United States, and in 1981 it contributed 4 percent to the Gross National Product. It

TABLE 1. Value of Shipments of Primary Wood Products

Product Class	Value of Shipments (millions of dollars)
Paper	$ 6,182.0
Softwood lumber	3,907.8
Paperboard	3,657.5
Softwood plywood	1,635.3
Pulp	1,132.4
Hardwood plywood	714.0
Hardwood lumber	516.0
Softwood veneer	304.3
Particleboard	292.8
Hardboard	258.5
Insulation board	219.7
Poles and Piling	196.7
Hardwood veneer	161.3
Shakes and Shingles (redcedar)	70.2
Total	$19,248.7

SOURCE: U.S. Bureau of the Census, *Census of Manufactures, 1972, Vol. II, Industry Statistics, Part I* (Washington, D.C.: Government Printing Office, 1976).

has consisted of many small firms, organized mostly as proprietorships or partnerships manufacturing comparatively homogeneous commodities from the severed stems of trees. The industry has migrated long distances to secure a stable, relatively inexpensive supply of timber: from New England to the Lake States in the nineteenth century; from the South to the Pacific Northwest and back to the South in the twentieth century.

The beginning of the paper industry in North America is marked by the establishment of a paper mill in Germantown, Pennsylvania, in 1690. The industry grew slowly until the introduction of the cylinder and fourdrinier paper machines in the early nineteenth century, which revolutionized the industry by making it possible to manufacture continuous sheets of paper.

In contrast to the lumber industry, the paper industry has been dominated by a small number of firms that have been comparatively large in size and mostly organized as corporations. When wood came into common use as a source of cellulose for papermaking during the late nineteenth century, the pulp and paper industries began to follow the geographical movements of the lumber industry. Because the industries can and do make complementary uses of the timber resource, close and frequent interactions between them soon developed and continue today.

The beginning of the plywood industry as it is currently understood can be marked with the manufacture of softwood plywood by the Portland Manufacturing Company in Portland, Oregon, in 1905. The industry grew slowly until shortly before World War II and the development of moisture-resistant and waterproof glues. After 1948, plywood grew at phenomenal rates, with new production records set almost yearly during the following two decades. The plywood industry was located principally in the Pacific Northwest until technology, developed in the mid-1960s, allowed the use of southern pine in the making of plywood. Subsequently, many plywood plants have been located in the South.

The plywood industry, like the pulp and paper industries, has been historically dominated by a small number of large firms, corporate in organization. Its products, like the lumber industry to which it has been closely tied, have been principally homogeneous commodities.

Census Data

The Bureau of the Census conducts a census of the manufacturing sector of the economy approximately every five years and subsequently releases the data it acquires in the *Census of Manufactures*. The agen-

TABLE 2. Wood Products Industries and SIC Industries

Principal Wood Products Industry	SIC Industry	SIC Industry Code Number
Softwood lumber industry	Sawmills and planing mills, general	2421
Softwood plywood industry	Softwood veneer and plywood	2436
Pulp industry	Pulpmills	2611
Paper industry	Papermills, except building paper	2621
Paperboard industry	Paperboard mills	2631

cy collects the data on the basis of industries defined in the *Standard Industrial Classification Manual,* a publication of the Office of Management and Budget. Standard Industrial Classification (SIC) industries do not correspond precisely with the principal wood products industries developed herein, in terms of their conceptual boundaries. Neither are they identified by the same names.

But since the industries do correspond generally and since census data are of good quality, widely accepted, and useful for describing and comparing industries, this analysis will make extensive use of these data. Relationships between principal wood products industries and corresponding SIC industries are listed in Table 2. Hereafter, the SIC industries will usually be referred to by their SIC code number.

The softwood lumber industry and SIC industry 2421 are not altogether comparable. The SIC industry is broader, including more products than softwood lumber. Nevertheless, in 1972, for example, softwood lumber made up 58.9 percent of the value of shipments of SIC industry 2421, and in turn, SIC industry 2421 accounted for 96.8 percent of the value of shipments of softwood lumber. Thus, considerable comparability between the two industries exists, and data with regard to SIC industry 2421 will be considered applicable to the softwood lumber industry.

The softwood plywood industry is also not completely comparable with SIC industry 2436. But since softwood veneer is a component of softwood plywood and since the manufacture of softwood veneer and softwood plywood are regularly integrated, differences are considered minor, and data with regard to SIC industry 2436 will be considered applicable to the softwood plywood industry.

Establishments, Companies, and Legal Form of Organization

Most of the companies and establishments in the principal wood products industries are engaged chiefly in softwood lumber manufacturing. An establishment, according to the Bureau of the Census, is not a mill but an economic unit in which goods and services are produced and which is located generally at a single site. Data on the number of companies and establishments in these industries are shown in Table 3. SIC industry 2421 contains 94.5 percent of the companies and 90.4 percent of the establishments.

Although the number of companies and the number of establishments in SIC industry 2421 are large, they have also sharply declined in the period since World War II. For example, the number of companies in SIC industry 2421 declined by 35.8 percent between 1963 and 1972, and the number of establishments by 33.8 percent. No comparable trend exists with regard to the other principal wood products industries.

Industries and markets are systematically described and compared on the basis of certain structural elements that affect the behavior of firms in conducting their business activities. These elements are seller concentration, product differentiation, barriers to entry, short-run cost structure, diversification, and vertical integration.

Seller Concentration

Seller concentration is used as a measure of competition between rivals and refers to the share of an industry's business accounted for by a given number of the largest firms. The Bureau of the Census calculates such shares in the form of concentration ratios for the four, eight, twenty, and fifty largest firms. The shares of value of shipments for the four and eight largest firms in SIC industries 2421, 2436, 2611, 2621, and 2631 are shown in Table 4. The eight largest firms account for 23 percent of the value of shipments in SIC industry 2421, 50 percent of the value of shipments in SIC industry 2436, 83 percent of the value of shipments in SIC industry 2611, 40 percent of the value of shipments in SIC industry 2621, and 54 percent of the value of shipments of SIC industry 2631.

TABLE 3. Establishments, Companies, and Extent of Corporate Form of Organization in the Principal Wood Products Industries, 1972

SIC Industry Code Number	SIC Industry	Establishments	Companies	Percent of Establishments of Corporate Form of Organization
2421	Sawmills and planing mills[1]	8,072	7,664	34
2436	Softwood veneer and plywood	232	121	96
2611	Pulpmills	60	46	83
2611	Papermills[2]	349	194	93
2631	Paperboard mills	273	135	98

1. For ease of exposition, "general" is deleted from the SIC industry title "sawmills and planing mills, general" and will continue to be deleted throughout the remainder of the discussion.
2. For ease of exposition, "except building paper" is deleted from the SIC industry title "papermills, except building paper" and will continue to be throughout the remainder of the discussion.
SOURCE: U. S. Bureau of the Census, *Census of Manufactures, 1972, Vol. I, Subject and Special Statistics* (Washington, D.C.: Government Printing Office, 1976).

A descriptive standard with regard to the eight-firm concentration ratio (CR-8) has been used in two recent studies of the structure of the wood products industries (see Table 5). This standard is applied to the date in Table 4 and presented with other information on elements of market structure in Table 6.

Particular interest centers on industries whose concentration ratios increase over time. Such is the case for the softwood lumber and plywood industries. All available evidence indicates that seller concentration in these industries has continued to increase during the postwar period.

Product Differentiation

Product differentiation refers to real or imagined differences in close substitute products through branding, packaging, advertising, quality variation, and design variations. Product differentiation is not a significant factor in the principal wood products industries, because generally they manufacture producer goods, as opposed to consumer goods, which are the final or end products. Product differentiation is not as prevalent among producer goods as it is among consumer goods, because industrial buyers are relatively more skilled at evaluating the products they buy. As a result, product differentiation for producer goods is more subtle than it is for consumer goods.

As producer goods, the demand for principal wood products is a derived demand—dependent upon the demand for other products. Demand for softwood lumber and plywood is derived from the demand for housing. Demand for primary paper products or grades is derived from the demand for newspapers, magazines, books, writing and printing papers, sanitary paper products, grocery bags, and wrapping papers. Demand for primary paperboard products or grades is derived from the demand for shipping containers, folding boxes, and shipping sacks and bags.

Accordingly, the principal wood products are usually sold on the basis of their being homogeneous commodities. They are sold more like wheat, beef, and coal than like automobiles, women's apparel, and breakfast cereal. Product differentiation is, therefore, considered insignificant in the principal wood products industries.

Barriers to Entry

The condition of entry into an industry is determined by the amount that sellers can raise prices above competitive levels without attracting new entrants. The concept is concerned with potential rather than actual rivals in an industry. An industry's "barriers to entry" are measured in principle by the highest price that will fail to attract new firms into an industry. Sources of such barriers include economies of scale in production or distribution, consumer preferences favoring estab-

TABLE 4. Concentration Ratio of Wood Products Industry

CR-8 (percent)	Descriptive Standard
0–32	Unconcentrated
33–49	Moderately concentrated
50–100	Concentrated

TABLE 5. Share of Value of Shipments Accounted for by the Four and Eight Largest Companies in the Principal Wood Products Industries, 1972

SIC Industry Code Number	SIC Industry	Value of Shipments (millions of dollars)	Percent Accounted for by the:	
			Four Largest Companies	Eight Largest Companies
2421	Sawmills and planing mills	6,420.8	18	23
2431	Softwood veneer and plywood	2,011.5	37	50
2611	Pulpmills	709.9	59	83
2621	Papermills	6,385.2	24	40
2631	Paperboard mills	4,153.5	29	54

SOURCE: U. S. Bureau of the Census, *Census of Manufactures, 1972, Vol. I, Subject and Special Statistics* (Washington, D.C.: Government Printing Office, 1976).

lished differentiated products, absolute cost advantages associated with the control of superior production processes or the possession of strategic raw materials, and capital requirements for entry.

A descriptive standard regarding the heights of barriers of entry is: (1) very high barriers that result in blocked entry; (2) high barriers that effectively impede entry; (3) moderate barriers that ineffectively impede entry; and (4) low or no barriers that allow easy entry into an industry.

The barrier to entering either the softwood lumber industry or the softwood plywood industry is the ability to purchase an adequate supply of timber or logs at competitive prices. No other barrier seems to exist with regard to economies of scale, product differentiation, or capital requirements.

Estimating the height of an entry barrier to an industry (estimating the significance of an entry barrier) always involves an element of conjecture. Nevertheless, the height of entry barriers for the softwood lumber and plywood industries seem to range, as indicated in Table 6, from moderate to high, depending upon the local market for timber. There can be no

doubt that this barrier effectively impedes entry into the softwood lumber and plywood industries in many timber markets in the Pacific Northwest.

Three barriers to entry are evident with regard to the pulp, paper, and paperboard industries. First, the capital requirements are so very large that they preclude entry for most firms. An investment of $150 million would be required for an integrated pulp and paper plant of minimum efficient size, and an investment of $115 million would be necessary for a comparable pulp and paperboard plant. Integrated plants are necessary, because of the economies connected with processing the pulp into paper or paperboard in one continuous operation. Such an arrangement avoids the costs of having to dry the pulp for shipment and then having to put it back into solution.

Economies of scale are a second significant barrier due to the proportion of the market an entrant would have to supply for efficient plant operation. Being able to purchase an adequate supply of timber or pulpwood at competitive prices constitutes a third significant barrier. The combined effect of the three barriers is that entry into the pulp, paper, and

TABLE 6. Characterization of Three Elements of Market Structure with Regard to the Principal Wood Products Industries

	Industry				
	Softwood Lumber	Softwood Plywood	Pulp	Paper	Paperboard
Seller concentration	Unconcentrated	Concentrated	Concentrated	Moderately Concentrated	Concentrated
Product differentiation	Insignificant	Insignificant	Insignificant	Insignificant	Insignificant
Barriers to entry	Moderate to High	Moderate to High	High	High	High

paperboard industries is effectively impeded. Accordingly, the combined height of the barriers is "high," as shown in Table 6.

Short-Run Cost Structure

Short-run cost structure is an important feature of industry structure. When fixed costs are high relative to total costs, the pricing behavior of firms is very cautious, and, as Scherer (1979) points out, "when tacit restraint fails, they have an unusually high propensity to scurry into formal collusive agreements." The reason for this behavior is that in an industry whose fixed costs are high and marginal costs low, there is a strong inducement toward price cutting with declines in demand to such a degree that it is destructive to some firms.

Data on the ratio of fixed to total costs are not available in Bureau of the Census documents. However, data on gross book value of depreciable assets and value of shipments are available, and their ratio is a good substitute for the ratio of fixed to total costs. Depreciable assets are tangible capital assets of two kinds: (1) structures and buildings; and (2) machinery and equipment.

Shown in Table 7 are the average ratios of gross book value of depreciable assets to value of shipments for the primary wood products industries, 1972 to 1976. The same ratio for all manufacturing industries taken together is also shown, and its value is 0.3557, less than any of the ratio values for the principal wood products industries. This ratio indicates that the principal wood products industries are relatively high-fixed-cost or capital-intensive industries.

The disparity within the principal wood products industries is also important. Values of the ratios for SIC industries 2611, 2621, and 2631 are about two and one-half times the values of the ratios for SIC industries

TABLE 7. Average Ratio of Gross Book Value of Depreciable Assets to Value of Shipments, 1972–1976

SIC Industry	Ratio
2421	.4445
2436	.4145
2611	1.1846
2621	1.0226
2631	1.0932
All Industries	.3557

SOURCE: U.S. Bureau of the Census, *Annual Survey of Manufactures* (Washington, D.C.: Government Printing Office, annually, 1973, 1974, 1975–1976).

2421 and 2436, as well as about three times the value of the ratio for all manufacturing industries.

Diversification

Diversification refers to the situation in which a firm is a seller of two or more products that are not substitutes for each other. An example of a diversified firm in the principal wood products industries is one that sells both paperboard and softwood lumber. The reason for concern about this element of market structure is that a diversified firm can use its profits from the sales of one product to subsidize its activities with regard to another. Such a capability provides a hedge for the firm against decreases in demand for individual products. It also gives the diversified firm an element of power in the market for the subsidized product over firms not similarly situated.

Many firms in the principal wood products industries are diversified, especially very large firms. Ten such firms are shown in Table 8, listed in order of the size of their holdings of domestic forestland, along with their respective rankings either in the production of or the capacity to produce softwood lumber, softwood plywood, pulp, and paper and paperboard. Also shown is their ranking in the 1977 "*Fortune* Directory of the 500 Largest Industrial Corporations." Every one of these firms manufactures each of the principal primary wood products. Five of them were among the ten largest lumber producers in 1977, five were among the ten largest manufacturers of softwood plywood, eight were among the ten largest manufacturers of pulp, and nine were among the ten largest manufacturers of paper and paperboard.

Vertical Integration

Vertical integration refers to the situation in which a firm operates in successive stages of production of a particular product. A lumber manufacturing firm which grows and cuts its own timber is vertically integrated. Three stages of production are involved: growing the timber, harvesting it, and processing it into lumber.

Cost reduction is one reason that firms integrate vertically. Savings associated with a vertically integrated pulp and paper mill have already been noted. Vertical integration may also give firms greater control over their economic environment. For example, vertical integration upstream (raw materials) may assure supplies at relatively stable prices, but vertical integration downstream (manufacturing processes) may assure a market for products that is especially important during a time of weak demand.

Vertical integration also gives the firm an opportunity for disciplining nonvertically integrated rivals.

TABLE 8. Largest Ten Wood Products Manufacturers in Terms of Forestland Ownership and Their Ranking in the Production of Principal Primary Wood Products, 1977

1977 Fortune Ranking among Largest Industries[1]	Company	Domestic Forestlands (thousand acres)	Softwood Lumber[2]	Softwood Plywood[3]	Pulp[4]	Paper and Paperboard[4]
57	International Paper Company	7,203	13	10	1	1
74	Weyerhaeuser Company	5,865	1	5	2	6
56	Georgia-Pacific Corporation	3,900	3	1	8	13
129	St. Regis Paper Company	3,151	14	(1)[5]	4	2
68	Champion International Corporation	3,024	7	2	9	7
259	Great Northern Nekoosa Corporation	2,705	48	(1)[5]	10	9
107	Boise Cascade Corporation	2,608	6	3	6	5
168	Scott Paper Corporation	1,848	84	(0)[5]	15	10
108	Crown Zellerbach Corporation	1,702	5	(2)[5]	5	4
225	Union Camp Corporation	1,680	36	(1)[5]	11	8

1. Terms of assets.
2. Terms of lumber production in the United States and Canada, 1977.
3. Terms of domestic installed capacity, 1977.
4. Terms of installed capacity in the United States and Canada, 1977.
5. The number in parentheses is number of plants. Ranking is unknown.
SOURCE: "*Fortune* Directory of the 500 Largest Industrial Corporations," *Fortune*, May 8, 1978: 238–265; "Ownership of Timber: A Critical Component in Industrial Success," *Forest Industries*, Aug. 1978: 30–32; "The Top 100 Lumber Producers," *Forest Industries*, May 30, 1978: 13; "Directory of Panel Plants, USA," *Forest Industries*, Mar. 1978: 106–130; "Financial and Production-Capacity Data for 76 Leading U.S./Canadian Companies," *Pulp and Paper*, June 30, 1978: 69–94.

When the latter firms are effectively precluded from alternative sources of supply of an essential raw material and the integrated firm raises the price of that raw material, the nonintegrated firms are subjected to a "price squeeze." This pressure becomes especially onerous during periods of low profit margins for the finished product.

Vertical integration is common among large firms in the principal wood products industries, and especially among the very large firms, as shown by their forestland holdings in Table 8. Acreages of lands under long-term lease and lands on which cutting rights are held are not included in the table; hence, lands under the control of the listed firms are understated.

The very large firms are also vertically integrated downstream from their operations producing primary wood products. For example, Boise Cascade, Champion International, Georgia-Pacific, and Weyerhaeuser each have extensive operations in wholesale building materials distribution. Furthermore, all of the firms listed in Table 8 are engaged in either paper or paperboard converting. In fact, all but three are engaged in both. Finally, Boise Cascade, Crown Zellerbach, and Great Northern Nekoosa each have a large network of facilities engaged in wholesale paper distribution. Much of the diversification and vertical integration in the principal wood products industries is the result of a large pervasive merger movement that began in these industries in the mid-1950s.

Structure of Timber Markets

Discussion of the structure of the principal wood products industries has been limited thus far to the structure of their respective product markets. For completeness, the structure of timber markets must be included. Of course, timber is the essential raw material in the manufacture of primary wood products. Three elements are pertinent: buyer concentration, barriers to entry, and vertical integration.

Timber has a low value per unit of weight, and hence, transporting it long distances is prohibitively expensive. Consequently, markets for timber are not as geographically broad as markets for primary wood products. Timber markets are local in nature, but markets for the principal wood products are regional or national.

Because timber markets are comparatively narrow, the number of buyers tend to be few. Expressed differently, since timber markets are geographically circumscribed, buyer concentration is typically high. Occasionally, seller concentration is also high. Markets with high seller concentration often occur in the West, where the federal government is a principal seller of timber and, in some places, virtually the only seller. Of course, the behavior of timber-selling agencies of the federal government, the FOREST SERVICE and the BUREAU OF LAND MANAGEMENT, is distinctly different from that of private enterprises. The former are motivated to meet their statutory obligations, the latter to earn profit.

When buyer concentration is high, firms can scarcely avoid recognizing their mutual interdependence. Decision making characteristically takes into account the likely effects of a proposed action upon competitors. Economic theory suggests that explicit and implicit agreements among competitors are likely; indeed, they have occurred. Theory also suggests that these agreements are subject to frequent breakdown, followed by a period of very destructive competition. Evidence of such breakdowns is ample.

It has already been pointed out that purchasing an adequate supply of timber at competitive prices is a significant barrier to entry in the wood products industries. Entry into a given timber market is difficult because existing firms recognize that the ultimate effect of a new entrant is higher timber prices and a destabilized market. It is to their advantage, then, to discourage potential entrants. One way established firms can do this is by paying entry-forestalling prices, that is, prices that are higher than necessary to attract adequate timber supplies. If a potential entrant actually does enter the market, the established firms can ensure, through competitive bidding, for example, that the new entrant does not purchase timber at a price at which profitable operation is possible over a sustained period of time.

The behavior of firms in timber markets is also affected by the common occurrence of vertically integrated firms. As noted before, a vertically integrated firm has some control over its economic environment. For example, a buyer who can supply part of his timber requirements from inventories on his own forestland can afford to be more selective in his timber purchases. If the price of a given sale is too high, he can pass it up and process his own timber instead. In contrast, the nonvertically integrated buyer who wishes to operate may be forced to buy timber at any price that allows covering his variable costs.

Summary

With the exception of the softwood lumber industry, the principal wood products industries are oligopolistic in structure, that is, a small number of firms account for a large proportion of production. The dominant firms are large, vertically integrated national corporations, which, with few exceptions, are diversified into all five of the principal wood products industries, including specifically the softwood lumber industry.

Timber is the critical raw material in the manufacture of wood products. Timber markets are comparatively local in their geographical reach and oligopsonistic in structure. That is, the number of buyers is small and their market actions are interdependent. The presence of vertically integrated firms is common.

Barriers to entry in timber markets range from moderate to high, and it is for this reason that entry into the softwood lumber and plywood industries is said to range from moderate to high. Two additional entry barriers exist for the pulp, paper, and paperboard industries, and the cumulative effect is that entry into these industries is effectively impeded. Therefore, the structure of the wood products industries is significantly different from the structure assumed in the competitive model of economic theory. Effective policy decisions must take this fact into account.

FURTHER READING: Paul V. Ellefson and Michael E. Chapp, *Systematic Analysis of the Wood-Based Industry* (1978). John A. Guthrie, *An Economic Analysis of the Pulp and Paper Industry* (1972). Lloyd C. Irland, "Do Giants Control Timber-Based Industries in North America?" *Forest Industries* 103 (June 1976): 40-41. Dennis C. LeMaster, *Mergers among the Largest Forest Products Firms, 1950–1970* (1977). Walter J. Mead, *Competition and Oligopsony in the Douglas-fir Lumber Industry* (1966). F. M. Scherer, *Industrial Market Structure and Economic Performance* (1979).

DENNIS C. LeMASTER

FOREST INFLUENCES

The effects of forests upon soil water, runoff, erosion, streamflow, flood, and climate are collectively called forest influences. Forest hydrology, which strictly applied deals only with water in the forest, is sometimes used loosely as a synonym. Forest influences have been recognized in Europe at least since the Middle Ages. Russian edicts to protect land from abuse and thus degrading influences date from the eleventh century. French forests have been subject to such regulation since 1215. In America, the first evidence of concern seems to be Massachusetts local ordinances passed in 1739 and later to protect a shoreline from shifting sand that buried pasture grass, the origin of the dune movement beginning with the harvest of the trees just inland.

Some eighteenth- and nineteenth-century observers believed that extensive clearing of timber affected climate. In the South, the relation of timber removal to malarial infection was so strongly presumed that settler migration routes were affected. Because of malaria (literally, "bad air"), settlers along the Atlantic and Gulf coasts were urged to settle on dry, airy ridges. Some attributed the disease to "vegetable putrefaction," which occurred most rapidly while forests were being cleared. Safety lay in dense, cool, uncut woods, for there pools of water were kept cool by sun-shading tree canopies. Completely clearing the land of trees to hasten drying of the pools also reduced the spread of infection, or so it was thought.

The attention of the federal government was drawn to the changing water flow brought about by forest removal in an 1849 report of the Patent Office (which then carried on the government's agricultural services). George Perkins MARSH's seminal study, *Man and Nature; Or, the Earth as Modified by Human Action* (1864), influenced governmental as well as popular opinion, and the GENERAL LAND OFFICE began advocating tree planting by homesteaders for the amelioration of the climate on the Great Plains. Congress responded by passing the Timber Culture Act of 1873. In 1876, $2,000 was allotted to study the forest situation at home and abroad and to make recommendations. The resulting report, by Franklin B. HOUGH, stressed "the connection between forests and climate." Cutting the forests was alleged to alter climate.

This emphasis on forest–climate relationships, taken up by the Bureau of Forestry and its successor, the FOREST SERVICE, generated considerable controversy within the government. The opposition was promoted by the GEOLOGICAL SURVEY, the Weather Bureau, and the ARMY CORPS OF ENGINEERS. Neither position could be proven; however, the effect of timber cutting upon soil water and upon soil and water separately could be shown, and from this time on, the subject of forest influences has been mostly concerned with hydrologic rather than climatic aspects. There is one notable exception: Russian hydrologists in the 1960s reported that precipitation increases under a cover of forest.

Massachusetts in 1882 apparently became the first state authorized to acquire land for watershed protection. Then, by an act of March 3, 1891, the U. S. Congress authorized the president to begin setting aside lands from the public domain, in part for a similar reason. The FOREST MANAGEMENT ACT of June 4, 1897, stated as a purpose of such reservations the "securing [of] favorable conditions of water flows." Soon the General Land Office's *Forest Reserve Manual* (1902) outlined how forests regulate the flow of water. Dense, vigorous stands of young trees were believed most advantageous.

Eventually the Forest Service undertook research to prove its assertions about the influences of the forest or its removal upon water flow. At Wagon Wheel Gap in southern Colorado about 1910, watersheds were marked out, cutting practices assigned to the watersheds, and the effects upon streamflow measured. As the slow growth of trees at that high elevation and the low precipitation in the growing season made data collection futile, the project was abandoned in 1926. Sixty years later an observer could locate the photographic points and, with old pictures in hand, note little change in vegetation.

No agreement was reached, even within government, over the relationship between forests and streamflow. Nevertheless, as land degradation attributed to overcutting worsened, Congress passed the WEEKS ACT in 1911 to permit additions to the national forest system "for the purpose of preserving the navigability of navigable streams." A year later, Raphael ZON summarized in the National Waterways Commission *Final Report* the scientific arguments for relating water production to forest protection (1912).

Even without the results of formal research, evidence was abundant that land degradation and the silting of rivers followed timber harvests and subsequent cultivation of cutover land. River siltation clogged shipping channels, important ports closed, and local economies suffered. Rivers, once the most important and least costly roads of commerce, were replaced by rails, not only because of economics but sometimes because of siltation.

Despite the inconclusive results of the Wagon Wheel Gap experiment, Forest Service experiment stations undertook forest influences research in the San Dimas watershed of the San Gabriel Mountains of California in 1933, at the Coweeta Hydrologic Laboratory in the southern Appalachians in 1934, and near Fraser, Colorado, in the Rocky Mountains in 1943. In the 1950s studies were under way at Hubbard Brook in New Hampshire's White Mountains; in the Poconos of Pennsylvania; and at Parsons, West Virginia, and Oxford, Mississippi. By the 1950s other government installations, universities, and industry were also involved in investigations of the influence of forests upon waters. The principal concern of these research groups is now to determine how to manipulate the vegetation to optimize production of water that is clear (free of sediment) and clean (free of microbes) for human consumption and industrial use.

Rapid infiltration of rain and snowmelt into the soil retards runoff and erosion and increases the amount of water recharging underground aquifers. Observers have long noted the relationships of tree species covering the land to rates of infiltration. For the development of a porous mull humus soil layer, eastern redcedar is greatly superior to red pine, and oaks are superior to southern pine. But any tree species is better than most forbs and any cover is better than a cultivated field.

These observations, and the publicity given to forest–watershed relationships, led to cities acquiring land on which to grow trees in order to improve the quantity and quality of water. The water company lands of New Haven, Connecticut, were early entrusted to the Yale School of Forestry to manage. Waynesboro, North Carolina, and Vancouver, British Columbia, own and manage watershed forests.

Federal involvement in the conservation of soil and water was furthered with the authorization of ten erosion experiment stations in 1930, the establishment of the Soil Erosion Service in the DEPARTMENT OF THE INTERIOR in 1933 (it later became the Soil Conservation Service of the DEPARTMENT OF AGRICULTURE), and the initiation of the Prairie States Forestry Project in 1934. Whereas the Soil Conservation Service encouraged tree planting to reduce erosion caused by rain, the shelterbelt program of the Prairie States Forestry Project was to reduce erosion caused by wind in those droughty, dust-bowl days. SHELTERBELTS, installed by the Forest Service on 30,000 farms from North Dakota to Texas from 1935 through 1942, were closely akin to the windbreak efforts of the Soil Conservation Service. Congress reaffirmed the importance of national forests for watershed protection when it passed the MULTIPLE USE-SUSTAINED YIELD ACT in 1960. Even so, appropriations and administrative concern for this function remained appreciably less than for other uses.

Although studies of the effects of forest upon rainfall, as a part of climate, have not been much further advanced than when Hough prepared his report in 1877, radiant energy aspects gained attention in the twentieth century with studies of the effects of the presence of forests of various kinds on summer evaporation, growing season transpiration, and winter snowmelt. Other recent concerns involving forest influences have emphasized drainage-basin morphology, vegetation control, windbreak removal for agricultural pursuits, microclimate, sewage disposal, the replenishing of the atmosphere with oxygen, and the effects of harvesting techniques upon water infiltration and runoff.

FURTHER READING: Wilmon H. Droze, *Trees, Prairies, and People* (1977). Joseph Kittredge, *Forest Influences* (1948). Ashley L. Schiff, *Fire and Water: Scientific Heresy in the Forest Service* (1962). United Nations Food and Agriculture Organization, *Forest Influences* (1962).

LAURENCE C. WALKER

FOREST INVENTORY AND VALUATION PRACTICES

At the close of the Revolutionary War, a committee that included Thomas Jefferson conceived the idea of dividing the vast wilderness of the West into thirty-six-square-mile townships and one-square-mile sections. Heavily in debt, the new nation had enacted the Land Ordinance of 1785 "for ascertaining the mode of disposition of Lands in the Western Territory." Surveys were executed by deputy surveyors operating under negotiated contracts, which included establishing section and quarter-section corners at half-mile intervals along north–south and east–west lines spaced one mile apart. Corners were set using wood stakes and other native materials, and the species and diameter of several "witness" trees at each corner were recorded in notebooks. These surveyors' notes, which also include descriptions of the vegetation and topography encountered along the lines, are the earliest records that systematically describe the presettlement forests of the United States. They are, however, far too sketchy to provide any idea of the volume or value of the timber in these forests.

During the 1800s, as the virgin forests began to fall under the lumberman's ax and sawmills spread across the countrysides of a growing nation, there was little if any interest in measuring the apparently limitless forests. Buyers and sellers of timber were much more concerned about the accurate measurement or scaling of the board-foot contents of logs. The board foot is a unit of sawn lumber equivalent to a plank one foot long, one foot wide, and one inch thick, and it became the custom to sell logs according to an estimate of the board feet of lumber they would yield in the mill. Estimates must take into account the portions of a log lost to saw kerf (the saw cuts between the boards) and slabs (the rounded edges of the log). By 1900, over forty log rules had been devised for obtaining board-foot estimates from measurements of the length of a log and the diameter, inside bark, of the small end. Most of these early log rules were very inaccurate, but two of them, the Doyle and the Scribner, achieved widespread acceptance.

In 1906, Judson Clark published his International Log Rule. He had been bothered by the inconsistent and radically different estimates that he obtained from the Doyle and Scribner rules. He concluded that these

Scaler measures diameter inside of bark. This dimension and log length are the two most important variables used to determine volume. American Forest Institute Photo.

rules grossly underestimated volume of long logs, because they did not take taper into account. The International Rule's allowance for taper and various kerfs makes it the most consistent rule yet devised, but the Doyle and Scribner continue to be used in many parts of the country.

The first estimates of the volume of standing timber in the United States were obtained by Charles S. SARGENT for the 1880 Census and were published in his *Report on the Forests of North America (Exclusive of Mexico)* (1884). His estimates were based primarily on the statements of timberland owners and state land agents. Few areas were actually surveyed. The total volume estimate of 856 billion board feet did not include important western species such as Douglas-fir and ponderosa pine, and it was far too low even for the species considered, as was revealed by later estimates.

The 1890s saw the beginning of scientific forest management in the United States. One of the first intensive inventories of a forest property, for the purpose of developing a management plan, was conducted by Carl A. SCHENCK in 1898 on the Pisgah Forest in

North Carolina. Schenck's inventory recorded the species, diameter, number of logs, and board foot contents of all trees having a diameter of eighteen inches or more. The woodsmen and rangers who assisted Schenck would tap each tree with their ax; a hollow sound indicated interior rot. Watching this, Schenck got the idea of making marks on the ax handles, so that the men could hold the ax horizontally against the tree and read directly from the handle the exact diameter of the tree. This idea led to Schenck's invention of the Biltmore stick (named after the Biltmore Forest, where Schenck worked as a forester), a widely used instrument for measuring tree diameters.

Periodic inventory of the volume of timber on a forest property is fundamental to management practices aimed at sustaining the yield of products from the forest. Unfortunately, the direct measurement of the volume of standing trees is a difficult and time-consuming task because of their irregular form, which varies with species, age, and locality. The latter half of the nineteenth century witnessed much research in the construction of volume tables for European tree species. These tables give the average volumes of trees of various species according to their diameter at breast height (in the United States, four and one-half feet above the base of the tree) and height, usually measured in sixteen-foot logs. When a volume table is available for a given species and locality, the forester or timber cruiser simply measures the diameter and height of a tree and looks up the average volume in the table. By 1903, very little had been done in the way of developing volume tables for the American species. Aside from some measurements on the Adirondack spruce and white pine, little was known of the average form and volume of the stems of the varied American silva. Foresters in the United States would have to wait many years before reliable source tables would be available for use in their forests.

The young forester of the early 1900s had to make do without tree volume tables, yet he usually lacked the experience of the lumberman in estimating timber by judgment. Unfortunately, the credibility of the forester and the value of his recommendations were often judged according to his skill as a timber cruiser. If he could closely approximate the volume of a stand of timber as known to the lumberman, his case was nine-tenths won. Many foresters devised "rules of thumb" to cover up for their inexperience. The "average log" rule would occasionally give acceptable results. According to this rule, the board-foot contents of the average log in a tree could be obtained by subtracting sixty from the square of the middle diameter and multiplying the result by eight-tenths. The volume of the tree could then be calculated by multiplying the average log volume by the number of sixteen-foot logs in the tree.

The timber cruiser often worked alone, carrying a staff compass, a Jacob's staff to support his compass, an aneroid barometer for measuring elevations, and a hand counter for counting paces. Starting from a known section corner and getting his direction from the compass and distances by pacing, the cruiser walked through a three-mile row of outer forty-acre blocks, tying in at each mile with a section corner. He then turned around and came back through the center of the adjacent row of forty-acre blocks. This resulted in six miles of cruise line and one and one-half square miles for the day. In each "forty," the cruiser estimated the timber volume on one or more sample acres by counting the number of sixteen-foot logs, estimating the average number of logs required to make a thousand board feet, and dividing the count by this ratio to get the number of thousand board feet for the sample area. The cruiser also made sketches to show natural features, forest type boundaries, and topography in each "forty."

Fieldwork demanded both innovation and stamina. The logistics of supplying isolated camps required careful planning lest the men had to do without certain food items or equipment. Traversing rugged terrain was arduous and being outdoors regardless of weather taxed constitutions. There were dangers, too, and even minor injuries remote from doctors could become serious.

By 1920, there had been no less than ten separate attempts to estimate the volume of standing timber in the United States. Most of these estimates proved to be grossly inaccurate and far too low. One reason for mistaken estimates was the tendency of private timber holders, who accounted for about 80 percent of the nation's timber, to understate either the acreage or the volume of timber belonging to them. This tendency was probably due to competitive considerations and the desire to avoid heavy taxation. The estimates of publicly owned timber may have been less biased,

With this hand-held level, calibrated to measure slope, the timber cruiser can determine heights of trees and also gather data essential for mapping and road location. Weyerhaeuser Company Photo.

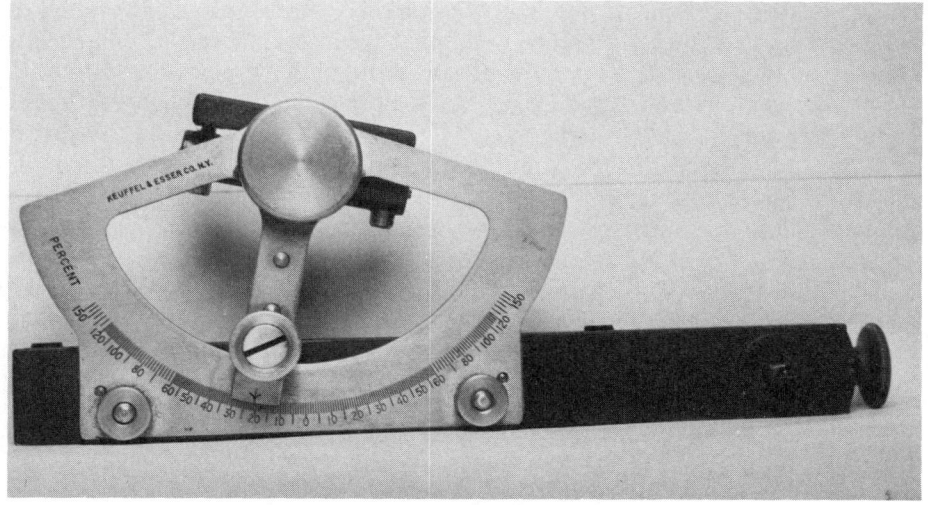

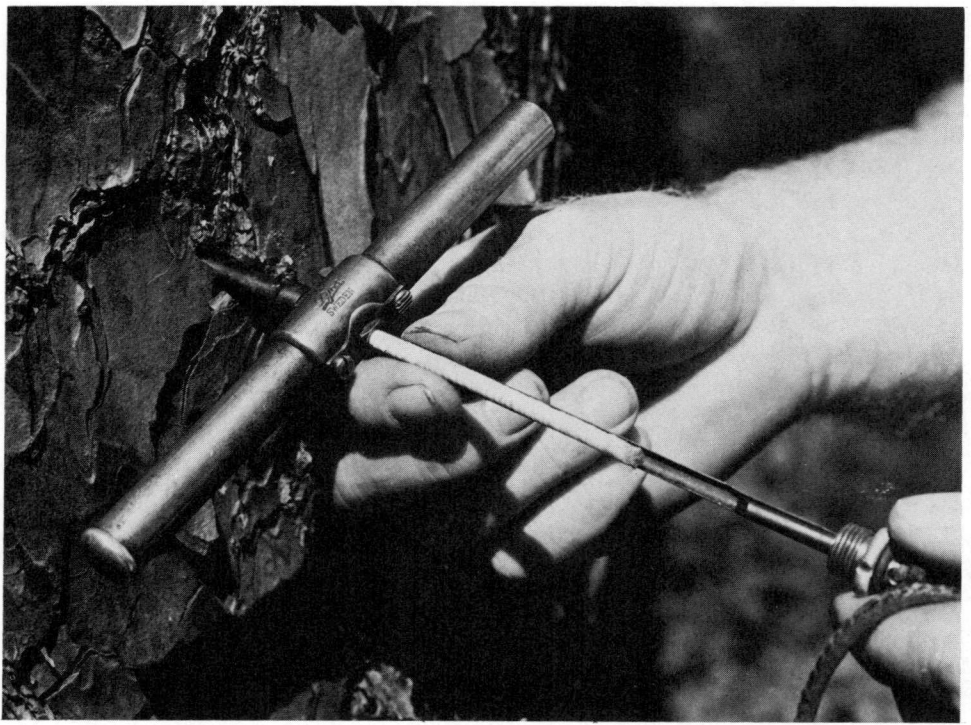

Forester pulls core out of an increment borer. The number of annual rings determines a tree's age and their spacing shows its rate of growth. The sample also reveals hidden rot or other defects. American Forest Institute Photo.

but they were based primarily on judgment and lacked scientific accuracy. Only a part of the estimate for national forest timber was based on thorough cruises.

On all ownerships, inaccuracy also stemmed from the practice of ignoring species that were of little commercial value or trees too small for milling. Thus, when small trees grew large enough to be counted or new markets pulled species onto the commercial list, earlier estimates were quickly proven to be low.

The Capper Report of 1920 gave a total volume estimate of 2,215 billion board feet of timber in the United States but pointed out that "thoroughly reliable data on such subjects as the remaining stand of timber . . . can be obtained only by a thorough-going timber survey. . . . Nothing of this character has ever been attempted in the United States."

In 1928, the first systematic and continuous inventory of the forest resources of the United States was made possible by the MCSWEENEY-MCNARY ACT. The project was assigned to the U. S. FOREST SERVICE with authorization to cooperate with state and private agencies. The objectives of the Forest Survey, as it came to be known, were (1) to make an inventory of the forestlands and the present supplies of standing timber and other forest products; (2) to ascertain the rate of growth of the forest stands; (3) to determine the rate of drain on the forests through industrial use and the ef-

fects of tree diseases, insects, and other natural agencies; and (4) to study the probable future requirements for timber and other forest products.

The Forest Survey was launched in the Pacific Northwest during the summer of 1930. To save time and money, it was decided to use the "compilation" method wherever possible. Under this method, existing data were assembled from private, county, state, and GENERAL LAND OFFICE timber cruises. These cruises were then checked by survey personnel to adjust them to the standards of the survey. Areas not covered adequately by existing data were blocked by forest type and condition. Field crews determined type boundaries by working along trails, using high points, and by a certain amount of cross-sectioning. Within each forest type, the crews measured the volume of timber on a number of well-scattered sample plots, either one-quarter-acre circles or one-acre rectangles. Based on these sample plots, an average volume per acre was applied to the type. Statistical studies, conducted by forest research scientists, had demonstrated that a few, carefully measured sample plots could provide more efficient estimates of timber volume than the long strip cruises. Forest scientists had also recently learned how to use statistical formulas to determine the exact number of plots required to obtain estimates within a specified margin of error.

In the South, the Forest Survey was initiated by the Southern Forest Experiment Station in January 1931. A 10 percent margin of error was considered to be the maximum permissible for items of major importance. Field data were gathered by foresters and expert timber estimators working in three-man crews on parallel compass lines ten miles apart. Along each line, one-quarter-acre sample plots were measured at ten-chain (660 feet) intervals. The plots were taken where they fell, some on forestland, some on agricultural areas, waterways, roads, and other nonforestlands. In this way, the proportional area of land in each category could be estimated from the systematic spacing of the plots. On each plot that fell on forestland, a count was made of the number of trees by species and two-inch diameter classes. The electrical sorting and tabulating machines, which were used for compiling and summarizing the field data, represent one of the first applications of automatic data processing for forest inventory.

While working on the Forest Survey in the South in 1933, James Girard devised a method of making tree volume tables that greatly increased their usefulness in the United States. Because of the widespread variation in tree form and volume, most volume tables were reliable only for certain species in a given locality. Girard's tables are based on the ratio of the diameter inside bark at the top of the first sixteen-foot log and the diameter at breast height. Once this average form class is determined for a stand of timber, Girard's tables can be used to obtain not only the volume of a tree but also the volume of each log in a tree. Thus, volumes by log grade can be estimated. Girard Form Class Volume Tables have been used in many forest types throughout the United States.

Beginning in the early 1930s, aerial photographs for much of the United States were made available by the Agricultural Adjustment Administration and other public and private agencies. However, these photos were seldom used for forest inventory until after World War II. During the war, many sophisticated instruments and procedures were developed for military applications of aerial photography. After the war, foresters who had received this training in the military quickly realized its usefulness in forest inventory work.

The Forest Survey in the Central States, initiated in July 1946, was well adapted to an aerial survey procedure, because much of the forest area is found in thousands of small, scattered farm woodlands, forming a checkerboard pattern throughout the region. Transparent dot grids were placed over each photo in a given county, and every fifth dot which fell

on a forested area was examined under a stereoscope (a device for three-dimensional viewing of aerial photos). Trained photo interpreters classified the area under each of these dots according to stand size and topographic site class. The forest area in each of these classes could then be determined by multiplying the total forest area by the proportion of forest dots falling in each class. A percentage of the forest photo dots were selected at random for field examination and timber volume measurement. The use of aerial photos in this manner greatly reduces the amount of field data that must be collected, thus reducing the overall cost of the forest inventory.

A rapid and ingenious method of estimating timber volume and related figures was devised in 1948 by the German forester Walter Bitterlich. However, it was generally overlooked in the United States until introduced by Lewis Grosenbaugh in a 1952 article in the *Journal of Forestry*. The method does not require the use of plots or strips of any kind: hence, it has been referred to as "plotless cruising." The cruiser views the diameter of every tree visible from a set of points selected in the forest. He then counts the number of trees appearing larger than a simple hand-held angle gauge. Dividing this count by the number of points and multiplying by a constant factor yield an estimate of the average volume of timber per acre. In 1955, David Bruce told the readers of the *Journal of Forestry* about a wedge-shaped prism that was a handy angle gauge for using Bitterlich's method. The prism became popular, and many foresters began referring to the method of "prism cruising." Whatever the nomenclature, Bitterlich's method has swept the United States and has significantly reduced the cost of many forest inventories.

High-speed digital computers arrived during the late 1950s, and foresters wasted little time adapting these powerful tools to their forest inventory data processing requirements. Development of a computer program for use in the Forest Survey began at the Northeastern Forest Experiment Station in the fall of 1961. The program was designed to compute the standard tables required of the Forest Survey and print them in a format suitable for publication. The final program was made as flexible as possible to accommodate different inventory objectives, methods of sampling, and required summary tables.

By 1970, all of the forests in the United States had been surveyed. Detailed statistics on timber volumes, growth, and depletion are available and are continuously updated for each state. Because of cooperative assistance contributed by forest industries, state forestry divisions, and other public agencies, the sampling errors achieved by the Forest Survey are much lower than the 10 percent maximum. As of 1977, the total volume of standing sawtimber in the United States (including Alaska and Hawaii) was estimated to be 2,569 billion board feet, International Log Rule.

FURTHER READING: Thomas Avery, *Natural Resources Measurements* (2nd ed., 1975). David Bruce, "A New Way to Look at Trees." *Journal of Forestry* 53 (Mar. 1955): 163–167. Donald Bruce and Francis Schumacher, *Forest Mensuration* (1935). Bertram Husch, Charles Miller, and Thomas Beers, *Forest Mensuration* (2nd ed., 1972).

GEORGE L. MARTIN, JR.

FOREST MANAGEMENT ACT OF 1897

On June 4, 1897, following six years of debate, Congress adopted an amendment to the Sundry Civil Appropriations Act that has been called the Forest Lieu Act, the Pettigrew Act, and most recently, the Organic Act. Generally, this law is known as the Forest Management Act. The act determined the basic purposes of the national forest system and did not have important revisions until Congress passed the MULTIPLE USE-SUSTAINED YIELD ACT in 1960.

The act contains several key clauses. "No public forest reservation shall be established, except to improve and protect the forest within the reservation, or for the purpose of securing favorable conditions of water flows, and to furnish a continuous supply of timber . . . ." Timber and water resources are among the several included in the Multiple Use-Sustained Yield Act, but until 1960, even though the U. S. FOREST SERVICE has interpreted its discretion broadly, these two resources were the only ones with official sanction.

The act authorized logging on the reserves. The timber was to be sold at or above appraised value and the operation supervised. "Dead, matured, or large growth trees" could be "marked and designated" for sale. This latter clause was instrumental to the so-called Monongahela case, a federal court decision in 1973 that made clearcutting illegal in the region under that court's jurisdiction. One of the most vigorous conservation conflicts of the century ensued, which was ultimately resolved by passage of the NATIONAL FOREST MANAGEMENT ACT of 1976.

Perhaps the most infamous sections of any public land law—lieu selection—was included in the Forest Management Act. Repealed in 1905, this section allowed land claims within a newly designated forest reserve to be exchanged for public land elsewhere. Although enacted in a mood of compassion for settlers who suddenly found themselves stranded in the midst of a vast, federal preserve, the lieu selection clause was ripe for abuse. It could be argued that these abuses did not exceed other abuses of land laws, but within seven years Congress had been convinced that the clause was a mistake, and repeal followed.

FURTHER READING: Harold K. Steen, *The U. S. Forest Service: A History* (1976).

FOREST OWNERSHIP

In the pattern of the more highly developed noncommunist countries, three-fourths of commercial timberland and five-eighths of all forestland in the United States is privately owned. All of this area was originally held by colonial, state, or federal governments. The development of present patterns of ownership can be traced to government land policies and subsequent private transfers.

Evolution of Forestland Ownership

When Europeans first came to what is now the United States, forests covered more than a third again as much land as today. Nearly one-half of the country was forest, extending over most of the East, the mountains and highlands of the West, and the Pacific Coast. The forest had already been noticeably altered by its Indian inhabitants, but these modifications paled to insignificance compared to those the newcomers made. Over the next three centuries, some 300 million acres were

TABLE 1. Federal Land Disposals, 1781–1980

		Million Acres
Cash sales and miscellaneous		303.5
Homesteads		287.5
Grants to states		328.4
Schools	77.6	
Swamplands	64.9	
Railroads	37.1	
Institutions	21.7	
Canals and river improvements	6.1	
Wagon roads	3.4	
Unclassified (mostly Alaska)	117.6	
Railroads		94.4
Military bounties		61.0
Private land claims		34.0
Timber and Stone entries		13.9
Timber culture		10.9
Desert land entries		10.7
Total		1,144.3

TABLE 2. Ownership of Commercial Forestland, 1977

	United States		North		South		Pacific		Mountain	
	1,000 acres	%	1,000 acres	%	1,000 acres	%	1,000 acres	%	1,000 acres	%
Public	136,602	28.0	31,318	18.3	17,742	9.4	44,374	62.7	43,167	74.7
Federal	105,744	21.7	12,244	7.2	14,485	7.7	38,125	53.9	40,890	70.8
State	23,642	4.8	13,129	7.7	2,519	1.3	5,791	8.2	2,203	3.8
Local	7,216	1.5	5,945	3.5	738	.4	458	.6	75	.1
Private	351,124	72.0	139,451	81.7	170,691	90.6	26,384	37.3	14,598	25.3
Forest Industries	67,976	13.9	17,777	10.4	35,754	19.0	12,349	17.5	2,096	3.6
Farms	116,785	23.9	45,384	26.6	57,217	30.4	5,872	8.3	8,311	14.4
Other	166,364	34.1	76,290	44.7	77,720	41.2	8,163	11.5	4,191	7.3
Total	487,726		170,769		188,433		70,758		57,765	

cleared, chiefly for farms, and most of the remaining forests, one-third of the nation's land area, were cut over one or more times. Standing sawtimber was reduced from perhaps 12.5 trillion board feet to 2.5 trillion.

Forests were felled both because wood was in demand and because they stood in the way of transportation, agriculture, and town building. The greater profits in land use came from crops, cattle, and commerce, not from timber. Consequently, Americans destroyed enormous quantities of growing timber while utilizing relatively little.

Most forestlands passed into private ownership for farms. Forest industries did seek out accessible, marketable softwood timber especially, but historically they owned little of the land they harvested, more often buying logs or stumpage or, particularly in the early years, cutting timber freely from vacant public and private land, the forest "commons." Later values —conservation, watershed protection, RECREATION, and wilderness appreciation—led to reservation of the remaining public forestlands, which contain most of the old-growth timber still left.

Colonial and State Land Disposition

One-third of all land in the United States was at one time owned by colonial or state governments. European sovereigns claimed title in fee simple to all lands in the New World by right of discovery or conquest. Both colonial and, later, American laws recognized Indian occupancy, and governments generally took care to buy out Indian claims.

Almost all land in the thirteen English colonies and the eighteen states carved from them was forested, and the great bulk of it was disposed of for farming. (Half of the commercial timberland in these states was still in farms in 1953.) In the middle and southern colonies the principal method of land disposal in the seventeenth century was the headright system. To induce immigration, stipulated amounts of land varying in time and place from fifty to several hundred acres were granted to anyone transporting himself or other persons to the New World. By the eighteenth century, sales replaced grants as the principal means of land disposition, including large tracts wholesaled to promoters and land companies.

New England colonial governments granted land in six-mile-square townships to groups of town proprietors, who in turn assigned or later sold lots to settlers. Much land in the Massachusetts province of Maine was granted and sold in large blocks to lumbermen and speculators. Even in heavily forested New England, which was poorly endowed for agriculture, most land went for farms. Over 90 percent of the colonial population lived by farming, much of it subsistence. Later, farming was abandoned on marginal lands as owners turned to other livelihoods, and cleared land frequently reverted to forest. Today in New England less than 8 percent of commercial forestland is on farms, but 54 percent is in private ownership other than farms and forest industries, most of it uncleared or regenerated forests on former farms.

Of the former colonies, only in upper New England have forest industries acquired a substantial portion of commercial timberlands (in 1977 nearly two-fifths; in Maine, one-half). Although sawmills were everywhere in the colonies and lumber and NAVAL STORES were important colonial exports, the white pine of upper New York and New England was especially in demand and supplied a flourishing New England SHIPBUILDING industry. There were few restrictions on cutting from government lands—one being the reservation of ship mast timbers for the Royal Navy; see BRITISH COLONIAL FOREST POLICIES—and these were largely ignored. Loggers and millmen did acquire some land to insure timber supplies, particularly as settlement advanced and the public lands were taken up. This area remained the nation's principal lumbering region until the 1850s. The coming of railroad transportation greatly stimulated lumbering and settlement, and the forests were largely cut over by 1900. Logged-off lands were sometimes resold for other uses or defaulted to state and local governments for tax delinquencies. Large areas were acquired for national and state forests. Spruce-fir forests and rehabilitated pinelands are increasingly being managed especially for pulpwood production.

Large areas of land in the colonies, especially in the western portions, were still unalienated when the Revolution broke out, and each state confiscated the remaining crown and proprietary lands, along with the properties of Loyalists, and passed laws for their disposition similar to colonial policies. Following the late colonial emphasis on revenue, most state lands were sold, including large tracts to western land companies. But lands were also granted free to frontier settlers, and large numbers of military bounty land warrants were issued to induce enlistments and reward veterans of the War for Independence. Again following colonial precedents, rights of squatters were widely recognized and lands were granted for support of schools and other public purposes. The new states gradually passed laws against timber trespass, but enforcement was sporadic.

Most lands in these eighteen states (including five carved from the original thirteen—Vermont, Kentucky, Tennessee, Maine, and West Virginia) were alienated during the colonial period and the half-century after independence. By the Civil War only marginal lands remained, such as the 2 million acres of swamps and mountaintops in North Carolina.

One other state controlled disposal of lands within its boundaries. The Republic of Texas retained its public lands when it was admitted to the Union in 1845. Under the Spanish, Mexican, and republican governments, 68 million acres had been granted to colonists and contractors, and in 1850 the new state ceded its claims to 73 million acres east of the upper Rio Grande to the United States for $10 million. Of the remaining 152 million acres of Texas public lands, 8 million were alienated as preemptions, homesteads, and military bounties, 32 million were granted to railroads, over 55 million were sold, and 52 million were "appropriated" to schools, the University of Texas, and other public buildings and institutions. All the appropriated lands,

except for the 2.3 million-acre university grant and scattered school lands, were in time sold. Currently, income from the remaining state lands comes from mineral leases and royalties and from grazing rentals.

Nearly all the 38 million acres of east Texas forestlands passed to private ownership under the state's general land laws. About 300,000 acres of remaining timbered school lands were sold under special timber legislation after 1879. Less than one-third of Texas's forestland can produce commercial timber, virtually all of it being east Texas pinelands and nearly all of it privately owned. Forest industries hold almost a third of the state's commercial timberland. The state owns 30,000 acres, and 650,000 acres have been acquired by the federal government for national forests.

In contrast to the situation in Texas, the Republic of Hawaii had no remaining public lands when it was annexed as a territory in 1898. Outside of the first eighteen states and Texas and Hawaii, all other lands in the United States—some 1,856 million acres—became federal public domain. Because of the heavy indebtedness of the national government and a strong sentiment that the trans-Appalachian lands were a common patrimony won from Great Britain by all the states, the seven former colonies with land claims west of the Appalachians gradually ceded most of those lands to the national government over the years from 1781 to 1802. This original public domain of 225 million acres between the Appalachians and the Mississippi River grew as the nation obtained new territory in the nineteenth century. The Louisiana Purchase was acquired in 1803, the Red River basin in 1818, Florida in 1819, the Mexican Cession in 1848, western Texas in the Compromise of 1850, the Gadsden Purchase in 1853, and Alaska in 1867.

Some 40 to 50 million acres of these acquisitions, however, were claimed as private grants, purchases, or settlement rights from predecessor governments —Britain, France, Spain, and Mexico. About 34 million acres of these "private land claims" were ultimately confirmed by the United States; nearly two-thirds were Spanish and Mexican grants in the Southwest. Only in Louisiana, New Mexico, and California, where about 10 percent of the land area was alienated before American acquisition, were the land policies of predecessor governments of much significance.

Even in the public-land states, much land was owned by state governments and administered under their laws. Following colonial precedents, Congress donated 328 million acres—18 percent of the public domain—to states for public purposes. Largest was the grant of one section in each township, later increased to two and then four sections, for support of public schools. Smaller in acreage, but often more valuable because they could be selected anywhere, were a wide variety of grants for support of internal improvements, higher education, and public buildings and institutions. States also received grants to subsidize construction of roads, canals, railroads, and river improvements, and 65 million acres of swamp and overflowed lands were donated to fifteen states to be reclaimed. Florida alone acquired 20 million acres of swamplands and Louisiana 9.5 million, these two states in federal grants receiving respectively 69 percent and 39 percent of their land areas. Upon its admission in 1959, Alaska was simply granted a lump-sum quantity of 105 million acres—28 percent of its land area—for public purposes.

States in general followed the federal example in disposing of their lands rapidly and cheaply. Lands were put into market early, at low prices, with easy credit or long-term leases. In later enabling acts, Congress restricted leases and prescribed high minimum prices or sale at appraised values, and the new states themselves avoided some of the mistakes made by older states. Like the federal government, states in the twentieth century moved away from the policy of land disposal to one of reservation and management, especially of nonagricultural lands. Outside of Alaska, which had yet to select most of its lands, the states in 1980 owned 80 million acres, 52 million of them the remainder of their original grants, the rest retained by nonpublic-land states, acquired through tax delinquencies or purchased for special purposes. A fourth of this state land is commercial timberland. State lands are most common in the West, and leases, mineral royalties, and timber sales constitute the major source of income from them. Land sales are negligible.

Congress from 1850 to 1870 also granted lands directly to transcontinental and other railroads. These grants consisted of the right-of-way plus alternate sections in a band 10, 20, or 40 miles wide on each side of the railroad line. The railroads ultimately earned title to 94 million acres, largely after completion deadlines. Another 37 million acres were forfeited for failure to build lines. Land-grant railroads sometimes alienated Westerners by their disposal policies as well as by their tardiness in building, which tied up huge swaths of public land. But in general, the railroads sold their lands rapidly and reasonably, having as much interest in generating settlement and traffic as in maximizing revenues from land sales. Large tracts were sold to cattle and timber companies. Railroad land grants were the principal source of large timberland holdings in the Pacific Coast states. The U. S. Bureau of Corporations' three-volume study of *The Lumber Industry* found in 1910 that the Northern Pacific, Southern Pacific, and Weyerhaeuser Timber Company (which purchased 85 percent of its holdings from the railroads) held almost one-fourth of all privately owned merchantable timber in that region. By 1940 railroads had sold all but 16 million acres of their land grants, and much of the remainder was of marginal value except for the chance of mineral discovery.

Federal Land Disposition

One-third of the nation's land was alienated directly under federal cash sale or settlement laws. At first, federal land policy, like that of the states, was based largely on the making of sales, though large quantities of land were granted to soldiers and veterans of the nation's wars. After survey on the New England model, lands were offered to the highest bidder at public auction, and unsold lands were available for "private entry" at the minimum price. Land sales produced very little revenue for the government, however, except during the speculative booms of the mid-1830s and mid-1850s, and Congress gradually abandoned the revenue policy, at least toward agricultural lands, in favor of promoting settlement. By 1820 it had reduced the minimum price to $1.25 per acre and the minimum purchase to fifty, and later forty, acres. The Graduation Act of 1854 lowered the price of land, in proportion to the length of time it had been on the market, to as little as twelve and one half cents an acre after thirty years. After a long struggle and a series of special and limited preemption acts, Congress in 1841 recognized a right of settlers to purchase at the minimum price 160 acres on which they had established a claim prior to the auction.

The culmination of the settlement policy was the Homestead Act of 1862, which gave 160 acres to any head of household who lived on and farmed a claim for five years. An entrant could obtain title after only six (later eighteen) months by commuting the residency requirement to a cash payment of $1.25 per acre. In 1912 the residency requirement was reduced to three years.

Because of marginal precipitation in many areas of the West, 160 acres was insufficient for farming on much of the public domain remaining after the Civil War. Partly to make larger farms possible and partly to promote forestation on the tree-scarce prairies, Congress passed the Timber Culture Act in 1873, granting 160 acres of land in return for planting trees on a portion of it. The Desert Land Act of 1878 permitted the purchase of 640 acres at the minimum price if the buyer would irrigate it. Besides these measures, settlers used preemption and private entry to supplement homesteads or even instead of them, since purchase was often preferable to the long residence requirement of homesteading. In 1891, however, timber culture, preemption, and private entry were repealed and the Desert Land Act tightened up to prevent abuses. In recognition of the need for larger economic units on semiarid lands, Congress later relented and enlarged homestead entries to 320 acres in 1909 for dry farming and to 640 acres in 1916 for stock raising. As a consequence of all these factors and of homesteading of federal reclamation projects, the great era of homesteading came in the first quarter of the twentieth century, long after original passage of the act.

In the last third of the nineteenth century the federal government began to abandon the policy of indiscriminate disposal in favor of classifying public lands according to their best use and developing separate policies for each type of land. The policy of disposal, chiefly by homesteading, was retained ostensibly for arable lands, but in fact lands valuable chiefly for other resources were often homesteaded. Disposal was virtually completed by the 1930s. Forest, mineral, and grazing lands, formerly subject to disposition under the general land laws, after the Civil War were dispensed under separate laws or reserved for public management. Scenic, recreational, and wild lands were gradually identified and set aside as national parks and monuments, recreation areas, and wildlife refuges.

Federal Timberland Policies

Most of the central hardwood and southern pinelands of the public domain were alienated for farms before the Civil War under the general sales laws—public auction, private entry, and preemption—or under state and railroad land policies. Much of the hardwood region was cleared for agriculture and most of the forest remaining in the late twentieth century was second growth occupying about 20 percent of the land area, much of it still on farms. The Southern forests were less extensively cleared for agriculture, and the sandy-soiled longleaf pinelands near the Gulf were passed over for farming and not alienated until the 1880s and after.

Because the eastern forests covered potential farmlands, the federal government in its first century never devised a separate policy for timberlands. It did not even prohibit timber cutting on public lands until 1831, except for the reservation of live oak and redcedar for naval construction. But cutting by settlers and miners and even small-scale commercial lumbering for local markets was still tolerated, and weak enforcement failed to protect even the naval reserves.

In the 1850s, with the advance of settlement onto the treeless central prairies and the rapid rise of midwestern cities, New England loggers and millmen migrated to the Great Lakes pineries and shipped lumber along the rivers and lakes to this burgeoning new market. At the same time, the California gold rush sparked lumbering on Puget Sound and the rivers and coastal inlets of Oregon and northern California. Much of the cut came from the public lands, which, outside of Michigan and Wisconsin, were largely unsurveyed and/or unoffered. This large-scale commercial cutting for export led to the first serious though not altogether successful federal efforts to suppress timber trespass. Because of political pressures and extenuating circumstances, timber protection quickly evolved into quasi-legal timber sales, allowing the trespasser to pay stumpage so as to yield to the government the price of the land. But compromise was never consistent, and in the late 1870s the government initiated another crackdown on timber depredation that helped accelerate the alienation of timberlands.

Large tracts of timberlands near waterways had been bought up under private entry by millmen and timberland dealers in Michigan and Wisconsin in the 1850s and in all the Lake States and the Pacific Northwest in the next decade as large areas of surveyed timberlands were proclaimed for sale. These offerings were justified in part as the best solution to the problem of protection, but the resulting large private holdings, along with state and railroad grants, were often plundered as much as federal lands.

In the 1870s and 1880s, railroads, new technology, and growing population expanded lumbering and, along with stepped-up timber protection, stimulated timberland disposals. Federal timberlands were by then mostly unoffered and available only through the settlement laws. Many preemption and homestead entrymen found a ready market for patented claims, and many "dummy" entrymen acted directly in behalf of timber companies. In the five southern public-land states, Congress in 1876 lifted the post-Civil War restriction of remaining public lands to homesteading; in the 1880s both Northern and Southern lumbermen bought several million reoffered acres of the heaviest and best located stands of the longleaf pine lands that had been passed over for agriculture. However, Congress discontinued virtually all private-entry sales in 1889 and repealed preemption in 1891.

Land officials had long urged the sale of public

timber or timberlands in reasonable quantities at appraised prices, but Congress declined to do either. Instead, in 1878 it softened the trespass laws and allowed free timber cutting on mineral lands of the mountain states and territories. From 1891 to 1898 even cutting for lumber manufacture from any public lands was permitted if the product was not exported from the state. Also in 1878, Congress provided for sale of 160-acre tracts of unoffered timber or stone land for $2.50 an acre in Washington, Oregon, California, and Nevada. The Timber and Stone Act promoted the same kind of speculative, sometimes fraudulent, entries that often characterized homesteads and preemptions on valuable timberland, though all these measures tended more to diffuse ownership of commercial forestlands in small uneconomic tracts than to promote forest industry ownership.

Extended to all the public land states in 1892, the Timber and Stone Act was thereafter the principal means of acquiring nonagricultural forestlands. Sales were greatest in the early and late 1880s, the early 1890s, and especially the first decade of the twentieth century. Entries dropped off sharply after sale at appraised value was initiated in 1908. When the law was repealed in 1955, 13.9 million acres had been sold, three-fourths of it in the Pacific states and Minnesota and most of the rest in the northern Rockies.

Turn-of-the-century Timber and Stone sales, as well as state and railroad timberland sales, were stimulated by expanding markets and the depletion of the Great Lakes timber stands and, perhaps most important, by the rapid withdrawal of more than 160 million acres of western timberlands from the public domain as forest reserves. Authorized under a provision of the General Revision Act of 1891, presidential withdrawals in the next two decades competed with private acquisition for possession of the remaining public timberlands. In 1907 Congress rescinded the presidential authority to withdraw lands in the six western states of Oregon, Washington, Idaho, Montana, Colorado, and Wyoming. President Theodore ROOSEVELT responded by adding 16 million western acres to the national forests before signing the new law. When in 1910 Congress approved the presidential power to withdraw land for water and power development and other public purposes, it specifically repeated the ban on proclamation of national forests (as forest reserves were by then called) in the six western states. Although by this time nearly all American timberlands had been cut over, reserved, or alienated, Congress extended the prohibition on presidential withdrawal of additional lands for national forests to California in 1912 and to Arizona and New Mexico in 1926. Montana was exempted from the ban in 1939.

Adjustments were made, both before and after 1907, to consolidate and rationalize landholdings in the national forests, including elimination of several million acres too hastily included. In 1897 private landowners within the reserves were allowed to relinquish their tracts and select unreserved land in lieu. This provision was extensively used, especially by land-grant railroads, to exchange inferior lands for valuable timberlands that were otherwise open only to 160-acre homestead or timber entries. The Santa Fe, Northern Pacific, and Southern Pacific railroads together sold a million acres of lieu scrip to large timberland buyers. A similar lieu provision in the 1899 act creating MOUNT RAINIER NATIONAL PARK enabled the Northern Pacific to exchange 450,000 acres of nearly worthless mountainside for timberlands in Oregon, 200,000 acres of which were sold to the Weyerhaeuser Timber Company. Congress abolished the practice of lieu selection in 1905, but by 1922 the burden posed by numerous requests for special acts authorizing land exchanges prompted the passage of the General Exchange Act. Under that law, Congress authorized forestland trades on an "equal value" rather than the earlier "equal area" basis, and only nonmineral national forest land, not unreserved public domain, was eligible for selection by the landowner.

The early national forests were located predominantly on public lands in the West and comprised mostly relatively inaccessible mountain forestlands. Under authority of the WEEKS ACT of 1911, which was broadened by the CLARKE-MCNARY ACT of 1924, more than 20 million acres were acquired for national forests, mostly in eastern states. Half of the land in the national forests contains commercially valuable timber.

By 1900 the Great Lakes forests were largely depleted. Much cutover land was sold to immigrant farmers and others or let go for taxes. Eighty years later, farms contained almost 29 percent of commercial timberland, and state and county governments in about equal shares owned a fourth of it, mostly acquired through tax delinquencies in the 1920s and 1930s. Alone of the nation's major timber regions, forest industry ownership in the Lake States is today insubstantial—less than 9 percent. Larger owners, especially in the PULP AND PAPER INDUSTRY, have in recent years, however, moved toward retention and expansion of holdings for forest management. Reforestation is widespread in the region for both timber and tourism.

With the depletion of Northern timber, the Southern and Pacific forests rose to primacy. The Southern pineries were heavily exploited for lumber in the early twentieth century and almost completely cut over by 1935. Reforestation has been stimulated by pulping, and 60 percent of the area is still commercial timberland, nearly a third of it in farms, a fifth of it owned by forest industries.

The Southern and Pacific forests each account for about 40 percent of the nation's timber harvest, on a third and an eighth respectively of the commercial timberland. The Pacific region is the only one in which old-growth timber harvest is still significant. It supports two-thirds of the nation's standing softwood sawtimber, half of it in national forests. Only 37 percent of commercial timberland is privately owned, nearly half by forest industries, which tend to very large holdings.

Because of difficult terrain and distance from markets, the Rocky Mountain forest has never developed as a major lumbering region. Only a fourth is privately owned, over half of that in farms and ranches and only one-seventh in forest industry holdings.

Present Patterns of Forestland Ownership

Largely as a result of clearing for farms, cities, and industries, and only secondarily as a consequence of timber harvesting, the original 1,070 million acres of forestland in the United States had been reduced by 1977 to 740 million acres. Of this present total, 488 million acres are capable of and available for growing trees commercially. Some 228 million acres are unproductive, and 24 million acres of productive lands are reserved from timber use, located mostly in state or national parks, wilderness areas, community watersheds, and the like. Four-fifths of the 252 million acres of noncommercial forestland is located in the Southwest and Alaska. These lands have value for recreation, watershed protection, grazing, and wildlife habitat; three-fourths is publicly owned, nearly all by the federal government.

In contrast, only 28 percent of commercial forestland is in public ownership. The federal government owns 21.7 percent of commercial timberland, three-fourths of it in the West. National forests alone account for 18.2 percent, and BUREAU OF LAND MANAGEMENT lands, Indian reservations, and other federal lands about 1 percent each. The states own 4.8 percent, and county and local governments 1.5 percent. The national forests alone contain over 40 percent of the nation's merchantable timber and over 60 percent of its softwood sawtimber, two-thirds of it located in the

heavy old-growth stands of the Pacific Coast. Federal forests play an increasing, perhaps ultimately dominant role in United States wood production. Since 1953 their share of production has grown from one-ninth to over one-third.

Nearly three-fourths of commercial forestland is privately owned. In the Northeast and Southeast, where three-fourths of the commercial timberland is located and where practically all lands at one time passed into private ownership, almost seven-eighths is privately held, compared with less than a third in the West. Forest industries own 13.9 percent nationwide, farmers 23.9 percent, and other individuals and companies 34.1 percent. Nine-tenths of farm and "other" private ownership is in the East, two-thirds of it hardwood timberlands.

Over half of all forest-industry-owned acreage is in the South, with the balance about equally distributed in the North and West. In no section of the country is forest industry the predominant private ownership in area, though it nearly equals farm and "other" private holdings in the Pacific Coast region. Two-thirds of the timberland held by forest industries is in large ownerships of more than 50,000 acres. Ninety percent of the 23,452 owners in 1953 were lumber manufacturers, but the 159 pulp companies owned two-thirds as much timberland, almost all of it in holdings of over 50,000 acres. In recent years pulp manufacturers especially have adopted aggressive land acquisition programs. From 1945 to 1977, forest industries increased their holdings by 15 million acres, mostly in the East. In the historical and doubtless permanent pattern, two-thirds of the annual cut still comes from non-forest-industry ownerships, but the industry has shown an increasing trend toward acquiring and retaining lands not just for harvesting but for tree growing. Although forest industry holdings comprise only 13.9 percent of the commercial timberland, they include some of the most accessible, productive, and well-managed forests.

In contrast with forest industry and public ownership, other private ownerships have been chronically underproductive and poorly managed, if managed at all, because of fragmentation and small size. Yet the bulk of commercial forestland is comprised of such holdings. In 1953, 60 percent of commercial forestland was in nonindustrial private ownership, with farmers holding 34 percent and "miscellaneous other private owners" 26 percent. There were 4.5 million owners of tracts considered small—less than 5,000 acres—and only 2,600 holdings of acreages larger than that. Over 54 percent of the commercial forest was in the hands of these small owners, with the average holding amounting to less than 100 acres.

By 1977, reflecting the long-term decline in number of farmers and land in farms, farm timberlands amounted to only 24 percent, and "other" private holdings had increased to 34 percent of the nation's commercial forest. Most of the decline in farm woodlands occurred in the Atlantic Coast states; often the owners had retained the land while abandoning marginal farming for other livelihood. Some of the former farm forests had been acquired by forest industries and other large private owners, but the pattern of small ownerships remains predominant. Despite the historical predisposition toward the small landowners and populist denunciations of the timber "barons," the "small forest ownership problem" is the most serious obstacle to efficient utilization of America's timber resources.

FURTHER READING: An excellent brief introduction to American land use and tenure is Marion Clawson, *Man and Land in the United States* (1964). The most authoritative, detailed treatment of federal land policies is Paul W. Gates, *History of Public Land Law Development* (1968). See also John Ise, *United States Forest Policy* (1920) and Harold K. Steen, *The U. S. Forest Service: A History* (1976). The Forest Service's periodic timber resource reviews are indispensable, especially *Timber Resources for America's Future* (1958). The American Forestry Association has initiated what it hopes will be a state-by-state study of forestland ownership, use, and management with three pilot studies: Kenneth B. Pomeroy and James G. Yoho, *North Carolina Lands* (1964); Samuel T. Dana, John H. Allison, and Russell N. Cunningham, *Minnesota Lands* (1960); and Samuel T. Dana and Myron Krueger, *California Lands* (1958).

FREDERICK J. YONCE

FOREST PATHOLOGY

Forest pathology is the study of diseases of forest trees and the biological degradation of wood in service. Most tree diseases found in the United States are native, although two of the most destructive—white pine blister rust and chestnut blight—have been introduced. As indicated in Table 1, fifteen major new diseases have been identified since 1900. Annual United States forest disease losses exceed the net forest growth and are greater than the impacts caused by fire, insects, and all other destructive agents. The *Timber Resources Review* reported that in the year 1952 disease reduced total growth in sawtimber by 45 percent, killing 2,242 million board feet and preventing the growth of another 17,647 million board feet. Of this growth impact, heart rot was the largest single cause, contributing about 33 percent of the total.

As early as 1887–1888, articles on tree diseases appeared in reports of the U. S. DEPARTMENT OF AGRICUL-

TURE, but systematic investigations of forest pathology in the United States began only in 1899 when the Department of Agriculture appointed the German-trained Hermann von Schrenk to study WOOD PRESERVATION. Von Schrenk's Mississippi Valley Laboratory in St. Louis was discontinued when he left government service for a career as a consultant to several railroads on wood preservation. In the same year, under the leadership of Haven Metcalf, the Division of Forest Pathology was started in the Bureau of Plant Industry in Washington, D.C. The division remained under the jurisdiction of the bureau until 1951, when responsibility for forest pathology was transferred to the U. S. FOREST SERVICE. For its first thirty years, the rapidly expanding division worked mostly on decay in old timber, native rusts, needle diseases, and the highly damaging dwarf mistletoes. In the East, it grappled with chestnut blight, blister rust, other cankers, and the prevention of decay in living trees and blue-stain in lumber.

During the 1930s, a growing team of experts trained in forestry and pathology at some fifteen universities, with the aid of manpower provided by the CIVILIAN CONSERVATION CORPS, ushered in a second productive thirty-year span for forest pathology. Fights against Dutch elm disease and phloem necrosis were major confrontations. Fusiform rust challenged Southern forest managers, as FIRE CONTROL decreased the acreage of rust-resistant longleaf pine and increased that of susceptible slash and loblolly pines and rust-carrying oaks. Littleleaf eliminated much of the piedmont shortleaf pine. Beech diseases, Dutch elm disease, birch dieback, and cankers plagued the North, and white pine blister rust, pole blight, root rot of Port-Orford-cedar, and poria and armillaria root rots of Douglas-fir added to the West's woes. Other diseases invaded nurseries, threatening to shut down some planting programs. Pathologists, mainly by employing soil fumigation, successfully combated these diseases and virtually revolutionized nursery practices.

Starting about 1960, there was much change in forest pathology emphasis. Research moved from remote experiment stations to land-grant universities. The McIntyre-Stennis Act of 1962 provided federal funds to land-grant colleges for forest research. Subsequently, university and federal pathologists working together produced more sophisticated and basic research than ever before. The results included gains in breeding for resistance, in preventing wood deterioration, in checking nursery diseases and air pollution, and in such areas as mycorrhizae, serology, and ultramicroscopy.

Pathology's contributions to forestry have been

The deadly blister rust infects young white pine. Forest Service Photo.

many. Pathologists predicted the course of chestnut blight and thus provided the ability to use killed trees for tannin extract production during World War II. The knowledge that half the hardwood fire loss was due to rot in damaged trees and that a rotation age under 100 years would eliminate most trunk rot had practical uses. Reducing southern pine rotations from 100 to under 50 years cut redheart losses from over 25 percent before the 1930s to 1 percent in the 1970s. Similar rotation-cull relationships have been shown for aspen, balsam fir, and Western species. Treating pine stumps with boron compounds reduced annosus root rot. Substituting other pines for shortleaf eliminated littleleaf in much of the piedmont. Nursery soil fumigation not only strongly decreased loss to disease, grubs, and nematodes but also cut weeding costs in the South. Lumber dips put a stop to annual losses suffered by the southern pine lumber industry from sapstain.

Pathology is highly integrated with other sciences.

Insects are involved in the spread of infection by most pathogens; meteorology and chemistry affect damage from air pollution and sprays; and nematodes lead to root rot. Reduction of disease losses depended upon pathologists working together with the other disciplines involved in forest pest management, fire, and, above all, SILVICULTURE. Pathologists work with silviculturists to lower rotation ages, reduce injuries, eliminate mature trees, and keep nurseries clean of pathogens. White pines are not planted where ribes abound nor loblolly and slash pines where oaks grow. Most pathology-based decisions must be made early in forest planning, for prevention is the key to disease control. The principles of control include avoidance, exclusion, eradication, protection, and resistance, all preventive measures. Therapy is hardly ever successful. Unlike animals, plants only rarely acquire immunity; trees are not cured of fungus-caused diseases. The futile hope of curing a sick tree thwarted plant science for centuries.

Major Introduced or New Diseases of Forest and Shade Trees in the United States since 1900

Disease	Main Species Attacked	Year First Reported
Blister rust	Five-needle species of *Pinus* (pines)	1897
Chestnut blight	*Castanea* (chestnut)	1904
Phloem necrosis	*Ulmus* (elms)	1918
Beech bark disease	*Fagus grandiflora* (beech)	1920
Larch canker	*Larix* (larch)	1927
Pole blight	*Pinus monticola* (western white pine)	1929
Birch dieback	*Betula* (birches)	1930
Dutch elm disease	*Ulmus* (elms)	1930
Littleleaf of pine	*Pinus echinata* (shortleaf pine)	1932
Persimmon wilt	*Diospyros virginiana* (persimmon)	1933
Mimosa wilt	*Albizia julibrissin* (silk tree)	1935
Phytophthora root rot	*Chamaecyparis lawsoniana* (Port-Orford-cedar)	late 1930s
Oak wilt	*Quercus* (oaks)	1942
Pitch canker	*Pinus elliottii* and *P. palustris* (slash pine and longleaf pine)	1945
Sweetgum blight	*Liquidambar styraciflua* (sweetgum)	1951

FURTHER READING: Warren V. Benedict, *History of White Pine Blister Rust Control—A Personal Account* (1981). John Shaw Boyce, *Forest Pathology* (3rd ed., 1961). George H. Hepting, *Diseases of Forest and Shade Trees of the United States,* Agriculture Handbook 386 (1971); "Death of the American Chestnut," *Journal of Forest History* 18 (July 1974): 60-67; and "The Threatened Elms: A Perspective on Tree Disease Control," *Journal of Forest History* 21 (Apr. 1977): 90-96. George H. Hepting and Ellis B. Cowling, "Forest Pathology: Unique Features and Prospects," *Annual Review of Phytopathology* 12 (1977): 431-450. National Academy of Sciences, *Plant Disease Development and Control* (1968).

GEORGE H. HEPTING

FOREST PRODUCTS RESEARCH

In the United States, forest products research carried on in scientific fashion got off to a slow start during the last decade of the nineteenth century. In 1887, the chief of the U. S. Division of Forestry, Bernhard E. FERNOW, deplored the lack of knowledge about most American woods. "Crude experience has been our guide," he said, "and crude has remained our knowledge."

During the period from 1890 to 1910, small amounts of money were apportioned by the federal forestry establishment to universities for forest products research. Mechanical property studies were begun at the universities of Washington, Yale, Purdue, California, and Oregon. Preservation and dry kiln studies were undertaken at Yale. NAVAL STORES research was started in the South. A small experimental pulp mill was erected in Boston, and wood chemistry and wood preservatives were also studied there in a small way.

Filibert Roth started his career by studying gross anatomy, shrinkage, and physical properties of pines at the University of Michigan in 1888. His publication, *Timber: An Elementary Discussion of the Characteristics and Properties of Wood* (Division of Forestry Bulletin No. 10, 1895), was a classic compilation of research-based knowledge about United States woods.

In 1907, McGarvey Cline, head of a section on wood uses in the U. S. FOREST SERVICE, proposed that improved efficiency and coordination in research could be obtained by bringing the far-flung federally sponsored products research scientists together in one laboratory. Accordingly, the Forest Products Laboratory (FPL) began operating in Madison, Wisconsin, on October 1, 1909. Scientists from various universities were moved to Madison and the cooperating University of Wisconsin provided a specially constructed laboratory building. Cline served as the first director of FPL, which formally opened on June 4, 1910.

There were a number of important early successes such as, for example, in the work of Harry D. Tiemann, who had been studying wood physics at Yale University since 1903. He was among the first of the university scientists to move to Madison in 1909. He

A technician at the Forest Products Laboratory in Madison, Wisconsin, applies water-resistant glue with a mechanical spreader. Forest Service Photo.

brought the benefits of considerable research already done on the concept of the critical "fiber saturation point" in wood drying. Tiemann received the first of a number of patents on the humidity-regulated dry kiln in 1911. His kilns were rapidly accepted in lumber manufacture to speed up and control the long and expensive process of drying lumber. Subsequently, wood physics studies related to moisture have probably yielded more doctoral theses than all other forest products research subjects together.

Timber mechanics studies were also continued at FPL, with the objective of providing a full array of engineering data about American wood species. About 200,000 specimens were tested during the laboratory's first decade. Compilations of strength properties of American woods were published by J. A. Newlin, L. J. Markwardt, T. R. C. Wilson, and other research engineers. Most important was the characterization of "stress grades" of lumber on the basis of strength, a concept rapidly accepted by the industry.

The FPL's pulp and paper research group was soon equipped with an experimental fourdrinier paper machine and pulping equipment suitable for studying mechanical as well as chemical pulping. Pulp variables were also studied in mechanical pulping at a full-size experimental groundwood mill constructed for research at Wausau, Wisconsin, before World War I.

Chemists at FPL studied the chemical composition of wood, wood distillation and extraction, and the manufacture of ethyl alcohol, glues, wood-preserving chemicals, and chemicals for stabilizing and moisture-proofing wood.

Forest products research boomed during the two world wars; the results were extremely important and useful for the war effort and far beyond. During World War I, the FPL staff rose from fewer than 100 employees to about 450. World War I caused many shortages. For example, paper requirements doubled. Scientists began planning research on a variety of tree species not then used for paper, notably the southern pines and hardwoods. FPL demonstrated a bleached sulfate pulping process in 1931, and nine years later a mill in Lufkin, Texas, began manufacturing newsprint from pulp produced by this process and mixed with groundwood pulp.

On May 18, 1928, Congress passed the MCSWEENEY-MCNARY ACT, which recognized research as an integral part of the nation's forestry program. It made special provision for continuation of products research at the FPL in Madison. FPL completed construction of a large, strikingly modern laboratory building in 1931. Over thirty years later, FPL added a large new pilot plant and two additional laboratory buildings.

During World War II, the FPL staff rose to about 700, in part to train wood processors, users, and inspectors, but mainly to conduct research and development work on the whole gamut of wartime uses, including airplanes, boats, structures, and containers; special papers were developed for greater wet-strength, durability, and stability for containers and maps, and for overlaying plywood. Adhesives for wood, permanently durable under all conditions of exposure, became commonplace.

During the two wars and the intervening period, the laboratory's reputation spread around the world, and it became the model for national laboratories in many industrialized as well as developing countries. Scientists from FPL accepted assignments abroad to assist in the establishment of these institutions, and young scientists from foreign laboratories spent lengthy training periods at FPL to prepare for research in their home countries. Through this long period from the beginning of World War I to the end of World War II, FPL was directed by Carlile P. "Cap" Winslow, a colorful, politically astute administrator.

By the end of World War II, a growing realization that the high-quality timber that had helped to build a wealthy nation was becoming scarce caused a shift of the emphasis in research to the utilization of hitherto lesser-used species and to the more efficient use of existing supplies. At the same time, forest products research began to be of greater interest to wood-using industrialists. In 1943, the NATIONAL LUMBER MANUFACTURERS ASSOCIATION (NLMA), through a subsidiary, the Timber Engineering Company (TECO), established a product development and research department with a laboratory in Washington, D. C., which studied a great variety of problems of interest to wood processors. In 1948, NLMA published a *Forest Products Research Guide*, listing 91 trade associations and 131 professional societies and commercial laboratories active in forest products research. The *Guide* also listed 209 forest products manufacturers and 507 processors, consumers, and material suppliers that participated in research.

Unfortunately, only a few industrial research groups were of any significant size, and the movement that developed at the time did not grow greatly, except at large forest products conglomerate companies and at firms that supplied chemicals, adhesives, and equipment to the industry. Even TECO's product development and research department was terminated in 1959. Furthermore, industry research was always of a proprietary and applied nature; very little of it was made public, although extensive and productive facilities were and have continued to be maintained by such firms as Weyerhaeuser, Potlatch, and Georgia-Pacific, among others.

Forest products research in universities before World War II was limited mainly to individual scientists at forestry schools. Notable exceptions were the Institute of Paper Chemistry established in 1929 at Lawrence College in Appleton, Wisconsin, where direction and financial support came from the pulp and paper industry, and the New York State College of Forestry at Syracuse, which early had strong faculties in wood technology, wood utilization, and pulp and paper.

Forest products research in state organizations dates from establishment of the Texas Forest Utilization Research Laboratory at Lufkin in 1937 and a similar laboratory at Corvallis, Oregon, in 1941. These and other such institutions, mostly at university locations, multiplied and grew in the decade after World War II. Graduate students at universities also contributed greatly to the research output at that time. However, after the postwar boom, difficulties in attracting students, high costs, and perhaps other problems caused some schools, notably Yale, Duke, and the University of Michigan, to withdraw from the forest products specialty. Nevertheless, there has been growth both in net numbers of research groups and in research output, and in the late 1970s at least a dozen sizable state or university forest products research laboratories were active in the field.

Following the pattern established for agricultural research and extension under the Hatch Act of 1887, the U. S. Congress in 1962 passed the McIntire-Stennis Act which authorized federal support for forestry (including forest products) research at land grant colleges. Funds subsequently provided and administered by the U. S. Department of Agriculture's Science and Education Administration helped to create a more favorable and more stable situation for research at most of the forestry schools. At the same time, the Forest Service emphasized greater cooperation and support for university research. The universities have concentrated on basic research, which has not always flourished in the government's own programs.

The Forest Service has always had a concern for problems of dissemination and application of its research. Before World War II, forest products officers were stationed at offices in Missoula, San Francisco, and Portland to provide liaison with timber processors. After the war this service was enlarged into the "Forest Utilization Service" with representatives at each of the experiment stations. During 1964 and 1965, these liaison offices were replaced by forest products research projects at each experiment station. These projects have since concentrated on regional problems in cooperation with the central laboratory in Madison. At the same time, the Forest Service enlarged its liaison effort through its program of state and private forestry, adding product specialists to assist industry in improving its technology on the basis of the latest research findings. Perhaps the most successful such project was the sawmill improvement program, which in cooperation with state officials helped hundreds of small sawmills to increase lumber yields. The FOREST AND RANGELAND RENEWABLE RESOURCES PLANNING ACT of 1974 and subsequent related legislation, especially in 1978, further promoted improvements in the Forest Service's long-range research planning process to increase the relevance of federal research to the overall forestry program of the country.

Recognition of research has come in part through the development of a profession of forest products science and technology and of publications specializing in this field. The professional organization of the forest products scientist and technologist is the Society of Wood Science and Technology founded in 1958 and numbering about 250 members in 1981. It publishes a quarterly journal and carries on other professional activities. The FOREST PRODUCTS RESEARCH SOCIETY, an information-disseminating organization formed in 1947 and dedicated to publicizing the results of research for the industrial practitioner, publishes two journals, conducts seminars, and otherwise stimulates the spread of new information about wood. In 1981, it claimed 5,000 members.

FURTHER READING: Charles A. Nelson, *History of the U. S. Forest Products Laboratory (1910–1963)*(1971). U. S. Forest Products Laboratory, *Wood Handbook: Wood as an Engineering Material*, Agriculture Handbook No. 72 (rev. ed., 1974).

HERBERT O. FLEISCHER

FOREST PRODUCTS RESEARCH SOCIETY

Organized in 1947, the Forest Products Research Society (FPRS) maintains offices and laboratories in Madison, Wisconsin. It is independent of but works closely with the U. S. Forest Products Laboratory in the same city and with the University of Wisconsin. It is supported in part by about 150 wood industry companies in the United States and Canada but generates the larger part of its income through its research and its publications: the monthly *Forest Products Journal* (1955), the quarterly *Wood Science* (1968), and occa-

sional books for both the industry and the general public.

The society grew steadily from about 2,500 in the early 1950s to 5,500 in 1980. The FPRS serves as a clearinghouse for new research in all aspects of wood processing "from logging operations through finished products and utilization of residue." In the late 1970s, the society expanded its programs to include practical industry problems as well as research in pure science. It sponsored up to five major international conferences a year.

FOREST RESERVE ACT OF 1891

On March 3, 1891, Congress passed a lengthy statute that reformed and codified many public land laws. The so-called Forest Reserve Act is actually Section 24 of the General Revision Act, added at the last minute by procedures that were at variance with parliamentary convention. The authorship of the Forest Reserve Act is still debated, with several contemporaries taking credit for this momentous law.

The Forest Reserve Act authorized the president to reserve certain forested lands from the public domain. This authorization reversed more than a century of federal land policy that singlemindedly had aimed to transfer public land to private ownership. The purpose of these reserves was not specified, and Congress failed to include provision for administration. It was not until 1897 that the FOREST MANAGEMENT ACT defined purposes and provided for administration of these reserves, which would be called national forests after 1907. Nonetheless, President Benjamin Harrison reserved 22 million acres by proclamations and began the 190-million-acre national forest system. In 1907, Congress amended the Forest Reserve Act to forbid creation or enlargement of national forests in the states of Washington, Oregon, Montana, Idaho, Wyoming, and Colorado, except by act of Congress.

FURTHER READING: Harold K. Steen, *The U. S. Forest Service: A History* (1976).

FORESTRY AS A PROFESSION

The task of a professional forester as articulated by Dana and Johnson (1963) is "the management of forest lands for the continuous production of goods and services—an art based on science and practiced with due regard to economic and social considerations" (p. 11). Although its prime objective is the growth and harvest of trees (SILVICULTURE), forestry also involves manage-

The heroic image of forestry attracted many young men to the profession, but they found themselves more often at a desk than in the saddle. Forest Service Photo.

ment of related renewable resources, such as water, wildlife, RECREATION, and forage.

Forestry means different things to people. To the hiker, the work of the forester is the rustic wooden sign on a trail. The rancher sees the foresters' output in terms of the number of livestock he may graze on a forested range. The farmer seeks a forester to mark the trees to be cut from his woodlot. The hunter recognizes the better access provided by logging roads and the improved wildlife forage and cover that can result from timber harvests. The homeowner drawing a glass of water and the fisherman may both unknowingly benefit from a forester's efforts to protect a watershed.

To many people, foresters are associated with fire lookout towers and Smokey the Bear fire prevention messages, both highly visible aspects of forest protec-

tion programs. Unless trees are allowed to live and grow, they cannot fulfill daily needs for homes, newspapers, and the myriad of paper and chemical products.

Forestry is more than growing trees, and Congress recognized that fact by enacting the MULTIPLE USE-SUSTAINED YIELD ACT in 1960. The law cites that production of wood, water, recreation, wildlife, and forage is the proper goal of national forest management. The law does not apply to private or other public forestlands but is regarded as an example to follow. To be practical, forestry must pay. The value of wood products can be termed in dollars, but social values such as clean water and recreation are harder to measure. That is why organic legislation such as the Multiple Use Act is important, for it assures that forestry will be broadly viewed.

Forestry is relatively young as professions go, but

A college-trained professional inventories Mississippi hardwoods in 1932, during the early stages of a nationwide, county-by-county tally of American forests. This ambitious program was authorized by the 1924 Clarke-McNary Act. Forest History Society Photo, Robert K. Winters Collection.

references to legal protection of game and trees for human benefit are found in records dating back to Roman times. Those who applied these early laws to the land were forerunners of the modern forester.

The first extensive regulation of the forest in western Europe was the royal banning of hunting in designated areas. In the twelfth and thirteenth centuries, forest ordinances of princes and barons limited forest cutting to the needs of family use. The timber was to be marked and cut at a specified time. Oak and beech were preserved to produce mast, an early recognition of wildlife habitat. Pastures were regulated with regard to young tree growth, a precursor of forest range management.

The period following the Middle Ages (1500–1800) brought the emergence of states and nations and the beginnings of applied forestry practices. More ordinances, often restrictive, evolved, and by the end of the 1800s, there was some interest in the continuous management of forestlands for firewood and building material. In the American colonies, the British Broad Arrow policy and a scattering of local colonial ordinances concerning timber cutting and fire control were signs of recognition of the importance of New World forests.

Modern management of forestlands for the continuous production of multiple goods and services emerged in Europe after 1800. In North America,

however, as long as resources of the frontier were thought to be inexhaustible, little consideration was given to maintaining forest stands for the future. In 1849, the commissioner of patents warned: "The waste of valuable timber in the United States will hardly be appreciated until our population reaches 50,000,000. Then the folly and shortsightedness of this age will meet with a degree of censure and reproach not pleasant to contemplate" (Dana 1956, p. 76).

By the last half of the 1800s, concern for the protection and wise use of forests aroused scientists and influential citizens. George Perkins MARSH defined man's responsibility to nature in his monumental *Man and Nature* (1864). In 1873, the American Academy for the Advancement of Science, in response to a paper presented by Franklin B. HOUGH, formed a committee with the charge to petition Congress and state legislatures upon the importance of promoting the cultivation of timber and preservation of forests. Three years later, Congress appropriated funds for the preparation of a study of the utility of forests and the best means for their preservation and renewal. The resulting four-volume *Report upon Forestry*, compiled by Hough and Nathaniel EGLESTON, remains a foundation of forestry in America.

During the last quarter of the century, the formation of the AMERICAN FORESTRY ASSOCIATION (1875), the establishment of a small Division of Forestry in the DEPARTMENT OF AGRICULTURE, the reservation of timberlands from the public domain, and the creation of several state forestry commissions revealed a growing recognition of the role of forestry. Forestry did not yet exist in America as a profession; however, by the turn of the century forest practitioners would be required to possess specialized knowledge, have undergone extensive training in methods and their underlying principles, and recognize common standards of achievement and conduct.

By the 1870s, forestry lectures were offered at Cornell University, the University of Michigan, and other American colleges, usually in departments of botany or horticulture. The courses stressed tree planting and the agricultural aspects of the subject. An opportunity to demonstrate forestry as it was practiced in Europe came in 1892, when George Vanderbilt hired Gifford PINCHOT to manage the extensive timberlands on his estate, Biltmore, in the Appalachian Mountains near Asheville, North Carolina. Pinchot, who attended the French National School of Waters and Forests and completed field studies in Germany, was the first native-born American to receive professional-level training in forestry.

Although Pinchot's attempt to apply silviculture at Biltmore was not profitable in monetary terms, it was a beginning for forestry in America. His successor as Biltmore forester, Carl Alwin SCHENCK, started a field forestry school there in 1898. Schenck's instruction concentrated on practical aspects of the subject and included considerable field work. (The site, now within the Pisgah National Forest, was commemorated in 1965 as the Cradle of Forestry in America.) A number of Biltmore graduates proved to be highly capable foresters, although the one-year curriculum's practical emphasis more nearly resembled a present-day forest technician program than a professional school of forestry. In the same year, 1898, Governor Black of New York requested a full four-year forestry curriculum at Cornell University. Bernhard E. FERNOW, the former chief of the U. S. Division of Forestry, who had been trained at Muenden Academy in Germany, was selected to develop the forestry curriculum at Cornell. The forestry courses in New York, as well as those in North Carolina, relied on German texts because there were as yet no American-authored forestry books, except for those that Schenck wrote for his students.

When forestry came to America from Europe, it carried German accents. The profession took root in a society with a manifest destiny based in part on the belief that forests were inexhaustible resources ripe for exploitation under laissez-faire capitalism. George

Perkins Marsh's *Man and Nature* was pivotal in setting the seeds for American conservation. Marsh pointed to nature's ability to renew and produce abundantly, provided resources were not depleted beyond their ability to regenerate. Evidence that Marsh's book was widely read led R. W. Behan (1975) to observe that "American forestry early on acquired an element lacking in German forestry, a well-argued scenario of the consequences of land abuse—and it proved to be politically potent."

Perhaps the real birth of forestry as a profession in America can be placed in the year 1900, with the founding of the SOCIETY OF AMERICAN FORESTERS (SAF) by Gifford Pinchot. He was joined in the venture by Henry S. GRAVES, Overton W. PRICE, E. T. Allen, William L. Hall, Ralph S. Hosmer, and Thomas H. Sherrard. "Seven in all, but enough," Pinchot recalled. In the same year, Yale University opened its graduate program in forestry, now the oldest forestry school in continuous operation in America. Schools of forestry were soon started in many states. In 1903, however, the curriculum at Cornell closed when Governor B. B. Odell, Jr., vetoed its appropriation in response to protests from owners of recreational camps who opposed the logging conducted on the school forest. Although the tree cutting undertaken by Fernow was probably justified in the pragmatic terms of European sustained-yield forestry, closing the school can be seen as a manifestation of the political and social aspects that would more and more influence the profession in America.

During the twentieth century, the practice of forestry in America evolved in an atmosphere of changing social objectives. This evolution, of course, was strongly influenced by available technology and scientific knowledge. Throughout, the durability of its sustained-yield foundation and the modifying influence of social concerns are in ample evidence.

Forestry's emerging period (1900–1925) began with the 1900 founding of the Yale University School of Forestry and the Society of American Foresters. Yale became an important source of faculty members for the many schools of forestry that opened at state land grant colleges during this period. Forestry was taught and practiced in the sustained-yield tradition of the European model. The nation was growing and was commodity oriented, particularly in the West. The forest reserves originally withdrawn from the public domain in the last decade of the 1800s, as a response to the concerns articulated by Marsh and others, were transferred in 1905 from the DEPARTMENT OF THE INTERIOR to the Department of Agriculture and placed under the management of the newly founded U. S. FOREST SER-

VICE, with Gifford Pinchot at its head. The agency remains one of the most important employers of foresters.

In 1916, the NATIONAL PARK SERVICE was organized, giving direction to the nationwide system of federal parklands, begun with the establishment of YELLOWSTONE NATIONAL PARK in 1872. The act in effect called for the protection of the forests within such parks by such means "as will leave them unimpaired for the enjoyment of future generations." Timber harvest was specifically limited to that necessary to control insect and disease outbreaks, or to conserve scenery. Foresters in the National Park Service had to work within these constraints and do so to this day.

In what can be thought of as a custodial period (1925–1950), the public concept of forestry was one of forest protection. This perception was influenced by the highly visible forest fire prevention programs, particularly in the South, and the advent of the CIVILIAN CONSERVATION CORPS (CCC). During this period, many state forestry agencies were organized, and the number of forestry schools and graduates grew. Toward the end of this quarter, however, it was becoming apparent that investment in sustained-yield forestry would be profitable for private landowners, as evidenced by the dedication of the first tree farm by the Weyerhaeuser Company in 1941. The end of the old-growth forests was in sight. America was approaching the equilibrium of wood scarcity and the demand for products that characterized German forestry a century ago. Sustained-yield became something more than a socially desirable public goal; it could pay its own way.

The promise of forestry as a career prompted thirty universities to establish four-year forestry programs by 1932. However, not all of them provided the same quality of education. Standards were needed, and in 1933 SAF established a Committee on Accrediting Schools of Forestry. Within two years fourteen forestry schools were accredited.

Adoption of a code of ethics is widely regarded as an indicator of professionalism. SAF began drafting a code as early as 1923. The membership adopted a twenty-five canon code in 1948, which was amended in 1971. In 1976, the code was revised to fifteen canons.

If there is a uniquely American contribution to forestry, it came in the period of rapid technological change following World War II. With the end of the war, American manpower and capital were ready to go to work. The resulting burst of activity drew heavily on natural resources, and foresters developed new innovations to increase productivity. Research in genetics led to the superior tree seed program, new

breakthroughs were made in insect and disease control, engineering advances permitted logging on difficult terrain, and improved milling procedures and the development of new industrial technology provided profitable markets for forest products that had not existed before. This burst of technology brought new opportunities as well as problems to foresters. Public concern over increased logging in national forests, conflicts over wilderness designations, difficulty in implementing the broad yet vague directives of the Multiple Use Act of 1960, and perceived abuses of some private forestlands led to a spate of national legislation which put constraints on forest management activities. The social implications of American forestry were again manifested.

The NATIONAL ENVIRONMENTAL POLICY ACT of 1969 mandated consideration of the environmental impacts of road building, timber harvest, and other forestry activities. The Federal Water Pollution Act of 1972 addressed the role of forestry as a source of water pollution and led to serious consideration of a model state forest practices act, although it was not adopted. The Clean Air Act of 1970 brought constraints to the use of fire as a forest management tool. The regulation of pesticides had an impact on efforts at tree release. The Endangered Species Act of 1973 added a new legal parameter to forestry operations. Although technological innovations would make wood products more competitive in the marketplace, meeting that demand was not to be at the expense of the amenities and other forestland products.

The broadening of social perception reflected in the national legislation enacted in the 1970s produced a holistic merger of Germanic roots and American ambitions. Such a balance is articulated in the NATIONAL FOREST MANAGEMENT ACT of 1976 and associated regulations. Holistic forestry holds the promise of successfully capturing the commodity (wood, water, forage) production potential made possible by technological progress through the skillful recognition of social values (protection of wildlife and fisheries habitat, outdoor recreation, and aesthetics). It is management of the whole forest environment, including both market and nonmarket resources. It is, to restate the definition of forestry cited in the opening paragraph, "the management of forest lands for the continuous production of goods and services—an art based on science and practiced with due regard to economic and social considerations."

By 1981, the Society of American Foresters had accredited forty-four professional forestry degree programs. Many foresters now obtain graduate degrees to acquire additional skills in other disciplines. As the profession grew in depth and complexity, a need for skilled field personnel became apparent. SAF developed suggested guidelines for forest technician curricula (two years), and by 1982, fifty-five schools in the United States and Canada, ranging from universities to community colleges, met these voluntary guidelines. Graduates of technician programs usually work under the supervision of professional foresters but do not receive the same level of training in mathematics, biological and physical science, and deductive disciplines.

Today's forester is as likely to be employed in the private sector as by a government agency. There is a trend toward increasing private employment, representing the profitable opportunities in forestry for corporate and other woodland owners. The days of a forester on patrol wearing a campaign hat are largely gone. The current version is more likely to be wearing a safety hard hat and carrying a pocket calculator. The once familiar forest fire lookout towers are coming down, replaced by aerial detection, citizen reports, and, in some areas, sophisticated electronic surveillance. As the management process has become more complex, specialization has occurred. Foresters now work beside other resource professionals: soil scientists, hydrologists, fish and wildlife biologists, range conservationists, recreation and park managers, and a variety of social scientists. But it is still the forester who must produce the integrated forest management plan providing sustained yield of desired commodities with due consideration of social and environmental values.

FURTHER READING: Keith A. Argow, "Professionalism and Ethics, A History within SAF," *Journal of Forestry* 73 (Aug. 1975): 460-463. R. W. Behan, "Forestry and the End of Innocence," *American Forests* 81 (May 1975): 16–19, 38, 40-49. Henry Clepper, *Professional Forestry in the United States* (1971). Henry Clepper and Arthur B. Meyer, eds., *American Forestry: Six Decades of Growth* (1960). Samuel Trask Dana, *Forest and Range Policy* (1956). Samuel Trask Dana and Evert W. Johnson, *Forestry Education in America Today and Tomorrow* (1963). Bernhard E. Fernow, *A Brief History of Forestry in Europe, the United States, and Other Countries* (1911). Gifford Pinchot, *Breaking New Ground* (1947). Stephen H. Spurr, "The Profession of Forestry: Today and Tomorrow," *Journal of Forestry* 78 (May 1980): 252, 254.

KEITH A. ARGOW

FORESTRY IN GENERAL EDUCATION

Forestry education in many collegiate institutions in the United States began with a single course designed to stimulate an interest in the care of the nation's woodlands. Such generalized instruction for the typical student was offered at Yale University in 1873 and at Cornell University in 1874. It dates to the 1880s at the universities of Michigan, New Hampshire, Massachusetts, Iowa, Missouri, and North Carolina. Courses were usually taught by botany or horticulture faculties. In some instances, the material was oriented toward wood anatomy, giving rise to interests in wood technology.

The Smith-Hughes Act of 1917, which provided federal funds for vocational agricultural instruction in high schools, encouraged the teaching of forestry in teachers' colleges. This has usually been, and still is, a single course accompanied by a library of supplementary material with which the teacher is able to instruct secondary school students. Under the Smith-Lever Act of 1914, the Agricultural Extension Service was authorized to appoint county agents, who would disseminate useful forestry information to farmers and farm owners. The need for collegiate forestry courses for these people encouraged the offering of such instruction in land-grant institutions and other colleges from which agents were likely to graduate. Yet, by 1959, only forty colleges listed such a course. Farm forestry courses mostly imparted information related to tree planting and had been offered since the 1870s.

Although a precise count is not available, perhaps a tenth of the nation's two- and four-year colleges now offer a course that emphasizes the various forest resources. Out of such instructional opportunities have recently emerged programs in environmental and conservation education—usually administered by education and environmental management departments.

Environmental education programs at both the university and high school levels, motivated by the environmental enthusiasm of the 1970s, have encouraged the development of field programs and the establishment of remote outdoor instructional facilities. Environmental institutes, sometimes cooperative consortiums of several colleges, are also recent innovations that may be catalysts for new concepts in natural resource education.

Correspondence schools have provided courses in forestry and conservation since at least 1958. A few universities have offered credit work by correspondence since before 1960.

College courses closely allied to forestry and encompassing uses of the forest apart from timber have been offered in wildlife biology (since 1931), watershed management (1947), range management (1917), and recreation management (1914).

Forestry emphasis in the secondary schools is generally assigned to vocational agricultural courses, Future Farmer of America (organized in 1928) activities, the 4-H clubs (organized around 1904 from a variety of school clubs), and biology instruction. In forested parts of the country, wood-using industries have allocated tracts of land for high school students to manage which serve as demonstration forests, beginning in the late 1940s. Companies also provide financial assistance and encourage their foresters to aid schools with instructional expertise.

FURTHER READING: Samuel Trask Dana and Evert W. Johnson, *Forestry Education in America Today and Tomorrow* (1963).

LAURENCE C. WALKER

FORESTRY RESEARCH

1876–1915

In 1876, Congress appropriated $2,000 for the DEPARTMENT OF AGRICULTURE to initiate "investigations and inquiries" into the use and condition of the forest resource. Over the next ten years, Franklin B. HOUGH and his successor as chief of the Division of Forestry, Nathaniel H. EGLESTON, collected, analyzed, and abstracted available information and published four voluminous reports and a number of short bulletins. Although there are earlier incidences that could be so considered, continuous forestry research began in the United States with these efforts.

In 1886, the Division of Forestry, established in 1881, was formally recognized by Congress, and Bernhard E. FERNOW, Prussian-trained and the first professional forester to practice in the United States, was named chief. He understood the nature and importance of research and felt that "the time seems to have come when direct original investigations should be undertaken with a view to furthering forestry practice." His 1887 annual report included a systematic plan for the research needed to provide a scientific, economic, and practical base for forestry. Early projects were conducted in cooperation with the University of Michigan and Washington University in St. Louis. Studies of major tree species and timber physics received initial attention.

The work of the division was concentrated in four areas: (1) description and measurement of the forest resources; (2) silvical characteristics and growth requirements of commercial species; (3) influences of forests on climate, soil, and streamflow; and (4)

Technicians mark a western white pine in Idaho after inoculating it against blister rust as part of an investigation on the spread of this damaging disease. Forest History Society Photo.

reforestation of denuded land. Nearly 100 publications were prepared by the division during Fernow's tenure, some of them—such as Charles Mohr's treatise on southern pines—of outstanding importance and lasting value.

Fernow resigned in 1898 to organize the forestry school at Cornell. He was succeeded by Gifford PINCHOT, under whom, according to Secretary of Agriculture James Wilson, "the work of the Division has been directed in distinctly different channels," that is, there would be increased emphasis on the protection and management of forestlands.

The first two forestry schools (Biltmore and Cornell) were established in 1898, and fourteen others followed over the next ten years. Research was recognized as an important adjunct to teaching, and schools at Cornell, Harvard, Iowa State, Michigan, Michigan State, Minnesota, and Yale were among those that conducted some research. Experimental and demonstration forests were set aside at several schools. But staffs rarely consisted of more than four professors, and heavy teaching loads plus other responsibilities left scant time for research.

State agricultural experiment stations, authorized by the 1887 Hatch Act, received little funding for forestry. From 1891 to 1900, less than 2 percent of the articles in the *Experiment Station Record* dealt with forestry. Perhaps the most important work was extensive research on tree planting in the arid and semiarid regions of the West.

Transfer of the forest reserves to the Department of Agriculture in 1905 made these vast areas available for experimental work. However, the small FOREST SERVICE research staff was centralized in Washington and could not cope with the multitude of urgent problems that the administrators of the new national forests faced, many of whom started their own studies. A step toward decentralization came in 1908 with establishment of the Fort Valley experiment station in Arizona under G. A. Pearson. Similar stations in Colorado, Idaho, California, and Washington soon followed. However, the field stations were poorly funded and could not completely supplant the investigative efforts of the national forests, a situation which created conflict.

Research did not prosper under Pinchot. He recognized its importance but was impatient and too busy with administrative affairs to pay much attention to it. Under the leadership of Henry S. GRAVES, Pinchot's successor, and with the urging of Earle H. CLAPP, the Branch of Research was created in 1915. Clapp was appointed chief of the new branch, responsible directly to Graves.

1916–1945

Designation of a separate Branch of Research allowed independence from but interaction with the national forests, the principal users of new information. It also spurred further decentralization. Between 1921 and 1927, six new regional forest experiment stations were set up in the East, and the five western stations were reorganized on a regional basis.

The dominant role of the Forest Service was strengthened. Virtually all federal forestry research centered in the Department of Agriculture, and although other USDA agencies carried on important work in related fields such as entomology and pathology, the Forest Service had by far the largest program.

Some foresters, especially educators, favored the European tradition of independent forest research units located at universities, with financial support from the central government. But the regional scope of most problems, the urgent needs of the national forests, and the leadership exerted initially by Fernow and continued by Clapp, Samuel Trask DANA, Raphael ZON, and others, all worked for a single federal agency. However, cooperation with forestry schools became a fixed Forest Service policy and six of the eleven regional stations, like the Forest Products Laboratory, were established in close cooperation with universities.

In 1926, the SOCIETY OF AMERICAN FORESTERS, the AMERICAN TREE ASSOCIATION, and the Forest Service collaborated on *A National Program of Forest Research*. This 232-page report examined the problem-solving potential of research, evaluated existing programs, analyzed problems requiring study, and discussed the institutional arrangements appropriate for an effective national program. It laid the foundation for the MCSWEENEY-MCNARY ACT of 1928, the organic legislation for Forest Service research.

The McSweeney-McNary Act bestowed legal status on the regional experiment stations and reaffirmed a policy of cooperation. It broadened the scope of Forest Service research responsibilities and authorized specific appropriations levels. It also called for a nationwide forest survey to inventory all ownerships, an undertaking that had been urged for years.

The Forest Service published the monumental COPELAND REPORT in 1933. Formally titled *A National Plan for American Forestry*, it included a forty-page section written by Earle Clapp on research policy, program direction, organization, and funding goals, all designed to move toward orderly implementation of McSweeney-McNary. In 1938, the National Research Council's Division of Biology and Agriculture published *Forest Research in the United States*, a comprehensive appraisal of the scope and quality of programs at various institutions.

The history of forestry research during this period is written mainly in laws, policies, national plans, and appraisals. The two world wars, with the Great Depression sandwiched between, allowed little progress in program expansion. In 1915, the Forest Service research budget was $286,000; in 1925, it was $764,000; in 1933, $1.7 million. By 1936, it had risen to $2.6 million but then remained almost static through 1945. Thus, over the thirty-year period, annual increments averaged about $80,000.

Most forestry schools were involved in research to some degree, and several maintained substantial programs. (Important contributions by individual scientists were also coming out of university departments of botany, zoology, agronomy, and related fields.) However, budgets did not generally exceed $10,000, and for the most part, the schools lacked faculty with adequate training or interest for scientific investigations. Graduate programs, essential to the training of researchers, developed slowly, with an average of only about fifty-five master's and four Ph.D. degrees in forestry granted annually from 1916 to 1945.

However, this period was important for another reason. Many of the fundamental concepts and principles necessary for the maturing of forestry research came into focus and gained acceptance. The critical role of the basic sciences, the inherent unity of forest problems, and the need for an interdisciplinary approach to research were recognized. The importance of continuity and precision in observations and measurements was stressed. The potential application of experimental design and statistical analysis became firmly established. The foundation was laid for systematic procedures to identify problems and set priorities, define research objectives, and document plans and results. The utility and integrity of later research owes much to the wisdom and vision of people like Earle H. Clapp, surely the outstanding research leader, Carlos Bates, Richard Boerker, Samuel T. Dana, Barrington Moore, James Toumey, and Raphael Zon.

1946–1980

Rapid expansion and intensification in the practice of forestry following World War II created unprecedented demands for research results. Although the Forest Service continued its leadership position, there was dramatic postwar growth in the programs of two other groups.

In the 1940s, some of the forest products companies with extensive timberlands saw the need to establish their own research units. Weyerhaeuser Timber Company in 1942 initiated a modest program of research in support of forestry operations on its Douglas-fir holdings. This effort was to grow uninterruptedly in the following years to include by 1980 a staff of approximately seventy-five scientists in most of the traditional forestry disciplines working on a wide range of problems in the Pacific Northwest and the South. In 1944, West Virginia Pulp & Paper Company set up a six-man project near Georgetown, South Carolina, to study protection and management problems of southern pines. In 1947, St. Regis Paper Company organized its Technical Forestry Department for research on SILVICULTURE, growth and yield, and chemical debarking of hardwoods in New York's Adirondacks. International Paper Company established its Southlands Experiment Forest at Bainbridge, Georgia, in 1956, which also marked the beginning of a continually expanding forestry research effort.

An alternative more commonly exploited by industry was the establishment of cooperative ties with universities and Forest Service experiment stations. Dozens of industrial forest owners made land, manpower, equipment, and dollars available for collaborative research efforts. In the 1950s, cooperative tree improvement programs involving industry and forestry schools were initiated at Texas A & M College, University of Florida, and North Carolina State University. Support was also widely given, by individual companies or in some cases industry-oriented associations, for expanded funding of public forestry research programs.

At universities, the era of sponsored research had dawned, and for the first time the research potential of the forestry schools began to be realized. In addition to forest industry cooperation, grants from public agencies and foundations became increasingly available, much of it in the form of graduate scholarships. These new funding sources had a profound influence on subsequent structuring of forestry schools and their role in national forestry affairs.

Coincident with the ascendancy of research at the universities was an acceleration and a broadening of the base of research training in forestry and related sciences. The number of master's degrees awarded at forestry schools jumped from 18 in 1945 to 275 in 1950, the number of doctorates from 7 to 29.

A new stimulus for the universities came with passage of the McIntire-Stennis Cooperative Forestry Act in 1962 which authorized federal matching funds to be apportioned among qualifying institutions. The act had two objectives—to produce research results and to educate forest scientists. From an initial appropriation of $1 million in 1964, this program made modest growth to $9.6 million in 1980. By contrast, only $1 million was available in 1980 under the Hatch Act.

A severe handicap at virtually all institutions had been hopelessly inadequate research facilities, but by the middle of the period this situation began to change. From 1959 to 1970, Congress appropriated $28 million to the Forest Service for research construction. Many state legislatures also recognized the need, and forestry schools began moving into new buildings where faculty and graduates had access to up-to-date space and equipment, usually for the first time. A measure of the impact of better working space are the 100 to 125 forestry doctorates awarded yearly.

Opportunities now were opening up for better deployment of teams of scientists who could launch multidisciplinary probes into related aspects of a problem. Wider use of laboratory technicians and student assistants allowed scientists to use their own time to better advantage. And, of course, the computer age was just around the corner.

Research emphasis also shifted. Forest genetics, which had made a modest beginning in the mid-1930s, gained support from industrial forest owners seeking to shorten rotations and maximize yields. By 1960, forest recreation research had become recognized as a distinct field, requiring attention from the biological, physical, and social sciences. The environmental revolution that burst upon the nation in the late 1960s resulted in initiation or expansion of research on biological control of insects and on safer methods of managing unwanted vegetation. The clearcutting controversy stimulated a new look at alternative cutting practices and prompted evaluation of long-term impacts on soil productivity, hydrologic values, aesthetics, and wildlife habitat. Concern about wasteful logging practices led to research and development by forest industries and equipment manufacturers on better harvesting systems.

Much of the great forward movement of forestry research in the United States during the 1950s and 1960s was attributable to the leadership of Verne L. Harper, who in 1951 replaced Edward I. Kotok as assistant chief for research in the Forest Service. Harper pushed vigorously for more effective cooperation with forestry schools. He engineered improvements in the organization and administration of research in the Forest Service and worked unceasingly for higher standards of planning and performance. He promoted policies and actions that markedly upgraded career development opportunities for research professionals and technicians. The impacts of Harper's fifteen years as head of Forest Service research extended far beyond the agency and will be discernible in the progress of research for years to come.

The legislative charter for Forest Service research was revised by the Forest and Rangeland Renewable Resources Research Act of 1978, which supplanted McSweeney-McNary. Research also benefited from the 1974 FOREST AND RANGELAND RENEWABLE RESOURCES PLANNING ACT, amended in 1976 by the NATIONAL FOREST MANAGEMENT ACT, which required the Forest Service to prepare for Congress detailed financial goals every five years.

From the beginning (Fernow's 1887 report), forestry research has been characterized by periodic plans and appraisals, which have helped promote balance, sophistication, and responsiveness to user needs. This tradition continues.

In 1977, the Renewable Natural Resources Foundation organized a national symposium to examine the structure and productivity of forestry research and subsequently published *A Review of Forest and Rangeland Research Policies in the United States*. In 1978, the Department of Agriculture and the Association of State College and University Forestry Research Organizations jointly sponsored a series of regional and national work conferences to identify and evaluate specific research needs. The findings and recommendations of these two projects are now being used to improve the coordination, content, and effectiveness of programs for the future.

FURTHER READING: I. W. Bailey and H. A. Spoehr, *The Role of Research in the Development of Forestry in North America* (1929). Earle H. Clapp, *A National Program of Forest Research* (1926). Frank H. Kaufert and William H. Cummings, *Forestry and Related Research in North America* (1955). U. S. Forest Service, *The Forest Research Program* (1950).

THOMAS F. McLINTOCK

FOREST SERVICE

The U. S. Forest Service is the largest agency in the DEPARTMENT OF AGRICULTURE. Headquartered in Washington, D.C., the agency is divided into three primary components: National Forest Administration, State and Private Forestry, and Research. Evolution of the Forest Service began in 1876, with the appointment of Franklin B. HOUGH as "forestry agent" who had the task of gathering statistics about the nation's forests. In 1886, Bernhard E. FERNOW was appointed chief of what was then called the Division of Forestry, and shortly thereafter Congress gave the small program permanent status. Gifford PINCHOT replaced Fernow

Constructed in 1899, this rude hut was the nation's first ranger station. Located within Idaho's Bitterroot National Forest, the cabin epitomizes the extreme isolation endured by rangers and their families as they worked to implement policies emanating from a distant Washington, D. C. Forest Service Photo.

in January 1898; his talent and zeal brought rapid growth and vastly expanded responsibilities. On July 1, 1905, the now Bureau of Forestry became the U. S. Forest Service. The growth of the agency in the century since 1876 closely parallels that of the CONSERVATION MOVEMENT. In fact, a strong case can be made that the Forest Service has been the movement's prime leader.

In 1873, Franklin Hough read a paper, "On the Duty of Governments in the Preservation of Forests," to a meeting of the American Association for the Advancement of Science. The scientists were impressed by the logic of Hough's paper and passed a resolution to petition Congress "on the importance of promoting the cultivation of timber and the preservation of forests." For the next several years, Hough labored in Washington, D.C., to gain congressional support, but the enabling legislation stalled in a reluctant or disinterested House Committee on Public Lands. Hough's congressional supporters then used the parliamentary tactic of attaching a $2,000 measure to support a forestry study to an agricultural appropriations bill. When this bill was passed on August 15, 1876, authorizing the commissioner of agriculture to appoint a forestry agent, the tradition of having a forestry program in the Department of Agriculture was begun, a tradition that would be repeatedly challenged in subsequent decades. Appropriately, Hough received the appointment.

Between 1877 and 1882, Hough compiled three volumes called *Report upon Forestry*, which brought together the best data available on American forests. Hough editorialized at length, passing severe judgments on past treatments of the forest, and recommended that the government retain forests on public land and adopt regulations to "*secure an economical use*" (emphasis in original). Nathaniel EGLESTON replaced Hough in 1883 and compiled the fourth *Report upon Forestry*. These four volumes provided a solid base of knowledge about forestry conditions for Congress and the Executive to heed.

Fernow replaced Egleston as chief of the Division of Forestry on March 15, 1886; on June 30, Congress gave full statutory recognition to the division. For the next twelve years, Fernow, a German immigrant trained in forestry, produced reports that expanded understanding of complex interrelationships between the trees of the forest and other forest resources, such as water.

Significantly, he added an economic dimension; private investors could not be expected to adopt conservation measures if costs could not be recouped. Like Hough, he advocated a federal forestry program for public lands and also included specific recommendations for the structure of the administering agency.

Halfway through Fernow's appointment, Congress enacted the FOREST RESERVE ACT of 1891, which authorized the president to establish federal forest reserves through withdrawal of land from the public domain. Although the GENERAL LAND OFFICE of the

DEPARTMENT OF THE INTERIOR had responsibility for the forest reserves created under this act, Fernow labored for increased acreage and more effective administration. When in 1898 Fernow accepted an appointment as director of the newly established forestry school at Cornell University, he left for his successor a legacy that was strongly scientific and a blueprint for effective administration of the federal forests. His successor, of course, was Gifford Pinchot.

A vital part of Fernow's legacy was the so-called

Early rangers often worked alone and had to take care of personal needs after a full day in the field. Rangers were notoriously underpaid, yet had to furnish two horses and even pay fees if the stock grazed on Forest Service land. Forest Service Photo.

The pine tree shield has been the official Forest Service badge since 1905. To Gifford Pinchot and his associates, the shape was a familiar symbol of power, often used by law-enforcement agencies, and would augment the ranger's authority. Forest Service Photo.

FOREST MANAGEMENT ACT of 1897, which would be used for the next sixty-three years as authorization for management. That Congress remained satisfied for more than six decades is a tribute to effective administration and an indication of how slowly attitudes changed until recent times.

Pinchot was well trained in forestry for the time, young and energetic, and a superbly skilled administrator. His personal wealth allowed him to be daring and ultimately to martyr himself. From 1898 to 1905, he was able to increase his staff manifold, develop cooperative programs in forest management and reforestation with scores of timber companies, and expand Fernow's timber-mechanics research program to include studies of the forest itself.

Undoubtedly in part because of Pinchot's friendship with Theodore ROOSEVELT, the president on February 1, 1905, approved the transfer of 63 million acres of forest reserves from the Department of the Interior to the Department of Agriculture, where Pinchot's Bureau of Forestry could administer them directly. To emphasize that the agency was committed to public service, its name was changed to Forest Service, and two years later, the forest reserves were renamed na-

tional forests, a gesture to show that the resources of these vast tracts were for use. At the time of transfer, Pinchot drafted a letter for the signature of Secretary of Agriculture James Wilson, establishing a management philosophy that still dominates Forest Service policy. The letter said in part, "In the management of each reserve local questions will be decided upon local grounds; the dominant industry will be considered first, but with as little restriction to minor industries as may be possible; . . . and when conflicting interests must be reconciled the question will always be decided from the standpoint of the greatest good of the greatest number in the long run."

Roosevelt aggressively used his presidential powers to expand the federal forest system; by 1907, there were 151 million acres, including 16 million acres of the so-called midnight reserves. This group was proclaimed in defiance of congressional constraints and were the last added in six western states without legislative approval. However, by the time Roosevelt left office in 1909, the fact that there were 195 million acres in the national forest system demonstrates that Congress too favored a large federal forestry program.

It is difficult to separate the Pinchot years with the Forest Service from the conservation movement itself, for he ranged far beyond the responsibilities of his appointment. He would often leave administration of the agency to his associate, Overton W. PRICE, while he would carry out lengthy presidential assignments. In fact, Pinchot's administrative genius was no more evident than in those many instances when the Forest Service seemingly ran itself during his long absences. To streamline his administration, Pinchot inaugurated new filing systems and budgetary processes that were adopted by other agencies, and he decentralized the agency so that personnel closest to a problem would have authority adequate to cope with it. This decentralized structure remains a matter of fierce pride within the Forest Service, a tradition that has suffered some erosion since enactment of the centralizing FOREST AND RANGELAND RENEWABLE RESOURCES PLANNING ACT of 1974 and the NATIONAL FOREST MANAGEMENT ACT of 1976. The *Use Book* was another innovation, a pocket-sized manual that contained rules and regulations supplemented with plain language and practical advice.

Effective administration of a decentralized operation requires inspections to assure that distant personnel are performing according to policy. Therefore, Pinchot divided the national forest system into inspection districts headed by district foresters. In 1930, the name was changed to region. Including Alaska, there have been ten regions, but when region seven was divided among its neighbors, it left a total of nine; there is a ten but no seven.

Each district (region) was comprised of several national forests, which were headed by forest supervisors. Since 1960, national forests have been the agency's basic planning unit. As of 1961, there were 155 national forests containing as much as 1 million acres each; frequently there are substantial inholdings of land owned privately or administered by another public agency. In 1981, 186 million acres of the 223-million-acre national forest system were under Forest Service jurisdiction; thus, there were 37 million acres of inholdings. These inholdings are largely a result of railroad land grants, mining claims, and homesteads and at times add greatly to administrative problems. Since 1960, the Forest Service has established nineteen national grasslands containing 4 million acres.

National forests are comprised of several districts headed by district rangers. In 1981, there were 640 ranger districts, down from 802 thirty years earlier, reflecting a centralizing tendency. The general public uses the title ranger for many different positions, but within the Forest Service, the ranger is in charge of the agency's smallest administrative unit. Each of the four administrative levels play a role in Forest Service programs, but especially in the earlier years, management decisions were made by the district ranger. It was he who sold the timber and supervised logging, or issued grazing permits and inspected the range, or took care of any and all of the myriad resources and services available on a national forest.

Pinchot set high standards for Forest Service personnel. Applicants were carefully screened and needed to demonstrate the proper mix of formal education and practical aptitude. During Pinchot's time, when only a few forestry schools existed, professional education was not required for rangers; but rangers did need to have the ability to write clear and accurate reports and have sufficient practical skills to accomplish assignments in a manner that would gain respect from grizzled frontiersmen. More recently, rangers and supervisors are graduates of four-year forestry programs, but more and more of the so-called professional positions are filled by engineers, landscape architects, and other specialists, reflecting the increasing complexity of Forest Service projects. In 1958, 90 percent of Forest Service professionals were foresters, but by 1973, only 50 percent had majored in forestry in college.

As measured by receipts, the Forest Service initially did more livestock business than timber. Often, when a forest reserve (national forest) was created, it included rangeland that, as part of the public land system, had been grazed regularly. Thus, Pinchot faced the rather substantial task of imposing regulations on areas that traditionally had been freely accessible. He recruited Albert F. POTTER, a stockman from Arizona, to head the Forest Service range program. The issues that Potter addressed remained for decades—were grazing permits a right or a privilege and should fees be based upon the cost of administering the resource or on the value of the resource?

Before these issues could be dealt with effectively, the Forest Service needed to establish that it had the authority even to issue permits and collect fees. Advised by legal officers George Woodruff and Philip P. Wells, Pinchot engaged in a patient and sophisticated effort to validate through a string of legal precedents the broad authorities he assumed he had under the Forest Management Act of 1897. Success was realized in 1911, after Pinchot had left office, when the U. S. Supreme Court ruled in favor of the government's contention in test cases brought by stockmen Fred Light of Colorado and Pierre Grimaud of California. The Court agreed that the secretary of agriculture had the right to issue rules and regulations for the national forests and to prescribe penalties for violation. That fundamental hurdle having been cleared, the Forest Service applied steady pressure to reduce the numbers of livestock on national forest ranges and to allow for rehabilitation; over the next half century, it achieved an average lowering of numbers of 2 percent each year.

Timber management was complicated, but in ways more subtle than that for range. Generally, there was little early demand for national forest timber, because private supplies were more than adequate. As late as the beginning of World War II, less than 2 percent of the nation's wood was derived from Forest Service timber sales. Therefore, early timber management was largely custodial. Except for localities that had depleted their private supplies, Pinchot adopted a policy, followed by his successors, of withholding federal timber to create scarcity in order to hold prices up. After all, if the national forest resources were placed on the market all at once, prices, at least in the short run, would plummet. He reasoned that a profit-making lumberman would be more likely to adopt better logging practices voluntarily; he ignored the irony of working to create scarcity while simultaneously predicting a timber famine. There is further irony in the historical fact that although fear of scarce resources was the basic pillar upon which the conservation movement was built, the reality that Pinchot and his successors had to deal with was a vast inventory of resources far in excess of the market's ability to absorb.

Pinchot labored to have his agency turn a "profit," that is, to have receipts exceed expenditures. The goal eluded him as it has all of his successors, for although receipts increased so did expenditures. In 1907, Congress instructed that all receipts be placed in the U. S. Treasury to be used for general purposes, rather than being earmarked to finance Forest Service operations. Congress has jealously guarded its prerogative to appropriate funds, regardless of revenues, since that time; there are exceptions, of course, and the ill-fated National Timber Supply Act of the 1960s was a near miss. This act proposed to create a revolving fund of timber sale receipts from national forests to support timber management. During the early 1950s, gross receipts briefly exceeded expenditures, and the Forest Service made much of its "business-like" operation. However, when the 25 percent of receipts that is returned to local government in lieu of property taxes not paid by the federal government is considered, the so-called profit quickly disappears. In 1981, the Forest Service received an appropriation of $2.3 billion while generating income through sale of timber and other resources of $1.1 billion.

If Fernow had not dealt with timber and range administration because the forest reserves were in another department, he had engaged in a limited way in cooperative programs, which under Pinchot were quickly expanded beyond timber testing for forest products firms. Even though Pinchot would have to wait until the 1905 transfer of the reserves to have forests of his own to administer, soon after he took office in 1898 the Division of Forestry issued two bulletins offering expert assistance to private forest landowners to develop management and reforestation plans. The landowner was required to pay travel costs only. In 1905, Pinchot reported that nearly 11 million acres had been or were being studied. However, his greatly increased responsibilities related to the reserve transfer and the economic depression of 1907 caused both him and the landowners to divert their attention from this cooperative venture. The growth of Forest Service cooperative programs continued, however, aided by the WEEKS ACT of 1911 and the CLARKE-MCNARY ACT of 1924. Since 1911, the Forest Service had provided matching funds to state forestry agencies in support of approved programs. The Clarke-McNary Act increased this support and broadened it to include assistance with nurseries and a major study of forest TAXATION. By the 1960s, there even was a deputy chief for the Division of State and Private Forestry to oversee the agency's cooperative programs. In regions where there was little national forest land, such as the South, this division constituted a large portion of Forest Service activities.

Even though Pinchot rarely missed an opportunity to belittle his predecessors, he often found himself following their lead. Research and cooperative programs are a good case in point; Fernow had emphasized the technical and theoretical aspects of forestry. By the end of Pinchot's first year in the Division of Forestry, he had established a research arm called the Section of Special Investigations. By 1902, it had become the Division of Forest Investigation with fifty-five employees claiming fully one-third of the agency budget. Six years later, Pinchot established the first of what would become many field research stations in Fort Valley, Arizona. In June 1910, after Pinchot left office, the Forest Products Laboratory was dedicated on the Madison campus of the University of Wisconsin and began a distinguished program of forest products testing and development.

Forest Service research efforts were given independence from its administrative branch in 1915, when chief forester Henry S. GRAVES established the Branch of Research. He named Earle H. CLAPP to direct the program and instructed him to "bring together . . . the various lines of research on investigative work conducted by the Forest Service." Clapp quickly became the architect of Forest Service research, and his legacy is much in evidence today.

In 1908, there was one field research station; by 1921, seven more were in operation. By the end of the 1920s, a basic network of twelve regional stations was in place and all major forest regions were represented. Clapp's *A National Plan of Forest Research* (1927) was a blueprint for what followed; the MCSWEENEY-MCNARY ACT of 1928 sailed through Congress and authorized $3 million for Forest Service research. The act also authorized a county-by-county inventory of the nation's forestlands.

The early years of Forest Service research saw investigators with little specialized training beyond a general education in forestry, and their publications emphasized the practical. In more recent times, the typical researcher has earned a Ph.D. degree in an esoteric specialty—insect physiology, soil chemistry, or fire physics—and although their publications still include practical offerings, they also write articles and monographs of a fundamental or theoretical nature.

On January 7, 1910, President Taft fired Pinchot for his insubordinate behavior in what historians call the BALLINGER-PINCHOT CONTROVERSY. In addition to the loss of Pinchot, the firing greatly weakened the agency's political base, and opponents quickly moved to capitalize on its vulnerability. From the advantage of more than a half-century distance, one might well describe the period 1910–1920 as the first "Sagebrush Rebellion." Federal ownership of the national forest system was challenged, and it fell to Pinchot's long-time friend and colleague, Henry S. Graves, to head the Forest Service during these years. He had been Pinchot's associate in the Division of Forestry, leaving in 1900 to be founding dean of forestry at Yale University. It is probably well for the Forest Service that his somber style stood in contrast to Pinchot's impatient flamboyance, as the agency might not have held its ground, both literally and figuratively.

In addition to placating the legion of adversaries inherited from Pinchot, Graves had to deal with the difficult issue of RECREATION, an issue that has yet to achieve consensus. In part because of Pinchot's utilitarian fundamentalism and in part because the political pressures of his time, especially in the West, required that the resources of the national forests be used, national park supporters advocated a new agency to administer the parks. When the NATIONAL PARK SERVICE was established in 1916 in the Department of the Interior, it was over the objections of Graves and Pinchot.

Historians disagree on the extent that the placement of the park agency in another department caused the Forest Service to bolster its own recreation effort, but the following year the agency asked Frank A. Waugh to make an intensive study of its recreational facilities. Waugh's inventory included an economic analysis, and he concluded that the public was well-served by national forest recreational opportunities. The primary concern of Graves and his successors was the erosion of national forest land base caused by creation of national parks. The Forest Service stoutly maintained, with little effect, that its recreation management was equal to that of the National Park Service. National forest lands of "park-like" quality tended to become national parks.

Wilderness was another matter, perhaps because the National Park Service initially focused on ways to attract visitors, requiring the construction of roads and tourist facilities. Chief Forester William B. GREELEY consulted at length with top staff, and in 1924 he used his administrative discretion to convert portions of the Gila National Forest in New Mexico into the nation's first wilderness (primitive) area. Greeley was wary of permanently reserving resources from commercial use, and he sought advice from a wide range of associates. Nonetheless, Greeley and his successors supported the establishment and protection of wilderness; in 1964, when the highly contested Wilderness

Act became law, there were nearly 14 million acres in the Forest Service wilderness system. The Park Service and the FISH AND WILDLIFE SERVICE would follow suit and create wilderness areas under their jurisdictions. By 1981, including 56.3 million acres in Alaska, the wilderness system for all agencies contained 85.4 million acres. This total can be broken down into 30.8 million wilderness acres for the Forest Service, 35.3 million for the National Park Service, and 19.3 million for the Fish and Wildlife Service. As of 1981, the BUREAU OF LAND MANAGEMENT had yet to establish wilderness areas, but in accordance with the Forest Land Policy and Management Act of 1976, the agency had selected areas to study.

Graves also had to lead his agency through the massive disruptions of World War I. Many of his personnel joined the Army and the Tenth and Twentieth Engineers—the forestry regiment. Graves himself and Assistant Chief William B. Greeley accepted commissions and served in France, working with French lumbermen to increase wood production in support of the war. In the United States, demands for wood, especially airplane-grade Sitka spruce, and sheep to produce wool for military uniforms placed heavy burdens on the diminished Forest Service ranks. Overseas experiences gave American foresters a more cosmopolitan view of the world, and increased activity on the national forests established an agency-clientele relationship that was never to return to its prewar state.

Graves resigned, and on April 15, 1920, Greeley was named his successor. Greeley ranks second only to Pinchot among those who have had lasting influence on the Forest Service. He defended the agency against the first overt effort to have it transferred to the Department of the Interior, worked effectively to blunt a Pinchot-led campaign to gain federal control over private logging, and stood firm against the relentless pressures from the livestock industry for a (to them) more liberal range policy.

As so often happens in history, concurrent events tend to obscure individual occurrences. Secretary of the Interior Albert B. Fall drafted an executive order for President Harding's signature that would have transferred the Forest Service to his department. However, Greeley had the good fortune of accompanying Harding on a 1923 tour of Alaska and was able to convince the president not to sign the order. The fact that the notorious Teapot Dome scandal broke into national headlines at this time and quickly discredited the secretary of the interior may have influenced the presidential change of heart more than Greeley's persuasive logic. Whatever the reasons, the

Forest Service's agricultural location would not be seriously challenged again until the next decade.

Stockmen took Greeley to task over grazing fees. They were adamant that fees should be pegged to the cost of administering the range. To charge them instead for the value of resource received, the stockmen complained, was to substitute commercialism for conservation. Greeley's chief of grazing, Will C. Barnes, studied the issue and recommended raising fees by 60 to 70 percent, which would reflect the true market value of the forage. Stockmen found strong support in Congress for the status quo, and only modest fee increases were imposed. But stockmen also wanted five-year instead of annual permits. They then asked for ten-year permits, which were implemented in 1926. For the time being, at least, stockmen were assured of stability, higher fees, and, not incidentally, reduced herd size. Although still yielding to the stockmen's superior political power, the Forest Service was gradually increasing its authority over the range.

Greeley's most lasting influence was the Clarke-McNary Act of 1924. About the time that Greeley was appointed to head the Forest Service, Gifford Pinchot began a crusade for legislation to regulate the forest industry. Earlier, Greeley had written that the industry was overcapitalized in timber and mills; lumbermen needed help not regulations. Pinchot branded Greeley's report as a "whitewash." Thus, the lines were drawn in a contest that was to last four years. Foresters, lumbermen, and conservationists debated the regulation issue; bills were introduced in Congress that represented the factions. However, Congress was not of a mind to impose regulations and instead adopted the Clarke-McNary Act, which opted for cooperation. The essence of this law—voluntary action inspired by cooperation—has since 1924 epitomized Forest Service posture. From that time, cooperation was to be the centerpiece of National Forest Administration, State and Private Forestry, and Research, although the issue of regulation was only quiescent. The next two decades would see two more concerted efforts to place the Forest Service in charge of logging on private lands.

Greeley resigned in 1928 to become secretary-manager of the West Coast Lumbermen's Association. Robert Y. STUART succeeded Greeley and brought the agency through the early years of the Great Depression and into Franklin ROOSEVELT's New Deal. Tragedy befell Stuart, who either fell or jumped to his death from his seventh-story office on October 23, 1933.

The New Deal years were atypical. For the Forest Service, it was a period of rapidly expanding programs, controversy, and preparation for war. The agency had four New Deal chiefs; Ferdinand A. SILCOX replaced Stuart, and he would die of a heart attack in 1939. Roosevelt named Earle H. Clapp to be acting chief, a position he held until 1943, when Lyle F. WATTS was moved into the top spot. It was in 1935 that the title of forester reverted to chief after thirty-seven years; in 1898, Pinchot had changed the title from chief to forester, because there were many bureau chiefs in Washington, D.C., but as forester, he would be unique.

The New Deal created jobs through conservation projects, and the Forest Service found its work load growing dramatically. The highly touted CIVILIAN CONSERVATION CORPS placed 3 million men in various projects, fully one-half administered by the Forest Service. These young men fought forest fires, planted millions of seedlings, and constructed roads, trails, and campgrounds. Decades later, the Forest Service would be straining its recreation resources to maintain and repair these aging works. Land acquisition, too, was a New Deal priority; nearly 8 million acres were purchased and added to the national forest system, or two and one-half times more than had been purchased in the years before the New Deal. The Prairie States Forestry Project (Shelterbelt) put thousands of unemployed men to work planting 18,000 miles of windbreaks between Texas and North Dakota.

These atypical times caused urgent recommendations to be superseded by even greater urgency. A backlog of planning helped the Forest Service to respond; the major planning document was *A National Plan for American Forestry*, the so-called COPELAND REPORT. The 1,677-page document was assembled in one year under Earle Clapp's supervision and was completed in 1933. It offers a state-of-the-art view for all aspects of American forestry—timber, water, forage, recreation, wildlife resources on all classes of land ownership—and the concept of multiple use was clearly articulated for the first time. When New Deal budgets and programs began to burgeon, the Forest Service had ready-made plans to be implemented.

Range received special attention. Under Clapp's supervision, the Forest Service began a major study of public ranges in 1932; in 1936, the Senate published *The Western Range*, technically as a favor to Senator George Norris. The report bluntly declared that all federal rangeland should be administered by the Forest Service, a clear criticism of the newly created Grazing Service in the Department of the Interior. The livestock industry also took exception to the report's conclusions, especially the estimate that 85 percent of private range was deteriorating. The Forest

Service challenge to Interior was not successful, but it did add animosity to their already wary relationship.

Secretary of the Interior Harold ICKES aimed to change his department's poor conservation image which was a holdover from earlier public land frauds, the Ballinger-Pinchot Controversy, and the Teapot Dome scandal. He proposed a new Department of Conservation, which would include transferring the Forest Service from the Department of Agriculture. An elderly Pinchot joined the ensuing fray, as the Forest Service energetically resisted the scheme. These efforts caused presidential anger, because Roosevelt's approval of Ickes's proposal was derailed by a supposedly subordinate agency. Historians generally concede that FDR deliberately kept Earle Clapp as acting chief as punishment for his obstinacy, rather than offering him a full promotion. Nonetheless, the Forest Service once again retained its place in the Department of Agriculture.

World War II altered priorities on a massive scale. Forest Service feuds with Ickes were shelved as all turned to the task of producing more resources with staffs depleted by the armed forces. Forest Service heavy equipment was used to complete or rehabilitate mine access roads in national forests, and the agency administered a project to grow a shrub called guayule to produce rubber. By war's end, the Forest Service was cultivating 200,000 acres of guayule but managed to produce only 1,500 tons of rubber. Looking ahead, the government established a Committee on Postwar Planning only six days after American entry following the Japanese attack in Hawaii. Throughout the war, Forest Service personnel made plans to absorb millions of returning servicemen in the work force and to provide vast quantities of resources to repair the war's damage. High on the Forest Service list was the halting of destructive logging practices that had been condoned as part of the total war effort.

In his introduction to the 1933 Copeland Report, Earle Clapp had written that public regulation of logging was a "quid pro quo in the public interest." Clapp, Pinchot, and others reasoned that the assistance lumbermen had received through the Clarke-McNary Act, tariffs on lumber, and similar benefits made it proper to assure "conservative" logging methods, even if imposed by force of law. The debate continued during the tumultuous New Deal years; in 1941, Senator John H. Bankhead introduced his Forestry Omnibus Bill, which contained regulatory sections. This too fell victim to war priorities, but in 1945, the Forest Service resumed its quest for legislation to regulate practices on private

forestlands. The forest industry countered with a carefully orchestrated defense coordinated by the American Forest Products Industries (since 1968, the AMERICAN FOREST INSTITUTE). Debates grew more heated year by year, but Dwight D. Eisenhower's 1952 election caused the Forest Service to shift its course abruptly, for the new president had promised a lessening of federal regulations. Cooperative programs replaced the quickly forgotten regulation issue.

The postwar years included range as well as timber controversy. Congressional supporters of the livestock industry had slashed Bureau of Land Management (BLM) budgets in retaliation for its recommendation of grazing fee increases. Grazing was important on two-thirds of the national forests, and the livestock industry, perhaps overconfident from its successful campaign to subdue BLM, made plans to acquire ownership of Forest Service rangelands. So clumsy and blatant were these tactics that the lumber industry, waging a concurrent campaign to stave off regulation, carefully disassociated itself from the effort. The conservation community rallied to Forest Service defense; significantly, author/historian Bernard DEVOTO began a waspish exposé of the livestock industry's "land grab." In retrospect, this episode was the precursor of the modern ENVIRONMENTAL MOVEMENT and yielded stockmen little for their efforts. Ironically, the Forest Service was the hero of this environmental piece; it would not be much longer before the environmentalists would begin to mistrust the agency.

Richard E. MCARDLE became chief in 1952, following Lyle Watts's retirement. It was McArdle's task to steer the Forest Service away from regulation, now that Republican Eisenhower was president, following two decades of FDR's New Deal and Harry Truman's Fair Deal, and focus on more politically acceptable programs. An inventory of the nation's forests was in order, and McArdle assigned Assistant Chief Edward C. Crafts to head the project. In 1958, *Timber Resources for America's Future* (TRR) began with McArdle's cautious claim, "There is no 'timber famine' in the offing, although shortages of varying kinds and degrees may be expected." The 715-page report saw no surplus of land, so utilization would have to be intensified and coupled with reforestation and combating forest fires, insects, and diseases. Reflecting their substantial political clout, lumbermen succeeded in preventing the Forest Service from including an action plan in TRR.

The capstone of McArdle's career was the MULTIPLE USE-SUSTAINED YIELD ACT of 1960. The Forest Management Act of 1897 had specified only timber and water resources, but Pinchot and his successors interpreted the act broadly, assuming that all resources found on the national forests were to be managed. The 1933 Copeland Report included the first articulation of multiple use, but still there was relatively little demand for national forest resources; such discussions bordered on the academic. However, following World War II, demands increased rapidly; for example, the prewar Forest Service supplied 2 percent of the nation's wood; now it supplied one-third. Recreational use burgeoned, too, and McArdle saw need for a congressional mandate to provide a balance of uses, lest the agency be whipsawn between special-interest groups. Skillfully overcoming opposition from the forest industries, the National Park Service, and the SIERRA CLUB, the Forest Service campaigned successfully for the Multiple Use Act, which decreed that timber, wildlife, range, water, and recreation were legitimate national forest resources.

The law also stated that wilderness use was consistent with multiple use. However, environmental groups had little faith that the Forest Service would safeguard their interests and campaigned in support of the Wilderness Bill. They reasoned that if the agency could create wilderness areas by administrative action, a similar action could eliminate the classification. The Wilderness Act cleared Congress in 1964, following eight years of controversy, and made the establishment of wilderness areas a matter for Congress to decide. The fact that the Forest Service on its own initiative since 1924 had created a multimillion acre wilderness system did not satisfy the environmental community, further testimony to the agency's loss of credibility in some circles.

It can be argued that the Forest Service fell victim to its own clever propaganda. In its earlier campaigns to attain legislation to regulate private practices, the agency portrayed logging as wasteful, even bad. This simplistic rhetoric seemed plausible to the general public; following World War II when the increasing numbers of recreationists "discovered" logging on national forests, they believed that a scandal had been uncovered. The controversy that began in the 1960s over clearcutting is a case in point; earlier, the Forest Service had carelessly classified clearcut logging as a form of devastation, when in fact foresters had long accepted the practice under appropriate conditions. Perhaps decades of support from the conservation community had made it complacent, but in any regard, the agency was stunned when in the 1960s and 1970s, its clearcutting practices prompted vociferous opposition. An overly defensive Forest Service dismissed its antagonists with the sarcastic epithet "well-meaning." But the environmentalists were much more than well-

meaning; they were intelligent, articulate, affluent, and effective. By the time the Forest Service realized the extent of its misjudgment, it, like so many institutions during the turbulent 1960s, found itself on the defensive. Edward P. CLIFF succeeded McArdle as chief in 1962; eight years later, he characterized Forest Service programs as being "out of balance to meet the public needs for the environmental 1970's."

John R. MCGUIRE became chief in 1972 and led the Forest Service through a period of regaining its balance. The Renewable Natural Resources Planning Act of 1974 (RPA) was a vote of congressional confidence in the agency's overall skills in planning and implementation. RPA was amended and expanded by the National Forest Management Act of 1976, which defined clearcutting as an acceptable silvicultural practice and also gave statutory status to the national forest system. Since 1891, most national forests had existed through a series of presidential proclamations.

During the 1970s, the Forest Service weathered two more efforts to dislodge it from the Department of Agriculture, as both Richard Nixon and Jimmy Carter envisioned a new Department of Natural Resources. R. Max PETERSON succeeded McGuire in 1979 and brought the agency into the 1980s.

FURTHER READING: Michael Frome, *The Forest Service* (1971). Glen O. Robinson, *The Forest Service: A Study in Public Land Management* (1975). Darrell H. Smith, *The Forest Service: Its History, Activities, and Organization* (1930). Harold K. Steen, *The U. S. Forest Service: A History* (1976).

HAROLD K. STEEN

FOREST SERVICE PLACEMENT

In engineering the 1905 transfer of the forest reserves from the DEPARTMENT OF THE INTERIOR to the DEPARTMENT OF AGRICULTURE, Gifford PINCHOT transformed the Bureau of Forestry (FOREST SERVICE) into a land-managing agency as well as a research organization. He also set up a target for all would-be government reorganizers since.

Whether or not the Forest Service's placement in Agriculture is good public policy, it is anomalous. Support of private ownership of intensively used private lands is the primary historic mission of Agriculture, but its Forest Service is the federal manager of extensively used publicly owned lands. In justification, adherents then and since have pointed to the croplike nature of the forest cycle as conferring the necessary generic connection between the Forest Service and Agriculture.

Interior's land management responsibilities in their

modern mode had not taken form by 1905. Except for a handful of national parks and one four-acre wildlife refuge, Interior's land responsibilities were centered in the GENERAL LAND OFFICE and pointed toward wholesale transfer of public land into private ownership—not its management.

After 1905, the federal land situation changed at Interior. The National Park Service was created in 1916, and Stephen MATHER, who directed its creation, was as energetic, resourceful, and successful in establishing national park administration by a professional corps as Pinchot had been for the national forests. The public lands were brought under public management in 1934. The long, slow process of forming a professional corps to manage them began with the creation of the Grazing Service in 1934 and continued after the Grazing Service was consolidated with the General Land Office in 1946 to form the BUREAU OF LAND MANAGEMENT (BLM).

The anomaly of having the Forest Service with its 187 million acres of federal lands in Agriculture, while Interior contains the Bureau of Land Management with 340 million acres, the National Park Service with 61 million acres, and the FISH AND WILDLIFE SERVICE with 96 million acres, frequently catches the attention of public administrators, management analysts, political scientists, and others called upon to study the federal organizational terrain.

In the 1920s, the Forest Service and Agriculture hoped to be assigned management of the public lands when federal management was finally extended to them, but the western livestock industry preferred the status quo and would not abide this. As a lame duck, President Herbert Hoover did recommend to Congress the transfer of the General Land Office to Agriculture, coupled with transfer of the ARMY CORPS OF ENGINEERS to Interior.

President Franklin D. ROOSEVELT selected Harold S. ICKES, a reform-minded Chicago lawyer, former Progressive Republican, and political ally of Gifford Pinchot, to be his secretary of the interior. With the National Park Service well established and with the beginnings of management of the public lands and the expansion of reclamation from irrigation to multipurpose water resource projects of monumental scale, Ickes was very proud of his efficient management of his department. He wanted to redeem it from the reputation that the BALLINGER-PINCHOT CONTROVERSY and the Teapot Dome scandal had bestowed upon it. Specifically, Ickes wanted Interior to be a department of conservation in name as in fact. As part of this plan, he worked to have the Forest Service transferred to Interior. Ickes succeeded to the extent that the President's Committee on Administrative Management

(Brownlow Committee) recommended renaming the Department of the Interior as the Department of Conservation, without specifying its components. When Ickes renewed efforts to have the Forest Service included in the proposed department, Forest Service leaders made a major effort to forestall the transfer, going almost to the point of outright presidential defiance. Ickes received much encouragement from Roosevelt, or at least thought he did, but never the crucial forthright presidential endorsement. Roosevelt disciplined Forest Service leaders for their lack of cooperation, including holding Earle CLAPP as acting chief for three years rather than promoting him to chief.

After World War II, President Truman launched a government-wide reorganization effort, calling ex-President Hoover back to public life to lead it. The Hoover Commission found reorganization of natural resources agencies to be its most controversial item. Its own task forces produced conflicting recommendations and consequently the commission made no overall or comprehensive recommendation for reorganization. It repeated recommendations that Hoover had made as president, namely, transfer of the Corps to Interior and transfer of the BLM to Agriculture. There was a second Hoover Commission in the Eisenhower administration, but it recommended coordination of natural resources agencies as a substitute for their reorganization.

With the proliferation of new programs and policies in the post-World War II years, there have been subsequent recurring efforts to reorganize the federal government in whole or in part, always seeking better alignment of organizational elements with policy and program elements. This effort naturally has kept Forest Service placement a live issue. Both the Johnson and Nixon administrations made numerous studies. President Nixon envisaged a grand reorganization that included a Department of Natural Resources. A bill embodying the concept of joining Interior's land management agencies and the Forest Service in the new Department of Natural Resources was introduced but never got beyond the stage of hearings in the 92nd Congress.

With reorganization success a highlight of his Georgia governorship, Jimmy Carter made government-wide reorganization an important element of his 1976 presidential campaign. In 1977, he formed a President's Reorganization Project. Its natural resources task force proposed a Department of Natural Resources, with the Department of the Interior as the matrix, but its superstructure reorganized for more effective management of its components. Its three major elements—all highly controversial—would have consolidated federal responsibilities in land management, water resources management, and ocean management. The most controversial proposal was transfer of the Corps of Engineers. At his first review, President Carter dropped the Corps from the design but approved the placement of the Forest Service in the Department of Natural Resources, where it was to be the core of a public lands administration. Finally admitting that the plan would have required more political effort than he wished to exert, President Carter halted the effort in May 1979, on the eve of its scheduled submission to Congress.

Shortly after his decision, President Carter ordered an acceleration of coordination between the BLM and the Forest Service. His goal was to accomplish many of the reorganization's objectives, including expansion and increase in exchanges of jurisdiction to simplify public dealings with these agencies and reduce administrative overhead.

In the 1960s and 1970s, Interior emerged from the shadows of the Ballinger-Pinchot affair and Teapot Dome scandal to bask in wider approval as an environmentally concerned federal agency. Thus, there was environmentalist support for Forest Service inclusion in the Carter Department of Natural Resources, but the hard fact about the Forest Service transfer was that there was no political constituency that wanted change sufficiently to make a high-intensity effort. Of equal significance, there were several constituencies that were very strongly opposed. In this situation, Forest Service transfer out of Agriculture could be brought about only by the emergence of a political constituency determined to wage a long campaign, or a president determined to use all his prestige and authority to neutralize or overcome opposition. In 1982, there were no signs suggesting the emergence of either force.

FURTHER READING: Louis Brownlow, *A Passion for Anonymity* (1958). Richard Pollenberg, *Reorganizing Roosevelt's Government: The Controversy over Executive Reorganization, 1936–1939* (1966). *The Secret Diaries of Harold L. Ickes*, vol. II, *The Inside Struggle* (1953). Harold K. Steen, *The U. S. Forest Service: A History* (1976). John C. Whitaker, *Striking a Balance: Environmental and Natural Resources Policy in the Nixon-Ford Years* (1976).

JERRY A. O'CALLAGHAN

FOREST SOILS

During the past fifty years, the concept of soils has evolved from something that bogged down tractors in the woods and stuck to the boots of loggers to recognition that it is the basic natural resource on forestlands. This change resulted from a research program that developed a body of knowledge on the relationship of soils to timber productivity in the major forest regions. In recent years, this research effort has been spurred by adoption of forest regulations and by environmental concerns. Of more importance, however, has been the longtime efforts of such pioneers in the field of forest soils as John Auten working in the Central States and the Southern pinery, S. A. Wilde at the University of Wisconsin, and T. S. Coile at Duke University. These men not only conducted a lifelong program of forest soils research but also trained a cadre of graduate students who themselves became teachers providing instruction and developing research programs in forest soils at most of the larger universities. Currently, there are courses of instruction in forest soils and graduate study programs at nearly all academic institutions that teach forestry.

It is now fully recognized that the ability of soil to support trees, to provide oxygen to root systems, and to store moisture and nutrients contributes greatly to forest productivity. Of course, climate influences productivity; nevertheless, within a climatic zone, the productivity of the forest is dependent on soil properties. The intensity of forestland management is directly related to productivity, because it is productivity that determines the return on the investment in various forest practices.

Most of the knowledge developed through forest soils research as well as operational experience are pertinent to the protection of soil productivity under the impact of timber harvesting or in seeking ways to improve soil productivity, such as providing drainage or adding nutrients. As land and wood values have increased in recent years, land managers have greatly intensified management practices in order to obtain maximum production from every acre of their forestlands. Effective application of these intensive practices requires a thorough and updated knowledge of the soil asset in order to obtain maximum returns.

In the following section, each of the major timber-producing regions will be discussed in relation to timber types, generalized soil productivity, and the degree of forest management in practice.

Douglas-fir Region of the Pacific Northwest

This region includes the area west of the Cascade Ranges to the coast and from southwestern British Columbia south into northwestern California. Geology and soils are varied throughout this region. Soils of northwestern Washington are mostly light-textured, since they are developing from gravelly, sandy

Forest researchers collect soil samples on the Coconino National Forest in Arizona, 1910. Forest Service Photo.

outwash and tills deposited by the last continental glaciation. Along the coast, deep friable soils are developing from relatively soft sedimentary rocks. To the east, in the foothills of the Cascades, soils are developing from volcanic rocks, primarily basalts and andesites, with extensive areas covered by a mantle of more recent pyroclastic materials, such as ash and pumice. There are some areas of serpentine rocks in southwestern Oregon and northern California with soils of poor productivity.

This region is characterized by a Mediterranean-type climate, with cool dry summers and relatively warm wet winters. Most of the region enjoys a summer drought, and tree growth is dependent on the ability of soil to retain sufficient moisture through the growing season. Precipitation ranges from about 40 to over 200 inches, most of which occurs in the winter. Above 2,000 feet in elevation, this winter precipitation is in the form of snow.

Along the coast and above 3,000 feet elevation in the Cascades, where the summer climate is cooler, the Douglas-fir type gives way to stands of western hemlock. Western hemlock productivity is high along the coast but low in the mountains. Soils in the coastal region developing from sedimentary rocks are among the most productive in the world. Douglas-fir productivity ranges widely throughout the region, with some coastal areas producing three times more growth than the steep mountainous areas in the Cascades.

Federal, state, university, and private research organizations have accumulated an extensive body of soil information for over thirty years. This research has provided guidelines for soil management to protect natural productivity for such forest practices as road construction, harvesting, thinning, and site preparation. Low-intensity soil surveys are completed for federal lands, and detailed soil surveys are available on much of the state and larger industrial holdings in the region. This region has one of the highest levels of forest management in the nation, especially on the larger industrial blocks where planting, thinning, and forest fertilization are routine forest practices.

Southern Pine Region

This is a large forest region, ranging from Maryland to Florida along the Eastern Seaboard and west along the Gulf Coast to eastern Texas, then north through southeastern Oklahoma and into Arkansas and portions of Tennessee. Southern pine forests, primarily loblolly, slash, and longleaf pines, cover nearly half of the region. A multitude of hardwood species occur in the more poorly drained areas.

There are four distinct physiographic provinces in this region: lower coastal plain, upper coastal plain, piedmont, and mountains, as one progresses inland from the coast. The lower coastal plain is relatively flat with poorly drained soils that are developing from relatively recent deposits of marine sediments. Soils are highly variable, with textures ranging from sands to clays with extensive areas of organic soils. The older marine deposits on the higher elevations of the upper coastal plain have soils with similar textures, and the relatively unconsolidated sediments are highly erodible. Erosion patterns have created some undulating and hilly topography.

The piedmont plateau lies between the coastal plain and the mountains. At one time, this area was part of the coastal plain but it has now been uplifted and exposed to weathering for a long period of geologic time. Soils on the piedmont are dense, heavy-textured, and in some places laced with gravels from more resistant rocks, such as quartzites and cherts. Erosion has created rounded drainage patterns on this plateau and in places has removed much topsoil.

The mountains, generally in the northern portions of the region from Oklahoma through Tennessee, are primarily hard sedimentary rocks of great geologic age that have been partially metamorphosed. Slopes are moderate and relatively smooth. Soils are shallow and rocky, except for some alluvial deposits in the valley bottoms.

In this region, the climate is characterized by long hot summers with a long growing season and mild winters. Annual precipitation ranges from forty-five to sixty-five inches, but most of the region receives about fifty inches, which is well-distributed throughout the year.

Although forest covers about half of the land, except for a few large blocks of industrial lands, it is widely scattered in small tracts interspersed with agricultural land. There is little federal ownership. A relatively high degree of forest management is practiced in this region, especially on the industrial forestlands of the coastal plains, using a large body of soil information. Common forest practices include providing drainage to poorly drained soils, site preparation and phosphorus application before planting, planting each harvested area with genetically improved seedlings, and fertilizing and thinning young stands.

Rocky Mountain Region

This region encompasses much of the western United States, including eastern parts of California, Oregon, and Washington to the west and from northern Arizona and New Mexico in the southwest to the Black Hills of South Dakota in the east. There is a wide range of commercial forest types throughout, with ponderosa pine being the most extensive at the lower elevations and combinations of Douglas-fir, Engelmann spruce, blue spruce, and western larch occurring at the higher elevations. Since some of this region is arid, there are extensive areas of rangeland, dry land farms, and noncommercial pinyon-juniper forests interspersed throughout the commercial forest areas. Commercial forests occur only where average annual precipitation is in excess of eighteen inches. All of the region has a continental climate, with hot dry summers and cold winters with heavy snowfall. Growing seasons are relatively short, especially at the higher elevations.

Much of the forestland is in large blocks of federal ownership. Shallow rocky soils in the mountains, restricted moisture at the lower elevations, and the relatively short growing seasons result in rather slow tree growth throughout much of the region. Most of the timber stands are old growth, and the emphasis is on harvesting rather than on growing timber. This emphasis, along with the economics dictated by relatively low productivity, results in a much lower level of forest management than in the Douglas-fir or southern pine regions. The soil information in this region is related primarily to hydrologic characteristics of watershed or range management.

Northeastern Coniferous Region

This region includes coniferous forests growing in the northern tier of states from Minnesota east through northern Maine. The forests are primarily stands of white spruce, balsam or red fir, white and jack pines, and scattered stands of quaking aspen and paper birch on recent cutovers and burns. Northern hardwood stands of yellow birch and sugar maple finger into these coniferous stands in places.

Topography is level to undulating throughout this region, a result of scouring by the latest continental ice sheet. Soils are primarily light-textured glacial outwash deposits. The ice sheet gouged many large depressions, which are now lakes or swamps. Although this region is relatively low in elevation, its northern latitude brings severe winters with deep snow and a short growing season.

Productivity is similar to that in most of the western pine region and much lower than for Douglas-fir or southern pine. There are several national forests in the Lake States, but the majority of the timberland is in larger industrial blocks. A great deal of soil information has been developed for this region, because forest management has been under way at a rather high level for many years.

Central Hardwood Region

This region ranges from Missouri through the southern portion of the Lake States, New England and Tennessee, and into the Appalachian Mountains. Although scattered conifer stands occur, most of the forest is made up of either central hardwoods (oaks and hickories and associated species) or northern hardwoods (yellow birch and maple).

The region has a continental climate with warm summers and cool winters. There is some snow pack in the northern portion but little in the southern area.

Soils are variable throughout, ranging from shallow rocky soils in the mountains, glaciate soils in the north, to loesal soils in the central portion.

Nearly all of the nation's hardwood lumber is produced in this region. Since most of these hardwood species are relatively slow-growing, productivity is lower than for southern pines, even though the soils and climate are favorable for tree growth. Because of the complexity of timber stands, they have been managed on an all-aged basis where only selected trees are harvested. Under this type of management, there is little need for regeneration, and only a minimum of soil protection is needed.

Summary

The amount of forest soil information is strongly related to the level of forest management. Both factors determine the inherent forest productivity of each region and whether the region is primarily "growing" trees or harvesting old-growth timber.

FURTHER READING: John W. Barrett, ed., *Regional Silviculture of the United States* (1962). S. A. Wilde, *Soils: Their Properties and Relation to Silviculture* (1958).

E. C. STEINBRENNER

FRENCH-CANADIAN IMMIGRANTS AND AMERICAN FORESTS

French-speaking and French-heritage workers have been prominent in the lumber woods and paper mills of New England and the Lake States since about 1860. Both Quebecois (French persons from Quebec province) and Acadians (French persons dispersed from Nova Scotia after 1755 into northern Maine, eastern New Brunswick, North Carolina, and especially Louisiana) have made a strong impact in these industries.

In the Northeast, these people often combined logging in winter with farming. By the 1860s, however, woods crews of French speakers were being recruited and were at work in New Hampshire and northern Maine. As migration westward diminished the numbers of Yankees in the woods, recruitment drives were made north of the border. Both Scotch-Irish and French Canadians responded in the decades of the 1870s and 1880s to this new source of income. By the turn of the twentieth century, they were a familiar sight in the woods; however, it was fairly unusual for mixed ethnic crews to be found. Where this was the case, the French were often used as teamsters, but in the ethnically separated crews there was no distinction of work. Occasional racial difficulties arose where mixed crews were found, or, as on the drive,

when the two groups met at work. In these same recruitment efforts, paper companies also began to employ French workers, and towns like Westbrook, Maine, took on a partially French flavor. French Canadians dominated woods work in the early days of logging in the Lake States and, despite being largely replaced by New England men, they remained active there as long as the pine lasted. By the height of Lake States lumber production, many French speakers there were second-generation Americans.

As the Yankees diminished in numbers in the Northeastern woods after 1900, more and more French workers were employed, many of them from the Acadian French towns in northern Maine. Certain Quebec towns near the border were recruitment depots for the large forest products companies. This source of income was a major economic force in such communities. When one combined the food and supplies provided for the woods, these towns found themselves as adjuncts to the lumber industry. In the 1920s many paper mills were located in Quebec itself (on the Saint Maurice and Saguenay rivers, and around Lac St. Jean), and the woods and mills had nearly all French employees below the administrative levels in these companies.

During the Great Depression, the numbers of French from Canada decreased sharply as Americans from the northern states returned to the woods to find work. This situation did not last long, however, and when a buildup for World War II occurred, French Canadians came into demand both in the woods and mills and in other war-vitalized industries of central Canada and southern New England. Migration increased rapidly.

The labor shortage of 1942 produced a diplomatic controversy between the United States and Canada over the numbers of French who could enter the United States to work in the woods. Political leaders from Maine, New Hampshire, and, to a lesser degree, Vermont worked with the U. S. State Department to increase these numbers, while Canada attempted to lower them. The situation was not resolved until new sources of labor, primarily prisoners of war, were utilized.

After 1945, the numbers of French in the woods diminished, largely because of increased mechanization in logging practices and enlarged employment opportunities in Quebec and other parts of Canada. Nevertheless, crews of imported labor, bonded to return to Canada, remain well known in the American woods.

FURTHER READING: David C. Smith, *History of Papermaking in the United States, 1619–1961* (1970), and *History of Lumbering in Maine, 1861–1960* (1972). Virginia K.

Thurner, *Origin and Development to 1860 of French Settlement in Wood County, Wisconsin* (1980). Walker D. Wyman, *The Lumberjack Frontier* (1976).

DAVID C. SMITH

FRENCH, SPANISH, AND MEXICAN FOREST POLICIES ON THE GULF COAST

Mercantilism characterized French and Spanish colonial policy toward the forest resources of the Mississippi and Tombigbee river valleys. The French maintained tar kilns on offshore islands in the Gulf of Mexico and produced wax candles from the bayberry (*Myrica cerifera*). Indians taught French and Spanish settlers how to make dugout canoes or pirogues from cottonwood or cypress. The French constructed coastal vessels at Biloxi as early as 1724. Shipbuilders made use of the white and black oak for ribs, knees, and curbs.

When Spain occupied French Louisiana in the late 1760s, vigorous government support developed trade between the French and Spanish islands of the Caribbean and Louisiana. Sailors sent out by the Havana arsenal in the eighteenth century, such as Juan Baptista Franco and Josa del Río Cosa, explored Florida for suitable stands of shipbuilding timbers. In an effort to maintain quality and durability, cypress cutting was banned except during the period from October through February. Francisco Luis Hector de Carondelet, governor of Louisiana from 1791 to 1797, outlawed the private cutting of any timber if the log measured more than seventy feet in length. Spain maintained shipyards at Bayou St. John on Lake Pontchartrain north of New Orleans, and wherever fresh water moved swiftly, French and Spanish colonists built sawmills to cut barrel staves, planks, and boxes to supply the Cuban and Santo Domingo sugar industry, an ideal exchange for the mercantilistic commercial system. Jacques Toutant-Beauregard had the box contract for a time, but he failed when the measures of a 1774 shipment were different from the specifications and Cuban box-buyers refused to pay. Disastrous fires of 1788 and 1794 destroyed most of the original French houses in New Orleans, and Spanish builders used cypress and sassafras lumber to rebuild the city.

Spain guaranteed the right of Indians to cut firewood in the mountains, and the *encomenderos* in charge of the Indians were ordered to plant suitable trees for that purpose. The only other evidence of conservation was the restriction on cutting seasons.

Because of the relative scarcity of fine timber in the northern provinces of Mexico, including Texas, the Mexican government after independence in 1821 did not adopt any notable variation in the Spanish colonial system of forest utilization. East Texas produced some cottonwood and pine, limited to local use because of the distance and difficulty in reaching the markets further south.

FURTHER READING: Jack D. L. Holmes, "Observations on the Wax-Tree in Colonial Louisiana and the Floridas," *Mississippi Quarterly* 20 (Winter 1966–1967): 47-52; "Naval Stores in Colonial Louisiana and the Floridas," *Louisiana Studies* 7 (Winter 1968): 295-309; and "Louisiana Trees and Their Uses: Colonial Period," *Louisiana Studies* 8 (Spring 1969): 36-67.

JACK D. L. HOLMES

FURNITURE INDUSTRY

Furniture making in America started before 1650 as a handicraft with individual pieces handmade from local woods by craftsmen with limited skills and tools. Wood has always been the most popular material. In addition to its natural beauty and warmth, wood can be shaped both by hand and by power-driven tools: it may be painted, glued, bent, and otherwise worked, and it was generally available near the centers of population during the growth of the nation.

Two characteristics of furniture influenced the changes in the kinds and amounts of wood used in its manufacture: the intended function limited the number of woods found suitable, and changing styles influenced the choice among the suitable and available woods at any particular time. Although a large number of tree species are usable for furniture making, a relatively limited number of woods, mainly hardwoods, have natural properties that make them preferable to others. Since colonial times, the most prized have been American walnut, true mahogany, rosewood, white oak, black cherry, maple, beech, and, to a lesser extent, gum. Preference for specific woods has varied from period to period, mainly due to changes in style, design, and availability.

There have been four major periods in the development of the American furniture industry: the Early Colonial (1620–1700); the Late Colonial (1700–1790); the Classical (1790–1900); and the Modern (1900 to the present). Each of these periods coincided with a stage in the history of the nation, and the furniture styles popular during each period had a strong influence on the selection of woods.

The Early Colonial Period

The isolation of the American colonies from Europe and the high cost of shipping bulky items on vessels with limited cargo space encouraged the manufacture of furniture in the colonies. The seventeenth-century

Wood Use in the Furniture Industry, 1928–1977

Form of Wood	1928	1940	1960	1972	1977
Hardwood lumber (billion bd. ft.)	1.12	1.08	1.59	2.59	2.59[e]
Softwood lumber (billion bd. ft.)	.09	.01	.37	.73	.67[e]
Hardwood plywood (billion sq. ft. ⅜")	.24	.26	.33	1.09	1.05[e]
Softwood plywood (billion sq. ft. ⅜")	.01	.03	.38	.59	.63[e]
Particle board (billion sq. ft. ¾")	—	—	.09	1.27	1.16[e]
Hardboard (billion sq. ft. ⅛")	—	—	.33	.96	.88[e]
Hardwood veneer (billion sq. ft., surface)	[a]	[a]	.80	1.39	1.30[e]

[a] = included in hardwood plywood   [e] = estimated
SOURCE: U. S. Forest Service, various reports.

furniture of the colonies was strongly influenced by styles in the home countries, but it was less elaborate and less bulky than the European originals, reflecting the scarcity of skilled wood craftsmen, the smaller colonial homes, and the more austere colonial lifestyle. In this sense, the development of American furniture is a microcosm of the development of America as a nation.

As the economic condition of the colonies improved and town dwellers began to build stylish houses, tastes in furniture began to change from the simple, unadorned early colonial styles to the more elegant William and Mary style. Smoother, richly grained walnut began to replace the coarse-textured oak.

The Late Colonial Period

The late colonial period encompassed the turbulent years before and after the Revolutionary War. The development of a primitive road network and coastal shipping encouraged commerce. Furniture was made in the North and traded for corn and tobacco from the South. The Southern colonies were agricultural and lacked craftsmen for making furniture; only Charleston among Southern cities had cabinetmakers producing fine furniture.

Mahogany from Santo Domingo, Cuba, and Honduras became the favored wood for furniture making, although it never completely replaced walnut. The use of mahogany for practically all of the fine furniture of this period, such as Queen Anne and American Chippendale, was attributable not only to its superb qualities as a furniture wood but also to the fact that it was probably more easily obtained than walnut, which did not grow in large quantity along the coastal plain. It often cost less to import hardwood logs from the West Indies than to haul domestic logs from forests thirty miles inland. Nevertheless, the increased skill of local cabinetmakers and the development of a demand for moderately priced furniture encouraged the use of maple, cherry, yellow-poplar, birch, and pine.

It is unlikely that furniture making contributed significantly to the depletion of forests during the colonial period. The limited size of the population, the crudeness of the housing, and the modest general standard of living meant that furniture making consumed only a minor volume of timber when compared with large-scale landclearing for settlement and farming, and cutting for fuelwood, SHIPBUILDING, CHARCOAL, and lumber. The FURNITURE INDUSTRY was more a victim of forest depletion than a cause.

The Classical Period

The rapid national growth following the Revolutionary War provided a new market for furniture. The bulky nature of furniture discouraged its shipment over long distances and encouraged western settlements to develop their own cabinetmaking shops, which produced crude furniture using whatever wood was available locally. The evolution of frontier towns into cities with elaborate new homes in need of fine furniture ushered in the golden age of American furniture making. This period produced American copies of the classical Hepplewhite, Sheraton, and Empire styles. The period was dominated by the work of Duncan Phyfe, perhaps the greatest of all American cabinetmakers.

Cabinetmakers living near the coast or along the inland canal system used mahogany as their principal wood. Phyfe used mahogany almost exclusively. Cabinetmakers further inland used walnut and cherry.

During the latter part of the classical period, the use of cast iron and brass in bed construction became popular and represents one of the earliest substitutions of metal for wood as a basic furniture material. The metal beds offered a relief from the massive wooden frames and were less likely to harbor bedbugs.

At first, the growth of the American furniture industry was limited by competition with imports from Europe, which, because of superior production methods, could compete on the American market despite transportation costs. This changed in 1812 when a 30

Chair backs are being glued together in this chair factory. American Forest Institute Photo.

percent tariff was imposed on all imported articles, and the interruption of trade by the War of 1812 gave American furniture makers the protection necessary to move from small-scale cabinetmaking to large plants specializing in specific pieces. It was during this period that the great furniture centers of Jamestown, Grand Rapids, and High Point were established.

Jamestown, New York. Almost from its founding in 1811, Jamestown, New York, began to produce furniture of high quality, and it soon became the furniture-making center of the East. As the eastern forests became depleted during the latter part of the nineteenth century, Jamestown turned increasingly to metal furniture making. Wood furniture making shifted further westward to Grand Rapids, Michigan.

Grand Rapids, Michigan. By 1880, Grand Rapids had attained national recognition as a furniture center. Grand Rapids manufacturers were leaders in the adoption of recent technical advances in woodworking machinery. With plentiful waterpower from the rapids of the Grand River, furniture making evolved from a handicraft to factory mass production. The river also provided low-cost transportation of wood from the forests of western and central Michigan.

Grand Rapids pioneered in the development of the furniture mart, held there first in 1878. A semiannual affair, the mart provided large department stores and retail chains with the opportunity of previewing furniture styles before entering into costly production runs.

Grand Rapids furniture manufacturers emphasized design. At the moment they were installing the latest woodworking machinery, the English Victorian style, with its ornate carved furniture and straight lines, became popular. Such a style was particularly adaptable to machine production, and Grand Rapids manufacturers were in a favorable position to capitalize on the trend.

By the beginning of the twentieth century, the hardwood forests of the north-central states were showing signs of depletion and the center of the furniture industry was beginning to shift from Grand Rapids to North Carolina. By 1920, high-grade hardwood timber supplies were limited to the more remote and inaccessible portions of the southern Appalachians and the lower Mississippi Valley.

High Point, North Carolina. The development of a furniture industry in the South lagged behind, reflecting the region's agricultural and plantation economy. The North Carolina furniture industry began in High Point in 1888, producing mainly low-quality furniture sold within the region. The establishment of the industry there is attributable to the availability of cheap labor, cheap raw material, and convenient local markets.

In 1921, the collapse of cotton prices triggered an economic recession in the South and the disappearance of the Southern market for the cheap North Carolina furniture. In the search for alternative markets, North Carolina manufacturers exhibited their products in New York, where they were ridiculed for their shabbiness and lack of style. North Carolina manufacturers responded by making medium-priced reproductions of high-grade furniture. This strategy marked the beginning of the rise of North Carolina as the nation's leading furniture state.

The rapid consumption of the high-quality hardwoods during the first quarter of the twentieth century forced Southern manufacturers to search for less expensive substitute woods such as gums in order to maintain their furniture in the medium-price range. In 1909, oak, poplar, and gum accounted for 74 percent, 13 percent, and 1 percent, respectively, of the total furniture lumber used; by 1919 gum had increased to 21 percent of the total, while oak and poplar had fallen to 60 and 6 percent respectively.

By 1926, oak had been supplemented by black walnut and mahogany veneers in finer pieces of furniture. Red gum, in turn, was substituted in moderately priced pieces for the finer cabinet woods such as black walnut and mahogany. Depletion of timber supplies also encouraged the substitution of veneer for solid wood, despite some public prejudice. Raw material hauls of 500 to 800 miles were not uncommon as early as 1920.

In response to the growing scarcity of fine-quality hardwoods, North Carolina furniture, plywood, and veneer men met with forestry leaders in 1953 and formed the Furniture, Plywood and Veneer Council of the North Carolina Forestry Association, since 1963 called the Hardwood Research Council. One of their objectives was to stimulate research on the growing of better-quality trees and the use of existing low-quality hardwoods.

The Modern Period

Modern furniture is largely devoid of carving and is simple in line. The emphasis is on functionalism and the use of newly developed materials and manufacturing techniques to develop styles and forms not previously practical. Most modern furniture design adheres to the dictum of modern architecture: "form follows function."

The modern period in America opened with the mission-style furniture (1895–1910), inspired by the simple, straight-lined furnishings of the Spanish missions in California. But perhaps the most striking phenomenon of twentieth-century furniture making was the development of the notion of modernism. A clean break was made with traditional lines and the emphasis was placed on displaying modern lifestyles, materials, and technology. Until 1925, almost all household furniture was made basically of wood, and other materials were but rarely used as a part of basic construction. Starting with the introduction of steel tubing in the 1920s, one material after another was adopted, including plastic, steel, and glass.

Wood continued to be the favorite material, but it was often used in unusual ways, emphasizing its natural color, grain, and form, frequently in conjunction with synthetic materials such as brightly colored plastic.

The American furniture industry in the second half of the twentieth century has been characterized by a shift to California, Texas, and Florida, following the general migration of the American population. Important market centers developed in Atlanta, Dallas, Los Angeles, San Francisco, and Seattle, although High Point-Hickory, North Carolina, continued to be the most important furniture market. Proximity to raw material remained significant in the location of furniture manufacturing, but the availability of cheap labor and access to markets became increasingly important.

The fact that woods preferred for furniture making typically are scattered in stands containing many noncommercial species and the relative ease with which other materials can be substituted for wood have discouraged either the ownership of timberland or the practice of forestry by furniture manufacturers. The economics of furniture manufacture dictate that the manufacturer's primary concern must be with the furniture market and labor costs. The kind and amount of wood in furniture manufacturing has continued to be a result, not a cause, of the forestry situation.

Twentieth-century trends in wood use in furniture making are shown in the table. The increasing use of hardwood plywood, veneer, and particle board reflects the combined effects of the growing scarcity of high-quality sawlog-sized hardwood trees as well as the structural and design advantages of plywood and other wood panel products in modern furniture making.

FURTHER READING: James Bradshaw, "Grand Rapids, 1870–1880: Furniture City Emerges," *Michigan History* 55 (Winter 1971): 321-342. Helen Comstock, *American Furniture* (1962). Eleanor Craig, "Recent History of the North Carolina Furniture Manufacturing Industry," Ph.D. dissertation, Duke University (1959). Philippe Garner, *Twentieth-Century Furniture* (1980). House and Gardens, Inc., *Interior Decoration* (rev. ed., 1970). John Kirk, *Early American Furniture* (1967). C. F. Korstian, *The Economic Development of the Furniture Industry of the South and its Future Dependence upon Forestry* (1926). Marvin Swartz, *American Furniture of the Colonial Period* (1976). Frances Watson, *The History of Furniture* (1976).

HAROLD W. WISDOM
CARMEN DEL CORO WISDOM

G

GENERAL LAND OFFICE

By an act of Congress, approved April 25, 1812, the General Land Office (GLO) was established as a bureau in the Treasury Department to superintend and execute all transactions concerning public lands except the work of surveying and mapping. In 1836 it was given responsibility for survey work with the placement and functions of the surveyors-general under its jurisdiction. It became a part of the newly created DEPARTMENT OF THE INTERIOR in 1849.

The GLO was charged with administering several laws relating to forests of the public domain. One of the earliest of these was the Timber Trespass Act of 1831, which became the basis for later legislation for the prevention of timber trespass on federal government land. Under the Timber Culture Act of 1873, the agency issued patents to settlers who planted and maintained forty acres of timber on any quarter section of public land; by authority of the Timber and Stone Act of 1878, the GLO supervised the sale of certain public lands which were considered to be valuable chiefly for timber and stone and unfit for cultivation; and under the Free Timber Act of 1878, it permitted people of nine western states to cut timber at will on mineral lands both for domestic and for mining purposes. With the passage of the FOREST RESERVE ACT of 1891 and the FOREST MANAGEMENT ACT of 1897, the GLO was given responsibility for protecting and managing forest reserves created from the public domain by presidential proclamation.

Due largely to inadequate and untrained staff members, inefficient administrative methods, and legal loopholes, the GLO did not have much success in protecting and managing the use of public forests under the legislation just mentioned. Antitrespassing legislation was widely violated with impunity. Timber-planting results under the law of 1873 were not very impressive. Under the act of 1878, large areas of timber were secured fraudulently by corporations through collusion with individual applicants. Following passage of the Forest Management Act of 1897, the Department of the Interior issued regulations for the administration of the forest reserves and set up a field organization which reported through the GLO's Special Service Division (Division P). In 1901 the reserves were assigned to the GLO's new Forestry Division (Division R) led by Filibert Roth. Fire prevention and fire suppression measures were used to reduce forest losses. Programs for timber sales and tree planting were launched. Technical forest management advice was sought from the DEPARTMENT OF AGRICULTURE'S Bureau of Forestry, then headed by Gifford PINCHOT and staffed with the federal government's only trained foresters. Criticism of the administration of public forestlands by the GLO, however, persisted for many years, in spite of the efforts of some GLO commissioners such as James A. Williamson (1876–1881) and William Sparks (1885–1887) to increase administrative efficiency and to check fraudulent practices in disposal of lands. The criticism led to the transfer of administration of the forest reserves to Pinchot's bureau in 1905.

After 1905, the GLO continued to supervise the management of the public domain as well as the survey and disposition of other federal lands and the minerals thereon. It executed all laws relating to the surveying, prospecting, locating, appropriating, entering, reconveying, and patenting of all federal lands

within national forests, grazing districts, and other reservations. It conducted scientific and professional work in land and mineral economics, maintained an organization for the prevention and suppression of fires on the public lands in Alaska, and prepared and issued the official map of the United States, in accordance with specific instructions of Congress.

The agency adjudicated all claims to public lands initiated under numerous public-land laws, including applications for coal, oil, and gas prospecting permits and leases; it also granted railroad and other rights-of-way over public lands. It administered the revested Oregon and California Railroad and reconveyed Coos Bay Wag-

Settlers wanting to acquire homesteads needed to file an application with the General Land Office and fulfill certain residency requirements. Shown here is a homestead claim in Oregon's Umpqua National Forest in 1909. Forest Service Photo.

Ferdinand V. Hayden leads a Geological Survey expedition through Wyoming Territory in 1871 as part of the Department of the Interior's responsibility for western lands. Geological Survey Photo.

on Road grant lands in Oregon. This responsibility included forestry and grazing activities, fire protection, development of sustained-yield forest units, land classification, and timber sale activities. It maintained numerous district land offices in the western regions of the United States to receive applications to enter public lands, take initial action thereon, render decisions, and keep tract-book and plat records showing the status of public lands.

By the President's Reorganization Plan No. 3 of 1946, effective July 16, 1946, the GLO was consolidated with the Grazing Service of the Department of the Interior to form the BUREAU OF LAND MANAGEMENT in the department.

FURTHER READING: Marion Clawson, *The Bureau of Land Management* (1971). Paul W. Gates, *History of Public Land Development* (1968). Benjamin H. Hibbard, *A History of the Public Land Policies* (1939).

HAROLD T. PINKETT

GENETICS

See Institute of Forest Genetics

GEOLOGICAL SURVEY

The sciences played an important role in the growth of forest conservation, and of the sciences, geology was dominant in the nineteenth century. Four post-Civil War scientific surveys preceded the U.S. Geological Survey (USGS). Popularly known for their leaders, three of them—the Hayden, King, and Powell surveys

One-armed John Wesley Powell, intrepid explorer of the Grand Canyon, served concurrently as director of the Geological Survey and the Bureau of Ethnology from 1880 to 1894. Here he talks to a Paiute Indian. Smithsonian Institution Photo.

—emphasized geological research, while the fourth, the Wheeler Survey, concentrated on mapping; all, however, carried out additional scientific investigations in the natural sciences. When the four were consolidated into the USGS in 1879, many of the old survey scientists continued their activities with the new bureau, forming a growing coterie of scientists in government.

The USGS was one of the first federal agencies to manifest a concern for the American land, including its forests. In its first hundred years this bureau with the seemingly restricted charge of making a geological survey of the United States carried out extensive assignments in the realms of land classification, forest surveys, hydrographic work, determination of areas of irrigable land, reservoir sites, power dam locations, and determination of the value of forests at the head of navigable rivers for the protection of those streams.

Some USGS contributions to forestry came about through the personal interests of its personnel. Arnold Hague became convinced that streamflow was best controlled by a heavy forest cover which held the mois-

ture and released it at a slow, steady rate. Hague wrote and lectured widely on this thesis as an argument favoring forest conservation. He influenced Secretary of the Interior John W. Noble into approving the Yellowstone Forest Reserve south and east of the park, the first such reserve established under the FOREST RESERVE ACT of 1891.

USGS involvement in forestry was greatest in the eight years following passage of the FOREST MANAGEMENT ACT of 1897. Until 1905, USGS carried out surveys of the forest reserves which later became the national forests. To accomplish this assignment the survey's Division of Geography was enlarged and renamed the Division of Geography and Forestry. Head of the unit was geographer Henry Gannett, who had written in disagreement with the theories of the head of the Forestry Division, Bernhard E. FERNOW, and had even suggested that a laissez-faire policy was best for American forests. Nevertheless, Gannett provided good leadership and his division did excellent work, reporting on the resources of more than 70 million acres of American forests.

Gannett set out to provide the geographic and economic information that until then had been lacking. "Of the amount of standing timber available for our use we know almost nothing," he wrote. He then made estimates and showed their degree of reliability. His work established a base from which future geographical and economic research could be conducted. His reports, which constituted parts of the USGS *Annual Reports*, included comprehensive essays describing such features as population, towns, farm areas, topography, climate, industries, extent and type of forests, forest fires, and extent of logging. Photographs and maps accompanied the reports. The General Land Office used these data in promulgating regulations during its administration of the reserves.

In 1910–1911, the USGS found itself involved in a controversy between the FOREST SERVICE and the ARMY CORPS OF ENGINEERS over the role of forests in the prevention of flooding, the corps taking the stand that forests played no role. The survey sided with the Forest Service, insisting that forests were vital for watershed protection. One facet of this controversy was passage of the WEEKS ACT of 1911 which created a NATIONAL FOREST RESERVATION COMMISSION authorizing the Forest Service to search for and purchase forestlands necessary for the protection of navigable rivers. The USGS was charged with checking upon such tracts and verifying the need. The Weeks Act was especially significant in Forest Service acquisition of forests east of the Mississippi River.

Much later, in 1964, the USGS was made responsible under the Wilderness Act for surveying forest wilderness areas to determine mineral values. To a small degree the USGS has always been involved in forest surveys and acquisitions. The nearly 9,000 employees of the USGS are still concerned primarily with matters geologic, but clearly the survey has made contributions to forestry and it will continue to do so.

FURTHER READING: Jenks Cameron, *Development of Governmental Forest Control* (1928). Samuel T. Dana, *Forest and Range Policy* (1956). Thomas G. Manning, *Government in Science: The U. S. Geological Survey, 1867–1894* (1967). Mary C. Rabbit, *A Brief History of the U. S. Geological Survey* (1979). Harold K. Steen, *The U. S. Forest Service: A History* (1976).

RICHARD A. BARTLETT

GEORGIA FORESTS

Georgia, largest state east of the Mississippi, is blessed with a variety of physiographic regions ranging from coastal marsh to mountains. Primeval forests once covered the entire state with the exception of Okefenokee Swamp grassy areas. Forest types ranged from oak-pine-hickory in the Blue Ridge Mountains in the northern part of the state to oak-loblolly pine in the piedmont region and pine-palmetto-wiregrass in the coastal plain, where longleaf pines grew thirty to fifty feet apart. Cypress grew in swamps in the southern and coastal regions and live oak covered the offshore islands. South Georgia bore a magnificent crop of longleaf and slash pine forest known as "pine barrens." Fire maintained these pine forests from Indian times to the present. In 1977, about 25.3 million acres, 67 percent of Georgia's total area, bore a forest cover. It was the largest forested area in any Southern state and the second largest in the nation.

Early European settlers, mainly Spanish and English, utilized Georgia's forests for local construction, but very little agricultural clearing was accomplished until Georgia became a colony in 1732 and English and Salzburger immigrants began removing the forest to make room for silk, rice, and indigo production. Sawmills existed in Savannah as early as 1744, and occasional cargoes of lumber and other wood products such as shingles, staves, headings, hoops, and oars were being exported to England and the West Indies. By 1762, the Savannah district was producing over 400,000 board feet of sawn longleaf pine lumber for domestic and foreign markets annually. After the Revolution, lumber exports increased significantly and in the early 1820s steam power replaced tidal power in the sawmills.

Between the 1790s and the 1840s, Georgia's expanding cotton plantations pushed the forest back to the mountains in the extreme northern section of the state. Throughout the antebellum period, however, Georgia's lumber industry maintained a larger output than any other Southern state, with Savannah one of the busiest lumber ports in the nation. By the 1840s, Georgia exported about 25 million board feet yearly. About half the lumber went to foreign ports, mainly in the West Indies. Since skilled white sawyers were scarce in Georgia, free blacks and slaves made up a good portion of the skilled and semiskilled labor force, particularly in the mills of the interior.

The Civil War destroyed Georgia's commercial system and recovery took many years, but during the Reconstruction period railroad expansion and the development of NAVAL STORES placed new importance on the state's forest resources.

The boom years for Georgia's lumber mills came at the end of the century. The state's annual lumber production peaked at 1.3 billion board feet in 1899 and again in 1909. In the early 1930s production dropped suddenly, reaching an estimated low of 460 million board feet in 1932. Lumber production revived later in the decade, passing a billion board feet again in 1936. It

A pure stand of pond cypress in the Okefenokee National Wildlife Refuge, Georgia. Fish and Wildlife Service Photo.

stayed above that mark thereafter, and for several years in the 1940s and early 1950s was above 2 billion. Yellow pine has usually supplied 80 to 90 percent of the annual yield.

Also helping to remove the gloom of the Depression years from Georgia forestry was the discovery by pulp manufacturers that, with the sulfate pulping process, second-growth pine provided excellent fibers. Beginning with the construction of a large Union Bag and Paper Corporation plant in Savannah in 1935, the pulp and paper companies began to move south, particularly to Georgia. The next few decades saw continued growth in the state's forest industry. By the 1950s, Georgia was harvesting 3.8 million cords of pulpwood annually, and since then it has been the South's leading pulpwood producer.

Although North Carolina remained the nation's chief supplier of naval stores until after the Civil War, by the 1820s the industry had entered the longleaf pine belt extending along Georgia's coastal plain. Locally, naval stores production boomed only after the Civil War, but by the 1870s the Savannah region was the nation's largest supplier of turpentine and rosins. The industry continued to grow to its peak in 1929–1930, when 318,770 barrels of turpentine were produced. In the 1950s, Georgia still produced 78 percent of the nation's naval stores and half of the world supply.

Perhaps one of the more positive events in the history of Georgia agriculture was the gradual demise of cotton as a primary cash crop during the twentieth century. Old cotton fields reverted to pine, providing the resource base for Georgia's resurgence to a position of prominence in forestry. In 1977, with 24.8 million acres of commercial timberland (over 98 percent of the state's total forest), forest products were Georgia's second leading industry. Other important products in addition to pulp, lumber, and naval stores have been veneer and plywood, poles and piling, posts, and crossties. A sizable furniture industry has made use of the state's hardwoods.

During the boom years of Georgia logging, the state's forests were quickly reduced by wasteful cutting and repeated burning. By 1920, Georgia's forestland reached an all-time low of 20 million acres, only 53 percent of the state's total area. Georgia's 18.8 million acres of cutover land was larger than that of any other state in the South. Early interest in conservation was reflected in the 1906 founding of the University of Georgia School of Forest Resources, the first Southern institution to grant forestry degrees.

The State General Assembly authorized a temporary board of forestry in 1921 to prepare a report on forest conditions. A Georgia Forestry Association (GFA) had been founded in 1907, but it had aroused little support then; revived in 1921 with the support of the Southern Forestry Congress, the GFA led the campaign for the creation of a state forestry agency as recommended by the board of forestry. In response, the assembly in 1925 created a permanent state board of forestry and the post of state forester, and provided for forestry personnel. Reorganized several times, the state forestry administration finally in 1949 was established as the Georgia Forestry Commission. The commission has provided a great service to the state, private citizens, and industry through its nursery programs, education, management advice, and excellent fire protection. In 1953, the assembly created the Georgia Forestry Research Council as a separate agency independent of the Forestry Commission. The council's function is to stimulate research projects carried out by other public and private agencies.

After its first legislative success in 1925, the GFA, representing forest industry and forestland owners, continued to serve as adviser to state officials and as the leading lobbyist for forestry legislation. After 1947, GFA sponsored Keep Georgia Green and in 1948

it launched the Georgia Tree Farm program. Among other forestry organizations of prominence organized in the state were the Southern Pulpwood Conservation Association (1939), the Southern Pine Inspection Bureau (1940), and the Forest Farmers Association (1941).

In 1925, in an effort to control forest fires, the first Timber Protective Organization (TPO) was formed. TPOs were composed of private owners holding over 60,000 acres each. These organizations worked in cooperation with the new State Forestry Department to construct firebreaks, telephone lines, and lookout towers, and to provide personnel to fight fires. Programs in fire prevention, vocational agricultural education, and tree planting were expanded in the 1930s. Aided by the CIVILIAN CONSERVATION CORPS, Georgia brought 4.3 million acres of forestland under organized fire protection by 1937.

About 94 percent of the commercial forestlands have long been in private ownership. Of this, well over half is in farm woodlots. Industry holds less than a quarter. The federal government in 1977 owned about 6 percent of the commercial forests. State-owned forestlands amount to only something over 100,000 acres. In addition to a state forest of 37,500 acres managed by the State Forestry Commission, considerable woodlands are included in areas held as parks and wildlife refuges. The Georgia Game and Fish Commission, established in its present form in 1943, administers unique wildlife habitats totaling 400,000 acres, which are home to several endangered species and include coastal marshes, barrier islands, parts of the Okefenokee Swamp, and areas in the Blue Ridge Mountains. State parks preserve Georgia's natural and historic heritage while providing for recreation activities such as fishing, shell collecting, hunting, birding, camping, hiking, swimming, and boating. The Georgia Division of State Parks administers thirty-five parks and related areas totaling 29,890 acres.

The earliest federal reservation of forestlands occurred in Georgia. As the state's coastal barrier islands were particularly rich in live oak, prized by the U. S. Navy for its warships, in 1799 the government purchased Grover's Island of 350 acres and in 1800 Blackbeard's Island of 1,600 acres as live oak timber preserves to provide shipbuilding material. However, it was the passage of the WEEKS ACT in 1911 and subsequent land purchases that made the federal government a major forest owner in Georgia. Acquired lands became the basis of the Cherokee and Nantahala national forests, established in 1920; the Georgia portions of these two forests were combined as the Chattahoochee National Forest in 1936. Similarly, retired marginal farmland purchased under the Bankhead-Jones Act was dedicated as the Oconee National Forest in 1959. Continual acquisitions brought federally owned land in Georgia's two national forests up to a total of 853,551 acres by 1980. Over 30,000 acres of it have been designated as wilderness.

FURTHER READING: J. C. Bonner, *A History of Georgia Agriculture* (1964). John A. Eisterhold, "Savannah: Lumber Center of the South Atlantic," *Georgia Historical Quarterly* 57 (Winter 1973): 526-543. G. Melvin Herndon, "Forest Products of Colonial Georgia," *Journal of Forest History* 23 (July 1979): 130–135. Ignatz James Pikl, Jr., *A History of Georgia Forestry*, Research Monograph 2, Bureau of Business and Economic Research, University of Georgia Graduate School of Business Administration (1966). G. L. Plummer, "18th Century Forests in Georgia," *Georgia Academy of Science Bulletin* 33 (1975): 1-19, and "Mulberries to Soybeans: Changing Vegetation Patterns," *Georgia Academy of Science Bulletin* 34 (1976): 182–191.

BOB IZLAR

GERMAN IMMIGRANTS AND AMERICAN FORESTS

The first large-scale German immigration to America occurred in 1719 when 2,800 Palatinate refugees were settled along the upper Hudson River in an unsuccessful attempt to develop a NAVAL STORES industry. Later in the century, other Germans worked as charcoal burners for iron furnaces in Pennsylvania. Halted during the Revolution, German immigration revived on a larger scale about 1820, and for the next century and a half, Germans provided more newcomers than did any other nationality, up to 15 percent of the total arrivals. Yet Germans contributed relatively little to the work force of the forest industries. Most of the German immigrants sought primarily to acquire farms. They usually settled in hardwood belts, sometimes taking up cutover lands but more often clearing the native forest. Thus they often engaged in logging either as an adjunct or as a prelude to agriculture. German farmers sold cordwood to nearby towns, to steamboats along rivers, and to railroads for use in locomotives. They also sold timber off their land, and when their farms were located near forests, they often found seasonal jobs in logging camps. But woods labor was only a temporary or part-time occupation for them.

During the 1840s and 1850s, many Germans obtained employment in the lumber mills of the Lake States, often saving their wages until they had enough capital to establish small businesses. Only a few Germans, generally young unmarried men, took jobs in isolated logging camps; fewer still entered the ranks of management. Nevertheless, the exceptions provided some of the leaders of American forest industry. Frederick Weyerhaeuser (*see* WEYERHAEUSER FAMILY), born in Neidersaulheim, entered the Minnesota woods in 1891. During the 1870s, Anthony Zellerbach, a Bavarian, established in San Francisco the paper firm that still bears his name. With the growth of southern yellow pine exports in the latter part of the nineteenth century, Germany became dependent upon American lumber. Several German lumber merchants were accordingly drawn to the United States, and one of them, Frederick Julius Schreyer, founded the German-American Lumber Company of Pensacola. Schreyer's firm from 1901 until World War I was one of the largest southern yellow pine producers.

Some Germans were also prominent as conservationists and foresters. Carl Schurz, who immigrated to the United States in 1852, attempted to protect the forests while he served as secretary of the interior from 1877 to 1881. Bernhard E. FERNOW, who trained in forestry at Münden, Germany, became chief of the U. S. Division of Forestry, secretary of the AMERICAN FORESTRY ASSOCIATION, and head of Cornell University's school of forestry. The first American forestry school was founded in 1898 at the Biltmore Estate near Asheville, North Carolina, by Carl Alwin SCHENCK, a native of Darmstadt.

GLACIER NATIONAL PARK

On May 11, 1910, President William Howard Taft signed the bill creating Glacier National Park. Legislation proposing protection of this region of northwestern Montana can be traced back to the 1880s, but it was not until President Grover Cleveland established the Lewis and Clark Forest Reserve on February 22, 1897, that the northern Rocky Mountain region was actually given governmental protection. Under pressure from copper mining interests, the mountainous and foothill region east of the Continental Divide from the Great Northern Railroad line to the Canadian boundary was acquired from the Blackfeet Indian Reservation for $1.5 million, added to the Lewis and Clark Reserve, and opened to mining in April 1898. Traces of oil were then discovered near Kintla Lake and in a few eastside valleys, while gold brought a boom to the Saint Mary region. None of the mineral deposits proved profitable, however, and by 1902 most mining activity had ceased. Some of the miners stayed to homestead, trap, or hunt within this region.

Montana residents proposed a national park in the Glacier area as early as 1883 and George Bird GRIN-

NELL, who explored the region later in that decade, publicized the park idea in a 1901 *Century Magazine* article. However, it was not until December 11, 1907, that Montana's Senator Thomas Carter submitted the first of several Glacier Park bills to Congress. The slight opposition came from a few local homesteaders, hunters, and loggers and from opponents of the Great Northern Railway, which favored park establishment as a boon to its tourist trade. Publicists such as Grinnell, politicians like Senator Carter, and railroad officials such as James J. Hill and Louis Hill promoted the park proposal. Allowances in the Glacier National Park bill for water projects, mining, and the continuance of private inholdings had mitigated most hostility by 1910 when the park was created.

On August 8 of that year, William R. Logan arrived as Glacier Park's first administrator, entitled superintendent of road and trail construction. With an appropriation of $15,000 in hand, Logan replaced FOREST SERVICE rangers with his own political appointees and initiated the formative period of the park. Roads, trails, ranger stations, telephone lines, and other administrative construction projects were built by Logan and his six successors during the next seven years, but government activity was meager in comparison with the vast number of hotels, chalets, camps, roads, and trails built by the Great Northern and its subsidiary, the Glacier Park Hotel Company. Many of today's structures, roads, and trails date from this first seven-year flurry of activity meant to make the park attractive to travelers.

The compromises made in the Glacier National Park Act left the park riddled with private and commercial developments for many years. In 1910, the park included 16,668 acres of legitimate private claims. Superintendent Logan proposed selling government-owned timber for revenue, and even after his time, park timber was provided for construction by concessionaires. A sawmill continued to operate on Lake McDonald in the park until 1925. Summer home leasing was permitted up to 1918, and existing leases were abolished only in 1931. Gradually, private holdings were reduced, however. In 1980, Glacier included over 1 million acres of government land, while within its boundaries little more than 1,000 acres remained in the hands of the railroad and other private owners.

Glacier's major construction project came during the tenure of Stephen MATHER as director of the National Park Service. This was the Transmountain or Going-to-the-Sun highway which bisected the park through Logan Pass. Completed and officially opened on July 15, 1933, this $3 million highway introduced a boom period in Glacier's history. Riding and hiking were quickly replaced by automobile trips as the most popular activity for park visitors. The Going-to-the-Sun road, with its adjacent campgrounds, picnic areas, and facilities, catered to a more transitory, hurried visitor. In 1936, Glacier had 200,000 visitors, up from only 15,000 in 1917. Except for a lull during World War II, annual visitation steadily climbed thereafter. By the late 1970s, nearly 1.5 million people visited the park each year. In 1969, however, the park service, facing both requirements of the Wilderness Act of 1964 and new demands from increasingly vocal preservationists, began to reconsider its traditional management policies and to place less emphasis on continual development for recreation centered on the automobile.

On June 30, 1932, Glacier National Park was proclaimed part of Waterton-Glacier International Peace Park.

FURTHER READING: C. W. Buchholtz, *Man in Glacier* (1976). John Ise, *Our National Park Policy: A Critical History* (1961), chap. 9. Donald H. Robinson, *Through the Years in Glacier National Park* (1962). James W. Sheire, *Glacier National Park, Historic Resource Study* (1970).

C. W. BUCHHOLTZ

GOODYEAR, CHARLES WATERHOUSE (1846–1911)

Charles Goodyear, born October 15, 1846, passed the New York bar in 1871 and succeeded Grover Cleveland as senior partner in Buffalo's leading law firm when Cleveland entered politics. Goodyear played an important role in Cleveland's election as governor in 1882 and was later a frequent guest of President Cleveland at the White House. Goodyear gave up his own political ambitions to devote his time to the lumber business.

Charles's brother, Frank Henry Goodyear, manager of a lumber firm in Buffalo, began acquiring hemlock timberland in north central Pennsylvania in 1872. Charles was drawn into lumbering when he was called on to run his brother's hemlock operation during Frank's recurring illness. Eventually, the Goodyears owned fifteen sawmills in Pennsylvania. They ran the biggest mills in the eastern United States, sawing up to 250,000 board feet a day, and operated the largest system of logging railroads in Pennsylvania. The Goodyears pioneered the use of the Barnhart steam logloader as a practical machine. They also sold hemlock bark to tanners as a sideline.

When the hemlock stands approached exhaustion in the 1890s, the Goodyear brothers hired James D. Lacey to inspect and purchase yellow pine timberlands in

Louisiana and Mississippi. Eventually, the brothers invested in the Great Southern Lumber Company $9 million of their own, out of a total capitalization of $15 million. They selected the site of their Great Southern Mill on the banks of Bogue Lusa Creek in southeastern Louisiana. The Great Southern's timber holdings, covering roughly a triangle 70 miles wide and 130 miles north and south in Louisiana and Mississippi, originally contained 7 billion board feet of virgin yellow pine. Frank died in 1907 before the mill was completed, and Charles then headed the business for four more years.

The Goodyears selected highly capable employees to whom they delegated great responsibility, making them feel like "part of the family team" instead of hirelings. The outstanding example was Colonel William Henry Sullivan who had been with the Goodyear operations in Pennsylvania and was made general superintendent of the Great Southern Lumber Company. Sullivan designed much of the mill. Because it was so much larger than any built previously, Sullivan at times had difficulty convincing manufacturers to meet his specifications. The mill had a capacity of 1 million board feet a day, making it one of the largest lumber mills in the world at that time. One innovation made by Sullivan was the reclamation of sawmill waste by the Bogalusa Paper Company, a subsidiary firm founded in 1918 and the earliest successful Southern paper manufacturer. Another subsidiary was the Bogalusa Turpentine Company, which distilled NAVAL STORES from slabs and other refuse. Sawmill waste also went into the making of LATH, shingles, box shooks, and other minor products, as well as supplying the fuel for running the mill.

The Goodyears intended to make their town of Bogalusa permanent, and in 1920 Great Southern undertook an extensive reforestation project, eventually planting trees over 200,000 acres of cutover lands. These lands became the largest privately owned and hand-planted forest in the United States. The Southern Forest Experiment Station made Bogalusa its planting research center in 1923.

With the exhaustion of the old-growth timber, the Great Southern mill closed in 1938. The paper company in 1937 merged with the Gaylord Container Corporation of St. Louis. Gaylord continued operations at Bogalusa and about 1949 began harvesting the second-growth forest planted by Great Southern. Gaylord merged with Crown Zellerbach Corporation in the mid-1950s.

FURTHER READING: Michael Curtis, "Early Development and Operations of the Great Southern Lumber Company," *Louisiana History* 14 (Fall 1973): 347-368. C. W. Goodyear, *Bogalusa Story* (1950). Thomas T. Taber, *The Goodyears:*

An Empire in the Hemlocks, Logging Railroad Era of Lumbering in Pennsylvania, Book no. 5 (1971).

ANNA C. BURNS

GRAND CANYON NATIONAL PARK

Grand Canyon National Park in Arizona in 1980 covered 1.2 million acres, including most of the chasm for which it is named and segments of the pine, spruce, and aspen forest on the Kaibab Plateau to the north and the pinyon-juniper and ponderosa pine forest to the south. The entire section of the Colorado River within the Grand Canyon, 277 miles in length, is part of the park.

The Desert Culture, Anasazi Pueblo, Cohonina, and other prehistoric peoples left remains in the Grand Canyon, and the Hopi, Paiute, and other modern tribes regard it as ancestral territory. Three Indian reservations include parts of the canyon: The Havasupai (created 1880; enlarged 1975), the Hualapai (created 1883), and the Navajo (extended into the canyon in 1884, 1900, and 1930). The Havasupai live inside the canyon.

Grand Canyon was first seen by Europeans in 1540, when Garcí López de Cárdenas and others of Francisco Vásquez de Coronado's men were guided there by Hopi. Pedro de Castañeda, their historian, spoke of the area as "full of low twisted pines," an apt description of parts of the South Rim. Other Spanish explorers and American trappers entered the canyon, and official American explorations began with Joseph Christmas Ives (1857–1858) and John Wesley Powell (1869 and 1871–1872). Powell's two expeditions used rowboats to run the length of the Colorado River from Wyoming to points within and below the Grand Canyon.

A sawmill began operation in the Kaibab forest in 1871. John Hance, the first white settler, built a cabin on the South Rim in 1883 and soon began advertising his services as a tourist guide. Prospecting, mining, grazing, and hotel-keeping were the major activities of Americans in the region in the 1880s and 1890s.

United States government administration began in 1893 with President Benjamin Harrison's proclamation of the 1.85 million-acre Grand Canyon Forest Reserve. Theodore ROOSEVELT, who visited the canyon several times, advised in 1903, "keep this great wonder of nature as it is now. . . . You cannot improve on it. The ages have been at work on it, and man can only mar it. What you can do is to keep it for your children, your children's children, and for all who come after you." He took several measures to see that this was done. The U. S. FOREST SERVICE, with Gifford PINCHOT as its head, in 1905 began administering the reserve, redesignated

A couple scans the awesome canyon in 1914. National Archives Photo.

Grand Canyon National Forest in 1907. Roosevelt had proclaimed an almost coextensive Grand Canyon Game Reserve in 1906, and he set aside part of the area as Grand Canyon National Monument on January 11, 1908. The Forest Service remained the agency in charge of all these reservations.

As early as 1898, local support for a national park was expressed by a Flagstaff, Arizona, newspaper; John MUIR and other national voices for conservation had already urged this. There was also opposition, but Arizona's Congressman Carl Hayden and Senator Henry Fountain Ashurst succeeded in getting Congress to create a park. The bill, signed by President Woodrow Wilson on February 26, 1919, established Grand Canyon National Park on most of the land formerly within the monument, which was abolished. The national park, covering approximately half of the area that it includes today, was placed under the jurisdiction of the recently formed National Park Service.

A new Grand Canyon National Monument, administered by the NATIONAL PARK SERVICE, was established to protect nearly 200,000 acres downriver west from the park in 1932. Lake Mead National Recreation Area, created in 1936, included a large segment of the lower Grand Canyon, and Marble Canyon National Monument, upstream to the north of the park, was set aside

at the urging of Secretary of the Interior Stewart L. UDALL in 1969. The park itself was enlarged in 1975 to embrace those parts of the canyon within these adjacent units. Most of the park was subsequently designated wilderness, pursuant to the Wilderness Act of 1964.

Among the many conservation issues that arose at Grand Canyon some reached national prominence. In the 1920s, Senator Ralph H. Cameron tried to gain private control of access along the South Rim through mining claims, operation of the Bright Angel Trail as a toll road, and political pressure, but Cameron's mining claims were ultimately invalidated by the Supreme Court. An agreement with Coconino County gave the trail to the park in 1928.

A classic mistake in wildlife management came to a crisis in the Kaibab forest in 1924–1925, after predators, especially mountain lions, had been almost eliminated by government hunters. "Uncle Jim" Owens alone killed at least 532 lions in twelve years. The deer, protected in the game refuge, increased from an estimated 4,000 in 1906 to about 100,000 only eighteen years later. They browsed so intensively that the forest looked like a carefully clipped city park. Then thousands died of starvation. This incident helped game managers understand the positive role of predators.

A chronic problem has been the destruction of native vegetation and competition with wildlife from feral burros, introduced by prospectors in the 1880s, which proliferated into every corner of the canyon and its tributaries. The National Park Service has tried to remove them, but legislation passed by Congress primarily to protect wild horses has hampered this effort.

The threat that dams might be built in the Grand Canyon produced one of the most far-reaching controversies over conservation. The upper end of Lake Mead, behind Hoover Dam, entered the canyon in 1936. Glen Canyon Dam, authorized in 1956, controlled the river above the national park, but a water plan proposed by the BUREAU OF RECLAMATION in 1963 included two more dams, Bridge Canyon (Hualpai) and Marble Canyon, both of which would have been inside the Grand Canyon itself. Environmentalist groups such as the SIERRA CLUB aroused public opposition to these dams, and Congress placed a moratorium on the projects in 1968.

Visits by tourists to the Grand Canyon National Park rose from 44,000 in 1919 to more than 3 million in 1976. Grand Canyon attracts more foreign visitors than any other national park.

FURTHER READING: C. Gregory Crampton, *Land of Living Rock: The Grand Canyon and the High Plateaus* (1972). J. Donald Hughes, *In the House of Stone and Light: A Human History of the Grand Canyon* (1978). Roderick Nash, ed., *Grand Canyon of the Living Colorado* (1970). Richard Reinhardt, "The Case of the Hard-Nosed Conservationists," *American West* 4 (Feb. 1967): 52-54, 85-92. Douglas H. Strong, "The Man Who Owned Grand Canyon," *American West* 6 (Sept. 1969): 33-40. Angus M. Woodbury, *A History of Southern Utah and Its National Parks* (1950).

J. DONALD HUGHES

GRAND TETON NATIONAL PARK

Few regions in the world have natural grandeur to compare with the unexcelled beauty of the precipitous mountains rising from the floor of Jackson Hole. Grand Teton is a park devoted to nature, but it is also a tribute to persons of vision who understood the psychological, ecological, economic, and social importance of keeping such areas pristine.

In 1882, only a decade after the establishment of YELLOWSTONE NATIONAL PARK, General Philip Sheridan suggested extension of the park's boundaries to include the adjacent Jackson Hole region. In 1898, Charles Wolcott, director of the U. S. GEOLOGICAL SURVEY, expanded on Sheridan's thoughts with the proposal that a separate Teton National Park be established. However, the first real effort to establish the region as a park awaited the creation of the National Park Service in 1916. Director Stephen MATHER and his assistant, Horace ALBRIGHT, wanted Jackson Hole and the Teton Range within their developing national park system; they could hardly have guessed that it would take thirty-five years of bitter struggle to accomplish that dream.

At first it seemed easy. In 1918, Congressman Frank Mondell of Wyoming introduced a bill to extend Yellowstone National Park southward to include the Tetons and the northern portion of Jackson Hole. Unfortunately, Senator John Nugent of Idaho killed Mondell's bill with a last-minute objection. Thereafter park possibilities crumbled before the opposition of ranchers, local businessmen, and the U. S. FOREST SERVICE, which administered the region as part of the Teton National Forest. Throughout the 1920s, Albright wooed local residents as well as writers and politicians of national stature. Prominent author Struthers Burt wrote eloquently for the preservation of the valley. Albright and Burt argued that the establishment of a park would serve the national interest while bolstering the local economy. By 1929, they had convinced enough people that Congress established a small Grand Teton National Park. However, the park included only the mountain range, leaving Jackson Hole to the mercy of chance development.

To save Jackson Hole, Albright teamed with philanthropist John D. ROCKEFELLER, Jr. In 1926 Albright guided Rockefeller and his wife through Jackson Hole. To remove the threatened lands from possible development, Rockefeller established the Snake River Land Company. Between 1927 and 1930 this firm purchased over 30,000 acres of key private lands in northern Jackson Hole astride the Snake River, intending to turn them over to the National Park Service.

Local residents were bitter toward both Rockefeller and the park service. Hence, for almost twenty years Congress refused to accept the offered land, while park proponents and opponents quarreled over the fate of Jackson Hole. At times the argument centered on the conflicting aesthetic and utilitarian conservation philosophies of the National Park Service and the Forest Service; at other times the issue was expressed in terms of a defense of the struggling western rancher against the power of eastern wealth. Then, in 1943, President Franklin D. ROOSEVELT established Jackson Hole National Monument and switched the debate to a question of the relative power of the executive and legislative branches of government and the rights of

Wyoming's Grand Teton Range reminds many visitors of the Alps. American Forest Institute Photo.

the states against the national government. Finally, in 1949, Rockefeller was allowed to sign over his land with the stipulation that it be used only for park purposes; in the following year congressional compromise let the enlarged Grand Teton National Park come into being.

Grand Teton National Park became one of the most popular parks in the country, and new problems emerged as in other crowded parks. Private landholdings within Grand Teton present a continuing source of conflict. Issues unique to Grand Teton include the Jackson Hole airport, an intrusion upon the sanctity of the park which, despite opposition, has been scheduled for removal in the 1990s; another is the seventy-year-old Jackson Lake dam, in need of major rebuilding, which raises questions of the propriety of artificial structures within a national park. A classic case in the difficulties of park making, Grand Teton serves as a reminder of the continuing difficulties of finding a balance between preservation and development.

FURTHER READING: William C. Everhart, *The National Park Service* (1972). Aubrey Haines, *The Yellowstone Story* (1978). John Ise, *Our National Park Policy: A Critical History* (1961). Robert W. Righter, *Crucible for Conservation: The Creation of Grand Teton National Park* (1982). Alfred Runte, *National Parks: The American Experience* (1979). Donald C. Swain, *Wilderness Defender: Horace M. Albright and Conservation* (1970).

ROBERT W. RIGHTER

GRAVES, HENRY SOLON (1871–1951)

Born in Marietta, Ohio, on May 3, 1871, Henry S. Graves was the son of a professor of natural science at Phillips Academy in Andover, Massachusetts. Graves attended Phillips and Yale University (B.A., 1892; M.A., 1900) where he achieved scholastic success and demonstrated a capacity for leadership. Among his first acquaintances at Yale was Gifford PINCHOT, a senior when Graves was a freshman. Upon Pinchot's advice, Graves took up forestry as a career, becoming the second native of the United States to study forestry abroad. On his return from Germany, Graves joined Pinchot as a private consulting forester. The two men were coauthors of *The White Pine* (1896). When Pinchot became chief of the U. S. Division of Forestry in 1898, he appointed Graves as his assistant.

Both men realized the need for forestry training facilities in the United States, and in 1900 Graves became director of the newly established Yale School of Forestry, where he remained for ten years. Funded by the Pinchot family, the Yale school was a graduate program; it included field work on the Pinchot estate in Milford, Pennsylvania. In addition to other academic duties, Graves wrote two of the earliest American textbooks on forestry, *Forest Mensuration* (1906) and *Principles of Handling Woodlands* (1911).

After Pinchot's dismissal as forester (chief) of the FOREST SERVICE, he was able to influence the selection of his erstwhile colleague Graves as his successor. Graves's appointment assured that the service would continue to be led by competent professionals rather than political appointees. As forester from 1910 to 1920, Graves quickly restored orderly relationships between his agency, the secretary of agriculture, and the

DEPARTMENT OF THE INTERIOR. He overcame internal morale problems and congressional suspicions remaining after the BALLINGER-PINCHOT CONTROVERSY; continued investigations of private land claims within national forests; promoted a policy for recreational use of forestlands; began the purchase of lands in the East as authorized under the WEEKS ACT; oversaw the opening of the Forest Products Laboratory in Madison, Wisconsin; and implemented cooperative fire-protection efforts with state and local agencies. During World War I, Graves and several of his staff went to France to direct logging to supply lumber to the United States Army.

In 1922, Graves returned to the Yale School of Forestry as dean, a position he held until 1939. During this period he worked on several committees to advance standards of forestry education and natural resources conservation, and he collaborated with Cedric H. Guise on the textbook, *Forest Education* (1932). Following World War II, Graves chaired the joint committee on forestry of the National Research Council and the SOCIETY OF AMERICAN FORESTERS; the committee's findings and recommendations were published in 1947 under the title, *Problems and Progress of Forestry in the United States*. Graves also chaired a committee which laid the plans for inclusion of forestry and forest products in the United Nations Food and Agriculture Organization program.

Graves served as president of the Society of American Foresters, of which he was a charter member and fellow; in 1944, that organization bestowed upon him its highest award, the Sir William Schlich Memorial Medal, and in 1950, it named him as the first recipient of the Gifford Pinchot Medal. Graves also served twice as president of the AMERICAN FORESTRY ASSOCIATION. His leadership in forestry was recognized by the award of honorary LL.D. degrees by Lincoln Memorial University (1922), Syracuse University (1923), and Yale University (1939). He died on March 7, 1951.

FURTHER READING: Henry Clepper, *Professional Forestry in the United States* (1971), pp. 124–128. William B. Greeley, "Henry Graves: The Great Conserver," *American Forests* 61 (Apr. 1955): 20-21, 40, 42, 44, 46-48. Harold K. Steen, *The U. S. Forest Service: A History* (1976), pp. 103–144.

JEAN M. PABLO

GRAZING ON FORESTLANDS

From the beginning of white settlement, American forests harbored domestic stock animals, which roamed freely in unsupervised frontier conditions. Competition from domestic animals drove native game

Sheep foraging in the Mescalero Indian Reservation in New Mexico, 1928. Forest Service Photo.

away from white settlements. Hardwood stands provided acorns and beechnuts for hogs, helping make pork the main domestic meat staple of the American table by the time settlement reached the Mississippi River in the nineteenth century. In the South, the "cow pens" of the pine barrens provided an early base for a Southern cattle-raising empire. In New England, sheepherding replaced crop farming, hindering reforestation in the wake of a farmer exodus to the West. In the treeless Great Plains, forests were not a factor in the raising of stock. As the Mormon and later the stockman's frontier reached the Rockies, high mountain valleys were grazed. The forests above the valleys protected watershed that nourished grass for summer grazing of both

cattle and sheep and provided refuge from the drought of desert summers in the lowlands. Various oak forests in California and the Southwest also gave small farmers opportunities to run hogs. The sparse pinyon-juniper lands of much of New Mexico sustained a goat culture indigenous to the area and, finally, the forest provided refuge for a growing number of wild horses in various parts of the West by the twentieth century.

The problem of grazing on forestlands confronted the United States government after it began establishing forest reserves in the last decade of the nineteenth century. Cattle interests, defenders of watershed, and preservationists such as John MUIR sought the prohibition of sheep from the reserves on the grounds that these animals were destructive to the plant cover. However, Gifford PINCHOT's investigations for the DEPARTMENT OF THE INTERIOR in 1898 brought him into contact with Arizona sheepman Albert F. POTTER and Oregon's John Minto who helped convince him that sheep could be permitted in forests in spite of Muir's charge that they were "hoofed locusts." From studies in the Cascades of the Pacific Northwest, DEPARTMENT OF AGRICULTURE botanist Frederick V. Coville drew conclusions similar to those held by Pinchot.

The Department of the Interior, which through the GENERAL LAND OFFICE (GLO) took up administration of the forest reserves in 1898, at first prohibited grazing of sheep on any reserve except those in Oregon and Washington, while the pasturing of cattle and horses was left virtually uncontrolled. In 1900, however, Interior adopted the recommendations of Pinchot and Coville and established a free permit system to control the number of animals grazing in the reserves; sheep were permitted on reserves where they would endanger neither timber nor water supply.

When the forest reserves were transferred to the Department of Agriculture in 1905, the FOREST SERVICE (now directed by Gifford Pinchot) inherited the GLO's loosely enforced free permit system. The service's utilitarian theme, "the greatest good for the greatest number," virtually ensured that grazing would continue to be regarded as a proper forest use. The service in 1906 announced that nominal fees for grazing privileges would be imposed for the forthcoming season, although on the lands of the newer forests created by President Theodore ROOSEVELT in 1907 a year's grace was allowed. Fees ranged from twenty to thirty-five cents per head for cattle and horses during the regular summer season and from thirty-five to fifty cents per head for the entire year. Sheep and goats drew lower rates, with an additional two cents per head on grown stock that entered the forest for the purpose of lambing and kidding. Fees for the grazing of hogs were not immediately announced, but several forests in the Southwest soon reported hog grazing detrimental to forest regeneration. Rangers designated areas for individual grazing allotments and set dates for the stock to enter and leave the forests.

The Washington office provided guidelines to local forests through regulations listed in the Forest Service *Use Book.* Each forest supervisor could be aided in his decisions by local stockmen's advisory boards, which could collectively and individually appeal local decisions to the final authority of the secretary of agriculture. As a matter of policy, the Forest Service relied upon the authority and ability of officers in the field to make decisions of administration. Still, the head of the Grazing Section within the Forest Service reviewed carefully the annual reports on grazing events and plans for the coming year's allotments.

Many landowning stock raisers of both cattle and sheep saw advantages for themselves in the establishment of government forest reserves. In many instances, they requested and worked for the creation of forests. The permit system worked to eliminate casual grazing by "tramp bands" of sheep whose immigrant herders possessed no property. Prejudice against Basque herders in the Southwest and Scottish herdsmen in the Northwest flared on this issue. At the same time, in the Pinchot-Roosevelt era, the government encouraged the private ownership of agricultural lands within the forests; the Forest Homestead Act of June 11, 1906, provided for 160-acre homesteads in the national forests with free access to limited amounts of forage by settlers (*see* FOREST OWNERSHIP).

However, challenges to the authority of the Forest Service to regulate grazing came quickly in Colorado and California. In 1907 Pinchot announced that the Forest Service intended to test trespass cases in federal courts against stockmen who refused to pay fees. The result was the *Light* case in Colorado and the *Grimaud* case in California. These two cases, decided by the U. S. Supreme Court in 1911, upheld the constitutionality of the 1891 and 1897 forest reserve acts and the validity of the regulations issued by the executive branch under the authority of these acts. Stockmen who continued to graze animals on Forest Service land without properly paying for permits were guilty of criminal trespass.

Forest Service administration proclaimed, in each forest, a "protective limit" in the categories of cattle, sheep, horses, or goats that could be allowed for an individual permittee. Also, a "maximum limit" (or in more recent terms "carrying capacity") was set for the total number of stock to be grazed in a forest. Class A permits were issued to graziers who owned land adjacent to the national forests; class B permits to those who owned property which was not necessarily adjacent to the forest but who had a record of grazing stock there; class C permits were for herders who owned no land but only stock, mostly sheep, and moved them continually from the public domain into the forests and back again. These tramp herds were the last to receive consideration from the service.

By 1911, it became clear that forest grazing privileges greatly enhanced the value of nearby ranches, and ranchers attached sale value to the permit when the ranch was sold. The Forest Service, however, refused to recognize the automatic transfer of permits to new ranch owners, lest permittees be tempted to assert a property right to the grazing lands in the forests. The service asserted that use permits must remain privileges which could be revoked or reduced in accordance with the need to protect forest resources.

The work of the Forest Service in range regulation made it a pioneer in range management research and techniques. In 1910, James T. Jardine headed the service's newly created Office of Grazing Studies, which began grazing reconnaissances or range surveys to determine the effects of grazing through analysis of vegetation. In 1911, regional offices of grazing studies were established in the Pacific Northwest, Intermountain, Rocky Mountain, and Southwestern districts. The first range experiment station (later called the Great Basin Research Station) was established in 1912 under the leadership of Jardine and A. W. Sampson on the Manti National Forest in Utah. Researchers studied grazing in relation to forest reproduction with a view to harmonizing competing resource values. Topics of research included the determination of range readiness and nutritional requirements of stock; rotational grazing advantages; herding and trailing methods for sheep and goats; improvements of watering facilities; reseeding; stock rationing; and, later, the use of fire in shrub control. The passage of the MCSWEENEY-MCNARY ACT of 1928 expanded research on forested and untimbered ranges, public and private.

Before World War I, the Forest Service won widespread approval for its regulatory grazing policies. The outbreak of war in Europe in 1914 increased demands upon American agricultural resources. The range resources of the forests were no exception. When the United States entered the war in 1917, the numbers of animals on forest pastures increased dramatically. Limited grazing was allowed in Glacier and Yosemite national parks. Later studies by the Forest Service revealed that numbers of stock did not increase the amount of meat production from the national forests. The forests suffered depletion of forage resources as a result of this attempt to achieve quantitative increases without regard to the nutritional base upon which stock fed. Many new graziers in the forests suffered bankruptcy because of the abrupt end of the war and the subsequent low prices for poorly fed stock.

Before the war, the service had begun moves to increase the "reasonable fees" charged for grazing privileges to a level that more resembled fair market value for the rental of similar private grazing lands. Although the service had gradually raised grazing fees since 1916, the Department of Agriculture received criticism from the House Committee on Agriculture in 1920 because the grazing fees were still far too low. Some members demanded an immediate 300 percent increase. In 1919, the service had agreed to five-year grazing permits and believed that a drastic change would jeopardize the good faith of the Forest Service in the grazing community. Also, the inflation of the period clouded the true forage values in the Western grazing industry.

Rather than consent to an abrupt raise in the fee schedule in 1920, the Forest Service undertook a comprehensive study of the range values on both national forests and private lands in the Western states, with the intention of determining a fair basis of compensation to the government. This report, by C. E. Rachford, raised severe objections from stockmen when it appeared in 1924. The new rates it proposed would have brought fees for the rental of government forest grazing land into line with rent charged for comparable private property.

The threat of a new fee schedule prompted the first of a series of congressional investigations into the Forest Service's administration of grazing lands. Senator R. M. Stanfield of Oregon conducted hearings in Western cities, where ranchers testified that they could not under present conditions afford higher fees. Many proposed that grazing lands be taken away from the Forest Service and returned to the public domain for ultimate disposal to ranching interests. Forester William B. GREELEY appointed Kansas City stockman Daniel Casement to review the Rachford recommendations. Meanwhile, the Forest Service held the Rachford recommendations in abeyance and in 1925 issued ten-year permits at the 1919 rates. In 1927, the Casement Report suggested year-by-year implementation of the Rachford rates. The coming of the Great Depression, however, halted gradual increases in 1932 when the Department of Agriculture agreed to tie grazing fees to market prices of the previous year. In most cases, this meant a 50 percent reduction in fees as stock prices had fallen drastically.

The Western drought in 1934 and the passage of the TAYLOR GRAZING ACT in the same year for the regulation of grazing on the unreserved public domain prompted the Department of Agriculture to authorize a study entitled *The Western Range,* which appeared in 1936. It concluded that the Forest Service had done a commendable job in protecting forage resources on the national forests and condemned the condition of the public domain that had been left unregulated. It implied that the Forest Service would be the best agency to handle all grazing lands. Instead, the Department of the Interior set up a new Grazing Service, which became the dominant government agency in administering grazing on the remaining public domain. Some of this domain included forested lands. Grazing under the new service largely fell under the influence of local boards composed of stockmen. This was true even after the Grazing Service was subsumed in the BUREAU OF LAND MANAGEMENT (BLM) in 1946.

Whereas the Forest Service saw an enlarged role for itself in the administration of all public grazing lands, Secretary of the Interior Harold L. ICKES proposed that all public grazing lands including those in national forests be consolidated under the administration of his department. This demand found favor among ranchers who were reacting adversely to the Forest Service's attempt at "redistribution" of grazing permits. Service policy sought a wider distribution of grazing privileges to more citizens or "little men" in the business. Although redistribution was an attempt to keep pace with the social trends of the time, it engendered the rage of the established stockmen who resented cuts in order to accommodate newcomers to the range. The controversies sparked a new investigation of grazing policies headed by Senator Patrick McCarran of Nevada in 1940.

The onset of World War II brought demands for the Forest Service to boost again the numbers of allowable stock for the purposes of increasing national meat production. With the disastrous experiences of World War I in mind, the Forest Service resisted efforts to increase numbers. In some instances it cautiously implemented adjustments downward. By the end of World War II, the service launched a program to upgrade managed ranges by reducing the numbers of permitted stock. Determined stockmen in some areas resisted any such reduction because of the value that their allotments had attained in terms of securing loans and enhancing the sale value of their ranch property. Many permittees resisted cuts even for urgent range protection. The Forest Service insisted that the carrying of preferences above grazing capacity was unfair to lending agencies, potential buyers, and the protection and revival of the forage resource itself.

Again congressional committees appeared in the West to investigate the regulation of public grazing lands and the alleged tyranny of the Forest Service over the stockmen. Senator McCarran, now chairman of the Senate Public Lands Committee, wanted the Forest Service to postpone all reductions while his investigations continued. Forest Service Chief Lyle F. WATTS replied that reductions were needed to protect water-sheds, halt range deterioration, and safeguard the interests of other forest users. From the standpoint of stockmen, other users were a growing threat to their range allotments. Graziers became increasingly sensitive to the rising demands from urban centers for wildlife and recreational uses of rangeland.

Rumors abounded in the press about plans for the federal government to sell the public grazing lands both in and outside of the forests to stockmen at nominal prices and on liberal credit. Congressman Frank A. Barrett of Wyoming, who headed a subcommittee of the House Public Lands Committee, called for a three-year moratorium on livestock reductions in Western national forests and for the establishment of appeal boards to "represent fully the interests of the general public as well as the permittees and the Forest Service." The secretary of agriculture rejected the moratorium because overgrazed conditions on the national forest ranges existed from the standpoint of both watershed and forage protection. Conservationists who denounced the efforts of livestock interests as a "great land grab" included the IZAAK WALTON LEAGUE OF AMERICA, Arthur A. Carhart of Denver, and Bernard DEVOTO, editor of *Harper's*. Inside the Forest Service and especially in the Rocky Mountain Region, severe administrative conflicts occurred as a result of the public debate. Difficulties over the methods and speed of introducing reductions caused transfers of personnel and ultimately a slowed program of reductions in the region.

The Granger-Thye Act of April 1950, which emerged from these postwar controversies about grazing on Forest Service lands, recognized the authority of the service to collect fees for grazing privileges and endorsed advisory boards for each national forest including appointed representatives of wildlife from the state game commissions. The act provided no vested grazing rights. It did allow cooperative range improvements and recognized the practice of issuing ten-year permits. The secretaries of agriculture under both the Truman and the Eisenhower administrations abandoned the controversial policy of distribution of forest grazing privileges to more and smaller users. This was hailed by stock organizations as a victory—a significant step in guaranteeing stability for the industry.

Grazing fees on the national forests also provoked dispute. In the 1950s the Forest Service still used the plan adopted in 1932, which based fees on market prices received by producers in the eleven Western states during the immediately preceding year. This was quite different from the declared intentions of the Rachford Report in 1924, which attempted to raise fees in accordance with the cost of renting similar private lands. In 1959, however, the Bureau of the Budget, conforming to an earlier directive from the attorney general, called for users of public resources to pay a fair and uniform market value for the use of resources based upon similar private costs. The Forest Service in 1966 participated in a Western grazing survey to determine grazing costs and values of grazing lands to the users. This study placed the service and the BLM on the road to charging equivalent market value for grazing privileges—a striking shift in the BLM practices that previously charged on the basis of administrative costs.

The 1960 MULTIPLE USE-SUSTAINED YIELD ACT, while recognizing grazing use of the forests, also asserted the legitimacy of recreation and wildlife claims to range resources. More and more, the stock industry began to feel the advances of the recreationists and wildlife and wilderness advocates. For a while in the 1950s and 1960s, relatively heavy investment in range improvement occurred, including seeding, water development, fencing, and the use of herbicides, but in the 1970s this improvement work came to a virtual halt as environmentalists expressed concerns about the long-term effects. Since then range management has stressed ecosystem approaches to research and management and greater understanding of plant, soil, and animal (including wildlife) interactions.

These considerations were reflected in the Renewable Resource Assessments required under the FOREST AND RANGELAND RENEWABLE RESOURCES PLANNING ACT of 1974. In 1976, two more important federal acts appeared. The FEDERAL LAND POLICY AND MANAGEMENT ACT called for renewed fee studies and reaffirmed the ten-year permits and the continued existence of advisory boards. The NATIONAL FOREST MANAGEMENT ACT continued the principle that the federal government's work on the public lands should serve as a catalyst for the improvement of both public and private lands.

In the late 1970s, Western legislatures in the intermountain region led a "Sagebrush Rebellion" calling for the cession to the states of the vast public lands held by BLM. Primarily, these lands were valuable for grazing. Some stock interests saw state governments as more amenable landlords than the federal government's environmentally conscious bureaucracy, and, historically, moves by Western states to claim the public lands within their boundaries have occurred periodically from the 1920s onward. Because of local opposition and the Interior Department's determination to retain the public lands, the Sagebrush Rebellion lost momentum by 1980.

At that time, grazing on forested lands contributed only a fraction (less than 3 percent) to the total meat production of the United States. Such enterprises became more important for the distinctive type of ranch life they supported than as an essential economic component of the nation's meat-producing industry.

FURTHER READING: Samuel Trask Dana, *Forest and Range Policy: Its Development in the United States* (1956). Daniel R. Mortensen, "The Deterioration of Forest Grazing Land: A Wider Context for the Effects of World War I," *Journal of Forest History* 22 (Oct. 1978): 224-225. Paul H. Roberts, *Hoof Prints on Forest Ranges: The Early Years of National Forest Range Administration* (1963). Harold K. Steen, *The U. S. Forest Service: A History* (1976). William Voigt Jr., *Public Grazing Lands: Use and Misuse by Industry and Government* (1976). *The Western Range: A Great But Neglected Natural Resource*, Senate Document No. 199, 74th Congress, 2nd session (1936).

WILLIAM D. ROWLEY

GREAT SMOKY MOUNTAINS NATIONAL PARK

The formation of the Appalachian National Park Association (ANPA) in 1899 marked the beginning of organized efforts to establish a national park in the Appalachian Mountains of Tennessee and North Carolina. Headquartered in Asheville, North Carolina, ANPA launched a crusade to win federal aid to preserve what was termed "the last of the Eastern wilderness." Because a national park in the southern Appalachians, unlike those in the West that had been carved out of public domain, would require federal purchase of privately owned lands, ANPA's campaign encountered strong opposition, especially in Congress where the attitude of "not one cent for scenery" was prevalent. Frustrated in its efforts to acquire a park, ANPA in 1903 shifted the focus of its crusade and concentrated thereafter on securing a national forest, a proposal ultimately supported by President Theodore ROOSEVELT.

Although the WEEKS ACT of 1911 paved the way for the creation of forest reserves in the southern Appalachians, the idea of a national park in the mountains of Tennessee and North Carolina continued to attract support. In the early 1920s, conservationists, promoters of tourism, and representatives of various other interests generally agreed that the most appropriate site for a national park in the area was the Great Smoky Mountains, a ridge along the North Carolina–Tennessee boundary, whose spectacular topography and "primeval forests" were the subject of much publicity. In 1924, favorable mention of both the Great Smokies and the Blue Ridge Mountains of Virginia in the report of a committee appointed by the secretary of the interior to recommend possible sites for "a great national park east of the Mississippi River" prompted park advocates in Tennessee and North Carolina to cooperate. In order to press the claims of the Great Smokies, both states created park commissions which later assumed charge of raising funds and purchasing lands in the park site. Intense rivalry developed between those who championed the cause of the Great Smokies and those who advocated the Blue Ridge site, but in 1926 a measure enacted by Congress cleared the way for the establishment of national parks in both areas on the condition that they "be acquired without cost to the United States Government."

In their efforts to acquire the minimum park acreage required by the secretary of the interior, the park commissions of Tennessee and North Carolina not only encountered serious problems in raising funds through private subscription campaigns but also became involved in costly and protracted legal battles with the owners of large tracts in the Great Smokies. Only a $5 million gift from the Rockefeller Fund and state bond issues at critical junctures made it possible for the commissions to continue land purchases. On February 6, 1930, after the two states delivered to the federal government deeds to 158,876 acres of land in the Great Smokies, the site assumed "limited park status." However, the onset of the Great Depression and a succession of political squabbles involving the state commissions seriously hampered completion of the park project. During the 1930s, an additional gift from the Rockefeller Fund and over $2 million in federal emergency relief funds enabled Tennessee and North Carolina to complete the required land purchases. When President Franklin D. ROOSEVELT dedicated the Great Smoky Mountains National Park on September 2, 1940, it contained 463,000 acres purchased at a cost of over $12 million. Although park advocates consistently emphasized the visual aspects of the Great Smokies, their repeated references to the area as a wildlife and botanical refuge anticipated ecological standards of a later era.

FURTHER READING: Carlos C. Campbell, *Birth of a National Park in the Great Smoky Mountains* (1960). Willard B. Gatewood, Jr., "Conservation and Politics in the South, 1899–1906," *The Georgia Review* 16 (Spring 1962): 30-41, and "North Carolina's Role in the Establishment of the Great Smoky Mountains National Park," *North Carolina Historical Review* 37 (Apr. 1960): 165–184. George W. McCoy, *A Brief History of the Great Smoky Mountains National Park Movement in North Carolina* (1940). Charles D. Smith, "The Appalachian Park Movement, 1895–

1901," *North Carolina Historical Review* 37 (Jan. 1960): 38-65.

WILLARD B. GATEWOOD, JR.

GREELEY, WILLIAM BUCKHOUT (1897–1955)

With the exception of Gifford PINCHOT, no chief of the U. S. FOREST SERVICE more effectively put his stamp on the agency than did William B. Greeley. In his ability to convey ideas forcefully and logically he was without peer. Born in Oswego, New York, on September 6, 1879, Greeley accompanied his family to California in 1890. Eleven years later, he graduated from the University of California with majors in English and history. His writing skills and ability to see forestry in its historical perspective were, in part, the result of these early interests. Greeley briefly taught in the California public school system but yearned for work in the woods, which he had enjoyed as a young boy. Accepting the advice of Bernhard E. FERNOW, former chief of the U. S. Division of Forestry, Greeley entered the Yale School of Forestry, receiving an M.F. in 1904 with the highest marks in his class and the unqualified recommendation of the school's director, Henry S. GRAVES.

That same year Greeley entered the Bureau of Forestry and in 1906 he became supervisor of the Sequoia National Forest in California. Two years later, he became the first district forester in the northern Rocky Mountains, where he pioneered in forging cooperative fire-protection agreements with and among private timber owners. In 1910, fires devastated the forests of his district and he became convinced that fire protection was the essential first step in the successful practice of forestry.

In 1911, Greeley was transferred to Washington, D.C., as chief of the Branch of Forest Management. In *Some Public and Economic Aspects of the Lumber Industry* (1917), he argued that severe competition, overinvestment, and inappropriate tax laws were largely responsible for overcutting. Greeley advocated federal cooperation with the states and the timber industry in order to remedy these problems. Former Forester Gifford Pinchot strongly opposed this view, favoring instead federal regulation of the timber industry. Thus the stage was set for a fundamental clash over forest policy. For two years, this clash was delayed by World War I, in which Greeley served with distinction as a lieutenant colonel in charge of ninety-five sawmills in France that provided lumber for the allied forces.

In 1920, Greeley succeeded Henry Graves to become the third head of the Forest Service, the first to have been promoted from within. He soon began to prepare his program of cooperative fire protection and reforestation with the states. Pinchot and his allies countered with a plan, sponsored in Congress by Senator Arthur Capper, to impose federal cutting regulations on private lands of the timber industry. After four years of vigorous debate among foresters and in Congress, Greeley prevailed when the CLARKE-MCNARY ACT was passed in 1924. During his tenure as forester, Greeley also promoted the passage of the MCSWEENEY-MCNARY ACT of 1928, which securely established the Forest Service's research program.

In May 1928, Greeley became secretary-manager of the West Coast Lumbermen's Association in Seattle, a position he held until his retirement in 1946, although he continued to participate in forestry as chairman of the board of the American Forest Products Industries, Inc. During the Depression of the 1930s, Greeley was successful in encouraging sound forestry practices in the North Pacific Coast lumber industry. He was a member of and held positions in several forestry organizations. He wrote *Forests and Men* (1951) and *Forest Policy* (1953), as well as numerous scientific and popular articles.

Greeley gave outstanding support to the Yale School of Forestry. He was an organizer of the school's graduate advisory board (1905) and a founder and first president of its alumni association. In his later years, he had a leading role in the planning and financing of the school's post-World War II development program, service for which he was honored posthumously in the naming of the William B. Greeley Memorial Laboratory. The university had previously (1955) awarded him its Yale Medal for outstanding service.

Greeley also served the SOCIETY OF AMERICAN FORESTERS (SAF) in various capacities, including president (1915) and member of its governing council (1944–1949). He was elected a fellow of SAF in 1918 and in 1946 received its highest award, the Sir William Schlich Memorial Medal. He was awarded an honorary LL.D. degree by the University of California in 1927. He died on November 30, 1955.

FURTHER READING: George T. Morgan, Jr., *William B. Greeley: A Practical Forester* (1961). Harold K. Steen, *The U. S. Forest Service: A History* (1976), pp. 173–195.

DENNIS M. ROTH

GRINNELL, GEORGE BIRD (1849–1938)

Although best known for his writings on the Plains Indian, it was in the conservation of natural resources that George Bird Grinnell made his greatest impact on American history. In his obituary, the *New York Times* described him as the "father of American conservation."

Born into an upper class Brooklyn family on September 20, 1849, Grinnell grew up in comfort, with the leisure to hunt and pursue nature studies. From Yale he received three degrees, a B.A. in 1870, a Ph.D. in paleontology in 1880, and an honorary Lit.D. in 1921. He served as a naturalist with several exploring expeditions to the unmapped West, including one led by paleontologist Othniel C. Marsh in 1870 along the line of the just completed transcontinental railroad, one with Colonel George A. Custer to the Black Hills in 1874, and one with engineer William Ludlow to YELLOWSTONE NATIONAL PARK in 1875. Grinnell became natural history editor of *Forest and Stream* in 1876 and was editor and owner of that journal from 1880 until 1911. He used this preeminent outdoorsmen's weekly to launch a series of conservation campaigns. Virtually all of his editorials were unsigned, because he felt that the viewpoint of a newspaper carried more weight than the opinion of a single individual.

Among these muckrakerlike campaigns was an effort, beginning in 1882, to secure proper protection and management for YELLOWSTONE NATIONAL PARK and to establish in law the concept that a national park should be an inviolate wildlife and wilderness sanctuary. This campaign succeeded in 1894 when Congress passed An Act to Protect the Birds and Animals in Yellowstone National Park. Grinnell and *Forest and Stream* deserved most of the credit for this success. In later years, he continued his efforts on behalf of the national parks. GLACIER NATIONAL PARK was set aside in 1910, because of a campaign initiated by Grinnell.

Another of his sustained editorial endeavors, starting in April 1882, was to have the European science of forestry adapted to American woodlands. In May 1884, for example, *Forest and Stream* demanded that the federal government immediately appoint "A Competent Forestry Officer," a "trained professional" to lead in "the inauguration of a system of forest conservancy." Editor Grinnell also encouraged the establishment of the NEW YORK STATE FOREST PRESERVE in the Adirondacks in 1885, as well as legislation granting the president of the United States the right to set aside forest reserves.

Grinnell was always most active in wildlife conservation. In 1886, he founded the first Audubon Society to preserve nongame bird species, and in 1887–1888, he joined with Theodore ROOSEVELT and others in establishing the BOONE AND CROCKETT CLUB, an organization made up mainly of patrician sportsmen dedicated to preserving big game and its habitat. Grinnell and Roosevelt coedited the Boone and Crockett Club book series on hunting, natural history, and conservation.

Grinnell had the greatest influence on the development of Roosevelt's conservation philosophy before the future president became well acquainted with Gifford PINCHOT.

Although he remained active in conservation activities after his retirement from *Forest and Stream* in 1911, nothing Grinnell did in later years matched in significance the accomplishments of his earlier career. He died on April 11, 1938.

FURTHER READING: John F. Reiger, "A Dedication to the Memory of George Bird Grinnell, 1849–1938," *Arizona and the West* 21 (Spring, 1979): 1-4; *American Sportsmen and the Origins of Conservation* (1975); and (ed.) *The Passing of the Great West: Selected Papers of George Bird Grinnell* (1972 and 1976).

JOHN F. REIGER

GYPPO LOGGING

Gyppo logging is a slang term used in the western United States forest industry to refer to timber harvesting or other woods work done on a piecework or small contract basis. A worker who is paid on this basis is called a gyppo (sometimes gypo).

One of the most colorful and individualistic workers in American industry, the gyppo works at almost any woods job. He negotiates piecework rates and contracts, often oral agreements, with mills and other owners of timber to do all or part of the work of cutting and moving timber from the stump to the mill. He is the independent operator of the industry, the small logger earning a living from handling the little jobs unsuited to larger, high volume enterprises.

Gyppo logging carried a derogatory connotation when it first became a widely accepted practice in the Western woods at the close of World War I. At that time, an increasing number of loggers opted for piecework to earn more money than was otherwise possible under the prevailing hourly and daily wage system. Labor leaders, union members, and woods workers believed these early pieceworkers "gypped" the wage workers and undercut the wage system by working longer hours at such low rates that no one benefited. (The term gyppo was borrowed from earlier days of western railroad construction when it was used to refer to crews laying ties and rails on a piecework basis.) Early gyppo loggers were thought to be interested only in "making a fast buck" and were believed to make shady deals and follow unscrupulous cutting practices.

Technological changes in the 1930s and 1940s, including the development of the crawler tractor, logging truck, and chain saw, and a greatly expanded mileage of forest roads, led to greater productivity and lower manpower requirements per job, gave the logger increased mobility, and spurred the development of truck and tractor logging that has become the hallmark of the gyppo. By the 1950s, the old-time lumberjack had virtually vanished, and the gyppo had evolved from the contemptible pieceworker of the post-World War I era to the independent, self-employed, often respected logger and family man that he is today. As the new technology favored smaller crews performing the complete stump-to-mill process, many small gyppo operations proliferated in areas of the western United States where earlier there had been large company crews.

FURTHER READING: Ralph W. Hidy, Frank E. Hill, and Allan Nevins, *Timber and Men: The Weyerhaeuser Story* (1963). Walter F. McCulloch, *Woods Words: A Comprehensive Dictionary of Loggers' Terms* (1958).

DAVID H. WILLIAMSON

HARDWOOD FLOORING INDUSTRY

Wood flooring has been manufactured from most species of softwoods and several of hardwoods, principally oak and hard (sugar) maple, but including limited quantities of birch, beech, pecan, and occasionally others. The manufacturing processes differ greatly. Softwood flooring is the product of planing mills, usually operated in conjunction with sawmills. Hardwood flooring, which requires a much higher degree of technology, is produced in plants designed exclusively for the purpose, with dry-kilns and highly sophisticated and specialized machinery. The hardwood flooring industry since the 1890s has been a separate and distinct entity within the forest products industries.

The first wood floors in the log structures erected by colonists in America were what are called puncheon floors, made up of split logs, flat sides up, fitted edge to edge, and smoothed with an ax or adz. The first major step toward turning out more refined flooring came with development of the whipsaw, which enabled the colonists to cut logs into wide planks. In the eastern states, there are a number of colonial homes and other buildings with original plank floors still intact. While oak flooring has been used since colonial times, maple flooring was not commercially manufactured until the late 1870s, when its hardness made it particularly suitable for certain mill uses. Only in the 1890s did maple become an important lumber tree, as Michigan lumbermen began harvesting their hardwoods after depleting the pine and hemlock on their lands. Early hardwood flooring had been made with straight sides, face-nailed, and butted in installation, with noticeable cracks often appearing between strips. The perfection about 1885 of the matching machine, which could cut a tongue on one side of planks and a groove on the other, made possible the modern hardwood flooring industry. The matcher produced flooring that would join snugly, with pieces interlocked at the sides and blind-nailed.

After 1890, Thomas Wilce's Chicago mill specialized in manufacture of maple flooring from lumber cut in Michigan. Specialized flooring machines were in use about 1896, and a few years later the Nashville Hardwood Flooring Company in Tennessee built the first factory designed for the exclusive manufacture of oak flooring. Other specialized flooring plants soon followed, primarily north of the Ohio River where oak, hard (sugar) maple, birch, and beech were indigenous, particularly in Wisconsin and Michigan. As supplies of desirable northern oak were depleted, the manufacturers of oak flooring moved south and located in an area extending from Virginia to Missouri, Arkansas, and east Texas. Hard maple producers continued in the North where supplies of that species were still available.

The next major technical advance in hardwood

Depletion of high-quality oak timber has virtually eliminated the manufacture of flooring in lengths as shown here in Chattanooga, Tennessee. Forest History Society Photo.

flooring production, introduced in 1898, was end-matching, which improved the appearance of floors, saved work (as the ends of flooring strips no longer had to meet directly over joists), and reduced installation time. This was followed in 1902 by the development of a side-matcher which permitted hollow backing. This device milled one or two grooves on the underside of the flooring. As the installation of subfloors became common, hollow backing, by straddling slight protruberances, enabled flooring pieces to lie on a level plane even though the subfloors were not perfectly flat. It also decreased the shipping weight of flooring.

The use of subflooring permitted thinner flooring strips, and in 1903, thicknesses of 5/16, 3/8, and 1/2 inch began to be stocked in addition to the old normal thickness of 7/8 inch. Five-sixteenths-inch flooring was square-edge and face-nailed, the others tongued and grooved.

Central heating, used in American homes in the early twentieth century, tended to dry out interiors in winter, adversely affecting wood surfaces. The answer to this problem was found in improved methods of kiln-drying to reduce the moisture content of flooring.

Special processes have been developed to enhance

the decorative effect of hardwood parquet flooring. Some mills, for example, have machines that bevel edges of planks to simulate the cracks which lend charm to the early colonial plank floors. Parquet floors include many different designs achieved by laying short pieces of flooring in varying patterns such as herringbone, squares, and more intricate arrangements. Unit-block flooring in the early 1920s reduced the cost of parquetry, which previously had to be laid painstakingly, piece by piece. Laminated blocks, composed of three plies of hardwood, could easily be installed in mastic. The 1930s saw the introduction of mass-produced flooring finished at the mill even to the final waxing and polishing. By 1940, strip as well as block flooring was available in prefinished style. In the mid-1950s, "finger blocks," consisting of five or six narrow strips five to six inches long and 5/16-inch thick, were offered for installation in mastic.

Since shortly after World War I, the production and use of strip-type flooring in oak has dominated the hardwood flooring industry, especially in residential construction. Flooring of hard maple was next in importance, with its chief markets in such buildings as stores, factories, textile mills, bakeries, and gymnasiums. Production of strip oak flooring peaked in 1955 at approximately 1.25 billion board feet. Following World War II, concrete slab construction steadily increased in popularity, particularly in warmer areas of the country. Other types of flooring, including wood blocks and parquetry that can be installed with an adhesive directly over concrete, wall-to-wall carpets, and (for a limited time) asphalt tile, took over much of the market that had been dominated by strip flooring. The worst blow to the market for strip flooring came in the late 1960s after the Federal Housing Administration approved the cost of wall-to-wall carpets over concrete or plywood as part of the value of homes for mortgage purposes. The use of strip flooring in 1979 was less than 10 percent of the 1955 peak. New types of thin planks and parquetry have since been developed for installation with adhesives. Hard maple flooring continues to have specialized uses, primarily for sport floors such as those for gymnasium, hand-ball, and racquet-ball courts.

Trade associations for the establishment of uniform grading rules and the compilation of industry statistics include the National Oak Flooring Manufacturers Association, founded in 1909, and the Maple Flooring Manufacturers Association, founded in 1897. Their activities include advertising and promotion programs. In 1925, the Supreme Court of the United States found that the distribution of statistical information by the Maple Flooring Manufacturers Association did not constitute restraint of competition under the Sherman Antitrust Act, a landmark decision which encouraged the use of trade associations as a force for economic stability throughout American industry in the later 1920s and 1930s.

HENRY H. WILLINS

HAWAII FORESTS

Hawaii's forest types vary with rainfall, elevation, and cloud cover. Rain forests predominate in windward areas; dry woodland, scrub, and savannas in leeward. Species tend to be tropical in origin, almost none of the indigenous plants being of temperate American derivation. Over the years, most attention has been directed to the rain forests, for as Ralph S. Hosmer, first territorial forester, put it, "in Hawaii water, not wood, is the principal product of the forest." Water was essential for domestic use and for irrigating sugar plantations, long the backbone of the islands' economy.

In precontact times, Hawaiians drew upon the forests for materials for buildings, weapons, clothing, utensils, and more. They introduced nonindigenous plants, such as the coconut, breadfruit, and mulberry, and they cleared and terraced various lowland areas for agriculture. Perhaps one-fourth to one-third of the forested area was significantly affected by precontact activities.

In 1778, Captain James Cook introduced Hawaii to the Western world and the goat to Hawaii. George Vancouver brought sheep and cattle in 1793. Overgrazing by domestic and feral herbivores could soon be seen. By 1856, Hawaii's pioneer botanist, William Hillebrand, was calling for conservation of native vegetation, but not until the reign of King Kalakaua did remedial action begin. By then, the sugar economy was booming, increasing the need for irrigation, and Honolulu was starting to outstrip its surface supplies of water. In 1876, the legislature passed a law that sought to prevent forest destruction and consequent diminution of water supplies through use of the power of eminent domain. In 1878, Kalakaua personally participated in the first governmental reforestation effort, helping plant eucalyptus trees in Honolulu's upper watershed. The first extensive reforestation was carried out in 1882 by the Lihue Plantation Company, which planted 300 acres on Kauai. That same year, the royal government established a tree nursery in Honolulu. By 1889, some 460,000 trees from the nursery had been planted. It continued to prosper under David Hughes, its director from 1893 to 1929.

In 1893, the Kingdom of Hawaii established a Bureau of Agriculture and Forestry that was continued under the Provisional Government and Republic. The Hawaiian Sugar Planters Association, established in 1895, worked closely with the bureau, setting up an experiment station in 1897, which, under Walter Maxwell, became a leading force in attempts to restore Hawaii's forests.

Success attended some early efforts—by 1902, the slopes behind Honolulu were largely reclothed—but overgrazing continued. Foresters from the mainland, brought in by Governor Sanford B. Dole to provide advice, criticized the practice of replanting while still letting out leases on damaged public lands. Act 44 of the Territorial Legislature, passed in 1903, cleared the way for forest reserves that would encompass both public and private lands and from which grazing would be barred. Hosmer, with the cooperation of the sugar planters, established the reserves without real opposition. Eventually, 30 percent of the land area of the islands (1.2 million of the state's 2 million forested acres) was included. Under Hosmer's successor, Charles Sheldon Judd, the reserves were fenced and the number of feral herbivores reduced. Restoration of Hawaii's forests could at last make significant progress. Work by the CIVILIAN CONSERVATION CORPS in the 1930s pushed it ahead, doing as much in eight years, Judd said, as the territory alone would have accomplished in forty. The control of feral herbivores was sufficiently successful for their status to be changed in 1950 from pests to game animals, although most environmentalists continued to view them as pests, and their destructive impact, although lessened, went on.

Commercial cutting was significant during the sandalwood boom of the early nineteenth century but seldom since. Damage to the forests from the cutting of scattered sandalwood trees was limited, but the sandalwood trade led to neglect of agriculture and to other problems, exacerbating the disintegration of native society. Also harmful to those engaged was the gathering of pulu fiber from tree ferns. Pulu was exported in the mid-nineteenth century for use as mattress and pillow stuffing. Gatherers often caught pneumonia working in the high, cool rain forests where it grew. From 1907 to 1914, mills sawed ohia and koa on the island of Hawaii, but most of the cut was of poor quality. Islanders continued to rely upon the West Coast of the United States for lumber. Cutting firewood for domestic use and for firing plantation boilers had a greater impact on the woods than did this short-lived logging. Planting eventually led to renewed but limited lumbering. In 1976, the state began a thirty-year program of tree planting, with the expectation of raising production some sevenfold (to 92 million board feet per year) by 2006. Most of the cut will probably go into wood chips for Japan.

Overgrazing wiped out numerous endemic plant species, making restoration of original biotic communities impossible. Botanists have played a major role in Hawaiian forestry through attempts to find nonindigenous species to use in creating healthy new plant communities. Unfortunately, some introductions have turned out to be pests.

Reforestation with native species began in 1901. Recently, new efforts have been made to save and bring back native species. In 1950, a Koai'a sanctuary was established and, in 1970, a system of natural areas for the preservation of other native flora and fauna. The need is great. Hawaii has more endangered plant and bird species than any other state; its forest habitats harbor some of the world's most unusual examples of evolutionary adaptive radiation. In 1973, the Endangered Species Act was employed to halt state foresters from bulldozing "unproductive forest land" and replanting it with commercial species. Public sympathy for such preservation efforts has grown markedly. In this, as in the recent establishment of greenbelts and marine parks, Hawaii reflects the shifting environmental concerns of the mainland.

Increasing recreational activity is occurring in Hawaii's forests, and state officials now talk of multiple use. At the same time, the burgeoning population of the islands has caused pressure to reduce the size of the reserves. The continuing need for water, coupled with the newer emphasis on endangered species, environmental quality, and outdoor recreation, seems sufficient to diffuse these pressures and keep the reserves at something close to their present size for the foreseeable future. Timber production will no doubt continue to be a secondary concern.

FURTHER READING: Sherwin Carlquist, "Beachheads for Life," in *The American Land* (1979), pp. 90-99. Thomas H. Creighton, *The Lands of Hawaii: Their Use and Misuse* (1978). William L. Hall, *The Forests of the Hawaiian Islands*, Bureau of Forestry Bulletin no. 48 (1904). Ralph S. Hosmer, "The Beginning Five Decades of Forestry in Hawaii," *Journal of Forestry* 57 (Feb. 1959): 83-89.

THOMAS R. COX

HERTY, CHARLES HOLMES (1867–1938)

Born in Milledgeville, Georgia, on December 4, 1867, Charles Herty was educated at Georgia Military and Industrial College, the University of Georgia, and Johns Hopkins University, where he received his Ph.D. in chemistry in 1890. His career began as a college professor, first at the University of Georgia and later at the University of North Carolina, Chapel Hill. He served as president of the American Chemical Society, was employed as a research chemist for the federal government and the State of Georgia, and was editor of the *Journal of Industrial and Engineering Chemistry.*

Charles Herty's contributions to the forest products industry began in the early years of the twentieth century. He did experimental work in 1902 for the U. S. FOREST SERVICE at Ocilla, Georgia. Herty's cup-and-gutter system to gather pine sap was a revolutionary process and eventually replaced the wasteful box method of gathering sap.

Herty's second contribution came in the late 1920s when he developed a vision of a Southern newsprint paper industry that would free the United States of Canadian dominance and provide Southern farmers with a market for pulpwood. Southern pine had previously been considered an unsatisfactory raw material for newsprint, as it contained too much resin and made a yellow-colored paper. Through experimentation, Herty proved that southern yellow pine pulp could provide a white paper. He secured financial assistance from various sources and established a laboratory for further investigation.

In 1933, after much frustration, Herty successfully produced a good grade of newsprint from Georgia slash pine. Commercial success came when a Canadian mill used Herty's wood pulp to produce the newsprint for the printing of several Georgia newspapers. Herty then launched a crusade to establish a Southern newsprint paper industry. He was a skilled publicist and his strategy was broad. Although he emphasized the need for a domestic newsprint paper industry to free the United States from Canadian dominance, he also pointed out the possibilities of reforestation, the profits of pulpwood as a second cash crop for farmers, and the potential development of secondary industries related to the paper industry. By 1936, his research indicated that sulfite pulp produced from southern pine was high in alpha cellulose and was excellent for the manufacture of rayon. He was quick to indicate what the economic impact of an extension of the rayon industry would mean to the South. Herty's speeches and papers appealed to a wide audience for support of Southern development, but they stirred resentment in the North and in Canada, areas that did not wish additional competition in an industry already overexpanded during this period of economic depression.

As a result of steadily increasing newsprint prices in 1937, the Southern Newspaper Publishers Association pursued the possibility of constructing a South-

ern newsprint mill. Meanwhile, Ernest L. Kurth, a Texas lumberman, became intrigued by Herty's research work and agreed to risk his money to build such a mill. This plant, Southland Paper Mills, Inc., located near Lufkin, Texas, began commercial operation on January 17, 1940. Its success, combined with the South's economic advantages for papermaking, eventually resulted in the establishment of many additional newsprint mills in the South. In subsequent decades, the region provided the bulk of the newsprint produced in the United States and enabled the nation to free itself from dependence on Canadian newsprint supplies.

Charles Herty, having died of heart failure on July 27, 1938, did not see his dream come true. This brilliant chemist not only helped establish a new papermaking technology but he also helped promote an industry based on that technology. Although most of his research was devoted to making newsprint by the sulfite process, he also recognized the use of bleached sulfate pulp, the type used at Southland and later mills. His crusade, moreover, had a profound impact on kraft pulp producers because they, too, were quite interested in the advantages of the South, which Herty had effectively dramatized.

FURTHER READING: Jonathan Daniels, *The Forest Is the Future* (1957). Jack P. Oden, "Charles Holmes Herty and the Birth of the Southern Newsprint Paper Industry, 1927–1940," *Journal of Forest History* 21 (Apr. 1977): 77-89. James I. Pikl, Jr., "Pulp and Paper and Georgia: The Newsprint Paradox," *Journal of Forest History* 12 (Oct. 1968): 6–16. David C. Smith, *History of Papermaking in the United States, 1691–1969* (1970).

JACK P. ODEN

HINES, EDWARD (1863–1931)

Edward Hines, founder of the forest products enterprise that bears his name, was born in Buffalo, New York, on July 31, 1863. Two years later, the Hines family moved to Chicago where Hines Lumber Company is still headquartered.

The only son in an Irish immigrant family of seven children, Edward at fourteen worked as an office boy for the lumber wholesale firm of S. K. Martin Company. Seven years later, he became secretary-treasurer of that firm. Soon, the energetic, dapper young man started his own business, Edward Hines Lumber Company, and astonished the gray-bearded lumbering fraternity of Chicago by outselling all his competitors in the city during his first year in business. He bought out his former employers in 1896.

Aggressive salesmanship, innovative merchandising, and a propensity for operating on an ever expanding scale accounted for his success. Hines first purchased lumber in boatloads and trainloads and then contracted for the entire output of sawmills, insisting that the type of lumber produced be geared to market demand. He encircled Chicago with a well-run branch-yard system offering on-the-spot purchases and prompt delivery. He acquired standing timber and sawmills, and at one time he owned or controlled seventeen mills in Wisconsin alone. Constant travel in the logging districts made Hines better informed than most of his competitors and established important business contacts. Hines purchased extensive holdings of southern pine and exported lumber to South America and Europe. He also leased timber-cutting permits on crown lands in Canada.

Hines's association with Frederick Weyerhaeuser (*see* WEYERHAEUSER FAMILY) began on a timber-buying trip to Louisiana and Mississippi in 1906. Weyerhaeuser was strongly impressed by the Irishman's ready wit and business acumen. Acting on a proposal from Hines, a number of Weyerhaeuser-associated companies agreed in 1908 to consolidate their holdings in northern Minnesota and Canada as the Virginia and Rainy Lake Company. Hines contributed $4 million cash and seventy-two square miles of timber permits in Canada. The Duluth, Rainy Lake & Winnipeg Railroad was organized to haul logs to sawmills at Duluth and Virginia, Minnesota. The Virginia plant, billed as "the world's largest sawmill" (capacity 1 million board feet daily), employed 1,500 men. Some 2,800 men and 900 horses logged the timber. Logs were hauled over 2,000 miles of sleigh roads and 3,000 miles of railroad track. Although the scale of this operation was stupendous, there were formidable obstacles, and the venture was unprofitable.

The dominant figure in the Virginia and Rainy Lake firm was its president, the flamboyant, decisive Edward Hines. On a tour of Italy in 1928, Hines was received by the king, the pope, and Mussolini in the space of two days. Two weeks later, Hines acquired a 67,400-acre tract of timber near Burns, Oregon. His firm erected a company town on the outskirts of Burns and pioneered selective logging and sustained-yield forestry in cooperation with the Malheur National Forest.

Edward Hines helped revolutionize lumber marketing. His sales promotion created a market for hemlock and birch; for example, he popularized birch kitchen cabinets. Hines was also known for his efforts to standardize lumber grades and for his leadership in lumber trade associations. He was an organizer of the NATIONAL LUMBER MANUFACTURERS ASSOCIATION. He married Loretta O'Dowd in 1895 and

had three sons, Edward, Ralph, and Charles, and a daughter, Loretta. Edward Hines, Sr., died on December 1, 1931.

Hines Lumber Company in the late 1970s operated eight midwestern wholesale yards, twenty-six retail outlets, seven forest products manufacturing plants, a plywood plant, and a wood-treating plant.

FRED W. KOHLMEYER

HISTORICAL SOURCES

Documentary and other historical sources relating to American forest and conservation history are varied and extensive. The sources available for public use, with which this article deals, are being preserved in several repositories of the National Archives and Records Service, in state archival agencies and educational institutions, and among the holdings of some historical societies, libraries, and business firms.

Federal Archival Repositories

Records divisions of the National Archives and Records Service, especially those in Washington, D.C., and to a lesser extent those in regional archives branches and presidential libraries, have the largest groups of archival materials in the United States relating to forest and conservation history. These records amount to several thousand cubic feet and are mainly the product of systematic activity of the federal government in forestry since 1876. They consist principally of records of the U. S. FOREST SERVICE, including correspondence dealing with program direction and activities, administrative directives, case files concerning national forest administrative transactions, annual and other periodic reports, minutes of staff meetings, program inspection reports, selected diaries of forest rangers engaged in representative forest work, organizational and functional charts, press releases, radio and television scripts, motion and still pictures of forest activities, title papers concerning national forest lands, and maps of national forest areas.

Records concerning the executive direction of the Forest Service and its predecessor agencies reflect changing concepts of the proper function of government in forestry, differing techniques in the planning and promotion of forest conservation, and varying public reactions to the conduct of government forest programs. Documentation of Bernhard E. FERNOW's administration (1886–1898), for example, reveals his efforts in initiating limited government assistance in timber testing, tree measurement, and tree identification activities. The development of the Forest Service under the leadership of Gifford PINCHOT (1898–1910) produced important documentary sources for study of the rise of scientific forestry in the United States. These sources reveal the advent and advance of a historic movement for the conservation of natural resources and the creation of a forest organization that became famous for its administrative efficiency and esprit de corps.

Records concerning the direction of federal forestry by Pinchot's successor, Henry S. GRAVES (1910–1920), reflect some moderation of the former's aggressive plans for conservation but reveal continuation of his basic forestry objectives. William B. GREELEY's administration (1920–1928) is documented by materials attesting to a stronger emphasis on federal cooperation in state and private forestry and to the growth of state forest organizations as well as the national forest system. Enactment and early implementation of the significant CLARKE-MCNARY ACT of 1924 are described in the records of the Greeley years. Archives focusing on the work of Forester Robert Y. STUART (1928–1933) are characterized by data concerning a great expansion of research to provide adequate timber supplies and more timber-growing lands.

The work of Stuart's successor, Ferdinand A. SILCOX (1933–1939), is shown in massive records relating to the general direction of forestry projects that employed the labor of nearly half of some 2,600 camps of the CIVILIAN CONSERVATION CORPS. The Silcox record of administration is also noteworthy for its association with the widely publicized shelterbelt project on the Great Plains, under which the Forest Service planted some 19,000 miles of tree belts on 33,000 farms. A vast documentary accumulation mirrors the direction of Forest Service work during World War II under the leadership of Earle H. CLAPP (1939–1943) and Lyle F. WATTS (1943–1952). Prominent in this material are reports concerning the proposed regulation of private forest management by the federal government, efforts to increase output of wood for war needs, and increasing participation of American foresters in international forestry organizations. Postwar administration of the Forest Service, which is beginning to be shown in accessioned archival materials, has produced significant records documenting the strengthening of national forest policy for multiple use of forestlands and sustained yield of forest products and services.

Cartographic and audiovisual records of the Forest Service in the National Archives Building provide especially useful supplements to textual records describing federal forestry and national forest resources. These include atlases and standard published maps of individual national forests and maps of fire-control activities, timber surveys and sales, and shelterbelt project areas and recreational facilities in national forests. The audiovisual records include photographs and posters illustrating Forest Service activities; pictures of forest cover, streams, fires, and reforestation projects; and photographs of the production of guayule rubber during the 1940s.

The historical sources produced by the Forest Service are supplemented for forest and conservation history purposes by important groups of records created by other federal agencies and preserved in repositories of the National Archives and Records Service. Especially noteworthy in this connection are varied files of the GENERAL LAND OFFICE (later, BUREAU OF LAND MANAGEMENT) relating to the creation of federal forest reserves, timber cutting and sales on the public domain, and management of Indian forestlands; records of the National Park Service concerning the creation and administration of parks and the preparation of master plans for the development of park areas; records of the U. S. GEOLOGICAL SURVEY relating to the survey and classification of public lands; records of the Civilian Conservation Corps pertaining to forest improvement and protection during the 1930s; and records of the Office of the Secretary of the Interior and the Office of the Secretary of Agriculture concerning policies and major programs in the administration of federal forestlands. Among the documentary materials in presidential libraries, especially those of the Franklin D. ROOSEVELT Library in Hyde Park, New York, and the Lyndon B. Johnson Library in Austin, Texas, are scattered series of papers relating to conservation projects and issues since the 1930s. They show how some conservation questions, such as regulation of private forestry and creation of recreational and scenic areas, were decided at the highest levels of the federal government.

State Archival Repositories

Although American state government agencies have been concerned with forest protection and improvement for many decades, state archival repositories usually have not acquired large quantities of records or personal papers relating to such work. There are, however, two notable exceptions, the State Historical Society of Wisconsin and the Minnesota Historical Society, which serve both as archival and as manuscript repositories. The Wisconsin repository has accessioned records of numerous lumber firms that operated in the state during the nineteenth and early twentieth centuries, an important body of personal papers of lumbermen, and records of state officials who were responsible for inspecting timber operations and forest conditions. The Minnesota repository has also acquired records of many lumber firms and the personal papers of several lumbermen and forest conservation advocates. Especially noteworthy are the personal papers of Christopher C. Andrews, an early advocate of forest-fire control and forestry training; of Raphael ZON, who helped plan the Prairie States Forestry Project; and the records of the Quetico-Superior Council. This repository also has large groups of records of the Minnesota State Division of Forestry and of state surveyors of logs and lumber.

University Repositories

University libraries in western and midwestern states have acquired important groups of archival and manuscript materials relating to the activities of lumber firms, lumbermen, foresters, and conservationists. Libraries at the University of California at Berkeley have obtained records of several lumber firms and of the SIERRA CLUB; personal papers of leading advocates of forest protection, such as George C. Pardee and Robert U. Johnson; and transcripts of oral history interviews with federal foresters such as Arthur C. Ringland, Edward C. Crafts, and Thornton T. Munger. Among the university's documentary holdings are also extensive notes of George B. Sudworth, an early dendrologist, presenting detailed descriptions of California trees. The University of Washington Library has a large body of records of lumber firms. This institution also holds the personal papers of Richard A. Ballinger, who as secretary of the interior was involved in the BALLINGER-PINCHOT CONTROVERSY; of Corydon Wagner, a leading lumberman; and of many other prominent figures concerned with forestry and conservation.

The University of Oregon Library has the personal papers of William B. Greeley, chief of the Forest Service and later secretary-manager of the West Coast Lumbermen's Association, and of numerous political figures who were involved in natural resource issues. The Michigan Historical Collections of the University of Michigan has acquired records of many lumber firms and the personal papers of a number of lumbermen. It is also preserving the personal papers of several former professors of the University of Michigan School of Forestry who were prominent in early efforts for the conservation of natural resources. Of special interest are the papers of Charles W. Garfield, a founder of the School of Forestry and a president of the Michigan Forestry Commission, and the papers of Samuel T. DANA, a noted forester and a former dean of

the School of Natural Resources, successor to the School of Forestry. The Forest History Archives at Stephen F. Austin State University Library in Nacogdoches has acquired records of several important lumber firms that were active in the pinewoods of east Texas, and the personal papers of W. Goodrich Jones, lumberman and founder of the Texas Forestry Association and the Texas Department of Forestry.

In the Department of Manuscripts and University Archives at Cornell University, there are records of New York State's first College of Forestry and of its director, Bernhard E. Fernow, from 1898 to 1903. Also in the department are the personal papers of two famous foresters, Jay P KINNEY and Ralph S. Hosmer. The Kinney papers are especially useful as a source of information concerning the administration of the Forestry Branch of the Indian Service, U. S. Department of the Interior, a unit in which Kinney served from 1910 to 1933. The Yale University Library is preserving the personal papers of Henry S. Graves, which document his direction of the School of Forestry (1900–1910, 1922–1939) and of the Forest Service, and the papers of Herman H. CHAPMAN, a distinguished professor of forestry at Yale for many years. The Baker Library at Harvard University has acquired accounting records of several lumber firms, mainly in New England. Many other university libraries have significant holdings of forest history sources, primarily of a regional orientation. Among them are the Southern Historical Collection at the University of North Carolina; the Manuscript Department of the Duke University Library; the West Virginia Collection at the West Virginia University Library; and the Conservation History and Research Center at the University of Wyoming.

Historical Societies

Reference has already been made to the forest and conservation history materials of the State Historical Society of Wisconsin and the Minnesota Historical Society. Similar materials are well represented among the holdings of the Oregon Historical Society. They include records of the Western Forestry and Conservation Association, a leading group in the movement for greater forest-fire protection in the Pacific Northwest; the personal papers of David T. MASON, a noted forester; and the records of many lumber firms. The Forest History Society of Santa Cruz, California, has acquired records of the AMERICAN FORESTRY ASSOCIATION, the oldest forest conservation organization in the nation; the SOCIETY OF AMERICAN FORESTERS, the leading professional forestry group in the United States; the NATIONAL FOREST

PRODUCTS ASSOCIATION (formerly the National Lumber Manufacturers Association); and the AMERICAN FOREST INSTITUTE (formerly American Forest Products Industries). The Society has also accumulated many transcripts of interviews with conservationists, foresters, and leaders of forest products industries as well as a useful collection of photographs and films relating to forest history.

Library of Congress

Personal papers of leaders of efforts for the conservation of forests and related natural resources constitute important collections in the Manuscript Division of the Library of Congress. Foremost among these are the extensive papers of Gifford Pinchot in more than 3,000 document containers. This material furnishes significant information concerning Pinchot's work as a private forester and as commissioner of forestry for Pennsylvania, and on his outstanding role in the conservation movement during the early decades of the twentieth century. There is hardly any issue of forestry or conservation during that period that is not discussed in the Pinchot papers. The Manuscript Division also holds personal papers of Carl Schurz, secretary of the interior (1877–1881) and an early advocate of forest protection; Myra L. Dock, Pennsylvania's first female forest commissioner (1901–1913); W. J. McGee, a noted geologist and anthropologist who has been considered to be the chief theorist of the early conservation movement; James R. Garfield, secretary of the interior (1907–1909) and supporter of Pinchot's conservation policies; Frederick H. NEWELL, director of the U. S. Bureau of Reclamation (1907–1914) and an influential figure in controversies concerning the management of water resources; and Harold L. ICKES, secretary of the interior (1933–1946) and strong advocate for the placement of all federal natural resource agencies into a Department of Natural Resources. The personal papers of Theodore ROOSEVELT, William Howard Taft, and Woodrow Wilson in the library also provide useful information concerning government conservation projects and policies during the administrations of these three presidents of the United States.

Another public library worthy of mention is the Conservation Library of the Denver Public Library, which has personal papers of some individuals and records of some organizations dealing with varied aspects of American forestry.

Business Archival Repositories

A few business enterprises have established archival or museum units for preservation of historical rec-

ords of the firms. For example, the Weyerhaeuser Company Archives in Tacoma, Washington, is preserving correspondence, journals, minute books, ledgers, audio-visual materials, and interviews relating to one of the nation's largest forest-products business organizations. The Georgia-Pacific Historical Museum in Portland, Oregon, has acquired photographs, minutes, correspondence, log books, and other records of its parent firm as well as other materials relating to the history of forest products in North America. The Armstrong Cork Company in Lancaster, Pennsylvania, has an archival unit that preserves annual reports, minutes, correspondence, and other records concerning the history of the company and its subsidiaries.

Guides to Sources

By far the most comprehensive and useful guide to varied sources concerning American forest and conservation history is *North American Forest History: A Guide to Archives and Manuscripts in the United States and Canada* (1977), compiled by Richard C. Davis. This publication of the Forest History Society describes the sources in repositories listed alphabetically by states. It has a detailed name and subject index. More recent acquisitions of forest history repositories are reported in the "Archival News" column of the *Journal of Forest History*. Less detailed but even more comprehensive is the *Directory of Archives and Manuscript Repositories in the United States* (1978), compiled by the National Historical Publications and Records Commission; it has a name and subject index that may help researchers to find repositories emphasizing sources relating to forest and conservation history. The principal description of records of the U. S. Forest Service in the National Archives Building is given in *Preliminary Inventory of the Records of the Forest Service* (1969), prepared by Harold T. Pinkett and revised by Terry W. Good. A descriptive treatment of these federal records also appears in Pinkett's article, "Forest Service Records as Research Material," *Forest History* 13 (Jan. 1970): 18-29. Federal archival holdings as a whole are described in the *Guide to the National Archives of the United States* (1974). Several nonfederal archival repositories mentioned in this article have prepared published and unpublished descriptions of their holdings.

HAROLD T. PINKETT

HISTORIC PRESERVATION

The National Historic Preservation Act of 1966 defines historic preservation in the United States as "the protection, rehabilitation, restoration, and reconstruction of districts, sites, buildings, structures, and objects significant in American history, architecture, archeology, or culture." The comprehensiveness of that definition reflects the culmination of over a century of developing thought about the nation's obligations to its man-made heritage, united inextricably with its changing attitudes toward the physical environment.

The earliest American preservation activities were chiefly attempts to memorialize people and events of the Revolution. Following the revitalization of Independence Hall during the 1820s, memorialization extended increasingly to sites and structures with historical associations. By the 1850s, private organizations had safeguarded George Washington's home at Mount Vernon and dozens of other places boasting some connection with revolutionary leaders. During the Civil War, a system of national military cemeteries was established, and, after the conflict, veterans' organizations erected thousands of monuments on battlefields. By the turn of the twentieth century, the growth of the system of national parks was matched by that of a system of national "military" parks protecting Civil War battlefields.

National interest in American history burgeoned in the post-Civil War period. Accompanying public concern about the destruction of the nation's forests was outrage over the looting and destruction of great Indian ruins in the Southwest and Midwest. In 1889, Congress took steps to protect the ancient ruins at Casa Grande, Arizona, and by the end of the century a movement was afoot to protect threatened historic and prehistoric resources in much the same fashion as was being devised for forests and other natural resources.

The historic preservation movement's most notable triumph on the federal level was the passage of the Antiquities Act of 1906 (later clarified and strengthened in part by the Archaeological Resources Protection Act of 1979), which provided for the protection of historic or prehistoric remains, "or any object of antiquity," on federal lands, and allowed the president to proclaim places of antiquity or scientific value on the public domain to be national monuments. On other levels, a number of states and communities took their first steps at protecting properties of historic value, and private programs in historic preservation mushroomed.

Historic preservation blossomed during the New Deal. In the interests of administrative consistency, national monuments and other historic properties administered by the departments of War and Agriculture were transferred to a unified National Park System managed by the National Park Service of the DEPARTMENT OF THE INTERIOR in 1933. Emergency work programs poured thousands of people and millions of dollars into the identification, investigation, recordation, preservation, and development of historic and prehistoric resources on state and federal lands. The Historic Sites and Buildings Act of 1935 lent such activities legislative support, provided for the designation of national historic sites to protect properties "of national historical or archeological significance," and authorized a number of wide-ranging programs in historic preservation. As one result of the Historic Sites and Buildings Act, the majority of the units of the National Park System in 1980 existed principally for historic preservation purposes.

Following World War II, growing public concern for environmental values threatened by large public works extended equally to natural and cultural resources. Massive programs of historical and archaeological survey and salvage were undertaken during the great river-basin development programs of the 1950s, and in 1960 the Reservoir Salvage Act made specific provision for the "preservation of historical and archeological data (including relics and specimens) which might otherwise be irreparably lost or destroyed" by the construction of dams and reservoirs. As amended in 1974, this provision applied to nearly all federal and federally assisted undertakings that may affect cultural values. As a result, most federal forest-management activities that disturb the terrain, including timber harvesting, are preceded by historical and archaeological investigations to locate and salvage historic or prehistoric resources in affected areas.

The National Historic Preservation Act of 1966 declared for the first time a national policy of historic preservation and inspired numerous programs in states and localities. Directing the expansion of a National Register of Historic Places to include resources of state and local as well as national significance, the act established the Advisory Council on Historic Preservation, whose comments are to be requested by any federal agency in the case of every undertaking that affects a property listed in the National Register. This introduced a major procedural step into virtually all federal land-management actions.

The NATIONAL ENVIRONMENTAL POLICY ACT of 1969 integrated concern for the cultural and natural aspects of the environment into a systematic package of procedures attending every federal activity. Implementing part of the act, Executive Order 11593 of

1971 laid down specific requirements for historic preservation upon all federal agencies, especially those managing lands and other properties. The advisory council's commentary procedures were extended to all properties qualified for the National Register, whether yet listed or not, and as a result federal land managers found themselves conjoined to consider the existence of cultural resources in project areas and take steps to minimize unnecessary harm to those values. Federal land-management agencies and their state and private counterparts broadened their staffs to include historians, archaeologists, and other preservation specialists, and concern for historic and prehistoric values became a substantial element of agency programs.

During the 1970s, the term "cultural resources" came into common usage to denote the various historic and prehistoric sites, structures, and objects affected by the protective legislation, and "cultural resources management" became, among land managers, the most common synonym of historic preservation. In actual practice, however, more attention went to the concerns of archaeology than to other historic preservation activities, although the imbalance was beginning to be adjusted by the decade's end.

Monumentalism, which focused on cultural resources for their inspirational value and assumed the public display of a site or structure, had by 1980 retreated to a minor role in land management, except in the National Park System and its state and local counterparts. More commonly, cultural resources demanded consideration for their inherent value rather than their developmental potential, and their existence in the public landscape was not to be denied or ignored. For the forest manager, cultural resources had become an environmental asset comparable to timber, wildlife, or water, requiring equal consideration in an integrated land management program.

DAVID A. CLARY

HISTORIOGRAPHY

Forest history is the study of mankind's continuing relationship to the forest ecosystem and the land and water surrounding it. Few fields of knowledge are more in need of the historical approach than forestry, since the forestland owner or manager must consider both the past and the present in planning for future use of the land. Forest history is a difficult field to define concisely. It starts with aboriginal man's impact on the forest and includes the application of science to the study of forestland, the development of technology for its utilization, the use of economics and law in its management, and the relevance of philosophy, literature, and aesthetics to the spiritual, mental, and emotional responses evoked by forests.

The American development of forest history consists of several interwoven strands of thought and study. First is forest history as an academic subject for professional foresters. Forestry education was modeled on that of the European schools, and these schools used a historical approach to forestry. In the volumes of Schlich's *Manual of Forestry* (3rd ed., 1906) and in Bernhard E. FERNOW's *A Brief History of Forestry: In Europe, the United States, and Other Countries* (1907, rev. 1911), early American foresters studied the historical development of forestry abroad as background to their own new profession.

In their study, *Forest Education* (1932), Henry S. GRAVES and Cedric H. Guise wrote of the value of history for the forestry student: the ability to consider historical developments was essential for solving many problems in forestry. They believed that "interest in history and the study of it is one of the most potent influences in education for developing the spirit of inquiry, tolerance, and breadth of view, which we are seeking to stimulate in the [forestry] student." A course in the history of forestry would enable the student to understand present conditions, policies, and methods as evolutionary steps. Because of the great amount of independent reading and the critical interest in study of the past required, a course in the history of forestry was seen as better adapted to the graduate student than the undergraduate. Several early forestry schools offered study in the history of forestry as part of the curriculum, and a number of graduate students selected historical themes for their theses. As early as 1920, Yale had produced four such theses, Cornell three, and Syracuse one. As time went on, courses in the history of forestry sometimes became integrated with courses in forest policy or law, while other universities, including Yale and Michigan Technological, instituted forest history as a separate subject.

Conservation education is related to forest history but is developed for a less specialized clientele. College courses in conservation of natural resources became popular after Charles R. Van Hise published his *Conservation of Natural Resources in the United States* (1910). They were strongly supported by the AMERICAN FORESTRY ASSOCIATION and by foresters: Shirley Allen, a professional forester, wrote the popular textbook *Conserving Natural Resources* (1955).

In many states these courses became mandatory for those engaged in teacher education. The courses varied greatly one from another but often had a historical orientation. A newer, related field is the growing one of environmental history. Although Roderick Nash, writing in "American Environmental History: A New Teaching Frontier," *Pacific Historical Review* (1972), asserts that he had invented this field in 1970, his claim seems slight when the long record of college courses dealing with man and his environment are considered.

Another source of forest history has been the graduate departments of history and cognate subjects, which have sometimes encouraged students to work on theses and dissertations related to forestry and natural resources. Joseph A. Miller, in "The Changing Forest: Recent Research on the Historical Geography of American Forests," and "Forests and the Regional Landscape," *Forest History* (1965), gives a valuable account of dissertations in the closely related area of historical geography. In the 1980s, with increased interest in the development of courses in public history and in interpretation of natural and cultural history, graduate participation in such research will probably increase.

Professionals in forestry and allied fields, journalists, and other writers have also taken forest history as a field of study. Jennie S. Peyton, who compiled guides to historical material in U. S. FOREST SERVICE files, wrote "Forestry Movement of the Seventies in the Interior Department, under Schurz," *Journal of Forestry* (1920). Gifford PINCHOT, former head of the Forest Service and governor of Pennsylvania, included important historical detail in his autobiography, *Breaking New Ground* (1947). Other retired foresters have written useful accounts, based in whole or in part on personal experience. An example is Paul H. Roberts, *Hoof Prints on Forest Ranges: The Early Years of National Forest Range Administration* (1963). A classic survey by a journalist is Stewart Holbrook's *Holy Old Mackinaw: A Natural History of the American Lumberjack* (1938). Recreationists have also contributed to the field in such books as Fred H. McNeil's *Wy'east "The Mountain": A Chronicle of Mount Hood* (1937).

Historical writings reflect the eras in which they were written. The early twentieth century, a time of keen interest in the birth of a new profession and in the development of a forest policy, produced two first-class books of forest history: John Ise's *The United States Forest Policy* (1920), and Jenks Cameron's *The Development of Governmental Forest Control in the United States* (1928). Cameron's book reveals

the influence of Frederick Jackson Turner's frontier thesis, just as Richard Lillard's *The Great Forest* (1948) is reminiscent in its approach of Walter Prescott Webb's *The Great Plains* (1931). Controversies over conservation issues encouraged historical studies to clarify the record or reinforce points of view, as George Patrick Ahern's *Deforested America* (1928) did in regard to the controversy over federal regulation of private cutting, or John T. Ganoe's "Some Constitutional and Political Aspects of the Ballinger-Pinchot Controversy," *Pacific Historical Review* (1934), which concerned a notorious political dispute over public resource policies in the early twentieth century (see BALLINGER-PINCHOT CONTROVERSY).

The period after World War II saw a flourishing of forest history, as it did of scholarly activity generally. The G.I. Bill of Rights increased the number of students engaged in graduate work. The National Archives and other libraries and depositories made ever increasing amounts of primary documentation available for research on historical topics. A number of biographies and autobiographies of old-timers in the forest and resource field were published. Gifford Pinchot, William B. GREELEY, Stephen T. MATHER, John MUIR, and others were the subjects of excellent studies in the 1940s and 1950s. The U. S. DEPARTMENT OF AGRICULTURE yearbook, *Trees* (1949), placed American forestry in historic perspective. The Forest Products History Society—forerunner of the FOREST HISTORY SOCIETY—was founded in 1946 and later began working for the preservation of archival and manuscript material from the forest products industries. Increasing numbers of articles dealing with natural resource history appeared in such magazines as *American Forests* and the *Journal of Forest History*, and in regional historical journals. The bulk of such writing by historians has focused less on the relationship of man to his physical environment than on the intellectual and political basis for natural resource policies and utilization. As Richard White commented in *Land Use, Environment, and Social Change: The Shaping of Island County, Washington* (1980), the success and substantial contributions of such books as Samuel Hays's *Conservation and the Gospel of Efficiency: The Progressive Conservation Movement, 1890–1920* (1959) and Roderick Nash's *Wilderness and the American Mind* (1967, rev. 1982) may have tended to make many historians overlook an earlier tradition reflected in the works of George Perkins MARSH, James C. Malin, and Walter Prescott Webb.

There remain numerous gaps in the study of forest history. Harold T. Pinkett, "Some Neglected Trails in

Forest History," *Journal of Forest History* (April 1976), lists a few overlooked topics worthy of study, including activities such as the observance of ARBOR DAY, the planting of school forests, and forestry education. Relationships of the United States to other countries in resource management have been relatively neglected, though two excellent recent books which take up aspects of this subject are Robert K. Winters, *The Forest and Man* (1974), and Thomas A. Lund, *American Wildlife Law* (1980). The legal history of the CONSERVATION MOVEMENT deserves more attention than it has received. Starting with a study of the work of the Taft-Wilson Supreme Court by E. A. Sherman, "The Supreme Court of the United States and Conservation Policies," *Journal of Forestry* (1921), a number of writers have explored parts of the subject. Studies in depth of the American Indian use of the forest are needed, such as those of Harold J. Lutz in his *Aboriginal Man and White Man as Historical Causes of Fires in the Boreal Forest, with Particular Reference to Alaska* (1959). Many good company histories have been written, such as Ralph W. Hidy, Frank Ernest Hill, and Allan Nevins, *Timber and Men: The Weyerhaeuser Story* (1963), but there is a need for more studies of the development of industrial forestry like George B. Amidon's brief *Development of Industrial Forestry in the Lake States* (1961) and David C. Smith's *A History of Lumbering in Maine, 1861–1960* (1972), to place the work of individual companies in regional and national perspective.

The subject of forest historiography is a field of immense complexity and rich variety. It is perhaps more than any other field of history a meeting place for the professional and the amateur, for those whose fields of interest are international and those whose concerns are local or regional. It has a distinguished past, an active and turbulent present, and prospects for the future.

Kurt Mantel, "History of the International Science of Forestry with Special Consideration of Central Europe," in John A. Romberger and Pietsa Mikola (eds.), *International Review of Forest Research* (1964), gives a taxonomy of forest history, defining nine separate categories. Evaluations of the literature appear in two articles by Gordon B. Dodds, "The Historiography of American Conservation: Past and Prospects," *Pacific Northwest Quarterly* (1965), and "Conservation & Reclamation in the Trans-Mississippi West: A Critical Bibliography," *Arizona and the West* (1971), in Lawrence Rakestraw, "Conservation Historiography: An Assessment," *Pacific Historical Review* (1972), and in Roderick Nash, "The State of

Environmental History," in *The State of American History*, edited by Herbert J. Bass (1970). Ronald J. Fahl, *North American Forest and Conservation History: A Bibliography* (1977) gives within its subject limits the most comprehensive listing of books and articles. Fahl's bibliography is kept up-to-date through book reviews and listings of recent articles in the *Journal of Forest History*.

LAWRENCE W. RAKESTRAW

HOUGH, FRANKLIN BENJAMIN (1822–1885)

Born on July 22, 1822, in Martinsburg, New York, Hough was a rural upstate New York physician. He became aware of serious forest depletion while directing the New York State censuses of 1854 and 1865 and developed broad interests in natural sciences and forest conservation. At the 1873 annual meeting of the American Association for the Advancement of Science (AAAS), he urged Congress and the states to act on behalf of forest protection. AAAS responded by petitioning Congress for the creation of a commission to investigate and report on forest conditions, wood products, future wood supplies, the influence of forests on climate, and European forestry practices. Somewhat later, in 1880, AAAS sent memorials to all the states urging the governors and legislatures actively to promote conservation and the economical use of forests, public and private, through legislation, the creation of forestry commissions, and the establishment of college forestry courses.

In 1876, Congress responded to the AAAS petition by appropriating $2,000 for a study to be undertaken by the DEPARTMENT OF AGRICULTURE. Hough was named to conduct this inquiry. Gathering data through wide reading and numerous mail inquiries and extensive travels in the United States, Canada, and Europe, he compiled three volumes and most of a fourth. This *Report upon Forestry* (1878–1884) contained Hough's recommendations for a strong policy for the reservation and management of federal lands, including the control of timber harvesting by leases similar to those used in Canada; the establishment of federal forest experiment stations and tree plantings; and a vigorous federal effort to educate the public on the need for forest protection and management.

Hough became chief of the Division of Forestry when it was created in 1881 and he spent the summer of that year in Europe gathering information about forestry practices and speaking with prominent forestry leaders. He wrote the first book on practical forestry in the United States, *Elements of Forestry* (1882). For a year (1882–1883), he also edited and published the monthly *American Journal of Forestry.* In 1882, in recognition of his tireless work to promote forestry, Hough was awarded a special diploma of honor by an international geophysical congress in Vienna. He took a prominent part in the young AMERICAN FORESTRY ASSOCIATION (AFA) and in its merger with the American Forestry Congress in 1882 at Montreal. He served AFA as its treasurer in 1880 and later as its recording secretary.

Hough also promoted the establishment of the Adirondack Forest Preserve and commission by New York State, as did Bernhard E. FERNOW, a German forester and a later chief of Hough's Division of Forestry. Fernow called Hough's first *Report upon Forestry* "by far the best and most useful publication on forestry in this country." Gifford PINCHOT, who succeeded Fernow in 1898, called Hough "perhaps the chief pioneer in forestry in the United States." Dietrich Brandis, the leading German forester of that period, also had high praise for Hough.

Despite his accomplishments, Hough was removed as chief of the Division of Forestry in 1883 by Commissioner of Agriculture George B. Loring. Hough remained, however, as an agent of the division until 1885. He died on June 11 of that year.

FURTHER READING: Dietrich Brandis, "The Late Franklin B. Hough," *Indian Forester* 11 (Oct. 1885): 429. Frank J. Harmon, "Remembering Franklin B. Hough," *American Forests* 83 (Jan. 1977): 34-37, 52, 54. Edna L. Jacobsen, "Franklin B. Hough, A Pioneer in Scientific Forestry in America," *New York History* 15 (July 1934): 317-321. Andrew Denny Rodgers III, *Bernhard Eduard Fernow: A Study of North American Forestry* (1951). Harold K. Steen, *The U. S. Forest Service: A History* (1976), pp. 9-20.

FRANK J. HARMON

I

ICKES, HAROLD LE CLAIRE (1874–1952)

Harold Le Claire Ickes was born on March 15, 1874, on a farm in Frankstown Township, Pennsylvania, of German-Scottish stock. When Ickes was sixteen, his mother died and he went to live with his aunt in Chicago. There he attended Englewood High School and the University of Chicago, where he received the B.A. degree in 1897. Following a brief stint as a newspaper reporter, he received a law degree from the university in 1907. By 1911, he was fully launched as a reformer and crusading politician and had married Anna Wilmarth Thompson, a wealthy widow with whom he had a son.

Ickes's first foray into politics began as a campaign organizer for reform-minded office seekers in Illinois. Although originally a Republican, Ickes often reversed his affiliations, preferring to cleave to principles rather than parties. In 1912, he enthusiastically endorsed Theodore ROOSEVELT's presidential candidacy on the Bull Moose ticket. Then, in 1920, after opposing the Republican presidential nomination of Warren G. Harding, Ickes cast his vote for the Democratic candidate.

Throughout the 1920s, Ickes promoted unsuccessfully a variety of reform causes including civic betterment, civil rights for blacks, and conservation. He was a shrill and persistent critic of Mayor William Hale ("Big Bill") Thompson of Chicago, of Samuel Insull and the private power companies, and of the Hoover administration's policy of promoting state control of the public lands. He developed a reputation as an embittered reformer, the champion of the underdog.

Ickes's fortunes rose in 1932 with the presidential victory of Franklin D. ROOSEVELT. He had helped by swinging liberal midwestern Republicans to Roosevelt's side. On February 22, 1933, after an extensive conference between the two men in New York City, Roosevelt appointed Ickes to the post of secretary of the interior, a move that signaled the president's determination to continue the old Bull Moose Progressive reform impulse in his administration.

Ickes immediately set out to remove the stigma of corruption and to restore public confidence in the DEPARTMENT OF THE INTERIOR, whose reputation had been severely damaged by the BALLINGER-PINCHOT CONTROVERSY and the Teapot Dome scandal of the 1920s. Like his predecessors, Ickes confronted the vexatious problem of determining priorities in resource access. With regard to national park policy, he adopted the preservationist concept of wilderness parks in a departure from the department's normal orientation, which had emphasized conservation for development and use. He also ended racial segregation in both the department and the parks. Despite bitter protests from

Westerners, real estate investors, lumber and mining interests, and the private power companies, he made the Department of the Interior the guardian of the nation's forests and public lands. He used his position as head of the Public Works Administration to channel funds into the BUREAU OF RECLAMATION's dam-building, power, and irrigation programs (such as Grand Coulee, Booneville, and Boulder dams). In the process, Ickes elevated the Interior Department into the largest generator and distributor of hydroelectric power in the world. He also broke Alcoa's monopoly of aluminum. In a few problems affecting the Western states, such as water pollution, he was willing to promote interstate compacts but, in general, Ickes placed national regulation before state or local initiative.

The most formidable challenge to the continuation of Ickes's policies came in 1940 and 1941 as the nation prepared for World War II. National defense and total mobilization greatly intensified demands for access to resources, especially to permit mineral exploration, lumbering, and grazing inside national parks. Rallying support from conservationists, Ickes resisted such demands. He was less successful in promoting his department's principal postwar objective: the further development of river basin systems for reclamation and hydroelectric power production. After 1945, he waged a fierce but losing battle to retain control of offshore oil lands for the federal government.

Ickes's substantial accomplishments as secretary of the interior were possible because he enjoyed the confidence of the president and because the American people, in the throes of the Great Depression, were receptive both economically and politically to resource policies that ensured large governmental expenditures and created jobs. At the close of his stewardship in 1946, he had amassed authority unequaled by any of his predecessors. In addition to his regular cabinet post, he was head of the Public Works Administration and oil administrator under the National Recovery Administration. As petroleum administrator during World War II, Ickes coordinated the conservation, acquisition, and allocation of the nation's oil resources. The only jurisdiction which eluded his grasp was the FOREST SERVICE, which remained firmly embedded in the DEPARTMENT OF AGRICULTURE.

Ickes's fighting temperament shaped the emphases and procedures involved in his distinctly imperial policies and caused his political enemies to refer to him sarcastically as "Honest Harold." He was a hard-driving administrative officer who assumed tasks that would have felled a lesser man. But he was often petty and suspicious and subjected his subordinates to harassment for the most trivial of infrac-

tions. This side of Ickes's personality was mostly concealed from the public who viewed him as the old curmudgeon: the terrible-tempered but honest figure so beloved in American folklore. If in some ways a flawed figure, Ickes nonetheless commanded respect for his invincible integrity and unabashed public assertion of New Deal principles.

Roosevelt's death in April 1945 was a deep personal loss to Ickes who took it upon himself to transmit the New Deal's legacy in resource policies to the Truman administration. But Ickes never really felt comfortable with the new president and, in 1946, when Truman nominated a California oil magnate to be undersecretary of the Navy, Ickes denounced the action. Fearing a recurrence of the Teapot Dome scandals, he lambasted the administration for its lack of interest in oil conservation and angrily resigned his cabinet position.

Ickes's first wife had died in an automobile accident in 1935. Three years later, he married the twenty-five-year-old Jane Dahlman, a graduate of Smith College, with whom he had two children. After leaving government service, Ickes lived in semiretirement with his family on his farm near Olney, Maryland. He wrote a syndicated column for the *New York Post* until 1949 and was a regular contributor to the liberal weekly *New Republic*. He died on February 3, 1952.

FURTHER READING: Ickes told his own life story in Harold L. Ickes, *The Autobiography of a Curmudgeon* (1948). *The Secret Diary of Harold L. Ickes* (3 vols., 1953–1954) is both a personal report of Ickes and an intimate history of the Roosevelt administration for the years 1933–1941, in which the author recorded skirmishes over public works, conservation, reclamation, power, slum clearance, and other subjects. A penetrating analysis of Ickes's tenure as secretary of the interior is contained in Elmo Richardson's *Dams, Parks & Politics* (1973); his early interest in park policy is delineated in Donald C. Swain, *Wilderness Defender: Horace M. Albright and Conservation* (1970). H. Judd Harmon places Ickes in the larger context of the New Deal in "Some Contributions of Harold L. Ickes," *Western Political Quarterly* 7 (June 1954): 238-252.

PHILIP J. FUNIGIELLO

IDAHO FORESTS

In 1805, when the Lewis and Clark expedition crossed the Lemhi Pass, the territory that the party observed—the future state of Idaho—was the last major region of the country to be explored by white men. In 1979, Idaho, the most heavily timbered of the Rocky Mountain States, still contained the longest stretches of wild rivers and the largest tract of roadless land in the contiguous United States. Its forests covered

Men are dwarfed by a grove of Idaho's famous western white pine. Forest History Society Photo.

21,727,000 acres, or 41 percent of the state's land area. Recreationists nationwide are attracted to premier resources, such as the Salmon and Selway rivers and the River of No Return Wilderness. Yet Idaho's forests also produce the fourth largest volume of lumber in the United States.

The state is roughly L-shaped, with coniferous forests occupying most of the vertical panhandle, the north and east edges of the horizontal base, and the great mountain mass where the two join. Sixty-nine percent of the total land area is publicly owned, with nearly seven of every ten acres of forested land in the fifteen national forests (20,375,171 acres).

Fire has been the most notable feature in the forests' growth history. Fire has always been part of the forest environment, but following discovery of gold in 1860, wildfire increase dramatically. It is estimated that man-caused fires destroyed 51 percent of the standing timber volume in one 4-million-acre area of northern Idaho between 1860 and 1900. After the turn of the century, recurring droughts brought particularly severe fire years in 1910, 1919, 1926, 1931, and 1934. Except for climate, fire has done more to shape the age, composition, and structure of Idaho's forests than any

other factor. One example is the large areas of lodgepole pine, a seral species, in country that would otherwise climax in subalpine fir or Douglas-fir; other examples are the abundant western larch and, in the lower country, ponderosa pine. One shade-intolerant, seral species—western white pine—occurred in extensive stands because of fire. It was this species that brought such lumbermen as Frederick Weyerhaeuser (*see* WEYERHAEUSER FAMILY) from the pine-depleted Lake States to northern Idaho and touched off a lumber boom after 1900.

Idaho's lumber industry began after the discovery of gold, with small mills supplying lumber for sluices and building construction. Rafting on the Clearwater River, the most important of Idaho's early logging rivers, reached its peak in the 1880s. From the Clearwater district, the industry moved into the better-timbered southern panhandle, particularly around Coeur d'Alene, in the 1870s. In the next decade, lumbering had spread throughout the mountainous northern region.

Early purchases from the Northern Pacific Railroad, homesteaders, and the state provided the land base for numerous combines and small companies, many of which later consolidated into the state's industrial giants, Potlatch and Boise-Cascade. Lumber production mushroomed from 65 million board feet in 1889 to a reported 846 million board feet in 1916, as supplies of white pine in the Lake States were depleted. Lumber production peaked in 1925 at 1.1 billion board feet. From a Depression low of 248 million board feet in 1932, Idaho's output again increased, reaching nearly 2 billion board feet in 1977. Douglas-fir, western larch, ponderosa pine, and white pine, respectively, provide most of Idaho's sawtimber, although since the 1960s, western redcedar has become an increasingly important source for decorative fences, shingles, and local construction lumber.

Idaho's fires also gave rise to two of the nation's earliest and most important combative aids—the lookout tower and the timber protective association. Both were the products of private enterprise. The first lookout tower was a dead tree with cross pieces nailed to it in the form of a ladder located on Bertha Hill in Clearwater County. A timber cruiser was assigned to the post during dry weather in 1903 with instructions to ride to the nearest logging crew or homesteader if he spotted smoke. The Clearwater Fire Protective Association, formed in December 1905, combined the forces of Clearwater Timber Company and other private landowners. Their pact was to fight all fires regardless of ownership, then to prorate expenses in proportion to the acreage held by each landowner. The effort led not only to more effective control of fires but also to their prevention and, as in other states, to other cooperative efforts, such as the Southern Idaho Timber Protective Association, formed in 1908. Nevertheless, these groups could not prevent the Big Blowup of 1910, which consumed 3,000,000 acres in Idaho and adjacent districts of Montana.

Conservation and natural resource management in Idaho originated with the Indians. Camas bulbs, an important food staple, were harvested annually using thinning techniques that left a significant portion of the plant to propagate the next crop. Anthropologists also report accounts from the Nez Perce of deliberately burning forest areas to promote the growth of grass and browse for deer and elk.

White settlement in the mid-nineteenth century brought an end to the balance of man and resources. In 1899, only nine years after statehood, legislation was necessary to protect the decimated herds of elk, moose, and caribou. The legislature authorized the first fish hatchery in 1907, but to a great extent this was to produce eastern brook trout to supplement the already abundant fishery. By mid-century, a series of dams tamed the great Columbia and Snake river systems, even bringing sea-going vessels to Lewiston, Idaho, in

1975. As a result, in addition to rearing the more abundant fish species, the focus of many hatcheries has now shifted to the effort of preserving the state's most spectacular fishes, the salmon and the steelhead.

Conservation efforts were stimulated statewide by the creation of the U. S. FOREST SERVICE, which led shortly afterward to the establishment of the Priest River Forest Experiment Station in 1911 and the Coeur d'Alene Forest Insect Laboratory in 1919. The College of Forestry at the University of Idaho opened its doors in 1909 and planted the West's first arboretum in 1911. Idaho acquired its first state park that same year.

Conservation activity underwent further expansion in the 1930s when CIVILIAN CONSERVATION CORPS camps were active in the woods, especially in white pine blister rust control. In the 1960s, a new state parks department, along with other agencies, sought to meet rising recreational demands in the state, much of which was and continues to be focused on forestlands. Recreation and resource-related tourism are considered one of Idaho's three most important industries. Much of this is due to the state's extensive wilderness areas which expanded from 989,000 acres before passage of the Wilderness Act of 1964 to over 3.8 million acres in 1980.

FURTHER READING: S. Blair Hutchinson, "A Century of Lumbering in Northern Idaho," *Timberman* 39 (Aug. 1936): 20-21, 26; 39 (Sept. 1936): 14–15, 28; 39 (Oct. 1936): 34-39. Beth Rhodenburgh and Dorine Goertzen, "The History of State Forestry in Idaho" (processed 1961). Clarence C. Strong and Clyde S. Webb, *White Pine: King of Many Waters* (1970). Ralph K. Widner, ed., *Forests and Forestry in the American States* (1963).

JAMES R. FAZIO

ILLINOIS FORESTS

In the so-called Prairie State, broad expanses of tall prairie grass were interspersed with "oak groves," and much of the southern portion and the uplands were covered with mixed hardwoods. Oak and hickory predominated; maple, walnut, elm, and basswood were common. Cypress, gum, and cottonwood grew along the rivers. Originally about 14 million acres (40 percent of the state's area) were forested.

Most of this pristine forest was cleared for agriculture and consumed for fuel and local construction. Coal producers also employed considerable quantities of both round timber and sawn lumber. In 1899, while lumbering in the Lake States was about at its height, Illinois's 372 sawmills reported 388.5 million board feet of lumber sawed, 66 percent of it hardwood. Oak provided 45 percent of the total, white pine 34 percent, which must have largely been sawn from logs rafted down the Mississippi and Rock rivers from Wisconsin. Lumber manufacture in Illinois thereafter declined, seldom reaching 100 million board feet annually again until World War II. As the domestic wood harvest fell, the great bulk of the raw material consumed by the state's wood-using industries came to be imported from other states. With the expiration of the commercial white pine stands, hardwoods increased their statistical dominance, reaching 99 percent in 1961. What little softwood lumber was produced was mostly shortleaf and loblolly pine. In 1978, with an estimated 126 million board feet of lumber manufactured, 8 percent was softwood.

Since the 1950s, forests have covered about 11 percent of the state, mostly in the southern part. Forest of commercial value in the 1970s measured 3,692,000 acres. Roughly 92 percent of the state's woodlands were in private ownership in farm woodlots and larger tracts along the principal rivers. There were some 250 sawmills, a dozen cooperages, and veneer, wood-treating, piling, charcoal, and pallet-fabricating operations. The largest growth in the state's production of primary forest products in recent decades came in pulpwood production.

Interest in forestry and conservation began about 1868 with an experimental planting, Illini Grove, at the newly founded state university at Urbana. A survey of the state's forest resources initiated by the U.S. Bureau of Forestry in 1904 was completed by the Illinois Natural History Survey in 1923. In 1926, the State Department of Conservation was established and R. B. Miller became the first state forester. The CIVILIAN CONSERVATION CORPS in the 1930s gave a tremendous impetus to forestry work. The state eventually established two tree nurseries, and the State Forestry Division added seventeen district offices for extension services and fire protection.

The largest public forest is the Shawnee National Forest with 250,000 acres of federally owned land in southern Illinois purchased since 1934 and established as a national forest in 1939. Cook County Forest Preserve, created in 1914, covers 65,000 acres in the Chicago area. The first state forest was created on 3,800 acres in 1929, followed by three others totaling 10,000 acres. Illinois's first state park was created in 1903. In 1975, there were 186 state park and recreation areas covering 287,000 acres. There are scores of county and municipal forests.

The Illinois Nature Preserve Commission, created in 1963, has established nature preserves throughout the state. Various individuals and groups, including sportsmen's clubs, maintain private forests and plantations, memorial forests, and virgin timber tracts.

The privately owned Sinnissippi Forest in Ogle County serves educational, recreational, and commercial purposes and received the state's first tree farm certificate in 1955. Nearby, White Pine State Park marks the southern boundary of that species. The U. S. FOREST SERVICE maintains a regional research center in Carbondale and an experimental forest at Kaskaskia.

The University of Illinois at Urbana began a preprofessional forestry program in 1938 and has offered professional-level training since 1958. Both the University of Illinois and Southern Illinois University in Carbondale currently offer undergraduate degrees in forestry, conservation, and wood technology and advanced degrees in forestry.

FRED W. KOHLMEYER

IMPORTED HARDWOODS

Since colonial times, lumber imports to America (excluding imports from Canada) have consisted of hardwoods and exotic woods brought to this country for the manufacture of the finest furniture, cabinetry, interior finish, trim, and veneers. Although for two centuries these imported hardwoods have composed less than 1 percent of the lumber used in the United States, they have been of great aesthetic importance to the woodworking and furniture industries. At times, such as during World War II when mahogany was used for torpedo boat shells and lignum vitae for ship bearings, certain imported species have been essential.

Of all the hardwoods that grow throughout the world, only those species with especially valuable qualities of durability, strength, and appearance have been imported to the United States. The chief imported species have been American mahogany (*Swietenia*) from Central America, which for decades represented the best in cabinet and furniture construction, and Philippine mahogany (*Shorea, Pentacme,* and *Parashorea*), which resembles true mahogany. Other significant imports have included Spanish cedar (*Cedrela*), once chiefly from Cuba; rosewood (*Dalbergia*) and purpleheart (*Peltogyne*) from South America; Gaboon ebony (*Diospyros*) and zebrawood (*Microberlinia brazzavillensis*) from Africa; teak (*Tectona grandis*) from Southeast Asia; satinwood (*Chloroxylon*) from Sri Lanka (Ceylon); and Japanese oak (*Quercus grosseserrata*) and ash (*Fraxinus sieboldiana*). Other hardwoods have been imported in more limited quantities. Countless species have been introduced in the United States market without gaining acceptance.

U.S. Department of Commerce figures for imported hardwoods before 1920 are sketchy at best, but they suggest that early in the twentieth century hardwood imports totaled slightly more than 50 million board feet annually. In the 1920s, hardwood imports averaged 80 million board feet annually, valued at $15 million. These imports fell to 56 million feet during the Great Depression. They increased during World War II, reaching 200 million board feet in 1946, and for the next twenty years rose slowly but steadily. Between 1960 and 1980, hardwood imports averaged about 380 million board feet annually, valued at more than $90 million.

American mahogany, which originated in Spanish Florida and the West Indies, was probably the first species imported by colonists. Its importation continued on a steady if limited basis throughout the nineteenth century. Later, the most generous supplies came from Mexico, British Honduras, and other areas of Central America. As the demand for mahogany increased, African mahogany (*Khaya ivorensis*), a species whose trade was controlled by British firms, was also imported.

In the early twentieth century, mahogany came to American ports as cants (logs hewn square). Cuban cants were relatively small, twelve to eighteen inches square, but cants from other regions could measure up to forty-eight inches square. These cants were sawn into lumber at such unlikely sawmill towns as Philadelphia, Staten Island, and New Orleans. Thompson Mahogany Company (Philadelphia), Robinson Lumber Company (New Orleans), and the Mengel Company (Louisville), were among the leading manufacturers of mahogany lumber.

In 1901, the United States imported 32 million board feet of mahogany, including 12 million feet from Mexico, 8 million from Nicaragua, 5 million from Cuba, and 5 million from the United Kingdom. During the next two decades, Mexico and the United Kingdom vied for the lead in shipping mahogany to America. While the Mexicans shipped their own production, the British supplied both Central American and African mahoganies, which they transshipped through Liverpool. Annual mahogany imports increased to 70 million feet shortly before the United States entered World War I. Following the war, mahogany imports stabilized at about 42 million feet per year.

In 1913, Ichabod T. Williams & Son of New York broke the British lock on African mahogany by shipping cants of that species on German ships directly from West Africa to the Staten Island sawmill. World War I halted this trade, but Williams & Son revived it after the war using their own vessels.

Since the exotic hardwood logs and cants imported to the United States were often sawn into lumber or sliced into veneers at the same mills that sawed mahogany logs, the exotic hardwood trade grew up alongside of the mahogany trade. Although many American firms have imported logs and lumber directly from Africa and Asia, British firms like William L. Marshall, Ltd., and J. H. Monteath Co. have tended to dominate this trade. Circassian walnut (*Juglans regia*) from Europe, snakewood (*Pithecolobium racemiflorum*) from South America, and prima vera (*Cybistax donnell-smithii*) from Central America were once among the significant exotic imports. After supplies of those woods were diminished in the 1950s, rosewood, African padauk (*Pterocarpus soyauxii*), and zebrawood became the most traded exotic woods in the United States.

During the first two decades of the twentieth century, 2,500 tons of Circassian walnut logs entered New York harbor annually to make veneer for expensive furniture and trim work. Ebony from the Congo, Java, and Madagascar arrived at the rate of 1,500 tons per year. Two thousand tons of balsa (*Ochroma lagopus*), used to fill life preservers and to serve as insulation, also came to New York annually. So did 3,000 tons of lignum vitae (*Guaiacum officinale*). Satinwood, at one time the choicest wood for fancy interior trim, came from Ceylon in lesser quantities. Snakewood arrived in New York from the Amazon River valley in the form of small logs, which were sawn for cane and umbrella handles. Brazilian and East Indian rosewood arrived at the rate of 100 tons per year, primarily for use in musical instruments. Teak, whose trade was dominated by British and Danish firms that had considerable control over the forests of Thailand and Burma, was imported for yacht building.

The exotic wood trade included the importation of a limited number of European species, including European oak (*Quercus robur*), elm burl (*Ulmus campestris*), and sycamore (*Acer pseudoplatanus*). Customarily, these species were sliced into veneer for architectural woodwork. Although botanically the same, the European oaks came from various countries. They varied in color due to differences in climate and soil, and they took their names from their origins, such as Russian, Austrian, or English oak. Since the oaks and sycamores have been largely cut out in Europe in recent years, imports of these species have become rare in America. The federal government placed a quarantine on elm logs from Europe in 1933 after discovery that some of them carried Dutch Elm Disease (*Cerotocystis ulmi*), a fungus that kills elm trees.

While these and other species of hardwood were being sawn on the East and Gulf coasts, the West Coast of the United States was developing a trade in hardwoods from the Pacific rim. The dominant species was Philippine mahogany. In the early years of this century, firms like the Robert Dollar Company of San Francisco and E. J. Stanton & Son and Cadwallader-Gibson of Los Angeles began importing sawn Philippine mahogany lumber. Cadwallader-Gibson specialized in lumber sawn on its own timber concession in eastern Luzon, marketing the product under its own copyrighted trade names—Bataan and Lamao. Other Philippine lumber came to the United States from sawmills that were partially owned and operated by Americans, such as the Johnson and the Insular lumber companies. Normally this lumber was kiln-dried after arriving on the West Coast. It was used in furniture plants and sold to consumers through retail lumberyards.

Apitong (*Dipterocarpus grandiflorus*), a dense, durable Philippine lumber, which Cadwallader-Gibson marketed as Bagac, was also sawn overseas and imported with the Philippine mahogany. Fisher Division of General Motors used millions of feet of apitong in automobile bodies throughout the 1930s. It was also milled for flooring and decking.

In the 1930s, before the Philippine veneer plants began buying up the best logs, Philippine mahogany lumber was available in widths up to forty-two inches and lengths to thirty-eight feet. At that time attractive intercoastal rates made it economical for large distribution yards in California to transship Philippine lumber to Gulf and East coast ports. This greatly expanded the Philippine mahogany market. In 1936, 30 million board feet of Philippine mahogany entered the United States. Shipments stopped during World War II, but otherwise Philippine mahogany became the dominant imported hardwood used in America.

After World War II, the Japanese began buying Philippine mahogany logs, processing them in Japan, and then exporting the milled lumber, moldings, and jambs to the United States. This lumber was all straight or ribbon grain because the Japanese customarily quartered their logs. In the 1960s, after labor costs had increased in Japan, Taiwan became the United States' major source for Philippine mahogany lumber and products, although South Korea took the lead in supplying millwork and plywood manufactured from Philippine mahogany. By 1963, hardwood plywood imports, principally Philippine mahogany plywood and door skins from Korea, rose to 1.6 billion square feet or more than 55 percent of the total United States consumption of plywood. By 1978, the quantity of hardwood plywood imported to the United States totaled 2.55 billion square feet.

Hardwoods from Japan, such as ash, oak, and birch, also ranked among the significant hardwood imports from the Pacific. The Robert Dollar Company began importing Japanese oak logs, which were sawn into railroad ties, as early as 1906. By 1912, White Brothers Lumber Company of San Francisco was sawing lumber from Japanese logs at its sawmill in Petaluma, California. About the same time, E. J. Stanton & Sons began importing Japanese hardwoods at Los Angeles. Short in length with a uniform texture, the Japanese hardwoods suited the furniture, fixture, and cabinet plants of California, but after the American dollar was devalued in 1972 these lumbers were no longer economical.

By the late 1950s, enterprising American importers were seeking new sources of foreign lumber to compete with Philippine mahogany and domestic softwood. Hamilton von Breton of Los Angeles was the first importer of South American virola (*Virola surinamensis*) and banak (*Virola koschnyi*), which were inexpensive substitutes for the mahogany used in moldings. Ramin (*Gonystylus*) from Malaysia also began arriving both in lumber and in cut parts for furniture. By the 1970s, meranti (*Shorea*), jelutong (*Dyera costulata*), and keruing (*Dipterocarpus*) were also arriving from Malaysia.

The 1970s brought dramatic changes in the worldwide hardwood market, which profoundly affected the United States market. By 1973, European nations, which had seen traditional African sources for hardwood lumber disrupted by political instability, began looking to Asian nations to meet their needs for hardwoods. Meanwhile, the exporting nations, including the Philippines, Malaysia, Thailand, and Burma, became more and more concerned about both utilization and conservation of their forest resources. These two factors, along with the rising cost of oil, the American dollar's poor performance on international money markets, and worldwide inflation, drove up imported lumber prices as much as 20 percent a year.

GAGE MCKINNEY

INDIANA FORESTS

At one time, hardwood forests covered about 20 million acres of the 23.2 million-acre land area in the State of Indiana. There were 134 tree species native to the state, of which 48 have had commercial importance. White oak was especially valuable to the early industries. Black walnut, other oaks, hickory, and hard maple were also of high quality and great value. By 1979, the state's forestland had declined to an estimated 3.9 million acres, about 17 percent of the land area. This loss was due to clearing for farms and, in more recent times, for industrial sites, homesites, highways, and airports. The decline was greatest in the northern part of the state. Woodlands could still be found in every county in Indiana, but they were concentrated in the northern third and the southern half of the state. Virtually the only remaining extended forest areas were the state forests and the Hoosier National Forest in the south.

More than 90 percent of the remaining forest was classified as commercial. Ninety percent of the forested lands were in private ownership, and of these private forests, more than two-thirds were in farm woodlots. The average woodlot holding measured less than 100 acres. Oak-hickory forest accounted for more than 60 percent and beech-maple-birch forest for 20 percent of the commercial timber. The elm-ash-cottonwood, with 14 percent, was most extensive in the lowlands and along streams in southern Indiana. There were smaller areas of commercially valuable oak-gum-cypress, loblolly-shortleaf pine, oak-pine, and aspen-birch. Elm was the only commercial tree species that had declined in growing stock volume in recent years; between 1950 and 1967 alone, mortality caused by Dutch elm disease and phloem necrosis reduced the standing volume of that species from 265 million to 96 million cubic feet.

In spite of disease and the conversion of forestland to other uses, the volume of timber growth in the 1960s and 1970s exceeded the loss in a ratio of about three to two. In the late 1970s, this favorable condition was threatened by new demands on the forest in the form of increased use of fuelwood and the perfection of hardwood particleboard.

From 1869 to 1900, Indiana led the nation in hardwood lumber production. Peak annual production came in 1899 with over a billion board feet, two-thirds of it oak. The Depression-era low was reached in 1932 when only 70 million board feet were produced. In more recent years, the state's lumber production has averaged about 200 million board feet yearly. Despite the decline in lumber production within the state, stability has been a hallmark of many Indiana wood-using industries. Some sites sustained large mills for more than 80 years. By the 1970s, such firms imported 85 percent of their raw material.

The state early became a center for fine face veneer manufactured from native walnut, maple, oak, and sweetgum; for cooperage, crossties, mine ties, and roofing; and for high-grade hardwood lumber produced by large sawmills. Veneer logs represented one-fourth of the value of all timber products in 1966, even though veneer-log volume was only 4 percent of the total cut. Cooperage log output peaked at 6.9 million board feet in 1960. The cooperage industry has been sustained by a law prohibiting reuse of barrels for aging bourbon whiskey. The four tool-handle plants in 1966 used 5.6 million board feet of material, of which 2.6 million were imported from the other hardwood states. Half the wood used was ash, the rest hickory and hard maple. The shift from underground to strip mining was responsible for the state's decline in mine timber production from 800,000 cubic feet in 1949 to 100,000 in 1966.

In 1871, when Indiana's forestlands had dwindled to fewer than 7 million acres, the State Horticultural Society issued a call for reforestation, but the legislature did not acknowledge forestry concerns until 1899. The forestry law of that year provided tax incentives for private woodland owners. Also in 1899, the Indiana Forestry Association and the Indiana Hardwood Lumbermen's Association were formed, and in response to their efforts the state created a board of forestry in 1901. In 1903, the board established Indiana's first state forest in Clark County. Two years later, Indiana's first fire protection legislation was passed. Charles C. Deam, state forester and secretary of the board after 1909, emphasized research in the Clark Forest and the identification and classification of Indiana's forests. His many publications also furthered the cause of conservation and forest policy in the state.

Indiana consolidated its resource agencies into a Department of Conservation in 1919. Richard Lieber, nationally known proponent of state park systems, was director of the department until 1933. During his administration, the 1921 Forest Tax Classification Act was passed, state nurseries were started, and land was purchased for state forests and parks. Forestry instruction has been offered within the state since 1926 when Purdue University established a forestry department.

As in other states during the Depression years, the CIVILIAN CONSERVATION CORPS (CCC) provided labor for conservation work and other improvements in the state parks and forests. In 1934, there were twenty-four CCC camps operating on state forests and game preserves and on soil erosion and flood control projects on private lands. The CCC grew, distributed, and planted 38 million seedlings that year, more than ten times the number provided by the state.

Federal forestry activity in the state dates from 1935, when the government began acquiring abandoned farmlands in southern Indiana. In 1951, these tracts became the Hoosier National Forest, which grew to include 185,127 acres of federal land by 1980.

While Lieber was director of conservation, Indiana became a leader in outdoor recreation. Its state parks, starting with Turkey Run established in 1921, increased eventually to twenty-one units by the 1970s, when the system totaled over 66,000 acres. Indiana's state forests (which measured about 25,000 acres in the late 1970s), the Hoosier National Forest, and the forested lands of the Crane Naval Depot have also been used in part for outdoor recreation. State forestlands measuring about 3,500 acres have been set aside in southern Indiana as backcountry areas where users may enjoy wilderness-type experiences.

ROY C. BRUNDAGE

INDIAN FORESTRY

The term Indian land as used here refers to land owned by an individual Indian (or his heirs) or by an Indian tribe. In either case, the land is held in trust by the United States to be managed for the benefit of the owners. The objectives of timberland management planning for Indian lands have been determined by the general Indian land policies of the United States government. Thus, the objectives in managing Indian forestlands differ in some respects from those applicable to publicly owned forests. Under provisions of the Dawes Severalty (or General Allotment) Act of 1877, it became policy to make allotments of tribally owned land to individual members of that tribe, and then to purchase from the tribe any of its lands remaining after allotments had been completed. This policy was ended with the Indian Reorganization Act of 1934, but in 1953, Congress adopted a policy of termination of federal trusteeship, although not specifically repealing the Reorganization Act. During the 1960s, termination was replaced by "self-determination" as the goal of government policy. The Indian Self-Determination and Education Assistance Act of 1975 committed the government to maintaining its "unique and continuing relationship" with Indian people while promoting an "early transition . . . to effective and meaningful participation by the Indian people in the planning, conduct, and administration of [federal] programs and services."

In 1977, there were more than 50 million acres of Indian lands, concentrated largely west of the Mississippi River and in the Lake States. Some 13.2 million acres were timbered. About 7.5 million of these timbered acres were classed as noncommercial forest, although they often provided rough wood products, grazing, and other values locally important. The 5.7 million acres classed as commercial forest produce sawlogs, pulpwood, and other salable forest products.

Timber volume on the entire commercial Indian forest was estimated to be nearly 40 billion board feet, and the allowable cut under sustained-yield management was set at about 1 billion board feet per year. Nearly 80 percent of the commercial forest had been logged at some time, beginning in the 1850s.

The first recorded sale of Indian timber was in 1857, by the Rabbit Lake Band of Chippewa Indians, in Minnesota. Although there were many more sales in subsequent years, most of them were of doubtful legality and were inadequately supervised by the government. The first important law governing the sale of Indian timber was an act of 1889 permitting the president to authorize the sale of dead and down timber on Indian lands, whether allotment or tribal lands, unless there was reason to believe it was intentionally killed. In the following year, however, Congress authorized the cutting of 20 million board feet of green timber on the Menominee Reservation in Wisconsin, and over the next twenty years it enacted legislation allowing cutting on other reservations. Logging under these acts was poorly supervised, although sometimes the Indian Service sought technical advice from the Bureau of Forestry. In 1909, Congress for the first time appropriated $100,000 specifically for forestry work on Indian reservations, and early in the following year Jay P KINNEY, a professional forester, joined the Indian Service to organize its forest administration unit. In June 1910, new legislation authorized the sale of "mature living and dead and down timber" on tribal lands generally and permitted allottees, with the consent of the secretary, to sell timber on their allotments. The work of the Indian Service's forestry organization was hampered by inadequate funding, except during the 1930s when emergency funds and CIVILIAN CONSERVATION CORPS labor were available. The Indian Reorganization Act of 1934 directed the secretary of the interior to make rules and regulations for the management of Indian forestry units on the principles of sustained yield —perhaps the earliest federal legislation to refer to sustained-yield management. This act applied only to reservations where the Indians voted to accept the act. Some 172 tribes accepted the act, but 73, including the populous Navajo, did not. In the 1950s, increased appropriations permitted new timber inventories and an enlarged volume of sales. The act of 1910 was amended in 1964 to provide that Indian forest management and timber sales must be in accordance with principles of sustained yield. Substantial improvements continued in the late 1970s, following studies by the American Indian Policy Review Commission, which showed that better financing was needed in order to provide acceptable levels of management.

In the sixty-one years from 1918 through 1978, 38.7 billion board feet of timber was cut on Indian lands, with a stumpage value of $894 million. Except in years of depressed markets, the annual cut increased rather steadily throughout this period, from 300 million to nearly 1 billion board feet. In the nineteenth century, treaties with many tribes provided that the United States would erect small sawmills on reservations to provide lumber for Indian use. In 1908, a sawmill with an annual capacity of 20 million board feet was erected at Neopit, Wisconsin, on the Menominee Reservation, financed largely with tribal funds and operated as a commercial enterprise. A smaller mill was erected at Redby on the Red Lake Reservation in Minnesota in 1916. Both mills were rebuilt, enlarged, and have continued to be commercially successful. Modern mills began operations on the Navajo Reservation near Fort Defiance, Arizona, in 1962; on the Fort Apache Reservation, Arizona, in 1963; and on the Warm Springs Reservation, Oregon, in 1967. These were integrated forest product enterprises using sophisticated manufacturing methods. Although differing in details, each of them was tribally financed and operated.

In the early 1900s, it became the policy to obtain tribal consent to the sale of timber from tribal lands, but this was at first little more than a formality. Meaningful Indian involvement in forest management decisions developed only gradually. By the 1940s, tribal officials were regularly included in discussions of forestry matters. It eventually became a requirement that tribal officers consent to forest management plans, timber sale schedules, and the forms of contract to be used. Indian participation was greatly strengthened by the Indian Self-Determination Act of 1975, which encouraged the Indians to perform many forest management tasks under contract with the federal government. Nevertheless, ultimate responsibility for the results of management will lie with the United States as long as the trusteeship exists.

After forest management was instituted on Indian lands in 1910, the Indian Bureau developed a fire protection system similar in most respects to those on other jurisdictions in the United States. In the early 1940s, the bureau became one of the pioneers in experiments with prescribed burning of ponderosa pine lands as a tool for fire hazard reduction and timber stand improvement. Most of the prescribed burning on Indian lands has been on the Colville Reservation (Washington), the Warm Springs Reservation (Oregon), and, especially, the Fort Apache Reservation (Arizona). On the Fort Apache Reservation, initial prescribed burns have covered more than 450,000 acres. One-third of the initial burn has been reburned once and about 10 percent of the initial burn has been covered a third time. The Indian Bureau has been an active participant in interagency fire management activities; its national-level staff is at the National Wildfire Center in Boise, Idaho.

FURTHER READING: J. P. Kinney, *Indian Forest and Range: A History of the Administration and Conservation of the Redman's Heritage* (1950).

GEORGE S. KEPHART

INDIAN FOREST USE

American Indians believed all nature to be sacred: every element of the forest possessed a soul and a spiritual power of which they were intensely aware. The Indians, an integral part of the forest, used, learned from, and found guidance and companionship in it, providing that the needs and desires of its natural beings were respected. The well-being of individuals and the community hinged upon a harmonious relationship with nature. Religious beliefs governed every aspect of Indians' interaction with the forest. Indians developed a personal relationship with the forest and a technology geared to gain the maximum benefit with minimal disturbance of the environment.

Trees, the most conspicuous component of the forest ecosystem, were important both economically and spiritually. As allies of humans, trusted and revered for their friendship, trees figured prominently in mythology. To the Cree in the north the tree was a mediator, a means of communication between humans and the supernatural. Western Abenaki of the Vermont-New Hampshire area had an even more personal tie to trees. Their creation myths related that in olden times the Owner made the first beings of stone, but, displeased with the result, destroyed them. He then made a man and woman from living wood who so pleased him that they became the first people, the ancestors of the Indians. Spiritual bonds with trees fostered by such myths strengthened indentification with the forest community. The Indians' technology reflected their belief that the forest's offerings must be harvested carefully in order to avoid any offense.

Indian technology combined an ingenious use of natural products with a thorough knowledge of the forest environment. Each tribe or band of hunter-gathers or horticulturists made skillful use of a vast array of raw materials to create tools and utensils appropriate to their subsistence mode. The forest type a tribe lived in—its particular plant and animal species, topography, and climate—influenced its technological devel-

Wigwam made of birch bark on the Lac du Flambeau Indian Reservation in Wisconsin, 1906. Forest Service Photo.

opment. The products needed by a northern group in a boreal-montane coniferous forest with cold, snowy winters differed substantially from those of Indians in deciduous forests in warmer southern climates. Regardless of geographical location, forest tribes used trees thoroughly; bark, leaves, nuts, roots, and wood were all incorporated into subsistence production, whether as binding material for bark canoes or as medical treatments.

In the northern forests where the white or paper birch (*Betula papyrifera*) grew in abundance, its bark was the preferred material for utensils, containers, shelter, and especially the streamlined, attractive birchbark canoes used by Hurons, Abenaki, Ojibwa, and others. Sheets of bark, stripped from the birch before the sap began to flow, were bound by spruce roots to a frame of cedar (*Chamaecyparis thyoides* or *Thuja occidentalis*). When green or damp, cedar was flexible but strong and, as the "Grandmother" tree, it also had religious importance. The seams of the canoe were sealed with a gummy substance made by chewing and heating black spruce (*Picea mariana*) resin. This same sealing method was used on birch-

bark buckets, cups, and bowls. Farther south, in the mixed mesophytic forests where birch grew too small to provide adequate strips of bark, Indians used the American elm (*Ulmus americana*) to make utensils, containers, and canoes. Elm was one of the primary climax growths employed by northeastern groups such as the Iroquois, who respected and propagated it for its economic and religious importance.

Wood itself was vital to the survival of Indian communities, particularly as the primary fuel source in forested areas. Deadfall and trees felled in slash-and-burn horticulture were the preferred fuels, and trees were seldom deliberately cut for firewood. The amount of available firewood was an important factor in the location of a village or camp and possibly affected a group's population growth. A large community in a thinly wooded area could quickly deplete easily accessible wood and had to be prepared to search far afield for fuel. Gathering firewood involved more transportation labor than any other subsistence production. In some groups, fuel gathering was of such significance that it was an integral part of ritual activities such as puberty rites.

For sedentary horticulturists, abundant lumber was essential in building sturdy, safe houses and palisades capable of withstanding inclement weather and attacks from hostile tribes. Huron and Iroquois, for example, were particularly reliant upon adequate lumber supplies for their longhouse villages. Conrad Heidenreich, a specialist on the Hurons, has estimated that a village of thirty-six longhouses required 16,000 poles for exterior walls and 250 more for inside support poles. Because of their limited technology for felling large trees and the amount of lumber needed to build a village, the size and age of a timber stand was probably more important than the tree species represented in it. Generally, secondary or successional growths were preferred because of workable girth and ease in hauling. Other tribes also used lumber to construct homes and buildings, The California Yurok used redwood (*Sequoia sempervirens*) to build large, solid split-plank homes, while farther up the Northwest Coast, cedar plank houses were common. In the Southwest, Pueblo Indians used ponderosa pine for rafters.

Trees were an important food source. Throughout New England and New York, aboriginal Indian women gathered maple sap in bark containers in the early spring. After being heated, sap could be added to food for flavoring, and it provided an additional source of calories. Fruits and nuts supplied a large percentage of the diets of most forest groups. For the California Indians, acorns from countless oak stands were a primary food. These nuts were leached or pounded and made into a flavorful mush or baked as bread. The oak woodland-grass areas in the foothills of the Coast Range and Sierra Nevada were the most important floral zones, abundant with oaks, seed grasses, and forage for deer. Tanoak (*Lithocarpus densiflorus*), black oak (*Quercus kelloggii*), blue oak (*Q. douglasii*), and valley oak (*Q. lobata*) produced the four most favored acorns and were found mainly in the northern part of the state. The sweet, oily digger pine nuts (*Pinus sabiniana*) were also relished; the nutritious buckeye nuts (*Aesculus californica*), however, generally were eaten only as an emergency food because of the work involved to prepare them.

Throughout the Southeast, acorns from the live oak (*Q. virginiana*) and nuts from several other oaks were regularly eaten. Chestnuts (*Castanea dentata*), pecans (*Carya illinoensis, C. pecan*) and other hickories, as well as black walnut (*Juglans nigra*) were particularly important to the diets of the Cherokee, Seminole, and other southern tribes. Fruits, eaten fresh or dried, included persimmons (*Diospyros vir-giniana*), papaws (*Asimina triloba*), crab apples (*Malus coronaria*), and wild plums (*Prunus nigra*).

It is possible that Indians deliberately promoted the growth of favored species of trees and plants to the extent that in some areas the actual composition of the forest changed. Nut-bearing trees, for example, are in unusually high proportions in present Eastern hardwood forests. Nuts were an important food source for aboriginal Indians there, and they were probably careful to leave preferred nut-bearers standing when they felled trees. In effect, they selected for nut-bearing trees and altered the species distribution of the forest. Iroquois are known to have planted Canada plum and to have encouraged the growth of medicinal plants, as other tribes undoubtedly did. Forest composition was also inadvertently shifted by the propagation of fruit-bearing and nut-bearing trees in the middens near Indian villages.

Trees and plants played a central role in Indian medicinal treatments, in both a practical and a religious sense, and gathering plants was a holy occupation. Plants which in myth had agreed to provide cures for disease were considered the special friends of humans. A Cherokee origin myth told how evergreen trees—cedar, pine, spruce, holly, and laurel—had been given the strongest curing powers because they successfully completed the first vision quest in this world. Because of similar beliefs in trees' power to cure, Iroquois face masks used in curing ceremonies were always carved in living basswood (*Tilia americana*), allowing the tree's healing power to become a part of the mask.

Each tribe had both a comprehensive knowledge of plants and herbs growing in the forest type they inhabited and a wide range of treatments for diseases and ailments. In the ecotone areas of the northern Great Plains, Indians took a boiled mixture of juniper berries and leaves (*Juniperus virginiana*) for coughs or inhaled smoke from the branches to relieve congestion. Rappahannock Indians of Virginia used a steeped infusion of chokecherry berries (*Prunus virginiana*) as a treatment for asthma. Some Indians used spunck (*Polyporus*), a growth found on black birch (*Betula nigra*), in a rather drastic cure for sciatica, burning the substance on the afflicted areas. Medicinal plants were valued for their use in reproductive problems. Arikara women drank chokecherry juice to stop postpartum hemorrhage, Ojibwa women used a powder made of blue cohosh (*Caulophyllum thalictroides*), also known as squawroot, to expedite parturition or menstruation, while the Omaha found it an effective febrifuge. The Penobscots of Maine as well as the Cherokees in the South used partridgeberry (*Mitchella repens*) to speed childbirth. Infusions, teas, and poultices, carefully compounded from a variety of plants and administered by women or men with special curing powers, could be found among every tribe. When combined with the spiritual ministrations of a healer or shaman, these medicines worked with an efficacy often not credited to them by white observers. Once again, the intertwining of physical and supernatural powers so innate in Indian cultures served the needs of the communities admirably.

One aspect of American Indian forest use that has long been a controversial topic is controlled, or cultural, burning. Seventeenth-century European explorers and travelers along the Eastern seaboard frequently reported that Indians fired the forests regularly in the spring and fall of each year to clear the woods of undergrowth or to drive game animals into enclosures for slaughter. This burning created vast, parklike expanses of widely spaced trees and grassy clearings. It is possible that fires mentioned by early travelers were the result of the Indians' carelessness or of natural causes such as lightning. Most evidence, however, suggests that deliberate burning was practiced by Indians, although the extent is uncertain. There were many practical reasons for Indians to fire the woods. Burning clears the forest of dense undergrowth conducive to conflagration and thereby prevents uncontrollable, crowning fires. Tender second-growth foliage, seed grasses, and berry production are encouraged by fire. Many economically useful plants do not occur in climax forests, and even climax forest species may do better in open areas. Important food animals such as deer thrive on the superior forage in the ecotone and pioneer forests of burned areas, and the decreased undergrowth from firing increases visibility and would have made hunting easier.

Many California tribes are known to have practiced cultural burning, some to increase seed yield and others to drive game or encourage the growth of wild tobacco. Areas such as the chaparral zone of the Sierra Nevada are dominated by broadleaf shrubs for which fire is a vital part of maintenance; at climax stage, the manzanita (*Arctostaphylos*), buck brush (*Ceanothus cuneatus*), and chamise (*Adenostoma fasciculatum*) become too heavy to provide forage for deer and so thick as to be impenetrable by humans and large animals. Only by regular burning, natural or cultural, can chaparral areas achieve their full economic potential.

Burning was not as common in the far northern areas where there was little agriculture, where canoe rather than foot was the primary summer mode of travel, and where snowshoeing in winter was not hindered by underbrush. There is little evidence that horticulturists such as the Hurons practiced burning other than to kill individual trees in slash-and-burn agriculture. A fire burning out of control would have had calamitous results in their wooden villages. Bands living in arid lands, such as the Gosiute of Utah, avoided using fire, since in their harsher environment brush regeneration was so slow that burning had a detrimental effect. Overall, however, many Indian groups used fire to manage land and wildlife resources when and where it was physically and ecologically feasible.

Indians influenced natural succession, species maintenance, and forest structure to their own advantage, yet they did so without exploiting the forest in the same sense as Euro-Americans later did. Indian forest use was based on a sympathy, kinship, and respect of humans for nature. The relationship satisfied the needs of both Indians and the forest. The Indians' technology and careful harvesting and use of raw materials embodied their spiritual identification with the ecological community of the forest.

FURTHER READING: Gordon M. Day, "The Indian as an Ecological Factor in the Northeastern Forest," *Ecology* 34 (Apr. 1953): 329-346. Robert F. Heizer, "Primitive Man as an Ecologic Factor," *Kroeber Anthropological Society Papers* 13 (Fall 1955): 1-31. Henry T. Lewis, *Patterns of Indian Burning in California: Ecology and Ethnohistory*, Ballena Press Anthropological Papers No. 1 (1973). Calvin Martin, "Fire and Forest Structure in the Aboriginal Eastern Forest," *Indian Historian* 6 (Fall 1973): 38-42, 54. William Christie McLeod, "Conservation Among Primitive Hunting Peoples," *Scientific Monthly* 43 (Dec. 1936): 562-566, and "Fuel and Early Civilization," *American Anthropologist* n.s. 27 (1925): 344-346. Joan M. Vastokas, "Architecture and Environment: The Importance of the Forest to the Northwest Coast Indian," *Forest History* 13 (Oct. 1969): 12-21. Virgil J. Vogel, *American Indian Medicine* (1970). Richard White, *Land Use, Environment, and Social Change: The Shaping of Island County, Washington* (1980).

CAROL DEVENS

INDUSTRIAL FORESTRY ASSOCIATION

The Industrial Forestry Association (IFA) was formed in 1949 as the Forest Conservation Committee of Pacific Northwest Forest Industries. It was renamed the Industrial Forestry Association in 1952. Its parent organizations were the West Coast Lumbermen's and Pacific Northwest Loggers associations.

IFA's purposes and objectives continue to focus on the "development of an adequate and permanent timber supply for the Douglas Fir Industry" (Hagenstein, 1979).

To achieve its objectives, IFA sponsors the West Coast Tree Farm Program, works on the persistent issue of forest taxation, and operates nonprofit tree nurseries to supply seedlings to members. The association also provides advice to its members on forest protection and on timber growing and harvesting. IFA testifies before federal and state legislative committees on behalf of its members and presents the industry's "story" through personal appearances and the media.

By 1979, IFA had certified 7.8 million acres of tree farms, which was 64 percent of the total private forestland in the Douglas-fir region. It had also provided 400 million seedlings for planting following the harvesting of 800,000 acres. That same year, IFA had 115 members that operated more than 400 wood-using plants and owned more than 5.5 million acres of forestland. Its professional staff of forty-five includes fifteen foresters.

FURTHER READING: William D. Hagenstein, "Informed Forestry Action," *Southern Lumberman* 239 (Dec. 15, 1979): 68H-68I.

INSTITUTE OF FOREST GENETICS

James G. Eddy was a well-to-do lumberman who was intrigued by Luther Burbank's experiments in plant genetics. In 1918, Eddy wrote Burbank to ask if he thought it possible to improve the growth rate and optimum size of conifers by the principles of hybridization with which Burbank had worked such miracles among smaller species. In addition to his scientific curiosity, Eddy was convinced that selective breeding was a necessary complement of reforestation programs if the nation was to meet its future demands for timber.

At first, Burbank discouraged Eddy. Although he had produced an improved walnut tree, Burbank feared that conifer growth was too slow for genetic experimentation to be practicable. Like most botanists of the time, he believed that conifers rarely flowered before they were twenty years old. Eddy rejoined with the testimony of numerous foresters that many species of pine flowered in five years and told Burbank that he had seen some individual trees prepared to reproduce at two. Burbank then approved and even nominated a director for Eddy's project, Lloyd Austin of the University of California.

Controlled pollination of western white pine is used to produce superior individuals. The bag prevents random pollination; syringe contains pollen from male flowers of selected individuals. Forest Service Photo.

Unable to interest government in funding such a study, Eddy tapped his own resources. The Eddy Tree Breeding Station was established in Placerville, California, in 1925. Over the next ten years, it cost its founder an average of $25,000 a year, rather more than he could readily afford, especially after the stock market crash of 1929 and the Depression that followed. As early as 1927, Eddy tried to affiliate the station with the University of California but he was unable to raise the exorbitant endowment demanded. In 1932, in order to appeal to other sources of funding, he renamed the station the Institute of Forest Genetics and secured stopgap support from the Carnegie Foundation and the Soil Conservation Service. Finally, after further negotiations, the U. S. FOREST SERVICE assumed control and responsibility for the institute and used it as a model for its forest genetics study programs elsewhere. The Forest Service also provided the institute with improved housing and laboratories constructed under the Works Progress Administration and CIVILIAN CONSERVATION CORPS.

Although Eddy's Station briefly continued Luther Burbank's research with walnuts and started a program with Austin's earlier interest, Douglas-fir, the governing board soon decided to concentrate entirely on pines. Within two years, over sixty different species of *Pinus* had been planted, the seeds secured all over the world. The station's first successful hybrid was a cross between the Monterey pine (*Pinus radiata*) and the knobcone pine (*Pinus attenuata*) of California, combining the rapid growth of the former with the knobcone's hardiness and resistance to fire. In addition to successfully breeding "bigger and better pines" for reforestation purposes, the institute also made important scientific discoveries about the evolution of the genus. Because of the problems anticipated by Burbank in the slowness of conifer growth, however, the ultimate contribution of the institute's research cannot be assessed until the distant future.

FURTHER READING: Lois C. Stone, "The Institute of Forest Genetics: A Legacy of Good Breeding," *Forest History* 12 (Oct. 1968): 20-29.

INTERNATIONAL FORESTRY

The participation of American foresters in forestry activities beyond the present boundaries of the United States began in 1902 when, at the request of Captain George P. Ahern of the United States Army, Gifford PINCHOT visited the Philippines and recommended a forestry program and organization for that nation.

The first organizational venture of American foresters internationally was participation in the International Union of Forest Research Organizations (IUFRO). This organization came into being in 1893 in Vienna, Austria, and was organized to stimulate and coordinate research in various European countries. Professor Filibert Roth, director of the Forestry Department of the University of Michigan, Ann Arbor, attended the VIth IUFRO Congress in Brussels in 1910. Following the VIIth Congress in 1929, Edward N. Munns of the U. S. FOREST SERVICE became an

active participant and served as vice-president, beginning in 1932. Since that time, American foresters have gradually increased their aggregate participation. After World War II, Verne L. Harper helped to reestablish IUFRO; in 1968, George M. Jemison assumed the presidency, and in 1971, the United States hosted the IUFRO Congress in Gainesville, Florida.

The first formal international effort of the SOCIETY OF AMERICAN FORESTERS, the official society of the profession, was the establishment of a Standing Committee on International Relations in 1925. Samuel Trask DANA was its first chairman, and its initial work was to plan America's participation in the First World Forestry Congress, held in Rome in 1926. The Fifth World Forestry Congress convened in Seattle, Washington, in 1960.

In 1927, Tom Gill organized the forestry work of the Tropical Plant Research Foundation. During the next three years, he made timber surveys of the Central American countries, plus Cuba and the Dominican Republic. His findings, presented in his book, *Tropical Forests of the Caribbean*, set forth the sum-total of what then was known about the forest resources of those areas. With the financial support of the CHARLES LATHROP PACK FORESTRY FOUNDATION, of which he was the chief forester, Gill was instrumental in establishing the International Training and Research Center for Tropical America at the University of the Andes in Merida, Venezuela. In 1939, the Forest Service established the Tropical Forest Experiment Station (currently designated as the Institute of Tropical Forestry) in Puerto Rico. Its objective was to serve as a center for the compilation and dissemination of information on tropical forestry to the entire Caribbean area.

In April 1943, President Franklin D. ROOSEVELT convened a conference in Hot Springs, Virginia, to consider ways and means to organize international cooperation in agriculture. From its deliberations came the Food and Agriculture Organization (FAO), later to become a member of the United Nations family of specialized agencies. Since the original charter did not include forestry, a group of internationally minded foresters, headed by Lester B. Pearson of Canada, obtained Roosevelt's approval for the inclusion of forestry in FAO activities.

The United States has also maintained a substantial bilateral aid program with developing nations through the Technical Cooperative Administration of the Department of State in 1950 and its successor agencies up to and including the Agency for International Development (AID). The modern program of

Indonesian technicians stand by containers of native *falcata* seedlings. Georgia-Pacific Photo.

international forestry assistance to developing countries resulted from the passage in 1939 of a law that authorized funds for United States technical assistance in Latin American countries, Liberia, and the Philippines. The Second Deficiency Appropriations Act of 1940 provided the first funds for the direct financing of agricultural and forestry experts in all foreign countries. This assistance has been financed by federal funds allotted to a succession of federal agencies. Through this cooperation, Forest Service personnel and other specialists were selected for assignment overseas, and arrangements were made for the education and training of foreign nationals in the United States. The Division of International Forestry was established in the Forest Service and staffed to administer this program as well as that derived from FAO.

The programs were very active from 1950 to 1974. During that period, more than 260 projects were in operation, and as many as 40 to 50 American specialists were on overseas assignments at any one time. In peak years, between 300 and 400 foreign participants were received and assigned to universities for education or to Forest Service field offices for training.

Other agencies, especially universities, served under contract to the several federal aid agencies. Over a number of years, the College of Environmental Science and Forestry at Syracuse, New York, provided a cadre of faculty members for the professional forestry school of Los Banos, Laguna, in the Philippines. Similarly, Purdue University assisted in staffing the faculty of a professional forestry school at Viscosa, Brazil; and Utah State University established a forest ranger school in Gurgan, Iran.

In 1958, Congress amended the Agricultural and Trade Assistance Act (PL-480) to permit use of foreign currencies to support forestry research in countries participating in the Surplus Agricultural Commodities program. In 1960, the Forest Service began developing research that eventually involved foreign scientists in many countries. This program produced significant new knowledge and strengthened ties among scientists around the world.

The Peace Corps has also made a considerable contribution to forestry in some of the countries in which it has operated. In 1982, it had forestry programs in a score or more nations of Asia, Africa, and Latin America. Nearly 100 graduate foresters are currently serving these programs for a two-year period. They have been especially active in reforestation projects.

Also in demand are foresters with skills in the field of outdoor recreation to help plan, establish, and maintain forest-park recreation facilities. Some of them work under the informal guidance of highly skilled professionals from FAO and AID. These senior officers make the initial surveys of the needs and resources of the developing nations, and the Peace Corps volunteers participate in the work program that implements the recommendations.

During the late 1960s, a sharp curtailment in bilateral forestry assistance funds developed. The explanation was that FAO had a large number of professionals from FAO and AID. These senior officers make the initial surveys of the needs and resources cordingly, it was in a better position to supply assistance than was the U. S. bilateral program, which did not have an adequate supervisory staff. Furthermore, since the United States contributed a substantial portion of funds administered by FAO, American officials saw little need for a duplication of forestry activities.

Until about 1970, the major portion of both multilateral and bilateral assistance consisted of projects under the direction of American specialists resident in the developing countries. Frequently, the nature of these projects required the expertise of specialists not assigned to the project. Therefore, a consulting specialist might be selected and assigned to the project for a few weeks. About 1965, the nature of these consultancies began to change. An increasing number of them were designed to review broad or specific forestry programs and to offer recommendations for improvement. These demands arose from two distinct sources. At that time, a number of foresters in some of the developing countries had, through the education and training that they had received abroad, become competent to originate programs in forestry and related fields. Their superiors, however, wished to have a review by outstanding foreign authorities. Accordingly, both AID and FAO financed consultancies for this purpose. In addition, the World Bank and similar institutions were receiving requests for loans from developing countries for purposes relating to land use, forestry, and forest-industrial development. They also began requesting the assignment of qualified experts for short periods to visit the countries under consideration and to evaluate the soundness of the loan requests and to assist in developing loan opportunities. Since 1965, therefore, the number of consultancy assignments has exceeded the number of project assignments, and this trend is likely to continue. The magnitude of both multi- and bilateral

forestry assistance programs is currently very much reduced from the peak years of the 1960s.

Tropical forestry is increasing in importance. The remaining virgin forests in the tropics and subtropics constitute a substantial untapped resource, and the wind and water erosion on the areas already cut over is serious. In an attempt to meet this situation constructively, the Department of State in 1978 organized in Washington a U. S. Strategy Conference on Tropical Deforestation. As an outgrowth of this conference, AID is increasing its staff of specialists (including foresters) in order to contribute to the effective management of the forest and nonforest lands in the tropics.

The current trend in international forestry involves a greatly accelerated participation in international congresses, conferences, and working groups of specialists. The Forestry Committee of the FAO meets biennially and recommends policy and programs for that organization. The International Union of Forest Research Organizations has six divisions and several hundred specialized working parties. Many of these latter have international meetings at intervals of two to three years, and the entire union holds international congresses at four- to six-year intervals. The orientation of their activities is toward forestry research to benefit the world and its important geographical subdivisions. In 1960, the International Union of Societies of Foresters was founded, largely by Verne L. Harper and Tom Gill, to foster the formation and support of professional forestry societies throughout the world. It holds an international congress at intervals of five to six years.

FURTHER READING: Grant W. Sharpe, Clare W. Hendee, and Shirley W. Allen, *Introduction to Forestry* (1976), especially pp. 193-209. Robert K. Winters, "How Forestry Became a Part of the FAO," *Journal of Forestry* 69 (Sept. 1971): 574-577, and 69 (Oct. 1971): 711; "U. S. Participation in International Forestry," *Journal of Forestry* 75 (Mar. 1977): 166–168; *The Forest and Man* (1974); and *International Forestry in the U. S. Department of Agriculture* (1980).

ROBERT K. WINTERS

INTERNATIONAL ORDER OF HOO-HOO

The International Order of Hoo-Hoo is a fraternal organization of lumbermen, trade association officials, trade journalists, and other men connected with the lumber industry. It was founded in Gurdon, Arkansas, in 1892 as the International Concatenated Order of Hoo-Hoo, the inspiration of Bolling Arthur Johnson

(1862–1925), a journalist and well-known lumber market editor who later became publisher of the *Lumber World Review*. Although there were a number of regional lumbermen's associations at the time, Johnson saw the need for a nationwide fraternal group in the increasingly integrated industry. He contrived the peculiar name in a moment of no doubt bibulous whimsy at the Southwestern Lumbermen's Association in Kansas City in 1891.

Throughout its history, Hoo-Hoo has been a purely social organization in the men's lodge tradition, replete with ornate ritual and paraphernalia. Johnson was something of an amateur Egyptologist and based Hoo-Hoo's flummery on Egyptian terminology and, curiously, Lewis Carroll's "The Hunting of the Snark." (The organization's president is known as "the Snark.") Its magazine, the *Hoo-Hoo Bulletin,* was devoted to personal news of members and general information on promoting sales of lumber. Although it reflected the conservatism of its businessman membership, the *Bulletin* avoided controversial issues.

Hoo-Hoo expanded in the booster atmosphere of the 1920s but virtually disappeared during the 1930s with the Depression-era demoralization of business and the decline of business culture. In addition, there was an episode of embezzlement, and the *Hoo-Hoo Bulletin* was not published for several years. During World War II, Hoo-Hoo was revived and it flourished again during the 1950s, reaching a membership high of almost 13,000.

However, as in other businesses, the new generation of lumbermen was less interested in the frivolous aspects of fraternal lodges than in service and public relations. "Concatenated" was dropped from the order's name and in 1955 the *Hoo-Hoo Bulletin* was renamed *Log and Tally.* Hoo-Hoo devoted considerable attention to the industry's competition with aluminum and plastics manufacturers and took a more active role in local parades and fairs in lumbering regions, sponsoring industry exhibits and promoting the use of wood and its products. Hoo-Hoo also initiated awards to forestry students and subsidized tree-planting projects by youth groups. Beginning in the 1960s, it sponsored educational programs in forest management and wood processing.

INTRODUCED FOREST TREES

Exotic trees were first introduced to North America by colonists in the eighteenth century. Among the earliest species brought from northern Europe were fruit trees, including varieties of apple, plum, and cherry. In the eighteenth century, trees from western America

and the coastal region of Asia were introduced to the Northeast, largely for ornamental purposes.

Cultivation of exotic species assumed a more scientific aspect with the founding of the Arnold Arboretum of Boston in 1872. Special expeditions, financed by the arboretum and similar institutions elsewhere, gathered seeds of woody temperate zone species from the rich interior forests of Asia. By 1920, several hundred trees had been introduced into the United States, most of them as seed from one to five individuals chosen for horticultural rather than wood-producing characteristics. Species introduced in the Northeast were disseminated quickly to other parts of the country, cultivated first in arboreta and later adopted for horticulture and shelterbelt uses. Among the most popular species used for SHELTERBELTS were Siberian elm (*Ulmus pumila*), Siberian pea (*Caragana arborescens*), and Russian-olive (*Elaeagnus angustifolia*).

Since the 1950s, a few species have been used for forestry purposes, although by 1980, exotics still accounted for less than 1 percent of the total planting program. The principal species used were European and Japanese larches (*Larix decidua* and *L. leptolepis*), Norway spruce (*Picea abies*), and Scotch pine (*Pinus sylvestris*) in the Northeast, and Australian eucalyptus (*Eucalyptus spp.*) in California (more common at the beginning of the century than in the 1980s) and southern Florida. Scotch pine, a native of Eurasia, now naturalized in some parts of Canada and the Northeast, accounted for two-thirds of the annual Christmas tree harvest by the 1980s. Paperbark tree (*Melaleuca quinquenervia*) from southeast Asia and Chinaberry (*Melia azedarach*) are often forest weeds in parts of the South.

In the United States, Hawaii has made the most extensive use of exotics for forestry purposes. Lacking native timber of high commercial value, Hawaii began introducing exotics in the 1880s. On mountain slopes in back of Honolulu, more than thirty species of eucalyptus were planted, and in the 1890s, extensive tracts of similar species were planted on Maui. In ensuing decades, foreign species came to dominate the forest, particularly below 2,000 feet. The trees were used for heating and fuel for home and industry, for fence posts, ties, timbers, lumber, and watershed protection.

America also exports trees. Northern Europe, with its limited native flora, has benefited especially. Species from eastern North America were introduced in Europe in the eighteenth century, with western trees following in the next century. Most of the species were confined to parks until the large-scale forest planting programs of the 1930s. By the 1980s, fores-

Eucalyptus from Australia was planted widely throughout California; shown here is a grove near Los Angeles. Forest Service Photo.

try in Denmark and the British Isles depended heavily on Douglas-fir (*Pseudotsuga menziesii*), western hemlock (*Tsuga heterophylla*), Sitka spruce (*Picea sitchensis*), and lodgepole pine (*Pinus contorta*). On the continent, red oak (*Quercus rubra*), Douglas-fir, and eastern white pine (*Pinus strobus*) were common. White pine also played an important part in the timber industry of Hokkaido in northern Japan.

Temperate parts of the Southern Hemisphere have also benefited from North American trees since the early 1800s. Species such as black locust (*Robinia pseudoacacia*) and sycamore (*Platanus occidentalis*) proved useful in urban forestry. In New Zealand, Douglas-fir and ponderosa pine (*Pinus ponderosa*) were planted for timber. Monterey pine (*Pinus radiata*) reached Australia in the 1850s and soon became known as the "miracle tree," due to its extremely rapid growth on mediocre sites. Extensive planting beginning in 1920 has made Monterey pine the most important tree, native or otherwise, in parts of Chile, New Zealand, and Australia with warm, moist winters and dry summers. In the twentieth century, southern pines reached the Southern Hemisphere where they played a minor role in the shadow of Monterey pine until foresters discovered them to be the best species for warm, temperate regions with moist summers. By 1980, plantations of slash and loblolly pine (*Pinus elliottii* and *P. taeda*) occupied several hundred thousand acres and comprised nearly all of the forestry efforts in southern Brazil; northern Argentina; Queensland, Australia; and parts of the Republic of South Africa.

FURTHER READING: R. J. Streets, *Exotic Trees in the British Commonwealth* (1962). J. W. Wright, *Introduction to Forest Genetics* (1976).

JONATHAN W. WRIGHT

IOWA FORESTS

The loess and glacial till plains of most of Iowa are unfavorable to forest growth. Under 7 million acres, less than one-fifth of the land area of Iowa, were forested before the 1800s. This native woodland, shaped by centuries of prairie fires, was most abundant in the east and southeast and thinnest in the north central and northwestern districts. Along rivers, pioneers found maple, hickory, oak, elm, walnut, ash, basswood, cottonwood, birch, hackberry, sycamore, willow, linden, and locust. In the northeast were scattered stands of white pine, low-growing yew, and juniper. After 150 years of occupancy by Europeans, almost 90 percent of the forest area, reduced to under 2.25 million acres, bears mixtures of oak and hickory (usually found on dry uplands) or of elm, ash, and cottonwood. Common upland trees include hard maple, wild fruit, juniper, butternut, aspen, and eastern redcedar. Throughout Iowa, the north and east slopes are most frequently wooded; the south and west slopes are comparatively treeless. White oak, northern red oak, and hickory are the most important species of sawtimber. Almost half the commercial growth is on less than 12 percent of the forestland and is fairly concentrated in the northeast.

The reduction of Iowa's forests was largely a byproduct of farming and pasturage. Until the 1840s, settlers wasted effort by locating farms in timbered areas. As farmland values increased, the appearance of the portable steam sawmill led to widespread clearing until, by the early twentieth century, virtually all of the state's forests were second or third growth. Local timber did not fulfill the needs of Iowa and its neighbors to the west, however; Iowa ranked as the

Forestry students at Ames, Iowa, work in the college tree nursery, 1914. Forest History Society Lantern Slide Collection.

ninth state in lumber production in 1869, but most of the wood was white pine and hemlock rafted downriver from Wisconsin.

Severe winters experienced on treeless prairies led to an interest in forest conservation. Tree planting was a major program of the Iowa State Horticultural Society formed in 1866. The society's secretaries served as forestry commissioners until 1924 when responsibility for state forestry was invested in the secretary of agriculture. After 1912, the head of the forestry department at Iowa State University, which had offered related instruction since 1872, served as deputy commissioner. In 1935, the new State Conservation Commission subsumed all state forestry activities. A campaign by the Iowa Park and Forestry Association led to passage of the Forest and Fruit Tree Reservation Act of 1906, which offered tax reduction incentives to keep the poorer agricultural land in tree growth, either natural or replanted. In 1919, the creation of a system of small state parks began. During the 1930s, four national forest purchase units were authorized in southern Iowa for the reforestation of submarginal farmland, but no significant holdings were ever acquired. In 1980, less than 2 percent of the state's forests were in public ownership, while farmers held 88 percent. Private owners did not generally practice scientific forestry until the 1970s. The Iowa climate can support mature forest, and cultivation (which destroys the prairie and reduces the high nitrogen content of the soil) is conducive to the future spread of the forest.

FURTHER READING: Jacob L. Crane and George Wheeler Olcott, *Report on the Iowa Twenty-Five Year Conservation Plan* (1933). Robert R. Davidson, "Comparisons of the Iowa Forest Resource in 1832 and 1954," *Iowa State Journal of Science* 36 (1961): 133–136. George Bernhardt Hartman, "The Iowa Sawmill Industry," *Iowa Journal of History and Politics* 40 (Jan. 1942): 52-93. National Association of State Foresters, "Iowa: Forestry on the Farm," *Forests and Forestry in the American States: A Reference Anthology*, ed. Ralph R. Widner (1968), pp. 380-388. Philip L. Thornton and James T. Morgan, *The Forest Resources of Iowa*, Central States Forest Experiment Station, Forest Survey Release 22 (1959).

GEORGE W. SIEBER

IZAAK WALTON LEAGUE OF AMERICA

It has been said that the Izaak Walton League of America (IWLA) was "born with fists doubled." Named for the author of *The Compleat Angler* (1653), the IWLA was founded in Chicago in 1922 by a group of angered anglers who feared that American attitudes and practices would soon destroy productive fishing waters. Through legislative, judicial, and oth-

er means, the IWLA sought to correct problems of water pollution, wetland drainage, and cut-and-run logging. At the start, IWLA declared itself the "Defender of Woods, Waters, and Wildlife," but in time, as its leaders learned more about habitat influences and ecological principles, the league also campaigned for soil conservation and air quality. Divided into state groups and local chapters, IWLA introduced three-level organization and unified action to the American CONSERVATION MOVEMENT.

Publicist Will H. Dilg is recognized as IWLA's founder and was its first president. Zeal, persuasive writings, and fiery speechmaking enabled Dilg and volunteer workers to make IWLA influential soon after its founding. However, Dilg's boast that the league would soon have a million adherents was not realized, the peak membership being about 100,000. When Dilg successfully sought the Illinois governor's help in outlawing the sale of black bass, an associate wrote that while there were then only seven chapters in the state, "Dilg made them look like 700." Although Dilg's methods worked, they were not acceptable to many members. When Seth Gordon, later IWLA's conservation director, chided him for giving a Pennsylvania audience inaccuracies, Dilg retorted, "Why worry . . .? They'll never know the difference." Dilg was replaced in 1926 and died the following year.

IWLA's forest-related activities have been many and varied. Its keen and continuing interest in Superior National Forest, especially in what became the Boundary Waters Canoe Area, began in 1923 when it opposed roads to the interior and urged that private inholdings be acquired. Soon, IWLA joined a coalition to oppose the schemes of E. W. Backus, an industrialist who wished to dam and control the border lakes of Minnesota and Ontario. The result was wilderness protection under the U. S. FOREST SERVICE after 1926 and, eventually, inclusion of the area under the Wilderness Act of 1964.

The league became aroused over the so-called Great Land Grab of the 1940s when livestock associations sought private ownership of national forest and public land ranges. It then opposed subsequent efforts to restrict Forest Service authority over grazing use of its rangeland. IWLA has participated in numerous legislative and judicial conflicts affecting forests. It has supported multiple use and sustained yield, establishment of a national wilderness system and wild and scenic rivers, the OUTDOOR RECREATION RESOURCES REVIEW COMMISSION of the 1950s and implementation of many of its recommendations, the PUBLIC LAND LAW REVIEW COMMISSION of the 1960s, and an Eastern system of national forest wild areas in the 1970s. The league opposed clearcutting of mixed hardwoods and large softwood areas.

The league's first and longest crusade has been for clean waters. At President Calvin Coolidge's request, it carried out the nation's first official pollution survey in 1927. From 1934 until success was achieved in the Water Pollution Control Law of 1948, it campaigned for federal abatement legislation. Subsequently, the league sponsored more effective pollution-control measures at all levels of government. IWLA also opposed undue exploitation of waterways, fought against construction of dams in units of the National Park System (such as Dinosaur National Monument), and sought legislation to encourage rebuilding the nation's damaged soil base.

IWLA's shortcomings have included failure to attract and hold large numbers of members and to accumulate an endowment sufficient to bolster its treasury and allow greater breadth and depth in staffing. Headquartered in Arlington, Virginia, since 1971, the IWLA in 1980 claimed 50,000 members organized in 22 state groups and 600 local chapters.

WILLIAM VOIGT JR.

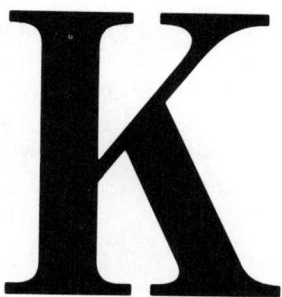

KANSAS FORESTS

About 85 percent of the natural woodland of Kansas is located in the eastern third of this prairie state, principally in narrow belts along valleys, side drainages, and adjacent slopes. In the west, forests are confined to river valleys and stream banks. Except for eastern redcedar, all Kansas's natural timber is deciduous. Bottomland forest is mainly elm-cottonwood, which produces the bulk of the commercial hardwoods. Upland forest is primarily oak-hickory of lesser value. Settlers converted much of the estimated 4,480,000 acres of original forest (approximately 8.4 percent of the state's land area) to cropland. Commercial harvest reduced the remainder to 1,508,700 acres of natural woodland before the 1981 inventory. Almost 89 percent of Kansas's forest acreage is ranked as commercial forest.

Early settlers in Kansas used trees along the streams and rivers mostly for fuel, although sawmills have existed in the state since 1843. The state's sparse timber supplies were quickly depleted and lumber production peaked in 1869 at 74 million board feet. Output in 1962 was 17 million board feet. Other Kansas forest products include box and crating materials, cooperage, pulpwood, gunstocks, and CHARCOAL.

Kansas began paying tree-planting bounties in 1865, and in 1887 it created the position of commissioner of forestry (later state forester). Kansas State University's Division of Forestry, established in 1909, offers teaching, research, and an extension service. In 1962, the university added a cooperative fire control program which assists rural fire districts with equipment and training. Federal afforestation activity in Kansas dates from the 1905 establishment of the Garden City Forest Reserve (later the Kansas National Forest). The plantings failed, and the reserve was abolished in 1915, but federal forestry revived with cooperation under the CLARKE-MCNARY ACT of 1924 and the SHELTERBELTS of the 1930s. Between 1935 and 1942, a total of 3,541 miles of windbreak was planted. Altogether, 250,000 acres of forests have been planted in Kansas, and another 2 million acres are special-purpose urban forests confined to villages and cities. Kansas hosts three federal wildlife refuges, totaling 51,098 acres; seven state refuges with 45,450 acres; and forty-one state parks and lakes comprising 55,893 acres.

Approximately 98 percent of the woodland in Kansas is owned by farmers and small private owners. Seventy sawmills and wood processing plants were operating in 1979, using 45 million board feet of timber. The stumpage was approximately $8.5 million and the value of wood products was estimated at $40 million annually.

FURTHER READING: Royal S. Kellogg, *Forest Planting in Western Kansas* (1909). Huber Self, *Environment and Man in Kansas: A Geographical Analysis* (1978). Willis C. Sorensen, "The Kansas National Forest, 1905–1915," *Kansas Historical Quarterly* 35 (Winter 1969): 386-395.

HUBER SELF

KENTUCKY FORESTS

From its discovery, Kentucky has been known for its dense forests and wide variety of trees. The swamps and bottomlands of the western counties were originally covered with cypress, gum, and oaks. The central region, which was largely cleared by the 1880s, grew a variety of oaks, walnuts, and hickories, while the dense forests of the eastern and southeastern counties, particularly along the Allegheny Mountains, contained valuable hardwoods such as black walnut, white oak, cherry, and yellow-poplar. Throughout most of the nineteenth century, these eastern mountains were protected from heavy timber cutting by the Cumberland Falls, which prevented log drives, and by inaccessibility to railroads. Forests once covered 24 million acres, or 96 percent of the state. In 1977, Kentucky's forestland still totaled over 12 million acres, nearly all of it of commercial value.

Wood was basic to the settlement of Kentucky. It was used for crude puncheon forts as protection from Indian attacks, for pole cabins, log houses, and the region's earliest public buildings. Between 1780 and 1900, prime timber was used extravagantly for fence rails and for the construction of flatboats to transport farm products to downriver markets, where the boats themselves were dismantled and sold as lumber or firewood. After 1811, Kentucky woods were used in the building of western river steamboats.

Kentucky's first frame houses were constructed with whip- or pit-sawn lumber, but the state's abundant streams were quickly harnessed to drive saw and grist mills. From 1820 onward, a large volume of prime white oak was used in making charred barrels in which bourbon whiskey was aged. After 1825, oak, hickory, hard maple, ash, and yellow-poplar were used by farm implement producers, including the well-known B. F. Avery & Sons and the E. C. Brinley plow manufacturers. Kentucky's strong, durable white oak and hickory lumber was also used in the manufacture of wagons and buggies, while furniture makers in Louisville and other Ohio River towns consumed walnut, cherry, maple, and poplar lumber. Elsewhere, independent nineteenth-century craftsmen created the fine hardwood cabinets that have become today's cherished antiques.

After the Civil War, Kentucky lumbering and wood-using industries expanded rapidly, and by 1880 annual output from Kentucky's 670 sawmills reached 306 million board feet. Small farmers in the Appalachian Highlands spent their summers cutting logs and running them in rafts down the lower Cumberland, Green, Barren, Tennessee, and Big Sandy rivers. Highland loggers riding the unruly, oblong Kentucky log rafts combined the exploits of legendary flatboatman Mike Fink and the northern woods' Paul BUNYAN. On the Kentucky River, logs were rafted to Louisville, Frankfort, Valley View, West Irvine, the Pan Bowl, and Quicksand (near Jackson). Big Sandy raftsmen steered their logs to Catlettsburg, at the confluence of the Big Sandy and Ohio rivers, while Cumberland loggers headed for Nashville and Paducah, and Green and Barren river raftsmen went to Henderson. In the last decades of the nineteenth century, portable mills permitted lumbermen to manufacture lumber closer to the standing timber. Such small "peckerwood" mills, cutting largely second-growth timber and supplying local markets, became common. As the Kentucky railway system was extended into the isolated forest areas, the combined big mill-peckerwood operations became major suppliers of crossties and bridging timbers.

Peak years for lumbering in Kentucky came in the decade between 1900 and 1910. In 1907, output reached a reported 913 million board feet, 94 percent of it hardwood. During the Depression, lumber production dropped as low as 47 million board feet, but in the decades after World War II, lumber production averaged 400 to 500 million board feet annually, about 1 percent of the national total. Lumber production became largely a stationary industry, with logs being hauled long distances from woods to mills. Forest products remained diversified, with native woods supplying crossties, heavy construction timbers, machine bases, wood mosaics, furniture, baseball bats, pallets, fence posts, planking, and cooperage.

In 1970, the state's 12 million acres of forestland grew an estimated 1.97 billion board feet of timber, of which only 30 million feet were softwoods. The South Cumberland region, with 11 percent of the state's land, held 47 percent of the sawtimber, including some of the finest hardwoods in North America.

Kentucky's early state foresters found it difficult to rally public support for their programs. The state's first efforts at fire control came with the creation of the State Board of Agriculture, Forestry, and Irrigation in 1906, and the designation of the first state forester, John Earle Barton, in 1912. Discouraged by inadequate

This high-quality white oak was logged near Lenox, Kentucky. Forest History Society Photo.

funding, lack of public support, and a generally ineffective forestry program, Barton resigned in 1919. However, by the mid-1920s, the public proved more receptive to forestry efforts, and federal programs provided encouragement and financial support for new state forestry initiatives. Lobbying by women's groups resulted in the establishment of the Forestry Division under the commissioner of agriculture in 1924. A year later, the state hired two foresters—Fred Merrill and William E. Jackson—to implement reforestation, protection, and tree nursery programs.

During the Depression, the CIVILIAN CONSERVATION CORPS (CCC) established over fifty camps in Kentucky and carried out programs in forestry, park development, and soil erosion control. The CCC brought some of the first roads, truck trails, bridges, and telephone lines to remote areas of eastern Kentucky, resulting in new opportunities for social, agricultural, and industrial development and greater public awareness of the value of the state's forests. The State Reorganization Act of 1936 established the Division of Forestry as part of the newly created Department of Conservation. Kentucky's first state forest, the 3,642-acre Kentenia State Forest Reserve, was established in 1919. Since then, six other state forests have been added to the system, bringing the total area to nearly 50,000 acres. A Department of Parks was added to the Division of Conservation in 1960, and Kentucky has acquired forty-five state park and recreation areas totaling 41,000 acres.

The 17,000-acre Land Between the Lakes Recreation Area in western Kentucky and Tennessee was created by dams built on the Tennessee River in 1945 and the Cumberland River in 1965. The recreation area itself, managed for multiple use by the TENNESSEE VALLEY AUTHORITY, was established in 1965. Barkley Dam, on the Cumberland River, inundated the 65,000-acre Kentucky Woodland Wildlife Refuge, which had been established in 1938. The refuge was replaced by the creation of the Cross Creek Wildlife Refuge in Tennessee, while the Land Between the Lakes has also been developed for wildlife habitats.

Federally managed forestlands in Kentucky include the 52,000-acre Mammoth Cave National Park, authorized in 1926 and established in 1941, and the Daniel Boone National Forest, known as the Cumberland National Forest from its creation in 1937 until 1966. In 1981, the Daniel Boone encompassed over 1.36 million acres, only 526,032 of which were in federal ownership. A small part of Jefferson National Forest is in Kentucky, but only 961 acres of it are federal lands.

THOMAS D. CLARK

KINGS CANYON NATIONAL PARK

See Sequoia and Kings Canyon National Parks

KINNEY, ABBOT (1850–1920)

As heir to half of the Sweet Caporal cigarette fortune, Abbot Kinney, born in New Jersey on November 16, 1850, and raised in Washington, D.C., received a European education and traveled the world. At the age of thirty, he settled on a citrus ranch, which he named Kinneloa, near Pasadena, California. Kinney quickly gained notoriety as a manufacturer, author, and regional booster. He later moved to Santa Monica where he undertook his most famous real estate promotion, Venice by the Pacific. In 1883, he and Helen Hunt Jackson wrote a report to U. S. Secretary of the Interior Carl Schurz which was sympathetic to the plight of the Mission Indians. In other publications, Kinney proposed reforms in education, morals, child-rearing, and politics.

Kinney was among the most influential advocates of forest and watershed protection in the region as well as in the state. In his book, *Eucalyptus* (1895), he promoted the commercial and decorative planting of this Australian hardwood. In *Forest and Water* (1900), Kinney expounded his basic tenet of the importance of watershed protection in semi-arid California, dependent on irrigation for its agricultural livelihood. Like his Pasadena friend Theodore Parker Lukens, who was a protégé of John MUIR and an agent of the

U. S. Division of Forestry, Kinney feared that forest destruction threatened to convert southern California into a desert. He wrote many technical and popular articles for national magazines such as the American Forestry Association's *Forester* and for regional journals such as the *Land of Sunshine, California Illustrated Magazine,* and his own *Los Angeles Saturday Post: Fruit, Forest, and Farm,* in which he described the local flora and argued for fire suppression and federal forest preservation. When Kinney was the chairman and dominant figure of the California State Board of Forestry (1886–1889), that agency carried out the first survey of the state's forest resources and urged that forestlands on the public domain be reserved from sale. Kinney also served the state as a Yosemite Valley Commissioner (1897–1901) and in that capacity tried to abolish toll roads. He served as president of such organizations as the Southern California Academy of Sciences (1890–1900), Southern California Pomological Society (1882–1892), and the Forest and Water Society of Southern California (1899) and its successor, the Forest and Water Association of Los Angeles County (1900–1909). Kinney supported forest conservation for aesthetic as well as utilitarian motives and was a member of the SIERRA CLUB. He promoted professional forestry, lecturing at the University of Southern California in 1887 and encouraging the establishment of a short-lived school of forestry there in 1899. The state established an experimental plantation on twenty acres donated by Kinney in Santa Monica Canyon in 1887 and 1890. When the State Board of Forestry was abolished in 1893, the Santa Monica station was transferred to the University of California's College of Agriculture. Kinney, who died November 14, 1920, has been called the father of the San Gabriel Timberland Reserve (later the Angeles National Forest), the first federal forest reserve established in California by presidential proclamation.

FURTHER READING: C. Raymond Clar, *California Government and Forestry* (1959). Ronald F. Lockmann, "Forests and Watershed in the Environmental Philosophy of Theodore P. Lukens," *Journal of Forest History* 23 (Apr. 1979): 82-91, and *Guarding the Forests of Southern California: Evolving Attitudes toward Conservation of Watershed, Woodlands, and Wilderness* (1981). John S. McGroarty, *History of Los Angeles County* (1923).

RONALD F. LOCKMANN

KINNEY, JAY P (1875–1975)

Jay P Kinney was born in Snowdon (town of Otego), New York, on September 18, 1875. He attended Cornell University, receiving the A.B. in 1902, and did graduate study in the College of Forestry in 1902–1903, although he did not receive an M.F. degree until 1913. He was the first recipient of the master of forestry degree at Cornell. He also earned the LL.B. in 1908 from National University in Washington, D.C. Kinney worked as a high school principal in Cooperstown, New York (1903–1906) and as assistant examiner in the U. S. Patent Office (1906–1910). In 1910, he joined the U. S. Indian Service with instructions to organize its first branch of forestry. Under various titles, he served as head of that unit until 1933 when he became general production supervisor in charge of CIVILIAN CONSERVATION CORPS activities on Indian reservations. In 1942, Kinney left that post to become associate director of soil conservation in the Office of Land Utilization of the DEPARTMENT OF THE INTERIOR. In 1945, under special exception to provisions for mandatory retirement at age seventy, Kinney was appointed adviser in forestry, U. S. Department of Justice. He retired from full-time duty in 1954, but continued as consultant in the Department of Justice. Only in 1967, after sixty-one years of distinguished service with the federal government, did Kinney retire completely. Thereafter, he continued his interest in forestry and Indian affairs and in the history of Otsego County, New York, where his forebears had been among the first settlers.

Kinney's master's thesis, *Forest Legislation in America Prior to March 4, 1789*, was published as Bulletin 370, Cornell University Agricultural Experiment Station (1916). In addition to numerous articles, Kinney wrote four scholarly books: *The Essentials of American Timber Law* (1917), *The Development of Forest Law in America* (1917), *A Continent Lost—A Civilization Won: Indian Land Tenure in America* (1937), and *Indian Forest and Range* (1950). In retirement, Kinney published four volumes that were less formal in style, including *My First Ninety-Five Years* (1972), *Facing Indian Facts* (1973), *Like Other Men: The American Indian Resented Restraint* (1974), and *Mental Elixir* (1975).

Kinney's dynamic personality revealed itself in these later writings and in his accomplishments during a lifetime that spanned a century. He possessed an instinct for close observation and thorough analysis. He had strong feelings of self-respect and self-confidence. His interest in and concern for others, regardless of race, creed, or station in life, was genuine but not idealistic. He demanded of himself and of his co-workers the best of which each was capable, and his loyalty to those around him was returned in kind. The esprit de corps within the Indian Service's forestry branch reflected the character of its chief, and this spirit counterbalanced the fiscal handicaps which restricted activities for many years.

When Kinney transferred to the Department of Justice, he used his training and experience in both law and forestry to great advantage in the preparation of cases and as a witness in claims brought before the U. S. Court of Claims and the Indian Claims Commission.

Kinney was a fellow of the SOCIETY OF AMERICAN FORESTERS and of the FOREST HISTORY SOCIETY. He died December 2, 1975, in Hartwick, New York, about three months after his hundredth birthday.

FURTHER READING: J. P Kinney, *The Office of Indian Affairs: A Career in Forestry*, an oral history interview by Elwood R. Maunder (1960).

GEORGE S. KEPHART

KIRBY, JOHN HENRY (1860–1940)

On November 16, 1860, John Henry Kirby was born on a farm in Tyler County, Texas, the son of John Thomas and Sarah Payne Kirby. Young Kirby struggled for an education, briefly attending Southwestern University and reading law in the office of Texas State Senator S. Bronson Cooper. Admitted to the bar in 1885, Kirby practiced law and purchased and managed properties for absentee landowners, especially a group of Boston investors headed by N. B. Silsbee. During this period, Kirby constructed his first sawmill and built a short-line railroad into the longleaf pine country. He later sold this road to the Atcheson, Topeka, and Santa Fe Railway on terms of mutual advantage. This friendly relationship with the Santa Fe continued throughout his life.

In 1901, Kirby joined with his Boston backers and other Eastern financiers to incorporate the Houston Oil Company at $30 million and the Kirby Lumber Company at $10 million. Between these firms he negotiated stumpage agreements and mineral leases based on nearly 1 million acres of pinelands. For these complex maneuvers the Houston press hailed Kirby as "the first citizen of Houston" and the "father of industrial Texas." The venture led to seemingly endless litigation, however, and eventually Kirby relinquished any claims to the Houston Oil Company but retained the lumber company and the vital stumpage contract.

Kirby Lumber Company was a large and complex organization. With headquarters in Houston, Kirby operated some fourteen sawmills and twelve to fourteen logging camps. COMPANY TOWNS housed his workers, company stores served their needs, and a company medical plan provided for their health. Like many other lumbermen of the Gulf Southwest, Kirby operated largely with tram roads and steam skidders and paid his workers with merchandise checks. With an annual cut of more than 300 million board feet, the Kirby Lumber Company was the largest lumber manufacturer in Texas and one of the largest in the South. He prided himself on his concern for his workers and their families, and many young men and women went to college because of loans or grants from John Henry Kirby. But he took the lead in defeating all efforts to unionize the mills in Texas and strongly opposed the principle of the eight-hour day.

Described as tall, charming, and ruddy-cheeked, Kirby became a powerful political and business leader. As an active Texas Democrat, he served in the state legislature, chaired the state convention, and was a delegate to the national convention in 1916. He was one of the organizers of the Southern Pine Association and served for four years as president of the NATIONAL LUMBER MANUFACTURERS ASSOCIATION.

During World War I, Kirby became lumber administrator for the South in the Emergency Fleet Corporation, U. S. Shipping Board. He resigned in August 1918 in the midst of a controversy over the fixing of lumber prices by the War Industries Board. In the postwar era, he was an adviser on Southern lumber questions to President Warren G. Harding and later to President Herbert Hoover.

The Great Depression hit Kirby and his lumber empire hard, and in 1933 he declared personal bankruptcy. The company continued to operate but eventually became a subsidiary of the Sante Fe. Kirby, though nearing eighty, remained as president of the company until his death on November 9, 1940.

FURTHER READING: There is no satisfactory critical biography of John Henry Kirby. Available accounts include *The Gulf Coast Lumberman*, July 15, 1951; John O. King, *The Early History of the Houston Oil Company* (1959); Mary Lasswell, *John Henry Kirby, Prince of the Pines* (1967); and George T. Morgan, Jr., "The Gospel of Wealth Goes South: John Henry Kirby and Labor's Struggle for Self Determination, 1901-1916," *Southwestern Historical Quarterly* 75 (Oct. 1971): 186–197.

ROBERT S. MAXWELL

LABOR IN THE PULP AND PAPER INDUSTRY

Through much of the twentieth century, the PULP AND PAPER INDUSTRY has expanded. In 1899, about 100,000 workers were employed. By the late 1940s, the figure had grown to about 450,000 and then increased nearly 25 percent by 1960. Since then, growth has been slower and less even: figures for 1976 showed a total of 676,000 employees, a rise of 14 percent as compared with 1960 employment, but a decline from the all-time high of 709,000 workers reported in 1970.

Over the course of the century, the percentage of workers in primary pulp and paper production has been decreasing, while the proportion performing converting operations has grown. In 1900, relatively few workers toiled in converting plants and shops; however, the proliferation of consumer and shipping goods after World War I expanded both production and employment in the converting sector. Thus, in 1929 converting shops employed almost 45 percent of paper workers. By 1960, amid vast industrywide expansion, the two segments reached parity in employment. In 1976, there were 269,000 workers in primary pulp and paper and 406,000, or just over 60 percent, in converting.

Wages in paper and allied products have traditionally ranked near the upper levels of the nondurable goods wage scale. Differentials between primary pulp and paper production, in which wages have been substantially above all-industry levels for many years, and wages paid in converting have traditionally been wide. Although many firms had introduced the eight-hour day starting as early as the 1870s, other pulp and paper workers, particularly those in conversion plants, were plagued with unusually long hours of employment until the 1930s, due in part to the industry's continuous processes. As an expanding industrial sector, however, pulp and paper usually was able to offer its workers relative stability and regularity of employment.

Throughout the twentieth century, the composition of the labor force of the industry has been changing. Until the 1930s, mills, located close to timber resources and waterpower, were usually situated in small towns and villages in Wisconsin, New England, and New York State. Aside from the small office staffs, virtually all workers were males. Unskilled workers cut and hauled logs, undertook debarking and chipping operations, and performed manual labor, servicing the pulp digesters and cookers in the pulp mills and the huge papermaking machines. Beatermen, digester cooks, and machine tenders performed skilled tasks, as did the machinists who kept the paper machines in repair and the electricians who manned the powerhouses. Skilled workers accounted for about 35 percent of the traditional labor force, which was largely Anglo-American and French Canadian.

The growth of the industry in the 1920s and afterward sharply modified traditional patterns of employment. Primary pulp and paper production expanded into the Pacific Northwest, and, especially after 1935, into the South. In addition, many of the finished paper products entering the stream of commerce were geared to urban markets, either as consumer goods or as packaging and shipping materials. Labor force composition shifted substantially as urban production centers drew upon ethnically diverse workers of both sexes to meet their ever-rising demand for relatively unskilled operatives. By World War II, well over 100,000 urban workers, at least 40,000 of them women, had joined the labor force.

Permanent labor organization in the industry dates to 1884 with the founding of the Eagle Lodge of machine tenders in Holyoke, Massachusetts. For the next twenty-five years, a variety of organizations struggled for identity. By 1909, two international unions had been chartered by the American Federation of Labor (AFL). These were the International Brotherhood of Paper Makers (IBPM), which represented primarily skilled machine tenders, beater engineers, and related workers, and the International Brotherhood of Pulp, Sulphite, and Paper Mill Workers (IBPSPMW), which sought to organize the less skilled woodyard, pulp, and common labor elements. Eventually, the IBPSPMW also laid claim to converting workers. The AFL paper unions made modest gains in the 1910s, winning a strike against the International Paper Company in 1910 and gaining membership throughout the World War I period. By 1918, the Pulp Workers could claim 15,000 members and the Paper Makers perhaps 10,000.

The 1920s were disastrous for the two organizations, however. International Paper imposed an open-shop policy in 1921, triggering a bitter strike that ended in 1926 with defeat for the unions. Strikes launched in 1922 against the St. Regis Paper Company and other papermakers resulted in a major setback for the pulp workers' union. These strikes laid bare the deep hostilities between the leaders and memberships of the two unions. Further devastated by the Depression, the unions barely survived into the 1930s. By 1933, together they could count no more than 5,000 American members.

A combination of factors led to the unions' dramatic reversal of fortunes in the 1930s. Section 7(a) of the National Industrial Recovery Act of 1933 stimulated organization. Both unions at least nominally retained a socialist orientation and both eagerly greeted the opportunity to grow. In 1933 and 1934, West Coast employers, impressed by the sobriety and conservatism of the two AFL affiliates, cooperated in laying the groundwork for an innovative regional bargaining arrangement that soon came to include strong union security provisions. After 1936, the sporadic activity of rival organizations associated with the Congress of Industrial Organizations (CIO) impelled aggressive organizing in the South on the part of the two AFL unions and in urban converting plants on the part of the Pulp Workers. By 1941, the Pulp Workers claimed 60,000 members, while the Paper Makers edged toward 50,000. Under the leadership of the widely respected John P. Burke, president-secretary of the IBPSPMW since 1917, and Matthew Burns of the IBPM, the organizations put the bitterness of the 1920s behind them. They cooperated closely, especially in the South and Pacific Northwest, and made good use of the provisions of the National Labor Relations Act of 1935 in securing recognition. The AFL paper unions found formerly hostile employers—most notably International Paper—sympathetic to the point of overt collaboration in the face of CIO organizing activities.

After several tentative starts in the paper industry, in 1944 the CIO launched a major effort to challenge the two AFL affiliates by chartering the Paper Workers Organizing Committee (PWOC). In that year, the PWOC ousted the IBPSPMW as bargaining agent for 4,000 workers of the West Virginia Pulp and Paper Company, but elsewhere between the end of World War II and the AFL-CIO merger in 1955 the older unions more than held their own. In 1957, the former CIO organization—since 1946 called the United Paperworkers of America—merged with the International Brotherhood of Paper Makers. Burke, however, continued to resist overtures to bring his Pulp Workers into the new United Papermakers and Paperworkers (UPP).

Throughout the 1960s, the two separate organizations, both affiliated with the AFL-CIO, continued to grow. The IBPSPMW, despite internal controversies and damaging charges of corruption leveled against key leaders, enrolled over 170,000 members by 1970, while the UPP counted about 140,000. The AFL-CIO organizations received a major blow in 1964 when forty-nine West Coast locals disaffiliated. Since 1934, these locals had been party to the Uniform Labor Agreement, a widely hailed regional bargaining system notable for the absence of strikes. The West Coast locals established the Association of Western Pulp and Paper Workers (AWPPW), defeating the older unions in a National Labor Relations Board election. By 1972, the AWPPW claimed over 20,000 members and was a permanent feature in the industry.

In 1972, the UPP and the IBPSPMW merged, creating the United Paperworkers International Union (UPIU) with a combined membership of 340,000. The selection as president of UPIU of Joseph Tonelli, who had succeeded John P. Burke in 1965 as president-secretary of the Pulp Workers, attested to the continuing strength of the IBPSPMW. In 1978, Tonelli pleaded guilty to embezzlement of union funds, while the union's treasurer, Henry Segal, who like Tonelli had risen to influence in the old IBPSPMW under the aegis of the personally unimpeachable Burke, was convicted of violations of federal labor law.

By the late 1970s, under the banners of the UPIU and the AWPPW, unionism was firmly established in the pulp and paper industry. But fluctuating employment, the separation of most Canadian locals, and the taint of corruption frustrated the ambitious hopes of expansion announced at the 1972 UPIU merger convention. In 1982, membership figures stood at 265,000.

FURTHER READING: Harry Edward Graham, *The Paper Rebellion: Development and Upheaval in Pulp and Paper Unionism* (1970). Clark Kerr and Roger Randall, *Collective Bargaining in the Pacific Coast Pulp and Paper Industry* (1948). Robert M. Macdonald, "Pulp and Paper," in Lloyd G. Reynolds and Cynthia H. Taft, *The Evolution of Wage Structure* (1956), pp. 99–166. Robert H. Zieger, "Oldtimers and Newcomers: Change and Continuity in the Pulp, Sulphite Union in the 1930s," *Journal of Forest History* 21 (Oct. 1977): 188-201.

ROBERT H. ZIEGER

LABOR ORGANIZATIONS IN THE LUMBER INDUSTRY

The earliest labor unions among forest and sawmill workers in the United States were founded in the Pacific Northwest in the 1870s under the aegis of the Knights of Labor. Although the Knights admitted workers regardless of craft, only shingle weavers seem to have joined. Although there was a great deal of job mobility between mills and woods, the loggers seem to have remained aloof. In the Lake States and in the South, the Knights had better luck organizing loggers. But, as with most K of L organization, the unions there were ephemeral affairs, sustained only by enthusiasm bubbling over in the wake of the Knights' victory over the Union Pacific and flagging just as quickly after disappointing local strikes or, sometimes, no strike at all.

In 1890, six shingle weavers locals in Washington attempted to unite into the West Coast Shingle Weavers Union, but it collapsed almost immediately during the serious depression of that decade.

After the turn of the century, the American Federation of Labor (AFL) chartered federal unions in several northwestern mill towns. ("Federal unions" were locals comprised of workers in various crafts. The AFL looked on them as temporary expedients, way stations until such time as sufficient members joined to justify chartering craft locals.) By January 1903, enough shingle weavers had signed up that the parent organization sanctioned the International Shingle Weavers Union of America (ISWUA).

Because wood industry workers tended to be footloose and mill owners were fierce in their opposition, the ISWUA grew very slowly. Brief periods of success in recruiting members were followed by aggressive anti-union campaigns. In 1905, the ISWUA felt strong enough to call a general strike of woods and town workers throughout the Pacific Northwest, but the employers countered by establishing a company-dominated Shingle Weavers' Bureau. When the loggers took little interest in the battle, the ISWUA tacitly surrendered and barely survived. Another AFL union founded in August 1905, the International Brotherhood of Woodsmen and Sawmill Workers, never took hold and formally dissolved in 1911.

Although employer opposition was strong, the failure of these early efforts is largely explained by the mobility of the labor force. The "timber beasts" and "sawdust savages" moved casually from job to job and were just as likely to take work in construction, mining, fisheries, or agriculture. They had little interest in improving conditions in any particular occupation.

By way of contrast, the Amalgamated Wood Workers International Union of America (AWWIUA), an AFL association of sedentary furniture and wood processing workers founded in 1895, had some success, claiming a membership of 31,230 in 250 locals in 1904. When the AWWIUA declined thereafter, it was because of jurisdictional raids by the United Brotherhood of Carpenters and Joiners rather than because of the opposition of employers.

Beginning about 1908, the Industrial Workers of the World (IWW) began to organize loggers and millhands in the towns of the Pacific Northwest where the workers gathered between jobs, and to a lesser extent in the Great Lakes region. In the South, especially in Louisiana, the Brotherhood of Timber Workers (BTW), a union sometimes associated with the IWW, succeeded for a time in bringing together black and white loggers, turpentine workers, and millhands.

The BTW was militant and revolutionary. But the employers in the pineys were just as stern and, after a series of bitter and sometimes bloody strikes at Grabow and Alexandria, Louisiana, succeeded in crushing the brotherhood.

In the Northwest, the "Wobblies" were sidetracked from striking by disputes with city officials of places like Missoula, Montana, and Aberdeen and Spokane, Washington, over their right to speak on the streets. The IWW won several of the highly publicized "free speech fights" and the sentimental loyalty of thousands of timber and lumber industry workers but no tangible bread-and-butter victories.

Nevertheless, the AFL responded to the IWW's popularity by reorganizing the ISWUA as the International Union of Shingle Weavers, Sawmill Workers, and Woodsmen (IUSWSWW), giving it jurisdiction over the entire industry. The new union launched a campaign to institute an eight-hour-day law in Oregon and Washington, but when the bills were defeated in both state legislatures, the IUSWSWW fell apart with the exception of the old established Shingle Weavers locals. In 1916, they were rechartered as the International Shingle Weavers Union of America.

In May 1916, the ISWUA called a strike in Everett, Washington. Supported by the IWW to which many ISWUA men also belonged, this conflict led to the infamous Everett Massacre when the sheriff of Snohomish County opened fire on a ferry carrying strike sympathizers from Seattle, killing at least seven men and wounding fifty or more. Widespread anger throughout the region caused a surge of pro-union sentiment, as many workers considered the sheriff the client of the mill owners. The AFL tried to profit from the situation by chartering the International Union of Timber Workers (IUTW) in August 1917, but it was to the IWW that most loggers turned. Many Northwestern workers were suspicious of AFL motives and the ISWUA had lost too many strikes in the summer of that year.

Sensitive to employer strength, the IWW advocated a policy of "sabotage," striking on the job, or the "conscious withdrawal of efficiency." Both employers and the Woodrow Wilson administration (which was particularly interested in the production of spruce for aircraft construction) grew concerned about the expansion of the revolutionary union. The Lumbermen's Protective Union suggested the formation of an anti-IWW association of employers and workers based on the issues of loyalty and patriotism. Responding to this, Colonel Bryce P. Disque of the U. S. Army organized the LOYAL LEGION OF LOGGERS AND LUMBERMEN (4L), a kind of industrywide company union partly funded and protected by the army's Spruce Production Division. The 4L enjoyed considerable success, claiming a membership of 70,000 within a few months. It published a newspaper and attempted to take credit for the general improvement of wages and conditions in the logging camps. However, most historians have attributed the dramatic change for the better in industry conditions to the combination of high wartime profits and fear of the Wobblies.

Lending support to this idea is the fact that the 4L declined rapidly after the armistice while, despite the disarray of the central office, the IWW actually grew to perhaps 20,000 members. However, the unionization of lumber was to be short-lived. The postwar depression in the industry killed all but a few IWW locals and also the IUTW which, having grown to 10,000 in 1920, dissolved itself in 1923. Likewise, a large strike for the eight-hour day in the Lake States in May 1920 failed when, short on orders, employers felt no pressure to accommodate their workers.

Timber and lumber unionism languished during the 1920s as a consolidated and integrated industry adopted paternalistic policies which contrasted sharply with its exploitative practices during the entrepreneurial phase of development. New, larger companies provided a wide range of social services in COMPANY TOWNS, and with the adoption of forestry and forest management techniques, the importance of the migrant worker, the mainstay of the Wobblies, declined.

The Great Depression and the national upsurge of industrial unionism led in July 1937 to the founding by the Congress of Industrial Organizations (CIO) of the International Woodworkers of America (IWA), headquartered in Portland, Oregon. With 70,000 members at the outset, the IWA was made up of several discontented AFL unions and fought a number of jurisdictional battles with the Federation's United Brotherhood of Carpenters.

Although mostly successful in these disputes, the IWA was plagued by the internal competition between communists and anticommunists that affected many CIO unions. The first president of the IWA was a "fellow traveler," Harold Pritchett of British Columbia, who had broad rank-and-file support. The anticommunist faction under the leadership of Don Helmick of the Columbia River district was equally strong, and the even split threatened to destroy the union at the same time that it was scoring major victories in winning recognition by employers.

However, the communists (led by O. M. Orter after 1940) lost support as a result of attempts to manipulate the union administration, and in 1941 the IWA voted to exclude "communists, nazis, and fascists" from membership. Vice-president Worth Lowery, who led the coup, was elected to the presidency.

Although always strongest in the Pacific Northwest, including Canada, the IWA also organized locals in the Great Lakes region and eastern Canada. After World War II, it expanded into the South where, in 1946, the IWA won representation rights in fifty-five National Labor Relations Board elections. In addition to maintaining high wages and good conditions for a membership that reached about 110,000 by 1980, the IWA took a serious interest in conservation and forestry. In 1941 and 1948, the union adopted a comprehensive forestry program and support for government programs of forest protection, insect and disease control, and appropriations for research.

FURTHER READING: Gary M. Fink, ed., *Labor Unions*, The Greenwood Encyclopedia of American Institutions (1977). Vernon M. Jenson, *Lumber and Labor* (1945).

LACEY, JOHN FLETCHER (1841–1913)

John F. Lacey, "Father of Federal Game Legislation," was born on May 30, 1841, to John Mills and Eleanor (Patten) Lacey in New Martinsville, Virginia (now in West Virginia), and moved to Oskaloosa, Iowa, in 1855. His education in local academies, interrupted by the Civil War, did not extend to college, yet intellectual keenness and self-sought study furnished a sound classical, literary, and historical awareness. Lacey's war record was exemplary. Enlisting as a private, he found time to read law while on parole after capture in 1861. He then served under his legal mentor, General Samuel A. Rice, and, after Rice's death in battle, as assistant adjutant general on the staff of General Frederick Steele, earning a final promotion to brevet major for gallantry at the siege of Mobile in 1865. Later that year, Lacey married Martha Newell, was admitted to the Iowa bar, and began to forge a distinguished legal and political career. His respect as a lawyer was enhanced by his authorship of *Third Iowa Digest* (1870) and *A Digest of Railway Decisions* (2 vols., 1875, 1884), which brought him a national reputation as an expert on railroad law. Early political service included membership in the Iowa House of Representatives (1869). He emerged on the national political scene in 1888, defeating General James B. Weaver for Iowa's sixth congressional district seat and served in Congress from 1889 to 1891 and again from 1893 to 1907. A staunch, regular Republican, he left politics after losing to a Progressive candidate, Governor Albert B. Cummins, in a race for the Senate in 1908, and returned to private law practice in Oskaloosa until his death.

Lacey's sixteen-year tenure in Washington coincided with and fostered the flowering of national concern over the conservation of national resources. Membership on, then chairmanship of, the House Committee on Public Lands helped to thrust him into the significant conservation issues of the time: the creation of the forest reserve system and its subsequent enlargement and protection under presidents Harrison, Cleveland, McKinley, and Theodore ROOSEVELT; the expansion and creation of national parks and monuments; the creation of wildlife refuges on the public domain; the protection of game and nongame wildlife in national parks, national forests, and in Alaska; the termination of all market hunting for hides, horns, food, and feathers; and the assertion of national (rather than state) authority over the taking of migratory bird species and the importation of harmful wildlife from abroad. Active in all these causes, Lacey was a dependable friend and ally of early conservation leaders such as George Bird GRINNELL, William T. Hornaday, Gifford PINCHOT, George Shiras III, and Theodore Roosevelt. A member of Roosevelt's BOONE AND CROCKETT CLUB, Lacey fully cooperated in its initiation and support of natural resource and game protection. Honest, energetic, approachable, quick-witted, and respected in debate, Lacey was the legislator chiefly responsible for important conservation enactments, including the first law to adequately protect the wildlife of YELLOWSTONE NATIONAL PARK (1894); the Lacey Act (1900), which prohibited interstate shipment of wildlife killed in violation of state laws and first cast the federal government in its now substantial roles of wildlife administration and wildlife law enforcement; and the Antiquities Act (1906) under which NATIONAL MONUMENTS have been established by executive proclamation. Lacey was an early advocate of the philosophy of the "wise use" of natural resources, later popularized by Pinchot, and on conservation issues, regardless of his conservative Republican label, Lacey held the Progressive faith in expanded federal control and regulation. Lacey died September 30, 1913.

FURTHER READING: Theodore W. Cart, "The Lacey Act," *Forest History* 17 (Oct. 1973): 4–13. Iowa Conservation Association, *Major John F. Lacey, Memorial Volume* (1915). John Ise, *Our National Park Policy* (1961). James B. Trefethen, *Crusade for Wildlife* (1961).

THEODORE W. CART

LAND CLASSIFICATION

Both physical and socioeconomic considerations are involved in categorizing land on the basis of inherent characteristics, present use, potential capacity, and recommended use. The general objectives of land classification are (1) to aid in the development of more enlightened and economically sound public and private land settlement policies; (2) to guide public-land purchase and development programs; (3) to assist planning for organization and distribution of local government services; (4) to guide policies for the distribution of public aid; (5) to determine real estate financing policies; (6) to promote the equalization of land assessments for taxation purposes; (7) to guide the development and administration of programs for improved land use practices or for soil conservation and erosion control measures; and (8) to aid in projecting the most effective type and size of operating units.

In the period immediately after Independence, interest in land classification focused on the segregation, measurement, and subdivision of land for sale since the new government needed a source of income and the public land was its major resource. In 1796, an act of Congress required surveyors in the Northwest Territory to describe the nature of soil, water, and vegetation. The GENERAL LAND OFFICE was made a repository for reports regarding the quality as well as the quantity of unsold public land. The addition of huge territories acquired in the 1840s, together with the discovery of gold in California, led to the desire for information on agricultural and mineral wealth potential and on possible routes for transcontinental railroads to speed the settlement of the West.

The four federal geographical and geological surveys of the West carried out between 1867 and 1884 under the direction of the War Department (George M. Wheeler), the DEPARTMENT OF THE INTERIOR (Ferdinand Hayden and Clarence King), and, jointly, the Smithsonian Institution and the Department of the Interior (John Wesley Powell) shared a concern with identifying agricultural and irrigable lands, timbered tracts, pasturelands, mineral lands, and "wasteland" areas. Wheeler emphasized the relationship between population distribution and water supply, while Powell advocated the classification of land according to best use, with separate land disposal programs to be established for each land type. Powell's recommendations, however, were generally disregarded in such land legislation as the Timber Culture Act (1873), the Desert Land Act (1877), and the Timber and Stone Act (1878). The surveys were superseded by the United States GEOLOGICAL SURVEY (USGS), established in 1879 and headed initially by Clarence King, aided by Henry Gannett as chief geographer. The land-classification work of the USGS had the double objective of providing data concerning the natural resources of the public domain and of furnishing information needed for administration and conservation of these resources.

Improvements were made in the techniques of land classification in the late nineteenth and early twentieth centuries. Frederick E. Clements's work in ecological plant succession and plant indicators for farm, forest, and rangeland highlighted the importance of using climax communities and soil indicators for describing land types. The United States Soil Survey under Milton Whitney developed the outline of a system of soil classification based on the assumption that there was a close relationship between the geological formations in a region and the characteristics of its soils. The land classification scheme developed by Henry Gannett for the USGS provided useful data for the Bureau of Forestry in identifying and mapping forest, cutover, burned over, and pasture or irrigable lands. Important breakthroughs were made in the regional categorization of landforms developed by Nevin M. Fennerman and the working out and testing of mapping methodology by Carl O. Sauer. The passage of the Forest Homestead Act of 1906 required an improved system of forestland classification. The Bureau of Plant Industry in the DEPARTMENT OF AGRICULTURE began gathering data for national land use inventories in 1912. Research would later be carried on by the Farm and Land Economics Divisions of the Agricultural Research Service. The creation of national parks and recreational areas called for studies and plans involving land classification. Partly due to the work of Russian soil scientists and of social scientists in the United States, soil came to be seen as a dynamic natural body in equilibrium with the environment and not merely as a geological formation.

Several states laid the groundwork for an improved land classification technology in the 1920s, a decade of inflated land values and speculation. The Michigan Land Economic Survey, begun in 1922, focused at first largely on the land type features of the cutover areas, but later came to include data on landownership, property, taxation, and trade and marketing conditions. Wisconsin and Minnesota followed a similar course. In New York, a regional plan for New York City indicated areas best suited for various land use purposes. Building upon the earlier pioneering survey of Tompkins County by George F. Warren, Cornell University helped develop a composite land classification system to guide further development in areas of the state where farm abandonment was of concern and where the possibility of state forest and recreational land purchases existed. In California in the 1930s, a scheme was developed for classifying land resources in terms of uses most likely to provide the greatest social return. By 1941, twenty-two states were contributing to land classification efforts by means of the work carried on in agricultural colleges, agricultural experiment stations, and state departments of conservation, with aerial photography increasingly supplementing ground observation in the gathering of base data.

On the federal level, technical improvement was stimulated by a Forest Survey, by FOREST SERVICE surveys of Western ranges, and by the soil survey work carried on by the Bureau of Plant Industry under C. F. Marbut's direction. The TENNESSEE VALLEY AUTHORITY's Rural Land Classification Project developed a fractional code classification system for describing physical conditions and land usage. Land classification became a practical tool for distributing Farm Security Administration Loans to farmers in need. Through the County Agricultural Land Use Planning Program, local groups in participating counties were encouraged to inventory and classify land resources and to use the data as a basis for recommending programs for more efficient land use. The National Resources Planning Board's land committee supervised an examination of rural land problems and in 1941 published a broad study of land classification in the United States. In the previous year, the first National Conference on Land Classification took note of the discrepancies in rural land use planning and wrestled with the question of whether to define land narrowly as soils or broadly to include both the physical environment and the full spectrum of land use.

In 1964, the Classification and Multiple Use Act and the Public Land Sale Act extended to the BUREAU OF LAND MANAGEMENT the authority to inventory and gather information about the land under its jurisdiction. As part of the same legislation package, Congress also authorized creation of the PUBLIC LAND LAW REVIEW COMMISSION, but the final recommendations of that agency, which proposed in 1970 that federal land be classified according to the "dominant use," were stillborn in the "environmental" climate of the new decade. Subsequent attempts to appropriate federal funds for state land classification died under fire from opponents who feared the threat of a "feudal system." THE FEDERAL LAND POLICY AND MANAGEMENT ACT of 1976, however, did provide for mutual land planning cooperation between the federal government and the states.

Since World War II, land classification procedures and data have become more and more sophisticated. An upsurge of interest in land use has taken place with the continuing encroachment of suburban development on previously rural areas, the need for urban redevelopment and transportation problem resolution, and the pressure for providing expanded outdoor recreation opportunities for the public. Three major outcomes were the cooperative drawing up of a land classification manual by the Urban Renewal Adminis-

tration and the Bureau of Public Roads, the inventorying of major uses of land by the Economic Research Service of the Department of Agriculture, and the gathering of soil and land use information by the Soil Conservation Service. Increasing use has been made of orbital and high-altitude remote sensory devices for the gathering of land information. The state of New York developed a Land Use and Natural Resources (LUNR) Inventory, later modified by a Land Related Information System (LRIS). Storage and retrieval of information was enhanced both by the development of tabular lists (Datalist I) and by the creation of computer graphic maps (Planmap II).

Nevertheless, formidable challenges have remained in land classification. The technical nature of the data has made it difficult to keep classifications simple, understandable, and practical. The long time span involved in accumulating data may require considerable rechecking of the older material. Collected data have tended to be more useful for description than for evaluation and prescription. More scientific information is needed for differentiating soil types and for describing the relationship between the nature of the soil and the quality of plants that may be grown. Greater coordination among agencies concerned with land use adjustment would help avoid both the disasters resulting from disregarding the limitations of the land and the narrowness of prospects that follows from the failure to recognize the potential of the land. Surely the trend toward multiple and integrated use of land resources will quicken interest in land classification.

FURTHER READING: James R. Anderson et al., *A Land Use and Land Cover Classification System for Use with Remote Sensor Data*, U. S. Geological Survey Professional Paper 964 (1976). Raleigh Barlowe, *Land Resource Economics: The Political Economy of Rural and Urban Land Resource Use* (1958). Marion Clawson, "Historical Overview of Land Use Planning in the United States," in Donald M. McAllister, ed., *Environment: A New Focus for Land Use Planning* (1973). Marion Clawson and Charles L. Stewart, *Land Use Information: A Critical Survey of United States Statistics, Including Possibilities for Greater Uniformity* (1965). Howard E. Conklin, "Principles of Land Classification," in Land Economics Institute, *Modern Land Policy: Papers of the Land Economics Institute* (1960). Howard E. Conklin and Sherwin O. Berg, *A Preliminary Report on Developments in Land Classification Methods*, Cornell University Agricultural Experiment Station, Agricultural Economics Report 688 (1948). Albert Z. Guttenberg, *New Directions in Land Use Classification* (1965). V. Webster Johnson and Raleigh Barlowe, *Land Problems and Policies* (1954). Charles E. Kellogg, G. Donald Hudson, and M. M. Kelso, "The Theory of Land Classification," in University of Missouri College of Agriculture, Agricultural Experiment Station *Bulletin* 421

(Dec. 1940): 164-200. National Resources Planning Board, Land Committee, *Land Classification in the United States* (1941). Marc J. Rogoff, *Statewide Computer Based Land Information Systems*, Council of Planning Librarians Exchange Bibliography 1490 (1978).

NORMAN J. SCHMALTZ

LATH

Lath is thin, narrow, unplaned stripping sawn from slabs, low-grade lumber, and occasionally from trimmings and edgings. Historically, its principal use has been as a base for plastering or hanging tiles. Although it was specifically sawed as early as medieval times, it was a practicable product only with the appearance of power-driven high-speed mills. Its most direct ancestors for Americans are the branches and other miscellaneous scrap used in wattle-and-daub building construction.

Lath was widely manufactured in the United States, and by the last quarter of the nineteenth century, a more-or-less standard dimension—3/8 inch by 1 1/2 inch by, usually, 48 inches—had emerged. Virtually every kind of commercial softwood was used for lath—pines, spruces, hemlock, and Douglas-fir—and even some hardwoods. In some parts of the country, plasterers insisted on a particular variety.

Production of lath peaked in the United States in 1905 when, in addition to imports from Canada, American mills produced 15 billion pieces of the standard lengths. After World War I, the substitution of more easily mounted and nonshrinking metal lath screens undercut the wood product, so that only 6 billion laths were produced in 1929 and 17 million in 1933. By the 1930s, plywood sheeting or plasterboard (sheetrock) was replacing lath and plaster construction, and the latter was almost completely abandoned with the mass-production home construction methods of the late 1940s and 1950s. Mills continued to manufacture lath from wastewood into the 1980s for use in cheap fencing, particularly snow and sand fences.

FURTHER READING: Nelson Courtlandt Brown, *Forest Products* (1937).

LAW AND ORDER IN LUMBER CAMPS AND TOWNS

Forest historians have suggested that one of the reasons loggers and lumbermen have frequently been ignored as part of America's frontier tradition was because the lumber camps and towns lacked the dramatic stories of the cattle towns and mining camps in terms of violence, excitement, and colorful characters. Authorities of lumber lore, though, can quickly point out that lumber camps and mill towns easily rivaled their wild west counterparts in action, mayhem, tragedy, violence, and legend.

The unique characteristics of the men who flocked to these lumber settlements have been both praised and condemned. One of the earliest descriptions, dating from colonial times, depicted them as debauched fellows, indolent, intemperate, powerfully built, "with a passion for a wild and toilsome life." Lumbering had always been perceived as a man's industry, involving heroic work. Physical prowess and an easy willingness to demonstrate it were traits that described every shanty boy. The lumberjack was coarse and rough and personified the extreme individualism of frontier life. Like the cowboy and the miner, he often boisterously celebrated his return from the log drive. It is not surprising that his style of life necessitated uncommon methods to preserve order.

Amos Todkill worked as a logger for Captain John Smith's Jamestown settlement in 1607 and described what was probably the first account of logging discipline in the New World. In order to correct the excessive use of profanity among the Jamestown logging crew, Captain Smith ordered a "canne of water" poured up each logger's sleeve for every profanity uttered. Accordingly, within a week, Todkill recorded that "a man would scarce hear an Othe."

Regulations on cutting trees came as early as 1691 in the New England colonies, where all land belonged to the Crown. Alarmed by local woodsmen who were cutting indiscriminately, the royal governor banned the cutting of the largest pines and oaks. An arrowhead-shaped blaze was cut on those trees designated for mast and naval timber. Although penalties for removing crown timber were severe, the colonists openly defied the regulations. In New Hampshire, early in the eighteenth century, efforts by the royal surveyor-general to suppress illegal activity and confiscate sawed pine met with violent resistance. Colonial loggers, disguised as Indians, attacked local authorities and drove them physically from the woods. Similar incidents involving violent resistance continued in Connecticut, Massachusetts, and the Maine District until the Revolutionary War. Very early, the habit of flouting authority that was perceived as unjust and unenforceable came to be characteristic of the men of the lumbering frontier.

Loggers were involved in the "Aroostook War." In February 1839, Maine lumberjacks camped along the Aroostook River in a region claimed by both New Brunswick and Maine. The Maine men attempted to dislodge trespassing Canadian loggers by seizing log rafts, shooting oxen, and setting several fires. Barroom brawls and periodic sniping along the river on both sides threatened to erupt into open combat. Both state and provincial militias were called out. Sensing the potential for an international episode, President Martin Van Buren sent General Winfield Scott to negotiate a truce with the New Brunswick authorities. The Webster-Ashburton Treaty (1842) determined the present boundary between the United States and Canada and ended the border controversy.

It was in the eastern states, particularly in Maine, that the traditional images of the lumberjack and the business of lumbering emerged. The lumber industry was migrant, speculative, and exploitative. The pattern was to take as much timber as one could, take it quickly, and get out. Its migratory patterns and its seasonal organization and operation were responsible for producing a homeless, womanless, and individualistic labor force. Here the legendary lumberjack with his distinctive dress, colorful language, and impetuous mannerisms developed and came to populate the northern tier of states for the next century.

Primitive living conditions and lack of emotional and psychological outlets shaped the shanty boys' lives. Furthermore, falling trees, rolling logs, swirling rapids, or powerful machinery meant that death was always close at hand. This combination of ever-present danger, isolated living, and poor working conditions gave the lumberjack a predilection to strong drink, wanton women, and more than occasional violence. Both in the camps and in the lumber towns, a rugged lifestyle often necessitated rugged methods of law, order, and discipline.

Discipline in the camps was strict and enforced by the boss or foreman often through sheer physical prowess. No drinking, no card playing, no gambling, and no talking during meals were unwritten rules. Any violations were handled typically by the boss-foreman in the manner recounted by Rex J. Dye who described how his father, Jacob, handled two card-playing jacks in Michigan: "My father . . . walked over to the table, grabbed one of them by the front of his shirt, and literally threw him across the room. The other fellow, who looked bigger than my father, had gotten up from the table and was ready to start fighting, but he started much too late as my father moved in fast, hit him, and he 'went to sleep' on the floor. My father did not fire these men and they were working the next day, but there were no more card games started." Dye concluded that this all "seems rather brutal, but in those days in that area you couldn't call a policeman, and 'law and order' was a matter of a man's will and ability to enforce it."

In the Southern industry, generalization about camp life and law and order are difficult because of the differences in the lumber industry. Slave labor and, later, the large number of tenant black workers, part-time lumberjacks, and a family-oriented work force did not produce a homeless, migratory, fiercely independent breed of lumberjacks. Many wage earners worked only part-time and readily shifted back and forth between agriculture and lumbering. In the large full-time operations, the company-owned sawmill town organized the workers' lives. Although conditions varied widely from one company town to another, discipline became the responsibility of the owners. The Southern tradition of paternalism determined the operation of these towns. Workers who were dependent on the owner for food and shelter for their entire families seldom challenged traditional guidelines of law and order. The relationships between workers and management in the South was vastly different from that found in the industry in general.

Despite its rather brief existence as a major lumber region, the Great Lakes area and its sawmill towns produced the romance and reputation that has come to characterize nineteenth-century lumbering. The Saginaw River's "catacombs," Muskegon's "sawdust flats," Seney's "stockades," St. Paul's "under the hill" region, Hibbing, and Hurley, among many others, developed infamous reputations. Shanty boys flocked to these towns after the long drive, and mill workers populated them year around. Prostitution, drunkenness, assault, and periodic deaths were the unsavory features that formed the reputations of these frontier communities.

Although legend implies that the lumber towns were at the mercy of marauding shanty boys, the settlements largely succeeded in containing the most threatening tendencies of the lumberjacks. Before the Civil War, eastern cities had already developed organized police forces. The larger and most notorious lumber towns, relying on these eastern precedents, readily established efficient police forces. They generally attempted to suppress violence without alienating the free-spending shanty boys. Homicide was rare and seldom went unpunished. Prostitution, gaming, and drinking were regulated but seldom successfully eliminated. "Red Ribbon" temperance crusades were common, and many states passed prohibition amendments; however, local option and persistent flouting of unpopular laws made it all but impossible to exclude drink. Likewise, prostitution flourished within these lumber settlements long after the shanty boy moved on. Authorities themselves frequently imbibed and invested in houses of ill-repute. Legal troubles only came to those who refused to pay local taxes or engaged in especially vile and violent aspects of the trade.

Law enforcement in the mill towns was carried out by sheriffs, marshals, and policemen, who frequently were hired because of their physical attributes. Fighting was the most common "sport" engaged in by the lumberjacks, and policemen had to be capable of defending themselves amidst almost constant turmoil. Pitched lumberjack battles, although not uncommon, were seldom disturbed by the police, as long as only the lumberjacks themselves seemed in danger. Mutual respect between police and lumbermen prevailed. A Saginaw police officer remembered that the shanty boys "weren't really thieves or crooks—just boys grown big and strong and out for a lark. . . . They were a decent lot."

Not everyone shared these feelings, especially when the shanty boy engaged in organized labor activity. As the lumber business moved west and some of the lumberjack's historic individualism dissipated, the shanty boys and mill workers were more willing to rely upon collective action and sporadic violence to secure decent wages, hours, and working conditions. "Riots" and "Ten Hours or No Sawdust" strikes occurred in Williamsport, Pennsylvania, in 1872, and in Eau Claire, Wisconsin, and Muskegon and the Saginaws in Michigan in the 1880s. Beatings and considerable violence ensued and necessitated the use of state militia to restore order.

Yet, it was in the Far West region that lumber and labor experienced its most violent confrontations. During World War I, the efforts of the Industrial Workers of the World to organize the western lumberjacks resulted in death and widespread violence in Everett, Seattle, and Centralia, Washington. The I.W.W. and the anti-red hysteria of the postwar period prevented judicious law enforcement. In several instances, "law and order" became the function of local vigilante organizations that sought to suppress all labor activity in the lumber camps and towns. The frontierlike conditions in which the lumber industry of the West developed led to tragic and violent labor relations.

Throughout most of the twentieth century, violence and unrest in the lumber industry has centered on issues of labor and conservation. No longer consisting of a group of individuals merely seeking a night out on the town, lumber agitation has become part of the fundamental economic and social problems of the nation that remain to be solved.

FURTHER READING: Freeman Coats, *Diary of a Department: A History of the Saginaw Police Department* (1965). Jacob and Rex Dye, *Lumber Camp Life in Michigan* (1975). Stewart H. Holbrook, *Holy Old Mackinaw*

(1937), and *Yankee Loggers* (1961). Vernon H. Jensen, *Lumber and Labor*, Labor in Twentieth Century America Series (1945).

JEREMY W. KILAR

LAW AND THE FOREST

Law has influenced every phase of American forest history, for it is law that defines private rights and duties, establishes the dimensions of governmental power and its uses, and expresses the values of society or, at least, of society's dominant groups and interests.

Before English settlement of North America, forests had held a unique place in the law of England. Forests traditionally had come under the king's protection—reflecting the interest of the state in the maintenance of wild game, both for food and for sport. By the seventeenth century, the concerns of forest law in England had extended as well to the goal of conserving the country's diminishing sources of wood. Forest-law enforcement comprised a judicial system separate and independent of the rest of English judicial organization; the special officers and courts that had jurisdiction over the forests wielded powers that significantly limited private owners' uses of their property. To protect wild game, for example, the forest officials enjoyed a power of easement to enter private forestland in winter to cut down brush for forage. Forest law also set limits upon the uses of forest by owners who herded livestock, and it restricted even the degree to which private owners could encroach on designated wooded areas with clearings or enclosures.

Traditional forest law was, then, a system of control founded on societal values that gave high priority to conservation of natural resources. Even when the regular common-law courts took over many of the functions of the independent forest courts and offices, communal values persisted. Surviving even the formal abolition of forest offices by Parliament in 1817 were legal concepts such as the prohibitions against "waste" (cutting timber in a manner damaging to a family estate which the prudent proprietor of the inheritance would not countenance), wanton burning, and even the cutting of mature ornamental or shade trees in proximity to a private residence. English law also continued to prescribe legal definitions of "timber" (wood that might be cut legally), applying standards of age and size according to variety. To be sure, enforcement was not always strict or effective. Still, communal values were never altogether lost in the heritage of English forest law.

The American colonies, by contrast, displayed little respect either for communal values or for royal

Regulation of splash dams and of the flood waters they released during log drives was the focus of much forest law during the nineteenth century. Forest Service Photo.

prerogative. The colonists in British North America viewed relentless incursions on forestland for settlement and commercial enterprise as an unmitigated good. English mercantilist legislation encouraged exploitation of forest resources by paying bounties for production of turpentine, tar, and pitch; and in a larger sense, English law spurred the rapid development of forest industries by its encouragement of SHIP-BUILDING and by commercial policies that opened rich West Indies markets to American forest products. As towns expanded in population and new farms were made, rising domestic demand intensified the pressure on American forests. Only in the broad-arrow policy, by which the tallest pines in New England's forests were reserved for the Royal Navy, did the imperial authorities introduce significant control over private uses of forest resources. Significantly, even this minor regulation was resented and sparked resistance. The same sort of opposition arose in response to early efforts of New England town proprietors to protect standing timber on common lands.

The lack of regulation attracted much comment from foreign observers who were accustomed to timber shortages and governmental controls in the Old World. Thus a German traveler, J. D. Schoepf, wrote in his 1783–1784 journals on the lack of effective "sovereign right" over game and forest in America: "Whoever holds new land, in whatever way, controls it as his exclusive possession, with everything on it, above it, and under it." It would be a long time, Schoepf believed, before "experience and necessity" would finally teach the value of a forest law that required people to "leave for their grandchildren a bit of wood over which to hang the tea-kettle"! Few indeed in colonial America were evidences of forest law that embodied the values of one New Englander who believed that wanton destruction of timber was "displeasing to Almightie God, who abhorreth all willfull waste and spoile of his good Creatures" (Carroll 1973, p. 126).

The commonly held individualistic values that had overwhelmed communal principles or conservationist goals in early America were expressed by a Georgia court in 1808, when it was asked to apply the traditional English law with respect to waste in the forest. How could English law, the court asked, possibly "ap-

This log boom in Minnesota (1888) was a collecting and sorting area where the ownership of logs floating down the river could be determined. Disputes over boom operation resulted in much litigation. Forest History Society Photo.

ply to a country which was but one extended forest, in which the liberty of killing a deer or cutting down a tree, was as unrestrained as the natural rights of the deer to rove, or the tree to grow?" (*State* v. *Campbell*, Georgia, 1808).

Nineteenth-Century Law: In Support of Productivity

In the nineteenth century, as the great forester William B. GREELEY has written, "Production became the god of lumber" in the United States. Sheer abundance of timber, together with successive additions to the territory under U. S. control in North America, militated against any basic changes in the laws of forest use. Law worked largely to expedite the application of technology to maximize short-term output from the forests. A ruthlessly exploitative style of enterprise and technology prevailed. Law was mobilized mainly to accomplish two things: first, through public policy and legislation, to allocate resources by transfer of forest property from governmental to private ownership; and second, through both legislation and judge-made rules (common law), to order and monitor private-sector relationships so as to make the private marketplace work smoothly. As the leading historian of forest law, Willard Hurst, has written, American law revealed a "common acceptance of what were taken to be the self-evident values of

releasing creative [entrepreneurial] energies through the market and through the law's related instruments of contract and property."

In the realm of public law, both federal and state policies operated to expedite transfer of forestlands ownership from public to private control. Although the agricultural frontier moved forward, federal law gave little consideration to the special character of forests. Until the 1870s, public wooded land was sold on much the same terms as agricultural land; in fact, lumbermen were required to purchase public timberland under an agricultural guise. Neither the states nor the federal government expended much in the way of public resources in the enforcement of rules against timber-poaching from public land. One might accurately say that a "trespass ethic" prevailed through much of the nineteenth century; people in newly settling regions viewed it as natural and ethically acceptable to take timber from public property. In the 1870s, moreover, Congress validated this ethic by formally allowing access to public lands to cut timber "for agricultural, mining, or other domestic purposes"; and abuse of the laws was endemic.

Neglect of the dangers and costs of forest fires was also endemic. Despite laws requiring care and diligence, there was no even minimally adequate policy of providing active governmental protection through fire-prevention, detection, or firefighting organization. The resultant losses, not only to timber but also to soil, were enormous.

Apart from making timberland available on liberal terms of sale, the legal system worked through resource allocation to expedite commercial lumbering in other ways. By legislation and by common law, waters in the logging regions were made available for drives and for milling. The public interest and private rights gave way to the needs of the lumber industry, so far as fisheries, navigation, and private property bordering streams were concerned. Both state and federal courts tended to take a pragmatic view of such priorities-ordering, designed as it was to promote economic development and maximum production (at least in the short run) from their forests. The state courts tended to defer to the judgment of legislators as to which interests should be favored in allocating resources. The U. S. Supreme Court, in turn, tended to accommodate regional differences and to validate the diverse state policies by deferring to resource-allocating decisions by the states, so long as Congress did not preempt decision making. In a leading case of 1877, in which the Supreme Court upheld state laws permitting dams, booms, and piers on streams important to the lumber industry, the Court's majority declared that it was the states' proper constitutional role to decide where such structures would "do more good than harm, and to impose such regulations . . . as will best reconcile and accommodate the interest of all concerned" (*Pound* v. *Turck*, 95 U. S. 464).

Because the national government did not enact regulatory or conservationist laws until creation of the forest reserves (national forests) in the 1890s, there resulted what Justice Brandeis called a "competition for laxity" among the states. That is, each state had an incentive to minimize the regulation of its business interests and to keep regulation in line with the level imposed in other states; to do otherwise would be to disadvantage its producers in the common national market. The result was a weak public sector relative to private interests, something clearly manifest in the relationship between government and the resource industries generally.

The other major function of law in the nineteenth century was the ordering of economic relationships in the private-law areas, especially through contract, tort, and property law. In effect, the state legislatures and courts helped establish the rules of the game so as to maximize certainty and predictability in the marketplace's contractual processes. Standard contracts in the trade thus depended on legal definitions of such terms as "merchantable timber" or

"sawlog timber." Rules of conveyance and passing title were set down by courts, and the obligations of boom operators were defined. The rules of liability and fault (that is, of torts) shaped the framework of private transactions and established the duties and obligations of private property ownership in the forest and in commercial life. Moreover, the state legislatures granted important franchises that included both corporate status for lumber companies and monopoly privileges for boom companies and stream use.

The police power of the states was invoked to justify positive regulation, though in a very limited way. When law imposed regulation for log-boom controls, or authorized public officials to undertake survey and scaling, it tended to be done for the purpose of keeping the wheels of enterprise running smoothly and enhancing production, not (as the police power would be used in the twentieth century) to assert a public interest in the conservation of forest resources. Indeed, the law tended to work in ways that attenuated protections formerly given to the public interest. For example, in the courts of many lumber states the forest industries were held immune from traditional common-law liability for water pollution, while air quality and noise were of little concern to the courts. Legislatures mobilized the state's power of eminent domain to aid in lumbering, devolving the power to take private property upon millers or log-boom operators who wished to flood adjoining lands held by others.

Taxation law was another major area of public law that affected the operations of the lumber industry and influenced forest use generally. In the nineteenth century, the rules of property taxation were never seen as a potential means of encouraging conservation of forest resources. On the contrary, the taxation of mature standing timber on the same basis as any ordinary real property operated as an incentive for clearcutting and abandonment.

Some scholars contend that because timber was an abundant resource in the nineteenth century, there was little real need for conservationist law or for adherence to communal values. Other analysts find the record deplorable because law failed to impose a calculus of long-term costs and benefits, instead yielding to "the god, Production" and working haphazardly, with little effort to define a public interest. Great decisions affecting the forests were made, as Willard Hurst has written, "largely by default, without material awareness or discussion"; Americans left such matters to the marketplace. (Hurst, *Law and Social Process*, 1960, p. 188). It remained for a later era, when unlimited abundance of timber no longer was a rational premise on which to base policy, for communal values to surface once again.

Twentieth-Century Law: In Pursuit of the Public Interest

Whereas nineteenth-century forest law reflected the premise that production should be maximized—a premise challenged rarely and to little effect—it has been different with law since the 1890s. Instead of the consistent dominance by producer interests, we have had a counterpoint of competing legal values; instead of single-minded devotion to private control and use of forest resources, we have had extensive debate and a line of important policy decisions in quest of "the public interest."

One question long at the forefront of policy debate concerns federalism: which level of government, the states or the national government, ought to control forest law? A second question embodies the classic confrontation of communal values versus private rights of property: how much control over private uses of forest resources is legitimate and constitutional? Finally, there is the question of competing premises and goals: what values should prevail in the controls that government at any level may exercise over private uses of the forest and other public resources—the air and water—that are affected by forest industries? Quite apart from regulation, to what extent should forests be devoted to such purposes as recreation, long-term protection of watersheds, or simply wilderness and its perpetuation?

The resolution of these problems is a process still under way, indeed a process that already has generated many intense confrontations of interests in twentieth-century legislatures and courts. Before the 1890s, the content of forest and forest-use law had been set as the result of legislative actions responsive to pressure from lumber interests, or else as the result of court decisions adjudicating well-focused disputes between firms, industrial versus labor interests, or other litigants. By contrast, the modern legal process has been much affected by the appearance of new categories of actors influencing policy outcomes. Among these new participants in lawmaking debate and decision are (1) the professional foresters, who by the 1890s were pressing for law to advance principles of scientific management and to achieve sustained yield; (2) associations of producers, organized both regionally and according to types of operation within the forest and wood-products industries, which in the early twentieth century emerged as

spokesmen for the industry; and (3) consumer-oriented public-interest groups, including many that are devoted primarily to litigation. Since World War II, the public-interest groups have joined with the old-line "naturalists" and their organizations to seek regulation of air and water quality, protection of game, WILDERNESS PRESERVATION, and other objectives embodying nonindustrial uses of the forests.

The problem of federalism—the proper allocation of functions to the national government and to the states—arose in the earliest phase of the organized conservation movement. Conservationists supported creation of national forest reserves, for they doubted the constitutionality of national laws regulating private forest use and they were certain such laws would not gain popular support. The FOREST RESERVE ACT of 1891 authorized the first forest reserves, but the initial effect of "locking up" resources was soon altered when the FOREST MANAGEMENT ACT of 1897 specified "favorable conditions of water flows" and a "continuous supply of timber" as the twin goals of national policy. The U. S. FOREST SERVICE's professional staff generally championed federal management of the reserved lands as the best way to achieve conservationist aims. Others, however, advocated the national regulation of privately owned forestland as the only effective means for attaining conservationist goals. A protracted debate followed in Congress in the 1920s, and the proponents of strong regulation lost. The dominant model of federal intervention became "cooperative federalism," involving grants-in-aid to the states for coordinated studies of forest use and policy, for assistance in fire protection, and for research and education, including extension work to encourage woodlot and windbreak planting.

National policy has not been limited, however, to the cooperative state–federal framework. In 1918, for example, federal legislation for protection of game birds introduced national regulation in a new dimension. Throughout the twentieth century, moreover, forest use has been affected indirectly by the enforcement of federal antitrust legislation, by federal labor laws, and by the tariff and other international trade policies of the national government.

In the 1960s and 1970s, a series of congressional enactments gave heightened importance to national law affecting the forests. These laws asserted minimum national standards as to air pollution, clean waterways, and occupational safety. Although they did not directly regulate private cutting practices or impose national regulation for purposes of timber conservation as such, they did express broad environmental and safety concerns that established new constraints upon private enterprise in the forest and wood-products industries. They were accompanied, moreover, by legislation concerning the principles and practices of federal management in the national forests. Congress revised in basic ways the objectives of national policy by enactment of the 1960 MULTIPLE USE-SUSTAINED YIELD ACT. Some viewed this law as a mandate for stepped-up timber harvesting by franchised private interests on the public lands; but exemplary of how complex law had become in establishing the framework of forest use was a 1975 federal appellate court decision (*Izaak Walton League* v. *Butz*, 522 f.2d 945), in which a conservationist organization successfully challenged contracts made by the Forest Service with private loggers in the Monongahela National Forest. The court ruled favorably on the Izaak Walton League's contention that harvesting sales and contracts within the forest should permit cutting only of mature, large-growth trees; should require individual marking of trees; and should require removal of all cut timber. Other decisions of federal courts interpreting the NATIONAL ENVIRONMENTAL POLICY ACT, the Wilderness Act, and other new statutes similarly have required federal agencies in their administration of public lands to take increasing account of environmental concerns.

The second great legal question in the modern period of forest law—what types of public control of private forest property uses are legitimate and constitutional?—has been confronted, in large part, in the arena of state legislation and adjudication. Failure of the movement for national regulation of private cutting and other forest-industry practices left with the states the initiative for regulation. They responded by resorting to a variety of means of control. There have been very great differences, from state to state, in degree of strictness; "competition in laxity" still is evident today. Early in the twentieth century, most states adopted laws designed to guard against forest fire dangers. Encouraged by federal aid measures, many states also augmented forestry research and extension work through the acquisition of land for state-managed forests dedicated to recreation, managed cutting, or, in a few cases, wilderness preservation. Reminiscent of British colonial law are bounties adopted by some states to encourage reforestation. More popular were reforms of state taxation, with fourteen states having adopted by 1940 a policy of exempting standing timber from tax assessment or otherwise seeking to avoid forced cutting by private owners.

In the decade of the 1940s, thirteen states went still further and adopted outright regulation of cutting practices, thus mobilizing the classic police power of the states. Few of the laws were strictly enforced, however; some actually relied upon voluntary compliance, while others (as in California) left definition of standards and enforcement to the counties. Momentum seemed lost, and by 1955 only four more states had been added to the roster of those imposing regulation.

Challenges to the laws that were enacted did, however, present an opportunity for courts to speak on the issue of how far the states' police powers could legitimately reach. Much the same pattern as was seen in the nineteenth century now prevailed once again: state courts deferred to the judgment of legislatures, and the Supreme Court upheld the preferences of individual states as to how their resources ought to be managed. This time around, however, it was regulation in the public interest and not priorities-ordering to foster industrial development and growth that the courts upheld. Thus, the toughest regulatory law in any state, enacted in the State of Washington in 1945 and requiring private landowners to obtain cutting permits and conform to reforestation goals and standards, was validated by the state's high court: in its decision of *State* v. *Dexter* (32 Wash. 2d. 551), the Washington court in 1949 declared that a "constitutional morality" required that lawmakers consider future generations and their claims on society's heritage of natural resources. The court held to a robust definition of police power to guard the public welfare and public interest, and the Supreme Court turned back a challenge to that decision. State courts generally have upheld regulatory efforts, giving operative meaning to the pronouncement of the Supreme Court seventy-five years ago that it is a legitimate function of state government to act "to protect the atmosphere, the water, and the forests within its territory, irrespective of the assent or dissent of the private owners of the land most immediately concerned" (*Hudson Water Co.* v. *McCarter*, 209 U. S. 349 [1907]).

Reform of state taxation laws has continued to the present day, with some states substituting yield taxes for regular property assessments, others specifically exempting standing timber from "highest and best use" assessment rules, and still others giving tax concessions in return for owners' agreement to apply forest-management standards. Local government has played an important role, too, in regulation through adoption of zoning laws. Special forestland zones were a legal form pioneered by Wisconsin in 1929. Greenbelt zones, restrictions on clearcutting along highways or waterways, and other legislative innovations have similarly affected private forest management and woodlot management in other states. In a few states, explicit constitutional amendments have introduced new regulatory powers and conservationist goals.

Withal, the legitimacy and constitutionality of regulation by the states have been given solid doctrinal underpinnings by the courts. How far the states will go, however, remains a vital political question—just as the future scope and reach of environmental regulation remains a major question for political decision at the national level of government.

Widely varying legal and philosophical views characterize the contemporary debate over forest law and policy. At one extreme are those who wish to sustain and revitalize the values of an uncompromising economic individualism. Typically, their preferences are linked to the notion that it is the national government's obligation to "unlock" the country's resources by giving renewed access to the forests on liberal terms. In several states, for example, paper-milling firms have put up a fierce legal fight against water-pollution and air-pollution controls; and commercial lumber interests have often been in the forefront of political battle against the designation of new wilderness preserves or the reservation of additional blocks of land as national forests. Entering a dissenting opinion in the State of Washington case, cited earlier, which upheld a law strictly regulating private cutting of timber, one of the court's judges expressed the old individualistic ethic. He angrily condemned arguments that the obligation to future generations justified restricting private uses of property today. "The ultimate end" of such laws, he declared, "is confiscation of property rights and the imposition of governmental decrees by political appointees" (*State* v. *Dexter* 32 Wash. 2d. 551, 569). For the most part, however, commercial interests in the forest industries have accepted the view that their private holdings have "common property" characteristics, being an exhaustible resource of vital importance to existing and future populations. In fact, at some periods in our recent history—the 1950s especially—commercial firms have taken the lead in introducing sustained-yield management, far in advance of compulsory legal requirements. Conservationist in orientation, such views derive from the major strain in reform thought associated with Gifford PINCHOT in the Progressive Era—the view that it should be the object of forest law "not to preserve the forests because they are beautiful . . . or because they are refuges for the wild creatures of the wilderness" but instead because they are the basis for "the making of prosperous homes."

A more strictly communal ethic comprises a second strain in legal thought regarding forest property. It is exemplified by claims that forests are a "public trust"; that is, they are a special kind of property, whether in private or public ownership, that must be passed on as the future generations' legacy—whether for economic sustenance, or for recreation, or for aesthetic qualities that transcend material concerns. Based on such a view, several courts have upheld the contention that the federal government and its agencies must consider environmental impact before proceeding with policies, programs, or construction that can cause permanent harm to forests or other natural resources, as in *Scenic Hudson Preservation Conference* v. *FPC*, 354 F.2d 608 (1966) — a holding that the Supreme Court declined to review on appeal. Moreover, the federal courts have wrestled with the question of legal standing to sue, first expanding that right so as to enable public-interest litigants such as the SIERRA CLUB to come to court on behalf of the public generally, later establishing some serious legal limits on such eligibility to sue.

More recently, some legal scholars and environmentalists, taking their cue from a dissent of Justice William O. Douglas in a 1973 case in which he contended that constitutional rights ought to extend to resources and not only persons, have challenged the entire utilitarian basis of even "public trust" legal concepts. It is not only that human population enjoys the forests, is uplifted in spirit by them, or needs them to build prosperous homes that justifies regulation and restraint in use of these resources, they claim. Rather, one should be concerned to sustain the integrity and functions of natural systems as a whole. "Persons are not the only entities in the world that can be thought to possess rights," lawyer Laurence Tribe has contended; he insists that one ought "to entertain seriously the notion that a mountain or a seashore has intrinsic needs and can make independent moral claims upon our designs."

Whether on the utilitarian ground that there is a set of important human needs (including economic needs) to be served by forest law, or on broader grounds that natural objects and creatures have rights, there is growing acceptance today of the concept of a "constitutional right to a habitable environment" and the related idea of "environmental due process." Recognition of these new precepts by courts and legislatures has exacted short-run economic costs, to be sure, and in times of economic stress or stagnation such ideas may prove fragile and vulnerable as governments seek out ways to maximize economic output. Still, the law of the American forests has moved far from nineteenth-century norms and practices. Although the debate over utilitarian premises continues and although the strictly economic calculus that underlies old-style individualism still finds voice in legal discourse and policy debates, the continuing quest for "the public interest" remains the central concern of contemporary legal discussion.

FURTHER READING: Charles F. Carroll, *The Timber Economy of Puritan New England* (1973). Harry W. Falk, Jr., *Timber and Forest Products Law* (1958). Paul W. Gates, *History of Public Land Law Development* (1968). Willard Hurst, *Law and Economic Growth: The Legal History of the Lumber Industry in Wisconsin, 1836–1915* (1964). J. P Kinney, *The Development of Forest Law in America* (1917). Charles Reich, "The Public and the Nation's Forests," *California Law Review* 50 (Aug. 1962): 381-407. Glen O. Robinson, "Wilderness: The Last Frontier," *Minnesota Law Review* 59 (Nov. 1974): 1-65. Joseph L. Sax, "The Public Trust Doctrine in Natural Resource Law: Effective Judicial Intervention," *Michigan Law Review* 68 (Jan. 1970): 473-566. Laurence H. Tribe, "Ways Not to Think about Plastic Trees," *Yale Law Journal* 83 (June 1974): 1315–1348.

HARRY N. SCHEIBER

LEAGUE OF CONSERVATION VOTERS

The League of Conservation Voters was founded by Friends of the Earth (FOE) in 1970. The organization was set up as an independent body, because FOE's charter has limited its role in raising funds for political purposes. Officials of many prominent conservation groups sit on the League's board: the SIERRA CLUB, IZAAK WALTON LEAGUE, NATIONAL WILDLIFE FEDERATION, WILDERNESS SOCIETY, Friends of the Earth, and others. The organization's purpose is to influence federal and state conservation policy by supporting the election of sympathetic officials and defeating those known to be hostile.

A nonpartisan organization (although in practice it has supported mostly Democrats), the League is a fund-raising action group modeled on the election committees of more traditional lobbies such as manufacturers' associations and labor unions. It collects funds from private and organizational contributors and donates them to environmentalist candidates for House, Senate, and gubernatorial seats, especially in elections with "high environmental stakes." By the late 1970s, the League was participating in from fifteen to twenty election campaigns a year.

Decisions are made by a steering committee which elects its own members. In practice, officials of the major conservation and environmentalist groups sit on it but not as official representatives of their organizations. In 1978, the League donated $80,000 to thirty-four candidates for public office, of whom eighteen were elected. This was its worst percentage in several years.

In addition to disbursing funds, the League publishes detailed analyses of the conservation records of candidates for national and state offices. These are distributed by local environmentalist groups and political committees. The League is not a membership organization. Its headquarters are in Washington, D. C.

LEONARD, RICHARD MANNING (1908–   )

Born in Elyria, Ohio, on October 22, 1908, Richard Manning Leonard graduated from the University of California's Boalt School of Law in 1932 and subsequently practiced law in San Francisco.

In the 1930s, Leonard made several first ascents in the Sierra Nevada. For maximum safety he used the rope-and-piton and mathematical planning techniques he described in his book, *Belaying the Leader* (1946). His emphasis upon such safety techniques in amateur climbing was a departure from the European tradition and influenced Western mountaineering. During World War II, Leonard helped revise the U. S. Army's clothing and equipment for artic and tropical survival.

Leonard has served the SIERRA CLUB as director (1938 –1973), secretary (1947–1953), president (1953–1955), and honorary president (since 1976). He has also been a SAVE-THE-REDWOODS LEAGUE director since 1954 and president since 1975; a WILDERNESS SOCIETY director since 1948 and vice-president in 1962–1963. He has acted as an independent adviser to federal and California state land use agencies.

Leonard's role in the history of increased citizen activism has been crucial. His term as Sierra Club president spanned the height of the club's successful national campaign to save Dinosaur National Monument from the Upper Colorado River Project. In 1963, Leonard formed the Conservation Law Society of America, the first such organization dedicated to environmental litigation in the nation. He argued, in a vein similar to that of William O. Douglas, that nature has rights that must be defended.

Leonard believed that citizen groups should press public agencies to ensure environmental protection but that they should never attempt to alienate or discredit public officials. He sought cooperation and open communications with public agencies and private industry. Upon occasion during the 1960s, this stance brought him into conflict with more militant leaders in the Sierra Club.

FURTHER READING: Richard M. Leonard, *Mountaineer,*

Lawyer, Environmentalist, an oral history by Susan R. Schrepfer (University of California Regional Oral History Office, 1975).

SUSAN R. SCHREPFER

LEOPOLD, ALDO (1887–1948)

Born on January 11, 1887, in Burlington, Iowa, and educated in Burlington, at Lawrenceville School in New Jersey, and at Yale (where he received the B.S. degree in 1908 and the M.F. in 1909), Leopold early acquired a lively interest in hunting, ornithology, and natural history. One of the earliest graduates of the Yale Forest School, he joined the U. S. FOREST SERVICE and was assigned to the newly organized Southwestern District, where he headed a reconnaissance crew on the Apache National Forest in Arizona Territory. He rose to the post of supervisor of the Carson National Forest in New Mexico in 1912, but in the following year was incapacitated by a near-fatal attack of nephritis.

After eighteen months of recuperation, he turned to his old interest in wildlife, organizing game and fish management for the Forest Service and founding game protective associations in New Mexico and Arizona. His efforts for law enforcement, predator control, and refuges won him the gold medal of W. T. Hornaday's Permanent Wildlife Protection Fund in 1917. Leopold served during 1918 as secretary of the Albuquerque Chamber of Commerce, then returned to the Forest Service as assistant district forester in charge of operations. In addition to developing more efficient personnel practices, fire-control procedures, and forest-inspection methods, he made special contributions in the realms of watershed management, WILDLIFE CONSERVATION, and wilderness protection. Through his work on the problem of soil erosion on Southwestern watersheds he began developing his philosophy of man's responsibility for maintaining the health of the land, and in his wildlife work he began applying traditional Forest Service concepts of wise use and sustained yield to the scientific management of game. He laid the groundwork for administrative designation in 1924 of over 500,000 acres of the Gila National Forest in New Mexico as wilderness, setting the pattern for the system of undeveloped areas that was given force of law in the Wilderness Act of 1964.

From 1924 to 1928, Leopold served as associate director of the Forest Products Laboratory in Madison, Wisconsin, then the principal research arm of the Forest Service. In 1928, he left the service to take the lead in establishing a new profession of game management, modeled on the profession of forestry. He began by conducting game surveys (published in 1931 as *Report on a Game Survey of the North Central States*) and authored a text for the new field, *Game Management* (1933), still a wildlife classic. He served as officer, director, or chairman for over 100 professional societies and conservation organizations, including the SOCIETY OF AMERICAN FORESTERS, the WILDLIFE SOCIETY, President Franklin D. ROOSEVELT's Committee on Wildlife Restoration, the WILDERNESS SOCIETY, the ECOLOGICAL SOCIETY OF AMERICA, and the Wisconsin Conservation Commission. Through a chair of game management created for him at the University of Wisconsin in 1933, he trained a generation of leaders in the wildlife field and inspired hundreds of students with his ethic of ecological responsibility.

Originally imbued like other early conservationists with the belief that man could rationally control his environment to produce desired commodities for his own benefit, Leopold slowly developed a philosophy of naturally self-regulating systems and an ecological concern with land health and a land ethic. His intellectual development may be traced through the nearly 350 articles that he published during his career. The capstone of his effort was *A Sand County Almanac* (1949), a volume of vignettes of his monthly activities at a run-down Wisconsin farm he was restoring to ecological integrity, together with more far-reaching philosophical essays such as "The Land Ethic," for which he is best known. Representing the distillation of a lifetime of thought on the interrelations of ecology, aesthetics, and ethics, the *Almanac* sold over a million copies and earned for Leopold the status of a prophet of the environmental movement of the 1970s.

Leopold married Estella Bergere of Santa Fe in 1912 and had five children, Starker, Luna, Nina, Carl, and Estella, all of whom became leading naturalists and three of whom gained election to the National Academy of Sciences, a unique achievement for a group of siblings. Leopold died on April 21, 1948.

FURTHER READING: Paul L. Errington, "In Appreciation of Aldo Leopold," *Journal of Wildlife Management* 12 (Oct. 1948): 341-350. Susan L. Flader, *Thinking Like a Mountain: Aldo Leopold and the Evolution of an Ecological Attitude Toward Deer, Wolves, and Forests* (1974). Susan L. Flader, with Charles Steinhacker, photographer, *The Sand Country of Aldo Leopold* (1973). Donald Fleming, "Roots of the New Conservation Movement," *Perspectives in American History* 6 (1972): 7-91. Roderick Nash, *Wilderness and the American Mind* (rev. ed., 1982).

SUSAN L. FLADER

LOG CONSTRUCTION

As here defined, log construction refers to walls built of horizontally laid logs or shaped beams, fas-

Lodgepole pine logs from an eastern Washington forest were used to construct a barn and the fence in the foreground. American Forest Institute Photo.

tened at the corners by any of several techniques. Although log construction is often thought of as an American frontier type, its origins lie in central, northern, and eastern Europe, and such carpentry methods reached the United States through multiple diffusions from diverse Old World sources.

The earliest and most notable implantation occurred in Delaware and adjacent parts of Pennsylvania and New Jersey, where the Midland style of American log construction developed between 1640 and 1750. Several immigrant groups introduced log carpentry techniques into the Midland hearth. Earliest to come were Swedes and Finns, who founded the New Sweden colony in the mid-seventeenth century. In the first half of the 1700s, they were joined by two groups of log-building Germans, one from Switzerland and the Black Forest and a second from Moravia, Bohemia, Silesia, and Saxony. The resultant Midland style which combined elements from these various sources subsequently spread through much of North America.

A second diffusion of log carpentry led into the American Southwest by way of Mexico, where the technique was likely introduced in the sixteenth century by German miners. The result was the distinctive Hispanic-Southwestern style of log construction, clustered mainly in the highland Spanish villages of New Mexico, particularly in the San Juan, Sangre de Cristo, and Manzano ranges. From across the Pacific, in a third diffusion, came the Russo-Siberian style of log construction, remnants of which can be observed in southern coastal Alaska and in California. Early colonists in Quebec introduced a fourth style, French Canadian-Hudson's Bay, in the seventeenth century, though log construction was seemingly never dominant in the Saint Lawrence Valley. Some French-

Canadian log buildings were erected in trading-post colonies in the American Midwest, and the style was later adopted and spread by the Hudson's Bay Company.

In the late nineteenth and early twentieth centuries, a Fenno-Scandian style was introduced into the north woods of Wisconsin, the Upper Peninsula of Michigan, and northern Minnesota, most notably by Finns. In the same period, Slavic immigrants in the Canadian west implanted the Prairie Ukrainian style in the provinces of Manitoba, Saskatchewan, and Alberta.

As a consequence of these introductions, log construction became known in most parts of North America, including the greater part of the United States. Only in New England and the Tidewater South, where few settlers familiar with log carpentry were found among the immigrants, and in certain unforested districts of the West, was log construction rare. New England's frame buildings prevailed over log construction even as far west as Ohio's Western Reserve. Most of the Hispanic-Amerindian Southwest similarly had few log buildings.

These separate introductions of log construction led to regional contrasts in building techniques. These contrasts can be seen in the major features of log carpentry, including shaping of logs, corner timbering, and spacing of logs in the wall.

Various methods, some crude and others requiring the expertise of skilled craftsmen, are employed to prepare logs for use in a wall. The simplest shaping technique is to leave the logs round, either peeled or with the bark intact, a method typical of log cribs, barns, and hastily built, first-generation cabins in most of the North American log construction styles. In the Midland region, a more skilled preparation of logs involves two-sided planking, accomplished by hewing off rounded sides with ax and adz to produce two flattened surfaces. More common in Hispanic-Southwestern, Fenno-Scandian, Russo-Siberian, and French Canadian-Hudson's Bay styles are logs flattened on four sides, producing squared or slightly rectangular timbers. This squaring is often achieved by use of the saw rather than the ax and adz. The sawn surfaces are smooth, lacking the tell-tale ax score-marks typical of Midland two-sided planking. Another shaping method, confined exclusively to the Midland style, is half-log construction, achieved by splitting round timbers in half lengthwise, producing a semicircular or half-moon shape. Sometimes, the outermost part of the remaining round side is hewn off, producing a planked half-log.

Closely related to log shape are the methods of corner timbering, the joints where logs from adjacent

walls are fastened to hold the structure together. These joints serve to prevent lateral slippage of the beams and to bear a substantial part of the building's total weight. Faulty corner timbering means a faulty structure, and carpenters therefore devote considerable attention to fashioning these joints. In most of North America, as in Europe, the typical means of corner construction is the notch, whereby timbers from adjacent walls are affixed directly to one another by a locked joint. The eight most common American types are the full-dovetail, half-dovetail, V, square, half, saddle, semilunate, and double notches.

The saddle notch, probably the most ancient of all types, normally occurs on round logs and is fashioned by cutting a rounded depression in the top or bottom (or both) sides, shaped to fit the rounded contour of the adjacent log. It is a common type in the Midland, Fenno-Scandian, Hispanic-Southwestern, and Prairie Ukrainian styles of construction. V-notching, so named because of its inverted V-shaped joint, apparently developed in Scandinavia as a variant of the saddle notch and is applied to round or planked timbers. In North America, V-notching appears to be exclusively a Midland type and is most common in Pennsylvania, the central Appalachians, the Ohio Valley, and interior Texas.

The full-dovetail notch resembles a cabinetmaker's joint and is characterized by two slants or "splays" cut at different angles on the end of the log, producing a locked joint of superior strength. Most commonly, full-dovetailing is seen in Fenno-Scandian, Russo-Siberian, and Prairie Ukrainian construction in North America, but it also occurs as a minority type in the Midland style, particularly in the Delaware Valley. Perhaps akin to the full-dovetail is semilunate notching, applied to half-round timbers. The natural curve of the semicircular log profile replaces the splays of full-dovetailing, and the end result is a firmly locked corner. In North America, semilunate notching is confined largely to the Gulf Coastal Plain portion of the Midland region. The half-dovetail notch also resembles the full-dovetail, differing in that it has a splay only on the top side of the tongue of the log. Overall, half-dovetailing is the most common Midland type, particularly for dwellings, and occurs widely, particularly in the southern Appalachians, Cumberland Plateau, Ozark-Ouachita highlands, and Texas.

Another exclusively Midland type is the square notch, a crude and easily fashioned joint that does not form a locked corner. It consists only of right angle cuts, with a rectangle of wood removed from the top and bottom of the log tongue. Pegs are needed to prevent lateral slippage. The half-notch is very similar to the square type, differing in that the carpenter removes a rectangle of wood only from the bottom side of each timber. Half- notching occurs infrequently in Midland construction but with considerable frequency in the Hispanic-Southwestern style. Both square and half-notching appear to be of Swedish origin.

The double-notch is also much like the square notch, differing by virtue of a projection at each corner which allows it to form a locked joint. In North America, double-notching is common only in Fenno-Scandian and Hispanic-Southwestern styles.

Another method of securing the corners of log buildings, not involving notching, is corner-posting, in which the horizontal logs from adjacent walls are tenoned and fitted into slots or mortices in vertical corner beams. Often, other vertical beams are placed at midpoints of the wall, allowing almost infinite expansion of the structure, an advantage not shared by corner-notching construction. Corner-posted buildings are a hallmark of the French Canadian- Hudson's Bay style, and some examples still survive in the scattering of French trading colonies in the North American interior. Corner-posting also appears very rarely in Midland construction.

Two different techniques for spacing logs within a wall are encountered in the United States. The carpenter can either fit the timbers tightly together by carefully shaping the tops and bottoms of adjacent beams, forming a solid fitted wall, or he can leave open cracks, called chinks, between the logs, so that the timbers touch only at the corners. The chink technique requires less skill and work, permits slightly crooked logs to be used, and accommodates a certain amount of warp and natural taper. Additional labor is needed, though, to fill the chinks with clay or some other substance, assuming the builder desires a tight wall. Chink construction is a hallmark of Midland construction in the United States, since all other styles are characterized by fitted timbers. It may be derived from Moravia, Bohemia, and Silesia.

To summarize, six styles of log carpentry occur in North America, at least five of which can be found in the United States. Most common is the Midland style, distinguished by two-sided planking, half-round, and round timbers; saddle, V, half-dovetail, square, and semilunate notching; and chink walls. The Hispanic-Southwestern style employs round and squared logs; saddle, double, and half-notching; and chinkless walls. Russo- Siberian buildings in Alaska and California normally consist of full-dovetailed, squared timbers without chinks; while French Canadian-Hudson's Bay log structures are corner-posted. Chinkless, double-

notched, or full-dovetailed walls and squared logs typify Fenno-Scandian log carpentry.

These log building techniques were applied to a great variety of floor plans and architectural styles, including dwellings, barns, churches, forts, courthouses, jails, stores, and other types of structures. Each of the six styles described above is related to a distinctive complex of floor plans and roof forms, but to describe these is beyond the scope of this article.

FURTHER READING: Terry G. Jordan, *Texas Log Buildings: A Folk Architecture* (1978). Fred B. Kniffen and Henry H. Glassie, "Building in Wood in the Eastern United States: A Time -Place Perspective," *Geographical Review* 56 (1966): 40-66. Hermann Phleps, *Holzbaukunst: Der Blockbau* (1942). Harold R. Shurtleff, *The Log Cabin Myth: A Study of the Early Dwellings of the English Colonies in North America* (1939). C. A. Weslager, *The Log Cabin in America from Pioneer Days to the Present* (1969).

TERRY G. JORDAN

LOGGING TECHNOLOGY AND TOOLS

Logging technology—which for purposes of this article will include only that associated with the felling, on-site handling, and yarding of logs—has evolved rapidly in the United States since the mid-nineteenth century. Change had occurred earlier, but at a slower pace. The details of early changes are obscure; pioneer observers seldom recorded the equipment and techniques used in woods operations.

Initially, colonists harvested America's forests using tools and methods from Europe. They had good hewing tools for making square timbers, but since Europeans had never been confronted with such large trees they lacked adequate felling tools. By 1789, the American felling ax evolved to meet the need. This single-bitted ax had a heavy poll to give greater balance to the ax and more power to the stroke. Its short, heavy, wedge-shaped blade was both durable and easily extracted from the wood. By 1816, the ax was being copied in England, and by the end of the century it was common in most parts of the world. In the 1830s, Americans were manufacturing it of cast steel rather than of iron with a steel cutting edge welded on. A variety of other modifications appeared; by 1863, one manufacturer's catalog listed thirteen types of American felling axes. During the nineteenth century, curved handles became standard, a development made possible by facsimile lathes similar to those developed for the mass production of gunstocks. At the Philadelphia Exposition in 1876, American felling axes won greater praise from foreign observers than perhaps any other tool. By this

Ax-swinging fellers place an undercut to control the direction in which this Douglas-fir will fall. They are standing on springboards, a commonly used aid during the handtool era, which placed fellers above obstructing brush and debris and also above the often defective lower portion of the tree. Forest History Society Photo.

time, the many plants of the American Axe and Tool Company—the "Axe Trust"—were supplying what one authority has estimated as 75 percent of the world's commercially produced axes, hatchets, and scythes. The Collins Company in Connecticut and the W. C. Kelly Axe Company in West Virginia were also major producers.

Some time before 1850, loggers began using a double-bitted ax— apparently first on a major scale in Pennsylvania. When loggers from Maine moved into western Pennsylvania after the opening of the Susquehanna Boom in 1850, they were initially suspicious of the double-bitted, straight-handled axes in use there. However, they were converted to them as the advantages of an ax with two cutting edges that still possessed the balance and durability of the "Yankee" ax became clear. Both forms have continued to be used, but in the United States the double-bitted ax has long

been the more common felling tool on lumbering operations. The single-bitted ax has become more of a utility tool, although it is still used on small operations in second-growth and hardwood timber, especially in the Northeast, the Central States, and the South. Since single-bitted axes could be used both to drive saw wedges and to chop, they eliminated the need to carry both an ax and a wedge hammer.

From the beginning in North America, colonists felled trees by chopping, but early on the English practice of "rounding up" a tree trunk so as to reduce splintering was abandoned. Americans also modified other European chopping techniques. Instead of making V-shaped cuts at almost the same level on opposite sides of the trunk, they made one cut considerably lower (the "undercut") and made both cuts flat on the bottom. This method gave greater control over the direction of fall and reduced the time-consuming use of wedges and levers, commonly resorted to in Europe to control the fall. These modifications left more wood on the stump and more unusable wood on the base of the trunk than did European techniques, but in America labor savings were more important that resource conservation.

Beginning in the 1870s, an even more important change took place. Crosscut saws, which had long been used once trees were on the ground, were adapted to felling. Two developments paved the way. First, the invention of raker teeth, which, coupled with cutting teeth and interspersed with gullets to carry away the sawdust, resulted in a saw that could cut standing, green softwoods quickly without binding on the sawdust produced. Second, the adoption of tempered steel blades yielded saws that would remain sharp through prolonged use and were less apt to snap in two than were earlier saws. The origin of these innovations is not clear. Shurley & Dietrich of Galt, Ontario, were turning out raker-toothed crosscuts by 1874; Henry Disston of Philadelphia produced the first crucible saw steel in the United States in 1855 and by the 1870s was using tempered steel in the crosscut—giving it, a company brochure later claimed, "its first great start." The two may, indeed, have been the first with their respec-

tive improvements. Use of the crosscut felling saw, especially two-man models, spread rapidly. It was in use on the Pacific Coast by the 1880s. Depending on the size and species of tree, the crosscut saw could save up to two-thirds of the time that it had formerly taken to fell a tree. Moreover, the new method gave fellers greater control over where trees would land than they had possessed before; fewer now fell where they were irretrievable and fewer trunks were shattered on impact. By 1900, saws with different types of teeth and different combinations of teeth and rakers had been developed for use on various types of trees. For pines the saws normally had broad teeth in twos between rakers; for Douglas-fir, solid lance teeth in sets of four between rakers; and for white oak, solid teeth in sets of three. Axes were now relegated to a support role; they were used in clearing the undercut and in other supplementary tasks, but the saw had become the main felling tool. Axmen had sharpened their own tools. The crosscut, more difficult to keep in good cutting condition, brought a new specialist to logging camps: the saw filer.

In the 1920s, the bucksaw replaced the crosscut in many pulpwood operations in the Northeast and Canada. Introduced by Finns and Swedes, who had

Fallen trees supported at their ends present problems for the bucker, who cannot cut from the top without having the settling logs bind his saw. Here the solitary bucker undercuts, using the springy handle of his ax as an assistant. The bottle, which is hanging by a hook, contains kerosene to splash on the saw whenever it gets too pitchy to pull easily. American Forest Institute Photo.

Before light-weight gasoline engines were available, fellers made use of pneumatic saws that were powered by a portable air compressor. Forest History Society Photo.

used it in Europe, the lightweight bucksaw could cut as fast as the crosscut, was easier to carry, and could be used close to the ground—thus leaving a short stump. However, since it was not suitable for large timber, the bucksaw's use was limited to pulpwood camps.

By the 1870s, when the Ransome steam tree-feller appeared, inventors were trying to develop mechanically powered saws. What may have been the first gasoline-powered chain saw was tested in Eureka, California, in 1905. This was followed by experiments with saws powered by portable air compressors and electric generators. Mechanically powered circular saws, reciprocating (drag) saws, and chain saws were all tried both for felling and for bucking. Without exception, these early devices proved too cumbersome, too undependable, or both, although in the 1920s some power saws did prove profitable when used on level terrain for bucking. Then, in 1927, Andreas Stihl of Stuttgart, Germany, built a portable, gasoline-powered chain saw; the great breakthrough had come. In 1930, the Eastman-Gardiner Company of Laurel, Mississippi, became the first American firm to use chain

saws on a large scale, but power saws remained relatively rare in the United States until after World War II. During the war, many American firms moved into the production of chain saws, often by copying Stihl's models (whose patents were released during the war by the United States government). In 1947, Joe Cox, a former logger from Portland, Oregon, began producing an improved saw chain, the chipper chain; other improvements followed. Except where terrain prevented use or timber was too small or scattered to make it feasible, the chain saw soon replaced the crosscut as the main felling tool of loggers. At the same time, it eliminated much of the remaining ax work. The power saw not only saved time, but it also made possible new felling techniques. In the big timber of the Far West, loggers began using the Humboldt undercut: they made their initial horizontal cut and then sawed up at an angle from below it. In this way the wedge of the undercut was taken from the stump, leaving the butt log with a square end that resulted in less waste in the mill.

Important though it was, the chain saw did not mark the end of the evolution of timber-harvesting techniques. In the 1940s appeared hydraulic shears that could cut through trees as a result of pressure applied to heavy-duty blades rather than by sawing action. By the 1960s, a variety of tractor-mounted single- and double-bladed hydraulic shears were in use; many combined cutting with handling and stacking capabilities. These devices were especially valuable in close stands of tall, small-diameter trees that would suffer much loss from breakage if harvested by traditional methods. Shears were faster than men with saws and could be operated day and night, but they are feasible only in small timber, with fairly uniform ground and slight slopes.

The general trend in logging was always toward less labor- intensive tools and techniques, but conditions sometimes required other adjustments. In the Northeast, where the finest white pines often went to the mast trade, much work was expended in preparing a bed of small trees and brush to cushion their fall. The value of long spars was such that this extra work to reduce breakage upon impact more than paid off. In the cypress forests of the South, woodsmen girdled trees before cutting them. Cypress thus killed gradually dried, eventually becoming light enough to be floated from the swamps in which they grew. The extra step of girdling made lumbering practical in stands that could not otherwise have been exploited. And in the Far West, loggers adopted the springboard (which was also used in cypress logging); this short, metal-tipped plank was inserted into notches chopped in the trunk and served as a platform allowing fellers to stand above the dense undergrowth rather than having to "swamp out" work space before starting to cut; more important, it raised them high enough so that they could cut above the swollen bases of the area's trees, for the lower trunks of old-growth timber were often so pitch-laden and afflicted with rot and shakes as to make cutting them difficult and their wood valueless in the mill.

During the earliest period of logging, little activity intervened between felling and transportation to the sawmill or other point of utilization. Trees next to waterways were felled, limbed, bucked into lengths, rolled into the water (if they could not be felled into it), and floated to market. A minimum of equipment was needed for such operations: jacks, cant hooks (later Peaveys), ring dogs, and blocks and tackle—all of which were used to wrestle logs into the water— and the ubiquitous saw and ax. Many woodsmen got by with even fewer tools.

As harvesting proceeded, lumbermen had to cut further and further from the water's edge. As they did so, the problems of moving bulky logs became greater.

Woodsmen responded with increasing on-site processing to reduce the size and weight of the materials being moved. This resulted in much wood being left in the forest. However, as improved methods of moving logs on land were developed, on-site processing—and its attendant waste—declined, largely because processing at the mill was more susceptible to mechanization and integration than was that done in the woods. Thus, although on-site processing has never completely disap-

A Sikorsky S-64 E Skycrane lifts a log on Oregon's Siskiyou National Forest, 1967. Forest Service Photo.

peared, it flourished primarily during lumbering's pre-industrial phase.

From colonial times until well into the nineteenth century, countless Americans worked in the woods riving boards, splitting shingles and rails, and in other ways reducing logs to objects that could be moved from the forest with relative ease. These same people normally felled the trees and then transported the end products of their labor to nearby markets. Woods jobs merged naturally into one another; the logger was also a manufacturer and merchandiser. Tools were simple— axes, mauls, and wedges being the mainstays—and the work was labor-intensive.

Of all on-site processing, none loomed as large or became so sophisticated as the preparation of square timbers and spar sticks. After a tree was down, a "liner" marked a cutting line along the trunk with a chalk line, a "scorer" roughed out the sides of the trunk with a standard ax, and a hewer then "hewed to the line," smoothing the sides with a broadax. Skillful hewers could cut fourteen inches with a single stroke, leaving the side as smooth as if it had been sawn. The process, repeated on each side of the stick, resulted in a long square timber of high value. Similar processes were used for producing octagonal spars, the largest of which were used as ship's masts and brought the best prices of all early forest products. Squared timbers frequently ran 40 to 60 feet long, but spars could run 100 feet or more. Their large size severely tested the skill and ingenuity of those who moved them to streamside for rafting to market. The square-timber and mast trade, which had begun in colonial times, was still strong on the Allegheny Plateau in 1850 and even later in Ontario. Thereafter, it declined rapidly as less skilled but more productive sawlog gangs moved into the woods to feed the rising steam sawmills.

Goosewing axes were the standard hewing tools in the early years, especially in Pennsylvania, but by the nineteenth century the simpler broadax had become almost universal. It was not only easier to make and lent itself more readily to mass production, but the same ax could also be made a left-handed or right-handed model by simply inserting the handle from different ends—something not possible with the goosewing ax. Both patterns were of European origin.

With the passing of the square-timber trade, on-site processing declined sharply. Sawlogs, being much shorter than timbers and spars, could be moved with less preparation. What processing now took place was aimed at making the logs easier to skid. They were limbed, bucked into lengths (usually sixteen feet) that were short enough not to jam during log drives, beveled slightly on the front end so as to reduce drag, and

at some times and places debarked to reduce friction. Much of this work was done with axes. Bucking was done with crosscut saws, and special tools were developed for debarking. With some of the larger species, such as redwood, logs were frequently split before being moved. Mauls, wedges, drills, and even dynamite were employed. Although less so than in the days of the square-timber trade, on-site preparation was still a labor-intensive process carried out largely with hand tools. Not until the advent of the chain saw and later of hydraulic shears was this to change. In the meantime, most strides toward increasing production and reducing costs of logging came not through improvements on-site but through those made in the yarding of logs— the process of hauling logs from the stump to yards or landings where they were gathered for transporting out of the woods by river drives, railroads, log trucks, or other means.

The most noticeable advances in the yarding of logs came with the adoption of better means of motive power. Initially, logs had been moved by manpower applied through block and tackle, jacks, and levers, aided wherever possible by gravity. But by the time logging had moved far enough from the waterways to make yarding a distinct operation, a better source of power was essential. It was found in oxen, which were in use in some woods operations before the end of the colonial period. These huge beasts were little affected by cold or wet; they could live on coarser food and were less excitable than horses; with their cloven hoofs (which were shod, unlike farm oxen) they could work in areas too swampy for horses; and their wooden yokes were inexpensive and easy to make. Above all, oxen were strong.

By the 1830s, horses were replacing oxen because they were faster, more maneuverable, and could work on steeper slopes and on ice roads. Even in the Douglas-fir and redwood forests of the Far West, where the huge size of logs gave oxen an advantage, horses were used more and more for yarding from the 1880s on, while oxen were being relegated to hauling long trains of logs out of the woods over skid roads.

When animal power first began being used in the woods, the hauling distances were relatively short. Landings were located on waterways, and logs were pulled directly to them. As distances became greater, landings were established in the woods; logs were hauled to them and then moved by some intermediate form of transportation (such as sleighs or skid roads) to railroads and waterways.

In the Northeast and Lake States, yarding was initially done only in winter, when ice and snow made skidding easier. The front ends of a few logs—or a single log if it was especially large—would be rolled onto a small sled known as a "go-devil." The trailing ends were left to drag. At first, the go-devil was nothing more than a Y-shaped fork of hardwood, but gradually it became more sophisticated in shape while continuing to serve the same function. With the friction reduced by raising the front end of logs onto the go-devil, horses could pull logs to the landings with relative ease. Go-devils were used mostly on bare ground or when there was little snow cover; when snow was deeper, logs were simply skidded on it.

But these techniques were inadequate for keeping up with the rising demand for sawlogs. A method of hauling logs in summer as well as winter was needed. It was supplied by high-wheel logging, a system using paired giant wheels with a connecting axle and long tongue to which teams of horses could be harnessed. Logs, the front ends of which were suspended from the axle of the big wheels (as these devices were called), could be dragged over rocks, brush, and stumps to the landings. At most, only the simplest of skid roads were needed. Developed in the Lake States in the 1880s, big wheels were subsequently used in relatively flat pine forests in both the South and the Far West. Over the years, equipment gradually improved. Iron wheels replaced wooden ones, thus making wheels twelve feet in diameter—and bigger payloads—practical. An improved tongue, known as the slip-tongue, came into general use about 1910; with it, the front end of logs could be raised from the ground at the start of a haul but let down to drag on the ground, serving as a brake, when on a down grade. When tractors proved their dependability in the 1920s, small units were attached to the big wheels, displacing horses. Various adjustments followed, including hydraulic means of lifting the logs. By 1927, the Red River Lumber Company, which operated in the pineries of northern California, was experimenting with smaller, crawler-type wheels combined with an arched steel axle that maintained the great clearance of the big wheels. So successful were these and similar devices that the logging arch soon replaced the big wheels. By the late 1930s, arched axles were beginning to be replaced by A-frames, although loggers continued to refer to the devices as logging arches. These and similar lineal descendants of the big wheels continue in use to the present day.

But the tractor was not the pioneer in power logging. Steam preceded the internal-combustion engine in the woods; indeed, its introduction was perhaps the greatest single advance in getting out logs. With steam, woods operations vaulted into the age of me-chanical power in which sawmills had already long been operating. The breakthrough came in August 1881 when John Dolbeer, a leading redwood lumberman, tried out what he called a steam donkey in yarding logs near Eureka, California. Dolbeer's original logging machine was little more than a steam-powered spool to which rope was attached for pulling logs to a landing. The engine and spool were mounted on skids so that they could be moved from one site to another. The power of this first donkey engine was so small that several blocks were used to increase pull. But it worked, and with improvements, it revolutionized logging first in the redwoods, then in the Douglas-fir forests of the Pacific Northwest, in the South, and elsewhere. Wire rope (cable) helped make the success possible. The wire rope available in the nineteenth century left a good bit to be desired, but it had greater tensile strength, was less bulky, and stretched less than hemp rope. At first, the steam engine was used only in yarding, but by 1891 it was also being used to replace oxen on the skid roads. The days of draft animals in the woods were clearly counted. By the 1930s, the oxen were virtually gone and horse logging was rapidly becoming an anachronism relegated to tiny operations in stands of small timber—mostly in the South and the Appalachians, where a shortage of investment capital exacerbated the difficulties of shifting to power logging.

Crawler tractors first entered the woods for log hauling, but by the 1920s, with the addition of power-driven winches, they came into widespread use for skidding as well. With gasoline and, after 1931, diesel tractors replacing horses in yarding, loggers in the pine country were following the path toward mechanization just as Dolbeer had in the redwoods decades before. By the late 1930s, diesel tractors were powerful and durable enough to handle the biggest redwood and Douglas-fir logs and the roughest terrain, but they represented not so much a fresh departure as simply one more step along the road of power logging.

Dolbeer's steam donkey had yarded logs by simply pulling them along the ground. Ground-lead logging, as this came to be known, was hindered by stumps, debris, and rocks. It was also destructive of young growth and dangerous to the loggers. In the 1880s, Horace Butters tried a modified system, high-lead logging, in the white pines of Michigan. Instead of dragging logs along the ground toward the steam donkey, Butters ran a haul-back line to the top of a spar tree near the donkey; in this way the front ends of logs being yarded were pulled above the ground so that they cleared many of the obstacles in their path. Butter's experiments met with indifferent success, but the idea quickly reappeared in Louisiana's cypress swamps where ground-lead logging was difficult or impossible. From the South it spread to the West Coast where it soon became popular, especially in the rugged terrain of western Washington, western Oregon, and northern California. The high rigger, who prepared the spar trees and rigged them, emerged with high-lead logging; his work (and frequent antics) 175 feet and more above the ground awed even hardened woodsmen.

One drawback of high-lead logging at first was that it required the presence of an appropriate spar tree near the landing one wished to develop; each time an operation moved to a new landing, a new spar tree had to be found, prepared, and rigged. In the early twentieth century, the Lidgerwood Manufacturing Company was a leader in introducing logging machines equipped with steel spars. These could be prepared for yarding more quickly than spar trees and gave loggers more flexibility in selecting sites for landings.

Another offshoot of high-lead logging was skyline logging. Skylines were cables suspended so that logs being retrieved along them were carried, for at least part of the distance they were being yarded, completely above the ground. Two or more spar trees were often used in rigging skylines. The system could not be used in flat country, but on extremely broken terrain it was sometimes the only feasible way of logging. It was an expensive and difficult method. As diesel tractors improved, offering a practical alternative, skyline logging declined; however, in the 1970s and 1980s it rebounded as road-building costs escalated and logging moved into steeper terrain where the damage to soil and vegetation needed to be minimized. Balloons have been used on some skyline operations, usually where spars were not practical. With or without such adaptation, skyline logging seemed destined for use on major logging operations for a long time to come, even though helicopters have also proved useful in selective logging in rugged country.

The steam engines used in yarding by John Dolbeer and his contemporaries have long since been replaced by diesel engines. Still, skyline logging is a lineal descendant far more closely related to the yarding techniques of Dolbeer than his methods were to those of pioneer loggers who first yarded logs using horses and a primitive go-devil carved from a hardwood tree. The mechanization that Dolbeer introduced into yarding—together with the mechanization of felling brought on by the chain saw—allowed logging to keep pace with the growing demand of ever

more modern sawmills. Most developments since have simply been improvements on the basic system.

FURTHER READING: Nelson C. Brown, *Logging* (1949). Steve Conway, *Logging Practices* (1976), and *Timber Cutting Practices* (1978). Henry J. Kauffman, *American Axes* (1972). Ellis Lucia, "A Lesson from Nature: Joe Cox and His Revolutionary Chain Saw," *Journal of Forest History* 25 (July 1981): 158–165. Donald MacKay, *The Lumberjacks* (1978).

THOMAS R. COX

LOG TRANSPORTATION

The movement of logs from stump to the point of manufacture into lumber is the oldest form of industrial transportation in American history. The expense of transporting logs has always been a major cost factor. Studies made as early as 1870 revealed that the cost of placing a log at the sawmill acounted for one-third to one-half of the total sawlog costs. Log transportation is divided into two distinct phases: skidding, or the movement of logs to a collecting site, and the movement of logs by one or more means from the landing to the mill. Skidding operations usually cover a distance of one-quarter of a mile or less, while the second phase, which forms the subject of this article, is usually measured in miles.

Early in the seventeenth century, Royal Navy captains rafted "Broad Arrow" mast trees down eastern rivers to the sea. Until the Civil War, four to eight oxen (called "bulls" in New England and "steers" in the Far West) hitched single file snaked logs up to 150 feet long to the riverbank. At this "landing," logs were sawed or "bucked" into various lengths with sixteen feet considered the norm. By the 1850s, Lake States loggers were decking logs into rollways. When the props securing the base logs were removed, the whole pile was supposed to roll neatly into the water, spreading out like a giant drop of oil. River drivers, called "pigs" in the Lake States and "hogs" in the Far West, labored from first light to dark. Laymen cast the river drive in a romantic role, but the driver's job was arduous and often wet. Even with four hearty meals a day, drivers' lives were full of hardship and discomfort.

When logs were cut on the upper reaches, streams needed to be improved for log navigation by the removal of obstacles. In 1828, the State of Maine granted authority to build a logging dam (sometimes called a splash, sluice, or flooding dam) in the Little Kezar River. Such dams created an artificial rise in the water. Since many drives coming downstream at the same

John Dolbeer patented this "donkey engine" in 1882, making the power of steam available to pull logs to a central loading site. Forest History Society Photo.

time created problems, Maine allowed loggers on the Kennebec River to organize and choose a master driver to supervise a joint drive. First organized as a primitive form of cooperation, by 1835 the Kennebec association had become a joint stock company driving all logs to the boom which, stretching across the river, stopped the logs, allowing them to be sorted and rafted to various sawmills. As early as 1789, Massachusetts and New Hampshire permitted a boom across the Androscoggin River. The most famous of the eastern booms was the Penobscot near Oldtown, Maine, chartered in 1825. Maine authorized two booms for the Kennebec River by 1831, and between 1836 and 1856 eight others were permitted there. The Susquehanna Boom Corporation of Williamsport, Pennsylvania, was incorporated in 1846, and the boom across the Hudson River at Glens Falls, New York, was in operation in 1851. When Maine men migrated to the Lake States, they constructed many booms modeled on the one at Penobscot. After the Civil War, almost every major river running out of the northeastern pineries had one or more booms across it. In 1896, there were twenty-eight major booms in Michigan, Wisconsin, and Minnesota. These boom companies spent a total of $2,367,691 on channel improvements that year and were handling more than 20 million logs each season.

Maine loggers attempted to solve the problem of log ownership by chopping identifying "bark marks" into the side of each log. Every owner had one or more specific marks, such as "S notch bar combine" or "Girdle Crowfoot Cross A." As the industry grew, the limited number of easily made bark-mark designs led the Michigan legislature in 1859 to enact a law requiring owners to mark the ends of the logs with a heavy marking hammer. These marks were registered to deter log "lifting" or "log rustling."

Lumbermen learned early that there was a difference between the number of logs entering a driving stream and the number reaching the boom. This "shrinkage," caused primarily by sunk or stranded logs, has been computed to have been 10 percent in the rivers of Montana, about the same on the Mississippi, Cumberland, and Tennessee rivers, 25 to 40 percent for Pennsylvania hardwoods, and 20 to 30 percent for southern yellow pine. Most Lake States lumbermen allowed for a 10 percent loss in white and Norway pine.

One well-publicized aspect of log driving was the jam, wherein some logs might strand on a snag or rock, or in a sharp bend, causing others to pile up. Infrequently, a jam would take weeks or months to clear. Legend held that somewhere at the bottom was the first log to hang up, which had caused the mischief, and if this "key log" could be found and removed, the whole jam would break.

At the boom, a collection and sorting site used by several mills, most logs were formed into rafts. Before

Only three teams of horses are needed to pull heavily loaded sleds over iced roads in Minnesota, 1904. Forest Service Photo.

the Civil War, river rafts were constructed rigidly with the parallel logs fastened to a cross log to create a "string," usually sixteen feet wide. A number of strings similarly fastened together formed a strong raft. Sometime in the 1880s, Lake States lumbermen constructed rafts more quickly and cheaply by "brailing." Floating logs were encased within overlapping boomsticks. A quarter-inch wire, stretched tightly across the brail from boomstick to boomstick, made the raft tighter and more compact.

In the northeastern United States, many driving streams ran through shallow lakes. Maine loggers solved this slack water problem by roping logs end-to-end into a large circle. This formed a boom around a free floating mass of logs which was towed across the lake by a "headworks" raft, upon which was mounted a winch or capstan. Three or four hundred feet of rope attached to an anchor allowed the power of the

capstan to kedge the boom across the lake. Southern loggers evolved other forms of rafts. Many of these were constructed by fastening strings or brails together stem to stern, allowing a hinging space between strings, and the long, spineless mass floated downstream guided by boats at head and rear.

As log transportation became more mechanized after the Civil War, the first major change was the bucking of tree trunks into sawlogs in the forest and their transportation to the landing on sleighs. This entailed a larger capital expense for road building, logging sleighs, and snowplows. Rut cutters were perfected and sprinkling sleighs created ice roads. West Coast lumbermen developed the skid road; relatively short logs were laid crosswise to the line of travel and oxen pulled the long trees downslope. Skidroads were expensive to build and could not reach all of the timber, even when the logs were bucked into shorter lengths and tied together end-to-end to form a "turn." By the 1850s, West Coast loggers were developing tramways and pole roads to move logs to the skidroad. In 1854, there was a reported twenty miles of tramway near Eureka, California. In 1852, a steam railroad was hauling logs to the Tioga River in New York using wooden rails, and about the same time a California pole road was equipped with steam power. On the eve of the Civil War, numerous loggers were experimenting with homemade steam locomotives on pole roads and tramways, none of which were particularly successful.

The first steam logging railroad using iron rails may have been the short-lived Arapahoe, Jefferson, and South Park Railways which, in 1868, hauled railroad timbers to Denver for the building of the parent Denver Pacific Railroad. This was followed in 1871 by the California lumbering firm of Smith and Dougherty in the redwoods. The Gualala Mill Company used a steam locomotive for redwood hauling a year later; the Humboldt Bay and Mad River Railroad began hauling in 1874; and the nearby South Bay Railroad started in 1875.

The droughts of 1872 and 1876 left millions of feet of timber stranded in Michigan streams, and lumbermen searched for alternative means of transportation. As one result, W. Scott Gerrish and his associates incorporated the Lake George and Muskegon River Railroad with ten miles of track laid with twenty-five-pound iron rails, two locomotives, and fifty logging cars. It started hauling a half million feet of logs a day in 1877 and was an instant success. Its first year's earnings returned 28 percent on the investment, and its success was widely publicized in the lumber trade journals. Only ten years later, the *Northwestern Lumberman* reported that there were 422 logging railroads in the nation, operating 486 locomotives on 3,042 miles of track, Michigan led with 89 railroads, Pennsylvania had 45, and Texas was third with 34. More than half of these were narrow-gauge roads, but by 1900 most logging railroads had standard-gauge tracks and equipment.

By 1870, some Lake States lumbermen made "milling-in-transit" contracts with nonlogging common carriers. Sawlogs were hauled to the mill at a cheap rate provided the lumber was shipped to market on the same carrier. Some millers extended the life of their sawmills by several years in the closing days of Lake States pine lumbering by sawing milling-in-transit logs often brought from as far as 200 miles away.

Steam power stimulated improvements in the more

A Shay locomotive, the woods workhorse of the railroad era, pulls a string of cars loaded with hardwood logs through West Virginia. Gears rather than pistons turned driver wheels, providing even power and the ability to negotiate the sharp curves common to mountainous country. Forest History Society Photo.

A caravan of trucks carry mammoth Douglas-fir logs through North Bend, Washington. American Forest Institute Photo.

traditional modes of log transport. In the early 1870s, a sleigh load of logs ran about 3,000 board feet. Wider sleighs and improved ice roads allowed an increase in average sleigh loads to about 8,000 board feet by the end of the century. Record sleigh loads included one in Michigan with 30,068 board feet in 1884, an 1892 Minnesota load of 31,480 feet, and, during that year, 36,000 feet hauled near Hinckley, Minnesota.

Since the 1840s, lumbermen had used steamboats to tow log rafts across Lakes St. Croix and Pepin. By the Civil War, they were advancing the steamboat one-half of its length into the rear of the raft, but oarsmen were still needed on the bow of the raft. By running a line from each of two capstans on the steamboat to the stern corners of the raft and varying the angle of the steamboat to the raft, the boat could act as a rudder. In

1864, Cyrus Bradley thus used the side wheeler *Union* to move a raft 250 miles to Clinton, Iowa. In 1869, R. A. Young introduced the steam capstan on his *Minnesota* and placed the towboat at the stern of the raft rather than partially in the raft. At that time, there were twenty-one raft boats on the upper Mississippi.

The proliferation of bridges, each a deadly enemy of oar-steered rafts, encouraged the rapid increase of raft boats on the Mississippi. Before 1868, raftsmen encountered only two bridges between the mouth of the St. Croix and St. Louis. By 1874, there were ten. That year, Chauncey Lamb invented the double-spooled steam winch with which one operator could control the relationship between the raft boat and the raft. Within three years, 95 percent of the Mississippi River log rafts were towed, and raft oarsmen were obsolete. The last major improvement in Mississippi River rafting was the use of a bowboat lashed across the head of the raft, which came into common use by the 1890s. The bowboat could steer the raft by coming ahead, stopping, or reversing. In 1887, ninety raft boats plied the river. Six years later, there were only sixty-three, though they were handling 25 percent more logs. The largest single-log raft, covering almost ten acres of water, was towed the 169 miles from Lynxville, Wisconsin, to Rock Island, Illinois, by Weyerhaeuser and Denkmann's *F. C. A. Denkmann* in 1896 with the *H. C. Brockman* as bowboat. It contained 2.25 million board feet of lumber. A double log raft (literally one raft lying on top of another raft) towed by the *J. W. Van Sant* with the *Lydia Van Sant* as bowboat contained more than 3 million board feet.

Until the 1880s, attempts to raft logs on the Great Lakes had been unsuccessful and transporting them in huge barges proved too expensive. Benjamin Boutell, of Bay City, Michigan, developed the "bag boom," using logs three feet or more in diameter, bored through the centers and strung on a chain. When towed, the boom trapped the floating logs and formed the shape of a balloon or bag. Bag booms were used to tow pulpwood logs across Lake Superior until 1963.

The development of salt water log rafting paralleled events on the Great Lakes. Early experiments at ocean log rafting on both the Atlantic and Pacific coasts of North America had been failures, the logs washing up on beaches and causing havoc with shipping. In the mid-1890s, after several unsuccessful tries, Hugh Robertson managed to get a cigar-shaped log raft from Coos Bay, Oregon, to San Francisco. Working for Pope and Talbot, Robertson monopolized the Pacific coast rafting until 1906 when Simon Benson designed a raft which was to be towed from the Columbia River to San Diego, California. A cradle or frame of logs was constructed in the water, then carefully filled with wired and chained sixty-foot logs. Thirty-five feet wide and 835 feet long, the Benson raft drew twenty-eight feet of water and contained 3 million board feet of lumber. Until World War II, several Benson rafts left the Columbia River for California ports each summer.

Steam-powered traction machines first replaced the ox and horse in yarding and skidding and were later found to have other uses in log transportation. In 1883, Horace Butters, of Ludington, Michigan, patented the first stationary steam skidder, and others, such as the Dolbeer, the Clyde, the American, and the monstrous Lidgerwood, followed. These machines could skid logs, haul logs through the air, load logs, and jockey railroad log cars into position, as necessary.

An unsuccessful steam crawler was built in Erie, Pennsylvania, as early as 1868; eight years later, Martin Mower introduced an unsuccessful steampowered iceboat and George Christian invented a walking beam sled. Grover and Chandler built a steam crawler tractor in 1888 but went bankrupt the following year. Alvin O. Lombard of Maine in 1900 began building a steam-powered log hauler with crawler treads and skids in front for steering on ice roads. This Lombard hauler remained in production for seventeen years. In 1907, the Phoenix Manufacturing Company of Eau

Log jam in Minnesota, 1937. Forest Service Photo.

A McGiffert loader was a self-propelled railroad device that could rest on skids and hoist its wheels to allow empty flatcars to pass underneath. American Forest Institute Photo.

Claire, Wisconsin, also produced a successful steam log hauler.

Two forms of transportation generally used to connect skidding sites to some other major form of log transportation were chutes and flumes. Chutes (or slides) had been used for centuries in Europe. In America they were employed in steep terrain and made usually of logs, laid parallel, with hewn faces for the easy sliding of logs, poles, ties, and bolts. Where the slope was not steep enough for movement by gravity alone, the logs were pulled along by horses, donkey engines, or, later, tractors. Earthen chutes, iced in winter, were used in Canada, New York, and the southern Appalachians. Log chutes were built extensively in Idaho, Montana, and British Columbia. During the early twentieth century, an estimated average of 250 miles of chutes was constructed each year in the Inland Empire, but they were gradually superseded by crawler tractors and trucks. Flumes were board troughs, generally V-shaped, carrying running water, and often built on high trestles in order to maintain an even gradient. Flumes carried logs, sawed lumber, crossties, bolts, poles, and posts from the woods to sawmill ponds, railroad sidings, or drivable streams. J. W. Haines developed the flume to transport lumber from the Sierra forests to Nevada's Comstock mines. Hundreds of miles of flumes were subsequently built in California's Sierra Nevada in the 1870s and afterward, although these usually transported rough-sawed lumber and square timber rather than logs. In the early twentieth century, flumes were chiefly important in logging in Idaho and other parts of the northern Rockies, but others were employed in eastern Canada, the Adirondacks, the southern Appalachians, the Pacific Northwest, and the Sierra Nevada.

The Michigan droughts that caused W. Scott Gerrish to build a logging railroad also stimulated Ephraim S. Shay of Haring, Michigan, to experiment with steam power. In 1880, the first lopsided Shay locomotive was built by the Lima Machine Works. Its piston engines, mounted vertically ahead of the cab on the right side of the boiler, powered an exposed gear and shaft system which drove the truck wheels. The first Climax locomotive, also gear-driven, was built in 1888 at Corry, Pennsylvania. Pistons were mounted on each side, somewhat like the traditional rod-piston locomotive, but tilted at about a forty-five-degree angle. A third geared steam logging locomotive was developed by Charles Heisler and first manufactured in Erie, Pennsylvania, in 1894. The Heisler had a pair of pistons opposed in a "V" shape with the boiler in the middle. Generally, the geared locomotives were used by small logging railroads or on the spur lines of the larger railroads. Mainline locomotives were usually the rod piston type as used by most railroads. Almost 1,000 Climax locomotives were built before the works folded in 1928; fewer Heislers were made, although manufacturing continued until 1945; the last Shay, number 2,761, was outshopped in 1945. These geared locomotives had a host of competitors and imitators, ranging from the fairly successful cogwheel Blackman to the so-called Willamette Shay manufactured between 1922 and 1929, but none was as popular as the Shay.

The rapid expansion of logging railroads after 1892 increased the rate at which forests were devoured. Water-transported logs declined in numbers, and in 1894 Michigan's Tittabawassee Boom Company ceased operations after handling more than 10 billion board feet of lumber in logs. Logging ceased on the Black River in 1897, and on the Chippewa in 1905, and by World War I, Mississippi River log rafting was over and every major boom in the Lake States was closed.

The logging railroad was the heart of log transportation from 1900 to 1940. Just as the logging railroad hastened the demise of the Lake States pineries, on the West Coast it enabled the lumbermen to triple their cut in twenty years. California had a total of about 270 logging railroads, Oregon about 450, and Washington about 1,000, the longest being the 194 miles of track that Weyerhaeuser started operating out of Longview in 1929. In that year, 1,000 steam locomotives hauled logs on 7,000 miles of track in the Western states, but the Great Depression, the widespread use of the internal combustion engine, and other changing conditions in the woods cut both figures by half in less than a decade. Miles of rails and hundreds of logging cars and locomotives were sold on the world market and, when that marked dried up, to the scrap metal market. Nevertheless, some roads continued to run, and as late as 1980 Weyerhaeuser still operated 55 miles of logging railroad from Longview, 29 miles at South Bay, and 10.3 miles at Chehalis, all in Washington.

Logging trucks were in the forest by 1913 and a two-wheeled semitrailer was in use two years later. As truck technology improved, their use expanded. In the 1920s, many logging operators built truck roads instead of logging railroad spurs. At the beginning of the Great Depression, trucks were hauling an estimated 6 percent of the logs cut; fifteen years later, they were hauling a majority of the logs. By 1938, the logging truck had helped make Oregon the principal lumber-producing state, for only trucks could reach many areas of the Cascades and Coast Range effectively.

Alongside the truck, another internal combustion-powered machine entered the woods: the crawler tractor. Many of these were employed in skidding, but they also pulled wagon trains of logs over primitive roads. By 1922, there were 2,000 crawler tractors, in some twenty models, clanking through the trees. The most popular was the "Caterpillar," a registered trade name of the Holt Manufacturing Company which became the Caterpillar Tractor Company. The name became generic so that all crawler tractors came to be called "cats," the crawler operator the "cat skinner," and his assistant the "cat chaser."

By the 1940s, the diesel engine had largely replaced the gasoline engine in both trucks and tractors. The small one-man or one-family logging operation had been almost eliminated after about 1874 by the high cost of stumpage and the capital investments required by logging railroads and mechanized logging equipment. During the 1930s, with the aid of the truck and the crawler tractor, the small logger began to reappear. Stimulated by the chain saw, rising lumber prices, and the availability of military surplus trucks at bargain prices after World War II, the small logger pursued scattered clumps of sawable timber that had been previously uneconomical to log.

The increasing impetus of environmental considerations since 1960, the requirement that loggers on national forests must submit environmental impact statements, and court challenges to logging have affected skidding rather than log transportation, but at least one suit (*Black Bear Ranch* v. *United States*,

1971), in addition to charging that environmental damage would be done by a proposed logging road, alleged that a logging road would "impair the aesthetic enjoyment" of the forest. By 1980, a number of interesting experiments were being conducted with log transportation methods intended to have less effect on the environment. One was a portable monorail system that could transport logs at the rate of twenty-five miles per hour. The Canadian forest service has experimented with an air cushion vehicle which would carry a log raft six feet above the ground surface. Balloons and helicopters have frequently been used to carry high-grade timber from normally inaccessible locations.

From the beginning of large-scale commercial lumbering, loggers have met resistance from other societal elements over the use of the common environment. Historically, the courts had ruled that all produce of a region enjoyed equal rights in a navigable stream. This meant that log drivers had as much right to river use as did steamboats, pleasure craft, and fishermen. By World War II, this attitude was changing. Lumbermen were losing power in society, while sportsmen and environmentalists were gaining influence. In the fall of 1957, two Coos River logging dams were burned in Oregon. They may have been the last active logging dams west of Maine in the United States.

FURTHER READING: There has been no historical treatment of log transportation on a national basis. Some works deal with it regionally, such as Alfred G. Hempstead, *The Penobscot Boom and the Development of the West Branch of the Penobscot River for Log Driving* (1931), and William G. Rector, *Log Transportation in the Lake States Lumber Industry, 1840–1918* (1953). Regional, state, and corporate lumber histories contain pertinent information; some, like Lynwood Carranco and John T. Labbe, *Logging the Redwoods* (1975), are transportation oriented. Kramer Adams, *Logging Railroads of the West* (1961), and Michael Koch, *Steam & Thunder in the Timber: Saga of the Forest Railroads* (1979), are both comprehensive treatments of their topics. The various editions of Ralph Clement Bryant, *Logging*, starting with the 1913 edition, and Steve Conway, *Logging Practices: Principles of Timber Harvesting Systems* (1976), are valuable. Nelson Courtlandt Brown, *Logging: Transportation* (1936), gives a good survey of methods in use during the early twentieth century.

WILLIAM G. RECTOR

LONG, GEORGE SMITH (1853–1930)

Operating manager of the Weyerhaeuser Timber Company from 1900 to 1930, George S. Long was one of the most influential lumbermen in the history of the Pacific Northwest. Born in Indiana on December 3,

1853, Long began working in his father's Indianapolis lumberyard while still in high school. He worked for a number of years in various lumbering operations in the Midwest and in the South. Long became sales manager of the Northwestern Lumber Company of Eau Claire, Wisconsin, in the early 1880s, serving in that position until the end of the century. In 1900, Frederick Weyerhaeuser and his associates (*see* WEYERHAEUSER FAMILY) purchased 900,000 acres of western Washington timber from the Northern Pacific Railroad and formed the Weyerhaeuser Timber Company. Long, with a reputation for hard work and personal integrity, was hired to manage the company, his salary supplemented with loans for the purchase of stock.

Arriving in Tacoma, Long admitted to lack of knowledge about Pacific Northwest timber stands and to inexperience in the purchase of timber. Nevertheless, he set to work to familiarize himself with the region and to add to the firm's already immense holdings. Blocking in the missing sections within the boundaries of the Northern Pacific purchase through acquisition of settlers' claims and additional tracts of railroad timber, Long increased Weyerhaeuser holdings to 1.3 million acres by mid-1903. Included in these transactions were extensive timberlands in southern Oregon and northern California.

Long also supervised a gradual move by Weyerhaeuser into the production of lumber. A small sawmill was purchased in Everett in 1902. A large new mill was eventually built on the site and, during Long's tenure, plants were erected at Snoqualmie Falls east of Seattle, at Longview on the Columbia River, and at Klamath Falls in southern Oregon. By the early 1920s, Weyerhaeuser's position as the largest owner of timberland was complemented by the leading position in manufacturing.

Long's leadership role in the Pacific Northwest industry resulted from factors other than the strength of Weyerhaeuser. Tall and lanky and with an ever present cigar, he was highly respected by all lumbermen. His word, it was said, was the equivalent of a signed contract, and he was always willing to spend time and money on the welfare of the industry. Long was the leading force in the West Coast Lumbermen's Association, securing the services of former FOREST SERVICE Chief William B. GREELEY as head of that organization. Long was also active in the Western Pine Association and in the WESTERN FORESTRY AND CONSERVATION ASSOCIATION.

Of most importance, Long worked for the adoption of conservation measures, recognizing that waste reduced the value of timber investments. Following disastrous forest fires in 1902, he secured the first effective fire-protection measures from the legislatures of Washington and Oregon. He also supported Gifford PINCHOT's campaign for fire prevention and tax reforms to encourage the practice of forestry, breaking with Pinchot only when the latter began to advocate federal regulation of cutting practices on private land.

After three decades of building Weyerhaeuser and providing leadership for the industry, Long died on August 22, 1930, while on an inspection trip to Klamath Falls. His death came in the first stages of the Great Depression, a crisis during which his abilities would be sorely missed by both his company and his industry. One of the great problems during those years was the absence of any figure with the ability to unify conflicting interests through the force of personality.

ROBERT E. FICKEN

LOUISIANA FORESTS

Over 23 million acres or 85 percent of Louisiana's land area was originally forested, largely in longleaf, slash, loblolly, and shortleaf pine. Broad belts along the lowlands of the Mississippi, Red, Ouachita, Pearl, and other rivers were covered with oak-gum-cypress forest. About 190 species of trees were native to the state.

Louisiana cypress (or baldcypress, *Taxodium distichum*) was logged by the French as early as the late eighteenth century, both for domestic construction and for export to the Caribbean. Antebellum Louisiana had an active lumber industry in both pine and cypress, although it was tiny by later standards. As late as 1879, when 133,472,000 board feet were cut in the state, Louisiana produced less lumber than any other Southern state. Perhaps the most notable incident in Louisiana lumbering up to this time was the Calcasieu "Log War" of 1877–1878, a dispute between local loggers and federal timber agents over the right to cut on public lands.

Two developments led to large-scale pine logging. Beginning in the 1870s, Louisiana was crossed with railroads linking it to Northern and midwestern markets. Then, foreseeing the exhaustion of the white pine around the Great Lakes, northern lumbermen invaded the South. In Louisiana they found that large blocks of fairly pure yellow pine stands were available cheaply, and the gentle terrain and climate were well suited to logging. Isaac Stephenson, Jr., James D. Lacey, and other Michigan lumbermen made Calcasieu Parish into Louisiana's first great lumber center by 1884. In the 1890s, operators of yards in the plains states, such as

Robert A. Long of the Long-Bell Lumber Company and Samuel H. Fullerton, began acquiring sawmills in the Louisiana pineries. A Pennsylvania lumberman, Charles W. GOODYEAR, opened the Great Southern sawmill at Bogalusa in 1908. Two other Pennsylvanians, Henry J. Lutcher and G. Bedell Moore, invested first in Texas pine starting in 1876 and then in Louisiana cypress during the 1880s. The cypress industry expanded chiefly after about 1890 when the pullboat was developed and extensive cutting of the swamp-dwelling trees became practical. Leading cypress magnates included native Southerners such as Robert H. Downman and Frank B. Williams.

During the first quarter of the twentieth century, the forests of Louisiana were largely cut out, and many of the pine operators moved to the West Coast. The Long-Bell Lumber Company, for example, began serious acquisition of Oregon and California timberland in 1918 and during the 1920s established its principal mill at Longview, Washington. In all but two of the seventeen years from 1905 through 1921, Louisiana ranked second among American states in total reported lumber production, trailing only Washington. (In 1914, Louisiana ranked in first place, and in 1920 it fell to third, behind Oregon.) Louisiana's peak reported production of 4,161,560,000 board feet was reached in 1913. This included 74 percent yellow pine, 18 percent cypress, and 8 percent hardwood. In addition to lumber, hardwood supplied staves, crossties, and distillation products. Turpentine production was a significant secondary use of pinelands.

Logging left vast areas of the state as blackened stump-wastes. Especially in the longleaf pine section of western Louisiana, residents customarily burned the woods to improve pasturage, preventing timber regrowth and diminishing wildlife. At least as early as 1904, Henry E. Hardtner of the Urania Lumber Company recognized the need for reforestation, protection, and tax incentives, but his ideas were too advanced for most of his fellow mill owners. Hardtner acquired and protected cutover lands in central Louisiana, depending upon the loblolly pine to reseed itself. Influenced in part by Hardtner, the Great Southern Lumber Company in 1920 began planting on its longleaf pinelands of eastern Louisiana what eventually grew into the largest privately owned man-made forest. Few other firms had any interest in following similar policies, however, and thousands of cutover acres reverted to the state for nonpayment of taxes.

Possibly at the urging of Henry Hardtner, Louisiana passed its first forestry legislation in 1904. This act would have established a state department of forestry, but lack of funding left it ineffective. In

1908, influenced by the White House, Louisiana created a Commission on Natural Resources with Hardtner as chairman. In response to the commission's recommendations, the state in 1910 created a permanent conservation commission (with Hardtner again as chairman) and passed the Timber Conservation Contract Law which authorized the state to enter into reforestation contracts with private owners, lowered property taxes on lands covered by such contracts, and imposed a severance tax upon harvesting. Hardtner's Urania Lumber Company signed the first contracts in 1913, but even so, few other owners were persuaded until the state set up an active forestry department in 1917.

Land acquisition began in 1923 for Louisiana's only state-owned forest, Alexander State Forest, located near Woodworth. Nevertheless, with limited funds and political interference, state leadership in forestry remained weak until 1940 when Louisiana reorganized its Division of Forestry. In 1944, constitutional amendments separated the Forestry Department from the Department of Conservation and allowed police juries, the local governing bodies, to tax land to support fire protection. The state forester henceforth was removed from politics and appointed not by the governor but by a forestry commission. Under James E. Mixon, state forester for the next thirty years, Louisiana forestry rose to a position of leadership in the South with advances in technology, foresty practices, fire fighting, and tree nursery production. A new state constitution in 1977 changed the Forestry Commission to the Office of Forestry under the Secretary of Natural Resources, but it retained the seven forestry commissioners. The state forester thereafter had the title of assistant secretary of natural resources.

Louisiana has also preserved a small state park system under legislation of 1934. By 1975, it totaled only 24,000 acres.

Federal forestry programs in Louisiana started when the U. S. FOREST SERVICE established its Southern Forest Experiment Station in New Orleans in 1921. The federal government became directly involved in forestland administration and reforestation after 1928 when, due largely to the urging of Caroline Dormon, it established three purchase units in the pinelands of central Louisiana under the CLARKE-MCNARY ACT. With additional lands, these units became the basis of the Kisatchie National Forest established in 1930. By 1978, the Forest Service owned 597,000 acres in the state. Another federal program that made a vital contribution to forest conservation in the 1930s was the CIVILIAN CONSERVATION CORPS which built fire towers, roads, and telephone lines, and suppressed fires and established tree nurseries and plantations.

Forestry education in the state dates from 1911 when Louisiana State University at Baton Rouge offered its first forestry course. In 1917, Yale University began sending its forestry students to Urania for field experience. LSU's School of Forestry began in 1925, making Louisiana the second Southern state to establish a forestry school. Louisiana Polytechnic Institute in Ruston (later renamed Louisiana Tech University) began its School of Agriculture and Forestry in 1946. McNeese State University started a forestry curriculum in its school of agriculture in 1954.

By the 1950s, Louisiana had 16.1 million acres of forested land, of which almost all was classed as commercial. Timber conservation contracts were in force with over fifty landowners, and annual forest growth was nearly double the annual timber harvest. Lumber production was only around 800 million board feet yearly, but pulpwood production of 1.5 million cords placed the state third in the nation. Most of the woodland was in the hands of small owners, with an average holding of less than 100 acres. By the 1970s, Louisiana was harvesting its second forest and planting its third. Timber was the state's major crop, accounting for 65 percent of its total agricultural income. With the return of pine timber and well-managed, multiple-use forests, there was a return of wildlife. Only in the hardwood bottomlands had the forestry outlook remained dim. Thousands of acres in the Mississippi delta had been cleared for soybeans, with dual loss of timber and wildlife. In 1977, there were only 14.6 million acres of forestland in the state, and about 90 percent of that was capable of commercial production. Over 13.5 million acres, 93 percent of the commercial forest, was in private ownership.

FURTHER READING: Anna C. Burns, *A History of the Louisiana Forestry Commission*, Louisiana Studies Institute Monograph Series no. 1 (1968); "Henry E. Hardtner: Louisiana's First Conservationist," *Journal of Forest History* 22 (Apr. 1978): 78-85; and "Frank B. Williams, Cypress Lumber King," *Journal of Forest History* 24 (July 1980): 127-133. "Golden Anniversary Forestry Edition," *Forest & People* 13 (First Quarter, 1963). Ervin Mancil, "Pullboat Logging," *Journal of Forest History* 24 (July 1980): 135-141. Donald J. Millet, "The Lumber Industry of 'Imperial' Calcasieu," *Louisiana History* 7 (Winter 1966): 51-69. George A. Stokes, "Lumbering and Western Louisiana Cultural Landscapes," *Annals of the Association of American Geographers* 47 (Sept. 1957): 250-266.

ANNA C. BURNS

LOYAL LEGION OF LOGGERS AND LUMBERMEN

When the United States entered World War I, federal civil and military officials feared that the army would have to keep a huge security force—estimated at a million men—in the Pacific Northwest in order to control Industrial Workers of the World (IWW) members. After both IWW and AFL timber workers struck for the eight-hour day and union recognition in the summer of 1917, odds seemed high that little of the essential spruce for aircraft and Douglas-fir for ships would be produced.

After conferences with Felix Frankfurter and Walter Lippmann, special assistants, respectively, to the attorney general and the secretary of war, the army sent to the West Coast a veteran of the Philippine occupation, Colonel Bryce P. Disque. He met there with lumbermen, including Mark Reed, and with University of Washington economist Carleton Parker. The latter was especially important in convincing Disque that "wobblies" were less ideologically radical, as most lumber operators claimed, than they were violently opposed to abysmal and unsafe conditions of life and labor.

Disque initially hoped to solve the labor problem with a new army unit, the SPRUCE PRODUCTION DIVISION (SPD), which would furnish soldier-lumberjacks to the logging camps. The SPD would thus give the army both a production force and a security reserve, though the latter was tiny compared to original estimates of what might be needed. The inability of the SPD to provide adequate manpower fast enough led to Disque's reliance on the Loyal Legion of Loggers and Lumbermen (4L), a cooperative effort among the army, lumbermen, and labor, as his primary instrument for reform in the woods and mills and for expansion of production.

Despite opposition from many operators and from AFL organizers, the 4L quickly made itself felt. Its staff appealed to patriotism and self-interest and won from employers the eight-hour day and working conditions at least equal to those endured by army privates. Employers gained production stability, a guaranteed market, and government aid in controlling dissident workers.

As Parker and others had argued, the wobblies proved to be remarkably susceptible to environmental improvements. They relished the attention of army doctors, dentists, and dieticians, and they welcomed the introduction of safety appliances into camps, not caring that it was cost-plus contracts that made operators willing to cater to workers' concerns. Many 4L members were wobblies, but almost all bought war bonds. Many formerly alienated migrant workers assumed unaccustomed respectability, joined churches, incurred mortgages, and began to vote. Lumber production soared.

Commentators hailed the 4L as a commendable ra-

tionalization of a long-chaotic industry. Canada was ready to imitate the experiment at the time of the Armistice. Nevertheless, in early 1919 the army dropped its connection with the 4L. Employers picked it up and during the 1920s made it into a barely concealed coalition of company unions. With the Depression and New Deal, many wartime 4L policies, including the eight-hour day and rigorous safety standards, became part of the National Industrial Recovery Act and other labor reform legislation. Already moribund because of competition from other unions, the 4L suffered a fatal blow when the Wagner-Connery National Labor Relations Act of 1935 outlawed company unions. Before the United States entered World War II, the 4L had died, largely unmourned. For its time, it was an innovative, moderate choice among generally unsatisfactory policy alternatives.

FURTHER READING: Robert E. Ficken, *Lumber and Politics: The Career of Mark E. Reed* (1979), chaps. 1-2. Harold M. Hyman, *soldiers and Spruce: Origins of the Loyal Legion of Loggers and Lumbermen: The Army's Labor Union of World War I* (1963). Robert L. Tyler, "The United States Government as Union Organizer: The Loyal Legion of Loggers and Lumbermen," *Mississippi Valley Historical Review* 47 (Dec. 1960): 434-451.

HAROLD M. HYMAN

LUMBER DISTRIBUTION AND MARKETING

Throughout much of the nation's history, lumber was the universal, indispensable building material. Demand for lumber was virtually insatiable, and the supply was considered unlimited. Expanding cities in the East as well as towns and farms on the prairies required enormous supplies of wood for nearly every form of public and private construction. Wood served such diverse and mundane purposes as picket fences, boardwalks, paving blocks, windmills, pails, tubs, farm implements, and furniture. Distributing and marketing this fundamental product during the so-called Age of Wood was relatively simple. Markets for most wood products were tied to local watersheds, and lumber shipped across regional bounds was confined almost entirely to one species—white pine. Price and quality were the two major competitive elements, with price clearly the most important. As markets broadened and new species became available in the post-Civil War period, more sophisticated marketing mechanisms developed. By the 1870s, manufacturers and wholesalers had begun placing notices in the few trade journals, sending mailing price lists to retailers, and handing out promotional cigars. In the ensuing decades, a nationwide system of marketing and distribution emerged.

Lumber is being loaded piece by piece for shipment by rail to distant markets. American Forest Institute Photo.

Throughout the colonial period, lumber markets remained primitive. Lumber for domestic use was typically sold directly from the innumerable small mills scattered throughout the colonies. Exports consisted mainly of raw or semiprocessed materials, such as squared pine timber, masts, and spars from New England; hickory hoops, white oak staves, and oak timber from the mid-Atlantic region; and longleaf pine timber and NAVAL STORES from the Southern colonies. Such commodities were generally handled by English or Scottish factors or large colonial merchant houses with connections overseas.

Marketing techniques changed little in the first half of the nineteenth century. Lumber, in effect, sold itself, since transactions were simple and relatively local. The process of marketing wood began at the sawmill located on an interior river. Here the rough, green, and ungraded lumber was assembled into "cribs" or rafts and floated downriver to urban centers or port cities. The sawmill owner might accompany the load in order to bargain directly with the wholesale distributor. The wholesaler dominated the market; he sorted the green lumber, dried it, finished it in his planing mill, and stored the product in his sheds. By advancing money under contract for a future delivery, he supplied the sawmill owner and logger with operating

capital. In addition, he extended credit to retailers. Larger wholesalers acquired their own retail yards. Thus, the wholesaler was a central figure with the rest of the industry dependent upon him.

By the early nineteenth century, at least one species—white pine—had entered markets beyond local watersheds. Key distributing points for white pine lumber shifted with changes in the accessibility of the timber itself. In the early decades of the century, Bangor, Maine, reigned as the premier lumber city, to be followed by Albany, New York. Construction of the Hudson River-Lake Champlain canal system in the 1820s and 1830s and the beginning of log driving on the rivers of Pennsylvania and New York brought new sources of white pine to eastern markets, first from the western sections of New York and Pennsylvania and then from the Lake States. New sources of supply enhanced the importance of distributing points, such as Albany and Tonawanda, New York; Williamsport, Pennsylvania; and later Burlington, Vermont. Throughout the period, the huge urban lumber markets of Boston, New York, Philadephia, and Baltimore established prices for domestic lumber.

As lumbermen moved into the Lake States, Chicago emerged as the nation's leading lumber market. For a period of fifty years after the Civil War, Chicago remained the foremost wholesale distribution center for both pine and hardwoods. As early as 1848, when the Illinois and Michigan Canal connected the city with the Mississippi, Chicago had thirty-five lumber dealers. The city's board of trade, also founded that year, dealt mostly in lumber. By 1871, the year of the great fire, over 100 lumberyards handled a total of 1 billion board feet. In 1885, Chicago boasted 115 pine dealers, 32 hardwood dealers, and 137 millwork and other lumber manufacturing plants. Lumber receipts reached a peak of 2.25 billion board feet in 1892, when Chicago distributed one-fourth of the pine lumber produced in the Lake States.

About 90 percent of Chicago's lumber supply in the 1880s arrived via Lake Michigan on cargo ships, and extensive wharf facilities were developed to handle it. Ships carrying lumber paid rental fees for dock space and additional fees for measuring, tallying, and grading lumber. Commission dealers met the ships and bid on the lumber. Water shipments to Chicago peaked in 1882 and were gradually replaced by rail shipments. By 1913, waterborne traffic amounted to less than 10 percent of the lumber handled, while thirteen railroads radiated from Chicago, connecting it with nearly every part of the Midwest. In 1869, lumbermen organized their own board of trade and negotiated advantageous railroad rates. Special "through" rates from Chicago, along with lumber shipped from Mississippi River sawmills, soon turned Kansas City into a major lumber outlet for the Prairie States. After creation of the Interstate Commerce Commission in 1887, attempts to pressure railroads to "equalize" freight rates brought only limited success or outright failure.

Around the turn of the century, other species and regions began invading the Chicago-dominated white pine market. The first Chicago yard dealing in southern yellow pine opened in 1884; the first sale of Pacific Coast Douglas-fir and western redcedar shingles came three years later. Meanwhile, the supply of Lake States white pine dwindled, and railroads built east and west of the pineries of Wisconsin and Minnesota bypassed Chicago as a distributing center.

Integration of lumber manufacturing and distribution at the headwaters of the Mississippi in the 1880s and 1890s also served to erode the position of the Chicago wholesale dealer. Typical of the growing presence of the sawmill owner in the industry was Orrin H. Ingram of Eau Claire, Wisconsin, who formed a permanent alliance with wholesalers at Winona, Minnesota, and Hannibal, Missouri, in an aggregation known as Empire Lumber Company. As improved

log-rafting techniques assured a reliable supply of logs, manufacturers located plants downriver in closer proximity to markets. Frederick Weyerhaeuser (see WEYERHAEUSER FAMILY), for example, started with a sawmill in Rock Island, Illinois, drawing his timber from regions far to the north.

Railroads widened the market for lumber and intensified interregional competition. The sawmill's sales territory expanded along railroad lines. Usually a retailer enjoyed a monopoly in his community, but where railroad lines intersected, he could anticipate competition. City lumber dealers formed "pools" to mitigate price competition, but these agreements were usually of short duration. Better transportation facilities permitted manufacturers such as the Laird, Nortons in Winona to establish their own retail outlets called lineyards. The typical lineyard was located near the railroad tracks and consisted of a yard, a shed, and a small, separate office. The yards stocked a diversified line of building materials: boards, dimension lumber, barn boards, fencing, pickets, stock lumber, shingles, lath, lime, plaster hair, window glass, paint, sandpaper, putty, tar paper, and felt. Millwork and other specialty items were ordered as needed.

By the 1890s, interspecies and interregional competition was a given in the industry. In 1899, the eleven Southern states, led by Arkansas, produced 32 percent of the nation's timber, while the Lake States accounted for only 25 percent (although Michigan and Wisconsin individually led the nation in production). By 1910, the major competitors were the western Douglas-fir and the southern longleaf pine. These two species, along with western ponderosa pine, reduced white pine to the status of a specialty wood, though still valued in the East as a superior form of lumber. By the 1920s, virtually the only genuine white pine marketed in large quantities was from Idaho; several related species—notably ponderosa and sugar pine from California and Norway (red) pine from Minnesota—were masqueraded as white pine. Idaho producers felt forced to identify each piece of their own product with a rubber stamp, until a U. S. Supreme Court decision in 1934 finally vindicated white pine's exclusive status.

The Pacific Coast, with its dense stands of big timber, was last to enter the competitive arena. Before the 1849 gold discoveries, the lumber industry of California and the Pacific Northwest was of little consequence. In the years following the Gold Rush, considerable lumber from as far away as Maine was marketed successfully in San Francisco. However, Maine lumbermen were also transplanting themselves and their techniques to the West Coast, particularly to

Puget Sound and the Willamette and Columbia river basins. The booming California market collapsed in 1854 and was followed by modest growth on the West Coast until the depression of the mid-1870s. During this time, trade routes were established with China and Australia. Special cargo droghers (single-decked schooners with large holds) were designed for the lumber trade. Later, during the railroad construction era, a ship might carry lumber to China and return with Chinese immigrants or a cargo of sugar from Hawaii.

Railroad construction stimulated a huge demand for ties and bridge timbers and at the same time opened up eastern markets to western lumber. The St. Paul and Tacoma sawmill on Puget Sound, founded by eastern lumbermen in 1889, was the first to specialize in production for eastern markets. In view of the large proportion of the price of delivered lumber consumed in freight charges, transportation was an important competitive factor. Railroads, eager to increase their traffic, offered special lumber rates. James J. Hill of the Great Northern in 1893 set a special rate of forty cents per hundredweight on lumber from the Pacific Northwest to St. Paul, ten cents additional to Chicago, and another thirty cents to the Atlantic seaboard. Other northern transcontinentals followed suit. Production soon outstripped demand and falling prices brought chronic complaints of car shortages, excessive demurrage charges, refusal to grant stopover privileges, and other forms of maltreatment by the railroads.

The Panama Canal, completed in 1914, brought the nation's lumber producers into closer competition. Previously, about four-fifths of the lumber manufactured on the West Coast had been consumed locally; as a rule only the higher grades were shipped east of the Rocky Mountains (or to foreign markets). After 1914, Pacific Coast lumber made conspicuous gains in eastern markets. By 1932, Oregon and Washington alone furnished half of the lumber requirements of the North Atlantic states. Ponderosa pine, Douglas-fir, and redwood progressively crowded out white pine, while holding their own against shortleaf pine, baldcypress, and other southern softwoods.

Foreign competition came almost entirely from Canada. Canadian imports fluctuated with changes in tariffs. A reciprocal trade treaty, in effect between 1854 and 1866, was followed by a tariff on lumber imports and a Canadian export duty on logs. A second brief interlude of free trade in forest products between 1894 and 1897 affected southern pine in eastern markets. Pacific Northwest lumbermen felt threatened by Canadian competition, but lumbermen along the Great Lakes, increasingly dependent upon

Canada for their log supply, called for free entry. The 1913 tariff placed lumber on the free list. Threatened imports from Sweden, Finland, and Russia led to renewed tariff protection in 1931, although the measure had little or no effect.

Since the 1870s, the forest products and building materials industries have spawned scores of trade associations and journals. The Chicago Lumbermen's Board of Trade was established in 1869 and, in the next decade, lumber exchanges or boards of trade were formed in lumber distributing centers through the East and Midwest. In 1893, wholesale lumbermen met in New York to form the National Wholesale Lumber Dealers' Association and prepared a broad program of activities of mutual concern. The nation's first lumber trade journal, the *Lumberman's Gazette*, was published in Bay City, Michigan, in 1872. The *Northwestern Lumberman*, published in Chicago a year later, became a model for others, including the *Mississippi Valley Lumberman* (Minneapolis, 1876), the *Southern Lumberman* (Nashville, 1881), and the *Timberman* (Chicago, 1886). *Hardwood*, a trade journal devoted to a single branch of the industry, appeared in Chicago in 1892.

The associations' first major effort was to establish uniform grading rules. Early grading rules were poorly defined and loosely interpreted. Attempts to set standards in the Northeast, dating from the 1860s, met with little success. Minneapolis grading rules, adopted in 1878, were likewise ineffective. Each sawmill owner graded lumber his own way, and dealers freely manipulated grades. Trade journals published market quotations, but these prices were of little value since they were not based on uniform grading practices and terms of sale. The major objective of the Mississippi Valley Lumbermen's Association, organized in 1891, was to standardize grades. By 1898, its Bureau of Grades, chaired by George S. LONG, established detailed grading rules enforced by association inspectors. These grading rules were adopted by the Northwestern Hemlock Manufacturers Association (founded 1894), the Southern Lumber Manufacturers Association (founded 1890), and later by the Western Pine Association (founded 1903). Every softwood lumber association has used these rules as a guideline.

Other association activity was concerned with market information, lobbying for tariffs, negotiating railroad rates, and pricing. Despite association backing, lumber producers had little success in stabilizing prices. Various association efforts to control production by curtailing log output or hours of mill run failed, as did joint marketing through central distributing yards. On the West Coast, a huge lumber export combine, including both manufacturers and wholesalers, collapsed within a few years. San Francisco wholesalers formed the California Lumber Exchange to try to bring order out of chaos, but with limited success.

Nationwide distribution and increasing competition brought changes in marketing patterns and techniques. By the early twentieth century, the larger lumber manufacturers succeeded to some extent in circumventing middlemen distributors. As early as 1902, the Weyerhaeuser-associated mills opened a joint sales office in Chicago. In 1919, Weyerhaeuser's Baltimore yard established a foothold among eastern wholesalers and jobbers. From Baltimore, Weyerhaeuser lumber (principally Douglas-fir) went directly to retailers, large building contractors, and industrial firms. In the 1920s, sales offices were opened in Toledo, Philadelphia, New York, Pittsburgh, and other wholesaling strongholds.

Lumber prices in the 1920s and 1930s sank to unprofitable levels, and aggressive merchandising by producers of nonwood building materials further depressed lumber markets. Statistics show a steady decline in per capita wood consumption since 1905. Rolled steel plate, steel girders, wire fencing, cement blocks, asphalt roofing and paving, cardboard boxes and cartons, aluminum, glass, gypsum, dry-wall construction, brick, tile, and finally plastics replaced wood in a variety of uses.

Lumbermen in turn resorted to trade promotion, advertising, product differentiation (Weyerhaeuser's 4-SQUARE packaging, for instance), and product development (such as Masonite hardboard, TECO truss connectors, and wood insulation) in the effort to improve sales. The coming of synthetic glues created a boom in plywood, laminated arches, and veneered paneling. Poles, posts, shingles, and boards were treated with preservative and fire-resistant chemicals. Prefabricated items, including modular housing, were developed. New materials, such as particleboard and bark products, increased the utilization of inferior tree species and sawmill waste. Numerous specialty items such as broom handles and stepladders managed to survive the competition.

During the Great Depression, no amount of price cutting or promotion could increase sales. Lumbermen recognized that curtailing production was the only remedy and agreed to cooperate with the National Recovery Administration (NRA) in an attempt to bring supply and demand into balance. Secret price rebates and frequent violations of NRA quotas, however, plagued the industry. Throughout the long depression, overproduction and low prices provided a buyer's market for lumber.

Lumber stacked on a pier awaits shipment by sea. Weyerhaeuser Company Photo.

Desperate lumber manufacturers catered to customers by selling mixed carloads, granting discounts, and extending credit. Under the pseudonym of "trade relations," they practiced reciprocity with favored customers. Trade associations, on the other hand, attempted to "stiffen" prices by compiling and distributing price and output information. Between 1938 and 1940, the entire building industry came under indictment for alleged antitrust violations, and on the eve of World War II, the leading lumber associations, companies, and individual lumbermen signed "cease and desist" consent decrees.

World War II completely reversed the situation. Wartime needs for cantonments, crating, dunnage, pallets, and general construction quickly emptied lumberyards of their surpluses. The abnormal demand produced such extreme shortages that even lesser species, such as Idaho's white fir, became merchantable. Lumber was designated a "critical" war material subject to War Production Board priorities and Office of Price Administration ceilings. The postwar building boom absorbed all the lumber that could be produced but, after a decade of capacity output, the demand slackened and manufacturers adopted new marketing strategies. Instead of merely selling lumber, industry giants shifted to more end-use forest products. Manufacturers and large wholesalers offered such items as laminated trusses, beams, and arches; prefinished paneling; pressure-molded, contoured, and curved products; insulation board, pre-primed siding, end-painted studs, industrial cut stock for millwork, toys, and furniture; and prefabricated roof trusses and exterior wall panels. They also differentiated their products with individual logos and trademarks.

Since the mid-1950s, most retail outlets have become building material centers offering a complete line, including many nonwood house furnishings and hardware. Many such building material supermarkets are chains managed from distant headquarters. Due to the tendency to bypass or cross traditional marketing channels, it is often difficult to classify wholesalers, retailers, manufacturers, and real estate developers. Some retailers, for example, build and finance room additions, garages, and other home remodeling projects using subcontracted crews, while others sell only to large builders. Manufacturers in some cases engage in prefabrication or have expanded into mobile homes and home financing. Some marketing intermediaries, such as cargo shippers and office wholesalers, tend to stick to lumber commodity lines.

FURTHER READING: Nelson Courtlandt Brown, *The American Lumber Industry* (1923). Wilson Compton, *The Organization of the Lumber Industry* (1916). Thomas R. Cox, *Mills and Markets: A History of the Pacific Coast Lumber Industry to 1900* (1974). George W. Hotchkiss, *Industrial Chicago: The Lumber Interests* (1894). Fred W. Kohlmeyer, *Timber Roots: The Laird, Norton Story, 1855–1905* (1972). Stuart U. Rich, *Marketing of Forest Products* (1970). Paul F. Sharp, "The War of Substitutes: The Reaction of the Forest Industries to the Competition of Wood Substitutes," *Agricultural History* 23 (Oct. 1949): 274–279. Charles E. Twining, *Downriver: Orrin H. Ingram and the Empire Lumber Company* (1975).

FRED W. KOHLMEYER

LUMBER INDUSTRY: CENTRAL STATES

Lumber production of the Central States of Illinois, Indiana, Ohio, Missouri, Kentucky, Tennessee, and West Virginia exceeded slightly over 18 percent of the United States total in 1879 and thereafter declined to about 8 percent in the 1930s. The utilization of these forested areas never competed in glamour and political and economic importance with the initial settlement of New England, New York, and eastern Pennsylvania, or even the southern Atlantic states. The lumber industry of the Central States did not experience the spectacular rise and then decline of production that was the story of the Lake States or the Gulf South, nor did it sustain the enormous production that was the hallmark of the industry in the Pacific Northwest.

The Central States contained elements of nearly all the major forest types in the eastern United States as well as prairie grasslands. Hardwoods predominated, with beech-maple-birch forest through the bulk of Indiana and Ohio; oak and hickory along the Ohio River, the western two-thirds of Kentucky and Tennessee, and southern Missouri; oak-gum-cypress along the Mississippi and Ohio rivers, and oak and pine in the mountains of eastern Tennessee and Kentucky. In West Virginia, with the rise in elevation in the Appalachians, oaks were dominant. In northern Illinois and western Missouri, declining rainfall gave rise to a mosaic of oak-hickory forest intermixed with bluestem grass prairie, the "oak openings" becoming more frequent and larger further west and away from the major rivers. Local soil and hydrographic conditions gave rise to similar "openings" in the Blue Grass region of Kentucky, south central Ohio, and southwestern Indiana. There were scattered stands of white pine in the extreme northern portions of Illinois and in the uplands of West Virginia and Tennessee. Hemlock existed in West Virginia, and there were extensive stands of yellow pine in southern Missouri and Tennessee.

There was a widespread distribution of wood-using industrial establishments in all the Central States. However, they were more an adjunct to a densely settled pioneer farming community than a conscious design to utilize the woodlands for commercial purposes. From the beginning of settlement in the Old Northwest in 1790, sawmills were constructed almost contemporaneously with the first farm settlements. The mills provided the material for a bewildering array of manufactures. The census for the State of Ohio in 1870 illustrates the density and ubiquity, yet relatively small-scale nature, of nineteenth-century wood-using industries in the Central States. Eighty-four out of the eighty-eight counties had sawmills, with 2,228 establishments (or an average of 26.5 per county), 8,225 persons employed (or an average of 98 per county), and the value of production at over $10 million surpassing that of any other manufacture. There were carriage makers, coopers, furniture makers, lumber-planers, and sash, door, and frame-makers present in large numbers in half or more of the counties.

Lumber output in the Central States climbed during the nineteenth century, reaching a fluctuating peak between 1899 (when 6 billion board feet were cut) and 1909 (when the total was 5.6 billion board feet), and then declined steadily until the Depression years of the early 1930s. The proportion of hardwood rarely if ever fell below 90 percent of the total. The Central States were the most productive hardwood region in the country from the mid- nineteenth century until surpassed by the South in 1916. Of the hardwood cut in the Central States, at least one-half was oak, with yellow-poplar and maple being the other main timbers, accounting between them for 10 to 20 percent of the total production. Between 1869 and 1919, the Central States supplied approximately 60 percent of the total oak production of the United States. After 1915, this proportion fell to about 40 percent as lumbermen in the Lake States and the South turned their attention to local hardwoods once the more easily obtained and profitable softwoods had been cut.

The destruction of the forests of the Central States owed more to the clearing of the land for agriculture than it did to commercial lumbering. Nevertheless, there were major centers of lumbering in the more broken terrain of eastern Kentucky and Tennessee and in West Virginia. Logs were floated singly or in rafts down all the westward-flowing rivers that were tributary to the Ohio, and down the Cumberland and Tennessee and their tributaries. In West Virginia, the Little Kanawha, Guyandotte, Coal, Elk, Gauley, and Big Sandy all carried hardwood logs to be caught and

Log rafts float down the Mississippi River at Memphis, Tennessee. Forest History Society Photo.

sorted out at booms on the lower reaches of the rivers. Cyrus G. Pringle wrote for Charles S. SARGENT's *Report on the Forests of North America* (1884) a description of the milling operations at the Parkersburg Mill Company, a small firm typical of many in the region. Pringle "was astonished and delighted to see how closely the lumber was worked up and the great variety of articles manufactured from slabs, edgings, culls, etc., which in other mills are so generally thrown into the waste pile." Useful items ranging from handles of many types to fly- trap bottoms were made from scraps of poplar, beech, maple, sycamore, black walnut, and cherry. The mill depended on log rafts brought down the Little Kanawha by settlers who had cleared farmlands.

Lumbering was carried out on a much larger scale on the Cumberland River. Beginning in the 1870s, rafts of up to 100,000 board feet were sent down from eastern Kentucky and Tennessee to mills at Martinsburg, Celina, and Nashville. In time, the upriver mills declined in importance as timber supplies were cut out, and the economics of scale favored the concentration of operations in Nashville, which became the region's major milling center. By 1930, most of the log rafting on the Cumberland had ended.

The Central States as a whole have remained a significant hardwood region. They provided 33 percent of the hardwood but only 11 percent of all lumber produced in the United States in 1946. Thirty years later, the corresponding figures were 27 percent of the hardwood but only 5 percent of all lumber.

Although not directly a part of the lumber industry of the Central States, the country's largest lumber exchange and market in the nineteenth century was situated in Chicago. Chicago was the collecting point for the lumber produced and sent out of western Michigan and eastern Wisconsin, and it was also the distribution center for lumber sold throughout the Midwest and the Prairie states. In 1847, receipts of lumber in Chicago were 32 million board feet; in 1851, 125 million board feet; in 1868, over 1 billion board feet; they never dropped below 1 billion again until the 1930s. The trade in lumber accounted for about three-quarters of all the vessels entering the port of Chicago, and as the years progressed the ships came from further afield—from Lake Superior and even the Michigan shore of Lake Huron. Between 60 and 65 percent of the timber was shipped out of Chicago in barges on the Illinois Canal and on bullock wagons that trundled out across the prairies for up to a 200-mile radius to supply the new farms and towns. But later, especially after the disastrous fire of 1871, Chicago's own growth was so great that about half the lumber that arrived was retained for construction within the city. After 1880, the railroads began to capture more and more of the inward and outward trade, and by 1895 waterborne movements had been reduced severely. But the position of the city as a lumber market and exchange was in no way diminished, and Chicago dominated lumber marketing in the Midwest and Great Plains as long as supplies from the Lake States continued. In a smaller way, a number of cities in the Central States along the Mississippi River, such as Rock Island and Moline in Illinois and Hannibal and St. Louis in Missouri, served as important sawmilling and distribution centers for white pine rafted down from the Lake States.

FURTHER READING: The lumber industry in the Central States has been little examined by historians. Specialized works include the following: Thomas D. Clark, "Early Lumbering Activities in Kentucky," *Northern Logger* 13 (Mar. 1965): 14–15, 42-43, and "Kentucky Logmen," *Journal of Forest History* 25 (July 1981): 144–157. Steven A. Schulman, "The Lumber Industry of the Upper Cumberland River Valley," *Tennessee Historical Quarterly* 32 (Fall 1973):

255-264. George W. Webb, "The Hardwood Lumber Industry of the Eastern Highland Rim," *Journal of the Tennessee Academy of Science* 32 (July 1957): 216-227.

MICHAEL WILLIAMS

LUMBER INDUSTRY: LAKE STATES

The Lake States, as they have been defined in the lumber industry, include Michigan, Wisconsin, and Minnesota—three states whose forests contributed mightily to a rapidly expanding post-Civil War America. In that connection, the last half of the nineteenth century merits discussion, not only because these were the only years of lumbering activity in the region but also because efforts before and since have been slender shadows of this period of peak activity.

Three basic features dictated the onset of large-scale lumbering. The first had to do with the forest itself. The original forested area of the Lake States totaled 97 million acres, or about 78 percent of the total land area. The most valuable of the Lake States' timber species was the white pine, which spread over the northern two-thirds of Michigan's Lower Peninsula and much of its Upper Peninsula; most of Wisconsin, ranging north of a line from Green Bay to the mouth of the St. Croix; and northern Minnesota east of the Mississippi. It is impossible to say just how much pine stood in the Lake States forests; estimates of the original stand of red and white pine range from 500 to 1,000 billion board feet.

Trees, however, were initially considered more an impediment to settlement than a resource to exploit. Therefore, the second factor in the development of the lumber industry was the development of a market for forest products. Large-scale lumbering in the Great Lakes region was a response to demand occasioned by the growth of great urban centers like Chicago, by increasing eastern dependence on western lumber, and, most important, by the surge of settlement onto the treeless prairies and plains.

The third factor was the means by which the resource could be efficiently harvested and marketed. Throughout the region, operators took advantage of an extensive network of rivers, streams, and creeks in the movement of their sawlogs. The Mississippi River system and the Great Lakes connected sawmills with markets from St. Louis, Missouri, to Tonawanda, New York. From the latter, as early as 1847, the Erie Canal carried Michigan lumber east to Albany. Thus forest products flowed from the pineries of the Lake States in two principal directions: on schooners, millions of feet of lumber moved annually across the lakes toward the south and east, while immense rafts of logs and lumber floated down the Mississippi and its tributaries to sawmills and railheads for shipment to the farms and new communities of the prairie West. Regardless of the direction or methods employed, the importance of economical water transport cannot be overemphasized. Timber areas lacking such natural transportation opportunities would not become productive until the construction of logging railroads beginning in the late 1870s.

The era of large-scale lumbering in the region was brief. Between 1869 and 1879, the Lake States' lumber output jumped 75 percent from a reported 3.6 billion to 6.3 billion board feet; by 1889, it had again increased about 60 percent to nearly 10 billion board feet. By 1899, however, production had declined to 8.7 billion board feet, and in 1909 to 5.5 billion. Regional lumber production reached a low of 289 million board feet in 1932; the period of intense activity had lasted less than five decades. The Lake States lumber boom had seen exploitation at both its most unattractive and most romantic extremes; by any subsequent standards, the methods were wasteful and destruction was wanton, yet the contribution to the construction of urban America and the farms of the trans-Mississippi West was remarkable.

As was typical of the American frontier, the progression of the lumbering industry in the Lake States was generally westward. Within each of the states, however, the frontier moved from south to north. Michigan's first sawmills, located on the edge of the forest in the 1830s, produced only for local purposes. But the state's excellent export opportunities permitted these local operations to expand quickly into an industry of primary importance. The first state census, that of 1837, counted some 450 sawmills, and by 1850 Michigan had climbed to fifth place among states in the production of lumber. Typical of this growth was the Saginaw Valley of Michigan's eastern shore. Only eight sawmills were operating in 1850, but in just five years the valley claimed as many as sixty. Along the western shore, accessible to the insatiable Chicago market, the industry expanded even more rapidly, with Muskegon dominating that district. By 1860, the lumber industry was clearly the most important in Michigan, with some 900 firms and more than 6,000 employees manufacturing products worth nearly double that of the second-ranking flour industry. By 1870, Michigan was the leading lumber producing state in the nation, its 1,600 mills employing more than 20,000 people and producing more than 2.3 billion board feet of lumber yearly. Michigan re-

tained its leading position almost until the end of the century.

While lumbermen were proceeding through Michigan pineries, activity was beginning in the Wisconsin woods. Lumbermen from the East, seeking new opportunities, looked beyond the established industry in Michigan to the undeveloped resources farther west. The pine of Wisconsin was, for the most part, accessible, and while most of Wisconsin's rivers had carried logs to frontier mills since the 1830s, the real exploitation of the state's forests had hardly begun before the Civil War.

Although the growth of the Wisconsin lumber industry approximated that of Michigan, there were differences in timing and marketing arrangements. While lumber manufacturing in Michigan reached its greatest volume in the 1890s, Wisconsin's mills increased their production steadily until 1904. Sawmills along streams that fed into Green Bay and Lake Michigan marketed lumber in Milwaukee and Chicago, as did the mills on Michigan's west shore. But the greater portion of Wisconsin was drained by river systems tributary to the Mississippi and therefore the bulk of the state's forest products were shipped to points south and west. Immense log and lumber rafts moved ponderously but economically from the pine regions downriver to feed the ever increasing market for lower-grade lumber associated with agricultural expansion into the prairies. Although Wisconsin pine was accessible and of good quality, the state's total resources were less extensive than those of Michigan. The era of large-scale lumbering was even briefer in Wisconsin than in Michigan. Wisconsin led the nation in the production of lumber at the turn of the century, but already its best pineries had been exploited, leaving only the remote areas in the northern part of the state. Wisconsin's subsequent decline was even more rapid than that of Michigan.

The Minnesota story was of relatively lesser importance. With smaller resources at hand, Minnesota was outranked by both Michigan and Wisconsin in lumber production even during its peak year of 1899. The industry in Minnesota shared its beginnings in 1840 with Wisconsin, since the St. Croix, Minnesota's first logging river, formed the boundary between the two states. As in Wisconsin, lumber was sent to market on the Mississippi. A difference soon developed, however; Minnesota, with extensive prairie farmlands within its borders, enjoyed a voracious home market for lumber. After mid-century, railroad construction extended this market westward into the Dakotas and the prairie provinces of Canada. Although mills along the St.

Croix and Mississippi continued to send large amounts of lumber downriver, rail transportation became the basis for much of the Minnesota industry.

Minnesota's decline was the most rapid of the three Lake States. Between 1902 and 1909, lumber production in Minnesota mills fell from 2.5 billion board feet yearly to 1.6 billion, and by 1919 it was only 699 million board feet. With the closing of Minnesota's last big mills at Cloquet and Virginia in the 1930s, the era of large-scale lumbering throughout the Lake States was brought to a close. In 1900, Wisconsin, Michigan, and Minnesota were the three national leaders in both value and volume of timber products. Just nine years later, the state of Washington ranked first, Louisiana second; Wisconsin had fallen to seventh place, Michigan to ninth, and Minnesota to eleventh. Lumbering did not cease altogether in the region; it continued to be of large local importance, and the Lake States became major producers of pulpwood. Nevertheless, the great days of the Lake States lumber industry lasted only as long as did the region's white pine.

FURTHER READING: Robert F. Fries, *Empire in Pine: The Story of Lumbering in Wisconsin, 1830–1900* (1951). George W. Hotchkiss, *History of the Lumber and Forest Industry of the Northwest* (1898). Agnes M. Larson, *The White Pine Industry in Minnesota* (1949). William G. Rector, *Log Transportation in the Lake States Lumber Industry, 1840–1916* (1953).

CHARLES E. TWINING

LUMBER INDUSTRY: NORTHEAST

Rapid land clearing and forest depletion characterized the early history of the northeastern United States, an area including New England and the Mid-Atlantic states of New York, Pennsylvania, New Jersey, Maryland, and Delaware. By the mid-nineteenth century, the valuable white pine had been culled from the forests. New tree species were utilized, technology was refined, and markets were expanded until the 1870s, when forest depletion and competition from the Lake States, the South, and the Pacific Northwest brought the rapid expansion of the northeastern lumber industry to an end. After 1870, the industry returned to a more limited commercial forest, became more specialty-oriented, and developed a thriving hardwood component. During the nineteenth century, abandoned farms grew back to red spruce in northern New England, white pine in central New England and New York, redcedar and yellow pine in the southwestern part of the region, and pitch and loblolly pine and Atlantic white-cedar in the southeast. These conifer-

ous forests were later reduced by portable sawmills. However, when lumber production tapered off in the 1920s, forest cover thereafter increased. Lumbering in the Northeast continued with a growing technological sophistication and a declining work force, and the pulp and paper industry dominated use of the commercial forest.

The lumber industry in this region dates from the arrival of the first settlers, who used local woods for housing, outbuildings, fences, and firewood. The original promoters of colonization hoped to profit from a trade in forest products, but most early efforts failed, since colonists had neither sufficient time nor experience to produce wood for export. The colonists' first permanent settlers concentrated on subsistence farming, fishing, and fur trading; lumbering remained an adjunct to farming throughout the colonial period.

Although settlers continued to make lumber with pit- or whipsaws, small waterpowered mills producing clapboards, planks, and timber were common throughout the Northeast by the 1640s. By 1701, there were forty mills in the Province of New York alone, most of them supplying lumber locally. Other than building construction, the first use for lumber in the colonies was for fishing vessels and, later, for ships carrying trade. As early as the 1630s, planks, spars, masts, ship's knees, and oak staves were being shipped to England, the West Indies, and the ports of the Mediterranean. A supply of New England white pine masts reached England in 1634, and by the 1650s the trade was well established. Demand for the majestic "mast pine," encouraged by commercial wars and a growing English merchant marine, resulted in 1691 in the so-called Broad Arrow policy, whereby the best white pine suitable for masts was reserved for the Royal Navy. SHIPBUILDING also stimulated a trade in oak timbers and NAVAL STORES. Although agriculture occupied most of the population during the colonial period, lumber ranked with fishing and shipbuilding as the northern colonies' most important product. In 1770, for instance, exports of masts, staves, boards, and other lumber products from the New England colonies amounted to 45,000 pounds. Exports of ships brought an income of 49,000 pounds, and potash, another forest product, returned 20,000 pounds.

After the Revolutionary War, development of the lumber industry was hampered by limited population, distance from trans-Atlantic markets, and primitive technology. Lumber production in the early national period was characterized by a large number of small mills using relatively simple technology and serving limited, localized markets. However, growing domes-

Approximately 18,000 cords of pulpwood have turned the East Branch of the Penobscot River near Medway, Maine, into a river of wood (1943). American Forest Institute Photo.

tic demand, steady population increase, and advances in lumbering technology permitted the industry to grow at a steady rate. The 1840 census listed 18,364 sawmills in the eleven northeastern states producing lumber valued at $8.6 million.

Markets for the northeastern lumber industry developed rapidly. Overseas trade in ship timbers and naval stores benefited from the Napoleonic Wars, which increased demand for North American wood products, especially in the Caribbean area, and reduced Britain's dependence upon Baltic timber. Large seaports such as Boston, New York, and Baltimore exported oak and pine timber to Britain, and sent timber, oak staves, and shook to the West Indies. The strongest demand for northeastern lumber, however, resulted from rapid urbanization along the Eastern Seaboard. Rivers in Maine, Vermont, and New Hampshire supplied lumber to New York and the industrial cities of Massachusetts; lumber from the Delaware and Susquehanna was used in Philadelphia and Baltimore, and the Allegheny River supplied Pittsburgh, the frontier along the Ohio River, and cities as far downriver as New Orleans. In the 1830s, the lumber trade concentrated in Maine around Bangor on the Penobscot and in New York at Albany on the Hudson. After mid-century, Burlington, Vermont, on Lake Champlain, and Williamsport, Pennsylvania, on the Susquehanna, took on increasing importance. Huge rafts of rough-sawn planks and squared timber were transported down the Mohawk, Delaware, Hudson, and other rivers in the Mid-Atlantic states in the 1840s; on the Penobscot, Androscoggin, and Connecticut rivers, logs were floated to the booms at tidewater and manufactured into lumber there.

Meeting the growing demand for lumber called for changes in the technology of forest exploitation. In the mills, new types of saws took narrower kerfs, moved at higher speeds, and processed more lumber, which increased the efficiency of the industry. The first waterpowered mills used upright saws held in heavy timber frames. Gang saws were introduced into the Northeast in the early 1830s, and, about the same time, steam-powered saws began to replace the older variety. Steam power also took the place of manual labor in much of the log-handling process in the mills. Circular saws were to be found in the Northeast in 1860 and were common by 1880. Band saws were introduced in 1889 and were used in most of the larger mills by the end of the century.

Advances in high-speed sawmilling called for changes in harvesting and transporting the raw material. Better supply roads permitted crews to remain in the woods throughout the winter; sharper axes made of superior grades of steel permitted faster felling. On the rivers, the use of distinctive log marks allowed lumbermen to intermingle their logs on the drive and later to unite their efforts to improve the rivers. A boom was chartered on the Kennebec River in 1789. The first large, permanent boom was constructed across the Penobscot River near Bangor, Maine, in 1832, and three years later, the Kennebec Log Driving Association, a mutual-benefit corporation, was organized. In 1846, the Penobscot Log Driving Company took control of the entire West Branch Penobscot drive. Such innovations made it possible to handle almost 3 billion board feet of lumber on the West Branch of the Penobscot between 1832 and 1855.

New methods of log transportation made operations on the more remote headwaters possible. Use of dynamite for channel clearing, along with splash dams and roll dams, made even small streams drivable. The first logging railroad in New York State was the Fox, Weston, and Bronson "Bull of the Woods," which carried logs to Steuben County, New York, over wooden rails as early as 1852. Becoming common by the late 1870s, logging railroads in the Adirondacks and Alleghenies allowed lumbermen to reach timber previously inaccessible. Waterslides and steam loaders also facilitated transportation in the interior regions. In 1858, Joseph Peavey refined the cant-dog, a ubiquitous woodsman's tool. Later in the century, double-bitted axes, crosscut saws, and the use of raker teeth in all saws sped the process of harvesting trees and made possible the delivery of more logs and lumber to markets around the world.

By the 1830s, a well-organized infrastructure had been created for the industry and was maintained by a court system that defined the limits of responsibility for individuals and corporations. Laws enacted in Massachusetts between 1796 and 1818, for instance, regulated such activities as constructing dams, setting fires in the woods, recovering stranded logs on the rivers, defacing or defrauding log marks, building and maintaining booms, and trespass committed while lumbering. During the 1820s, additional regulations defined log scales and regulated the quality of timber and logs. An 1804 act inspired by lumbermen prevented pirating timber floating on the Hudson River. The Ausable received similar legislation in 1825. Throughout the region, the common law concept of navigable streams was extended after 1750 to include not only tidewater but all streams suitable for transporting boats, logs, or rafts of timber. Thus, operating on public waterways, lumbermen were no longer subject to tolls, man-made obstructions, or confiscations of their stranded logs or rafts. In 1806, the Salmon River was the first waterway declared a public highway in New York. The Raquette River, in eastern New York, was so designated in 1810. These and similar laws established a general legal code for the logging industry in the Northeast.

During the first quarter of the nineteenth century, state lands and the large colonial land grants in the Northeast fell into the hands of land speculators and large timberland owners. Among the largest of land sales was the Bingham Purchase, by which over 2 million acres in the District of Maine were purchased by William Bingham in 1793. The Macomb Purchase in New York conveyed to Alexander Macomb and Daniel McCormick almost 4 million acres in 1782. By the middle of the nineteenth century, ownership patterns were stabilized, as most of the lands falling under such large purchases were dispersed among a widely scattered group of lumbermen and timber owners. The latter sold stumpage to the logger, who hired crews, took most of the risks, and often remained in debt to the landowner until the logs were driven to market.

Logs were milled and sold to commission merchants or marketed directly by the mill owners. As markets broadened on a national and international scale, lumbermen took steps to refine marketing procedures. The greater lumber markets, such as New York, Boston, Providence, Liverpool, and Glasgow, registered price quotations for various grades of lumber, and these were widely published in journals and newspapers in the lumbering districts. Such measures helped to bring some predictability to the industry.

During the nineteenth century, the colorful river

drives served as the hallmark of the lumbering industry in the Northeast. Every major river had its log drives. The extensive and well-timbered watersheds of the Penobscot, Kennebec, Connecticut, and Susquehanna rivers provided inexpensive transportation systems that sustained huge mills at tidewater and gave these regions a competitive advantage for a time. In Maine, the Saint John River, famous for its squared pine or "ton" timber before the Civil War, was an international waterway. The Webster-Ashburton Treaty of 1842 allowed Maine logs to be manufactured into lumber in Canada and marketed duty free in Britain or the United States. By the 1880s, the great drives of sixteen-foot sawlogs had largely given way to drives of four-foot pulpwood. Portable steam mills located near the timber supplies and the extension of railroads through the region hastened the demise of the river-driving era, although as late as the 1930s and 1940s some operators continued to bring long logs down the Saco, the Machias, and the Saint John. Pulp mills began phasing out river drives after the introduction of the internal combustion engine into the woods, beginning in the 1920s. River driving lingered in the Northeast until the 1970s, when increasing relative costs, pressures from recreational and environmental organizations, increasing obstruction by dams, and a shift back to harvesting and transporting tree-length logs ended the drives.

By 1839, New York had eclipsed Maine as the leading lumber producer in the nation, and twenty years later New York was outpaced by Pennsylvania. The census of 1870 reported Pennsylvania as still the largest producer in the Northeast, but the state already ranked second to Michigan nationwide. The lumber industry on the Susquehanna peaked in 1873. Older lumber manufacturing centers, such as Burlington and Albany, retained their prominence through the 1870s and 1880s but increasingly drew their timber supplies from outside the region. In 1880, two-thirds of Albany's pine came from Michigan and one-third came from Canada. New York pine then manufactured in Albany was negligible.

The Northeast as a whole reported nearly 4.6 billion board feet produced in 1869 and still ranked first among the nation's regions. By 1879, the region had fallen behind the Lake States in production and ten years later ranked third after the Lake States and the South. In absolute terms, however, the Northeast continued to increase its lumber output until 1907, when its mills reported production approaching 5.7 billion feet. After 1909, production dropped sharply, reaching a regional low of 387 million board feet in 1932. Lumber production in the Northeast increased

steadily after the Depression, with the exception of a slight dip in the late 1950s. In 1970, regional production estimates approached 1.7 billion feet.

Until the 1840s, the lumber harvest in the Northeast was mostly white pine, along with some birch and larch. Much of this product was exported as square timber. Other species began to replace pine in the 1850s and 1860s, particularly hemlock in Pennsylvania and New York, and spruce in New England. In 1869, for instance, 53 percent of the lumber produced in the Northeast still came from white pine, 15 percent from hemlock (in Pennsylvania 30 percent), 10 percent from spruce (in Maine 21 percent), and 17 percent from hardwoods. By the end of the century, the figures were only 21 percent white pine (and that largely from New England), hemlock furnished 36 percent (in Pennsylvania 65 percent), spruce 20 percent (in Maine 52 percent), and hardwoods 20 percent. Other woods continued to be harvested for special purposes; cedar from New England and northern New York was used extensively for shingles, and larch was cut for ship's knees and other construction demanding strong, durable wood.

After 1880, steam sawmills freed lumbermen from sites with available waterpower and allowed lumber manufacturing to move nearer the timber. Small portable steam and, later, internal-combustion-powered mills exploited the second growth, often on abandoned farmland. In such operations, usually all the merchantable timber was cut, leaving only a few seed trees to restock the cutover areas. Use of portable sawmills declined in the 1920s when much of the old-field pine was depleted and markets for lumber declined. By the 1970s, most of the mills in the Northeast—84 percent in New England and 72 percent in the Middle Atlantic states—were located on permanent sites, made possible in part through the use of log trucks to tap scattered stands.

Beginning in the 1880s, the lumber industry faced increasing competition for available timberlands from the growing pulp and paper industry. In addition, the northeastern industry's markets were threatened by competition from West Coast softwoods, particularly after the completion of the Panama Canal in 1914. Consequently the Northeast after 1900 began shifting toward hardwood production, which by the end of the 1920s accounted for 45 percent of the lumber manufactured in the region. Hardwoods were used locally for furniture, particularly near urban centers in Massachusetts, New York, and New Jersey. Specialty items, such as coffins, spools, croquets sets, toys, dowels, toothpicks, and clothespins, were manufactured in small hardwood mills. Furniture and novelty industries continued to grow slowly in the interwar period, as the dimension lumber industry slowed substantially. Hardwood operations were usually handled on a small scale in the Northeast, often organized by farmers during their slack winter season. Hardwoods were also used extensively for fuelwood until the end of World War I, and fuelwood production again increased in the 1970s.

In 1938, a great storm blew down more than 2 billion board feet of commercial second-growth pine in the Northeast. Although market conditions were unfavorable, lumbermen, with the aid of the federal New England Salvage Administration, harvested 600 million feet of the blowdown by 1940. When lumber markets recovered during World War II, lumbermen and the government were more than able to make up losses from the disaster.

Since 1938, lumber production, handled mostly by small mills, has been increasing, although the quality of the timber itself has decreased. Rising production figures have largely been the result of better forestry practices and more intensive use of remaining timber stocks. After World War II, the lumber industry in the Northeast began experimenting with integrated production of various types of hardwood and softwood products, including veneer, wood pulp, and sawlogs and, increasingly, the use of waste from sawmills for wood pulp. During this period, pulp mills began to diversify, producing studs and lumber in addition to pulp, thus utilizing the available wood resources more effectively.

Little consolidation has taken place in the lumber industry in the Northeast. Although a number of combinations were attempted in the second half of the nineteenth century, they tended to founder in difficult economic times and increasing competition from Western and Southern lumber sources. The most important lumber trade association in the region has been the Northeastern Lumbermens Association, organized in 1933 under the National Recovery Administration and covering Pennsylvania, New York, and New England. There has been little labor organization among northeastern woodsmen, although sawmills in some cases have been unionized. In 1979, 73 percent of the mills in the region produced less than 1 million board feet annually. The lumber industry in the Northeast has remained dominated by a large number of relatively small, fiercely independent firms.

FURTHER READING: James Elliott Defebaugh, *History of the Lumber Industry*, vol. 2 (1907). William F. Fox, *A History of the Lumber Industry in the State of New York* (1901). Robert E. Pike, *Tall Trees, Tough Men* (1967). David C. Smith, *History of Lumbering in Maine, 1861–1960*

(1972). Richard G. Wood, *History of Lumbering in Maine, 1820–1862* (1935).

DAVID C. SMITH

LUMBER INDUSTRY: PACIFIC COAST

Lumbering began in what is now Washington, Oregon, and California before the area belonged to the United States. Spaniards shipped lumber from Monterey in northern California to missions further south beginning in 1776. The Hudson's Bay Company erected a waterpowered sawmill on the Columbia River near Vancouver in 1827, shipping the cut primarily to Hawaii. Thomas O. Larkin, American consul in California during the Mexican period, developed an export trade in lumber. He bought the production of whipsawyers and primitive sawmills in the Santa Cruz Mountains, chartered vessels, and dispatched cargoes to Hawaii, Latin America, and elsewhere. In 1844, Captain Stephen Smith erected a steam sawmill, the first on the West Coast, at Bodega Bay. He sold most of his cut in nearby San Francisco and in Hawaii. For all this activity, lumbering was extremely limited before California's gold rush. One authority has estimated production in 1848 at a mere 10,000 board feet.

Burgeoning demand during the gold rush led to greatly increased production. Sawmills sprang up along the redwood coast, in western Oregon, and around Puget Sound. Initially, mills on the lower reaches of the Columbia and Willamette rivers had the largest share of the market, but gradually mills on Puget Sound, which was easier and safer for sailing ships than were the rivers, pulled ahead. Sawmills along the northern California coast also prospered, benefiting from their relative nearness to San Francisco, the entrepôt to the mines. When the gold rush bubble burst in 1854, lumber sales plummeted, but many sawmills survived thanks to sales in markets scattered around the Pacific Basin. Gradually, San Francisco regained its position as the primary market of the West Coast lumber industry, a position it held until near the end of the century. The huge size of available timber eventually was to give lumbermen in the Far West a competitive advantage, but initially it was more of a problem than a benefit, pushing imagination and existing technology to their limits.

While the cargo mills, serving maritime markets, were the most noticeable part of the industry, they were not the only sawmills in the Pacific Coast states during the last half of the nineteenth century. In Oregon's Willamette Valley, a host of small mills catered to local demand, as did mills east of the Cascades in Oregon and Washington and in the Sierra Nevada of

California—the latter frequently sending their cut down elaborate systems of flumes to yards in the Central Valley or in the Comstock Lode country on the eastern side of the range.

During the nineteenth century, railroads played a growing role in West Coast lumbering. They were primarily important at first as a means of tapping new log supplies. Gradually, they began to open new markets, too, especially after 1893 when James J. Hill's Great Northern Railway inaugurated a rate of only forty cents per hundred pounds on lumber shipped from the Northwest to St. Paul and fifty cents to Chicago. Dwindling supplies in the upper Lake States helped open the way to midwestern markets, and West Coast lumbermen were soon engaged in a head-to-head struggle with lumbermen from the South for control of the Midwest. At first, producers in and around Portland benefited the most from these new outlets, but after 1908, when lumbermen in western Washington won equivalent freight rates in the Portland Gateway case, Washington's mills came to the forefront. By contrast, California's redwood producers sent little east, for the areas of production lacked convenient railroad connections. Indeed, beginning about 1900, sizable shipments began to move from Oregon to California by rail, which resulted in a boom in production in southern Oregon and weakened the redwood producers and other cargo mills by cutting into markets they had previously controlled through San Francisco.

As timber stands in the upper Lake States became depleted, more and more lumbermen transferred operations to the West Coast. By the end of the nineteenth century, the influx had become a flood. Pioneer firms, such as Pope & Talbot and the Port Blakely Mill Company, found it increasingly difficult to compete with these aggressive, well-financed newcomers. Many sold out. The greatest of the new arrivals was Frederick Weyerhaeuser (see WEYERHAEUSER FAMILY), who put together a consortium that in 1900 purchased 900,000 acres of land-grant forests from the Northern Pacific Railroad for six dollars per acre. It was years before Weyerhaeuser commenced major lumber production in the Pacific Northwest, where these lands were located, but simply through his huge purchase Weyerhaeuser had assumed a position of primacy in West Coast lumbering.

Demand for timberland rose sharply with the arrival of newcomers from the Lake States and, subsequently, from the South. The creation of federal forest reserves reduced available acreage. Buyers scrambled for the rest. Timber speculation rose sharply, forcing prices higher, and timber frauds, perpetrated by per-

verting the Homestead and other federal land laws, grew in frequency until they culminated in the Oregon land fraud cases of 1903–1910 that touched high state and federal officials. Through it all, timber ownership in the Far West was growing more concentrated and sawmills became larger.

For all these changes, many of the old cargo mills continued to prosper, shipping to southern California, Japan, north China, Australia, South Africa, and the Atlantic Coast. But their time was running out. In 1920, passage of the Jones Act restricted the coastal and intercoastal trade of the United States to American-owned vessels. The act barred West Coast lumbermen from shipping to the East Coast on cheaper foreign bottoms; as a result, competitors in British Columbia wrested the lion's share of this important trade from them. Japan soon withered as a market as the silk trade collapsed and other problems buffeted its economy. The great days of the old cargo trade were clearly over even before the Depression of the 1930s administered the *coup de grâce*.

In spite of the difficulties faced by the cargo trade, the West Coast continued to grow in importance as a lumber-producing region. A West Coast state entered the ranks of leading lumber producers for the first time in 1899 when Washington ranked sixth. By 1905, it had risen to first place, and production was increasing rapidly in Oregon and California. In 1920, Washington was still first (producing over 5.5 billion board feet); Oregon had climbed to second and California to fifth spot. By 1940, the three states stood first, second, and third in production and were turning out 40 percent of the nation's total. Oregon was now in the lead, a position it has held ever since, with an annual output of some 20 percent of the nation's lumber production—this in spite of the fact that, since the end of World War II, Oregon's industry has had to shift from dependence upon old-growth forests to sustained-yield forestry and second-growth trees. California has regularly been the nation's second largest producer during this period.

A key factor in Oregon's rise to primacy was the development of truck logging, which opened vast stands in the Cascades and other parts of the state that could not be economically tapped by the railroad logging that preceded the use of trucks and dominated in much of Washington. Few stands were too small or too remote to escape truck loggers, especially after cheap, war-surplus trucks became available following World War II. Hundreds of small operators, known as gyppo loggers (*see* GYPPO LOGGING), entered the woods with converted military vehicles searching for stands overlooked by major firms. Between the gyp-

After clearcutting an area of Douglas-fir, broad-scale reforestation produces an even-aged stand, one of the goals of this timber-harvest method. Radiating lines are skid trails, marking routes of logs hauled to central loading areas or landings. Forest Service Photo.

pos and the established companies, which also turned to trucks, railroad logging was soon pushed into a minor position.

Oregon's rise was also a result of the opening of major operations in the pine forests of southern Oregon and east of the Cascades. Grants Pass, Bend, and Klamath Falls became lumbering centers of the first rank. Sizable mills also sprang up in Burns, Lakeview, Prineville, Medford, and other places. Similar developments were taking place in the pineries of northeastern California and east of the Cascades in Washington, but Oregon had the greatest pine stands and there the greatest increases came.

Whether old or new, lumbering centers in the Pacific Coast states as elsewhere were hard hit by the Great Depression. Indeed, for lumbermen the Depression began in 1926. During the early 1930s, housing starts, the greatest generator of demand for lumber, hit their twentieth-century low. Many firms were forced into bankruptcy. Some of the more fortu-

nate, such as the Simpson-Reed interests in Shelton, Washington, managed to continue on a reduced scale thanks to integrated operations and an absence of significant debts. The owners of timberland could at least take consolation from the fact that although there were few buyers for their trees, the stands were growing, adding more wood each year. World War II brought renewed demand, and the postwar housing boom kept it high. However, the industry remained vulnerable to swings in housing starts, which responded to interest rates and other factors beyond the control of lumbermen. Production has fluctuated widely since World War II, just as it did before the war. The boom of the West in the postwar period had made the region its own largest market, taking up some of the slack caused earlier by the Jones Act.

Lumbering on the West Coast has grown ever more capital-intensive since the 1880s. As planing mills, dry kilns, molding plants, and labor-saving machinery became necessary during the late nineteenth century in order to remain competitive, the need for investment capital rose. Further integration of operations pushed capital needs even higher. Plywood, introduced commercially in Portland in 1905, became a major use for high-quality Douglas-fir logs, and plywood plants absorbed much capital. By 1936, Oregon's four plywood mills were turning out 69.8 million square feet of plywood per year; twenty-five years later, there were 117 plants, producing 5.6 billion square feet annually. Plywood production that year, in 1961, was valued at $405.5 million, compared to $574 million for lumber and $116.9 million for pulp, which was also rising rapidly in importance. Conversion to sawmills designed for smaller, second-growth timber also was expensive, often prompting smaller operators to sell out. Concentration of ownership and outside control have increased as a result of the rising need for investment capital, but the West Coast's lumber industry, like that in other parts of the country, continues to be more decentralized than most American manufacturing industries.

The lumber industry has played an important part in the shift to sustained-yield forestry in the Pacific Coast states. George S. LONG, of the Weyerhaeuser Timber Company; William B. GREELEY, of the West Coast Lumbermens Association; and David T. MASON, a private consulting forester, were key advocates in the struggle to win acceptance for modern scientific forestry in the region. The Western Pine Association and the INDUSTRIAL FORESTRY ASSOCIATION, both made up of lumbermen, successfully pushed for tree farms on private holdings. Although the lumber industry of the Pacific Coast is decentralized, timber holdings are, nevertheless, much less fragmented there than in the Gulf South, and success in bringing good management therefore came more readily.

In western Oregon, the BUREAU OF LAND MANAGEMENT, through its handling of O & C LANDS, played a leading role in furthering sustained-yield management. The U. S. FOREST SERVICE was less important at first, but it became increasingly significant in the region as time passed. Underfinanced state forestry agencies long had relatively little impact on management practices, but state regulation of cutting on private land had a significant effect beginning in California in the 1940s.

Since the 1960s, log exportation from the West Coast to Japan has been a continuing source of friction. The owners of small mills, facing increasing difficulty in obtaining sawlogs, have frequently blamed their problems on the exports. Workers laid off when mills have closed have protested that exporters are sending jobs as well as logs to Japan. Exporters and some analysts have countered that the smaller saw-

mills are often obsolete, uneconomical units that would be in trouble with or without exports; that log sales to the Japanese at high prices are important to the United States, with its unfavorable balance of trade; that exporting generates many jobs in communities such as Coos Bay, Oregon, and Hoquiam and Tacoma, Washington; and that sales to the Japanese bring needed capital into the region. Various large timber owners, including Weyerhaeuser, have invested heavily in log export facilities. In spite of restrictions on the exportation of logs from federal lands, the trade seems destined to continue.

Large or small, sawmills and other forest products plants have been affected more and more since the 1960s by rising nonindustrial demands on West Coast forests. Operators dependent upon timber sales from national forests have felt especially vulnerable. They and their spokesmen have been active in trying, on the one hand, to limit withdrawals of timber for wilderness and other recreational and aesthetic uses and, on the other hand, to have the allowable cut on national forests increased. Their actions have led to counterattacks from environmentalists. As with debates over the exportation of logs to Japan, there is no reason to predict an early end to these differences. If it ever existed, the day when the West Coast's lumber industry could simply cut logs while ignoring public issues is clearly past.

FURTHER READING: Edwin T. Coman, Jr. and Helen M. Gibbs, *Time, Tide and Timber: A Century of Pope & Talbot* (1949). Thomas R. Cox, *Mills and Markets: A History of the Pacific Coast Lumber Industry to 1900* (1974). Ralph W. Hidy, Frank Ernest Hill, and Allan Nevins, *Timber and Men: The Weyerhaeuser Story* (1963). Edmond S. Meany, Jr., "The History of the Lumber Industry in the Pacific Northwest to 1917," Ph.D. dissertation, Harvard University (1936). Howard Brett Melendy, "One Hundred Years of the Redwood Lumber Industry," Ph.D. dissertation, Stanford University (1953).

THOMAS R. COX

LUMBER INDUSTRY: ROCKY MOUNTAIN REGION

Scarcity of timber in the Rocky Mountain Region, which includes Idaho, Montana, Wyoming, Utah, Colorado, New Mexico, Arizona, and all but the Sierra forests of Nevada, can be attributed to meteorological conditions and the interference of mountain ranges situated upwind on the storm track. With few exceptions, it is only in the high mountains, where annual rainfall reaches at least twenty inches, that there are large forests of Douglas-fir, larch, and ponderosa pine.

Even there, most precipitation occurs during the winter months, a dormant season for trees. Thus, the Rocky Mountain Region is mostly barren of trees. Heavily timbered areas occur largely in the northern states, particularly Idaho and Montana, where over 70 percent of the forestland is deemed commercial, compared to 30 percent of that in the southern section.

Native American use of Rocky Mountain forests was limited to what the land produced naturally. Forests were perceived as sacred places rather than as resources for economic exploitation. However, Indians employed fire to clear undergrowth and to increase browse for deer and elk. Use by early European trappers and explorers was also minimal, but the miners who arrived in the 1860s exploited the region's timber resources extravagantly. Timber was used for cribbing and shoring, and as a fuel to fire smelting furnaces and maintain homes. It is estimated that during the 1860s and 1870s, the Comstock mine in Nevada used 70,000 board feet per year for props and cribbing to shore up the mine's ceiling and walls and 250,000 cords for smelting.

Settlers who followed the miners into the region used timber for homes, outbuildings, fences, and corrals. People were few enough, however, so that no real overuse of timber resources resulted. Utah settlers, who actually arrived before the miners, adapted to the extreme scarcity of trees that characterized the southern Rocky Mountain Region by using other building materials, such as cut stone, fired brick, and adobe. Railroad construction, beginning with the Union Pacific Railroad in 1867–1868, consumed substantial amounts of wood for ties and timbers. In the last quarter of the nineteenth century, "tie-hacking" operations extended throughout the region. Expert hewers, or tie-hacks, squaring forty or more ties a day, perpetuated a tradition of broadax skills going back to colonial times. Consuming approximately 2,500 ties per mile, the two northern transcontinental railroads, in addition to opening the territory for settlement and providing access to eastern markets, themselves created a significant demand for forest products.

Generous land policies, including the Homestead Law of 1862, the statehood grants, extensive railroad land grants, the Timber and Stone Act of 1878, and the Forest Homestead Act of 1906, led to a liberal disposition of public forestlands. Ultimately, much of the timberlands in the Rocky Mountain Region, particularly the extensive railroad land grants, fell into the hands of large lumber companies.

The turn of the century was a time for consolidation of sawmills, timberlands, and lumber operations in the states of Idaho, Montana, and Arizona, as lumber markets in the East were opened to Rocky Mountain lumbermen. Previously, long freight hauls left western timber uncompetitive with timber supplies closer to eastern markets, but in 1890 the Great Northern Railroad dropped its rates to attract freight on its eastern run. Moreover, as pine was depleted in the Lake States, prices for eastern timber increased. Between 1869 and 1899, lumber production in the Rocky Mountain Region increased from 59 million to 656 million board feet annually. Lumbermen from the east migrated to the Rocky Mountain states, forming groups to buy cheap forestland from mining and railroad companies. Among the arrivals was Frederick Weyerhaeuser (see WEYERHAEUSER FAMILY), who combined the finances and contacts of friends and relatives to acquire Idaho lands. In 1903, Weyerhaeuser's Potlatch Lumber Company—later Potlatch Forests, Incorporated—was founded. The company, centered around Coeur d'Alene, became one of the largest timber and paper products companies in the West.

Difficult transportation problems in the rugged country, combined with costly logging techniques and competition from West Coast and southern lumber, left many firms operating at a loss for several years. The influence of their Lake States experience led lumbermen initially to concentrate upon moving logs by river and stream and upon the construction of elaborate flumes to bring timber from high ridges. These forms of transportation in the steep watercourses of the west resulted in a great deal of damaged timber. The first substantial logging railroad in the region was Weyerhaeuser's Washington, Idaho & Montana Railway Company, running from Palouse, Washington, to Bovill, Idaho, with connections to the Great Northern, Northern Pacific, and Chicago, Milwaukee & St. Paul railroads. Development of motor trucks during the same period led to trucking roads that facilitated timber transport to the railroads for shipping.

Lumber production in the Rocky Mountain Region increased rapidly after 1900, reaching a peak of 1.9 million board feet a year in 1925 and dropping to a Depression low of 554 million board feet in 1932. Output again increased during the post-World War II construction boom. In 1952, the region produced a reported 2.4 billion feet of lumber, a figure that reached 4 billion in 1964, and 4.4 billion in 1977, when the region produced 14.1 percent of the nation's total softwood lumber. Output for individual states, however, suggests that only two are major producers. In 1977, a peak production year for all western states, Idaho output reached nearly 2 billion board feet—6.3 percent of the nation's softwood production—and Montana produced 1.3 billion board feet. Wyoming and Utah, on the other hand, produced only 225 and 58 million board feet, respectively. Other Rocky Mountain states ranged between the two extremes, supplying under 400 million board feet each. Douglas-fir provided 25 percent and 50 percent of the softwood lumber output in Idaho and Montana, respectively, while over half of Wyoming's production was lodgepole pine, and nearly half of Utah's was ponderosa pine. Timber products not reflected in these production statistics include railroad ties (which are still used in tremendous quantities), juniper fence posts (known locally as "cedar posts"), firewood, and EXCELSIOR—shavings commonly made from soft woods such as poplar or quaking aspen and used for packing.

In the 1980s, the timber industry in the Rocky Mountain Region is a vital industry to Idaho and Montana and is important in Arizona. In other Rocky Mountain states, the lumber industry is of small significance.

FURTHER READING: Merrill G. Burlingame and K. Ross Toole, *A History of Montana* (1957). F. Ross Peterson, *Idaho: A Bicentennial History* (1976). Edward H. Teplow, Jr., *History of Arizona* (1958).

JAY M. HAYMOND

LUMBER INDUSTRY: SOUTHERN STATES

At the opening of the seventeenth century, forests blanketed most of the territory that would become the southeastern states of Virginia, the Carolinas, Georgia, Florida, Alabama, Mississippi, Arkansas, and Louisiana, together with the eastern parts of Oklahoma and Texas. Timber was Virginia's first principal export before the rise of tobacco. However, when the white pine of New England became available in the 1630s, English demand for southern yellow pine lumber declined, and it thereafter was manufactured mainly for domestic use or for export to the West Indies. Of the British colonies on the south Atlantic coast, only Maryland (with heavy demand for shipbuilding timber) remained a net importer of lumber. Colonists produced lumber with whipsaws or pit saws. Their buildings were often made of lumber intermixed with hewn timbers. As the Southern interior was settled, local forest industries expanded. The Dismal Swamp area along the Virginia-North Carolina border yielded cypress (or baldcypress) shingles and shakes. Large amounts of wood were used in cooperage to ship tobacco abroad and in fencing to keep roaming animals out of croplands. The many rivers flowing into the Atlantic supplied power for the operation of sash saws (the first waterpowered sawmill in Virginia was constructed in 1620). By the end of the colonial period, North Carolina led the South in lumber manufacture.

England imported masts from Virginia as early as 1609, but interest shifted to white pine masts from New England after 1634. Early sad experience with northern white oak blinded English shipbuilders to the virtues of the live oaks that grew along the Southern coast. Americans successfully used live oak for SHIPBUILDING as early as 1750, and after 1799 the federal government took measures to ensure a continued supply. However, the development of forest industries in the Southern colonies was so far behind that of the Northern and middle colonies that by the mid-eighteenth century only Virginia, North Carolina, South Carolina, and Georgia had not troubled to enact timber trespass laws. The Southern forest was viewed primarily as an obstacle to be cleared before agriculture could begin.

Along the Gulf Coast, the French harvested pine and cypress for shipment to the West Indies and Europe up to 1757, when trade was disrupted by Spanish, and later English, occupation. Toward the end of the eighteenth century, the rise of New Orleans as a port, the need for replacement of buildings consumed in conflagrations there, the development of the sugar industry with its demand for boxes and other wood materials, together with the renewal of some of the West Indian and European trade, revived the market for Gulf Coast lumber.

After 1794, American settlement in the Old Southwest placed demands on pine, hardwood, cedar, and cypress stands. Unauthorized logging on public lands in southern Alabama and Mississippi led in part to passage of the Timber Trespass Act of 1831, the first general law concerning forest conservation to be enacted by the U. S. Congress.

Many Southern cities of the antebellum era grew as export centers of lumber and other forest products, among them Norfolk, Virginia; Wilmington, North Carolina; Charleston, South Carolina; Savannah, Georgia; Pensacola, Florida; Mobile, Alabama; and New Orleans. The use of steam engines freed sawmills from dependence upon locations near flowing water. Steam-driven sawmills were introduced in the South shortly after the beginning of the nineteenth century. Better saws (especially the circular saw introduced after 1840), carriages, and other equipment also speeded the production of lumber and gave wider range to the types of timber that could be produced.

Introduction of railroads into the South in the

R. F. Learned & Sons sawmill and lumberyard at Natchez, Mississippi, began operation in 1824, when it was founded by Andrew Brown. American Forest Institute Photo.

1830s increased demands for timber, crossties, and lumber for the construction of boxcars, but not until after the Civil War did railroad transportation really assist the growth of the Southern forest products industries. Only after the Civil War did such important furniture manufacturing centers as Highpoint, North Carolina, come into being. There were no really important manufactories of farm implements and wagons and carriages south of Kentucky. Such publicists as William Gregg and James B. D. DeBow decried the willingness of their fellow Southerners, living amidst great virgin forests, to import objects made of wood by non-Southern craftsmen.

In the half-century following the Civil War, timbermen in all sections of the South expanded their operations. As the supplies of white pine dwindled, first in the Northeast and subsequently in the Lake States, Northern lumbermen turned their attention to southern yellow pine. Greenleaf Johnson and E. L. Tunis,

Baltimore lumbermen, began selling North Carolina pine in the North shortly after the Civil War. William E. Dodge of New York purchased pineland in Georgia in 1875. By the 1880s, Northern shipbuilders used as much Southern pine lumber as northern woods. Later in that decade, Southern pine found a market in the plains states. Kansas lumber dealers Samuel H. Fullerton and Robert Fullerton purchased timberlands in Louisiana in 1894 and later in Arkansas. In the same period, through such ports as Pensacola, Escambia, Mobile, Jacksonville, Georgetown, Savannah, Biloxi, New Orleans, and Galveston, Southern lumber was shipped to Europe, the Middle East, and South and Central America. Improvements in woodworking machinery, especially introduction of the band saw, aided by steam yarding equipment and railroad log transportation, sped the destruction of the Southern forest. The South was dotted with hundreds of sawmill towns and villages such as Laurel, Hattiesburg, Selma, Bogalusa, Electric Mills, Weycross, and Hammond. Big mill operators not only became tremendous economic forces in the South, they also exercised a strong influence on the region's politics. By 1880, according to Charles S. SARGENT's *Report on the Forests of North America*, prepared for the U. S. Census Office, the South produced 13 percent of the lumber cut in the United States, with 4,360 sawmills which had a capital value of $16,344,401 and manufactured 2,377,700,000 board feet of lumber (the nation's totals for that year were 25,708 sawmills, valued at $181,186,122, producing 18,091,356,000 board feet of lumber). At that time, the South was just entering the first phase of heavy exploitation of its vast expanse of virgin pine stands. By 1910, Southern lumber production had approached 44 percent of the national figure, and it remained near that proportion until the 1940s.

The first lumber trade association in the South was the Missouri and Arkansas Lumber Association, formed by pine manufacturers in 1883. The South's first regionwide trade association, the Southern Pine Association, was formed in 1915 from various regional groups.

The era of the great sawmills and the exploitation of the Southern woods lasted approximately from 1890 to 1920. One giant band sawmill succeeded another as the largest: the Camp Mill in Virginia produced 12 million board feet in 1887, the Gulf Lumber Company mill in Louisiana sawed 120 million feet in 1906, and in 1908 the Great Southern plant built by the Pennsylvania lumbermen Frank and Charles GOODYEAR at Bogalusa, Louisiana, could produce 1 million board feet in one day. Southern lumber production peaked between 1908 and 1916 and descended rather sharply after that date. In 1899, the region's 6,342 sawmills produced 11,115,988,000 board feet of lumber, and a decade later this was increased to 17,712 mills and 19,972,822,000 feet. By by 1920, production of the 6,353 surviving mills had declined to 11,490,713,000 board feet. Nevertheless, from the end of the nineteenth century to 1950 southern yellow pine provided more of the lumber cut each year in the United States than any other species.

By 1930, the heart of the Southern pine and hardwood stands had been destroyed. Tragically, too many sawmill operators had operated on the policy of "cut-out-and-get-out." Behind them they left large areas of woodlands in cutover and smoldering devastation. Fires often destroyed prospects of recovery by native commercially important species. Social life in the lumbering South suffered serious displacement. Even at the height of lumber prosperity, sawmill villages had been crude affairs of two and three-room shanties, jammed close together. Sanitary facilities were rudimentary. Lumber workers' wages were low, hours long, and working conditions dismal. Company stores charged high prices and extended credit at high interest rates, and many companies issued tokens of scrip redeemable only in their commissaries. However, conditions did vary from town to town and company to company; some residents of lumber COMPANY TOWNS compared life there favorably to life in nonmill towns nearby. Even a company town could offer a life better in some respects than that in an isolated, rural farmstead.

When big mills closed and moved on, they often left the mill-town segment of the Southern population economically and sociologically stranded. In the case of the thousands of tiny, independent "peckerwood" sawmills, which carried the burden of the Southern lumber manufacturing from the 1920s through the 1930s, workers nearly always combined logging with farming or other seasonal employment without upsetting either function or suffering serious social displacement when the little mills cut through their timber boundaries.

Henry E. Hardtner of Urania, Louisiana, introduced scientific forestry to the Southern lumber industry. A Louisiana native of German immigrant parents, Hardtner began experiments on the timberlands of his Urania Lumber Company in 1904 to test the feasibility of growing and harvesting timber in successive crops. Hardtner served as the first chairman of the Louisiana State Conservation Department from 1908 to 1912. He invited U. S. FOREST SERVICE investigations on his land, in 1913 signed a reforestation contract with the state, and inaugurated the first forest fire protection on any large Southern property. Hardtner toured the South as a missionary of scientific forestry, and his example prompted the Great Southern Lumber Company also to undertake large-scale reforestation projects in 1920; others followed. Also important in the adoption of conservation by industry were the evolution of taxation policies that would encourage landowners to defer the harvesting of growing timber and the rise of stumpage prices to values which made an investment in forestry seem worthwhile.

In the 1930s, as the second growth of yellow pine sprang up in the cutover, the remaining large companies began to adopt management policies that would permit timber harvest on a sustained-yield basis. Sawmill operations became more stationary, carrying on continuous operations acquiring logs from renewable, forest-managed stands. Crawler tractors and logging trucks replaced steam equipment. With the building of modern highways and truck transportation, the territory of individual mills was extended. One of the claims for improvement in its section of the South by the TENNESSEE VALLEY AUTHORITY was that it speeded up scientific forest management to the point that sawmills could operate at permanent stands as did other industries. With the discovery of a chemical process for neutralizing the heavy resin content of southern pine, the pulpwood industry of the South grew to the extent that by 1979 the region was supplying approximately 65 percent of the nation's paper stock. Large forest landowners since the 1950s have raised pine trees like crops of cotton or corn, using machinery, such as hydraulic shears and feller-bunchers, that is well adapted to mass harvesting of relatively small second growth.

The hardwood lumber industry was much smaller than the yellow pine industry. In 1916, the year that hardwood production in the South surpassed that of the Central States, hardwood accounted for less than 14 percent of Southern lumber output. All Southern states supplied some hardwood but the major producers were Arkansas, Mississippi, Virginia, Louisiana, and North Carolina. As an important industry, Southern hardwood lumber manufacture dates from the late nineteenth century, when lumbermen from the Ohio Valley moved into the border states. By 1920, much of the southern Appalachians had been logged. Hardwood mill operators sought particular woods for specific purposes. The first to be cut by Northerners was walnut; then, as the available supply of walnut dwindled, poplar, which became the preferred wood for wagon and carriage bodies and later for automobile bodies. As poplar was used up, lumbermen turned to cottonwood and later to red gum. White oak was used first for tight cooperage and later for quartersawed lumber. Cottonwood was heavily used for boxes. As sawing and seasoning techniques and facilities improved, many hardwoods which previously had been regarded as worthless came to be of value. Among them were gum, elm, hackberry, tupelo, soft maple, magnolia, pecan, willow, and many more, often for purposes for which their decorative qualities made them particularly attractive, such as interior finish, furniture, and venetian blind slats. Hickory and ash have been used largely for wooden handles. Many hardwoods have gone into DIMENSION STOCK, a waste-reducing process of cutting to the precise size needed in secondary manufactures. North Carolina with its Appalachian hardwoods became a center of the furniture industry in the early twentieth century, while Memphis was an important center for hardwood flooring manufacturing. Over 27 percent of the national hardwood production in 1909 came from the South, and this proportion increased thereafter. Southern hardwood fluctuated widely, but the crest of 3,637,405,000 board feet, reached in 1929, was not approached again until World War II.

Another specialized segment of the Southern lumber industry was cypress (baldcypress) lumber manufacturing. Baldcypress (*Taxodium distichum*) grows in swamplands near the coast and in scattered "brakes" inland. The "tidewater red" has generally been considered more desirable than the inland-growing "yellow cypress," as the latter contains a wider band of less durable sapwood. Cypress is technically a softwood, but it has been cut, manufactured, and sold by both hardwood and softwood manufacturers. Cypress may have been the first lumber sawed in North America when the Spanish settled St. Augustine, Florida, in 1577. In the eighteenth and nineteenth centuries, cypress was the preferred wood for shingles, and bored cypress logs were used for water mains. Both the English colonists on the south Atlantic Coast and the French in Louisiana used cypress extensively in building and ship construction. Not until the 1880s was cypress lumber widely distributed, however. Early producers awaited floods in order to float cypress logs out of their swamps to the nearest bayous where they could be made up into rafts for removal to sawmills. In 1889, William Bristol of Harvey, Louisiana, developed the pullboat—a steam skidder mounted on a scow—and a system of canals dredged through the swamps. Cypress, because of its durability and resistance to decay, was employed in building construction, vats and tanks, boats, and greenhouses. Cypress lumber production, virtually all in the South, peaked at just over 1 billion board feet in 1913.

FURTHER READING: John A. Eisterhold, "Colonial Beginnings in the South's Lumber Industry: 1607–1800," *Southern Lumberman* (Dec. 15, 1971): 150–153, and "Lumber and Trade in the Lower Mississippi Valley and New Orleans, 1800–1860," *Louisiana History* 13 (Winter 1972): 71-91. James E. Fickle, *The New South and the "New Competition": Trade Association Development in the Southern Pine Industry* (1980). C. W. Goodyear, *Bogalusa Story* (1950). Nollie Hickman, *Mississippi Harvest* (1962). Stanley F. Horn, *This Fascinating Lumber Business* (1951). Walter W. Kellogg, *The Kellogg Story: Fifty Years in Southern Hardwoods* (1969). John Hebron Moore, *Andrew Brown and Cypress Lumbering in the Old Southwest* (1967).

THOMAS D. CLARK

LUMBERMAN'S FRONTIER

In 1893, Frederick Jackson Turner introduced into the writing of history the idea of the frontier as a central, shaping force. He turned away from European antecedents to find the mainsprings of the United States democracy and institutions in its frontier experience. For a time, the frontier thesis dominated the thought and writing of American historians. Although it came in for increasing criticism during and after the 1930s, it continues strong today.

Turner spoke not of a single frontier, but of a series of frontiers sweeping westward one after another, each bringing a more advanced social and economic state. Oddly, although Turner had grown up in Portage, Wisconsin, and later reminisced about loggers and timber raftsmen who came through the town during his boyhood, neither he nor his many disciples gave much attention to the lumberman's frontier. They focused on explorers, fur trappers, miners, farmers, and others but seldom wrote of loggers. In spite of this oversight, the lumberman's frontier was one of the most important of the nation's many frontiers.

From the first European settlements, forests played a vital role in American life. Lumbering was a leading activity in the colonies and young nation, and the use of wood was so widespread that the period down to 1850 has been called "America's Wooden Age." But not all places where lumbering took place or wood was used were parts of the lumberman's frontier. Much timber harvesting and lumber manufacturing was incidental to or supplementary to other activities, especially farming. Much lumbering was done where other enterprises dominated the economy. Not until demand was such that lumbering would pay when carried out far from the point of consumption—that is, not until forests could draw men and money for the purposes of timber harvesting and lumber manufacturing—and not until they did so on such a scale that the resultant activities dominated the areas involved, can a lumberman's frontier be said to have truly emerged. Other specialized forest operations, such as the production of NAVAL STORES and masts for the Royal Navy, and much lumber production took place earlier, but the real lumbering frontier made its initial appearance in Maine early in the nineteenth century.

The lumberman's frontier was central in opening and developing major parts of New England; portions of the interior of New York and Pennsylvania; much of Michigan, Wisconsin, and Minnesota; vast stretches of the South; and large parts of the Far West. Lumbering opened to settlement many areas bypassed or as yet unreached by farmers, miners, and others; and it turned resources into the capital that, through investment in other enterprises, gradually built a modern, diversified economy in place after place. In other cases, where natural conditions lent

themselves to ongoing timber production better than to other economic pursuits, lumbering gradually evolved from its extractive, frontier stage into a continuing operation. The capital generated during the extractive stage helped to make the transition possible.

But the lumbering frontier was also a frontier that failed. Clearcut logging—"cut-out-and-get-out" practices—removed the resource base from vast reaches of the upper Lake States and elsewhere and left in its wake not a diversified economy but a poverty belt. Capital generated by these operations was transferred to regions where better investment opportunities awaited. Since the farmland in the area was submarginal for the most part and other resources were limited, many decades were to pass before tourism and a rising emphasis on outdoor recreation would finally bring some economic vitality back to the cutover region.

The lumberman's frontier did not bring the first settlement to Maine. At first, residents of Maine depended upon fishing and the fur trade for their livelihood, but these trades soon declined. Since agriculture held out little promise in most places, many residents had by the end of the eighteenth century turned to the woods to eke out a living. Initially, most woodsmen were primitive resource gatherers, like their trapper forerunners. Their harsh life and crude, irresponsible behavior shocked educated observers. But as markets grew in Boston and elsewhere along the Atlantic seaboard as well as in the West Indies and Europe men of substance were attracted to the forests. Sawmills sprang up at favored sites; speculation in timberland grew rife. An economy based on lumbering quickly emerged. Bangor, its development spurred by the success of the Penobscot boom built in 1828, became the great center. Henry David Thoreau described the community in 1846: "There stands the city of Bangor . . . like a star at the edge of night, still hewing at the forest of which it is built, already overflowing with the luxuries and refinements of Europe, and sending its vessels to Spain, to England, and to the West Indies for its groceries— and yet only a few ax-men have gone 'up river' into the howling wilderness which feeds it." Thoreau underestimated the number of workers in the woods, but he certainly was correct in his assessment of Bangor. It was the main entrepôt to the first lumbering frontier.

As Maine's white pines dwindled in number, some lumbermen turned to spruce, a less valuable species, while others moved westward to new stands of pine. Some migrated to Pennsylvania, where they and their associates commenced operating a large boom at Williamsport in 1850. Within two decades, Williamsport had outstripped Bangor to become the world's leading lumber-producing center.

The quest for farmland had drawn people into Pennsylvania's interior at an early date, but not until the mid-nineteenth century—when forest resources drew a new wave of settlers and entrepreneurs—could the lumbering frontier be said to have reached the area. Moving as it did into a region with a pre-existing population and established economic patterns, friction between the old and new soon resulted. Violent clashes occurred, especially in Clearfield County in 1857.

By 1880, Pennsylvania's pine stands were showing signs of severe depletion. In response, lumbermen followed the pattern set in Maine: some turned to cutting another species (hemlock, in this case), while others migrated. Most went either to the Lake States, where lumbering was booming, or southward along the Appalachians, where logging techniques developed in the mountainous areas of Pennsylvania and upstate New York could be applied. This southward movement constituted a secondary lumbering frontier, one generally overshadowed by the larger movement westward.

Migration into the Lake States from Maine and elsewhere had begun by 1830 and gained momentum thereafter. The opening of the Erie Canal in 1825 provided access to eastern markets for the major lumbering center that soon arose around Saginaw and Bay City, Michigan. As settlement in the Midwest grew, Chicago became a great lumber emporium, and other centers developed along the Mississippi River and its tributaries. Previously, most settlement in the Lake States had been on the prairies or in the lightly timbered, mixed forests of the southern parts of Michigan, Wisconsin, and Minnesota. When migrating lumbermen moved into the pine forests to the north, they repeated the pattern of Maine, invading an area largely unsettled. Log drives, booms, and skidding techniques perfected in Maine were well adapted for use in the Lake States. As a result, loggers from Maine were highly prized by operators, some of whom recruited heavily in Bangor and other lumber towns of the Pine Tree State. Pennsylvania, New York, eastern Canada, and Europe added to the influx.

As lumbermen cut the pine forests of the Lake States, they moved further north and west in search of stands. Many crossed into Ontario; logs floated across Lake Huron kept Saginaw and Bay City mills sawing long after nearer forests had been depleted. By the 1880s, many were looking at even more distant timberland in the Gulf South and the Pacific Coast states.

Major migrations into the South's pineries and the West's Douglas-fir and redwood forests were soon under way.

In the South, railroads opened many previously inaccessible stands, untapped during earlier operations that had been carried out either in conjunction with agrarian undertakings or along the coastal waterways to supply the export trade to the West Indies. As nowhere previously, the lumberman's frontier in the South was a frontier dependent upon railroads. Since rail lines could be laid relatively cheaply in the often gentle terrain of the South, lumbering expanded rapidly there. Earlier settlers who had depended upon simple semisubsistence agriculture chafed under the new conditions that the influx of men and capital brought to the piney woods, but at the same time they welcomed the growing number of economic opportunities.

By 1909, lumber production had peaked in the South. Some lumbermen moved once more, joining those who had gone to the West Coast earlier. While most previous lumbering in the Far West had been in the Douglas-fir and redwood regions, during the first decades of the twentieth century more and more woodsmen transferred to the pine forests of the Sierra Nevada, to the areas east of the Cascades, and to northern Idaho. This was the last major phase of the lumberman's frontier. Save in Alaska, there were no vast, untapped softwood forests in the country left to invade; and those in Alaska were such that they could be efficiently tapped only with modern technology and large investments. The lumberman's frontier never moved on to Alaska's forests. When lumbering developed there on a significant level it was of the postfrontier type and, in any case, 90 percent of Alaska's forestland had commercial potential only for pulpwood production.

As the frontier phase passed, lumbering turned from being an extractive industry to one based on sustained-yield management. It became less resource and labor intensive, but more capital intensive. As a result, lumbering continues in many districts where the lumberman's frontier once swept through. But for other areas, the industry's reorientation came too late. With the resource base badly depleted, the resumption of major production in such areas remains years away.

Many writers have decried the waste and environmental destruction of the lumbering frontier. Both were real enough. Yet not until new systems of taxing timber holdings had been devised, the threat of forest fires had been reduced, and the price of timberland had risen above the cost of growing a second crop on old land was it economically feasible for lumbermen to do other than cut out and get out. They were both products and prisoners of the socioeconomic order in which they operated, and the lumbering frontier—with all its costs—was the natural result.

But during its heyday in the nineteenth century, Americans were not much given to decrying what the lumberman's frontier wrought. It provided cheap building materials for a rapidly growing nation, furnished a source of badly needed foreign exchange, and served to generate essential investment capital. By the time the lumbering frontier closed shortly after World War I, the nation's needs had changed. Nostalgic old-timers might mourn the passing of the lumbering frontier; but the nation, having gained from its earlier presence, was now ready to gain even more from the sustained-yield, multiple-use forest utilization that was to replace it gradually.

FURTHER READING: Stewart H. Holbrook, *Holy Old Mackinaw* (1938). David C. Smith, "The Logging Frontier," *Journal of Forest History* 18 (Oct. 1974): 96–106. Numerous state, regional, and company histories touch on the industry's migration, especially Ralph W. Hidy, Frank Ernest Hill, and Allan Nevins, *Timber and Men* (1963).

THOMAS R. COX

LUMBER, PLYWOOD, AND PAPER PRICES

Lumber, plywood, and paper may reasonably be classed as semiprocessed raw materials. That is, they stand midway, in a technical and economic sense, be-

tween a natural resource on the ground and a finished article in the hands of the final consumer. The forest industries start with trees in the forest, cut them for logs, haul them to a mill, process the wood to form various products, transport these products to markets, and sell them to consumers. The whole process is a complex one, with many technical aspects. It also has many business-organizational complexities, as title to the products changes hands and as men, machines, and management skills are combined with the resource to form the desired products. Thus, the point at which prices are measured and the form of the material to which they apply is basic to an understanding of the meaning of the prices.

Wholesale lumber prices are available by year since 1800 (Figure 1). These prices for the earliest years naturally apply only to Eastern markets, for much of the Midwest and West was not then settled. Prices for later years are more national in scope. Many foresters, economists, and others have called attention to the fact that lumber prices are almost alone among raw materials prices in exhibiting a sustained upward trend in real terms—that is, in terms of prices of all commodities and services as a whole. Many observers expect that lumber prices will continue to rise more or less indefinitely and at more or less the past rate; but this may not be a sound projection for the future.

This apparently steady upward movement of lumber prices is composed of several rather diverse price trends. There have been rather extensive periods of

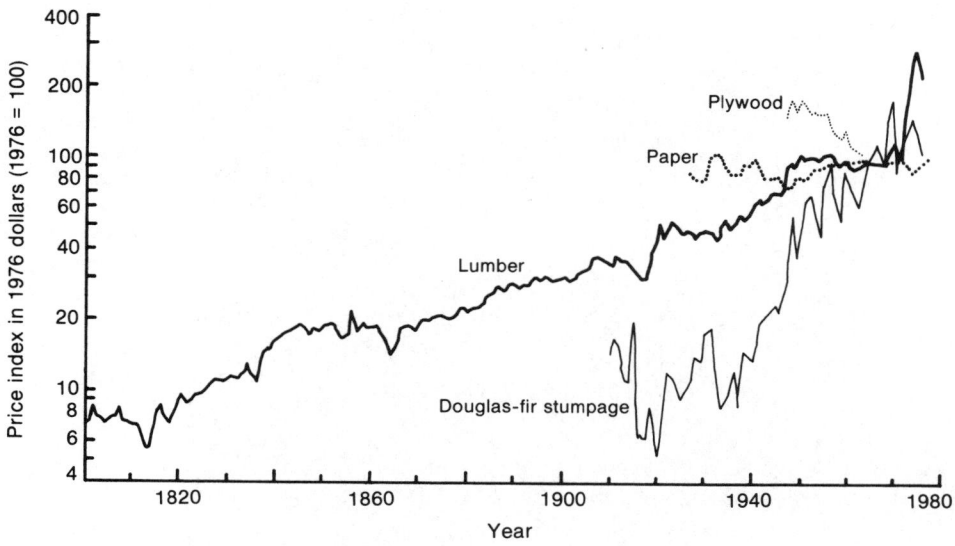

FIGURE 1.   Price indices (1976 = 100) for lumber, paper, plywood, and Douglas-fir stumpage, for years of record, 1800 to 1975.

years with near-stability of prices, a few periods with rather noticeable downward price trends over several years, and other periods of sharply rising prices.

The trend in lumber prices differs sharply from the trend in plywood prices. The latter, in real terms, has been more downward than upward. These divergences in price trends have surely been a major factor in the substantial substitution of plywood for lumber over the past fifty years, although the relatively higher productivity of labor when using plywood in construction, as compared with the use of lumber for the same tasks, has also had an influence.

To a substantial extent, these differences in trends of lumber and plywood prices reflect a depletion of the original virgin stands of timber as well as the development of new technologies. At one time, much stumpage was at extremely low prices, with the less accessible stands having no value. Gradually, as the higher quality and more accessible older stands were harvested, cutting proceeded into lower quality or less accessible timber stands, in either case with a rise in costs compared to value created. Price rises of lumber were a typical outcome. This probably would have happened for plywood except that new technologies have been developed whereby plywood could be made more cheaply, or from lower-grade logs, or both.

Paper prices show a still different trend—downward in some short periods of years, upward in other periods, and for the whole period of ready price record (since about 1925) no distinctive overall trend. Paper prices reflect, among other factors, the development of pulp growing in pine plantations in the South particularly but in other parts of the country as well. Techniques of growing pulpwood and of paper manufacture have also changed over the years, with consequent effects on paper prices.

As the great volumes of mature virgin timber are used up and as forestry moves from simply letting trees grow naturally to methods of managing forests more intensively, the prices of timber in the woods will come to reflect more closely the costs of growing it than has often been the case in the past. These costs and the costs of manufacture will affect the supply potential for the different wood products and such supply costs will interact with market demands to determine market prices.

FURTHER READING: Marion Clawson, "Forests in the Long Sweep of American History," *Science* 204 (June 1979): 1168–1174. William A. Duerr, *Fundamentals of Forestry Economics* (1960).

MARION CLAWSON

LUMBER PRODUCTION

A tree and the logs cut from it are rough cylinders, measurable by diameter and length; pieces of lumber, whether simple boards, beams, or two-by-fours, are rectangular prisms measurable by breadth, width, and length. From these simple geometrics spring much of

Logs entering sawmills are often debarked to decrease wear on saws, to allow a better view of log quality, and to make it easier to produce bark-free wood chips for the paper industry. Here high-velocity water literally blasts the bark off. Mills also use mechanical means to remove the bark. Weyerhaeuser Company Photo.

Until bandsaws were introduced, millwrights needed ingenuity to handle the extra large logs of the Pacific Coast. In 1869, David Evans of Eureka, California, patented a four-saw headrig to handle oversized logs. As the log was carried forward into the saws, the combination of a horizontal blade at left and the vertical blade at right cut out full-length wedges. Reduced to size, the log could then be accommodated by the conventional double circular saw headrig at center. Forest History Society Lantern Slide Collection.

the work, drama, and value of lumber manufacture and use.

Whole logs were used extensively in the colonial and early national periods of American history to build cabins, houses, and other structures. Logs could be trimmed flat on two sides with simple hand tools and thus be made to fit somewhat better into a structure than unmodified, round logs, but even today whole logs are used for piling and as poles for power and telephone lines.

Sawing of logs into lumber began early in American

history, at first by simple hand methods. Early lumber varied considerably in width, breadth, and uniformity of thickness. In time, waterpower, then steam power, and still later electricity and internal combustion were used to drive saws for lumber manufacture. As more complex methods were applied, with typically larger and more powerful installations, the precision of size measurements of lumber improved. Today, computers and other sophisticated equipment are used to enable the sawing of the log to yield the most valuable lumber.

In the nineteenth century wood fiber began to be

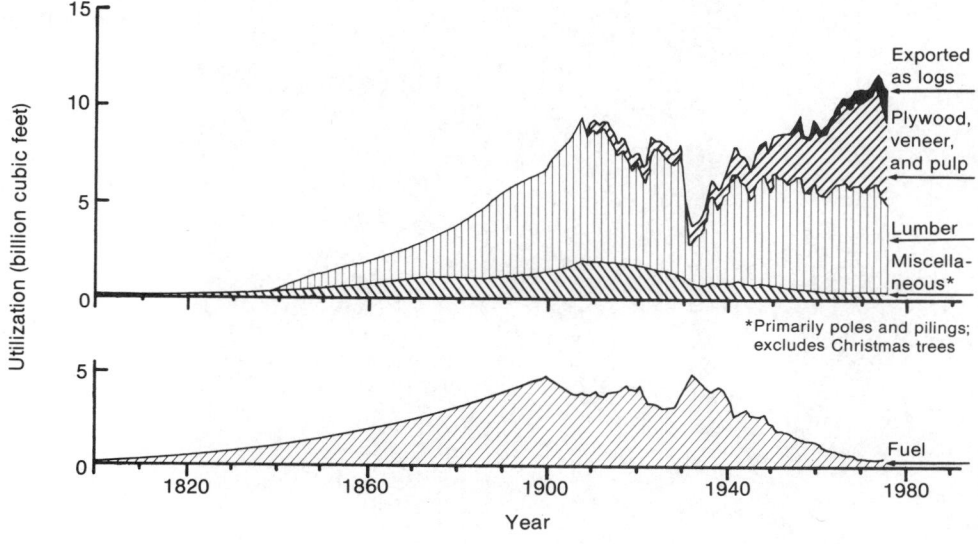

FIGURE 1. Total utilization of U.S.-grown wood (in roundwood equivalent), by major form of use, 1800 to 1975.

SOURCE: *Science* 204 (June 15, 1979): 1171. © AAAS. Reprinted by permission.

A bandsaw headrig cuts a thick slab from a Douglas-fir log. These blades are less wasteful than circular saws because they are thinner and also more accurate. Weyerheuser Company Photo.

A worker guides slab to conveyors for resawing into various lumber products. American Forest Institute Photo.

used to make plywood and paper. Manufacturing processes of these wood products are more complex, hence more expensive, than simple lumber sawing, but the products are of greater value and wider usefulness than boards. Plywood has tended to replace lumber in many uses, especially for construction, in part because it has much of the same ease of use (being readily nailed and cut to any desired size and shape) and because it is lighter and easier to put in place. Paper, too, has tended to replace lumber in some uses, especially in packaging. But lumber is far from outmoded; it continues to be useful for furniture, structural frameworks, and many other parts of buildings.

Lumber production (and consumption) in the United States expanded throughout the nineteenth century as population rose and as settlement of the Midwest and Far West proceeded. The period from 1890 to 1910 was in a sense the great age of lumber. Total annual lumber production reached a peak of 46 billion board feet

A worker sharpens the replaceable teeth of a circular saw headrig. Generally replaced by less wasteful bandsaws, this large blade made the first cuts after the log entered the mill. Invention of replaceable teeth greatly increased the saw's life expectancy, since teeth break when striking large spikes or other hard objects. Forest History Society Photo.

Multiblade gangsaw produces many boards simultaneously. These saws are often used to mill smaller logs of relatively uniform quality. Weyerhaeuser Company Photo.

around 1907. It stayed relatively high until the end of the 1920s, but it nose-dived to a low of 13.5 billion board feet in 1932 during the Great Depression, when construction of new buildings virtually ceased. Lumber production rebounded after 1940, first to meet the needs of war and then of the postwar building boom. Since 1940, total annual lumber production has stayed nearly constant, well above 30 billion board feet, with only a slight, irregular trend downward. On a per capita basis, the trend has been downward, of course, since total population has increased. But by any measure, lumber is still an important building material in the United States. The two-by-four is ubiquitous in almost every construction project, either in temporary structures or in the finished building.

The replacement of lumber by plywood and paper (and by plastics and lightweight metal alloys) has been substantial, and it seems likely that this trend will continue. Lumber production and consumption are likely, however, to remain high for a great many years.

FURTHER READING: Henry B. Steer, comp., *Lumber Production in the United States, 1799–1946*, U. S. Department of Agriculture Miscellaneous Publication No. 669 (1948). U.S. Bureau of the Census, *Current Industrial Reports: Lumber Production and Mill Stacks* (1959-).

MARION CLAWSON

LUMBER STANDARDS AND GRADING

The development of American lumber standards is due to individual and industrywide efforts, in cooperation with departments of the federal government, to provide a consistent basis for the classification of wood products. It was not an easy task because of the variations in the growth characteristics of trees, the needs of different markets, and the manner in which lumber is produced and distributed. Close uniformity in sizes, as well as quality, was needed to assure interchangeability, regardless of the mill that produced the lumber.

One of the earliest known lumber grading rules was developed in 1754 by a Scandinavian named Swan Alverdson. By 1833, the State of Maine had four official grades for white pine; the Saginaw Rules for Michigan provided for six grades. Grading rules were only a step behind the lumberman's westward march, and there were rules for Douglas-fir by 1906.

The 1890s witnessed a pronounced trend in the development of lumber grading rules in all producing regions. From the very beginning, the need for standardization of grades and manufacturing practices seemed to be the biggest influence in causing lumbermen to band together for the common good. The

grading and inspection of lumber was the most important function of the associations of lumber manufacturers that were formed in each of the producing regions—the Northeast, Lake States, South, and West. The National Association of Lumbermen was formed in 1874 in an attempt to replace regional standards with a national system of grading lumber, but the time was not right.

Early classification of quality was relatively simple but fully met consumer requirements at that time. Trees were large and plentiful, and there was no need from either a conservation or an economic standpoint to segregate the qualities in a way that would make the product suitable for particular uses. Frequently, clear lumber was used for studs, joints, and other items where appearance was a secondary consideration.

In 1897, the NATIONAL HARDWOOD LUMBER ASSOCIATION was formed to bring uniform standards to that important segment of the lumber industry. As for softwoods, at the turn of the century, the Northern Pine Association established twelve lumber classes for the Lake States, with three for clear, four for select, and five for common grades. Southern associations issued rules for their members, too.

It was not until the years immediately following World War I, however, that there was a major effort to bring about uniformity in lumber size and grade standards. Although definite strides had been made in the establishment of grading rules for the different species, there had been little success in coordination between the producing regions. Because of the increasing extent to which various species were competing in common markets, it seemed imperative that coordination be achieved.

Concurrent with this private effort, the Department of Commerce under Herbert Hoover was actively encouraging industries to use the facilities of its Simplified Practices Division. The lumber industry, through its American Lumber Congress, was quick to take advantage of this opportunity to establish basic provisions applicable to all regions. The industry in the late 1920s arrived at agreements on sizes and basic grading provisions that would be suitable for all softwoods, which became known as the American Lumber Standards (ALS). Hardwoods were not included in this program.

Representatives of the manufacturers, retailers, wholesalers, specifiers, and consumers of softwood lumber, such as architects, contractors, railroads, and millwork factories, participated in the movement. This coordination assured that the conclusions reached would be fair to all branches of the industry

Lumber is hand-sorted by grade on a conveyor belt called the "green chain." Forest History Society Photo.

and acceptable to consumers. The secretary of commerce appointed a Central Committee on Lumber Standards, on which all of these interested groups had representation. It functioned as a medium through which revisions of the ALS could be achieved. In recent years, there has been a complete and improved revision of the ALS, and the Central Committee was renamed the American Lumber Standards Committee.

By 1939, the standardization program of the lumber industry was well established. Lumber buyers, including departments of the federal government, required their lumber purchases to be supplied according to the grading rules for the species involved and to be properly marked as to grade. The Federal Housing Administration required all framing lumber in FHA-financed homes to bear the grade mark of the lumber association under whose rules the lumber was graded. In the interest of fair trade and honest dealings, this regulation was particularly important in the field of government purchases, where a contract is awarded to the lowest bidder. Through promotion and close supervision of the performance of mills authorized to grade mark with an association symbol, buyers generally were assured of quality.

When grading standards were first adopted by the lumber industry, it was quickly found that coordination under some form of authoritative supervision was vital. This coordination was accomplished through regular visits, examinations, and instructions by a corps of competent association inspectors. It was only in this manner that the manufacturers found it possible to produce uniform grades.

The practice of grade marking always has been important to lumber consumers. At the outset, it was realized that the promiscuous marking of lumber by the individual producer or seller would have little significance. If the mark is to mean anything, it must offer assurance that the lumber was graded properly under the applicable rules, and the grading behind the mark must be supervised. The basic pattern for this was established in the first ALS, and since then the mark has indicated the rules under which the lumber was graded. It also shows the symbol of the supervising association or other approved inspection agency.

The ALS Committee supervises all approved grading agencies and checks lumber bearing their grade marks at destination points to assure its conformance to the rules. Other refinements in the ALS include provisions for definite stress ratings to be assigned to the structural grades indicated in the mark, which offers further protection to lumber specifiers and buyers.

The standardization program of the lumber industry had become so effective by 1939 that some members of the industry began to complain about excessive

Lumber is graded piece by piece according to specific rules. Weyerhaeuser Company Photo.

controls. The Department of Justice responded with a thorough investigation of the activities of the several larger associations in the West and the South, as well as the NATIONAL LUMBER MANUFACTURERS ASSOCIATION (NLMA), the predecessor of the NATIONAL FOREST PRODUCTS ASSOCIATION (NFPA). This investigation culminated in consent decrees entered into by several of the larger regional associations and the NLMA. There was no charge of abuse, but the Department of Justice contended that benevolent restraint should not be relied upon, and the decrees explicitly stated the manner in which grading and inspection agencies must function. Thus, the industry was relieved of liability for restraint of trade as long as it conformed to these requirements. The pattern established in the first decree, which related to southern pine, was largely followed throughout.

From time to time, there have been proposals to have the federal government take control of lumber standards. However, the industry's program was judged effective, and the consent decrees kept it free of restraint of trade. The standardization program does not interfere with buyers and sellers as they negotiate contracts, and there is no requirement in any of the organizations for members to make only standard grades. The prime requirement is the maintenance of established size and grade standards, when standard grades are ordered or sold.

It was not until the mid-1960s that the ALS Committee succeeded in getting the concurrence of all producing regions to the inclusion of requirements that minimum ALS sizes apply at a specific moisture content. Previously, the grading rules of some regions permitted lumber to be dressed to ALS sizes whether green or dry, which more and more was unsatisfactory to specifiers and buyers. The current ALS provisions protect all branches of the trade as well as lumber consumers. Uniform standards contribute to product stability, which is of great value to producers, distributors, and consumers alike.

FURTHER READING: A. S. Boisfontaine, "Grading: Lumber's Quality Insurance," *American Lumberman* (Sept. 11, 1948): 236-240. Rodney C. Loehr, "Softwood Lumber Grading," *Southern Lumberman* 180 (May 1, 1950): 50, 52;

(May 15, 1950): 48, 50; (June 1, 1950): 50, 52. L. W. Smith and L. W. Wood, *History of Yard Lumber Sizes* (1964).

A. S. BOISFONTAINE

LUMBER TARIFFS

After the United States adopted its Constitution in 1789, the first important act of the first Congress was to pass a law establishing a schedule of duties on imports. Such legislation had proven a practical impossibility under the Articles of Confederation previously in force. This first tariff act, signed by President George Washington on July 4, 1789, included a 5 percent levy on imports of logs and lumber. This duty remained in force until May 2, 1792, when Congress placed "unmanufactured wood" (apparently including rough lumber) on the free list. However, neither such legislative acts nor foreign competition itself were serious concerns for American lumber manufacturers during the early years of the Republic, for imports of both logs and lumber were negligible. Early tariffs on logs and wood products were for revenue, not for the protection of an infant industry that, with growing markets and an ample store of raw materials, had little to fear from abroad. Canada was the only potentially significant source of competition, and until Great Britain's trade policies underwent basic changes in the 1840s, the vast bulk of the Canadian cut was drawn to British markets.

The early tariffs shifted repeatedly. In 1794, Congress placed ad valorem duties ranging up to 15 percent on "cabinet wares, and all manufactures of wood, or of which wood is the material of chief value," but unmanufactured wood continued to enter duty free. An act in 1812 raised the tariff on the dutiable items to 30 percent ad valorem. Not until 1833 did Congress for the first time specifically place boards and planks on the list of taxed items, initially setting the tariff at 25 percent but reducing it to 20 percent nine months later.

Gradually, laws became even more specific. In 1842, Congress placed a 30 percent levy on boards, planks, staves, and scantling, as well as on hewed and sawed timber; a 20 percent tax on rough boards, staves, and scantling, and on rough sawn timbers; and a 15 percent tariff on rosewood, satinwood, mahogany, and cedar. Unmanufactured wood not otherwise specified continued to enter free of duties. Congress revised this law in 1846. Among other changes, it placed a 30 percent ad valorem tax on all logs (most of which had been allowed duty-free entry since 1792).

By mid-century, Canada had become the focal point in discussions of the lumber tariff. The Reciprocity Treaty of 1854 both settled disputes over the fishing privileges of British and American citizens in each other's waters and provided for duty-free trade in a number of items, including logs and lumber. In response, imports from Canada grew. Sawmill owners in the United States soon felt the impact of this competition and therefore welcomed American abrogation of the treaty in 1866. Thereafter, they took an active interest in the tariff question, going so far as to actively oppose proposals for the remission of duties on Canadian lumber sent to facilitate the rebuilding of Chicago following the disastrous fire of 1871.

Responding to these new concerns of lumbermen, Congress revised the duties on wood products in 1872. This legislation was the first to contain a separate schedule for lumber. It increased tariffs on planed or finished lumber (fifty cents per thousand board feet for each side finished) and further increased the duty if the product was tongue-and-grooved (another fifty cents per thousand board feet). A tax of one dollar per thousand board feet was placed on rough sawn lumber of hemlock, whitewood, sycamore, and basswood, and two dollars per thousand on all other kinds. Shingles were charged thirty-five cents per thousand pieces, laths fifteen cents. Logs remained on the free list. Clearly, legislation was now being shaped to protect American manufacturers; a lumber tariff for revenue only was a thing of the past.

Canadian producers were hard hit. The crash of 1873 and the ensuing depression would have led to a dwindling of lumber shipments to the United States in any case, but the new tariff exacerbated the problem. Exports to the United States declined from a high of $29 million in 1873 to $13 million in 1878. Production and employment fell, many firms failed, crown revenues shrank, and emigration to the United States rose. In response, the Conservative party adopted protectionism in the form of its so-called National Policy. Through import duties of their own, Canadians pushed up the cost of essential supplies while doing nothing to reopen outlets in the United States, but the approach was widely acclaimed in Canada nonetheless. The return of prosperity in 1878 led to rising demand, and the Conservative party's policies received undue credit for the improvement.

From early in the nineteenth century, logs had been exported from Canada to the United States, where they were sawn and where the lumber was sold. Residents north of the border were complaining by the 1850s that this amounted to an exporting of jobs. By the 1880s, exportation of logs had become a major issue. Lumbermen in Michigan were importing huge rafts of logs from the Georgian district in Ontario in order to supplement their own dwindling supplies. In 1886, Michigan lumbermen reportedly held rights to 1.75 billion board feet of standing timber in Canada. Millmen north of the border, unhappy that their American counterparts could take logs home to be sawn and sold behind a tariff wall in competition with the Canadian product, turned to their government for redress. In 1886, Canada increased its export duty on logs to two dollars per thousand. In 1888, the rate was raised to three dollars per thousand, but it was returned to two dollars a year later. These levies were a severe blow to manufacturers who had bought timber in Canada to supply mills in Saginaw, Michigan, and elsewhere in the United States. Some now moved their plants north of the border, but the massive influx of men and capital that Canadian policymakers anticipated (and desired) failed to materialize. While the log export duty made the sawing of Canadian logs in the United States relatively unprofitable, the continuing American tariff on lumber imports meant that Americans sawing in Canada still faced difficulties in trying to compete for markets in the United States. Most of those who were running out of timber in Michigan simply chose to move on to Wisconsin, Minnesota, and other timbered areas on the American side of the border.

Accommodation between the two nations was needed to resolve this mutually unsatisfactory situation. It came in 1890 when the United States adopted the McKinley tariff, which reduced the duty on lumber imports to one dollar per thousand; in return, Canada revoked its export duty. Brief but significant expansion resulted on both sides of the border. Log shipments from Canada to the United States rose from 80 million board feet in 1891 to 301 million by 1894; shipments of sawn products also increased dramatically. But in 1894, a massive depression struck, and trade soon fell to the level of 1880.

President Grover Cleveland was a firm believer in low tariffs. True to the platform on which he had won election in 1892, he pushed for a reduction of duties even though he knew that the tariff was a politically divisive issue. The legislation that finally resulted, the Wilson-Gorman tariff of 1894, was a product of compromise and maneuver. Many schedules were actually increased, but a few items were placed on the free list in at least partial fulfillment of Democratic promises. Lumber was among them. In response, many American millmen moved their operations to Canada rather than continue the expensive towing of logs across the Great Lakes. Log exports from Canada quickly gave way to lumber exports.

No doubt the main reason lumber went on the free list in the Wilson-Gorman tariff, while most other

things did not, was that the lumber interests in the United States were deeply divided on the tariff question. They mounted no effective or unified lobbying effort. Millmen with plants or extensive timber holdings in Canada saw advantages in free entry; those operating solely in the United States feared it. Many lumber dealers in Chicago, the largest wholesale center, favored free entry, which they saw as promising cheaper products in their competition for markets. Most Southern lumbermen also appear to have favored (or at least agreed to) duty-free lumber. Apparently, they considered Canadian competition too distant to be dangerous, or believed that anything that weakened their rivals in the Lake States might help them, or simply went along with the deeply entrenched low tariff tradition of their region. Moreover, a new argument had appeared in behalf of free entry for lumber. In the 1870s and 1880s, concern over a coming "timber famine" became widespread in the United States. Many now stepped forward to argue that free entry would help save trees in the United States by diverting demand to the forests of Canada. These forces, together with the influence of President Cleveland and the efforts of people like Congressman William Jennings Bryan of Nebraska (who saw in cheap Canadian lumber inexpensive building materials for his constituents on the treeless plains), combined to ensure that lumber would be kept on that short list of items which were allowed duty-free entry into the United States.

Subsequent widespread mill closures were the result more of a deep, general depression than of the Wilson-Gorman tariff, but the latter provided a convenient scapegoat. One West Virginian claimed that free lumber caused the closure of 90 percent of the mills in his state; others held similar beliefs. As a result, lumbermen were soon demonstrating unprecedented unity on the tariff question.

The issue was, of course, highly partisan. When F. C. A. Denkmann commented that he was "a Republican, just as every good lumberman should be," he inadvertently indicated where most mill owners stood on the question after 1894. By then even the staunch Democrats in their ranks, such as Orrin Ingram, came to oppose free entry for lumber. When free-trader Bryan won the Democratic nomination for president in 1896, lumbermen marshaled their strength to defeat him. One warned, "if Bryan is elected our firm will not put in a log next year."

After Bryan's defeat, leading lumbermen met in Cincinnati to plan a campaign for restoring the duty on lumber. Although the meetings revealed the persistence of some division in their ranks, the protectionists clearly dominated. They adopted a strong statement in favor of restoring duties and dispatched a delegation to Washington, D.C., to lobby for the change. They were not disappointed; the Dingley tariff that emerged from Congress in 1897 restored the two dollar duty on rough lumber, while leaving logs on the free list. In an effort to prevent Canada from reciprocating by restoring the export tax on logs, Congress added a retaliatory clause which provided that any such export duty would be added to the tariff on lumber entering the United States. Canada responded not with an export duty but with an outright ban on the exportation of logs that had come from crown lands. Since these lands were the main source of Canadian sawlogs, the flow of logs from Canada was reduced to a trickle, and a number of mills in the United States had to close for lack of raw materials. However, the tariff was not sufficiently high to shut off the movement of Canadian lumber into the United States. In the first year under the Dingley tariff, imports were down 60 percent from the preceding year, but lumber dealers soon reversed themselves. From 1898 to 1909, when the Dingley tariff was replaced by new legislation, Canadian lumber shipments to the United States rose an average of 13 percent a year.

Attacks on the tariff continued. Plains congressmen argued that it fostered a lumber trust—a charge that gained credence because of rising lumber prices, although those increases in fact stemmed from other causes. Republican ranks were now deeply divided on the tariff question, and after President William Howard Taft called a special session of Congress to revise the duties, a major battle was soon under way. Lumbermen dispatched another delegation of lobbyists to Washington. They proved assiduous supporters of the industry's interests. As one historian put it, "it is doubtful that there had ever been in Washington a more aggressive lobby than the committee of lumbermen."

They were not alone. Gifford PINCHOT, frequently critical of the industry, stepped forward to champion a protective tariff. He argued that higher lumber prices meant that more expensive conservation practices could be adopted; so long as cheap Canadian lumber could come into the United States, American producers would have to respond by skimming the most profitable trees by the cheapest (and most destructive) means. Rather than seeing the tariff as the mother of trusts, Pinchot had come to see it as at least the godparent of careful management of the nation's forests.

Edward HINES, then president of the NATIONAL LUMBER MANUFACTURERS ASSOCIATION, went beyond lobbying for a lumber duty. Through bribery and influence peddling, he sought to get the Illinois legislature to name his ally, William Lorimer, to the United States Senate. In the end, although Lorimer was elected, Hines's role was exposed, and after months of haggling the Senate voted to expel Lorimer because of "corrupt methods and practices" used in his election. By then, however, the Payne-Aldrich tariff of 1909 was already law.

Like its predecessors, the Payne-Aldrich tariff's lumber schedule was a compromise between different views, both in and out of the industry. The *New York Lumber Trade Journal* admitted that it "never felt it advisable to take part in any controversy concerning the tariff . . . whichever [side] we took would not be representing a part of our constituency whose claims are absolutely legitimate."

The Payne-Aldrich tariff set a minimum duty on lumber of $1.25 per thousand, but it also contained provisions for an additional levy of up to 25 percent ad valorem on lumber from any country discriminating against the United States through its own import duties or through export bounties or duties. The threat of an added levy was aimed directly at Canada, but Taft hesitated to invoke its terms, fearing a tariff war between the two nations. Instead, he sought to renew reciprocity with Canada. Toward this end, a reciprocity bill was pushed through Congress in July 1911. Under its terms, duties were to be reduced more than 50 percent. In the Canadian elections that September, however, the Liberals lost control of the government. Chances of a new treaty of reciprocity vanished as protectionists came to power north of the border.

In the United States, the elections of 1912 returned the Democrats to power, adding new strength to the drive for lower tariffs. The Underwood-Simmons tariff of 1913 put lumber once more on the free list; logs stayed there as well. Lumber remained duty free until the Hawley-Smoot tariff of 1930 restored a levy of one dollar per thousand, with a proviso for exemption if Canada accorded reciprocal treatment. Since Canada did not tax either rough lumber or that planed on only one side, these items continued to enjoy free entry into the United States.

Although overall the Hawley-Smoot tariff was the highest in American history and set off a worldwide wave of retaliatory legislation, protectionists among the lumbermen were not satisfied. The global surge of economic nationalism gave strength to their cause, however, and in the Revenue Act of 1932 they belatedly won what they sought. The act set a tax of three dollars per thousand, over and above duties already being levied, on all lumber entering the United States except for maple flooring, birch, and beech.

But the tide was already turning. In 1936, Canada and the United States entered into a reciprocal trade agreement that reduced tariffs on up to 250 million feet of lumber by as much as 50 percent. A second agreement, effective in 1939, removed the quota and granted additional concessions to Canadian lumbermen.

The agreements with Canada reflected a larger trend that was just beginning. By this time it was clear that the economic problems facing the industry were far too great for protectionism to solve or even significantly alter. Throughout the Great Depression and World War II, attention was focused on other questions. Subsequently, economic nationalism, which had played an important role in bringing on the war, was in disrepute. The United States, as one of the moving spirits behind the General Agreement on Tariffs and Trade (1947), set about trying to lower international barriers to commerce.

Other aspects of foreign trade now loomed larger in the eyes of lumbermen than did tariffs. Shipments to the East Coast of the United States by sea from British Columbia took more and more of that market from producers in Oregon and Washington. Under the Jones Act of 1920, trade between ports of the United States had to be in American-flag vessels. British Columbia's producers, free to use less expensive foreign bottoms, enjoyed a cost advantage of fifteen to eighteen dollars per thousand over their American competitors. Tariffs sufficiently high to overcome this were clearly unattainable, so American millmen turned to seeking an exemption from the Jones Act for shipments of softwood (as of the end of 1981, unsuccessfully).

At the same time, growing log exports from the West Coast to Japan deeply divided the lumber industry and had a severe impact in the Pacific Northwest. Unlike Canada, which earlier had taxed log exports, the government of the United States was not free to do so because of a constitutional ban on export duties. As Americans debated log exports, the issue of import duties for lumber drifted ever further from the mind, except in the case of specific items such as plywood (and even here it failed to generate the widespread intensity of feeling of an earlier day). It now seems clear that the health of the lumber industry is far more closely tied to that of the economy as a whole and to interest rates than it is to tariffs. Under the circumstances, the bitter conflicts over the lumber tariff of the 1890s seem unlikely to return.

FURTHER READING: Ralph Clement Bryant, *Lumber: Its Manufacture and Distribution* (1922), pp. 429-437. James Elliott Defebaugh, *History of the Lumber Industry of America* (1906), vol. 1: 437-472. A. R. M. Lower, *The North American Assault on the Canadian Forest* (1938). Frank W. Taussig, *The Tariff History of the United States* (8th ed., 1931).

THOMAS R. COX